Subscribe to DIVER MAGAZINE

THE LONGEST-ESTABLISHED SCUBA DIVING MAGAZINE IN NORTH AMERICA

D0166975

MONTHLY COLUMNS   **DEPARTMENTS**   **SPECIAL REPORTS**

THOUGHT PROVOKING FEATURES

- **EXPLORED:** INTRIGUING DIVE SITES
- **REVIEWED:** RESORTS & CHARTERS
- **EXPLAINED:** SEA LIFE MYSTERIES
- **SHOWCASED:** GEAR INNOVATIONS
- **REVEALED:** CELEBRITY SECRETS
- **INFILTRATED:** DIVERS EVERYWHERE
- **SCOOPED:** HIGH TECH FOR DEEP SEA
- **DISCOVERED:** TREASURES OF HISTORY
- **EXPRESSED:** YOUR POINT OF VIEW
- **FOR:** DIVERS WHEREVER YOU ARE

DIVER Magazine is published 8 times a year.
To subscribe call 1.877.974.4333 **or** 604.948.9937
Email mail@divermag.com **Web** www.divermag.com

Canada (except NL, NS, NB): 1 year $26.50, 2 years $4770 (NL, NS, NB: 1 year $28.50, 2 years $51.30 - Prices include taxes)

" To me, it seems unique, it seems like something that is done for the profit of the diver. It's done so that we can dive and feel good when we dive ... and so that we're protected ... **"**

José Negroni
Attorney, Fort Lauderdale, Fla.
New diver & aspiring underwater photographer
DAN Member*

Divers Alert Network is a buddy like no other to tens of thousands of divers around the world, just like José. As a non-profit medical and research organization, we are dedicated to the safety and health of all recreational scuba divers. Our membership, insurance services and product sales all support the unique resources we offer to our community. So join us and you'll help us to keep helping divers just like you ... and José.

That's being a real buddy.

www.**DiversAlertNetwork**.org

For more information contact
Divers Alert Network, 6 West Colony Place , Durham, NC 27705
Toll Free 1-800-446-2671
* Testimonial given April 2006

Divers Alert Network is a 501(c)(3) not-for-profit organization.
Priority code: B01DAY2007

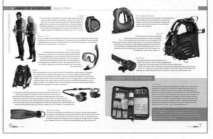

Dive into an interested target group with *duiken*

Duiken is the most widely read underwater sports magazine for the Netherlands and Flanders and is geared to the scuba diver and snorkelling enthusiast. It offers a perfect mixture of information as well as beautiful photoreports, making Duiken an inspiring magazine for every underwater sport fan. The team of editors comprises divers boasting years of diving experience, so it's only natural that they write about their passion for the underwater world with great enthusiasm and knowledge. The diving hotspots featured are both exotic places as well as national spots. In addition to topical news, every month the magazine features articles on subjects such as biology, underwater photography, archaeology, wreck diving and diving equipment.

For more information please contact Rob Keersmaekers, Magazine manager Duiken, 0031 76 530 17 16 or rob.keersmaekers@vipmedia.nl

At AKR, every day is a new adventure. Make that two or three new adventures.

Anthony's Key Resort

Roatan • Bay Islands
Honduras

www.anthonyskey.com

A PADI 5-Star Gold Palm Resort

Call and mention promotion code DAY07
800.227.3483 / 954.929.0090

> What will it be today? Snorkel with dolphins? Dive an endless wall or a massive wreck? Gallop horseback on the beach?
Fly through the jungle canopy? Watch a fiery sunset from your private hammock? > Then there's tomorrow to think about.

THE 2007 DIVING ALMANAC & YEARBOOK

Jeffrey J. Gallant
Editor-in-Chief

www.divingalmanac.com

Porbeagle Press Inc.
Drummondville

The 2007 Diving Almanac & Yearbook
By Jeffrey J. Gallant

Publisher:
Porbeagle Press Inc.
P.O. Box 483
Drummondville, QC
Canada J2B 6W3
www.porbeaglepress.com

Editor-in-Chief: Jeffrey Gallant
Senior Editor: Patricia Hay
Reviewers: Chris Harvey-Clark
Mack Sprague
Sylvia Watterson
Researchers: Jeffrey Gallant
Patricia Hay
Art/Design: Jeffrey Gallant

Cartography: CIA Book of Facts, D.A.Y.

Photography: Various sources including: D.A.Y., Aqualog, NOAA, OAR/NURP, U.S. Navy, & Canadian Archives.

Advertising & Sales:
sales@porbeaglepress.com
1 819 477 3374

International Standard Book Number: ISBN 0-9781078-0-2

The Diving Almanac & Yearbook may be accessed on the Internet at www.divingalmanac.com

Printed in Canada

When we think of the sea bed, abandoning ourselves to its fantasy, we become poets of childlike wonder. We roam around like divers in colored shadows overhung with liquid skies.

– PAUL VALÉRY (1871-1945)

Editor's Note

This book is the first known compilation of such diverse and far-ranging information on the diving world. Much of the information was obtained directly from the source or from verified references. However, getting the latest information on records and what may appear as simple data is far from easy. Even in this day and age of the Internet and satellite communications, language and cultural barriers, as well as the absence of a central body of information, make it very difficult to gain access to all of the latest news on the diving community.

The first edition of the Diving Almanac & Yearbook may thus contain factual errors and omissions, none of which are deliberate or meant to ignore the accomplishments of any individual or group. If you discover any mistakes or omissions, please accept our apologies and forward the correct information to us for inclusion in the 2008 edition.

We also ask for your assistance in obtaining new information such as missed records or world firsts, and we will gladly receive suggestions for inclusion in the 'Personalities' section. The Diving Almanac & Yearbook is an inclusive publication meant to showcase the accomplishments of the world diving community. If you or anyone you know should be presented in our Who's Who of diving, or if you know of any event that could be of interest to our readers worldwide, please contact us.

info@divingalmanac.com

Safety Note

Although the Diving Almanac & Yearbook may well complement a scuba training program, it is not meant to be used as a training manual. Any person who wishes to become a certified diver must register in a course offered by one of the many professional training agencies based around the world and dispensed by certified instructors.

Individuals attempting to dive without proper training or supervision do so at their own risk.

Like the millions of certified divers around the world, ensure your diving experiences are safe and pleasurable by signing up in a recognized training program before your first dive. Your life depends on it.

TRIBUTE

Clifford J. Simoneau (1959-2005)

Clifford Simoneau, whose life was all about diving, passed away at age 46 November 13, 2005, after a brief but spirited fight with cancer. To countless friends and associates he was simply 'Cliff,' a dynamic go-getter with an insatiable appetite for learning and for sharing knowledge. His passion for the underwater world was ever present in a can-do attitude that affected so many people over the course of his diving career.

A diver at age 12, he became an instructor at 18 and quickly gained a high profile in the New England dive community. Cliff went on to become one of the most successful dive industry entrepreneurs in the United States. Over the years he owned and operated several dive shops, a charter boat operation and he represented a multitude of high-profile product manufacturers. His latest brainchild was Silent Diving Systems, which he founded with Mike Fowler, his friend and associate from Brockville, Ontario.

Cliff training divers off Boston, Massachusetts
Photo: J. Gallant / D.A.Y.

Cliff was a natural teacher and as founder of SDI/TDI with Bret Gilliam, he became one of the most influential dive instructors in the world. He helped develop dozens of training manuals that covered everything from basic open water techniques to staged decompression and Trimix diving. He left his mark on the thousands of divers – sport, technical and military – to whom he taught these same skills.

What set Cliff apart was his ability to treat every student with the same level of care and respect. An openwater student was just as important as a Trimix student. No matter how technical the subject, he always emphasized getting into the water and having a good time. And Cliff certainly had a lot of fun. His many training programs and expeditions took him to the far corners of the world to teach or to lend expertise to divers shooting documentary films or engaged in research projects, such as one aimed at protection of whale sharks in the Galapagos.

When rebreathers hit the recreational market, Cliff was one of the first to embrace the concept of 'silent diving' and he and Mike set up what is today the largest rebreather operation on this side of the Atlantic. Today, Inspiration rebreathers are the most widely recognized units in North America due largely to Cliff's incomparable marketing skills and knack for being in the right place at the right time. Cliff made his presence felt at all of the trade shows and big events. When he didn't show up at DEMA in October, everyone knew something was seriously wrong.

Cliff's influence inevitably crossed over the border into Canada where he led several training programs in Ontario, Quebec, and Nova Scotia. It was through one of these programs that I befriended Cliff, in Halifax five years ago. Cliff, who was also an officer of the Shark Research Institute (SRI), based in New Jersey, took an immediate interest in the Greenland shark and became involved in Operation Skalugsuak, a study of this animal in the St. Lawrence Estuary. True to his generous nature, he supplied rebreather training and materials at no charge and never asked for anything in return. In recent years, I had the good fortune to visit Cliff and his wife Kathy at their home in Wolfeboro, New Hampshire, where he continued to dive in Lake Winnipesauke. His many adventures and worldliness notwithstanding he was always close to his roots and home. This is how I will remember him.

Everyone who knew Cliff will remember him for his friendly, outgoing nature. He was the embodiment of positive attitude and it was not unusual for him to share the words of Charles Swindoll who wrote: *"The longer I live, the more I realize the impact of attitude on life...I am convinced that life is 10 per cent what happens to me and 90 per cent how I react to it...and so it is with you...we are in charge of our attitudes. "*

Cliff, this book is dedicated to you.

- JG

FORWARD

By Dr. Phil Nuytten (OBC, L.L.D.)

It is a relatively modern myth that man is tough, resilient, and (like the cockroach) can survive anywhere. What nonsense! We are actually the most fragile of creatures: big soft jellyfish full of chopsticks, arranged in a physical design that is millions of years old. Our cranial software has evolved at quite a respectable rate but our chassis' – the vehicle we use to truck the hard-drive around – has barely changed, and is very specific and inflexible.

We 'tough', 'resilient' humans can't survive anywhere close to the extremes of our home planet, as we were designed. We can't go to the top of Mount Everest as we were born – naked and without oxygen – and we sure as hell can't breathe water, nor survive the crushing pressure of the Challenger Deep. But we *do* go there – just as we routinely fly from continent to continent and, less routinely, walk on the face of the moon!

We do it by using the armor of technology to allow us to venture far outside of our primitive design specifications. We build devices, contraptions and 'stuff' that allows us to carry our optimum temperature, breathing gas, and sometimes, even our pressure, with us. Our ability to adapt simple things to complex purposes surrounds us with a life-preserving layer of that warm, sea-level, swamp where we were conceived.

And that's what I (and others like me) do: build the 'stuff'. I've spent most of my life developing and building everything from saturation systems to one-atmosphere pressure suits – from deep submersibles to submarine rescue systems. In the course of doing so, I've reached some conclusions, the most important of which is that we haven't yet even scratched the surface of the bottom! The real exploration of the major part of Planet Ocean is just starting and I have no doubt that some of you younger readers will be 'deeply' involved.

While my day job is as a blacksmith, building the armor that allows scientific, military and commercial divers to dive deep, stay long and come back safely, in my heart of hearts, I'm simply a diver. The thousands of hours that I've spent underwater working, testing or just simply drifting and looking, have confirmed what I knew the first time I swam through a kelp bed and watched the sunbeams revolve and refract as the kelp fronds shifted: this is the most beautiful part of our planet.

This almanac has placed its emphasis on diving activities around the world. By knowing what *has* happened and what *is* happening, you have the best possible perspective on what's *likely* to happen - and that's what almanacs are all about.

We divers are a curious lot (and I mean that in both of its senses!). Curious and eager to see what lies beyond the next bend in the road, and the next bend in the galaxy.

This work by Jeffrey Gallant promises to satisfy some areas of your curiosity even as it piques others.

Enjoy yourselves!

Acknowledgements

It took nearly 25 years of diving for me to find the courage to undertake what has proven to be a challenging endeavor in producing this book. Had it not been for many great people I have encountered over these years, I could not have accomplished the task. They shared their knowledge and experience, they gave me their trust and they offered me their friendship. They were all in my thoughts while I was writing this book.

Most profound thanks to my good friend Chris Harvey-Clark, who took me under his wing in 1997. Rather than hitting the pub with the rest of the crew after a dive in Lunenburg, Nova Scotia, he offered to take me snorkeling in nearby Lahave River, where we admired empty eel pots surrounded by their intended – and witty – prey. I never would have guessed that our relationship would lead to so many incredible adventures and discoveries; most recently the study of the Greenland shark.

Many many thanks to John Batt, Paul Boissinot, and Marjorie Maury whose unrelenting support and boundless passion for the underwater world have been my inspiration.

To the Royal Canadian Sea Cadets who initiated me to scuba diving at the Quadra Cadet Camp near Comox, British Columbia, in 1982.

To the late Jacques-Yves Cousteau who fired my imagination and my passion for exploring the unknown depths through his many films and books.

To the Divers Alert Network (DAN), CMAS Québec (AMCQ), AIDA International, CAFA & Performance Freediving who contributed much technical and educational material.

Special thanks to NOAA for making available an unending supply of invaluable information and photos on the marine environment and research. Aidan R. Martin, for sharing his passion and expertise on sharks. Neil McDaniel, Graham Dickson, Patrice Strazzera, for their amazing images.

Leonard and Beatrice Hay, my grandparents.

Anthony's Key Resort (Haydee and the Galindo Family), Vania Atudorei, Terri Batt, François Bourret, Dr. José Castro, CEGEP de Drummondville, Joe Choromanski, DIVER Magazine (Canada), Rachel Gobeil, Alec & Deany Hay, Jean-François Joly, Kirk Krack, Yan Labrie, Solange Lebel, Alexandre Leclerc, Loïc Leferme, Val Leferme, Éric Michaud, Constantin Mihaï, Alison Mills, Ionel Miron, Liviu Miron, Phil Nuytten, Marc-André Saint-Laurent, Carl Savoie, Franck Seguin, Jo Shadbolt, Guylaine Simard, Kathy Simoneau, Mack Sprague, Ralph Tomilson, Peter Vassilopoulos, Éric Vigneault, Sylvia Watterson and everyone else that has encouraged, supported, and put up with me over the years.

Last but not least, loving thanks to my parents, André and Patricia, for their lifelong support and devotion to their sons. When I was a child, they let me spend days on end by the Saint-François River where I instinctively took to observing the aquatic creatures of my native Drummondville, Québec. My parents also took my brother Davy and I on our first trips to the St. Lawrence Estuary and to the Atlantic Ocean where my love for the sea took root in the land of my Maritime Acadian ancestors.

INTRODUCTION

It is the dawn of a new D.A.Y. The Diving Almanac & Yearbook 2007, first edition, is the realisation of a long time dream.

Author, Jeffrey Gallant, has given D.A.Y. the mandate of making up-to-date diving information of all kinds available to the diving community in one reference book. D.A.Y. will please avid divers, occasional divers, new divers, professional divers as well as non-divers interested in the underwater world. It is unique with its compilation of international diving data at your fingertips. This first edition with its 500 plus pages has something for everyone. The chronicle will keep readers posted on what happened in the diving world in the past year. The feature destination section will tantalize divers with its colourful view and description of diving sites. It is the author's hope and intent that D.A.Y. will be a diver's reference *par excellence*.

The past two and some years have been challenging and interesting. D.A.Y. staff have been speaking and writing to people in the diving industry around the world. Federations, associations, organizations, dive clubs, dive shops, to name but a few, have been contacted for statistics and dive regulations in their respective countries, as well as favourite dive sites and other information of interest to divers and the dive industry.

We are so grateful to all the people who took the time to reply and give us what information they could. As our contacts increase, we expect D.A.Y. to get bigger and better every year. Each edition will be updated to give our readers information that is essential, correct and timely. Expanded sections on technical diving, archaeology and underwater photography are already in the works for 2008. We expect to hear from our readers and welcome your comments, corrections, and suggestions.

Canada is the featured dive destination in this first edition. As a Canadian publication destined for national and international markets, we want to show the world the underwater beauty of this country. The feature destination will be in a different world location every year. Depending on the size of the country, it may cover only one or two areas or the entire country, but be assured, the beauty and diving attractions of the feature destination will entice us one and all.

The chronicle is another feature that will be of particular interest to our readers from one year to the next. Our researchers compile data from media sources and our own personal contacts in countries around the globe.

The D.A.Y. website updates world records and posts corrections for other sections until they are incorporated into the next edition.

Every year our creative staff will continue to bring in new ideas and developments that will make each edition of D.A.Y. a valuable tool for all divers and a welcome addition to every present, past and future diver's library.

AUTHOR'S PREFACE

Transcendental Saturation / Diving Into the Womb of Mother Earth

Transcendency is a state of being untainted by everyday limitations imposed by the conscious mind and our fast-paced environment. This voyage out of our 'experience' imbues us with a level of serenity unattainable in our daily lives. How many of us have entered this state of bliss during a dive, where everything we know disappears and we feel in perfect harmony with the liquid world around us and perhaps even the whole universe as we understand it?

I rang in the new millennium at a depth of 30 ft (9m) off the dock at Les Escoumins, Quebec. Along with a few friends, we waited for the arrival of the year 2000 doing what we most love. Once the moment had passed, we just hung off the wharf for a few minutes shaking hands and then started to head back to shore. On this one very rare occasion, I wasn't on a photo hunt nor did I have any plans other than to be in the water at midnight. That's when it hit me, literally. I felt suddenly and acutely present. Turning away from the dock I faced the dark void, dive light off, attention focused on my place in time and space. Hanging suspended in the chilly ocean with all of my senses now investigating the featureless surroundings, I realized that I wasn't alone. Through the noise of bubbles, a distinct sound emerged, unlike any I had heard at this site before. I slowed my breathing and tuned into it, oblivious to the festivities still unfolding behind me.

Soon I recognized the chirps and squeals as the singing of beluga whales. The sounds became very clear and seemingly from all around. Drifting in the slight current I felt a pull from my reality and time into another, into that of the ocean. For a fleeting moment, I felt a part of the sea, no more and no less than the white whales whose song enveloped me in the darkness. I sensed a connection and I felt safe. It was comforting and instinctive, as though I had experienced it before, 33 years before to be exact. When I 'awoke' from this intense and dreamlike state of awareness, the idea of a new millennium suddenly seemed silly and artificial, an absurd human concept.

Cousteau's 'silent world' is primal and as it turns out, ideal for divers interested in the idea of communion with the living world. It's been said that diving into the sea is like a return to the womb, with its enveloping, tactile nature. This vital source of life, by virtue of its immense size and absolute reign over our planet, is a place of reverence that invites us to connect with our inner-selves, far from the 'noise' of accumulated life experience, by reaching into the abyss of the soul.

Renowned psychologist, Abraham Maslow, studied the phenomenon of this inner experience, which he called the peak experience:

> "They come from moments of intense love and sexuality, of great artistic moments - music in particular - of intense bouts of creativity and inventiveness - great inspiration - of intense moments of intuition and discovery, of women giving birth naturally and loving their child, of instants of fusion with nature - in the forest, by the sea, in the mountains, etc. - of certain sporting activities such as **scuba diving**, dancing, etc."

Maslow clearly identifies the sea as an ideal location to sense a peak experience, something many divers have understood for a long time, maybe since their very first immersion. Maslow also believes that these experiences are within reach of every person, and that many have already experienced such an event without realising it on a conscious level, since they are practically impossible to relive or describe with words. I occasionally meet other divers who have also sensed a connection with the sea and although none of us can effectively articulate our experiences, we feel rather than understand what the other is saying.

Maslow explored the characteristics of the peak experience and its effects on the human mind; they are moments of pure ecstasy, where everything seems interrelated, in harmony, and of a serenity that is completely reassuring. These experiences are instinctive and can be shared between living creatures. Returning to reality, to the rational world, from such experiences can be jarring. A dive buddy tugging on your fin is all it takes to be yanked from a euphoric state.

Diving with dolphins in the open sea off Roatan was everything I had imagined, and more. The setting was ideal: nothing but blue water on a flat and apparently endless sandy bottom. The ocean had never appeared so vast and the dolphins, repeatedly, would swim by us within arm's reach. With every pass we looked deeply into each other's eyes and I sensed a mutual effort to connect on a higher level. Although the professional and conflicting urge to take photos prevented me from completely letting go of my reality, this sense of connecting beyond mere visual contact seemed very real.

Sensing a peak experience requires particular environmental conditions, physical awareness, and a very open mind. And yet it really isn't as complicated as it appears. Nor is it dangerous. This is nothing like nitrogen narcosis and you will immediately be aware of any safety hazards such as loss of buoyancy control the moment they appear. I have often planned or even improvised attempts at peak experiences and have enjoyed considerable success without ever putting my safety at risk. Much like a shark uses its lateral line to detect vibrations, so can we use our bodies to detect the pulse of the sea. Being approximately 60 per cent water, the adult body is an ideal receptacle and transmitter of sounds and pulsations when immersed. Water is 800 times denser than air, making the body more attuned to sensing distant and profound vibrations and frequencies during a dive. And like all life in the sea, we receive and send out signals that announce our presence; however faint, these signals are sensed around the ocean world.

My long search for the Greenland shark not only led me to the discovery of an elusive and relatively unknown Arctic predator, but also to more than one peak experience with an animal not known for its superior intelligence and, frankly, with a low charm factor. Unlike the dolphin, the shark has not endeared itself to humans. Still, on occasion I have experienced feelings looking into the eyes of these very large and emotionless fish, not unlike those experienced swimming with dolphins. In fact, I have repeatedly sensed a connection with all marine animals regardless of form or size; whether animated seals, schooling fish or even the stationary anemone, encounters with the sea's living creatures always leave me with a profound sense of my existence, individuality, and of being part of a whole.

The bigger the body of water, the bigger the effect of signals we emit. Much in the same way the largest parabolic antennas pick up the faintest signals emanating from space, the largest bodies of water detect and diffuse the most vibrations and signs of life. Famed German diver and explorer Hans Hass wrote in 1959 that he "imagined the whole sum of the seas as one immense, vibrating being which, as it were, lies prone and embraces the whole world…" He goes on to say that the primeval nucleus of creation must have contained "all the stupendous evolutionary possibilities which led from the first piece of living matter right up to man with his immense potentialities of spiritual development…" Hass noted that he was "never free of such thoughts and (that) they have led me to regard with redoubled reverence and curiosity what I have seen and experienced in the seas."

Life came from the sea, humankind's ancestors included, and thus we are inextricably linked with this most dominant feature of planet 'earth' and its inhabitants. Although terrestrial beings we spend our first nine months growing and developing in a liquid environment. To me, all this means is that the sea is a natural choice for those who seek to make a deeper spiritual connection within themselves. Experiencing the sea passively, in a sense 'surrendering' to it momentarily, can be rewarding.

In *World without Sun* (1964), Jacques Cousteau states that "undersea exploration is not an end in itself, although it is spiritually rewarding merely to be an onlooker." Hence to associate diving with spirituality is not a new concept. Surprisingly though, at a time when we are, perhaps, more receptive than ever before to our spiritual nature (not to be confused with religion), you won't find any trace of the subject in even the most exhaustive scuba training manuals.

In Canada, the fact is our often bulky cold water diving gear inhibits peak experiences. The less equipment worn, the better the chances are of aligning the necessary conditions to sense a peak experience. For northern divers, the cherished dry suit is likely the most troublesome piece of gear for its ability to absorb the sea's vibrations, insulating us from the experience we seek. Having your skin in direct contact with the water, even in a wetsuit, is much more conducive to feeling the ocean. The noise of bubbles from open-circuit scuba also causes interference. Rebreathers produce none or far less making it easier to listen.

Practically devoid of all this (interfering) gear, the freediver is better equipped to sense a peak experience. In fact, this is what keeps a lot of them coming back and going ever deeper. "To be able to swim like a fish and breath hold like an orca is a feeling of being at one with the ocean that you get no other way that I know of," says Phil Nuytten[1], one of the earliest freedivers on the west coast of Canada. Direct bodily contact with water also helps to hear sea creatures, which is a definite mood setter. When trying to home in on the chirping of beluga whales in the St. Lawrence, never mind the cold, flood your hood and let the ocean make its way to your eardrums. Then adjust your buoyancy to neutral, slow and synchronize your breathing with your partner and you will hear whales, as well as countless other mysterious voices speaking to you. Privacy is a rare commodity under water.

In order to condition your mind for a peak experience, you must be aware of your place in this world. No matter how well equipped and trained we are, the sea is not our realm. As Hans Hass put it, "when we are surrounded by the fish and the waving tendrils of sea plants, we may regain a little of our lost humility." Human arrogance will shut out the pulse of the sea more effectively than the thickest drysuit. Leave your ego on shore or the boat deck along with your scientific, technical or other training, before entering the water. Think of yourself as a helpless and insignificant piece of plankton drifting at the mercy of the tide, itself under the influence of cosmic powers. Open your mind to the biggest picture imaginable.

Timing a peak experience is crucial. Dawn and dusk are stressful times in the ocean. They are transition periods when animals are either scurrying to seek shelter or are still too nervous to come out of their day or nighttime hiding places. There's too much excitement and little peace. Stormy or intense surge conditions will frustrate efforts to enjoy a peak experience. Waves breaking on the shore and the constant churning of bottom sediment resonate and echo in all directions thus creating a cacophony that drowns out even the ocean's deepest vibrations. Diving near busy sea lanes also makes it difficult, if not impossible, to sense a peak experience. The propellers of seagoing vessels can be heard dozens of kilometers away even if the vessel is far out of sight. The steady rhythmic thumping of a

[1] Grierson, Bruce, **Take a Deep Breath**, Saturday Night Magazine, August 11, 2001

propeller is completely unnatural and trains the brain to tune into the beat rather than be attentive to the unexpected. Unlike mechanical or musical sounds produced by humans, sounds coming from the sea are not subjected to the rhythm of a metronome. Ocean sounds fluctuate greatly and are as unpredictable as the Northern Lights.

Although diving is one of the best ways to sense a peak experience, it is still possible, although a little more difficult, to connect with the ocean when the sea is too rough to dive or if you aren't a diver. One of my favorite techniques requires a very large and smooth rock that protrudes above the waterline. The immense rock formations that make the shoreline at Peggy's Cove, Nova Scotia, or at Cap-Bon-Désir, Québec, are ideal. Such large rocks are very good at amplifying sounds or vibrations coming from the ocean. If conditions are right, you may even hear the sound of whales emanating from the rock. Find a quiet spot where you can sit and place your bare hands with open palms facing downwards directly onto the rock face. Keep your eyes open or slightly closed and look to the open sea while keeping anything human out of sight. If you are able to free your mind, the rock will eventually feel as though it is an extension of the sea, and you will sense its power.

Maslow's theory of the peak experience helped me understand a little more the character of Jacques Mayol, the aloof protagonist of the cult movie *The Big Blue*, who ultimately fins into oblivion to forever be in this universe without words. For the most passionate of us, the attraction of the sea is exactly of this nature. While diving, we are complete.

- JG

ABOUT THE AUTHOR

Jeffrey Gallant started diving in 1982 at the age of 14. He has led several research and training expeditions around the world, most notably in Canada where he is co-director of the Greenland Shark and Elasmobranch Education and Research Group (GEERG). Among his most memorable accomplishments, Gallant was trained as an aquanaut in Romania in 1995. An award-winning underwater photographer and videographer, he has contributed to several dive publications, books as well as natural history documentaries. He has been a columnist of Vancouver-based DIVER Magazine since 1997. Gallant lives in Drummondville, Quebec, where he teaches at the local CEGEP.

www.aqualog.com / www.geerg.ca

TABLE OF CONTENTS

Chapter 1

DIVING AT A GLANCE

For as long as history has been recorded, Man has been diving to get food, to fight and to explore. Today, millions of people around the world dive for the sheer pleasure they get when they cross into the underwater world. They dive in all kinds of environments from the frozen polar oceans to the warm waters of the equator in search of adventure and discovery.

A diver explores the Belize Barrier Reef in the Caribbean Sea. Photo: J. Gallant / D.A.Y.

Once a sport for the toughest and fittest of men, diving today is accessible to all, including people with disabilities who find new freedom when released from the bonds of gravity.

Technological advances have led to the development of safe and reliable equipment and diving is now safer than ever before. Formerly a stealth tool of the military, bubbleless rebreathers have ex-

tended the range of sport divers much to the delight of technical divers and underwater photographers.

Thousands of businesses offer exotic excursions to all parts of the world. Formerly forbidding places like the Arctic Ocean are now prized destinations for the more adventurous seeking to discover new environments and cultures.

Freedivers keep going deeper and deeper on a single breath of air far surpassing depths that were once believed fatal to humans. Professional divers now work at depths well below 1,000 ft (305 m) with a sophistication befitting even the most farfetched adventure novels written when diving was in its infancy.

Gone are the days when visitors needed a boat to get to the best dive sites. Today, one can simply swim through a hatch at an underwater resort to get a closer look at sea life swimming by the bedroom window.

Even non-divers can explore the deep by hitching a ride on one of the many sightseeing submersibles operating in every ocean. Beautifully designed websites and glossy magazines as well as underwater cinematography of a quality unheard of only 5 years ago entice millions of people around the world to appreciate and care for the underwater world and even to take up diving themselves. For millions of people around the world, diving has been a life-changing experience, a source of sustenance or discovery, and has become a way of life.

STATISTICS

The definitive number of divers around the world is impossible to fathom. In 2005, PADI alone certified 913,419[1] divers worldwide for a total of 14,730,658* since 1967[2]. Of these 535,286 were entry level divers trained in 2005.

According to PADI, 2 out of every 3 new divers in the U.S. and over 1 out of 2 in the world are PADI certified annually. This makes PADI by far the largest dive training agency in the world.

A group of divers from all over the world awaits dolphins at Anthony's Key Resort in Honduras. Photo: J. Gallant / D.A.Y.

A study[3] done for DEMA revealed that there were 2,321,000 active divers in the United States in 2000. Of these, 65.8% were male and 34.2% were female. The same study also revealed that there were 6,330,000 snorkelers of which 53.5% were male and 46.5% were female. Two other surveys came up with similar numbers of active divers: 2,901,000 (Sporting Goods Manufacturers Association) in 2000, and

2,985,280 (Mediamark Research) in 1998. If we average the three, it is safe to assume the approximate number of active divers in the U.S to be 2,735,760.

A study released by the Diving Equipment and Marketing Association in 1998[4] reveals that nearly half of the adult population of the U.S. is interested in scuba diving, and that 8% of the adult population, or 16,184,240 Americans, have tried scuba diving and plan to dive again. By tallying the number of divers we have researched to produce the Diving Almanac & Yearbook, our own estimate is that there are at least 20 million divers in the world today.

The following numbers were compiled from official sources[5] by the _Diving Almanac & Yearbook_ within each country or territory. See 'Countries' section for details on each country. Numbers include active and non-active divers.

Algeria	2,500
Argentina	3,200
Australia	34,600
Barbados	500
Belgium	21,500
Bosnia & Herzegovina	143
Brazil	190,000
Bulgaria	87
Cambodia	40
Canada	619,000
China	8,000
Cook Islands	500
Djibouti	250
Dominica	70
East Timor (Timor-Leste)	250
Finland	50,000
France	340,000
French Polynesia	7,000
Greece	600,000
Guatemala	12,300
Haiti	100
Hong Kong	20,000
Iceland	1,400
Indonesia	2,000
Iran	3,200
Israel	120,000

---

[1] Represents total entry level and continuing education diving certifications for all PADI Offices combined. Divers may have multiple certifications. Does not include introductory scuba diving experiences or non-diving experiences.
[2] PADIcom – PADI Worldwide Certification History
[3] Sports Participation in 1999 – Scuba & Snorkeling, National Sporting Goods Association
[4] Track on Scuba Diving (January 1998) / The Leisure Trends Group
[5] Sources listed in 'Countries' section.

Japan	1,000,000
Jordan	500
Latvia	70
Lebanon	7,000
Lithuania	2,250
Luxembourg	700
Maldives	600
Malta	2,500
Micronesia	250
Moldova	58
Monaco	250
Monteserrat	110
Namibia	50
Netherlands, The	20,000
New Zealand	320,000
Nicaragua	200
Oman	3,500
Palestine	60
Panama	7,000
Romania	2,300
Russia	3,250
Samoa	70
Serbia	15,000*
Seychelles	650
Slovenia	5,000
Solomon Islands	150
Spain	50,000
Sri Lanka	10,000
Sweden	130,000
Taiwan	4,000
Tonga	50
Tunisia	800
United Arab Emirates	6,000
United Kingdom	100,000
United States	16,184,240**
Vanuatu	300
Vietnam	200

Total number of divers:

19,513,748

* Includes Montenegro
** Active divers (Dive & will dive again)

TRAINING

Safe diving is only possible with diver training. Training organizations exist which will give people the training they require for the type of diving they wish to do. Training will consist of courses to obtain basic certification, required in most countries around the world, to training in cave diving, wreck diving, commercial diving and other types of diving.

Divers are trained to give certification and other diving courses by scuba diving training agencies such as PADI, Professional Association of Diving Instructors; NAUI, National Association of Underwater Instructors; GUE, Global Underwater Explorers; ACUC, American and Canadian Underwater Certifications, SSI, Scuba Schools International, BSAC, British Sub Aqua Club; CMAS, Confédération Mondiale des Activités Subaqualiques and others. A list of associations in the Diving Community section of D.A.Y. includes the many different training organizations for recreational diving as well as organizations that specialize in the more advanced technical and commercial diver training.

Reputable dive shops will often be able to provide basic diver training for people interested in recreational diving. Some will be able to provide the more advanced courses. It is very important to be sure that the courses you are getting are up to the standards of the aforementioned diver training agencies, in both the theoretical and practical aspects of diving. Depending on the course, a certain number of hours diving is required, and exams are two-fold, one part theory, one part practical. The entry level certification course can be given in a pool or in open-water but the more advanced courses will often be given in open-water as close as possible to conditions that the diver will encounter in the type of diving he is training for.

Another aspect of diving is the equipment used, whether personally owned or leased from the dive shop. It should be up to par. Training will include how to use this equipment and keep it in good working condition. While it is not necessary to have the latest equipment when diving, it is in the best interests of the diver to have equipment which will keep him safe because it is functioning as it should and because the diver knows how to use it.

Each agency issues manuals which are required as part of the training and are kept by the trainee at the end of the course. They contain the technical information that a person must master in order to attain the certification in question. At no time can general information such as that contained in magazines or in publications such as the Diving Almanac & Yearbook substitute for these essential training manuals.

Learning how to use dive tables in Ghana, Africa.
Photo: J. Gallant / D.A.Y.

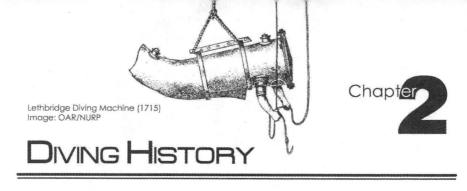

Lethbridge Diving Machine (1715)
Image: OAR/NURP

Chapter 2

Diving History

Man has been exploring the sea from the beginning of time, first in his search for food and later, for commercial and military exploits. Up until the invention of the diving bell, these early dives consisted of holding one's breath and diving to depths of up to 100 ft (30 m). Evidence of breath-hold diving is found in drawings as well as in ornaments and other artifacts made from mother-of-pearl and other seashells. Much of this historical evidence connects man to the sea as far back as 3,000 BC and earlier.

Food was probably the first attraction man had for diving followed by the collecting of sponges, oyster pearls and seashells used to make ornaments. Sponge diving dates back to ancient times and while it was a great source of economy, it was also very difficult and dangerous work for the divers. Small boats would bring the divers out to sea where they would use a glass bottomed cylinder to spot the sponges on the ocean bed.

海女 Ama (sea woman) divers in Japan have been diving for pearls and food for over 2,000 years. Photo obtained under GNU General Public License.

The divers would go down holding a heavy stone which was roped to the boat. This stone allowed a fast descent to the bottom where the diver would harvest sponges into a net for as long as he could hold his breath. Divers could go about 100 ft (30 m) deep and, depending on lung capacity, could stay under for 3 to 5 min.

So that sponge fishers may be supplied with air for respiration, vases are lowered in the water with the mouth downward so they fill not with water, but with air; these vases are forced steadily down, held perfectly upright, for if tipped slightly, the water enters and knocks it over.

Aristotle

In 1599, Samuel de Champlain noted in his West Indian Journal, that pearl diving had already established itself in the New World.

From this port, Margarita, more than three hundred canoes leave every day, going a league offshore to fish for pearls in ten or twelve fathoms. The fishing is done by Negro slaves of the king of Spain, who take a little basket under their arm, and with it plunge to the bottom of the sea, and fill it with oysters, and climb back into their boats.

Divers were often involved in military activities. Historical documents and drawings show divers performing underwater operations in the 5th century BC, during the Persian wars, in the siege of Tyre in 332 BC and at other battles.

There was some skirmishing in the harbor around the palisades the Syracusans had planted in the sea so that their ships could not be reached by the enemy. The Athenians sent a 250-ton ship with wooden towers to pull up the palisades or they dived and sawed through them underwater, at length destroying most of the stakes. There were some stakes out of sight in the water, the most dangerous of all, and these were sawn off by hired divers.

Thucydides, Siege of Syracuse

Aristotle writes, in his work *Problemata* about Alexander the Great himself going underwater in a diving bell during the siege of Tyre.

16th century painting of Alexander the Great, lowered in a glass diving bell. Image: OAR/National Undersea Research Program (NURP); "Seas, Maps and Men"

Around 100 A.D., the business of underwater salvaging was so well organized that a

set salary rate was instated: at 26 ft (8 m), a diver could keep half of what he recovered; at 13 ft (4 m), one third; at 3 ft (1 m), one tenth.

Since the diver was limited by the air he could carry in his lungs, staying submerged for extended periods required the invention of devices that would make air available underwater.

THE DIVING BELL

The first diving bell was open at the bottom and was simply lowered into the water. Weights kept it down and divers could exit from the bottom and return to breathe the trapped air, compressed by the water pressure, inside the bell. This could go on for as long as the air was breathable.

A more sophisticated device appeared in 1531 when Italian Guglielmo de Lorena constructed a small glass bell encompassing the diver's head which was used to recover Caligula's pleasure galleys in Lake Nemi.

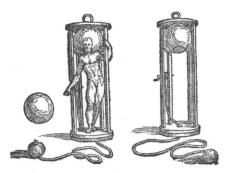

An early diving bell used by 16th Century divers during salvage operations from *Regola generale di soleuare ogni fondata naue & nauilii con ragione*, by Niccolo Tartaglia (1562). Image: National Undersearch Research Program (NURP) Collection

In 1690 Edmond Halley perfected the bell by adding weighted barrels connected to the diving bell. These air filled barrels allowed the divers to stay under for longer periods and records show dives of 90 min. at 60 ft (18 m). Eventually an improved version supplied with fresh air brought in barrels allowed Halley himself to stay under for over 4 hours.

Innovations and creations in the 1700s to the bell, helmet and suit were the starting point to many of the advances made in diving that have brought the industry to where it is today. Many scientists and engineers worked on and improved the diving bell and helmet during this period of time. In 1715, John Lethbridge constructed a wooden cylinder with arms and a glass window that allowed divers to salvage goods from the bottom of the sea. The diver could work inside for periods up 30 min. at a depth of 60 ft (18 m) without the supply of fresh air.

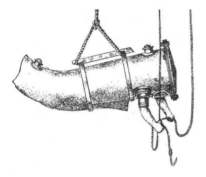

Lethbridge Diving Machine (1715)
Image: OAR/NURP

By the end of the century the diving bell was made of cast iron. Fresh compressed air was hand pumped and kept in the bell through the use of a non-return valve.

DIVING SUIT AND HELMET

After the diving bell came variations of the helmet. In 1772, French scientist Freminet invented the hydrostatergatic machine a helmet fitted with an air hose allowing the diver to remain submerged for up to 45 min.

A diving suit was created in 1797 by a German mechanic, Karl Heinrich Klingert. The suit was made of waterproof leather and was connected to a reservoir allow-

ing the diver immediate access to the air for a limited period of time.

In 1828, an invention for fire fighting patented by Charles Anthony Deane and his brother John five years earlier was used for diving as well. A helmet was fitted over the divers head and held on with weights. Air was pumped to the helmet directly from the surface. The helmet, however, was not attached to the suit which forced the diver to remain upright or risk drowning. In 1840 the helmet was sealed to a watertight, air-contained rubber suit by inventor Augustus Siebe.

Early hard hats were heavy in air, but buoyant underwater. Photo: OAR/National Undersea Research Program (NURP)

Siebe Deane helmet (1840) and weighted boots (circa 1900). Photos: *Association Les pieds lourds -* **www.pieds-lourds.com**

The German-born inventor was later described as the father of diving. This improvement to the original diving helmet allowed divers more safety at greater depths. It revolutionized diving and was used in both salvage operations and underwater engineering. This design also included weighted boots and an over-pressure valve in the suit.

In the early 1900s, new innovations including an oxygen re-breather from Draeger (Germany) and a self-contained underwater breathing unit by Yves Le Prieur (French) would forever change Man's explorations of the sea. Le Prieur's compressed air bottle carried on the diver's chest supplied air to a face mask controlled by an on/off switch to extend bottom time. SCUBA had come into being.

Photo: NOAA Ship Collection

SCUBA[7]

The 19th Century also saw inventors develop autonomous diving equipment that did not require surface-supplied air. In 1825, Englishman William James created a device in which a container carried a diver's air supply around his waist. In 1831, American Charles Condert built a similar device made of copper but died after several successful dives when his air hose broke.

[7] SCUBA: Self Contained Underwater Breathing Apparatus

In 1865, two Frenchmen, Rouquayrol and Denayrouze improved on the self-contained air supply device through the use of a metal canister containing compressed air that was carried on the back.

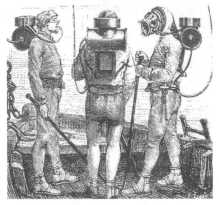

Rouquayrol and Denayrouze self-contained air supply device

Rouquayrol and Denayrouze *Aerophore* helmet (1865). Photos: David Dekker / www.pieds-lourds.com

A valve connected the air supply to a mouth piece and air was delivered when the diver inhaled. The *Aerophore* was the forerunner of modern scuba equipment. It appeared in Jules Verne's 1870 novel *20,000 Leagues under the Sea*.

Hardhat diver inspects a shipwreck in the Mediterranean. Photo: Patrice Strazzera

This was followed in 1876 by the development of the first diving rig using compressed oxygen instead of compressed air by Henry A. Fleuss.

The invention of rubber goggles with glass lenses, face masks, snorkels and fins came in the early 1930s. American Owen Churchill developed the first fins made of vulcanized rubber in 1940.

The Aqua Lung was invented in 1943 by Frenchmen Émile Gagnan and Jacques-Yves Cousteau. They connected a cylinder of compressed air to a variable pressure regulator enabling divers to remain underwater without any link to the surface for over an hour. Their invention has since been improved by several companies around the world.

PHYSICS & PHYSIOLOGY

Thanks to the development of new equipment and techniques, depths and the amount of time spent underwater increased dramatically. Coincidentally, the number of divers afflicted by a strange malaise became commonplace. Researchers therefore spent a lot of time studying what came to be known as decompression sickness. One of the first stud-ies on pressure changes was by Frenchman Paul Bert who suggested that gradual ascent would prevent the problem and recompression would relieve the pain of divers who had surfaced too quickly. In the early 1900s, detailed studies were published by John Scott Haldane, Arthur E. Boycott and Guybon C. Damant. These studies included tables recommending decompression stop times based on depth and duration of dives which were later tested by the U.S. Navy.

In the early 1900s, many of the contributions and innovations in diving equipment were made by the U.S. Navy. Among them was the Mark V Diving Helmet. Testing the dive tables and stage decompression, American divers went from diving 60 ft (18 m) to eventually reaching 274 ft (84 m).

The U.S. Navy also experimented with helium-oxygen mixtures and studies showed that these mixtures were advantageous for deep dives, leaving divers without undesirable mental effects while shortening decompression time. From these studies came reliable decompression tables and specialized apparatus.

Today, the causes and treatment of decompression sickness are still the focus of much research and discussion.

UNDERWATER PHOTOGRAPHY

Modern underwater cameras come in all shapes and sizes. In the early days, camera housings were leaky behemoths and lighting systems were as huge as they were ineffective. Taking even one photo took much preparation and required a great deal of hard work wearing cumbersome dive gear. The first photo taken underwater was by Englishman William Thompson (1822-1879) in February, 1856. The idea came to him while watching a wave battered bridge from a public house. Thompson used the collodion process to take the single photo during which the camera flooded. Although the resulting image was by no means a masterpiece, it was nonetheless a technical success.

> ... I knew that, could we sink a glass plate, prepared with collodion, to the bottom of the sea, in theory there was no reason why we should not obtain as good an image as we do on land, provided the sea water could be kept from the camera, and that the light was sufficient. I was not, sufficiently versed in optics and chemistry to know whether or not the water obstructed any and what light ray.

> Following my idea, we made a box as nearly watertight as we could, and large enough to enclose the camera.

> This box is fitted, in front with a piece of plate glass and on the outside is a wooden shutter, heavily leaded, and which is raised by a string attached to it and communicating with the boat...

> ... Up to the present point everything has been done on land. We now lash the whole of the apparatus, properly set, to the stern of the boat, and, when we arrive at the proper spot, sink the camera. By means of the lowering rope we can find when the camera is upright at the bottom. When satisfied on this point, we raise the shutter in front of the camera box, by means of the string attached to it, and the other end of which communicates with the boat. The camera is now in action...

> ... When I opened the camera and found it full of water, I despaired of having obtained a view; but it would appear that salt water is not so injurious as I had feared. I took the precaution of washing the plate gently with fresh water, and then of dipping it, for an instant in the silver bath. The

> plate was exposed for ten minutes on an ordinary day in the month of February*; it took nearly the same time to develop with pyrogallic acid, using Horne and Thornthwaite's collodion; you will see the negative is a weak one...

> ... This application of photography may prove of incalculable benefit to science. We may take (to a reasonable depth) sketches of submarine rocks, piers of bridges, outlines of sand-banks, in fact, everything that is required under water. Should a pier of a bridge require to be examined, you have but to suit your camera, and you will obtain a sketch of the pier, with any dilapidations; and the engineer will thus obtain far better information than he could from any report made by a diver...

> - William Thompson
> Weymouth, May 6, 1856[8]

After taking a single photo, Thompson made no further attempts with his crude device and nearly 40 years went by before Frenchman Louis Boutan designed and repeatedly used a sturdier and more reliable system in 1893. Boutan's housing weighed approximately 400 lbs (180 kg) in air. It was constructed with the help of his brother Auguste, an engineer, and Joseph David, a mechanic in the French navy.

> ... The boat being anchored securely to the bottom and kept stationary with the help of a series of cables fixed to the rocks of the coast, I put on my diving suit (hard hat – Ed.) and went in at the point chosen in advance as the center of operations. After having landed at the desired depth, I signaled the captain to lower the different parts of the photographic equipment. On the end on a line I received the iron platform, the cop-

---

[8] From William Thompson's Original Paper of 1856

per-covered camera, and a weigh to anchor everything.

The view chosen, I would set up the base of the apparatus at leisure and arrange the camera in such a way as to have only to press a button to open the shutter. This done, I sent another signal to the captain who held the life line in his hand. This signal indicated that the exposure had begun, and I would wait patiently for the captain to indicate the end of the operation.

You understand, of course, that it is impossible or, at least, very difficult without a special gadget, to take a watch down in a diving suit to time the exposure. Thanks to the method that I had adopted, this difficulty was overcome; the captain's job was to consult his watch and warn me in time.

It was thus that the photographs were obtained, after exposures that lasted up to a half-hour...

- Louis Boutan (Date unknown)

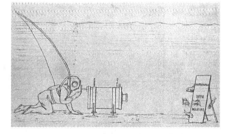

Boutan's 3rd underwater camera system (1898).
Photo: NOAA Ship Collection

The first underwater color photos were taken by ichthyologist Dr. William Longley and National Geographic photographer Charles Martin off Florida's Dry Tortugas for the January 1927 issue of the magazine. Lighting was supplied by means of magnesium powder explosives set on a pontoon and discharged by the diver. During one such exercise, Dr. Longley was badly burned and incapacitated for six days by an untimely explosion.

Not before 1958, would underwater photography become accessible to sport divers, when Belgian engineer Jean De Wouters and Jacques-Yves Cousteau designed the Calypsophot camera. In 1963, Nikon marketed an improved version of the Calypsophot under the name Nikonos.

Over the years, advancement in technology and the abundance of literature have made underwater photography one of the most popular specialties in diving.

EXPLORATION & SCIENCE

The 1900s was a time of great explorers in the diving industry. In 1930, William Beebe descended to 1,427 ft (435 m) using Otis Barton's *Bathysphere*, a diving vessel which was attached by a steel cable to the mother ship. Otis Barton and William Beebe tested the bathysphere at even greater depths to eventually make a record descent of 3,028 ft (923 m) off Nonsuch Island in Bermuda in 1934.

This and further records would all be eclipsed on January 23, 1960, when Swiss inventor Auguste Piccard and Don Walsh (USN) descended to the deepest point on earth, the Challenger Deep (Mariana Trench, Guam) at the depth 35,797 ft (10,911 m) aboard the Bathyscaph *Trieste* (Project Nekton). Many of the principles used in the building of the bathysphere and bathyscaph are incorporated in submersible research vessels today.

The development and subsequent availability of scuba equipment led to an era of exploration and scientific discovery beginning with the explorations of famous teams led by Hans Hass and Jacques-Yves Cousteau. Their many discoveries, books and films would be the inspiration for many more explorers of the underwater world. If humans were now able to admire the wonders of the sea from below the surface, they would later be the first to become aware of the effects of pollution, unbridled development, and overfishing. This led people such as Cousteau to contribute to the development of the environmental movement in the 1970s. Today, divers all over the world, including scientists and sport divers, continue to make discoveries and promote environmental awareness.

PUBLICATIONS

At the turn of the millennium, a multitude of websites catering to divers could be found on the Internet. Unfortunately, much of the enthusiasm for web-based diving information was short-lived as webmasters couldn't keep up with the countless hours of work required to keep their website updated and esthetically pleasing. Much of the initial wave of dive-related websites are now inactive or have gone offline.

Since the advent of the Aqua-Lung, long after American Charles Deane published what is considered by many the first diving manual in 1836, diving has become accessible to more and more people. Its popularity increases with publications on the beauties of the underwater world, such as *Diving into Adventure* published by Hans Hass in 1951, followed in 1952 with *The Silent World* by Jacques-Yves Cousteau, Frederic Dumas and James Dugan. The first national diving magazine in the U.S., *The Skin Diver*, appeared in December, 1951. The inaugural issue contained only 16 pages and catered mostly to underwater fisherman. By comparison, the June 1990 issue contained 270 pages and had a paid circulation of 223,077 copies. Skin Diver was to become the longest-lived diving publication in the world (51 years) until its last issue in November, 2002. The longest established diving publication in North America still in print is Canada's Diver Magazine (est. March 1975 under the name *Pacific Diver*). In 2006, over 100 diving magazines were published around the world in several languages.

Today, the diving publishing industry is composed of large publishers, small companies and self-publishers that put out a steady number of new book titles every year, ranging from specialty items on underwater photography and technical diving, to coffee table books containing award-winning photos from around the world.

DVDs sales are also flourishing as more and more divers produce their own films on marine biology, wreck diving, history, training and travel.

DIVE TRAVEL

Dive travel has established itself as a major staple of the tourism industry. The industry began to take hold in the 1960s in Florida and the Caribbean. Today, resorts and liveaboards offer diving venues on every ocean and major bodies of water in the world. Much information is available on the Internet where divers can plan trips based on the type of diving (sport, technical, rebreather, expedition, etc.), or other considerations (gay & lesbian, singles, etc.).

DIVING TIMELINE

While researching historical data for the following timeline, several discrepancies were found with names, dates and places. If you find errors or if you would like to suggest historical events that we have missed, please contact us so that we may further research historical items prior to printing the next edition: **info@divingalmanac.com**

ANTIQUITY

4000- 4500 B.C.
Seaside communities in many parts of the world, including the Mediterranean, the Middle-East, Asia and the Pacific, dive for sustenance and to conduct war.

1194 B.C.
Homer tells of divers attacking ships during the Trojan War in the Iliad.

500 B.C.
Herodotus tells of Cyana and her father Scyllias, a pair of divers who recovered sunken treasure for the Persian King Xerxes. When he refused to let them return home, they cut the anchor ropes of the entire Persian fleet under the cover of darkness and fled to aid the Greeks.

DIVING EQUIPMENT

332 B.C.
Aristotle describes a diving bell in his *Problematum*. The bell has an open bottom and is lowered upright into the water. It is used by sponge divers in the Aegean. It is also used by Alexander the Great during the siege of Tyre in 332 B.C.

The diving bell was by far the most used method of diving for the next 21 centuries.

Original drawing from Da Vinci's *Codex Arundel*

Circa 1500
Leonardo Da Vinci designs a diving-suit and flexible snorkel system for breathing at depth. The snorkel was made of cane tubes joined by pig leather and reinforced with steel rings to counteract the effects of water pressure. The system was successfully tested in shallow water in the

Venetian Lagoon by Jacquie Cozens in 2003 for BBC's *Leonardo's Amazing Inventions*. Da Vinci also developed the first-known self-contained diving system using a leather wineskin to hold air and a urination bottle within the suit for prolonged immersions. The drawings appear in his *Codex Arundel*[9]. There is no evidence that the apparatus was ever built.

1535
Italian Guglielmo de Lorena successfully uses a diving bell equipped with a glass port to recover Caligula's pleasure galleys in Lake Nemi.

An early diving device used by 16th century divers during salvage operations. Photo: OAR/National Undersea Research Program (NURP)

1551
Nicholas Tartaglia builds a bell device resembling a weighted hour glass. The entire air supply was contained in a small dome at the top which made the design impractical. Al Giddings had a replica built which was tested by Pete Romano to a maximum depth of 30 ft (9 m).

---

[9] Codex Arundel is a collection of Da Vinci's papers put together by Lord Arundel (1630) including descriptions of sea-monsters and designs for a submarine and underwater breathing apparatus.

1597
Lorini describes a square diving bell made of wood and bound with iron bands. The bell also has glass ports to enable the diver to scout his surroundings.

1616
German inventor Kessler designs an unstable diving bell with glass ports.

1620
Lord Francis Bacon describes a diving bell made of metal in *Novum Organum* used to recover items from submerged vessels.

1626
A Spanish salvage operation in the Florida Keys locates the wreck of the *Santa Margarita* (sunk in 1622) using a bronze diving bell with glass view ports at a depth of 25 ft (8 m). They also discover that Native Americans have already salvaged part of the treasure, an indication that the natives have some knowledge of diving. Nine natives are hired by the Spanish in 1628 when they are found to be better divers than the Europeans.

Circa 1640
American Edward Bendall builds two wooden diving bells to salvage the wreck of the *Mary Rose* off Charlestown, England.

1650s
The first air pump for diving is developed by German physicist Otto Von Guericke.

1667
The diving bell is now being used at greater depths. It is still open at the bottom and kept down by weights. Divers can exit the bell and return for air until it becomes unbreathable.

1680
Physicist Giovanni Borelli unsuccessfully attempts to recycle his own breathing air. Borelli also designs claw-like footwear to enable the diver to pull himself along the bottom with his feet. Despite the fact that the footwear was not designed for swimming, Borelli is credited by some to be the inventor of swim fins.

1687
William Phips' salvage of a Spanish galleon using a diving bell off San Domingo earns him a knighthood and eventually makes him High Sheriff of New England. Phips unsuccessfully tries to take the city of Quebec (New France) in 1690. The remains of one of his ships, the *Elizabeth & Mary*, are discovered in the St. Lawrence Estuary at depth of 10 ft (3 m) by diver Marc Tremblay in 1994.

Physicist Giovanni Borelli - Photo: OAR / National Undersea Research Program (NURP)

1689
French physicist Denis Papin designs but never builds a surface-supplied diving bell.

1690
English astronomer Edmond Halley - of Halley's Comet fame - improves the diving bell. Additional air is available in weighted barrels connected to the diving bell to replenish the air supply. Dives of 90 minutes to depths of 60 ft (18 m) are recorded. An improved version later allows Halley to stay immersed for over 4 hours.

1715
A fully enclosed diving 'machine' is developed by Englishman John Lethbridge. The Lethbridge Diving Machine consists of a leather-covered barrel of air with a glass porthole and two watertight sleeves. Di-

vers can thus use their arms for salvage work. An air pipe connected to the barrel supplies it with compressed air.

Lethbridge Diving Machine (1715). Photo: OAR/National Undersea Research Program (NURP); Smithsonian Institution

1715
English inventor Andrew Becker also develops a leather diving suit complete with metal helmet and window. The helmet has three tubes for air to enter and exit. The air is pumped into two of the tubes from the surface.

1720
Jacob Rowe designs a diving barrel of his own which is successfully used to salvage a wreck off the Cape Verdes.

1771
French inventor Freminet makes a helmet out of brass. Air is pumped into the helmet from the surface. He dies in 1772 after breathing untreated exhaled air.

1773
American Benjamin Franklin recalls the use of wooden fins in his youth.

> When I was a boy, I made two oval palettes, each about ten inches long and six broad, with a hole for the thumb, in order to retain it fast in the palm of my hand. They much resembled a painter's palette. In swimming, I pushed the edges of these forward, and I struck the wa-

ter with their flat surfaces as I drew them back. I remember I swam faster by means of these palettes, but they fatigued my wrists. I also fitted to the soles of my feet a kind of sandals; but I was not satisfied with them, because I observed that the stroke is partly given by the inside of the feet and the ankles, and not entirely by the soles.

1775
Scottish inventor Charles Spalding builds a wooden bell that can be maneuvered by its occupants. The air supply is based on Halley's barrel system.

1786
Freminet's helmet is improved by other inventors including Englishmen John and William Braithwaite and German Karl Heinrich Klingert in 1787.

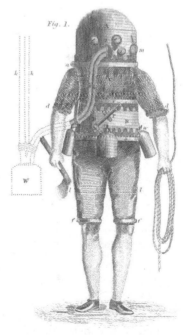

Klingert diving apparatus tested in the Oder River in 1787. (Original Plan)

1788
Major improvements to the diving bell are made by American John Smeaton. The biggest change is the cast-iron bell, a hand-operated pump for the supply of fresh compressed air, and the air reservoir system with non-return valves which keep the air from going back up the hoses.

Early 1800s
Inventors try to find ways to get air to the diver without being connected to the surface. In 1825 a device is created by Englishman William James. His invention consists of a container of air which is tied to the diver's waist. American Charles Condert builds a similar device but dies during testing. Other inventers in the early 1800s include English brothers Charles Anthony and John Deane and Englishman William H. James.

1808
German mathematician Friedrich von Drieberg (1780-1856) develops the 'Triton' apparatus which consists of an air reservoir worn by the diver. The system is not self-sufficient since the reservoir is supplied by surface hoses. To breath air from the reservoir, the diver operates a valve by nodding his head.

1812
British engineer James Rennie designs a surface-supplied rectangular diving bell made of cast-iron equipped with 12 glass ports. The air hose feeding the bell is equipped with a leather non-return valve to prevent the air from escaping and water from entering the bell should the hose rupture.

1823
A fire-fighting helmet and air supply system are modified for use underwater. The helmet is held in place with weights and air is supplied from the surface. This invention by Englishmen Charles and John Deane is used in salvage work but limits the diver's movements as it is not connected to the suit. Should the diver not remain in an upright position, he is at risk of drowning. In time, the helmet is sealed to the suit by German inventor Augustus

Siebe. The Deanes run a successful salvage operation and are later credited with producing the first diving manual.

1825
The first successful self-contained underwater breathing apparatus is designed by Englishman William James. The limited supply of slightly compressed air is worn around the waist in a cast-iron belt.

1828
Lemaire d'Augerville designs a swimming belt that enables divers to control their buoyancy.

1829
Russian E.K. Gauzen, designs a surface-supplied helmet strapped to a full-body leather suit. Gauzen's design and later modifications were used by the Russian Navy for more than 50 years. The final version of Gauzen's invention was known as the three-bolt suit.

1831
A self-contained system consisting of an air-filled copper pipe worn around the body is developed by American engineer, Charles Condert. He drowns in the East River (Brooklyn, New York) in August 1832.

1836
John and Charles Deane publish the first diving manual.

1837
Deane's diving suit is further improved by German inventor Augustus Siebe. The watertight diving suit with the helmet now sealed to it revolutionizes diving enabling safer dives to greater depths. Siebe comes to be known as the father of diving.

1839
Siebe's improved diving suit becomes the standard diving dress of the British Navy and is used for salvage work. The British warship HMS *Royal George* is salvaged by divers working as a team. Symptoms of decompression sickness are recorded for the first time during the salvage operation.

1864
Frenchmen Benoit Rouquayrol and Auguste Denayrouze improve Siebe's design. Now the diver can detach himself from the hose and breathe from an air reservoir equipped with a demand valve for brief periods.

French engineer Ernest Bazin develops the first underwater electric lights.

1865
An apparatus for underwater breathing is designed by Frenchmen Benoit Rouquayrol and Auguste Denayrouze. A tank of compressed air is carried on the diver's back and equiped with a valve connected to a mouthpiece. Called the 'Aerophore', it is the first demand regulator and delivers air only when the diver inhales.

Rouquayrol & Denayrouze Aérophore (1865)

1867
Auguste Denayrouze replaces the Aerophore helmet with a three-bolt hardhat.

1872
French engineer Ernest Bazin develops a closed underwater observatory equipped with electric lighting. It is used successfully during the salvage operation in Vigo Bay.

1876
Englishman Henry Fleuss designs a closed-circuit rebreather that uses pure compressed oxygen instead of compressed air. The unit is used in air and for brief periods underwater. His design is later commercialized by Siebe Gorman.

Denayrouze three-bolt helmet (1867). Photo: David Dekker - www.pieds-lourds.com

1892
Frenchman Louis Boutan, a pioneer of underwater photography, develops a closed-circuit diving system good for three hours at shallow depths.

1909
Draeger, a German manufacturer, develops a self-contained diving system which connects a helmet to a compressed gas cylinder.

1911
A diving oxygen rebreather is developed by Draeger of Germany. The design is based on a previous model used for mine rescue.

Sir Robert Davis improves the Fleuss system by developing the Davis False Lung. The self-contained rebreather is used by several nations as an escape device for submarine crews.

1912
Westfalia Maschinenfabrik of Germany manufactures a diving apparatus which combines scuba and surface-fed devices using mixed gas.

The Davis Submersible Decompression Chamber (SDC) is developed by Sir Robert Davis.

1914
An oxygen rebreather is invented by Sir Robert Davis. This rebreather called the 'Submarine Escape Apparatus' is used to escape from sunken submarines.

ogy capable of attaining depths up to 130 ft (40 m).

The MK V diving helmet is introduced by the U.S. Bureau of Construction & Repair. It becomes the standard for the U.S. Navy until replaced by the MK 12 in 1980.

1918
The Ohgushi Peerless Respirator, an air supply cylinder carried on the back of the diver is developed by Japanese Ohgushi. Air flow into the mask is controlled with the diver's teeth. The device was successfully tested to 324 ft (99 m).

1919
C. J. Cooke develops Heliox, a gas mixture of helium and oxygen for use by divers. This invention greatly extends the depth range of divers while reducing the risk of nitrogen narcosis.

1925
Frenchman Yves Le Prieur introduces a 150-bar (2,176 PSI) self-contained underwater breathing unit. The Fernez/Le Prieur diving system supplies air from a cylinder to a full-face mask.

MK V dive helmet. Photo: D.A.Y.

Draeger rebreather (1909).
Photos: David Dekker - www.pieds-lourds.com

1917
Draeger markets a self-contained system combining tanks and rebreather technol-

1927
The combined weight of the MK V helmet and breastplate are reduced to 56 lbs (25 kg).

1930
American Guy Gilpatrick develops the first pair of diving goggles to explore the Mediterranean off the coast of France.

1933
A demand valve with a high-pressure air tank that eliminates hose connections to the surface is developed by Yves Le Prieur.

1935
Broadbladed swim fins are patented by Frenchman Louis de Corlieu.

1937
A diving suit with a self-contained mixed-gas helium and oxygen rebreather is developed by The American Diving Equipment and Salvage Company (now known as DESCO). Max Nohl sets a world record dive to 420 ft (128 m) while using the system in Lake Michigan.

A two-cylinder open-circuit apparatus with demand regulator is developed by Georges Commeinhes for use by the French Navy. WWII impedes its development and Commeninhes dies in 1944. The system is showcased in a pool at the Paris International Exposition.

Danish-American Niels Christensen invents the o-ring to seal hydraulic equipment.

1938
The Mousquemers (Cousteau, Dumas & Tailliez) begin diving with a single-glass dive mask, the 'monogoggle.'

While serving in Indochina in 1951, Tailliez observes Vietnamese divers using a single-glass dive mask with skirt made of buffalo skin. It is based on an earlier Chinese model used by climbers collecting sparrow nests. Both designs likely preceded the 1938 monogoggle.

1939
The first rebreathing device to be called SCUBA is designed by Dr. Christian Lambertsen in the USA.

1940
Swim fins made of vulcanized rubber are hand-made by Owen Churchill.

1943
The first scuba incorporating an automatic demand valve to release air as the diver inhales is developed by Jacques Cousteau and Émile Gagnan. The 'Aqua-Lung' is born and it revolutionizes the diving world. Initial testing of the equipment in January in the Marne River ends in failure. The system is then modified by Gagnan and successfully used for the first time in a tank several weeks later. Its first use in a natural environment takes place in the Mediterranean Sea during the summer. Frédéric Dumas dives to the depth of 210 ft (64 m) in October, 1943.

1946
Jacques-Yves Cousteau patents the first constant volume drysuit.

1947
Jordan Klein founds Marine Enterprises, Inc., a manufacturer of spear guns and housings for underwater cameras.

1948
The first Aqua-Lung regulators are imported to the USA by Rene Bussoz.

Canadian production of the Aqua-Lung begins in Montréal, Québec after Émile Gagnan emigrates to Canada.

Jacques-Yves Cousteau develops the first DPV (Diver Propulsion Vehicle) for combat divers.

Early 1950s
Gustav dalla Valle imports diving equipment manufactured by Italian Eduardo Cressi to the United States.

1950
The first neoprene wetsuit is introduced in the United States by Hugh Bradner at Lake Tahoe.

1951
The Reserve Valve commonly known as J valve is developed. This valve allows the

diver access to the last 500 psi of air in the tank as he comes to the surface.

E. R. Cross designs the 'Sport Diver,' one of the earliest single-hose regulators developed in the United States.

1952
The U.S. Navy Emerson-Lambertsen closed-circuit oxygen rebreather is developed.

1953
California-based U.S. Divers is founded by *La Spirotechnique*, a subsidiary of *Air Liquide* and manufacturer of the Aqua-Lung.

1954
The prototype Mark V semi-closed circuit mixed-gas rebreather is developed.

1955
Dacor founder Sam Davison, Jr. designs the Dial-A-Breath, a two-hose, double-diaphragm regulator, that includes a low-pressure reserve and variable breathing resistance.

1956
Other types of breathing equipment are developed by Submarine Products Ltd in Northumberland, England.

The red and white Divers Down flag is introduced by Ted Nixon.

Jordan Klein (Marine Enterprises) begins manufacturing compressors under the MAKO name.

1958
Sherwood markets the first piston regulator.

Sam LeCocq of Sportsways designs the Waterlung, the first single-hose regulator widely used in the United States.

1961
Ed Replogle develops an audible alarm that warns a diver of low air pressure.

Maurice Fenzy patents a device invented by the underwater research group of the French navy. The device includes an inflatable bag with a small attached cylinder of compressed air. It rapidly becomes the first commercially successful buoyancy compensator. Within a few years, divers throughout Europe, and a few well-traveled Americans, are wearing Fenzys.

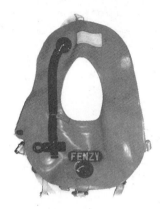

Fenzy buoyancy compensator. Photo: D.A.Y.

1968
Walter Starck develps the Electrolung, the first rebreather with electronic parts.

1971
The stabilization jacket (BCD) is introduced by Scubapro.

1972
Captain Don Stewart of Bonaire develops the concept of sea tethers, concrete blocks and lines known today as mooring buoys. The device is meant to protect reefs from anchor damage.

1979
Dr. Phil Nuytten begins work on a revolutionary one-atmosphere diving suit that results in a patented breakthrough in rotary joint design, and forms the basis for the world-famous *Newtsuit*. The *Newtsuit* is rated to 1,000 ft (300 m) and it completely protects the wearer from outside pressure and eliminates the need for decompression while still maintaining mobility and dexterity. It is now standard equipment in many of the world's navies.

Draeger version of Newtsuit 2000

1980
Optical fiber technology is used by scientist Dr. Robert Ballard to transmit video footage in real time to the surface.

1983
Orca markets the first dive computer (Orca Edge) for recreational divers. The computer is developed by Craig Barshinger and Carl Huggins.

1997
Nuytco produces the two thousand foot-rated micro-submersible *DeepWorker 2000*.

2000
Nuytco produces an ultra light weight, swimming hard suit called the 'Exosuit'.

DECOMPRESSION & DEPTH

1839
Symptoms of decompression sickness are recorded for the first time during the salvage operation of HMS *Royal George*.

1860s
English physicist, Robert Boyle, studies compression and decompression in animals. A gas bubble is observed in the eye of a snake after decompression. This observation is the beginning of studies in decompression sickness.

1869-1883
Several divers working on the Brooklyn Bridge in New York are crippled by 'caisson disease' which reporters dub as 'the bends' due to the signs of the illness.

1873
Dr. Andrew H. Smith recommends chamber recompression after workers suffer from the bends while working underwater on the Brooklyn Bridge.

1878
A study entitled *La Pression Barométrique* is published by Paul Bert. This study on pressure changes details decompression sickness caused by the formation of nitrogen gas bubbles in the body. He suggests gradual ascent to prevent decompression sickness.

1908
A paper on decompression sickness, *The Prevention of Compressed-Air Illness*, is published by John Haldane, Arthur Boycott, and Guybon Damant. This lays the foundation for further studies and, as a result, decompression tables from this research are adopted by the British Navy and later the United States Navy.

1912
The U.S. Navy tests decompression tables published by Haldane, Boycott and Damant.

Sir Robert Davis develops the *Davis Submersible Decompression Chamber* (DSDC).

1915
U.S. Navy Chief Gunner's Mate Frank W. Crilley dives to over 300 ft (91 m) during the salvage of the submarine *F-4* (SS-23) off Honolulu, Hawaii.

1924
Experimental dives using helium-oxygen mixtures are jointly sponsored by the U.S. NAVY and Bureau of Mines.

1925
The U.S. NAVY Air Decompression Tables are developed by EDU and become the accepted world standard.

1937
American Max Nohl sets a world record dive to 420 ft (128 m) in Lake Michigan using a self-contained mixed-gas helium and oxygen rebreather.

Charles B. Momsen and Karl R. Wheland of the U.S. Navy's Experimental Diving Unit (NEDU)) make a simulated dive to 500 ft (152 m) breathing a helium-oxygen mixture.

1938
Edgar End and Max Nohl make the first intentional saturation dive. They spend a total of 27 hours at a simulated depth of 101 ft (31 m) in a Milwaukee hyperbaric chamber. Nohl subsequently suffers the bends despite a five-hour decompression period.

1943
Frenchman Frédéric Dumas dives to 210 ft (64 m) using the newly-invented Aqua-Lung.

1945
Arne Zetterström dives to 525 ft (160 m) in the Baltic Sea breathing a hydrogen mixture. He dies during decompression.

1948
Frédéric Dumas dives to 307 ft (64 m) using the Aqua-Lung.

Wilfred Bollard (Royal Navy) dives to 540 ft (165 m) in Scotland's Loch Fyne breathing a helium-oxygen mixture. He dies during decompression.

1954
Zale Parry makes a record dive to 209 ft (64 m) near Catalina Island, California.

1956
The USN Standard Decompression Tables are published by NEDU.

A Royal Navy diver reaches 600 ft (183 m) using a helium-oxygen mix.

1957-62
U.S. Navy Genesis Project sets standards for saturation diving and eventually leads to the SeaLab habitat programs.

1961
Swiss Hannes Keller and Kenneth MacLeish dive to 728 ft (222 m) in Lake Maggiore, Switzerland.

1962
The first practical saturation dive takes place in Edward A. Link's Man-in-the-Sea program. A diver breathing helium-oxygen at 200 ft (61 m) stays under for 24 hours in a specially designed diving system.

1967
The Undersea Medical Society (now known as the Undersea and Hyperbaric Medical Society, UHMS) is founded in Maryland.

1968
Record dive to 1,025 ft (312 m) is made from a saturation depth of 825 ft (251 m) by NEDU in a joint venture with Duke University.

Early 1970s
The Office of Naval Research (ONR) conducts experiments simulating dives to depths between 1200-1600 ft (366-488 m). Along with respiratory-circulatory and neurological studies. The mental, visual and auditory functions of the divers are also measured. World record dive to 850 ft

(259 m) using the DDS MK-1 Deep Diving System.

1972
World record dive to 1,010 ft (308 m) using the DDS MK-2 Deep Diving System.

COMEX[10] divers make a simulated dive to 2,001 ft (610 m).

1975
Depths of 1,148 ft (350 m) are reached using the MK 1 Deep Dive System.

1977
COMEX divers make an open-water dive to 1,644 ft (501 m).

Diver undergoes deep diving tests. Photo. U.S. Navy.

1979
NEDU divers complete a 37-day, 1,800 ft (549 m) dive in the Ocean Simulation Facility.

1980
Divers at Duke University Medical Center make a simulated dive to 2,132 ft (650 m) breathing a helium-oxygen-nitrogen mixture.

1981
A British dive team conducts the deepest ever diver-assisted salvage operation by recovering 431 gold ingots from the wreck of HMS *Edinburgh*, which sank at a depth

of 803 ft (245 m) during World War II off Norway.

1988
COMEX divers make an open-water dive to 1,752 ft (534 m) off Marseille, France, breathing a helium-oxygen-nitrogen mixture.

1992
COMEX divers make a simulated dive to 2,300 ft (701 m) breathing a helium-oxygen-nitrogen mixture

2005
Frenchman Pascal Bernabé dives to 1,083 ft (330 m) on open-circuit scuba.

See section on *Diving Records and Aquatic Superlatives* for complete listing and details of depth records.

MODERN FREEDIVING

Freediving history contains only milestone records and important events.

1911
Greek fisherman Yorgos Haggi Statti dives more than 200 ft (60.96 m) to help salvage the anchor of an Italian ship in the Aegean Sea.

1949
Raymondo Bucher (Italy) reaches the depth of 98 ft (29.87 m) in the Bay of Syracuse using a weighted speargun.

1951
Ennio Falco (Italy) is the first to freedive beyond 100 ft (30.48 m) when he reaches the depth of 115 ft (35.05 m) off Napoli, Italy.

1960
Americo Santarelli (Brazil) is the first to dive beyond 150 ft (45.72 m) when reaches the depth of 151 ft (46.02 m) off Santa Margherita Ligure, Italy.

1966
Enzo Majorca (Italy) is the first to pass 200 ft (60.96 m) when he reaches the depth of 203 ft (61.87 m) off Syracuze, Italy.

---

[10] COMEX - *Compagnie maritime d'expertises* (Marseille, France) - www.comex.fr

1975
Jacques Mayol (France) is the first to freedive beyond 300 ft (91.44 m) when he reaches the depth of 302 ft (92.05 m) off the island of Elba, Italy.

1989
Angela Bandini (Italy) surpasses even the men when she is the first to freedive beyond 350 ft (91.44 m) by reaching the depth of 351 ft (107 m) off the island of Elba, Italy.

1992
Establishment of AIDA (International Association for the Development of Freediving), an international body that oversees the recognition of records and organizes competitions. AIDA International has since officiated over 165 world records. (aida-international.org)

1993
Umberto Pelizzari (Italy) is the first to freedive beyond 400 ft (121.92 m) when he reaches the depth of 404 ft (123.14 m) off Montecristo, Italy.

Loïc Leferme – First freediver to go beyond 500 ft (152.40 m). Photo: Franck Seguin Deadline / Press Agency / www.deadline-press.com

2000
Loïc Leferme (France) is the first to freedive beyond 500 ft (152.40 m) when he reaches the depth of 505.25 ft (154 m) off Saint-Jean Cap Ferrat, France.

2000
Francisco "Pipin" Ferreras (U.S.A.) crushes all previous records by reaching the depth of 528.22 ft (161 m) off Cabo San Lucas, Mexico. (Not recognized by AIDA)

2002
Tanya Streeter (U.S.A.) beats the women's and men's records (AIDA) by reaching the depth of 525 ft (160 m) off Providenciales, Turks and Caicos.

Audrey Mestre (France) dies while ascending from a depth of 561 ft (171 m) off La Romana, Dominican Republic.

2003
Francisco "Pipin" Ferreras (U.S.A.) reaches the depth of 557.74 ft (170 m) off Cabo San Lucas, Mexico. (Record not recognized by AIDA)

2005
Patrick Musimu (Belgium) is the first to freedive beyond 600 ft (182.88 m) when he reaches the depth of 687.66 ft (209.6 m) off the coast of Egypt. (Record not recognized by AIDA)

Herbert Nitsch – Current AIDA No Limit record holder 600.39 ft (183 m). Photo courtesy Harald Lautner / www.freediving.at

2006
Herbert Nitsch (Austria) sets the last No Limit AIDA record before the Diving Almanac & Yearbook goes to press, by reaching the depth of 600.39 ft (183 m) off the coast of Croatia in August.

SUBMARINES
& SUBMERSIBLES

1570s
William Bourne, an English mathematician draws the first plans for an underwater boat powered by oars.

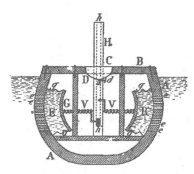

Bourne original drawing.

1620s
Dutch physician Cornelis Drebbel builds the first submarine made of wood reinforced with iron and leather. Like Bourne's earlier design, it is oared from the inside by a 12-man crew. The sub was operated successfully in the Thames River at depths of up to 15 ft (4.6 m).

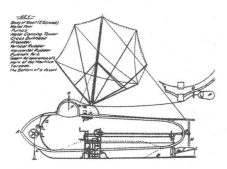

From original plans for Robert Fulton's *Nautilus* (1798)

1775
American David Bushnell builds the first submarine ever used in combat. The *Turtle* is used unsuccessfully against British ships blockading New York Harbor.

Bushnell's *Turtle* used in attempts to bore holes and insert time-delay explosives into British ships in 1776. Image: OAR/National Undersea Research Program (NURP)

1800
A submarine, the *Nautilus*, is built by Robert Fulton, inventor of the steamboat.

1856
Wilhelm Bauer successfully dives aboard his second submarine, the *Seeteufel*.

1900
John P. Holland designs a submarine for the U.S. Navy.

Crewman exits the USS *Narwhal*'s escape hatch wearing the "Momsen Lung" emergency escape breathing device during sea trials in July, 1930. Photo: U.S. Navy

1929
An escape lung is developed by submariner and diver, Lieutenant C.B. "Swede"

Momsen. It is tested with success to bring 26 seamen to the surface from a bottomed submarine.

1932
The bathysphere, a round steel craft with several windows that is lowered by cable into the sea, is developed by Americans William Beebe and Otis Barton. In 1934 they successfully submerge to 3,028 ft (923 m) and set a world record.

1939
The McCann-Erickson Rescue Chamber is used to rescue 33 men from the USS *Squalus* that sank at a depth of 243 ft (74 m).

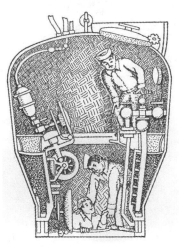

McCann-Erickson Rescue Chamber cutaway drawing of the device used to rescue 33 crewmen from the sunken submarine *Squalus'* (SS-192) in May 1939. Image: U.S. NAVY / U.S. Naval Historical Center.

1947
German prisoner of war Heinz Sellner claims to have escaped from a prison camp in Murmansk by building a submersible buoyed by gas. During his successful escape, Sellner claims to have reached a depth of 7,874 ft (2,400 m). In 1951, Sellner, Philippe Taillez, Jacques-Yves Cousteau and Canadian Paul Thuot begin construction of *Aquarius* based on Sellner's design. The first test of the submersible ends in failure in 1959. The project is never completed until it is finally abandoned in 1971. Sellner dies in 1960 taking with him his unproven record.

1948
Otis Barton reaches 4,500 ft (1,372 m) in a modified bathysphere.

1950
Swiss scientist August Piccard, a record-setting balloonist, and his son Jacques design the bathyscaph.

1954
A manned bathyscaph reaches a depth of 13,287 ft (4,050 m) breaking Barton's 1948 record.

1958
USS *Nautilus* nuclear-powered submarine cruises below the ice at the North Pole.

1959
Jacques-Yves Cousteau launches the *DS-2* (Diving Saucer), also known as *Denise* and *La Soucoupe*. The *DS-2* is propelled by two water jets and can carry two passengers to depths reaching 1,000 ft (305 m). Its cruising speed is one knot.

Cousteau's *DS-1* (a.k.a. *Denise*) is lowered into the Pacific Ocean off the coast of California in 1964. Photo: U.S. Navy

1960
Jacques Piccard and Lieutenant Don Walsh (USN) reach the deepest known point in the ocean aboard the bathyscaph *Trieste*.

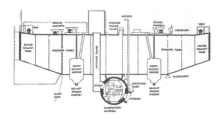

General arrangement drawing of the *Trieste*. The two occupants take place in the sphere at the bottom center of the illustration. Image: U.S. Naval Historical Center

USS *Triton* circumnavigates the world entirely underwater.

1962
Hannes Keller and Peter Small dive to 1,000 ft (305 m) in a diving bell off Santa Catalina Island, California. Small dies during decompression.

1963
USS *Thresher* (SSN-593) nuclear-powered submarine is lost with all hands at a depth of 8,400 ft (2,560 m) about 220 miles (354 km) east of Boston. Photographs taken by the USN bathyscaph prove that *Thresher* broke up after sinking beyond its crushing point.

Photo mosaic of sail and other debris from the USS *Thresher* taken by the bathyscaph. Photo: U.S. Navy

1964
The Deep Submergence Systems Project (DSSP) is created.

Jacques-Yves Cousteau launches the *Sea Fleas*. Like the *DS-2 Diving Saucer*, the *Sea Fleas* are propelled by two water jets and can carry their single passenger to depths reaching 1,640 ft (500 m).

1979
American explorer Sylvia Earle walks untethered on the sea floor at the depth of 1,250 ft (381 m) in a *Jim Suit* for two-and-a-half hours.

1985
Dr. Robert Ballard uses an ROV to discover the wreck of the RMS *Titanic* which lies at a depth of 12,460 ft (3,798 m) off the coast of Newfoundland.

Dr. Sylvia Earle prepares to dive in a *Jim Suit*. Photo: OAR/National Undersea Research Program (NURP)

HABITATS

1960s
Experiments are conducted with people living in underwater habitats from which they can leave for sea exploration using scuba equipment.

1962
Conshelf I: Cousteau divers Albert Falco and Claude Wesley spend seven days at the depth of 33 ft (10 m) in the *Diogenes* habitat near Marseilles, France.

1962
Man in the Sea: Ed A. Link spends 24 hours at 200 ft (61 m) breathing a heliox mixture. The *Floating Instrument Platform* (FLIP), a 355-ft (108 m) long floating oceanographic instrument platform goes on its first assignment. The platform is towed by

a ship to the research site in a horizontal position and then its ballast tanks are flooded to make it tilt to an upright position. All but 55 ft (17 m) of its length disappears below the water. FLIP is used for research by the Scripps Institution of Oceanography.

The **Floating Instrument Platform (FLIP)**. Photo: U.S. Navy.

1963

Conshelf II: Two underwater habitats are lowered into the Red Sea where 8 Cousteau aquanauts live for one month. The larger habitat houses 6 divers at 33 ft (10 m) while the second structure is used by 2 divers at 82 ft (25 m).

1964

Sealab I: Four aquanauts man the habitat for 11 days at the depth of 193 ft (59 m).

1965

Conshelf I: Six Cousteau aquanauts spend 27 days at the depth of 328 ft (100 m) off Nice, France.

1965

Sealab II: Three teams of ten men spend 15 days at the depth of 205 ft (62 m). Scott Carpenter remains below for 30 days and makes radio contact with fellow astronaut Gordon Cooper orbiting the earth in a Gemini spacecraft. A dolphin named Tuffy ferries supplies from the surface.

1967

The *L.S.-1 Underwater Laboratory* is launched in Lake Bicaz, Romania. It is operated by the Salmo Ecological Diver Association (APES) of A.I. Cuza University.

It is fixed to a mobile platform and can be positioned at desired depths above or below thermoclines to study captive fish behaviour for aquaculture.

Aquanauts emerge from Tektite I in 1969. Photo: OAR/National Undersea Research Program (NURP)

1969

Tektite I: Four Scientists under the direction of the Office of Naval Research spend 60 days at a depth of 50 ft (15 m) in Lameshur Bay, U.S. Virgin Islands.

1969

Sealab III ends tragically with the death of diver Berry Cannon at 610 ft (185 m) off San Clemente Island, California. Cannon is killed while making repairs to a leak during an early test dive. No new habitats are built by the U.S. Navy.

Tektite II all female team in crews quarters, including Sylvia Earle (2nd from left). Photo: OAR / National Undersea Research Program (NURP)

1970

Tektite II: Ten missions coordinated by the Department of the Interior and lasting 10-20 days with four scientists and an engineer on each mission. Dr. Sylvia Earle leads an all-female two-week research expedition at a depth of 42 ft (13 m).

1971

USN divers using SeaLab techniques successfully retrieve Soviet test missiles. The divers are deployed from a submarine – USS *Halibut* – which carries a pressure chamber in the Sea of Okhotsk. They also tap several underwater communications cables (Operation Ivy Bells) that run from the Soviet submarine base at Petropavlovsk to Fleet headquarters near Vladivostok.

1971

The research habitat *La Chalupa* becomes operational off Puerto Rico. It is operated by the Marine Resources Development Foundation.

1984

The *MarineLab Undersea Laboratory*, operated by the Marine Resources Development Foundation, becomes operational at a depth of 27 ft (8.23 m) off Key Largo, Florida.

Marine Resources Development Foundation Lab entry lock is an acrylic sphere. Photo: OAR / National Undersea Research Program (NURP); Marine Resources Development Foundation

1986

The *Aquarius* underwater habitat devoted to scientific research becomes operational off St-Croix in the U.S. Virgin Islands.

In the *Aquarius* main lock looking aft towards the entry lock. Photo: OAR / National Undersea Research Program (NURP); Univ. of North Carolina at Wilmington

1986

The research habitat *La Chalupa*, operated by the Marine Resources Development Foundation, is transformed into the world's first underwater hotel, *Jules Undersea Lodge*, in the Key Largo Undersea Park (Florida). The habitat can accommodate up to 6 guests at a depth of 21 ft (6.4 m). (www.jul.com)

1993

The *Aquarius* is relocated off the Florida coast.

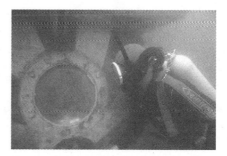

Aquanaut Constantin Mihaï peers into the L.S.-1 Underwater Laboratory in Lake Bicaz, Romania. Photo: J. Gallant / D.A.Y.

1994

Romanian aquanauts Liviu Miron and Constantin Mihaï set the European record for the longest uninterrupted stay in an underwater habitat by living in the *L.S.-1 Underwater Laboratory* (Lake Bicaz) for 36 days.

2007
Currently in the final design stages, the *Poseidon Undersea Resort* is also vying to become the world's first seafloor luxury resort complex. The resort will be a unique, intimate and exclusive, five-star destina-tion providing the highest possible levels of luxury and service. The earliest antici-pated opening date is late 2007. (www.poseidonresorts.com)

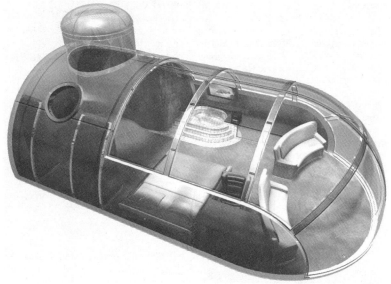

artist concept ©2005 by chris huf. contact: spatial@huf.org

Room of the Poseidon Undersea Resort. Image © Chris Huf / www.huf.org

DIVING FOR TREASURE

vage treasure from the Spanish fleet of 1715 off the coast of Florida.

500
Earliest records of diving for treasure go back to Persian King Xerces during the Persian Greek wars.

1685
A diving bell is used by *Sir William Phips* to recover treasure from the wreck of the Spanish galleon *La Nuestra Senora de Almiranta* in the West Indies.

1964
Universal Salvors (later known as Treasure Salvors,) Mel and Deo Fisher, Rupert Gates, Demosthenes "Mo" Molinar, Dick Williams, Walt Holzworth, Arnold McLean, and Fay Field work alongside Kip Wagner to sal-

1968
Mel Fisher discovers several wrecks from the 1733 fleet during his search for the *Nuestra Señora de Atocha.*

1970
Kip Wagner's salvage of the 1715 Fleet off Vero Beach, Florida, reaches an estimated $6,500,000 USD in coins, jewellery and pre-cious metals.

1985
Mel Fisher finds the cargo of the 1622 wreck *Nuestra Señora de Atocha* which contains an estimated $400 million in gold, silver and emeralds.

1988
Tommy Thompson and the Central America Discovery Group find the wreck of the SS *Central America* at a depth of 8,500 ft (2,591 m) off the Carolina coast. The vessel was carrying 21 tons of gold estimated today at one billion dollars when it sank in a hurricane in 1857.

2002
Florida-based Odyssey Marine Exploration identifies the wreck of the HMS *Sussex* which sank in a storm off the Straits of Gibraltar in 1694. When the 80-gun warship went down it took all but two of the 500-man crew and the equivalent of nine tons of gold coins, worth $4.54 billion USD in 2006. Salvage operations by Florida-based Odyssey Marine Exploration are currently underway.

MILITARY

1834
Royal Navy divers recover canons from the wreck of the HMS *Royal George* at a depth of 65 ft (20 m).

1843
The first diving school is established by the Royal Navy.

1912
The U.S. Navy tests decompression tables published by Haldane, Boycott and Damant.

1915
U.S. Navy divers using the MK V system salvage the submarine USS *F-4* at a depth of 304 ft (93 m).

1916
The U.S. Navy Dive School is established at Newport, Rhode Island.

1917
The MK V helmet and dress becomes the standard helmet diving system for the U.S. Navy till 1985.

1927
The Navy School of Diving & Salvage (a.k.a. Navy Deep Sea Diving School) and the Experimental Diving Unit are relocated to the Washington Navy Yard.

1936
The Italian Navy develops a diver-operated torpedo system.

1939-1945
Italian divers use midget submarines and rebreathers to place explosive charges under British warships. The British also use similar devices to try to sink the German battleship *Tirpitz*.

1942
The Naval Training School is established in New York to train salvage divers.

Establishment of the Admiralty Experimental Diving Unit (AEDU).

1942-43
Navy and civilian divers clock over 16,000 hours during salvage operations in Pearl Harbor, Hawaii.

1944
Naval Combat Demolition Units (later known as UDTs) are formed and take part in the Normandy invasion on June 6. Frogmen clear paths through underwater obstacles for landing craft in the Anglo-Canadian sector.

1945
Philippe Taillez, Frédéric Dumas and Jacques-Yves Cousteau create the GRS, *Groupe de recherches sous-marines* (Underwater Research Group) under the auspices of the French Navy in Toulon. Taillez commands the unit till 1949.

1946
Establishment of the The British Admiralty Experimental Diving Unit

1948
Jacques-Yves Cousteau develops the first DPV (Diver Propulsion Vehicle) for combat divers.

1949
Jean Alinat and Guy Morandière create the SISM, *Section d'intervention sous-*

marine (Underwater Intervention Section) under the auspices of the French Navy in Saigon. Philippe Taillez joins the unit in 1951.

1950
Establishment of the Home Station Clearance Diving Team (Royal Navy). Clearance Diving Teams are also established to support the Mediterranean Fleet and the Far East Fleet.

1950-53
U.S. Navy Underwater Demolition Teams (UDT) are deployed to Korea.

1952
Establishment of the Clearance Diving (CD) Branch (Royal Navy).

1962
U.S. Navy Seal Teams 1 and 2 are formed.

1964
The U.S. Navy adopts the MK 6 UBA semi-closed circuit rebreather.

1966
Establishment of the Minewarfare and Clearance Diving (MCD) Branch (Royal Navy).

Establishment of U.S. Navy Harbor Clearance Unit One (HCU-1).

1967
Deep Diving System (DDS) placed in Fleet Service by Harbor Clearance Unit One.

1967-71
U.S. SEAL Teams 1 & 2 deploy to Vietnam

1972
U.S. Navy commissions the first Deep Submergence Rescue Vehicle (DSRV)

The U.S. Navy Los Angeles attack submarine USS *La Jolla* (SSN 701) with the deep submergence rescue vehicle *Mystic* (DSRV-1). Mystic was specifically designed to fill the need for an improved means of rescuing the crew of a submarine immobilized on the ocean floor. It can operate independently of surface conditions or under ice for rapid response to an accident anywhere in the world. Photo: U.S. Navy Journalist 3rd Class Wes Eplen.

1974-75
Operation Rheostat: The Fleet Clearance Diving Unit (Royal Navy) clears the Suez Canal of ordnance following the Arab-Israeli 6-Day War.

1975
NEDU relocates to Panama City, Florida.

Naval Diving and Salvage Training Center instructor stands ready to offer assistance to a diver student if he is not able to regain his own air supply during a problem solving exercise at the pool confidence-training portion of the student's course. The school is located in Panama City, Florida and is the center for navy diver training. Photo: U.S. Navy Photographer's Mate Chief Andy McKaskle

1978-79
Royal Navy clearance divers and Egyptian divers help relocate Egyptian monuments

submerged during the construction of the Aswan Dam.

1979
U.S. NEDU divers spend 37 days at 1,800 ft (549 m) in the Ocean Simulation Facility.

1980
U.S. Naval Diving & Salvage Training Center (NDSTC) is opened in Panama City, Florida.

1982
Draeger LAR V (MK-25) rebreather replaces the MK 6 Emerson-Lambertsen rebreather for U.S. combat swimmers.

1982
Operation Corporate: Royal Navy clearance divers conduct mine disposal operations in the Falklands.

1983
Operation Urgent Fury: U.S. Navy SEALs deployed for the invasion of Grenada.

1984
Operation Harling: Royal Navy clearance divers conduct mine disposal operations in the Red Sea.

1985
MK 12 officially replaces the MK V diving helmet (U.S. Navy). The MK V has been in service for 68 years since 1917.

1987
Operation Cimnel: Royal Navy clearance divers clear Iranian mines in the Gulf of Oman and the Persian Gulf.

1989
Operation Just Cause: U.S. Navy SEALs deployed for the invasion of Panama.

1990
Operation Desert Storm: U.S. Navy SEALs deployed in Kuwait.

1991
Operation Granby: Royal Navy clearance divers conduct mine disposal operations off Kuwait.

1993
MK 21 Superlite helmet replaces the MK 12 (U.S. Navy)

1997
U.S. Navy diving and salvage units assist the recovery of flight *TWA 800* off Long Island, New York

1998
Canadian Navy diver LS Culliford recovers flight recorder of *Swissair Flight 111* off Peggy's Cove, Nova Scotia.

2000
Operation Allied Harvest: Royal Navy clearance divers remove allied bombs jettisoned into the Adriatic during the Bosnian and Kosovo conflicts.

USN tests Advanced Swimmer Delivery System (ASDS) dry sub off of Hawaii.

U.S. Navy divers assist NOAA divers in recovering the turret of the Civil War ironclad USS *Monitor* off Cape Hatteras, North Carolina.

Hull Technician 1st Class John Coffelt works on a hydraulic ram on the sunken Civil War Ironclad, USS *Monitor*, which rests 230 feet (70 m) below the ocean's surface. Photo: U.S. Navy Chief Photographer's Mate Eric J. Tilford

2001
Operation Cleanex: Royal Navy clearance divers conduct remove wartime ordnance in the Baltic.

Members of SEAL Delivery Vehicle Team Two (SDVT-2) huddle together inside a flooded Dry Deck Shelter mounted on the back of the Los Angeles-class attack submarine USS *Philadelphia* (SSN 690). Dry Deck Shelters (DDS) provide specially configured nuclear powered submarines with a greater capability of deploying Special Operations Forces (SOF). DDSs can transport, deploy, and recover SOF teams from Combat Rubber Raiding Crafts (CRRCs) or SEAL Delivery Vehicles (SDVs), all while remaining submerged. Photo: U.S. Navy Chief Photographer's Mate Andrew McKaskle

DIVING COMMUNITY

1844
A. Schrader's Son Inc. Diving Equipment Company is founded in Brooklyn, New York.

1933
The *Bottom Scratchers of San Diego* dive club is founded by Ben Stone, Jack Prodanovich, and Glen Orr. They are later joined by Jack Corbley, Bill Batzloff and Wally Potts.

1934
Le Club des sous-l'eau, a sport-diving club is founded in France by spearfishing enthusiasts.

1936
The world's first scuba diving club is founded by Yves Le Prieur.

Jacques-Yves Cousteau, Philippe Tailliez and Frédéric Dumas, known as the three *Mousquemers* (Musketeers of the Sea) dive together for the first time in the Mediterranean.

1937
Diving Equipment & Salvage Company (now known as DESCO) is founded by divers Max Nohl & Jack Browne and hyperbaric physiologist Edgar End, MD.

1950
The International Underwater Spearfishing Association (IUSA) is founded and holds its first national skin diving competition at Laguna Beach, California.

Dick Anderson becomes the first Aqua-Lung instructor at U.S. Divers.

The *Calypso*, the ex-Royal Navy minesweeper HMS *J-026*, is converted into an oceanographic research vessel by Jacques-Yves Cousteau.

1953
The British Underwater Centre at Dartmouth in Devon (England) is founded by Captain Trevor Hampton.

The British Sub Aqua Club (BSAC) is founded.

1954
The Los Angeles County Department of Parks and Recreation under the direction of Al Tillman and lifeguard Bev Morgan holds the first U.S. scuba certification course.

1955
The first formal instructor certification program is introduced by Al Tillman and Bev Morgan.

1956
Jordan Klein (Marine Enterprises) begins manufacturing compressors under the MAKO name.

1957
Bob Soto's Diving becomes the first full-time dive operation on Grand Cayman Island.

Jacques-Yves Cousteau retires from the French Navy to become Director of the Monaco Oceanographic Museum.

1958
Sunset House opens on Grand Cayman and soon becomes a popular dive resort.

Voit, U.S. Divers, Healthways, Dacor, and Swimaster create the *Organization of Underwater Manufacturers*.

1959
The *Confédération mondiale des activités subaquatiques* (CMAS) - *World Underwater Federation* - is founded.

The first nationally organized course for scuba certification is developed by the YMCA.

The Underwater Society of America is formed.

1960
The *National Association of Underwater Instructors* (NAUI) is formed by Al Tillman and Neal Hess.

The first Public Training Agency and Underwater Instructor Certification Course (UICC) is formed.

Small Hope Bay Lodge, owned by Dick Birch on Andros Cay in the Bahamas, becomes the first dedicated dive resort. The resort has welcomed thousands of guests for over 45 years.

1961
NASDS, the *National Association of Skin Diving Schools*, is founded by John Gaffney.

COMEX (*Compagnie maritime d'expertises*) is founded by Frenchman Henri G. Delauze in Marseille.

1963
Scubapro is founded by Dick Bonin and Gustav dalla Valle.

Voit, Scubapro, Dacor, U. S. Divers, Healthways form the *Diving Equipment Manufacturers Association* (DEMA) "to promote, foster and advance the common business interests of the members as manufacturers of diving equipment."

1964
On October 12, a CMAS delegation aboard an improvised fleet of vessels throws a cylinder into the Mediterranean Sea off Genoa. The cylinder contains the declaration of humanity's ownership of the ocean depths. The ceremony is greeted by rough seas and a loud clap of thunder resonates when the cylinder touches the water.

Richard Adcock launches *Marisla*, the first dedicated liveaboard, in La Paz, Mexico.

1965
UNEXSO is created by Al Tillman in Freeport, Grand Bahama Island. It becomes a prototype for the complete and environmentally-friendly diving resort.

Kirby-Morgan Inc., which later produces the MK 1 and MK 21 for the U.S. Navy, is formed by Bob Kirby and Bev Morgan.

1966
PADI, the *Professional Association of Diving Instructors* is founded by John Cronin and Ralph Erickson.

1969
Travel agent Dewey Bergman founds *Sea and Sea Travel* in San Francisco. The travel agency for divers offers trips to destinations such as Bonaire, Grand Cayman, and Cozumel.

1970
Scuba Schools International (SSI) is founded by Bob Clark.

A dive boat cruises past Anthony's Key Resort on Roatan. Photo: J. Gallant / D.A.Y.

1971
Peter Hughes opens the first dedicated dive resort on the island of Roatan, Honduras. Now owned by the Galindo family, Anthony's Key Resort has since become one of the best known and most popular Caribbean resorts. (anthonyskey.com)

1974
The *Cousteau Society* is founded in the U.S. as an international, not-for-profit, environmental and educational organization.

1977
The first DEMA trade show is held in Miami, Florida.

1979

Bonaire designates its waters as a marine park and requires the use of mooring buoys at all dive sites in order to protect its reefs from anchor damage.

1980
Divers Alert Network is founded at Duke University.

The International Diving Museum (known today as the *Museum of Man in the Sea*) opens in Panama City, Florida.

1981
The *Fondation Cousteau* is founded in France as a not-for-profit organization.

1982
Jacques-Yves Cousteau, Lucien Malavard and Bertrand Charrier develop and test the *Turbosail* on the converted catamaran *Moulin à Vent* (Windmill). The Turbosail breaks off and is lost in rough weather during the vessel's first Atlantic crossing from France to the U.S.

Cousteau's windship *Alcyone* sails past Percé Rock off the Gaspé Peninsula in Québec, Canada. Photo: J. Gallant / D.A.Y.

1984
Jacques-Yves Cousteau launches the windship *Alcyone* (a.k.a. the *Daughter of the Wind*) which is equipped with two Turbosails. *Alcyone* will serve on several Cousteau expeditions around the world and becomes the flagship of the Cousteau Society after the *Calypso* is sunk by a barge in Singapore in 1996.

1988
Captain Cousteau is elected to the prestigious *Académie française* in Paris in honor of his lifetime achievements.

1992
The *Womens Scuba Association* (WSA) is founded.

Richard Stewart founds and directs to this day the *B2B Dive Travel Association*, a networking trade organization for travel agents, resorts and liveaboard charter companies.

1994
TDI, *Technical Diving International*, is founded by Bret Gilliam and Mitch Skaggs.

1996
The Cousteau Society's flagship *Calypso* is sunk in Singapore harbor after a collision with a barge.

1997
Jacques-Yves Cousteau dies from pneumonia on June 25 at the age of 87.

1998
NASDS merges with SSI.

Scuba Diving International (SDI) is created.

2001
Richard Stewart founds the *Planet Ocean Society*.

2003
Richard Stewart founds *Ocean Realm Media* to create the *Ocean Realm Channel* (cable), the *Ocean Realm Journal* (print/DVD publication), *Ocean Realm Broadband* (Internet news network) and *Ocean Realm Radio* (AM and Internet broadcasting).

PUBLICATIONS
MOVIES & MEDIA

1869
Scuba divers take to the depths in *20,000 Leagues under the Sea* by Frenchman Jules Verne.

1878
A study entitled *La Pression Barometrique* is published by Paul Bert. This study on pressure changes details decompression sickness caused by the formation of nitrogen gas bubbles in the body. He suggests gradual ascent to prevent decompression sickness or 'the bends'.

1880s
French priest Abbé Jean de Hautefeuille publishes *The Art of Breathing Underwater*.

1916
The film version of *20,000 Leagues under the Sea* is released. It includes the first underwater cinematography used by the movie industry. Divers use modified Fleuss/Davis rebreathers.

1938
The *Compleat Goggler* by Guy Gilpatric is published and becomes a popular inspiration for skin divers.

1939
Hans Hass' publishes his first book: *Jagd unter Wasser mit Harpune und Kamera* (Hunt under water with harpoon and camera).

Other titles by Hans Hass:

1941 - *Unter Korallen und Haien* (With corals and sharks)
1942 - *Fotojagt am Meeresgrund* (Photo-hunt at the sea-bottom)
1947 - *Drei Jäger auf dem Meeresgrund* (Three hunters on the sea-bottom)
1949 - *Menschen und Haie* (Humans and sharks)
1952 - *Manta, Teufel im roten Meer* (Manta, devil in the Red Sea)
1954 - *Ich fotografierte in den 7 Meeren* (I photographed in the 7 seas)
1957 - *Wir kommen aus dem Meer* (We come from the sea)
1958 - *Fische und Korallen* (Fish and corals)
1961 - *Expedition ins Unbekannte* (Expedition into the unknown)
1968 - *Wir Menschen. Das Geheimnis unseres Verhaltens* (We humans. The secret of our behavior)

1970 - *Energon: Das verborgene Geheimnis* (Energon: The hidden secret)

1971 - *In unberührten Tiefe. Die Bezwingung der tropischen Meere* (In unaffected depth. Conquest of the tropical seas)

1972 - *Vorstoss in die Tiefe. Ein Magazin über Abenteuer bei der Erforschung der Meere* (Raid into the depth. A magazine over adventures with the study of the seas)

1973 - *Welt unter Wasser. Der abenteuerliche Vorstoss des Menschen ins Meer* (World under water. The adventurous raid of humans in the sea)

1976 - *Eroberung der Tiefe. Das Meer - seine Geheimnisse, seine Gefahren, seine Erforschung* (Conquest of the deeps. The sea - its secrets, its dangers, its research)

1976 - *Der Hans-Hass-Tauchführer. Das Mittelmeer. Ein Ratgeber für Sporttaucher und Schnorchle.* (The Hans Hass dive guide. The Mediterranean. An adviser for sport divers and snorkelers.)

1977 - *Der Hai. Legende eines Mörders* (The shark. Legend of a killer)

1978 - *Die Schöpfung geht weiter. Station Mensch im Strom des Lebens* (The creation continues. Station of humans in the river of the life)

1979 - *Wie der Fisch zum Menschen wurde. Die faszinierende Entwicklungsgeschichte unseres Körpers* (How fish became humans. The fascinating history of the development of our body)

1980 - *Im Roten Meer. Wiederkehr nach 30 Jahren* (In the Red Sea. Return after 30 years)

1985 - *Stadt und Lebensqualität* (City and quality of life)

1986 - *Abenteuer unter Wasser. Meine Erlebnisse und Forschungen im Meer* (Adventure under water. My experiences and research in the sea)

1987 - *Der Ball und die Rose* (The ball and the rose)

1988 - *Der Hai im Management. Instinkte steuern und kontrollieren* (The shark in the management. Instincts steer and control)

1991 - *Vorstoss in unbekannte Meere* (Push into unknown seas)

1994 - *Die Hyperzeller. Das neue Menschenbild der Evolution* (The Hyper-cellars. The new human picture of evolution)

1996 - *Aus der Pionierzeit des Tauchens. In unberührte Tiefen* (From the pioneer time of diving. Into untouched depths)

2004 - *Erinnerungen und Abenteuer* (Memories and Adventures)

1942
John Wayne stars in Cecil B. de Mille's *Reap the Wild Wind*. Wayne is killed by an Academy-Award-winning squid at the end of the movie.

1943
Frenchmen Jacques-Yves Cousteau and Frédéric Dumas produce their first underwater film, *Par dix-huit mètres de fond* (Sixty Feet Down). Other films and TV series by Cousteau:

1943 - *Épaves*

1944 - *Paysages du silence*

1948 - *Les phoques du Sahara*

1949 - *Autour d'un récif*

1949 - *Une plongée du Rubis*

1949 - *Carnet de plongée*

1951 - *La fontaine de Vaucluse*

1955 - *Station 307*

1955 - *Récifs de coraux*

1955 - *Le monde du silence*

1956 - The Silent World

1957 - *La galère engloutie*

1958 - *Histoire d'un poisson rouge*

1959 - The Golden Fish

1960 - *Vitrines sous la mer*

1960 - *Prince Albert 1er*

1963 - *Le monde sans soleil*

1965 - World Without Sun

1965 - *Précontinent III / L'Odyssée sous-marine de l'Équipe Cousteau*

1965 - Voyage to the Edge of the World

1966 - The World of Jacques-Yves Cousteau
1967 - *Les requins*
1967 - *La jungle de corail*
1967 - *Le destin des tortues de mer*
1968 - Sharks
1968 - The Savage World of the Coral Jungle
1968 - Search in the Deep
1968 - Whales (1968)
1968 - *Baleines et cachalots*
1968 - *Le voyage surprise de Pépito et Cristobal*
1968 - *Le trésor englouti*
1968 - *La légende du lac Titicaca*
1969 - The Unexpected Voyage of Pepito and Cristobal
1969 - Sunken Treasure
1969 - The Legend of Lake Titicaca
1969 - The Desert Whales
1969 - *Les baleines du désert*
1969 - *La nuit des calmars*
1969 - *Le retour des éléphants de mer*
1970 - The Night of the Squid
1970 - The Return of the Sea Elephants
1970 - Those Incredible Diving Machines
1970 - *Ces incroyables machines plongeantes*
1970 - The Water Planet
1970 - *La mer vivante*
1970 - The Tragedy of the Red Salmon
1970 - *La tragédie des saumons rouges*
1970 - *Le lagon des navires perdus*
1971 - Lagoon of Lost Ships
1971 - Dragons of Galapagos
1971 - *Les dragons des Galápagos*
1971 - Secrets of the Sunken Caves
1971 - *Cavernes englouties*
1971 - The Unsinkable Sea Otter!
1971 - *Le sort des loutres de mer*
1971 - *Les dernières sirènes*
1971 - Octopus, Octopus
1972 - *Pieuvre, petite pieuvre*
1972 - The Forgotten Mermaids
1972 - A Sound of Dolphins
1972 - *Le chant des dauphins*
1972 - The Smile of the Walrus
1973 - 500 Million Years Beneath the Sea
1973 - *500 millions d'années sous la mer*
1973 - *Le sourire du morse*
1973 - Hippo!
1973 - *Hippo ! Hippo !*
1973 - The Singing Whale
1973 - *La baleine qui chante*

1973 - South to Fire and Ice
1974 - *La glace et le feu*
1974 - The Flight of Penguins
1974 - *Le vol du pingouin*
1974 - Beneath the Frozen World
1974 - *La vie sous un océan de glace*
1974 - Blizzard at Hope Bay
1974 - *Blizzard / Esperanza*
1974 - Life at the End of the World
1975 - *Le voyage au bout du monde*
1975 - *La vie au bout du monde*
1975 - Beavers of the North Country
1975 - *L'hiver des castors*
1975 - The Coral Divers of Corsica
1975 - *Les fous du corail*
1975 - The Sleeping Sharks of Yucatan
1975 - *Les requins dormeurs du Yucatan*
1975 - The Sea Birds of Isabella
1976 - *Coups d'ailes sous la mer*
1976 - Mysteries of the Hidden Reefs
1976 - *Au cœur des récifs des Caraïbes*
1976 - The Fish That Swallowed Jonah
1976 - *Le poisson qui a gobé Jonas*
1976 - The Incredible March of the Spiny Lobsters
1976 - *La marche des langoustes*
1977 - What Price Progress?
1977 - Grain of Conscience
1977 - Troubled Waters
1977 - Population Time Bomb
1977 - The Power Game
1977 - Visions of Tomorrow
1977 - *Calypso*'s Search for the Britannic
1977 - *L'énigme du Britannic*
1978 - Diving for Roman Plunder
1978 - *Le butin de Pergame sauvé des eaux*
1978 - *Calypso*'s Search for Atlantis, Part I
1978 - *À la recherche de l'Atlantide (1re partie)*
1978 - *Calypso*'s Search for Atlantis, Part II
1978 - *À la recherche de l'Atlantide (2e partie)*
1978 - Blind Prophets of Easter Island
1978 - *Le testament de l'île de Pâques*
1978 - Time Bomb at Fifty Fathoms
1978 - *Ultimatum sous la mer*
1979 - Mediterranean: Cradle or Coffin?
1979 - *Le Sang de la mer*
1979 - The Nile, Part I
1979 - *Le Nil (1re partie)*
1979 - The Nile, Part II
1979 - *Le Nil (2e partie)*

1980 - Lost Relics of the Sea
1980 - *Fortunes de mer*
1981 - *Les pillages de la mer*
1981 - Clipperton: The Island Time Forgot
1981 - *Clipperton : Ile de la solitude*
1981 - *Les pillages de la mer*
1982 - Warm-Blooded Sea: Mammals of the Deep
1982 - *Sang chaud dans la mer*
1982 - Cries from the Deep
1982 - Saint Lawrence: Stairway to the Sea (*Du grand large aux grands lacs*)
1982 - Calypso Countdown: Rigging for the Amazon (*Objectif Amazone : Branle-bas sur la Calypso*)
1983 - *Au pays des mille rivières*
1983 - *La rivière enchantée*
1983 - *Ombres fuyantes : Indiens de l'Amazonie*
1984 - Journey to a Thousand Rivers
1984 - The Enchanted River
1984 - River of Gold (*La rivière de l'or*)
1984 - Shadows in the Wilderness
1984 - *Tempête de neige sur la jungle*
1984 - Blueprints for Amazonia (*Un avenir pour l'Amazonie*)
1984 - Legacy of a Lost World (*Message d'un monde perdu*)
1984 - *L'Équipe Cousteau au Mississippi*
1985 – The Mississippi - The Reluctant Ally (*Un allié récalcitrant : Le Mississippi*)
1985 – The Mississippi - The Friendly Foe (*Allié et adversaire : Le Mississippi*)
1985 - Jacques Cousteau: The First 75 Years (*Jacques-Yves Cousteau : les premiers 75 ans*)
1985 - Riders of the Wind (*Alcyone, fille du vent*)
1985 - *À la redécouverte du monde*
1986 - Haiti: Waters of Sorrow (*Haïti : L'eau de chagrin*)
1986 - Cuba: Waters of Destiny (*Cuba : Les eaux du destin*)
1986 - Cape Horn: Waters of the Wind (*Cap Horn : Les eaux du vent*)
1986 - Sea of Cortez: Legacy of Cortez (*L'héritage de Cortez*)
1987 - Marquesas Islands: Mountains from the Sea (*Iles Marquises : Les montagnes de la mer*)
1987 - *Les îles du Détroit : Les eaux de la discorde*

1987 - *Les îles du Détroit : À l'approche d'une marée humaine*
1988 - Island of Peace
1988 - Tahiti: Fire Waters (*Tahiti : L'eau de feu - Mururoa*)
1988 - *Les requins de l'île au trésor Cocos*
1988 - Pacific Northwest: Land of the Living Totems (*Au pays des totems vivants*)
1988 - New Zealand: The Rose and the Dragon (*La rose et le dragon*)
1988 - New Zealand: The Heron of the Single Flight
1988 - *Au pays du long nuage blanc*
1988 - The Land of the Long White Cloud
1988 - Channel Island: Waters of Contention
1988 - Channel Island: Days of Future Past
1988 - *Le péché et la rédemption*
1989 - Cocos Island: Sharks of Treasure Island
1989 - Australia: The Last Barrier (*Australie : L'ultime barrière*)
1989 - Borneo: The Ghost of the Sea Turtle (*Bornéo : Le spectre de la tortue*)
1989 - Bering Sea: Twilight of the Alaskan Hunter (*Le crépuscule du chasseur en Alaska*)
1989 - New Zealand: The Smoldering Sea
1989 - *Les forçats de la mer*
1989 - *Bornéo : La forêt sans terre*
1989 - Papua New Guinea: Into the Time Machine (*La machine à remonter le temps*)
1989 - Papua New Guinea: River of Crocodile Men (*La rivière des hommes crocodiles*)
1989 - *Le centre du feu*
1990 - Papua New Guinea: Center of Fire
1990 - *Îles Andaman : Les îles invisibles*
1990 - Australia: Out West, Down Under (*Australie : À l'ouest du bout du monde*)
1990 - Australia: A Continent at Odds
1990 - Thailand: Convicts of the Sea
1990 - Borneo: Forests Without Land
1990 - Andaman Islands: Invisible Islands
1990 - Outrage at Valdez (*Scandale à Valdez / Anatomie d'un accident*)

1990 - Lilliput in Antarctica (*Lilliput en Antarctique*)
1991 - Australia: People of the Dry Sea (*Australie : Le peuple de la mer desséchée*)
1991 – Australia: People of Fire and Water (*Australie : Le peuple de l'eau et du feu*)
1991 - Australia: A Continent of Dreams
1991 - *Les vergers de l'enfer*
1991 - *Le cœur de la mer Sumatra*
1991 - *Palawan : Le dernier refuge*
1991 - Australia: Fortunes in the Sea (*Australie : Les trésors de la mer*)
1991 - Tasmania: Australia's Awakening Island (*Tasmanie : Une île s'éveille*)
1992 - Indonesia I: The Devil's Orchard
1992 - Indonesia II: Sumatra, the Heart of the Sea
1992 - The Great White Shark: Lonely Lord of the Sea (*Le grand requin blanc : seigneur solitaire des mers*)
1992 - Nauru: The Island Planet (*Nauru : Ilot ou planète*)
1992 - Palawan: The Last Refuge
1992 - The Mirage of the Sea
1992 - *Lever de rideau*
1992 - *Le rêve de Charlemagne*
1992 - *Les cris du fleuve*
1992 - *Les débordements du fleuve*
1993 - Streams of Life
1993 - Danube: The Curtain Rises
1993 - Danube: Charlemagne's Dream
1993 - Danube: The Cries of the River
1993 - Danube: Rivalries Overflow
1993 - The Secret Societies of Dolphins and Whales (*Les sociétés secrètes des cétacés : Dans l'intimité des baleines*)
1993 - *Mékong : Le don de l'eau*
1993 - *Vietnam & Cambodge : Le riz et les fusils*
1994 - Mekong I: The Gift of Water
1994 - Mekong II: Vietnam/Cambodia: Children of Rice and Guns
1995 - My First Eighty-Five Years
1995 - Madagascar: The Island Bleeds *L'île des esprits I*
1995 - Madagascar, Island of Spirits (*L'île des esprits II*)
1995 - *La légende de Calypso*
1995 - *Profond, loin, longtemps*

1995 - *La mer illuminée*
1996 - South Africa: Diamonds of the Desert (*Diamants du desert*)
1996 - South Africa: Sanctuaries for Life (*Sanctuaires pour la vie*)
1996 - Across China with the Yellow River (*À travers la Chine par le fleuve Jaune*)
1996 - *Les promesses de la mer*
1997 - Lake Baikal: Beneath the Mirror (*Derrière le miroir : Lac Baïkal*)

The first issue of *The Skin Diver* magazine in 1951.

1951
Hans Hass' fourth book, *Diving to Adventure*, published in German in 1947, is the first of Hass' books translated into English.

The Skin Diver (later known as Skin Diver Magazine) is published by Chuck Blakeslee and Jim Auxier. The magazine initially caters to spearfishers but soon switches over to scuba diving.

The movie *The Frogmen* set in the Pacific Ocean in WWII and starring Richard Widmark and Dana Andrews is released.

Rachel Carson publishes *The Sea Around Us*.

John Steinbeck publishes *The Log from the Sea of Cortez*. His original report on his expedition was published in 1941 as The Sea of Cortez: A Leisurely Journal of Travel and Research.

Hans Hass wins Biennale Prize

1952

The Silent World is released by Jacques-Yves Cousteau, Frédéric Dumas, and James Dugan. The subsequent documentary film won the top award at the Cannes Film Festival in 1956.

Jacques-Yves Cousteau and André Laban develop the first underwater television equipment.

1953

Underwater Safety is published by E.R. Cross. The book eventually sells over 100,000 copies.

Dr. Eugenie Clark publishes *Lady With a Spear*.

Robert Wagner, Gilbert Roland and Peter Graves star in *Beneath the 12 Mile Reef*, a film about sponge diving in the Florida Keys.

First live undersea television broadcast by Jacques-Yves Cousteau.

1954

A textbook for diver education, *The Science of Skin and Scuba Diving*, is published by the Council for National Cooperation in Aquatics. Three more editions are published (1959, 1962 and 1974). Total sales of the book later published as *The New Science of Skin and Scuba Diving* exceed over one million copies.

Kirk Douglas, James Mason, Paul Lukas, and Peter Lorre star in the Walt Disney version of *20,000 Leagues under the Sea*. It wins the Academy Awards for art direction and special effects.

Kingdom of the Sea, the first underwater television series, starring Zale Parry is aired on TV.

Philippe Taillez publishes his first book *Plongée sans câble* (To the Ocean Depths),

which tells the story of the *Mousquemers*, the *FNRS 2*, of Cousteau's first films in 1943, and of Taillez's experiences in Indochina.

1955

Jane Russell, Richard Egan, and Gilbert Roland star in *Underwater*, produced by Howard Hughes.

1956

Jacques Cousteau and co-director Louis Malle win the Palme d'or at the Cannes Film Festival for *Le monde du silence* (*The Silent World*).

1957

The first international underwater film festival is organized by Al Tillman and Zale Parry in Los Angeles, California.

1958

The TV series *Sea Hunt* begins. The show starring Lloyd Bridges creates a great interest in scuba diving.

Underwater Warrior by Ivan Tors stars Ross Martin and Dan Daily. The film is about underwater demolition technicians.

1959

Don't Give up the Ship stars Jerry Lewis.

Hans Hass wins Oscar for u/w photography for the film *Unternehmen Xarifa*.

1963

Flipper is produced starring Chuck Connors, Luke Halpin and a bottlenose dolphin. The film later becomes a popular television series.

1965
Thunderball, a James Bond spy thriller including several underwater action scenes, is released and increases the interest in scuba diving. The film's underwater special effects win an Academy Award.

1968
Launch of the television series *The Undersea World of Jacques Cousteau*.

1971
Jacques-Yves Cousteau publishes the 20-volume encyclopedia *The Ocean World of Jacques Cousteau*.

1975
Peter Benchley's blockbuster film *Jaws* terrifies beachgoers and divers around the world.

1976
Richard Stewart founds *Florida Diver* magazine.

1977
Richard Stewart founds *Sport Diver* magazine.

1980
Ocean Realm Television, founded by Richard Stewart, pioneers the design and construction of the television industry's first underwater EFG (electronic field gathering) underwater video camera system for *Sony Video Products*, and in the mid 80's for Panasonic's RECAM video production system.

1981
Richard Stewart launchs the first ocean nature magazine titled *Ocean Realm* and remains publisher and editor until 1987.

1983
DEMA produces *I'd Rather Be Diving*, a promotional film on recreational diving. It is followed by three sequels: *Treasure Diving* (1984), *The Seven Wonders of the Diving World* (1985) and *Scuba Diving in America* (1986).

1985
Jacques-Yves Cousteau launches the *Rediscovery of the World* television series.

1989
James Cameron's *The Abyss* creates more interest in scuba diving.

2000
Richard Stewart creates *Big Grouper Media* to publish specialty titles that include *Splash Adventures, Destination Adventures, Caribbean Island Adventures, Out Island Adventures,* and the trade journals *Adventure Travel Specialist, Scuba Industry Professional, Dive Travel Specialist* and *Watersports Retailing.*

Men of Honor showcases the life of Carl Brashear, the first African American and later the first amputee U.S. Navy Diver.

PHOTOGRAPHY

1856
The first underwater picture is taken by William Thompson and underwater photography is born.

1870s
Eadweard Muybridge, whose chronophotography of moving subjects lead to the development of motion pictures, takes underwater photos in San Francisco Bay.

1893
The first underwater camera is invented by Louis Boutan.

The first ever flash bulb is designed by Frenchman Chauffour in 1893 for underwater photographer Louis Boutan. The glass bulb contains pressurized oxygen and magnesium which is ignited by a wire carrying an electrical discharge.

1915
Jack Williamson films the underwater images for *20,000 Leagues under the Sea* from inside a submersible sphere.

John Ernest Williamson produces the first underwater movie in which he kills a shark.

1926
W. H. Longley takes the first underwater color photographs. They appear in the January 1927 issue of National Geographic.

1948
The U.S. Atlantic Expedition photographs the seafloor at a depth of 1,181 ft (360 m) using a remote controlled ˪magnesium flash.

1949
Hans Hass and German company Franke & Heidecke develop the Rolleimarin underwater housing.

Dimitri Rebikoff develops an underwater electronic strobe flash for still and movie pictures.

1954
Dr Harold Edgerton develops an underwater still camera equipped with an electronic strobe.

1956
Harold E. Edgerton and Jacques-Yves Cousteau take the first photos of the deep ocean floor while anchored over the Romanche Gap off the coast of Africa. The *Calypso* is anchored at a record depth of 24,928 ft (7,600 m) using a 700-lb (318 kg) anchor, 100 ft (30 m) of heavy chain, a 550-lb (250 kg) pig iron, a 200-ft (61 m) steel cable and a quarter-inch braided nylon line 32,800 ft (10,000 m) long.

1958
Belgian engineer Jean De Wouters and Jacques-Yves Cousteau design the *Calypsophot* camera.

1962
A Plexiglas underwater housing is developed by *Life* Magazine photographers Elgin Ciampi and Peter Stackpole.

1963
Nikon markets an improved version of the Calypsophot under the name *Nikonos*.

1968
Nikon launches the *Nikonos II*.

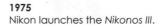

1975
Nikon launches the *Nikonos III*.

1980
Nikon launches the *Nikonos IV-A*.
* Automatic

1984
Nikon launches the *Nikonos V*.

1992
Nikon launches the *Nikonos RS* 35mm SLR.

1996
Nikon retires the Nikonos RS 35mm SLR due to poor sales.

2000
Mass production of inexpensive housings for consumer-level digital cameras begins.

2002
Nikon ends production of Nikonos V and accessories.

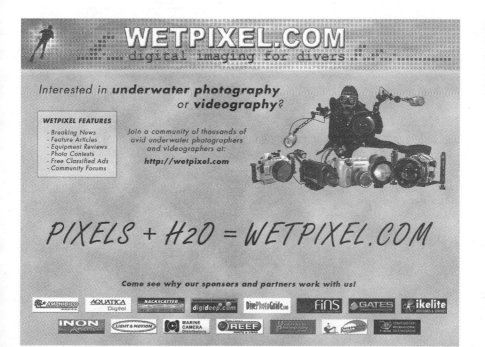

INFORMATION IN THIS SECTION
PROVIDED IN PART BY CMAS/AMCQ
AND ADAPTED BY D.A.Y.

Chapter **3**

DIVING ESSENTIALS

In order to explore the aquatic universe, a diver has to adapt to the underwater environment. The human body is designed to function on land. Because the aquatic environment is very different from our own, all of our senses are affected. This is largely due to the fact that water is a liquid and that it is much denser that air and cannot be breathed.

The diver has to adapt to new sensations. Vision, hearing and touch are modified. Communication, propulsion, heat conservation and breathing are also affected. In addition, changes in the surrounding pressure have physiological effects on a diver.

The information presented in this section offers only a brief overview of the information presented during a typical scuba course and in no way should be used to replace proper training manuals such as those developed by CMAS Québec (AMCQ)[11] and other recognized training agencies.

PHYSICAL EFFECTS

VISION

The vision of a diver is modified underwater. Light hitting the surface is subjected to four phenomena: refraction, reflection, absorption and diffusion.

REFRACTION

Light rays are greatly modified as they pass through water, the glass panel of a dive mask, and air before they reach a diver's eye. Objects appear enlarged at a rate of 4/3 and closer at a rate of 3/4. The refraction rate of water is 1.33. Objects thus appear larger and closer than they are in reality.

REFLECTION

Light rays are affected by the angle at which they hit the surface of the water. Rays that 'bounce' off the surface are reflected. Light penetration is best between 11:00 AM and 1:00 PM when the sun is at its zenith.

DIFFUSION

Light disperses when it hits water molecules, sediment or plankton. Sediments greatly affect visibility as well as lighting conditions.

ABSORPTION

Light is absorbed by water and colors are gradually filtered out by depth. A dive light, strobe flash or video lights restores absorbed colors at any depth.

[11] CMAS/AMCQ – www.cmasquebec.org

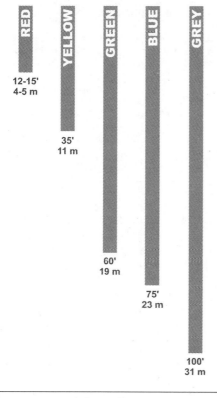

12-15'
4-5 m

35'
11 m

60'
19 m

75'
23 m

100'
31 m

BUOYANCY

Water is 800 times denser than air. The buoyancy of a diver is affected by the amount of water his body displaces.

Archimedes' Principle is the law of buoyancy. It states that *"any body partially or completely submerged in a fluid is buoyed up by a force equal to the weight of the fluid displaced by the body."*

The weight of an object pulls it downward, and the buoyant force provided by the water it displaces pushes it upward. If both forces are equal, the object is neutrally buoyant. Density is defined as weight per volume. If the density of an object exceeds the density of the water it displaces, the object will sink.

These huge tankers float because their weight is less than that of the water they displace. Photo: U.S. Navy Photographer's Mate 1st Class Richard J. Brunson

HEARING

Water is a great sound conductor as long as the sound is produced underwater. Sound travels four times faster underwater: 4,921 ft/sec (1,500 m/sec) in water compared to 1,083 ft/sec (330 m/s) in air. Because sound travels faster under water, it is difficult to detect its point of origin.

COMMUNICATION

Because of the density of water, human vocal communication underwater without a two-way radio system is virtually impossible. Divers must therefore use hand signals. (See charts on following pages)

PRESSURE

Pressure is one of the words most commonly associated with diving.

❖ **Atmospheric pressure** is the force exerted by air on the surface of the planet. This pressure is equal to 14.7 PSI (1 kg/cm^2) or 1 BAR. It is also referred to as 1 Atmosphere (ATM) of pressure.
❖ **Hydrostatic pressure** (a.k.a. relative pressure) increases by 1 ATM with every 33 ft (10 m) of water depth.
❖ **Absolute pressure** (a.k.a. ambient pressure) is the combination of atmospheric and hydrostatic pressure. Absolute

pressure affects the entire body and equipment of a diver. The air within his lungs, sinuses, ears, mask, buoyancy compensator and drysuit is compressed to absolute pressure.

BOYLE-MARIOTTE LAW

At a constant temperature, the volume of a gas is inversely proportional to the surrounding pressure.

In other words, the more a diver descends, the more the pressure increases and the volume of compressible materials decreases.

DEPTH	HYDROSTATIC PRESSURE	ATMOSPHERIC PRESSURE	ABSOLUTE PRESSURE	PRESSURE PSI / kg/cm²	VOLUME
0	0	1	1	14.7 1	12x
33 ft 10 m	1	1	2	29.4 2	6x
66 ft 20 m	2	1	3	44.1 3	4x
99 ft 30 m	3	1	4	58.8 4	3x
132 ft 40 m	4	1	5	73.5 5	2.4x
165 ft 50 m	5	1	6	88.2 6	2x

PRESSURE KEY VALUES

33 ft / 10 m
1 ATM = 1 BAR = 14.7 PSI = 1 kg/cm²

1 ft / 0.30 m
0.03 ATM = 0.03 BAR = 0.445 PSI = 0.03 kg/cm²

1 m / 3.28 ft
0.1 ATM = 0.1 BAR = 1.46 PSI = 0.1 kg/cm²

Use the preceding values to calculate the pressure at any depth.

Absolute pressure at 130 ft:
(Hydrostatic press.) + Atmospheric pressure

(0.03 ATM x 130) + 1 ATM = 4.9 ATM
(0.03 BAR x 130) + 1 BAR = 4.9 BAR
(0.445 PSI x 130) + 14.7 PSI = 72.55 PSI
(0.03 kg/cm² x 130) + 1 kg/cm² = 4.9 kg/cm²

Absolute pressure at 30 m:
(Hydrostatic press.) + Atmospheric pressure

(0.1 ATM x 30) + 1 ATM = 4 ATM
(0.1 BAR x 30) + 1 BAR = 4 BAR
(1.46 PSI x 30) + 14.7 PSI = 58.5 PSI
(0.1 kg/cm² x 30) + 1 kg/cm² = 4 kg/cm²

PHYSIOLOGICAL EFFECTS

BAROTRAUMA

Barotrauma is an injury sustained due to the inability to equalize the pressure of body air spaces with that of the surrounding environment.

DURING DESCENT

Due to the increase in pressure, the air volume in the inner ear decreases making the eardrum bend inwards. The Valsalva maneuver is the most common technique to equalize the pressure. You simply need to pinch your nose, close your mouth, and try to exhale. The pressurized air in your throat is thus forced into your inner ear via Eustachian tubes which instantly returns your eardrums to their normal position.

Sinuses are also subjected to a pressure increase during descent. Since they are directly connected to breathing passages, they equalize automatically, unless they are congested. Unfortunately, there is no technique to equalize the sinuses if they are congested. In most cases, the dive must be aborted due to extreme pain at very shallow depths.

Pressurized air entering a tooth cavity or filling can cause intense pain.

Lungs are compressed during descent. They are inflated to their natural volume by breathing compressed air.

The airspace inside a dive mask is also compressed. By blowing compressed air through the nose, a diver can avoid discomfort and injury.

DURING ASCENT

- Excess air pressure in the ears evacuates automatically through the Eustachian tubes.
- Excess air pressure in the sinuses evacuates automatically through the breathing passages.
- Pressurized air spaces inside a tooth cavity or filling can cause intense pain or force a filling to pop out. A very slow ascent may help the pressurized air to escape gradually.
- Compressed air within a mask will escape automatically between the mask skirt and the diver's skin.
- Pressurized air within the lungs causes the lungs to expand upon ascent. If the air is not allowed to escape by surfacing slowly and breathing regularly, the lungs may sustain serious injuries or rupture.

Injuries to the lungs include the following:

- **Embolism** - Air from the alveoli enters blood vessels in the form of bubbles and can block blood flow.
- **Pneumothorax** - Air gets between the lungs and the rib cage. Lungs may collapse.
- **Mediastinal emphysema** - Air enters the tissues located near the heart, the lungs and large blood vessels in the center of the chest.
- **Subcutaneous emphysema** - Swelling caused by the presence of an air pocket under the skin. Often appears in the area of the neck.

PARTIAL PRESSURE

Pressure affects the concentration of gases inhaled by a diver. The deeper a diver descends, the higher the partial pressure of every gas that composes his breathing mixture.

COMPOSITION OF AIR

Nitrogen	N_2	78.084%
Oxygen	O_2	20.946%
Argon	Ar	0.934%
Carbon dioxide	CO_2	0.033%

Rare gases:		
Neon	Ne	
Helium	He	
Krypton	Kr	
Hydrogen H_2		→ .003%
Xenon	Xe	
Radon	Rn	
Carbon monox.	CO	

DALTON'S LAW

The total pressure exerted by a homogenous mixture of gases is equal to the sum of the partial pressures of the individual gases.

Although the percentage of each gas remains unchanged during descent, the quantity of breathing mixture required to fill the lungs to full capacity increases. With more breathing mixture comes more of each gas that composes the mixture. The percentages are unchanged, but the partial pressure of each gas increases.

NITROGEN NARCOSIS

Certain gases like nitrogen (N_2) have adverse effects of the human body when their partial pressure is too high. Too much nitrogen leads to a condition called Nitrogen Narcosis, a.k.a. *Rapture of the Deep*. A diver suffering from Nitrogen Narcosis may feel or exhibit the following symptoms or signs: abnormal feelings of happiness, euphoria and drunkenness, or feel overly anxious and nervous for no apparent reason. The diver may also have problems with vision, feel dizzy or confused, and feel sleepy. All of these sensations increase with depth. Reducing depth once the symp-toms appear usually makes them disappear.

Other gases such as CO_2 and CO are soon fatal when their partial pressure reaches a certain level. Getting tanks filled with a well-maintained and certified filling station usually prevents this from happening.

Too much of a good thing can be dangerous. When breathing regular air with an oxygen percentage of 20.946%, the partial pressure of O_2 may cause a diver to lose consciousness at a depth of 297 ft (90 m). Breathing pure oxygen will have the same dramatic effect at a depth of only 20 ft (6.1 m). During WWII, Royal Navy divers discovered that partial pressure could be used as a deadly weapon. British commandos on rebreathers using a gas mix containing between 45% and 60% O_2 would grab hold of enemy divers using 100% O_2 re-breathers and drag them deeper until the partial pressure of O_2 would cause their opponents to go into convulsions and drown.

TEMPERATURE

Being cold is often what forces a diver to end a dive. Staying warm is key to enjoying your dive.

HYPOTHERMIA

Hypothermia is a drop in temperature in the body core. In extreme cases, hypothermia is very dangerous to a diver's health.

Normal body core temperature is 37.5°C. Critical body functions degrade as the core temperature decreases:

36°C	Chills
35°C	Loss of tactile sensitivity
34°C	Mental functions slowed; delayed response time and impaired judgment
32°C	Ventricular fibrillation (Usually fatal)
30°C	**Loss of consciousness**

The following chart applies to a person of average weight without dive suit.

WATER TEMPERATURE	EXHAUSTION OR UNCONSCIOUSNESS
70 - 80°F 21 - 27°C	3 - 12 hours
60 - 70°F 16 - 21°C	2 - 7 hours
50 - 60°F 10 - 16°C	1 - 2 hours
40 - 50°F 4 - 10°C	30 - 60 min.
32.5 - 40°F 0 - 44°C	15 - 30 min.
<32°F <0°C	<15 min.

Recommended thermal protection

>70°F >20°C	None
68 - 77°F 20 - 25°C	Minimal 3 mm wetsuit
39 - 68°F 4 - 20°C	Full wetsuit
32 - 50°F 0 - 10°C	Drysuit

DECOMPRESSION

Human beings are adapted for living at the surface of the planet under atmospheric pressure. When diving under water, the human body has to adapt to the increased ambient pressure. Upon returning to the surface, it must cope with a drop in pressure which may result in physiological trauma.

GAS ABSORPTION

When underwater, a diver breathes pressurized air from his tank. This compressed air is mainly composed of nitrogen (N_2) and Oxygen (O_2).

During the breathing process, an exchange is established between the air that the diver breathes and his circulatory system. During this exchange, oxygen and nitrogen enter the body through the blood stream via diffusion. The oxygen is consumed by living cells unlike the nitrogen which remains intact and in fact, accumulates in the blood and body tissues. Therein lies the root cause of decompression sickness.

HENRY'S LAW

At a constant temperature, the amount of gas dissolved in a given type and volume of liquid is directly proportional to the partial pressure of that gas in equilibrium with the liquid.

In other words, the more the pressure increases, the more dissolved nitrogen enters the body. In addition to pressure, time spent underwater also affects the accumulation of nitrogen in the body. Nitrogen first enters the blood stream before squeezing its way into body tissues which include muscles, fat and bones. The speed at which nitrogen is absorbed and eliminated depends on the type of tissue. The deeper you go and the longer you stay underwater, the more nitrogen accumulates in your body.

GAS ELIMINATION

When a diver starts his ascent back to the surface, the surrounding pressure decreases, therefore the gases that have accumulated in the diver's body come out of solution and need to be eliminated.

During ascent, nitrogen makes its way back to the lungs through blood vessels where it is progressively exhaled as the pressure decreases. If enough time is not allowed for this process to take place, the nitrogen will take a gaseous state and be released in the form of bubbles.

This phenomenon is often compared to the opening of a bottle of soda. When the cap is in place, pressure within the bottle keeps the gas (CO_2) under solution in the liquid. When the cap is removed, the gas comes out of solution and instantly changes into a gaseous state. In extreme cases, the same phenomenon can take place inside the human body when a diver makes an uncontrolled ascent to the surface after prolonged exposure to pressure.

DECOMPRESSION SICKNESS (DCS)[12]

Ascending too quickly from a dive without making the required stops to eliminate accumulated nitrogen exposes the diver to decompression sickness (DCS).

CAUSES OF DCS

- Too rapid ascent;
- not respecting dive tables

FACTORS INCREASING RISK OF DCS

- Poor physical condition, fatigue and oveexertion;
- drinking or substance abuse;
- dehydration, seasickness, excessive exposure to sun; hypothermia;
- recent trauma or surgery;
- obesity;
- smoking;
- intense physical effort during dive;
- cold water;
- residual nitrogen from a previous dive.

[12] Go to section on Diving Medicine for detailed information on DCS

SYMPTOMS OF DCS

- Fatigue;
- itching or skin rash;
- pain in joints (the bends);
- dizziness, vertigo, vomiting;
- state of choc, spasms and convulsions;
- loss of speech, hearing or vision;
- paralysis;
- difficulty breathing, coughing, bloody expectorations.

These symptoms mostly appear after the diver has surfaced:

First half-hour:	50%
First hour:	85%
First 6 hours:	99%
More than 12 hours:	Very rare cases

DCS TREATMENT

The only effective remedy for DCS is immediate recompression in a hyperbaric chamber. Any other treatment, including breathing pure oxygen, is only palliative and incomplete. Even minor DCS that isn't treated properly can affect a person for the rest of his life.

DIVE TABLES

The purpose of dive tables is to measure the quantity of nitrogen dissolved in the body according to the time and depth of a dive, in order to avoid or plan decompression stops before entering the water. Divers presenting any of the risk factors mentioned previously may still be affected by decompression sickness despite careful planning and meticulous observance of dive tables. Traditional dive tables normally include the following:

1. Gas decompression table
2. Surface interval table
3. Repetitive dive table
4. Depth correction table

Different breathing gases require different dive tables. Depending on their training agency, most new divers learn how to use tables during their openwater training under the supervision of qualified instructors. As a general rule, it is recommended that divers never rely solely on the use of dive computers and should stay proficient in the use of dive tables.

COMMUNICATION

Speaking underwater is practically impossible and speaking at the surface may be hampered by environmental conditions and distance. Therefore most divers use hand signals to communicate both underwater and at the surface. Several signals are used around the world with only minor variations. Others are local inventions. Most importantly, divers must go over hand signals when diving with new partners in order to avoid any misunderstandings. The following pages illustrate some of the most common signals used around the world.

OK

OK
(AT THE SURFACE)

OK
(AT THE SURFACE)

ASCEND
(GO UP)

DESCEND
(GO DOWN)

NOT OK
(TROUBLE)

LOW ON AIR

OUT OF AIR

I NEED AIR

SLOW DOWN

STOP!

LOOK

I'M COLD

TROUBLE
EQUALIZING

VERTIGO

HELP!

HOLD HANDS

OUT OF BREATH

FOLLOW ME

STAY CLOSE TO
YOUR BUDDY

OBSTACLE AT
THE SURFACE

I'M TIRED

INFORMATION
(TIME, DEPTH, AIR)

HOW MUCH AIR
DO YOU HAVE?

TANK HALF-EMPTY

COME HERE

I LOST MY
BUDDY

CMAS QUÉBEC

Are You Prepared?

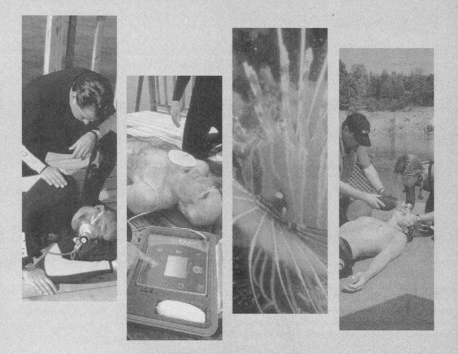

DAN Training Programs
Designed specifically with divers in mind.

www.DiversAlertNetwork.org
1-800-446-2671

INFORMATION IN THIS SECTION ·
PROVIDED BY DIVERS ALERT NETWORK
(DAN) AND ADAPTED BY D.A.Y.

Chapter 4

DIVING MEDICINE

DIVERS ALERT NETWORK
Your Dive Safety Association

Divers Alert Network (DAN) is a 501(c)(3) Non-profit medical and research organization dedicated to the safety and health of recreational scuba divers and associated with Duke University Medical Center (DUMC). DAN is supported by the largest association of recreational divers in the world.

HAZARDOUS MARINE LIFE

Marine Life Trauma
By Paul S. Auerbach, M.D., M.S. DAN

CORAL SCRAPES

Coral scrapes are the most common injuries from marine life incurred by divers and snorkelers. The surface of coral is covered by soft living material, which is easily torn from the rigid (abrasive) structure underneath, and thus deposited into the scrape or cut. This greatly prolongs the wound-healing process by causing inflammation and, occasionally, initiating an infection. Cuts and scrapes from sharp-edged coral and barnacles tend to fester and take weeks or even months to heal.

THE TREATMENT

1. Scrub the cut vigorously with soap and water, and then flush the wound with large amounts of water.

2. Flush the wound with a half-strength solution of hydrogen peroxide in water. Rinse again with water.

3. Apply a thin layer of bacitracin, mupirocin (Bactroban), or other similar antiseptic ointment, and cover the wound with a dry, sterile, and non-adherent dressing. If no ointment or dressing is available, the wound can be left open. Thereafter, it should be cleaned and re-dressed twice a day.

If the wound develops a pus-laden crust, you may use "wet-to-dry" dressing changes to remove the upper non-healing layer in order to expose healthy, healing tissue. This is done by putting a dry sterile gauze pad over the wound (without any underlying ointment), soaking the gauze pad with saline or a dilute antiseptic solution (such as 1- to 5-percent povidone-iodine in disinfected water), allowing the liquid to dry, and then "brutally" ripping the bandage off the wound. The dead and dying tissue adheres to the gauze and is lifted free. The pink (hopefully), slightly bleeding tissue underneath should be healthy and healing. Dressings are changed once or twice a day. Wet-to-dry dressings are used for a few days, or until they become non-adherent. At that point, switch back to #3 above.

4. If the wound shows any sign of infection (extreme redness, pus, swollen lymph glands), the injured person (particularly one with impairment of his or her immune system) should be started by a qualified health professional on an antibiotic, taking into consideration the possibility of a Vibrio infection. Vibrio bacteria are found more often in the marine environment than on

land, and can rapidly cause an overwhelming illness and even death in a human with an impaired immune system (e.g., someone with AIDS, diabetes or chronic liver disease).

Coral poisoning occurs if coral abrasions or cuts are extensive or are from a particularly toxic species. Symptoms include a wound that heals poorly or continues to drain pus or cloudy fluid, swelling around the cut, swollen lymph glands, fever, chills and fatigue. If these symptoms are present, the injured person should see a physician, who may elect to treat the person with an antibiotic or corticosteroid medication.

SEA URCHIN PUNCTURES

Some sea urchins are covered with sharp venom-filled spines that can easily penetrate and break off into the skin. Others (found in the South Pacific) may have small pincerlike appendages that grasp their victims and inoculate them with venom from a sac within each pincer. Sea urchin punctures or stings are painful wounds, most often of the hands or feet. If a person receives many wounds simultaneously, the reaction may be so severe as to cause extreme muscle spasm, difficulty in breathing, weakness and collapse.

Red sea urchin (*Strongylocentrotus franciscanus*), British Columbia. Photo: J. Gallant / D.A.Y.

THE TREATMENT

1. Immerse the wound in non-scalding hot water to tolerance (110 to 113 F / 43.3 to 45 C). This frequently provides pain relief.

Other field remedies, such as application of vinegar or urine, are less likely to diminish the pain. If necessary, administer pain medication appropriate to control the pain.

2. Carefully remove any readily visible spines. Do not dig around in the skin to try to fish them out - this risks crushing the spines and making them more difficult to remove. Do not intentionally crush the spines. Purple or black markings in the skin immediately after a sea urchin encounter do not necessarily indicate the presence of a retained spine fragment. The discoloration more likely is dye leached from the surface of a spine, commonly from a black urchin (Diadema species). The dye will be absorbed over 24 to 48 hours, and the discoloration will disappear. If there are still black markings after 48 to 72 hours, then a spine fragment is likely present.

3. If the sting is caused by a species with pincer organs, use hot water immersion, then apply shaving cream or a soap paste and shave the area.

4. Seek the care of a physician if spines are retained in the hand or foot, or near a joint. They may need to be removed surgically, to minimize infection, inflammation and damage to nerves or important blood vessels.

5. If the wound shows any sign of infection (extreme redness, pus, swollen regional lymph glands) or if a spine has penetrated deeply into a joint, the injured person (particularly one with impairment of his or her immune system) should be started by a qualified health professional on an antibiotic, taking into consideration the possibility of a Vibrio infection (see #4 under "Coral Scrapes).

6. If a spine puncture in the palm of the hand results in a persistent swollen finger(s) without any sign of infection (fever, redness, swollen lymph glands in the elbow or armpit), then it may become necessary to treat the injured person with a seven- to 14-day course of a non-steroidal anti-inflammatory drug (e.g., ibuprofen) or, in a

more severe case, oral prednisone, a corticosteroid medication.

FISH ENVENOMATIONS

Lionfish (as well as scorpionfish and stonefish) possess dorsal, anal and pelvic spines that transport venom from venom glands into puncture wounds. Common reactions include redness or blanching, swelling and blistering (lionfish). The injuries can be extraordinarily painful and occasionally life-threatening (in the case of a stonefish).

Volitan lionfish (*Pterois volitans*) in the Red Sea. Photo: NOAA Coral Kingdom Collection

THE TREATMENT

Soaking the wound in non-scalding hot water to tolerance (110-113 F / 43.3-45 C)

- may provide dramatic relief of pain from a lionfish sting,
- is less likely to be effective for a scorpionfish sting, and
- may have little or no effect on the pain from a stonefish sting, but it should be done nonetheless, because the heat may inactivate some of the harmful components of the venom.

If the injured person appears intoxicated or is weak, vomiting, short of breath or unconscious, seek immediate advanced medical care.

Wound care is standard, so, for the blistering wound, appropriate therapy would be a topical antiseptic (such as silver sulfadiazene [Silvadene] cream or bacitracin ointment) and daily dressing changes. A scorpionfish sting frequently requires weeks to months to heal, and therefore requires the attention of a physician. There is an antivenin available to physicians to help manage the sting of the dreaded stonefish.

STINGRAY ENVENOMATION

A stingray does its damage by lashing upward in defense with a muscular tail-like appendage, which carries up to four sharp, swordlike stingers.

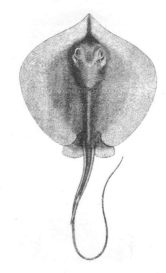

The southern stingray (*Trygon Sabina*). Illustration: Historic NMFS Collection

The stingers are supplied with venom, so that the injury created is both a deep puncture or laceration and an envenomation. The pain from a stingray wound can be excruciating and accompanied by bleeding, weakness, vomiting, headache, fainting, shortness of breath, paralysis, collapse and occasionally, death. Most wounds involve the feet and legs, as unwary waders and swimmers tread upon the creatures hidden in the sand.

THE TREATMENT

1. Rinse the wound with whatever clean water is available. Immediately immerse the wound in non-scalding hot water to tolerance (110 to 113 F / 43.3 to 45 C). This may provide some pain relief. Generally, it is necessary to soak the wound for 30 to 90 minutes. Gently extract any obvious piece of stinger.

2. Scrub the wound with soap and water. Do not try to sew or tape it closed - doing so could promote a serious infection by "sealing in" harmful bacteria.

3. Apply a dressing and seek medical help. If more than 12 hours will pass before a doctor can be reached, start the injured person on an antibiotic (ciprofloxacin, trimethoprim-sulfamethoxazole or doxycycline) to oppose Vibrio bacteria.

4. Administer pain medication sufficient to control the pain.

PREVENTION OF STINGRAY INJURIES

1. Always shuffle your feet when wading in stingray waters.

2. Always inspect the bottom before resting a limb in the sand.

3. Never handle a stingray unless you know what you are doing or unless the stingrays are definitely familiar with divers and swimmers (e.g., the rays in "Stingray City" off Grand Cayman Island in the British West Indies). Even then, respect them for the wild creatures they are - the less you handle them the better for them and for you, too.

SKIN PROBLEMS

SEA BATHER'S ERUPTION

Often misnamed "sea lice" (which are true crustacean parasites of fish, and which inflict miniscule bites), sea bather's eruption occurs in sea water and involves predomi-nately bathing suit-covered areas of the skin, rather than exposed areas. The skin rash distribution is very similar to that from seaweed dermatitis, but no seaweed is found on the skin.

The cause is stings from the nematocysts (stinging cells) of the larval forms of certain anemones, such as Linuche unguiculata, and thimble jellyfishes. The injured person may notice a tingling sensation under the bathing suit (breasts, groin, cuffs of wetsuits) while still in the water, which is made much worse if he/she takes a freshwater rinse (shower) while still wearing the suit. The rash usually consists of red bumps, which may become dense and confluent (i.e., run together in a mass). Itching is severe and may become painful.

THE TREATMENT

Treatment consists of immediate (for decontamination) application of vinegar or rubbing alcohol, followed by hydrocortisone lotion 1 percent twice a day. Topical calamine lotion with 1 percent menthol may be soothing.

If the reaction is severe, the injured person may suffer from headache, fever, chills, weakness, vomiting, itchy eyes and burning on urination, and should be treated with oral prednisone. The stinging cells may remain in the bathing suit even after it dries, so once a person has sustained sea bather's eruption, the clothing should undergo machine washing or be thoroughly rinsed in alcohol or vinegar, then be washed by hand with soap and water.

SEAWEED DERMATITIS

Sea bather's eruption is easy to confuse with "seaweed dermatitis." There are more than 3,000 species of algae, which range in size from 1 micron to 100 meters in length. The blue-green algae, Microcoleus lyngbyaceus, is a fine, hairlike plant that gets inside the bathing suit of the unwary aquanaut in Hawaii and Florida waters, particularly during the summer months. Usually, skin under the suit remains in moist contact with the algae (the other skin dries or is rinsed off), and becomes red and itchy, with occasional blistering and/or weeping. The reaction may start a few minutes to a few hours after the victim leaves the water.

THE TREATMENT

Treatment consists of a vigorous soap-and-water scrub, followed by a rinse with isopropyl (rubbing) alcohol. Apply 1 percent hydrocortisone lotion twice a day. If the reaction is severe, oral prednisone may be administered.

SWIMMER'S ITCH

Also called "clamdigger's itch," swimmer's itch is caused by skin contact with cercariae, which are the immature larval forms of parasitic schistosomes (flatworms) found throughout the world in both fresh and salt waters. Snails and birds are the intermediate hosts for the flatworms. They release hundreds of fork-tailed microscopic cercariae into the water.

The affliction is contracted when a film of cercariae-infested water dries on exposed (uncovered by clothing) skin. The cercariae penetrate the outer layer of the skin, where itching is noted within minutes. Shortly afterwards, the skin becomes reddened and swollen, with an intense rash and, occasionally, hives. Blisters may develop over the next 24 to 48 hours.

Untreated, the affliction is limited to 1 to 2 weeks. Persons who have suffered swimmer's itch previously may be more severely affected on repeated exposures, which suggests that an allergic response may be a factor.

THE TREATMENT

Swimmer's itch can be prevented by briskly rubbing the skin with a towel immediately after leaving the water, to prevent the cercariae from having time to penetrate the skin. Once the reaction has occurred, the skin should be lightly rinsed with isopropyl (rubbing) alcohol and then coated with

calamine lotion. If the reaction is severe, the injured person may be treated with oral prednisone.

Because the cercariae are present in greatest concentration in shallow, warmer water (where the snails are), swimmers should try to avoid these areas.

JELLYFISH STINGS

"Jellyfish" is the term commonly used to describe an enormous number of marine animals that are capable of inflicting a painful, and occasionally life-threatening, sting. These include fire coral, hydroids, jellyfishes (including "sea wasps") and anemones. The stings occur when the victim comes into contact with the creature's tentacles or other appendages, which may carry millions of small stinging cells, each equipped with venom and a microscopic stinger.

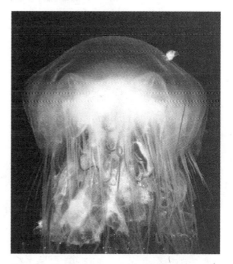

The highly potent lion's mane jellyfish, Nova Scotia. Photo by J. Gallant / D.A.Y.

Depending on the species, size, geographic location, time of year and other natural factors, stings can range in severity from mild burning and skin redness to excruciating pain and severe blistering with generalized illness (nausea, vomiting, shortness of breath, muscle spasm and low blood pressure). Broken-off tentacles that are fragmented in the surf or washed up on the beach can retain their toxicity for months and should not be handled, even if they appear to be dried out and withered.

Close-up look at the lion's mane's tentacles. Photo by J. Gallant / D.A.Y.

The dreaded box jellyfish (Chironex fleckeri) of northern Australia contains one of the most potent animal venoms known to man. A sting from one of these creatures can induce death in minutes from cessation of breathing, abnormal heart rhythms and profound low blood pressure (shock).

Fire worm. Photo: J. Gallant / D.A.Y.

THE TREATMENT

Be prepared to treat an allergic reaction following a jellyfish sting. If possible, carry an allergy kit, including injectable epinephrine (adrenaline) and an oral antihistamine. The following therapy is recommended for all unidentified jellyfish and other creatures with stinging cells:

The tentacles of the fish-eating anemone (*Urticina piscivora*) are lined with stinging cells. Photo by J. Gallant / D.A.Y.

1. If the sting is believed to be from the box jellyfish (Chironex fleckeri), immediately flood the wound with vinegar (5 percent acetic acid). Keep the victim as still as possible. Continuously apply the vinegar until the victim can be brought to medical attention. If you are out at sea or on an isolated beach, allow the vinegar to soak the tentacles or stung skin for 10 minutes before attempting to remove adherent tentacles or to further treat the wound. In Australia, surf lifesavers (lifeguards) may carry antivenin, which is given as an intramuscular injection a first aid measure.

2. For all other stings, if a topical decontaminant (e.g., vinegar, isopropyl [rubbing] alcohol, one-quarter-strength household

ammonia or baking soda) is available, apply it liberally onto the skin.

If it is a liquid, continuously soak a compress. (Be advised that some authorities advise against the use of alcohol because of scientific evaluations that have revealed that some nematocysts discharge because of this chemical's application.) Since not all jellyfish are identical, it is extremely helpful to know ahead of time what works for the stingers in your specific geographic location.

Apply the decontaminant for 30 minutes or until pain is relieved. A paste made from unseasoned meat tenderizer (do not exceed 15 minutes' application time, particularly upon the sensitive skin of small children) or papaya fruit may be helpful. Do not apply any organic solvent, such as kerosene, turpentine or gasoline.

Until the decontaminant is available, you may rinse the skin with sea water. Do not simply rinse the skin gently with fresh water or apply ice directly to the skin. A brisk freshwater stream (forceful shower) may have sufficient force to physically remove the microscopic stinging cells, but nonforceful application is more likely to cause the cells to fire, increasing the envenomation. A non-moist ice or cold pack may be useful to diminish pain, but take care to wipe away any surface moisture (condensation) prior to the application.

3. After decontamination, apply a lather of shaving cream or soap and shave the affected area with a razor. In a pinch, you can use a paste of sand or mud in sea water and a clamshell.

4. Reapply the primary decontaminant for 15 minutes.

5. Apply a thin coating of hydrocortisone lotion (0.5 to 1 percent) twice a day. Anesthetic ointment (such as lidocaine hydrochloride 2.5 percent or a benzocaine-containing spray) may provide short-term pain relief.

6. If the victim has a large area involved (entire arm or leg, face, or genitals), is very young or very old, or shows signs of generalized illness (nausea, vomiting, weakness, shortness of breath or chest pain), seek help from a doctor. If a person has placed tentacle fragments in his mouth, have him swish and spit whatever potable liquid is available. If there is already swelling in the mouth (muffled voice, difficulty swallowing, enlarged tongue and lips), do not give anything by mouth, protect the airway and rapidly transport the victim to a hospital.

CIGUATERA POISONING

Ciguatera fish poisoning involves a large number of tropical and semitropical bottom-feeding fish that dine on plants or smaller fish, which have accumulated toxins from microscopic dinoflagellates, such as Gambierdiscus toxicus. Therefore, the larger the fish, the greater the toxicity. The ciguatoxin-carrying fish most commonly ingested include the jack, barracuda, grouper and snapper.

Black grouper (*Mycteroperca bonaci*). Photo: J. Gallant / D.A.Y.

Symptoms, which usually begin 15 to 30 minutes after eating the contaminated fish, include abdominal pain, nausea, vomiting, diarrhea, tongue and throat numbness, tooth pain, difficulty in walking, blurred vision, skin rash, itching, tearing of the eyes, weakness, twitching muscles, in coordination, difficulty sleeping and occasional difficulty in breathing. A classic sign of ciguatera intoxication is the reversal of hot and cold sensation (hot liquids seem cold, and vice versa), which may reflect general hypersensitivity to temperature.

Persons can become severely ill shortly after they are poisoned, with heart problems, low blood pressure, deficiencies of the central and peripheral nervous systems, and generalized collapse. Unfortunately, many of the debilitating, but not life-threatening, symptoms may persist in varying severity for weeks to months.

THE TREATMENT

Treatment is for the most part based upon symptoms without any specific antidote, although certain drugs are beginning to prove useful for aspects of the syndrome, such as intravenous mannitol for abnormal nervous system behavior and abnormal heart rhythms. A physician must undertake these therapies.

Prochlorperazine may be useful for vomiting; hydroxyzine or cool showers may be useful for itching. There are chemical tests to determine the presence of ciguatoxins in fish and in the bloodstream of humans, but not yet a specific antidote. If a person displays symptoms of ciguatera fish poisoning, he/she should be see a physician promptly.

During recovery from ciguatera poisoning, the injured person should exclude the following from the diet: fish, fish sauces, shellfish, shellfish sauces, alcoholic beverages, nuts and nut oils.

DIVING WHILE ON MEDICATIONS FOR STINGS

In general, it is safe to dive while taking an antibiotic or corticosteroid medication. If a wound infection is more than minor or is expanding, however, diving should be curtailed until it becomes minor, is no longer progressing and can be easily covered with a dressing. In or out of the water,

corticosteroid medication should always be taken with the understanding that a rare side effect is to cause serious deterioration of the head ("ball" of the ball-and-socket joint) of the femur, the long bone of the thigh.

Most injuries from animals result from chance encounters. Be an alert diver, and respect their personal space. If you're injured, follow the advice you find here, and call DAN.

HEADACHES

By Dr. Frans Cronje, M.D., President & Medical Director, DAN Southern Africa

DAN gets many inquiries regarding headaches and diving. Probably very few divers who dive regularly have not left the water at least once with some cranial discomfort. This piece reviews the common causes of headaches in diving and offers some simple advice that should solve the problem in most cases.

Finding the cause of a headache is probably unnecessary if it only happens once or twice, occurs in the absence of any other symptoms and clears spontaneously or with only mild analgesics. However, a few divers complain of frequent and more troublesome headaches, and it is for these individuals that the following considerations and suggestions are intended.

One way to find the cause of a headache is to run through a checklist of possible causes and eliminate them one by one. While not an exhaustive list, these may include:

- Anxiety / Tension
- Sinus or Ear Barotrauma
- Sinus and Ear Infections
- Cold
- Saltwater Aspiration
- Mask Squeeze
- Temporomandibular Joint Pain (TMJ)
- Dental Problems
- Gas Toxicity (especially high CO2)
- Decompression Illness

- Migraine
- Hyperextension of the Neck
- Cervical Spondylosis
- Caffeine and Other Drugs

By simply looking at the list, one can already see that the origins of headaches are truly diverse. However, important clues can usually be found in the history taken from someone who develops headaches regularly. These five key questions may provide an answer to the causes of headaches:

Have you had previous head or neck problems, injuries or regular headaches, even when not diving? Divers who develop headaches regularly above water are also very likely to get them underwater. Such headaches, especially if they are associated with symptoms of nausea, vomiting, abnormal sensations, vision, abnormal smell or even paralysis, may be serious and require assessment by a specialist neurologist.

Migraine, a relative contraindication to scuba diving, requires expert assessment. Headaches may also result from tension, large caffeine intake and menstrual changes, among other reasons. A bad-fitting mouthpiece can also cause headache: Some regulators are quite heavy in the water and require a constant "bite" to stay in place. Swapping regulators or trying different mouthpieces may spell the end of a continuous string of headaches. In the end, it is always better to own your own equipment once you have found what works for you.

Divers with previous neck or upper back problems or injuries are very prone to develop headaches underwater or even as a result of a bumpy boat trip. The underlying bony problems lead to muscle spasms, which in turn cause the headache. A medical specialist such as an orthopaedic surgeon should assess these problems. Physiotherapy and muscle strengthening exercises are often of value. Some report improvement after visiting a chiropractor. Back surgery is usually a last resort.

What is the position of your tank on your back? Is the diver constantly avoiding the pillar valve by bending the part of the neck closest to the shoulders downwards, and then having to hyperextend the part closest to the skull to curl around the valve? As odd as this may sound, it is a very common cause of headache in divers. The solution is to ensure that the neck, when extended normally, does not bring the head against the pillar valve by simply adjusting the position of the cylinder as needed.

Where is the pain, and what does the pain feel like? Pain related to neck problems is usually a persisting non-throbbing pain that gradually spreads from the back of the head to the temples. Sinus pain is usually over the forehead or cheekbones or sometimes behind the eyes or on top of the head. Ear pain is mostly quite obvious, but it is always worth asking whether ear equalizing was easy and effective during a dive.

What is your surface air consumption? Many divers boast about low air consumption or try to artificially reduce their air consumption by skip breathing. The truth of the matter is that removing carbon dioxide from the lungs is very analogous to rinsing dye out of a carpet. The bigger the spill (in our comparison, this would be the amount of exercise which produces more carbon dioxide) and the bigger the carpet (in our example, the size of the person's lungs), the more water you would need to rinse it clean - that is, the more air you will require to wash the carbon dioxide out. Larger lungs require larger breaths and consequently an increase in air consumption. That is why female divers typically have better air consumption than males.

The only way to effectively reduce breathing requirements without building up carbon dioxide is to reduce underwater exercise, ensure adequate thermal protection and to relax; take slow deep breaths (better gas exchange - good rinsing) rather than shallow ones. A healthy breathing pattern is the key to solving many headaches. **What was the dive profile?** Long or deep dives, rapid ascents, breath-holding and panic ascents followed by headache all raise the suspicion of decompression illness (DCI) as a possible cause. Although fortunately uncommon, DCI is a cause that would require immediate treatment. Abnormal symptoms following any exposure to compressed air should always prompt a suspicion of DCI. Don't deny symptoms; when in doubt call DAN.

Some quick-fix solutions that may be useful (and are good diving practice anyway) include:

1. Loosen your mask strap to avoid pressure on the nose, forehead or cheekbones. If necessary, change your mask to a more comfortable one.
2. Relax during your dives. After all, you are on holiday.
3. Take slow deep breaths. These relax you and provide a more efficient way of removing carbon dioxide.
4. Relax your neck during dives. Even though it spoils your trim momentarily, rotating the body rather than the head to look at objects underwater may avoid the strain and the discomfort of hyperextending the neck.
5. Stay in shape. Exercise reduces the incidence of headaches.
6. Avoid caffeine and tobacco with diving.
7. Always follow safe diving practices. Spend three to five minutes at a safety stop at 3-5 meters (10-15 fsw) below the surface. It is relaxing (weather and conditions permitting) and allows time to reduce the carbon dioxide built up from finning to the surface.
8. Wear adequate thermal protection.
9. Go for regular dive medical examinations: at least every two years for those younger than 40, and annually for those older than 40.

Headaches can spoil a dive trip or vacation and detract from the wonderful underwater experience. Fortunately, once the cause has been determined, many headaches are simple to cure. Those who experience frequent, severely incapacitating, or chronic headaches may require an intensive evaluation by a physician to determine the underlying problem.

PSYCHOLOGICAL CAUSES

Psychological Causes
By Dr. Allan Kayle

Anxiety is a common cause of headaches in tense novice divers. It shows up as a classic tension headache, with pain over both sides of the head and at the back of the neck. It is due to insecurity about being exposed to a potentially dangerous underwater environment. With increasing experience and underwater skill, it invariably disappears.

New divers with a fear of losing their air supply under water often bite too tightly on the regulator mouthpiece. This may cause spasm of the temporalis muscles in the temples and produce headache. A maligned bite or a filling that is riding too high may result in uneven stress of the joints between the jawbone and the skull. This will also cause headache when clamping a mouthpiece tightly between the teeth.

PSYSICAL CAUSES

Tight gear is another common cause of headache in inexperienced divers. Adjusting mask straps too tightly in the hope of avoiding mask leakage during the dive causes pressure right around the head, exactly like a very tight hat or glasses that are too small for the wearer. This pressure effect of the mask straps starts some minutes into the dive and gets worse the longer the dive. It is relieved by removing the mask after the dive and pain usually disappears rapidly.

Wetsuit collars fitting too tightly around the neck is another cause of headache. Tight collars compress the veins that drain blood from the skull and brain and can cause retention of carbon dioxide in the brain. This can precipitate a typical carbon dioxide headache (see below). If the collar is very tight, compression of the carotid sinuses in the carotid arteries in the neck can occur with a reflex drop in blood pressure and even sudden unconsciousness - the so-called carotid sinus reflex. Headaches can also occur with wetsuits, straps or buoyancy compensators that are too tight-fitting around the chest and restrict easy breathing. This again can cause carbon dioxide build-up and headache.

Sinus squeeze causes headaches that are referred to the sinuses involved. Nasal and sinus allergy, polyps or infection can easily cause obstruction to the small openings between the sinuses and the nose. This makes it difficult or impossible for air to pass freely between the sinuses and nose and, with the increasing pressure of descent, Boyle's Law[13] operates and sinus baro-trauma occurs.

The most common site of sinus squeeze is the forehead, relating to the frontal sinuses. Pain over one or both cheeks or even the upper teeth is referred from the maxillary sinuses. Pain in the eyeballs is due to eth-moid sinus squeeze, and pain at the back of the head on descent often relates to sphenoid sinus squeeze. The pain is usually relieved by ascent. The reverse can also occur. Compressed air trapped in a sinus after a successful descent will cause headache on ascent. Management is obviously avoidance of diving in the presence of significant nasal obstruction and having allergy or infection treated.

Neck problems related to previous motor vehicle accident whiplash injuries to the cervical spine, or other head or neck trauma, quite commonly result in headaches while diving. The pain is usually right at the back of the head and neck and can radiate to the forehead and shoulders.

It is caused by the extended neck position that all divers have to adopt in order to see in front of them while swimming horizontally under water. It is equivalent to walking on land and looking up at the sky for up to an hour. Neck muscle spasm or compression of neck spinal nerves can occur. This causes headache. The diver may be totally

pain-free at all other times, the pain only occurring when assuming the abnormal neck position under water. It usually occurs in divers with a history of neck injury and it can last for minutes, hours or even days after diving.

It is often helped by swimming forward with the body axis at a 30-degree angle to the sea bed. This allows the diver to see in front and progress forwards without excessive extension of the neck. However, divers assuming this position must remain vigilant to the environment around them: kicking may damage fragile marine organisms.

Some divers may choose to substitute ankle weights for some of the belt weights to help them in adopt this position underwater. Other divers may find them fatiguing, so make this choice with particular care.

Cold causes a severe throbbing headache in cold-sensitive divers, occurring in the forehead or back of the head. It is very similar to the "brain-freeze" experienced when rapidly eating ice cream. This type if headache is variable: it can occur right away or some some minutes into the dive, usually gets worse the longer the dive, and persists for a while after leaving the water.

This type of headache can be mitigated by wearing a hood, but not always. For frequent cold headaches, combine the hood with habituating the skin prior to immersion. Try wetting the face with progressively colder water before entry: this usually help eliminate cold-water headaches.

Carbon dioxide build-up, in the whole body due to skip breathing or contamination of the air supply, or locally in the brain due to the congestive effect of a tight neoprene wetsuit collar, results in a headache that gradually develops during the dive as the amount of retained carbon dioxide slowly increases, or occurs almost immediately after surfacing and breathing atmospheric air with the resultant sudden decrease in blood carbon dioxide, one of the carbon dioxide "off effects." Some divers develop high CO_2 in the blood even without these factors.

---

[13] Boyle's Law states that at a constant temperature and mass, the volume of a gas is inversely proportional to the pressure exerted on that gas. This means that when the pressure is doubled - as in descending in the water column - the volume is reduced to one half of its original amount.

Carbon dioxide headaches are severe and throbbing, are not always relieved by painkillers and can last for hours after the dive. Other gases responsible for headaches are carbon monoxide following air supply contamination, and CO2 toxicity following deep diving on oxygen-enriched mixes or after using pure oxygen rebreathers.

Saltwater inhalation that occurs inadvertently during a sea dive can cause headaches. These headaches generally commence about half an hour after diving, are usually accompanied by body aches and pains and are worsened by exercise and exposure to cold.

Acute neurological decompression illness usually occurs within minutes of surfacing. It is manifested by a headache following a long or deep dive with a heavy nitrogen or other inert gas load, or it may be due to arterial gas embolism following lung barotrauma. Headache is an extremely serious symptom when it's due to inert gas overload. It is usually accompanied by other manifestations of central nervous system bubble injury such as weakness or paralysis, confusion and abnormalities of sensation. For treatment, immediate surface mask oxygen, urgent contact and discussion with a diving doctor, and emergency recompression therapy are absolutely essential.

Looking into the sun or glare on the water for prolonged periods during a diving cruise can cause headache due to spasm of the scalp and forehead muscles. The solution is obviously to wear dark glasses, preferably with polarized lenses, when exposed to prolonged glare.

All of the above causes of headache in divers can precipitate an underwater migraine, a potentially dangerous event. This type of headache, whether contracted above or below the waterline, can cause nausea and vomiting. Some people experience neurological abnormalities in association with a migraine, such as partial blindness, weakness and numbness. A blindingly painful headache can result in confusion, inability to react to the challenges of the underwater milieu, vertigo and vomiting through a regulator.

Individuals with frequent migraine headaches should not dive, especially if there are accompanying neurological manifestations. Migraine is sometimes precipitated by diving. Furthermore, severe headache after a dive, especially associated with neurological symptoms, may be impossible to distinguish from acute cerebral decompression illness including arterial gas embolism.

Should a migraine sufferer with headaches of this type insist on diving, trio or double buddy pair teams may be helpful to ensure that a diver totally incapable of saving his or her life if a migraine hits can safely be returned to the surface and professional help. The best advice, however, is to avoid diving.

Headaches remain a problem in divers. The causes are manifold, and proof of the exact cause can be difficult to determine. In many cases, the exact cause is never clearly determined. If you are an underwater headache sufferer, consider the above causes clearly and honestly.

If the reason for your pain is still a mystery, consult a diving doctor or request an opinion from a neurologist - there are many less common causes for headache and you could fit the bill. Enjoy diving, and do it with care.

DIVING & WOMEN

MENSTRUATION

Are women at greater risk of experiencing decompression illness (DCI) while menstruating? Theoretically, it is possible that, because of fluid retention and tissue swelling, women are less able to get rid of dissolved nitrogen. This is, however, not definitively proven.

One recent retrospective review of women divers (956 divers) with DCI found 38 percent were menstruating at the time of their injury. Additionally, 85 percent of those taking oral contraceptives were menstruating at the time of the accident. This suggests, but does not prove, that women taking oral contraceptives are at increased risk of decompression illness during menstruation. Therefore, it may be advisable for menstruating women to dive more conservatively, particularly if they are taking oral contraceptives. This could involve making fewer dives, shorter and shallower dives and making longer safety stops. Four other studies have provided evidence that women are at higher risk of DCI, and in one study of altitude bends, menses also appeared to be a risk factor for bends.

Are women at an increased risk of shark attacks during menstruation? There are few reported shark attacks on women, and there are no data to support the belief that menstruating females are at an increased risk for shark attacks. The average blood lost during menstruation is small and occurs over several days. Also, it is known that many shark species are not attracted to the blood and other debris found in menstrual flow.

In general, diving while menstruating does not seem to be a problem as long as normal, vigorous exercise does not increase the menstrual symptoms. As long as the menstrual cycle poses no other symptoms or discomforts that affect her health, there is no reason that a menstruating female should not dive. However, based upon available data, it may be prudent for women taking oral contraceptives, particularly if they are menstruating, to reduce their dive exposure (depth, bottom time or number of dives per day).

PREGNANCY

There is little scientific data available regarding diving while pregnant. Much of the available evidence is anecdotal. Laboratory studies are confined to animal research and the results are conflicting. Some retrospective survey type question-

naires have been performed but are limited by data interpretation.

An issue to keep in mind is the risk of decompression illness to the mother due to the physiological changes which occur while pregnant. During pregnancy, maternal body fluid distribution is altered and this redistribution decreases the exchange of dissolved gases in the central circulation. Theoretically, this fluid may be a site of nitrogen retention. Fluid retention during pregnancy may also cause nasopharyngeal swelling, which can lead to nose and ear stuffiness.

In regards to diving, these may increase a pregnant women's risk of ear or sinus squeezes. Pregnant women experiencing morning sickness, which could then couple with motion sickness from a rocking boat, may have to deal with nausea and vomiting during a dive. This is an unpleasant experience and could lead to more serious problems if the diver panics.

Due to the limited data available and the uncertainty of the effects of diving on a fetus, diving represents an increased exposure for the risk of injury during pregnancy. There's a baseline incidence of injury including cases of decompression illness in diving. One must consider the effects on the fetus if the mother must undergo recompression treatment.

MOTION SICKNESS

By Dan Kinkade, DAN Medical Information Specialist

Motion sickness - it goes by terms both descriptive and outlandish: mal de mer, seasickness, hurling, chumming for sharks, upchucking, tossing your cookies, blowing chunks. Divers know all about it; even if they haven't experienced it firsthand, they've likely been witness to this form of involuntary fish feeding. Seasickness is not life-threatening, even though you might think - or wish - it were, when it's happening. The good news: you are not alone.

Ninety percent of all people will suffer from motion sickness at one time or another.

This article will explain motion sickness and offer ways to avoid or manage it while diving.

WHAT IS MOTION SICKNESS?

Seasickness results when the eyes are seeing one thing - e.g., the inside of the boat - while the balance organ (the semicircular canals) detects another - your movement up and down. The brain gets confused, figuring out why your eyes tell it you are stationary, but your inner ear tells your brain you are moving.

A diver about to feed the fishes. Photo: J. Gallant / D.A.Y.

Other factors can compound the problem: they include alcohol ingestion, anxiety, fatigue, odors (e.g., diesel fumes), being overheated and inner ear injury or infection. Signs and symptoms include sweating, nausea, headache, drowsiness, increased salivation and a sensation of spinning or dizziness. Vomiting may make you feel better, but the symptoms will not resolve until the inner ear acclimates to the motion or you use another form of treatment.

Seasickness tends to diminish after a few days without treatment. Generally, the more time you spend on a boat, the less severe the sickness becomes. When some individuals become acclimated to the

motion, readjusting once they're back on land may take some time.

AVOIDING MOTION SICKNESS

Positioning - If the boat is rocking bow to stern, seek out a spot in the middle of the boat for the least movement. A lower cabin may be more suitable than a top deck outer cabin. And remember, the smaller the boat, the larger your potential for sickness, as smaller boats tend to rock more quickly.

Fix on an object - Look beyond the boat: use the horizon as a reference point. This helps your brain to adjust more easily to the unstable environment. Avoid focusing tasks like reading, setting up equipment and writing.

Fresh air - If you're feeling ill, nothing worsens it like diesel fumes. Find a spot away from the fumes, where fresh air blows. Keep a reference point by looking at the horizon.

Keep something in your stomach - Stay well hydrated before and during your trip. Sip water, juice or sports drinks, but avoid carbonated drinks, alcohol and caffeine. If you are nauseated, don't drink lots of water since it will create an unpleasant sensation of sloshing in your stomach. Eat saltines or bread to absorb stomach fluids.

Some Remedies for Prevention
Plainly stated, there is no cure for motion sickness, but a plethora of medications, devices, procedures and herbal remedies are touted to alleviate its symptoms. If you have discovered a safe system that works, stick with it.

Over-the-Counter Medications
The classification of these medications is "antinausea." The most common over-the-counter antiemetics are antihistamines: i.e. Bonine (meclizine), Dramamine Less-Drowsy (meclizine), Dramamine (dimenhydrinate), Marezine (cyclizine), and Benadryl (diphenhydramine). These medications work by affecting nerve pathways between the vomiting center in the brain and other control centers. These effects are

associated with relief of nausea and vomiting.

Side effects of these medications may impair your ability to dive safely. Some cause drowsiness, the most common side effect. Because of this, they carry warnings about operating heavy equipment or performing hazardous tasks. Before using antinausea medications, always read the accompanying information. To evaluate for side effects, take your dosage well before the dive. If you feel drowsy while taking it on land, the effects may worsen underwater.

Medications by Prescription

Many divers have used Transderm Scop (the patch with scopolamine as its main ingredient) to relieve seasickness. With few reported problems, this patch releases the drug slowly through the skin; it can be very effective against motion sickness for as long as three days.

Since the medication affects the central nervous system, however, it can have side effects that may impair your ability to dive safely. The most common side effects are dry mouth and blurred vision. Fingers that contact the medication side of the patch and touch the eye will cause the pupil to dilate. After handling the patch, wash your hands thoroughly.

Other side effects, more common in children and the elderly include hallucinations, confusion, agitation or disorientation. The dosage is fixed and cannot be altered by cutting the patch.

You can get SCOPACE, a tablet form of scopolamine, by prescription. Taken an hour before travel, each dose will last up to eight hours. Benefits of the tablet over the patch can include a faster onset, flexibility with dosages and fewer side effects. For more information on Transderm Scop, see the upcoming November/December issue.

OTHER FORMS OF PREVENTION

Other non-drug remedies might help relieve symptoms of motion sickness. Ginger, sometimes recommended for motion sickness, has been found to reduce electrical activity in the stomach, reducing contractions and thereby the nausea. A study conducted at University of Michigan in Ann Arbor proved ginger's effectiveness in relieving motion sickness symptoms. Participants were spun in a large drum. When compared to those taking a placebo, those taking ginger had significantly less nausea.

According to the authors of the study, anti-motion sickness medications have significant side effects, such as dizziness and dry mouth. "Ginger appears to be an effective herbal alternative to the medications," the authors concluded. Take 1 gram of ginger orally, followed by eating gingersnaps, drinking ginger ale or candied ginger.

The ReliefBand, made by Woodside Biomedical of Carlsbad, Calif., is advertised to relieve nausea and vomiting with gentle, noninvasive stimulation on the underside of the wrist. This battery-powered stimulator looks like a wristwatch; electrodes on the underside are positioned over the P6 acupuncture site. This is one inch toward the heart from the wrist, between the two-finger flexor tendons. When positioned properly, the wearer will feel a pulsed tingling sensation across the palm and in the middle two fingers.

The ReliefBand is the only device that has been cleared by the FDA for over the counter use for the treatment of nausea and vomiting due to motion sickness. It was also recently cleared for morning sickness. A similar device has been used as a prescriptive device for relief of post-operative nausea and vomiting.

The ReliefBand operates on the theory that the electrical impulse travels the median nerve and interrupts the nausea-related messages that are being transmitted between the brain and stomach. It can be used before or after symptoms begin. Although anecdotal, there have been reports of people receiving relief from the device even after being sick. The device is water-resistant but it's not submersible, so divers should take off the device before entering the water. The band presents no side effects to interfere with a diver's mental performance.

Another similar product is the Sea-Band, made in England and distributed worldwide. The Sea-Band is an elastic band with a button that applies pressure to the acupuncture site, much like the ReliefBand, but without electrical stimulation.

Motion Eaze, manufactured in Grand Rapids, Mich., is a concoction of natural oils that are applied topically behind the earlobe. These oils, which are absorbed, reportedly calm the inner ear, relieving the symptoms of motion sickness. It has no known side effects and, like all these remedies, its effectiveness can vary from person to person.

What Should You Do?

Before traveling, be adequately hydrated, nourished and rested. However, if you start to feel apprehensive about the boat ride or plane trip, don't eat a large meal before departure. Munch on crackers and sip water or a sport drink.

Before you leave the dock or get into open water, set up your dive gear. This will keep you from looking down while moving through swells. Find a spot on the boat with the least amount of motion, good ventilation and visual references.

Believe in what you use, medication or non-medication; that means testing it for side effects before a trip. You don't want to get out on a boat and find out you are too drowsy to dive - ruins a perfectly good dive trip. Dive safely.

DIVING & MEDICATION

Some of the more common questions to DAN medics concern the use of OTCs and their compatibility with safe diving.

By Daniel A. Nord, AEMT-CC, CHT, DAN Medical Information Specialist

As open-water students, we all were drilled about the perils of alcohol and diving. To be sure, there is no exception to the rule that drinking and diving don't mix.

But what about other drugs and diving - specifically over-the-counter medications? Is the line so clear-cut with OTCs?

This is the stuff many dive medical questions are made of - some of the more common questions to DAN medics concern the use of over-the-counter (OTC) medications and their compatibility with safe diving.

The fact that these drugs are easily available over the counter versus a more controlled dispersal as with prescription medications carries with it a sometimes faulty assumption - that all OTCs are completely safe, whether you're topside or underwater.

Not true, say doctors, diving medical specialists - and anecdotal experiences of divers. All drugs are capable of producing some side effects, and even untoward effects in some people when above water. So what happens when you use OTCs underwater - when you're subjected to the pressures of depth? The answer is not so clear, because little empirical evidence is documented - there has been scant research conducted on the effects of drugs used in a hyperbaric environment. Diving while using most medications is, at best, a matter for you, your doctor and DAN to discuss - before you dive.

CAN'T LIVE WITHOUT 'EM?

Three-fifths of the medications purchased in the United States are nonprescription over-the-counter (OTC) drugs, widely viewed as a cost-effective segment of personal health care. The OTC drug system supports a trend toward self-care and self-medication and is experiencing, on average, an 8- to 10-percent annual growth. Given the popularity of recreational scuba, there is often a concern that some OTCs may not be appropriate for use while diving.

By definition, OTCs are that classification of drugs considered safe for consumer use, based solely on their labeling. When used as directed, they present a minimum risk and a greater margin of safety than prescription (Rx) drugs. They are typically used to treat illnesses which can be easily recognized by the user, in contrast to conditions treated by prescription drugs, which are generally more difficult to assess. Additionally, there are about 300,000 OTC drugs currently on the market, far outnumbering the 65,000 prescription drugs. The most commonly encountered OTCs - and probably of greatest concern for the sport or recreational diver - fall within the following categories:

- Antihistamines
- Decongestants and cough suppressants
- Anti-inflammatory agents
- Analgesics
- Anti-motion sickness preparations

PRESCRIPTION FOR THOUGHT

A diver considering the use of any medication should first give serious thought to the underlying need or reason to take the drug. Does the underlying condition disqualify the individual from diving, or does it compromise his general safety and that of other divers?

The diver, for instance, who requires decongestants in order to equalize his ears and sinuses, has increased risk of serious injury from barotrauma. Another example is the seasick diver who, medicated or not, may experience in-water episodic disorientation, vomiting, loss of buoyancy control and embolism as a result of breath-holding or violent diaphragmatic movement.

No drug is completely safe, regardless of the environment. Drugs are chemicals and by design, alter body functions through their therapeutic action. Moreover, they all may have undesirable effects that vary by individual or environment - with sometimes unpredictable results.

BACKGROUND INSIGHTS

What's the first step to take in researching your medications? Review and familiarization with the active ingredients, warnings and directions provided by the manufacturer may offer good insight to the potential for a problem. Here are some examples to learn from.

ANTIHISTAMINES

Most often used to provide symptomatic relief of allergies, colds and motion sickness are antihistamines, with the active ingredients diphenhydramine hydrochloride, triprolidine hydrolochloride and chlorpheniramine maleate. The word "antihistamine" literally denotes a drug with characteristics which are antagonistic to the actions of histamine.

Histamine, in turn, is a powerful stimulant of gastric secretion, a constrictor of bronchial smooth muscle, and a dilator of capillaries and arterioles. Antihistamines, then, counteract the symptoms of allergies, colds and motion sickness, but may have side effects. In therapeutic doses, these side effects may include dryness of the mouth, nose and throat, visual disturbances, drowsiness or an undesired sedation or depression - all significant factors that, together or separately, can affect the safety of a dive. Antihistamines can also depress the central nervous system (CNS) and impair a diver's ability to think clearly and react appropriately when the need arises.

Decongestants - These are vasoconstricting drugs that cause narrowing of the blood vessels, which often gives a temporary improvement of the nasal airways. Common active ingredients include pseudoephedrine hydrochloride and phenylpropanolamine hydrochloride. Decongestants may cause a mild CNS stimulation and can also offer numerous side effects such as nervousness, excitability, restlessness, dizziness, weakness and a forceful or rapid heartbeat.

Medications known to stimulate the central nervous system may have a significant and/or undesirable effect on the diver. Additional precautions or warnings may advise against use by individuals suffering from diabetes, asthma or cardiovascular disease.

ANTI-INFLAMMATORIES & ANALGESICS

As with any drug, it is wise to consider the underlying condition for taking anti-inflammatories or analgesics. These drugs are generally taken for the temporary relief of minor aches and pains, and although they may provide temporary relief, remember that the injury itself is still present. Limitations in range of movement because of the injury, swelling or pain can place a diver at risk of additional injury. In addition, they may mask mild pain due to decompression sickness, and the diver may subsequently delay seeking treatment.

Active ingredients include naproxen sodium and ibuprofen, with notable side effects such as heartburn, nausea, abdominal pain, headache, dizziness and drowsiness. Standard precautions discourage their use by those with medical disorders involving heartburn, gastric ulcers, bleeding problems or asthma.

With anti-inflammatories or analgesics, perhaps one of the most significant considerations is potential adverse drug interactions in individuals treated with anticoagulants, insulin and nonsteroidal anti-inflammatories (NSAIDs).

ANTI-MOTION SICKNESS PREPARATIONS

It's best not to self-medicate here; specific warnings regularly prohibit the use of these medications prior to consulting a physician. It's generally agreed that - at any time - recreational divers should use these medications with caution.

As with some antihistamines, these medications may typically contain meclizine hydrochloride, dimenhydrinate, diphenhydramine hydrochloride and cyclizine. Common side effects are drowsiness and fatigue. Coupled with impairment of a diver's ability to perform hazardous activities requiring mental alertness or physical coordination, these side effects will definitely not enhance the pleasure of a dive.

PRESSURE

Any medication that affects the CNS, such as anithistamines, decongestants anti-motion sickness medications, has the potential to interact with increased partial pressures of nitrogen. How? The effects of the medication may increase the chance of nitrogen narcosis. In addition, nitrogen may have a synergistic effect in enhancing the sedative or stimulant quality of the drug.

Furthermore, because of the increased intensity of these effects, a new and unexpected reaction such as panic may occur in an otherwise rational diver. These side effects will vary from diver to diver and from day to day within the same diver - it's simply not possible to predict who will have a reaction while diving.

What does this all mean for the recreational scuba diver? From a medical perspective, many doctors knowledgeable in diving medicine will quickly advise anyone who requires medication in order to dive to wait the illness out. Other maxims to heed follow below.

Consult your physician when you are ill - your doctor may be able to provide you with a more effective medication and counsel you on diving fitness.

Study all the information supplied with your medication and understand the warnings, precautions and what effects it may have on your body. A trial exposure of at least one or two days prior to diving may help you assess your individual reaction to the drug.

As we often experience in other day-to-day matters, the decision of whether or not to dive is personal and one of acceptable risk. The choice of acceptable risk is a matter of judgment, with careful attention given to the risk versus the benefits, as well as the ability and willingness to deal with possible negative consequences.

Diving should be a positive experience. Dive with care. Remember that both your doctor - and DAN - are there to answer any questions you may have about diving and your health.

EAR INJURIES

By Bruce Delphia, DAN Training Staff Specialist

NOTE: No article can give you the same degree of information as an experienced medical practitioner. DAN suggests all persons with any ear discomfort should be examined by a trained medical practitioner as soon as possible after the complaint develops.

What's the most frequent diving injury? Decompression illness, right? No, it's ear injuries. The most common injury divers experience is some form of barotrauma to the ear. Barotrauma means injury from pressure (baro = pressure + trauma = injury). This type of injury occurs for a variety of reasons, but generally it develops when the pressure in the middle ear is not equal to

the pressure of the outside environment as the diver descends in the water column. Because of the rapid relative gas volume change as the diver descends at the beginning of the dive, the first 14 feet / 4.2 meters of the descent is where the ear is at most risk of injury.

ANATOMY OF THE EAR

No discussion of the examination of any part of the human body could be complete without a working knowledge of the anatomy of that part. The ear is made up of three compartments: the external ear, the middle ear and the inner ear.

The External Ear Auricle and the External Ear Canal - The auricle (pinna) is the first and most obvious view of the ear. It's what we generally refer to as the ear, although it is just the outside section of it. Funnel-shaped and mostly cartilage covered by a thin layer of skin, it channels sound (and water) into the ear.

Directly behind the tragus, the cartilaginous prominence in front of the external opening of the ear, the ear canal curves inwards approximately 24 mm in the average adult. The outer portion of the ear canal contains the glands that produce earwax (cerumen). The inner portion of the ear is covered by thin, hairless skin. Pressure on this area can cause pain.

The Middle Ear - At the inner end of the ear canal, separating the external ear from the middle ear, is the tympanic membrane, or eardrum. The middle ear is an air-filled space that contains the ossicles - three tiny bones that conduct sound. (many of us learned them as the hammer, anvil and stirrup: in medical terminology they are the mallus, incus, and stapes.)

The Eustachian tubes, one in each ear, connect the middle ear and the back of the throat (nasopharynx). They keep the middle ear "equalized" by keeping the air pressure on both sides of the eardrum the same. Because they are surrounded by cartilaginous tissue they don't allow for expansion. Therefore a diver must equalize his or her ears by gently "opening" the tubes—that is, by introducing air through them and into the middle ear.

The Inner Ear - Separating the middle ear from the inner ear are two of the thinnest membranes in the human body, the round and oval windows. These membranes embody one of the reasons diver are taught to gently blow to equalize their middle ears—damage to the round or oval windows may cause a leakage of fluid from the inner to the middle ear. This can cause a ringing or roaring in the ears, and even hearing loss. Window rupture can also cause sever vertigo and vomiting, a dangerous—even deadly—combination when underwater.

OTITIS EXTERNA
SWIMMERS EAR

This is an inflammation of the external ear caused by infection. Some people are prone to developing this kind of infection. If the ear remains moist from immersion in the water, this moisture, coupled with the warmth of the body, creates an inviting growth are for many microorganisms, especially opportunistic bacteria.

Signs & Symptoms - The ear canal can become inflamed and may partially close. The external ear canal is red and swollen and may itch. Touching the outer ear may cause intense pain.

THE TREATMENT

Prevention is key, especially in those persons who have previously shown they are susceptible. Domeboro Otic , solution, available at drugstore, may function as a prophylactic and treatment for otitis externa when it is used as directed.

BAROTITIS MEDIA
MIDDLE EAR BAROTRAUMA

This is by far the most frequently reported injury among divers. People with barotitis media generally develop symptoms im-

mediately following the dive, but delays of up to one day or longer have been reported. When the diver descends, the pressure can cause injury to the middle ear. This overpressure of the middle ear can cause serious fluid and blood to leak into the middle ear, partially or completely filling it.

Signs & Symptoms - A feeling of fullness in the ear may develop, like the feeling of fluid inside the ear. Muffled hearing or hearing loss are other indications of middle ear barotrauma. On examination with an otoscope (a special device medical personnel use when examining the ear) fluid may appear behind the tympanic membrane, causing it to bulge and appear red. In other cases, the eardrum may be retracted or sunk in. Either condition warrants immediate medical attention.

THE TREATMENT

First, diving must stop. Also, changes in altitude—as with flying—must be considered a concern as well. See a medical practitioner. The combination of drugs and time will usually allow this injury to heal in a few days, but cases have lasted up to several months. If you have been on decongestant therapy for seven days and have experienced little or no relief, it's time to see your otolaryngologist, an ear, nose and throat (ENT) specialist.

OTITIS MEDIA (MIDDLE EAR INFECTION)

This is not a diving malady, but may look the same as middle ear barotrauma to a non-dive-trained medical practitioner. Because the treatments can vary, it is important to realize that an ear problem immediately following a dive outing usually signals a pressure-related injury rather than an infection.

INNER EAR BAROTRAUMA

This injury generally occurs when divers attempt to forcefully equalize their ears. This "hard" blowing over-pressurizes the middle ear and can result in implosive or explosive damage to the round and oval windows.

Signs & Symptoms - Vertigo, vomiting, hearing loss, loud tinnitus (a ringing or roaring sound in the ear).

THE TREATMENT

Place the injured diver in a sitting head-up position. Get the injured diver to medical help right away, preferably to someone knowledgeable in diving medicine since inner ear barotrauma may be difficult to distinguish from inner-ear decompression ickness.

TYMPANIC MEMBRANE (TM) RUPTURE

Barotraumatic injuries to the ear may result in perforation or rupture of the tympanic membrane. This may occur in as little as 7 feet / 2.1 meters of water.

Signs & Symptoms - Generally there is pain and bleeding from the ear. This may no always be the case, as a number of dive-related traumatic TM ruptures have reported no pain at all. Hearing loss and tinnitus may also be present, but not always. A discharge from the ear of commingled fluid and blood may be a sign of TM rupture.

THE TREATMENT

Go to the nearest medical practitioner immediately for an examination. Do not re-enter the water if you suspect TM rupture: water entering the middle ear cavity may cause severe and violent vertigo. Do not put any drops of any kind in your ear. Do not attempt to equalize your middle ears.

VESSEL RUPTURE

This occurs more often in divers who wear hoods. Occasionally, the overpressure may rupture a blood vessel inside the external ear canal, causing some minor bleeding.

Signs & Symptoms - A minute trace of blood trickling from the ear canal. Later, the injured diver may find drops of blood on his/her pillow or bedclothes.

THE TREATMENT

In order to distinguish between this injury and other, more severe injuries, it is necessary to stop diving and seek evaluation by a medical practitioner. On a general note, a physician should examine any ear problem that drains purulent material (pus) or has a foul or disagreeable odor.

SUMMARY

Ear injuries are the most commonly encountered injuries to divers. Permanent hearing loss may result from barotrauma to the ears. The likelihood of injuries is reduced by preventive measures such as:

- properly equalizing
- never diving with a cold or other congestion, and
- abstaining from diving if you cannot clear your ears.

Several types of ear injuries can occur. All ot these injuries should be examined by a qualified medical practitioner. If in doubt regarding the practitioner's knowledge of diving medicine, bring this article with you or encourage them to call +1-919-684-2948 and ask for the Medical Department here at DAN for a consult. Otoscopic examination of the ear by a qualified medical practitioner knowledgeable in diving and emergency medicine may be useful in determining what type injury has occurred. In remote areas of the world or on board liveaboard dive vessels you may have to wait a while until you can get medical help. DAN's advice is to encourage you to get to a medical facility as soon as possible.

DIABETES

Diabetes mellitus (DM) is a disorder of the endocrine system, manifested by one of two things: an insufficient production of insulin or the resistance of the body's cells to the actions of insulin despite normal or high levels. People with DM often have excessively high blood glucose (BG), called hyperglycemia, or an excessively low BG, better known as hypoglycemia.

Diabetes mellitus itself has two major forms: Insulin-requiring diabetes (IDDM, Type 1),* for which insulin must be given by injection to control blood sugar levels; and non-insulin-dependent diabetes (NIDDM, Type 2), which may be controlled by diet or by oral medications (oral hypoglycemic medications).

The main risk to the diver is the occurrence of hypoglycemia that can manifest itself as confusion, sweating, rapid heartbeat, unconsciousness and even death. High blood sugar levels, or hyperglycemia, may also cause unconsciousness, although this usually develops much more slowly than hypoglycemia. Impaired consciousness underwater leads to almost certain death. Although hypoglycemia occurs most commonly in Type 1, it can also occur in individuals taking oral hypoglycemic medications. Hypoglycemia experienced during a deep dive may be wrongly perceived as nitrogen narcosis.

Although hypo- or hyperglycemia can occur daily, other problems can develop over the long term, in persons with diabetes. These maladies include: retinopathy (alterations in visual acuity); disorders of the kidneys; coronary artery disease; and changes in the nervous system, including abnormal nervous conduction and atherosclerosis that can cause poor circulation in the limbs.

Fitness and Diving - Divers with diabetes are at risk of sudden loss of consciousness. This carries the ultimate risk of drowning and implies additional risks for their dive buddies. Individuals with diabetes, however well the diabetes is controlled, should not be deemed as fit to dive without restriction. Those who meet certain criteria can dive provided they dive in accordance with detailed, specific procedures

(See Diabetes & Diving: Current practices demonstrate that many with diabetes do take the plunge; By Guy de Lisle Dear, M.B., FRCA, Alert Diver, January / February 1997). Divers with diabetes should be examined periodically for complications of their disorder that may disqualify them on the grounds of additional risk.

Medication Used in Treatment - Sulphonylureas (drugs that posses hypoglycemic action) such as glipizide, glibenclamide, chlorpropamide and tolbutamide may interact with numerous other drugs used to lower BG.

Biguanides (metformin) may cause self-limited (gastrointestinal side effects and may cause problems[14] in individuals with renal, liver or heart diseases.

Acarbose (an alpha-glucosidase inhibitor) is also used in conjunction with other agents when the more simple sulphonureas do not work adequately to control blood glucose. Insulin acts to lower BG. In general, diving with diabetes is not recommended. An additional consideration: insulin requirements may change substantially with demands of exercise and diving.

There is a small risk of lactic acidosis which is markedly increased by any condition that reduces metformin clearance (acute or chronic renal impairment) or compromises oxygen delivery and predisposes to tissue hypoxia (acute or chronic respiratory or cardiovascular insufficiency) in persons with renal, liver or heart diseases.

ASTHMA

By Guy de Lisle Dear, M.B., FRCA, DAN Assistant Medical Director

One of the most frequently asked questions DAN's medical department tackles each week involves asthma and diving. Specifically, DAN medics are often asked to ex-

---

[14] Bayer ceased manufacture of Otic Domeboro in December 2000.

plain why there may be problems for a person with asthma who wishes to dive.

In this short article, DAN describes the nature of asthma and some aspects of its treatment as well as a review of current thinking on this issue in the dive medicine community. Keep in mind, however, this is still a hot topic — with a substantial amount of controversy — even among diving medical specialists.

Whether you have asthma or another medical condition, the consideration and acceptance of the risks involved in scuba diving should be an informed decision. This article provides basic information on where you can obtain additional guidance on asthma — for yourself, for prospective divers and for personal physicians.

OVERVIEW

The topic of asthma and diving has long been a controversial subject in the recreational diving community. Traditionally, divers with asthma have been excluded from diving.

Asthma is a disease characterized by narrowing of the breathing tubes (bronchi) in response to a variety of stimuli. It is not a fixed response, and a patient can have a sudden worsening in lung function, called an "attack." An asthma attack can be triggered by pollen and other so-called "allergens," cold air, irritants in the atmosphere, colds or flu.

The bronchial narrowing in asthma has two effects: one is to decrease the amount of air that can be moved in and out of the lungs. This can reduce exercise capacity — especially for a diver, who already has reduced breathing capacity due to the external resistance of his breathing apparatus and the increased internal resistance due to higher breathing gas density at depth. Secondly, reduced airway caliber could cause trapping of gas in the lung during ascent. If trapped gas expands at a rate greater than it can be exhaled through the narrowed airways, lung rupture

can result, causing arterial gas embolism or pneumothorax (collapsed lung).

Another related concern with asthma and diving has been the increased propensity of airways in asthmatics to narrow when exposed to the conditions implicit in diving: inhalation of cold, dry air and/or sea water (the latter by losing the mouthpiece or from a leaky regulator). Dr. Mark Harries from the British Medical Olympic Center has pointed out that asthmatics who dive are at risk from exercise limitation, not just peripheral gas-trapping. While exercising on land it is easy enough to stop, rest and catch one's breath; this may not be possible underwater.

DISCUSSIONS ON DIVING WITH ASTHMA

What do dive physicians think about diving with asthma? This subject has generated much discussion worldwide, and many physicians hold opposing viewpoints.

Perhaps the most liberal guidelines are from the United Kingdom, which states that well-controlled asthmatics may dive — within two guidelines:

1. Provided they have not needed a bronchodilator within 48 hours; and
2. If they do not have cold-, exercise- or emotion-induced asthma.

In Australia, the most conservative country in this respect, all divers are expected to pass a spirometry (lung function) test, to exclude asthma, prior to certification.

As a general overview, DAN statistics show that several divers with asthma have died. It is unclear, though, from examination of their accident reports whether asthma was actually the cause of death or merely an unrelated finding. Data from the British Sub Aqua Club (BSAC) indicate that few divers die with asthma or as a result of asthma.

In addition to DAN's own research, the issue of diving with asthma was discussed at the 1995 annual meeting of the Undersea and Hyperbaric Medical Society

(UHMS), the international organization comprised of diving physicians from around the world. The symposium "Are Asthmatics Fit to Dive?" was an important agenda item at that meeting.

On the general assessment of the risks of diving with asthma, the South Pacific Underwater Medical Society (SPUMS) has stated that diving may precipitate an asthma attack. Asthmatics are at risk of shortness of breath, panic and drowning on the surface.

Information from the DAN database on divers with asthma suggests that there may be a slight increase in the risk of decompression illness, but there are insufficient numbers as yet to assess the risk accurately.

The incidence of asthma in the general population is approximately 4-5 percent. Records indicate that about the same percentage of the diving population has asthma, whether or not they admit so on their diving medical forms. It appears, then, that a percentage of divers with asthma are diving safely. Bear in mind that this only represents divers who took up diving against medical advice, and who probably have mild asthma only. The true risk for all asthmatics may well be significantly higher than is currently appreciated by the statistics.

The treatment of the four forms of asthma.is relevant in determining its severity (see below) and therefore the associated risk of diving. According to UHMS discussions, the first three types of asthma (mild, intermittent, and mild-to-moderate persistent asthma), if well-controlled, may allow carefully selected divers to continue diving.

CATEGORIZING RISKS

The next question involves assessing a diver with asthma, with these two qualifications:

- Is the asthma of a mild nature; or

- Is the treatment working sufficiently to prevent an acute asthmatic attack while underwater or on the surface?

If the treatment regimen can return the pulmonary function tests to normal, especially those taken post-exercise, divers may be safe to dive and undergo the severe exercise they may need to perform while diving. Potential divers with asthma should undergo both an assessment of lung function and an exercise test to gauge asthma severity. A physician knowledgeable in diving as well as the treatment of asthma might be in a position to offer the best advice.

One consistent theme from all the medical agencies involved was the lack of good information about asthma and diving. DAN is presently working on an assessment of the whole issue. We hope to develop guidelines as to whether individuals with asthma can dive safely and under what circumstances. The best source to help you decide on the issue of diving and asthma for yourself is your physician.

FLYING AFTER DIVING

Revised Flying after Diving Guidelines for Recreational Diving - May 2002

Photo: J. Gallant / D.A.Y.

The following guidelines are the consensus of attendees at the 2002 Flying After Diving Workshop. They apply to air dives followed by flights at cabin altitudes of 2,000 to 8,000 ft (610 to 2,438 m) for divers who do not have symptoms of decompression sickness (DCS). The recommended preflight surface intervals do not guarantee avoidance of DCS. Longer surface intervals will reduce DCS risk further.

For a single no-decompression dive, a minimum preflight surface interval of 12 hours is suggested.

For multiple dives per day or multiple days of diving, a minimum preflight surface interval of 18 hours is suggested.

For dives requiring decompression stops, there is little evidence on which to base a recommendation and a preflight surface interval substantially longer than 18 hours appears prudent.

DECOMPRESSION ILLNESS (DCI)

Decompression Illness: What Is It and What Is The Treatment?

By Dr. E.D. Thalmann, DAN Assistant Medical Director

With Reports by Renée Duncan, Editor, and Joel Dovenbarger, Vice President, DAN Medical Services

Decompression illness, or DCI, is a term used to describe illness that results from a reduction in the ambient pressure surrounding a body. A good example is what happens to your body when you're surfacing after a dive.

DCI encompasses two diseases, decompression sickness (DCS) and arterial gas embolism (AGE). DCS is thought to result from bubbles growing in tissue and causing local damage, while AGE results from bubbles entering the lung circulation, traveling through the arteries and causing tissue damage at a distance by blocking blood flow at the small vessel level.

WHO GETS DCI?

Decompression illness affects scuba divers, aviators, astronauts and compressed-air workers. It occurs in approximately 1,000 U.S. scuba divers each year. Moreover, DCI hits randomly. The main risk factor for DCI is a reduction in ambient pressure, but there are other risk factors that will increase the chance of DCI occurring. These known risk factors are deep / long dives, cold water, hard exercise at depth, and rapid ascents.

Rapid ascents are closely linked to the risk of AGE. Other factors thought to increase the risk of DCI but for which evidence is not conclusive are obesity, dehydration, hard exercise immediately after surfacing, and pulmonary disease. In addition, there seem to be individual risk factors that have not yet been identified. This is why some divers seem to get DCI more frequently than others although they are following the same dive profile.

Since DCI is a random event, almost any dive profile can result in DCI, no matter how safe it seems. The reason is that the risk factors, both known and unknown, can influence the probability of DCI in myriad ways. Because of this, evaluation of a diver for possible decompression illness must be made on a case-by-case basis by evaluating the diver's signs and symptoms and not just based on the dive profile.

DECOMPRESSION SICKNESS (DCS)

Decompression sickness (DCS, also called the bends or caisson disease) is the result of inadequate decompression following exposure to increased pressure. In some cases, the disease is mild and not an immediate threat. In other cases, serious injury does occur; when this happens, the quicker treatment begins, the better the chance for a full recovery.

During a dive, the body tissues absorb nitrogen from the breathing gas in proportion to the surrounding pressure. As long as the diver remains at pressure, the gas presents no problem. If the pressure is reduced too quickly, however, the nitrogen comes out of solution and forms bubbles in the tissues and bloodstream. This commonly occurs as a result of violating or approaching too closely the diving table limits, but it can also occur even when accepted guidelines have been followed.

Bubbles forming in or near joints are the presumed cause of the joint pain of a classical "bend." When high levels of bubbles occur, complex reactions can take place in the body, usually in the spinal cord or brain. Numbness, paralysis and disorders of higher cerebral function may result. If great amounts of decompression are missed and large numbers of bubbles enter the venous bloodstream, congestive symptoms in the lung and circulatory shock can then occur.

SYMPTOMS OF DCS

- Unusual fatigue
- Skin itch
- Pain in joints and / or muscles of the arms, legs or torso
- Dizziness, vertigo, ringing in the ears
- Numbness, tingling and paralysis
Shortness of breath

SIGNS OF DCS

- Skin may show a blotchy rash
- Paralysis, muscle weakness
- Difficulty urinating
- Confusion, personality changes, bizarre behaviour
- Amnesia, tremors
- Staggering
- Coughing up bloody, frothy sputum
- Collapse or unconsciousness

Note: Symptoms and signs usually appear within 15 minutes to 12 hours after surfacing; but in severe cases, symptoms may appear before surfacing or immediately afterwards. Delayed occurrence of symp-

toms is rare, but it does occur, especially if air travel follows diving.

DENIAL AND RECOGNITION

The most common manifestations of DCS are joint pain and numbness or tingling. Next most common are muscular weakness and inability to empty a full bladder. Severe DCS is easy to identify because the signs and symptoms are obvious. However, most DCS manifests subtly with a minor joint ache or a paresthesia (an abnormal sensation like burning, tingling or ticking) in an extremity.

In many cases these symptoms are ascribed to another cause such as overexertion, heavy lifting or even a tight wetsuit. This delays seeking help and is why it is often noted that the first symptom of DCS is denial. Sometimes these symptoms remain mild and go away by themselves, but many times they increase in severity until it is obvious to you that something is wrong and that you need help.

What happens if you don't seek treatment? In severe DCS, a permanent residual handicap may result: this can be a bladder dysfunction, sexual dysfunction or muscular weakness, to name a few.

In some cases of neurological DCS, there mat be permanent damage to the spinal cord, which may or may not cause symptoms. However, this type of damage may decrease the likelihood of recovery from a subsequent bout of DCS.

Untreated joint pains that subside are thought to cause small areas of bone damage called osteonecrosis. Usually this will not cause symptoms unless there are many bouts of untreated DCS. If this happens, however, there may be enough damage to cause the bone to become brittle or for joints to collapse or become arthritic.

PREVENTION OF DCS

Recreational divers should dive conservatively, whether they are using dive tables or computers. Experienced divers often select a table depth (versus actual depth) of 10 feet (3 meters) deeper than called for by standard procedure. This practice is highly recommended for all divers, especially when diving in cold water or when diving under strenuous conditions. Computer divers should be cautious in approaching no-decompression limits, especially when diving deeper than 100 feet (30 meters).

Avoiding the risk factors noted above (deep / long dives, exercise at depth or after a dive) will decrease the chance of DCS occurring. Exposure to altitude or flying too soon after a dive can also increase the risk of decompression sickness.

ARTERIAL GAS EMBOLISM (AGE)

If a diver surfaces without exhaling, air trapped in the lungs expands with ascent and may rupture lung tissue - called pulmonary barotrauma - which releases gas bubbles into the arterial circulation. This distributes them to body tissues in proportion to the blood flow. Since the brain receives the highest proportion of blood flow, it is the main target organ where bubbles may interrupt circulation if they become lodged in small arteries.

This is arterial gas embolism, or AGE, considered the more serious form of DCI. In some cases the diver may have made a panicked ascent, or he may have held his breath during ascent. However, AGE can occur even if ascent appeared completely normal, and pulmonary disease such as obstructive lung disease may increase the risk of AGE.

The most dramatic presentation of air embolism is the diver who surfaces unconscious and remains so, or the diver who loses consciousness within 10 minutes of surfacing. In these cases, a true medical emergency exists, and rapid evacuation to a treatment facility is paramount.

On the other hand, air embolism may cause less spectacular symptoms of neurological dysfunction, such as sensations of tingling or numbness, a sensation of weakness without obvious paralysis, or complaints of difficulty in thinking without obvious confusion in individuals who are awake and easily aroused. In these cases, there is time for a more thorough evaluation by a diving medical specialist to rule out other causes of symptoms.

Like DCS, mild symptoms may be ascribed to causes other than the dive, which only delays treatment. Sometimes symptoms may resolve spontaneously and the diver will not seek treatment. The consequences of this are similar to untreated DCS: residual damage to the brain may occur, making it more likely there will be residual symptoms after a future bout of AGE, even if the later bout is treated.

SYMPTOMS OF AGE

- Dizziness
- Visual blurring
- Areas of decreased sensation
- Chest pain
Disorientation

SIGNS OF AGE

- Bloody froth from mouth or nose
- Paralysis or weakness
- Convulsions
- Unconsciousness
- Cessation of breathing
- Death

Currently cerebral gas embolism is responsible for approximately 10 percent of all DCI cases annually. AGE has decreased significantly over the past decade, however, moving from 18 percent of all cases in the late 1980s and early 1990s to much lower numbers. By 1997, the fraction had fallen to 7-8 percent.

In 2001, AGE was still cited in 7-8 percent but by 2002 it had fallen to 6.6 percent of the total diving population reporting DCI. It has been speculated that one of the reasons for this decrease is the advent of dive computers, which help chart the rate of ascent, thus reminding divers to slow down.

PREVENTION OF AGE

Always relax and breathe normally during ascent. Lung conditions such as asthma, infections, cysts, tumors, scar tissue from surgery or obstructive lung disease may predispose a diver to air embolism. If you have any of these conditions, it warrants an evaluation by a physician knowledgeable in diving medicine.

TREATMENT - CALL DAN!

The treatment for DCI is recompression. However, the early management of air embolism and decompression sicknessis the same. Although a diver with severe DCS or an air embolism requires urgent recompression for definitive treatment, it is essential that he be stabilized at the nearest medical facility before transportation to a chamber.

Early oxygen first aid is important and may reduce symptoms substantially, but this should not change the treatment plan. Symptoms of air embolism and serious decompression sickness often clear after initial oxygen breathing, but they may reappear later. Because of this, always contact DAN or a dive physician in cases of suspected DCI - even if the symptoms and signs appear to have resolved.

Treatment involves compression to a treatment depth, usually 60 feet(18 m), and breathing high oxygen fraction gases at an oxygen partial pressure of between 2.8 ata (atmospheres) and 3.0 ata. Delays in seeking treatment have a higher risk of residual symptoms; over time, the initially reversible damage may become permanent. After a delay of 24 hours or more, treatment may become ineffective and

symptoms may not respond to treatment. Even if there has been a delay, however, consult a diving medical specialist before drawing any conclusions about possible treatment effectiveness.

In some cases, there may be residual symptoms after a treatment. Soreness in and around a joint that was affected by DCS is common and usually resolves in a few hours. If the DCI was severe, significant residual neurological dysfunction may be present, even after the most aggressive treatment. In these cases, there may be follow-up treatments, along with physical therapy. The good news is that the usual outcome is eventual complete relief from all symptoms, provided treatment was begun promptly.

RETURNING TO DIVING AFTER DCI

The U.S. Navy has set down rules for returning to diving after treatment. For pain-only DCI where there are no neurological symptoms, divers may begin diving two to seven days after treatment, depending on the treatment table used.

If there are neurological symptoms, the diver may resume diving two to four weeks after treatment, depending on symptom severity. For very severe symptoms, the diver must be reevaluated three months after treatment and cleared by a Diving Medical Officer.

The Navy's guidelines are for professionals, where time off must be minimized so operations are not compromised.

GUIDES FOR SPORT DIVERS

For recreational divers, where diving is not a livelihood, a more conservative approach is called for to further minimize the chance that a diving injury will recur.

- After pain-only DCI where there are no neurological symptoms, a minimum of

two weeks without diving is recommended.
- If there are minor neurological symptoms, six weeks without diving is recommended.
- If there are severe neurological symptoms or any residual symptoms, no further diving is recommended.

Even if symptoms were not severe and they resolved completely, a diver who has had multiple bouts of DCI must take special considerations. If DCI is occurring where other divers on the same profile are DCI-free, the diver may have an increased susceptibility to DCI. In these cases, a Diving Medical Specialist must be consulted to determine if diving can be resumed safely.

Remember, your good health needs to last as long as you do.

DAN

Founded in 1980, DAN has served as a lifeline for the scuba industry by operating diving's only 24-hour emergency hotline, a lifesaving service for injured divers. Additionally, DAN operates a diving medical information line, conducts vital diving medical research, and develops and provides a number of educational programs for everyone from beginning divers to medical professionals.

Divers Alert Network is supported by membership dues and donations. In return, members receive a number of important benefits including $100,000 emergency medical evacuation assistance, DAN educational publications, a subscription to Alert Diver magazine, and access to diving's first and foremost accident insurance coverage.

DAN'S MISSION STATEMENT

DAN helps divers in need with medical emergency assistance and promotes diving safety through research, education, products and services.

DAN, a non-profit organization, exists to provide expert information and advice for the benefit of the diving public. DAN's historical and primary function is to provide emergency medical advice and assistance for underwater diving injuries, to work to prevent injuries and to promote diving safety. Second, DAN promotes and supports underwater diving research and education particularly as it relates to the improvement of diving safety, medical treatment and first aid. Third, DAN strives to provide the most accurate, up-to-date and unbiased information on issues of common concern to the diving public, primarily, but not exclusively, for diving safety. DAN is *Your* Dive Safety Association.

DAN'S VISION STATEMENT

Striving to make every dive, accident- and injury-free.

DAN's vision is to be the most recognized and trusted organization worldwide in the fields of diver safety and emergency services, health, research, and education by its members, instructors, sponsors, and recreational diving community at large. "Your Dive Safety Association," DAN currently has more than 200,000 members.

INTERNATIONAL DAN

International DAN (IDAN) is comprised of several independent DAN organizations based around the world to provide expert emergency medical and referral services to regional diving communities. These local networks have pledged to uphold DAN's mission and to operate under protocol standards agreed to by the IDAN Headquarters. Each IDAN organization is a non-profit, independently administered organization. Each DAN depends on the support of local divers to provide its safety and educational services, such as emergency hotlines. In addition, each country has its own rules and regulations regarding insurance. DAN America complies with U.S. regulations only. Each regional DAN is cognizant of the insurance regulations of its territory.

DAN AMERICA

Divers Alert Network (DAN) America serves as the Headquarters for IDAN. Regions of coverage include North America, Central America, South America, and the Caribbean.

The Peter B Bennett Center
6 West Colony Place
Durham, NC 27705-5588 USA
1-800-446-2671 Toll-Free
1-919-684-2948 General Inquiries
1-919-490-6630 Fax
1-919-493-3040 Medical Fax
Diving Emergencies

DAN America
1-919-684-8111
1-919-684-4326 (accepts collect calls)

DAN Latin America
1-919-684-9111 (accepts collect calls)

Non-Diving Emergencies & TravelAssist Services

1-800-326-3822 (1-800-DAN-EVAC)
1-919-684-3483 (Call collect if outside the USA, Canada, Puerto Rico, Bahamas, British or U.S. Virgin Islands)
www.diversalertnetwork.org

DAN EUROPE

Regions of coverage include geographical Europe, the countries of the Mediterranean Basin, the countries on the shores of the Red Sea, the Middle East including the Persian Gulf, the countries on the shores of the Indian Ocean north of the Equator and West of India and Sri Lanka, as well as the related overseas territories, districts, and protectorates.

DAN EUROPE
P.O. Box DAN
64026 Roseto (Te) ITALY
39-085-893-0333
39-085-893-0050 FAX

Diving Emergencies
DAN Europe

39-039-605-7858
Non-Diving Emergencies and TravelAssist Services
39-039-605-7858
www.daneurope.org

DAN JAPAN

Regions of coverage include Japan, Japanese islands, and related territories.

Japan Marine Recreation Association
Kowa-Ota-Machi Bldg, 2F, 47 Ota-Machi 4-Chome, Nakaku, Yokohama City, Kagawa 231-0011 Japan
81-45-228-3066
81-45-228-3063 FAX

Diving Emergencies
DAN Japan
81-3-3812-4999
www.danjapan.gr.jp

ASIA PACIFIC

Regions of coverage include Australia, New Zealand, South Pacific Islands, Southeast Asia, India, China, Taiwan, and Korea.

P.O. Box 384
Ashburton, Victoria 3147
AUSTRALIA
61-3-9886-9166
61-3-9886-9155 FAX

Diving Emergencies
Australia
1-800-088-200 (within Australia)
61-8-8212-9242 (outside Australia)
New Zealand
0800-4DES111
Singapore Naval Medicine & Hyperbaric Center
67-58-1733
DAN AP - Philippines
02-632-1077
DAN AP - Malaysia
05-930-4114
DAN AP - Korea
82-010-4500-9113
www.danseap.org

DAN SOUTHERN AFRICA

Regions of coverage include South Africa, Swaziland, Lesotho, Namibia, Botswana, Zimbabwe, Mozambique, Angola, Zambia, Zaire, Malawi, Tanzania, Kenya, Madagascar, Comoros, Seychelles, and Mauritius.

Private Bag X 197
Halfway House, 1685
SOUTHERN AFRICA
2711-254-1991 or 2711-254-1992

2711-254-1993 FAX

Diving Emergencies
DAN Southern Africa
0800-020111 (within South Africa)
27-11-254-1112 (outside South Africa)
www.dansa.org

CMAS QUÉBEC

INFORMATION IN THIS SECTION
PROVIDED IN PART BY CMAS/AMCQ
AND ADAPTED BY D.A.Y.

Chapter **5**

DIVING EQUIPMENT

In order to explore the aquatic universe, a diver has to adapt to the underwater environment. The human body is designed to function on land. Because the aquatic environment is very different from our own, all of our senses are affected. This is largely due to the fact that water is a liquid and that it is much denser that air and cannot be breathed. Diving equipment is required to enable human beings to see, breathe, move, and stay warm underwater.

Knowing how to use diving equipment does not in itself make a diver safe or proficient. A diver must understand the underwater environment, remain calm at all times, and use the skills learned during his training.

DIVE MASK

Because the human eye is made for seeing clearly in air, a diver must create an air space between his eyes and the water to be able to see. A dive mask like the one at the top of this page enables the diver to see and it also protects his eyes and a good portion of his face against the cold, water impurities and salt.

Most masks today are made of silicone while a few are still made or rubber. Certain masks come with a purge valve; others can be fitted with corrective lenses. All masks encompass the nose which can be compressed with fingers to equalize using the Valsalva maneuver.

Low-volume masks are easier to clear when flooded. They are preferred by freedivers who do not carry an air supply.

The air inside the mask is warmer than the surrounding water which causes condensation to form on the inside of the glass. To eliminate condensation, divers use a non-irritating solution commonly known as defog, or use spit on the lense in order to ensure clear vision throughout the dive.

Full face masks protect the diver's skin from the cold or from contaminants in the water. Certain models also enable the diver to breathe through his nose and use a communications system.

Poseidon full face mask. Photo: Poseidon www.poseidon.se

SNORKEL

The snorkel is required to breathe at the surface without emerging the head from the water. This enables a diver to swim at the surface without losing sight of his underwater surroundings.

Many snorkels are equipped with purges so the diver can easily clear any water that has entered the snorkel due to waves or immersion. Certain models have dry features that prevent water from entering the snorkel while at the surface.

The one-way purge valve on this snorkel is located below the mouth to keep the mouthpiece clear of water. Photo by J. Gallant / D.A.Y.

Snorkels are rarely longer than 12 in. (50 cm) because the pressure exerted on the human body at that depth makes it nearly impossible for a person to fill his lungs.

FINS

Water is 800 times denser than air and thus offers much resistance to a diver trying to move forward. Since the diver is essentially floating in mid-water without solid footing, the diver needs a surface more effective than his arms and legs to propel him through the water.

Fins offer a flat and solid surface that enables the diver to move effectively. Fins come in many designs with varying surface areas. They are made of plastic, rubber or various fibers. Larger blades offer more power but demand more energy in return.

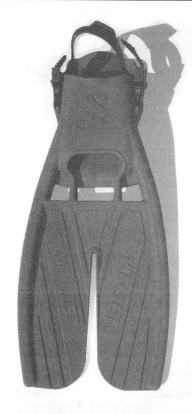

The Scubapro Twinjet combines modern split-blade technology with a more traditional design. Photo: D.A.Y.

A full-footed fin. Photo: Leaderfins
www.leaderfins.com

Long fins give more power while smaller fins offer great maneuverability for photographers that need to approach their subject from just the right angle to get that perfect shot.

Forcefins – Photo: D.A.Y.

REGULATOR

A diver can only breathe air at a pressure equal to ambient pressure, that is, the pressure which surrounds him. A diving regulator is used to release the compressed air in the tank to the diver at ambient pressure and at any depth.

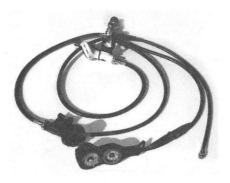

First and second stage regulators, depth and tank pressures gauges, and BCD and drysuit inflators. Photo: D.A.Y.

The regulator releases the pressure in two stages. The first stage is to supply air to the diver upon demand, when the diver inhales or applies pressure on a demand valve. The first stage is usually designed to release the gas at a constant rate despite the pressure in the cylinder becoming less as the gas in the cylinder is used, i.e. the diver never has to make an effort to breathe.

Poseidon Technika second stage regulator. Photo: D.A.Y.

Royal Mistral single-stage regulator (circa 1965) Photo: D.A.Y.

GAUGES

The pressure gauge, a.k.a. tank gauge, measures the air pressure in the scuba tank to allow the diver to know how much air is available at all times.

The depth gauge is indispensable to the diver as knowing the depth of the dive is essential. The depth gauge can be worn on the wrist or fixed in a console with the pressure gauge. Measurements are shown in feet or meters. The scales will differ from one model to another, with some being more precise at low depths and others at high depths.

The depth gauge with a diaphragm is the most precise and resistant depth gauge for deep dives. For recreational dives, the depth gauge with a scale of 0 to 160 ft (50 m) is typical.

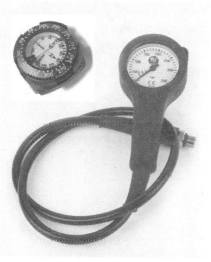

Poseidon compass and analog tank pressure gauge.
Photo: Poseidon / www.poseidon.se

Becoming more popular over the past few years is the electronic depth gauge. It works with a lithium battery and measures depth plus dive time, maximum depth reached, water and air temperature. It will also save data from previous dives. Some models have a visual or audio alarm should the diver go beyond the normal resurfacing speed.

Not a gauge at all but often mounted on a gauge console, the dive compass is the same as a land compass. It is very practical for mapping a dive site or simply to avoid swimming in circles, especially when the visibility is poor.

DIVE COMPUTER

The dive computer practically eliminates the need for a watch or dive tables. They are becoming more popular with divers since their arrival in the early 80s. The dive computer keeps track of the maximum depth, present depth, dive time, resurfacing speed, the number of dives made, dive parameters, surface time between dives, amount of nitrogen in the diver's body, delay time to be respected before flying, and more.

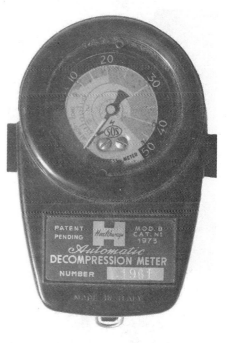

Dive 'computers' have come a long way since the Automatic Decompression Meter (1973). Photo: D.A.Y.

Computerized depth tracking has resulted in deeper and longer dives however, the measurements are theoretical and do not take into consideration the personal physiology of the diver, nor the conditions of the dive (current, water temperature, fatigue, etc.). For the sake of safety, it is highly recommended to stay clear of the preset non-decompression limits of dive computers.

Aeris dive computer. Photo: www.diveaeris.com

DIVE WATCH

A dive watch is used to calculate the time and duration of the dive as well as to monitor the diver's rate of ascent. A dive watch should be water and pressure resistant to over 300 ft (100 m). A good dive watch will indicate depth in feet or meters or the pressure that it can withstand. A rotating bezel enables the diver to measure the time spent underwater from the start of the dive. The strap should be adjustable and long enough to fit over a dive suit. In addition to current depth, digital models may also indicate water temperature.

CITIZEN
ECO-DRIVE

Digital/analog dive watch. Photo courtesy Citizen Watch Company of America - www.citizenwatch.com

Analog dive watch. Photo courtesy Citizen Watch Company of America - www.citizenwatch.com

BUOYANCY COMPENSATOR

The buoyancy compensator or buoyancy control device (BCD), serves a double purpose. It permits the diver to adjust his buoyancy as it constantly changes during his descent and ascent. Buoyancy must be kept as neutral as possible throughout the dive. This will enable the diver to keep safe his energy, use less air and move more easily on the sea bottom. It is also a potential life saver which will allow the diver to ascend easily in problematic situations and to float on the surface.

Poseidon BeSea W100 BCD. Photo: www.poseidon.se

The vest buoyancy compensator is an inflatable vest with a harness going over the shoulders and which buckles at the chest level. It also has a Velcro belt that attaches at the waist. The vest has various valves: an inflation valve, easily accessible to the diver for fast air entry; a vent valve to allow gas to exit rapidly; a mechanical valve that allows for immediate and fast air entry from the diving cylinder; and an overpressurization valve to vent an excess of air quickly and automatically. There are pockets and D rings used for carrying or

clipping on various equipment including pocket weights in the case of a weight-integrated BCD. Technical BCDs usually are normally back inflated and include a metal back plate for extra strength and to reduce the amount of weight carried in pockets or the harness.

WEIGHTS

A wet or dry suit increases a diver's positive buoyancy making it difficult to descend to the sea bottom. To compensate for this, the diver wears a weight belt, a weight harness or weights pockets in his BCD.

The weight belt is made of strong woven nylon and has a one-hand release buckle that is quick and easy to snap on or off when required. Lead bullets or other shapes are tightly threaded into the belt and the weight neutralizes the diver's buoyancy. Weights come in different sizes, shapes and materials. The most common is the lead weight "brick" which is unfinished or coated with plastic. Another weight is the pouch filled with lead shot. The traditional weight belt requires keepers to ensure that the weights stay in place on the belt. Another type of weight belt has pockets all around it for placement of the weights. It is very important for weight to be distributed evenly around the diver's body. Proper weighting is a crucial safety factor for all types of diving. Too much or not enough weight can be dangerous.

Poseidon lead packets. Photo: www.poseidon.se

DIVING SUIT

A diver protects himself from losing excessive heat when diving in cold water by wearing an insulated thermal suit. The suit reduces or totally eliminates direct contact of the skin with the water. The length of time this protection will last depends on different factors, including the type and fit of the suit, the depth of the dive and the water temperature. The suit also provides protection against minor injuries and scratches that can occur on contact with the sea bottom, flora and fauna.

A diver wearing a 3 mm wetsuit in the Caribbean. Photo: J. Gallant / D.A.Y.

There are two types of insulated thermal suits on the market: wetsuits and drysuits. The wet suit is a protection against the loss of body heat. This suit does not stop water from penetrating; however, it only allows a limited quantity of water between the diver's skin and the suit itself. This small amount of water, isolated from its cold source, will warm to the body temperature and provide a thermal protection.

A wet suit is made of neoprene covered with a coating of nylon or Lycra on the outside and/or the inside. Neoprene is a soft rubber composed of thousands of tiny closed cells. The gas-filled cells in neoprene cause it to tighten as the diver descends which reduces the thermal protection.

Rescue Swimmer Cory Lawrence wearing a "shorty" suitable for rescues in the warm waters off eastern Florida and the Gulf of Mexico. Photo: U.S. Navy Chief Photographer's Mate Chris Desmond.

The thickness of the neoprene material, measured in millimeters, will play a role in the protection against heat loss. Of equal importance is the fit of the wet suit. A suit should not be overly tight so as to restrict circulation however, a well fitted suit, thickness 7 mm will allow in very little water thus resulting in better thermal protection than a thicker ill-fitting suit. The nylon or Lycra covering the neoprene will protect the suit from tears and snags.

Wet suits come in various shapes and thicknesses: one-piece, two-piece, and shorty with or without a hood.

When the water is very warm, some divers wear only a bodysuit which provides protection from the sun and abrasions.

A dry suit, as its name clearly states, keeps the diver dry. The suit keeps the diver from any skin contact with the water. As a result, the loss of body heat is greatly diminished. The diver's protection is enhanced from the air inside the suit as well as thermal clothing which is worn under the dry suit.

Chris Harvey-Clark rinses his self-donning drysuit in a freshwater river after a dive in the cold North Atlantic. Photo: J. Gallant / D.A.Y.

A dry suit is made of latex, neoprene rubber, or a tri-laminated rubberized nylon thus making it waterproof. Booties are generally attached to the suit and seals around the neck and wrists render it watertight. Thermal clothing is worn underneath. On some suits, the zipper is located in the back between the shoulder blades and help is needed to zip it up. Other suits are self-donning and require no assistance. A dry suit should fit properly and allow for thermal clothing to be worn underneath. The hood can be separate from the dry suit or attached.

A hood, gloves or three-fingered mitts are worn with a drysuit. Depending on water conditions, they are optional with a wetsuit or skin. The valve used for inflating air into a dry suit is located on the chest of the suit. Air is inflated as the diver descends for buoyancy as well as for keeping warm. An

exhaust valve will permit the diver to deflate the suit on ascent. Most manufacturers warn that a dry suit should not be used as a buoyancy compensator and that the diver should also wear a BCD.

DIVE TANK

A diver on scuba needs a supply of compressed air in order to breathe under water. This air supply is carried in a compressed state within a metallic cylindrical container. The tank is made of either steel or aluminum. A steel container is generally 4 to 5 mm (+/- 3/16 inches) thick; an aluminum tank can be up to 11mm (+/- 3/8 inches) in thickness. Aluminum tanks are thus larger than steel tanks holding an equal volume of gas.

Rows of aluminum tanks at a dive resort. Photo: J. Gallant / D.A.Y.

Because they are larger and weigh less, they become positively buoyant as the gas inside is progressively released. Steel tanks remain negatively buoyant throughout the dive.

In America, the scuba tank capacity is measured in pressurized cubic feet (ft^3), the number of cubic feet of air that the tank can contain at 3,000 psi. The average recreational diver will use one tank with a capacity that can vary from 65 ft^3 to 120 ft^3. This is equivalent in size to the air in a small telephone booth. In Europe the tank capacity is measured by the number of litres of water that the tank can contain.

An average recreational diver will use a tank with a volume of 10-12 litres.

A diver heads for the ocean wearing a twin set of tanks. Photo: U.S. Navy Mass Communication Specialist 2nd Class Jennifer A. Villalovos

In America air pressure is measured in lbs/in³ (psi) and is usually between 2,250 psi and (+/- 156 bars) and 3,000 psi (+/- 208 bars). In Europe, pressure is measured in bars and is usually 200 bars (2,880 psi) or 230 bars (3,300 psi).

High pressure DIN[15] adapter. Photo: D.A.Y.

Yoke adapter. Photo: D.A.Y.

The size of the scuba tank is determined by the amount of air you need for a particular dive. The standard tank is 80 ft³; however tanks come in various sizes from the 15 ft³ pony tank to tanks of more than 100 ft³. The standard 80 ft³ measures approximately 29 in. (74 cm) in height excluding the valve, 7 ¼ in. (18 cm) in diameter, and weighs 35 lbs 15 kg more or less. Scuba tanks generally have a polyurethane paint finish. The paint color provides visibility and optimal contrast which allows the diver to be spotted more easily under water and at the surface.

The enriched air decals on these tanks indicate that they contain a higher percentage of oxygen. Photo: J. Gallant / D.A.Y.

Scuba tanks are regulated in the United States by the U.S. Department of Transportation, in Canada by the Department of Transport, and similar agencies in other countries. Visual inspections are required every year, and hydrostatic (pressure) tests

[15] Deutsches Institut für Normung eV (German Institute for Standardization)

are required every 5 years or when damage is suspected.

An old steel tank serves a new purpose at the water taxi stand at Anthony's Key Resort. Photo: J. Gallant / D.A.Y.

DIVE KNIFE

The dive knife is an essential tool for a diver however it is not a weapon. It is mostly used for cutting fishing lines, ropes, and nets when a diver becomes entangled. It is also a useful tool for lifting or digging.

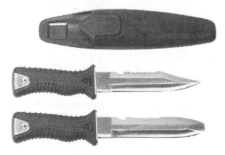

Oceanic dive knives with sharp and blunt edges. Photo: www.oceanicworldwide.com

A dive knife has to be made from good quality stainless steel to keep it corrosion free; it should be thick enough to be used as a lever; one side should have a straight cutting edge, the other a serrated edge. The handle should enable a firm grip and have a guard to keep the hand from sliding towards the blade. The knife has a sheath to hold it secure and allow easy access to it.

DIVE BUOY

A diving buoy marks areas where scuba diving is in progress. Its display is meant to keep the diver safe from injuries caused by sailboats, outboard motors, and fishing hooks or lines. Boaters are expected to keep a certain distance from the area. The distance can vary from one country to another and even within a country.

The diver's flag used in recreational diving is red with a white diagonal stripe. It warns all motorized and non-motorized vessels to keep a distance of at least 100 ft (30 m) and to slow down when near this zone.

The Alpha flag is blue and white and indicates that the vessel flying it is unable to maneuver because diving operations are in progress. Boaters must keep a distance of at least 100 ft (30 m). Both flags should not be displayed when the boat is traveling to or from the dive site.

A dive flag must be present and clearly visible to boaters whenever divers are under. Divers should resurface as close as possible to the buoy or dive vessel.

For more on dive flags and regulations:
➤ www.dive-flag.com

REBREATHERS

NURP (NOAA Undersea Research Program) is along the leading edge in advances in rebreather technology. According to Derek Smith, dive officer at NURP's Caribbean Marine Research Center (CMRC), "Dive technology has improved in two key areas - equipment and procedures. Equipment such as closed-circuit rebreathers was at one time only used by the U.S. Navy.

Inspiration fully-closed rebreather. Photo: D.A.Y.

Scientific divers tried them frequently over the past two decades, but they have been difficult to use and had technical problems - you don't want to mess around with your life-support unit. Recently they've benefited from computer developments and from debugging that comes with time." "It's kind of a strange thing," says Smith, "because rebreathers have been around longer than regular open-circuit scuba; they've been around since the 1800s.

... Since then, rebreathers have been used commercially, but they never came to the forefront of the scientific diving community, except for with a select group of people who were trained to use them and had unlimited checkbooks with which to gain access to the equipment and to the training."

"But now there are more and better rebreathers being manufactured and marketed," Smith says. "One of the biggest pushes in scientific diving right now is bringing rebreathers to the scientific communities. Although their cost per unit is relatively high, once you own one, the cost per dive is phenomenally low."

The manner of diving Captain Jacques-Yves Cousteau introduced to the world is called open-circuit scuba and uses compressed gas and a breathing regulator. A lot of the gas is wasted in this process, more and more the deeper you dive. Rebreathers employ a breathing loop that recycles the gas.

Inspiration fully-closed rebreather. Photo: D.A.Y.

Rebreather technology is computer controlled and it can keep your partial pressure of oxygen at a very set level," Smith explains, "whereas with trimix you might need six different mixtures of gas to get yourself to different depths, and they're either worn on the divers themselves or sent down on a line. You have to keep switching gases to make sure you're breathing the right amount of oxygen at different depths. "But a rebreather can be computer controlled such that it keeps the oxygen at the exact right place you want it no matter what depth you're at." Smith says the gas-management capability of rebreathers is impressive. "Eight dollars of helium, for example, can be stretched in a rebreather over many, many dives.

"Most people think of rebreathers in terms of deep and long dives," says Smith. "You can do long-duration dives at great depths with a lot fewer decompression obligations. But we're also talking about using rebreathers in perhaps ten feet (3 m) of water." The advantage here is nearly unlimited bottom time without having to change tanks and the absence of bubbles, which can affect fish behavior.

SOURCE: NOAA Research / Taylor Sisk, Advancing Diving Technology

FULLY-CLOSED REBREATHER

Fully closed-circuit rebreathers (CCR) are used for both shallow decompression and no-decompression diving, as well as deep decompression diving.

Photo © Søvcernets Operative Kommando (Denmark)

CCRs use oxygen and a diluent gas (air, nitrox, trimix, etc.) in a closed breathing loop, and a CO_2 scrubber to extend gas supply and bottom time. The partial pressure of oxygen in the breathing loop is monitored and maintained at a preset level throughout the dive. The optimum gas mix to minimize decompression, avoid oxygen toxicity, and maximize bottom time can be maintained at all times with this system. Gas is vented from the breathing loop only during ascent. Adequate open-circuit bail-out capability (reserve gas capacity) must be maintained in case of breathing loop/scrubber failure.

Cliff Simoneau trains a group of divers in the use of semi-closed rebreathers off Boston, Massachusetts. Photo: J. Gallant / D.A.Y.

SEMI-CLOSED REBREATHER

Semi-closed rebreathers (SCR) are typically used for shallow (<130fsw) no-decompression diving. SCRs use nitrox or mixed gas injected into a breathing loop, and a CO_2 scrubber to extend gas supply and bottom time. Injected gas fraction remains constant during the dive, but gas partial pressure varies with depth and exertion level. During operation SCRs emit a small stream of bubbles or gas "burp." SCRs are more efficient than open-circuit (in terms of gas usage), but less efficient than closed-circuit.

SOURCE: NOAA

MANUFACTURERS

Scuba equipment manufacturers from around the world. Please contact us at **info@divingalmanac.com** to suggest additional listings.

ACCESSORIES

Aquamax
Florida USA
Tel.: 800 278 2629
www.aquamaxadvantage.com

Bright Weights
Capetown South Africa
Tel.: 27 21 788 9343
Fax: 27 21 788 1973
www.brightweights.com

Carter Lift Bag
Washington USA
Tel.: 360-886-2302
www.carterbag.com

Cetacea
California USA
(650) 571-9411
Toll Free: 800 223 2833
Fax: 800 314 2844
www.cetaceacorp.com

Deep See
washington USA
Toll Free: 800 367 2626
www.deepseeinc.com

Dive Tech
Ontario Canada
Tel.: 613 562 0373
www.ncf.ca/~ep050

Highland
Massachusetts USA
Tel.: 508 429 4509
Fax: 508 429 9047
www.highland-millwork.com

Leonard Maggiore
New York USA
Toll Free: 800 567 5339
Tel.: 718 386 5339
Fax: 718 386 5339
www.rxdivemask.com

Mac
Maniago Italy
Tel.: 39 0427 71357
Fax: 39 0427 700634
www.italpro.com/maniago

Mask Connection System
Dorset UK
Tel.: 44 01 305 776037
Fax: 44 01 305 769977
maskconnectionsystem.com

Nordic Blue
Höganäs Sweden
Tel.: 0046 42 349244
Fax: 0046 42 333455
www.nordic-blue.com

Prescription Dive Masks
California USA
Tel.: 619 299 2878
Toll Free: 800 538 2878
Fax: 619 297 9500
prescriptiondivemasks.com

Prolift
Florida USA
Tel.: 850 892 6466
Tel.: 877 369 3553
Fax: 850 892 5611
www.proliftbags.com

SpecialFins Ltd.
Estonia
Tel.: 372 522 6034
Fax: 372 646 5121
www.specialfins.com

Underwater Kinetics
California USA
Tel.: 858 513 9100
www.uwkinetics.com

BAGS

Armor
Florida USA
Toll Free: 800 487 9485
Tel.: 813 764 8855
www.armorbags.com

Atlantis
California USA
www.atlantis-intl.com

StahlSac
North Carolina USA
Tel.: 800 521 2247
Fax: 828 645 3006
www.stahlsac.com

Watchful eye designs
Utah USA
Toll Free: 800 948 9433
www.splashcaddy.com

COMPRESSORS & GAS MANAGEMENT

Airdive
Victoria Australia
Tel. : 03 9544 4735
Fax : 03 9544 5108
www.airdive.com.au

American AirWorks
West Virginia USA
Tel.: 304 683 4595
Fax: 304 683 3257
www.americanairworks.com

Aquavit
Texas USA
Tel.: 281 364 8323
Fax: 281 364 1258
www.aquavitinc.com

Bauer Compressors
Virginia USA
Tel.: 757 855 6006
Fax: 757 857 1041
www.bauercomp.com

CompAir
Ontario Canada
Tel.: 905 847 0688
Fax: 905 847 8124
www.compair.ca

Eagle Compressors
North Carolina USA
Tel.: 336 398 8000
Fax: 336 398 8001
www.eaglecompressors.com

Max Air
Texas USA

Tel.: 830 257 5006
Fax: 830 257 3720
www.max-air.com

Nitrox Technologies
California USA
Tel.: 707 538 7598
Tel : 888 648 7692
Fax: 707 538 0850
www.nitroxtech.com

RIX
California USA
Tel.: 707 747 5900
Fax: 707 747 9200
www.rixindustries.com

Techno Divers
Arizona USA
Tel.: 877 838 1300
Fax: 480 838 1300
www.technodivers.com

Undersea Breathing Systems
Florida USA
Tel.: 561 588 7698
Fax: 561 588 0608
www.dnax.com

Vandergraph
West Yorkshire UK
Tel. :44 (0) 1535 634900
Fax: 44 (0) 1535 635582
www.vandagraph.co.uk

COMPUTERS & GAUGES

Liquivision
www.liquivision.ca

Uwatec
Worldwide
www.uwatec.com

VR3
Dorset UK
Tel.: 00 44 (0)1202 624478
Fax: 00 44 (0)1202 625308
www.vr3.co.uk

CYLINDERS

Catalina Cylinders
California USA
Tel.: 714 890 0999
Fax: 714 890 1744
www.catalinacylinders.com

Luxfer
USA/Europe
Toll Free: 800 764 0366
www.luxfercylinders.com

Pressed Steel
Wisconsin USA

Toll Free: 800 811 4530
Fax: 800 811 4701
www.pstscuba.com

DETECTORS & SONAR

JW Fishers
Massachusetts USA
Tel: 508 822 7330
Toll Free: 800 822 4744
Fax: 508 880 8949
www.jwfishers.com

Marschall Acoustics
New South Wales. Australia
Tel.: 61 2 4732 3208
Fax: 61 2 4731 4323
www.marschall-acoustics-
instruments.com.au

DIVE GEAR

A.P.Valves
Cornwall UK
Tel.: 44 01326 561040
Fax: 44 01326 573605
www.apvalves.com

Aeris
California USA
Tel.: 510 346 0010
Fax: 510 346 0015
www.diveaeris.com

Alpha Diving
Australia
Tel.: 613 9555 5000
Fax: 613 9555 5999
alphadiving.com

Apeks
Lacanshire UK
Tel. : 01254 692200
Fax : 44 1254 692200
www.apeks.co.uk

A-Plus Marine
Florida USA
Toll Free: 800 352 2360
Tel.: 850 934 3890
Fax: 850 934 3895
www.aplusmarine.com

Apollo
Washington USA
Toll Free: 800 231 0909
Tel: 425 290 7665
www.apollosportsusa.com

Aqua Sphere
Genoa Italy
Tel.: 39 0105 4451
Fax: 39 0105 445245
www.aquasphere.it

Aqua-Lung
Worldwide
www.aqualung.com

Atomic Aquatics
California USA
Tel.: 714 375 1433
Fax: 714 375 1435
www.atomicaquatics.com

Cressi Sub
Genoa Italy
Tel.: 39 010830791
Fax: 39 01083079220
cressi.it

Dacor
Italy
www.divedacor.com

Deca Diving
California USA
Tel.: 805 928 4500
Fax: 805 928 4570
www.decadiving.com

Deepoutdoors
California USA
Tel.: 858 513 1064
Tel.: 866 867 7739
Fax: 858 5131046
www.deepoutdoors.com

Dive Rite
Florida USA
Tel.: 386 752 1087
www.diverite.com

DiVex
Aberdeen UK
Tel.: 44 (0)1224 740145
Fax: 44 (0)1224 740172
www.divex.co.uk

Dutton
Taiwan ROC
Tel. : 866 2 8990 2100
Fax : 866 2 8990 2103
www.duton.com.tw

Force Fin
California USA
Te.l: 900 346 7946
Tel.: 805 966 9628
Fax: 805 564 8240
www.forcefin.com

Genesis Scuba
www.genesisscuba.com

H2O Odyssey
California USA
Tel.: 760 599 4097
Toll Free: 800 999 0019
Fax: 760 599 4096
www.h2odyssey.com

Halcyon
Florida USA
Tel.: 386 454 0811
www.halcyon.net

Hollandse Nieuwe
Groningen, Netherlands
Tel.: 31 594 614218
Fax: 31 594 614219
www.leadweights.nl

Hydro Optix
California USA
Tel.: 310 636 1700
Fax: 310) 390 8401
www.hydrooptix.com

Interspiro
Lidingö Sweden
Tel.: 46 8 636 51 00
Fax: 46 8 765 48 53
www.interspiro.com

Manta
New Jersey USA
Toll Free: 800 397 3901
Fax: 908 241 0721
www.mantaind.com

Mares
Worldwide
www.mares.com

Mar-Vel
New Jersey USA
Tel: 856 488 4499
Toll Free: 800 325 5711
Fax: 856 488 4343
www.mar-vel.com

Northern Diver
Lancashire UK
Tel.: 01257 251234
www.ndiver.com

Omersub S.P.A.
Italy
infosales@omersub.it

O.M.E.R. Technosport
Virginia USA
Toll Free: 800 853 1911
www.omerdiving.com

Ocean Management Systems
New York USA
Tel.: 845 692 3600
Fax: 845 692 3623
www.omsdive.com

Ocean Master
California USA
Tel.: 888 207 6404
www.oceanmaster.com

Ocean Reef
Genoa Italy
Te.l: 39 010 65986 11

Fax: 39 010 65986 22
www.oceanreefgroup.com

Oceanic
California USA
Tel.: 510 562 0500
Fax: 510 569 5404
www.oceanicworldwide.com

Patco
Maryland USA
Tel.: 410 444 4010
Fax: 410 254 9566
www.patcoinc.com

Picasso America
California USA
Tel.: 310-937-5660
www.picassoamerica.com

Poseidon
Sweden
info@poseidon.se
www.poseidon.se

Procean
Leek Netherlands
Tel.: 31(0) 594 580070
Fax: 31(0) 594 580090
www.procean.nl

Promate
California USA
Tel.: 626 401 2039
Fax: 626 4012069 •
www.promateusa.com

ProSub
Aschau i.Ch.Germany
Tel.: 49 0 8057 904674
Fax: 49 08057 904676
www.prosub.com

Ralf Tech
Worldwide
www.ralftech.com

Riffe
California USA
Tel.: 949 361 2818
Fax: 949 361 2885
www.speargun.com

Saekodive
Taiwan ROC
Tel.: 886 22 982 2660
Fax: 886 22 982 2662
www.saekodive.com.tw

Scubapro
California USA
Tel.: 619 402 1023
www.scubapro-uwatec.com

Sea Hornet
Sydney Australia
Tel.: 61 2 9948 0273
Fax: 61 2 9948 7209

www.seahornet.com

Seac Sub
Italy
Tel.: 39 0185.356301
Fax: 39 0185.356300
www.seacsub.com

SeaQuest Scuba
Worldwide
www.sea-quest.com

SeaSoft Scuba
Washington USA
Tel.: 1 800 939 5510
Fax: 1 253 939 2129
www.watermark1.com

Seeman Sub
Wendelstein Germany
Tel.: 49 09129 90 99 5 0
Fax: 49 09129 90 99 5 50
www.seemannsub.com

SepaDiver
Triest Italy
Tel.: 39 04 023 2573
Fax: 39 04 023 2648
www.sepadiver.com

Sherwood
California USA
www.sherwoodscuba.com

SMP
Lacanshire UK
Tel.: 44 (0)1772 687775
Fax: 44 (0)1772 687774
www.smp-ltd.co.uk

Sommap
Aubagne France
Tel.: 33 4 42 82 28 38
Fax: 33 4 42 82 13 27
www.sommap.com

Sopras sub
Czech Republic
Tel.: 00420 312 699 790
Fax: 00420 312 699 792
www.soprassub.com

Subacqua
Madrid Spain
Tel.: 34 91 151 02 50
Fax: 91 365 76 02
www.subacqua.es

Tabata Tusa
Worldwide
www.tusa.net

Tigullio
Genoa Italy
Tel.: 39 0185 362422
Fax: 39 0185 362445
www.tigullio52.com

Tilos
California USA
Tel.: 909 348 0130
Toll Free: 800 475 5703
Fax: 909 348 0134
www.tilos.com

XS Scuba
California USA
Tel.: 714.424 0434
Tel.: 866.XS SCUBA
Fax: 714 424 0454
www.xsscuba.com

Zeagle
Florida USA
Tel.: 813 782 5568
Fax: 813 782 5569
www.zeagle.com

DIVE SUITS

Abyss
Nova Scotia Canada
Tel.: 902 826 2954
Fax: 902 826 7921
www.abyssdivingsuits.com

American Wave
Idaho USA
Tel.: 866 434 0692
www.americanwave.com

Andys Dry suits
Maryland USA
Tel.: 410 957 4414
Fax: 410 957 4415
www.andysdrysuit.com

AquaFlite
California USA
Toll Free: 800 581 7916
Tel.: 530 596 4867
www.aquaflite.com

Aquala
Los Angeles USA
800 Dry Suit
www.aquala.com

Aquata
Berlin Germany
Tel.: 49 (0) 3302 81984 5
Fax: 49 (0) 3302 81983
www.aquata.de

Aropec Sports
Taiwan ROC
Tel.: 886 4 2569 3850
Fax: 886 4 2569 3842
www.aropec.com

Bare
British Columbia Canada
Tel.: 604 533 7848
Fax: 604 530 8812
www.bare-wetsuits.com

Beaver Sports
Huddersfield UK
Tel.:: 00 44 1484 512354
www.beaversports.co.uk

C Bear
Cornwall UK
Tel.: 44 (0)1566 777 636
Fax: 44 (0)1566 777 636
www.c-bear.co.uk

Camaro
Mondsee Austria
Tel.: 43 6232 4201 0
Fax: 43 6232 3545
www.camaro.at

Dolphin Wetsuits
Texas USA
Tel.: 281 367 7834.
www.dolphinwetsuits.com

DUI
California USA
Tel.: 619 236 1203
Fax: 619 237 0378
www.dui-online.com

ELIOS Sub
via Cattaneo, 5
47841 Cattolica Italy
Tel.: 39 0541 963831
Fax: 39 0541 954790
www.eliossub.com

Henderson
New Jersey USA
Tel.: 856 825 4771
www.hendersonusa.com

Hotline
California USA
www.hotlineonline.com

Hot'n'Dry
Ulladulla Australia
Tel.: 612 4454 0686
Fax: 612 4454 0696
www.hotndry.com.au

Hotwave
Phuket, Thailand
Tel.: 66 76 280787
Fax: 66 76 280788
www.hotwavephuket.com

IST Sports
Taiwan
Tel.: 886 2 2627 2516
www.istsports.com

Kettenhofen
California USA
Tel.: 714 997 0148
www.kettenhofenwetsuits.com

KME

Washington USA
(800) 800*8563
www.kmedrysuits.com

Liquid Fit
USA
Toll Free : 800 785 8362
Tel.: 305 453 3251
Fax: 305 453 3251
www.liquidfit.com

Lomo
Scotland UK
Tel.: 44 141 334 7271
www.ewetsuits.com

Marea
Brindisi Italy
Tel.: 39 0831 516 515
Fax: 39 0831 516 515
www.mareasub.it

Mobbys
California USA
Tel.: 510396 0635
www.mobbys.com

Namron
Rotherham UK
Tel.: 44 (0) 170 937 1006
Fax: 44 (0) 170 936 7295
www.scubauk.com

O.S. Systems
Oregon USA
Tel.: 503 543 3126
Fax: 503 543 3129
www.ossystems.com

Oceaner
British Columbia CA
Tel.: 604 434 0069
Fax: 604 434 0092
www.oceaner.com

Oceanray
Florida USA
Tel.: 850 892 6466
www.oceanray.com

O'Neill
California USA
www.oneill.com

O'Three
Dorset UK
Tel.: 44 (0) 1305 776754
Fax: 44 (0) 1305 778162
www.othree.co.uk

Otter Watersports
West Yorkshire
Tel.: 44 (0) 1274 307555
Fax: 44 (0) 1274 730993
www.drysuits.co.uk

Polar Bears
Cornwall UK

Tel.: 44 01566 773 654
Fax: 44 01566 776 065
www.polarbears.co.uk

Predator
Hants UK
Tel.: 01 425 620 571
www.predator-wetsuits.co.uk

Promotion
Oregon USA
Toll Free: 800 798 1628
Tel.: 541 386 3278
www.wetsuit.com

Rubber Jungle
Gold Coast Australia
Tel.: 07 5572 4099
Fax: 07 5572 0087
www.rubberjungle.com.au

Sea Dreams
California USA
Tel.: 949 338 0748
Fax: 949 759 8661
www.seadreamswetsuits.com

Spartan
UK
Tel.: 44 (0)1992 893889
www.spartan.uk.com

Swissub
Belmont Switzerland
Tel.: 41 21 791 41 41
Fax: 41 21 791 42 56
www.swissub.ch

Typhoon
Cleveland UK
Tel.: 44 (0)1642 486104
www.typhoon-int.co.uk

Undersea Designs
California USA
Tel.: 760 434 8508
Fax: 707 897 7834
www.underseadesigns.com

USIA
Oregon USA
Toll Free: 800 247 8070
Tel.: 503 366 0816
www.usia.com

Waterproof Diving AB
Partille Sweden
Tel.: 46 31 33 68 270
Fax: 46 31 33 68 271
www.waterproof.se

Weezle
Yorkshire UK
Tel.: 44 (0)1535 655380
www.weezle.co.uk

Wetwear
Florida USA

Toll Free: 800 771 8081
Tel.: 954 458 0400
Fax: 954 458 0333
www.wetwear.com

Whites
British Columbia Canada
Tel.: 250 652 8554
Fax: 250 652 8553
www.whitescoldwater.com

Xcel
Hawaii USA
Tel.: 808 637 6239
Toll Free: 800 637 9235
Fax: 808 637 9233
www.xcelwetsuits.com

DIVER PROPULSION VEHICLES (DPV)

Cayman Dive Gear
Florida USA
Tel.: 239 594 7997
Toll Free: 800 282 8725
Fax: 239 594 3080
www.caymandivegear.com

Farallon USA
Ontario Canada
Tel.: 613 822 1876
Fax: 613 822 3431
www.farallonusa.com

Gavin Scooters
Florida USA
Tel.: 954 328 2611
www.gavinscooters.com

JetBoots
California USA
Tel.: 626 449 1960
www.jetboots.com

Torpedo
Florida USA
800-489-6774
Tel.: 727 733 2218
Fax: 727 736 8748
www.torpedodpv.com

LIGHTING

Duo-Light
Forel Switzerland
Tel.: 41 021 781 11 23
Fax: 41 021 781 19 09
www.duo-light.ch

FA & MI
Angera Italy
www.fa-mi.com

Green Force
Erembodegem Belgium
Tel.: 32 (0) 53 64 72 72

Fax: 32 (0) 53 66 27 28
www.green-force.com

Hartenberger
Köln Germany
Tel.: 49 221 41 50 00
Fax: 49 221 41 50 50
www.hartenberger.de

Keldan
Switzerland
Tel.: 41 (0) 32 333 16 28
Fax: 41 (0) 32 333 16 26
www.keldan.ch

Kowalski
Berlin Germany
Tel.: 49 30 7715930
Fax: 49 30 77103096
www.taucherlampen.de

mb sub
Köln Germany
Tel.: 0221 9762140
Fax: 0221 9762142
www.mb-sub.com

Nite Rider
California USA
Toll Free: 800 466 8366
Fax: 800 465 8366
www.niterider.com

Pelican Products
California USA
Tel.: 310 326 4700
Toll Free: 800 473 5422
www.pelican.com

Princeton Tec
New Jersey USA
Tel.: 609 298 9331
Fax: 609 298 9601
www.princetontec.com

SeaLamp
Dorset UK
Tel.: 44 (0) 1202 677128
Fax: 44 (0) 1202 671047
www.sealamp.com

TekTite
USA
Toll Free: 800 540 2814
www.tek-tite.com

PHOTO/VIDEO

10 bar
Hong Kong
Tel.: 852 2573 3228
Fax: 852 2811 9180
www.10bar.com

Aditech
Girona
Tel.: 34 972 661 661

Fax: 34 972 660 735
www.aditech-uw.com

Amphibico
Montreal Canada
Tel.: 514 333 8666
Fax: 514 333 1339
www.amphibico.com

Aquatica
Montreal Canada
Tel.: 514 737 9481
Fax: 514 737 7685
www.aquatica.ca

Aquatix
USA
Tel.: 877 581 5660
Tel.: 314 487 3406
Fax: 314 487 3406
www.aquatix.com

AquaVideo
Florida USA
Tel.: 954 660 0062
www.aquavideo.com

Bonica
British Columbia Canada
Toll Free: 800 220 8463
Tel.: 604 270 7278
www.bonicadive.com

DeepSea Power & Light
California USA
Tel.: 858 576 1261
Fax: 858 576 0219
www.deepsea.com

Desert Star Systems
California USA
Tel.: 831 384 8000
www.desertstar.com

Ewa Marine
Geretsried Germany
Tel.: 49 8171 4185 0
www.ewa-marine.de

Gates
California USA
Toll Free: 800 875 1052
Tel.: 858 272 2501
Fax: 858 272 1208
www.gateshousings.com

Ikelite
Indiana USA
Tel.: 317 923 4523
Fax: 317 924 7988
www.ikelite.com

Inner Space Developments
Wierda Park, South Africa
Tel.: 27 82 444 5841
Fax: 27 12 668 1614
www.isdsa.co.za

Kabot
Berlin Germany
Tel.: 030 843 09 766
Fax: 030 833 94 73
www.kabot.de

Leone
Torino Italy
Tel.: 011 72 07 54
Fax: 011 72 00 31
fotoleone.netsurf.it

Light & Motion
California USA
Tel.: 831 645 1525
Fax: 831 375 2517
www.uwimaging.com

Multitec
Nesselwang Germany
Te.l: 49 08361 925943
Fax: 49 08361 3961
www.multitec.net

Nexus
USA
Tel.: 858 481 0604
www.usanexus.com

Night Sea
Massachusetts USA
Tel.: 978 685 6410
Tel.: 877 436 9262
Fax: 978 689 3232
www.nightsea.com

Nikon
Worldwide
www.nikon.com

Pace
California USA
Tel.: 818 565 0005
Fax: 818 565 0006
www.pacetech.com

Remote Ocean Systems
California USA
Tel.: 858 565 8500
Fax: 858 565 8808
www.rosys.com

SarTek
New York USA
Tel.: 631 924 0441
Fax: 631 924 2959
www.sarind.com

Sea & Sea
Saitama Japan
Tel.: 81 48 256 2251
Fax: 81 48 256 2276
www.seaandsea.com

Seacam
Voitsberg Germany
Tel.: 43 3142 22 88 50
Fax: 43 3142 22 88 54

www.seacam.com

SeaLife
New Jersey USA
Tel.: 856 866 9191
www.sealife-cameras.com

Shark Marine
Ontario Canada
Tel.: 905 687 6672
Fax: 905 687 9742
www.sharkmarine.com

Subal
Steyr Austria
Tel.: 43 7252 464240
Fax: 43 7252 464246
www.subal.com

Subatec
Mont-sur-Lausanne, Switzerland
Tel.: 41 21 653 23 62
Fax: 41 21 653 23 67
www.subatec.ch

Submerge
Florida USA
Tel.: 561 747 3640
Fax: 561 741 0046
www.silent-submersion.com

Subspace
Geneva Switzerland
Tel.: 4122 823 14 60
Fax: 4122 823 14 61
www.subspace.ch

Ultralight
USA
Tel.: 805 984 9104
Fax: 805 984 3008
www.ulcs.com

UnderSea Video Housings
California USA
Tel.: 916 989 5438
Fax: 916 989 0298
www.usvh.com

REBREATHERS

Ambient Pressure Diving
Cornwall, UK
+44 (0)1326 563 834
+44 (0)1326 565 945
www.apdiving.com

Carleton
New York USA
Tel.: 716 662 0006
Fax: 716 662 0747
www.carltech.com

Divematics
California USA
Tel.: 714 776 6330
Fax: 714 867 0455

www.divenet.com/divematics

Innerspace Systems
Washington USA
Tel.: (360) 330-9018
www.customrebreathers.com

OxyCheq
Florida USA
Tel.: 772 466 4612
Fax: 772 293 9657
oxycheq.com

Rebreather Technology Inc.
California USA
Tel.: 408 776 1657
www.frogdiver.com

Silent Diving Systems
Ontario Canada
Tel.: 613-345-6382
Fax: 603-297-0047
www.silentdiving.com

Steam Machines
Tennessee
Tel.: 615 374 0202
Fax: 615 374 9193
www.steammachines.com

ROVs

Video Ray
Pennsylvania USA
Tel.: 610 458 3000
Fax: 610 458 3010
www.videoray.com

SOFTWARE

Cyber-Strategy
Oregon USA
Tel.: 503 545 2686
www.scubase.net

De-Ox
Milano Italy
Tel.: 39 02 846 3648
www.temc.it

Sea Wolf
New York USA
Tel.: (516) 931-3955
www.seawolff.com

SPEARGUNS

Collins Spearguns
Australia
www.collinsspearguns.com

JBL
California USA
www.jblspearguns.com

SUBMERSIBLES

International VentureCraft
British Columbia Canada
Tel.: 604 436 5653
www.ivccorp.com

Odyssea Submarine
USA
www.odyssea-sub.com

UNDERWATER COMMUNICATIONS

DiveLink
British Columbia CA
Tel.: 250 479 4868
Toll Free: 800 348 7815
Fax: 250 479 5980
www.divelink.net

Orcatron
British Columbia CA
Tel.: 604 945 0916
Fax: 604 945 0917

www.orcatron.com

WATCHES

Casio
www.casio.com/products/Timepiece/

Citizen Watch Company of America, Inc.
1000 West 190th Street
Torrance, CA 90502-1040
www.citizenwatch.com

Luminox Watches
7501 N. Harker Drive
Peoria, IL 61615
Tel.: 309 683 8609
www.luminox.com

Rolex (Watches)
www.rolex.com

Seiko Watch Corporation
www.seikowatches.com

Suunto
Finland
Tel.: 358 2 284 1160
www.suunto.com

Timex Canada
445 Hood Road
Markham, Ontario
L3R 8H1
www.timex.ca

WATERCRAFT

BuddyBoats
California USA
Tel.: 707 575 1625
www.buddyboats.com

CMAS QUÉBEC

INFORMATION IN THIS SECTION
PROVIDED IN PART BY CMAS/AMCQ
AND ADAPTED BY D.A.Y.

Chapter 6

DIVING ACTIVITIES

Once you have become a certified diver, you may pursue your training in order to take part in dozens of diving activities accessible to recreational divers. Here are but a few possibilities.

NIGHT DIVING

At night, the underwater universe undergoes big changes. Animal activity switches to a nocturnal cycle where you can observe species not seen during the daytime hours. Certain lifeforms only appear at night to feed while species active during the daytime rest and may be more easily approached. Sensations are different from a day dive because of your field of vision which is limited to the range of your dive light. You find yourself observing smaller details on the sea bed and the many colors your light reveals.

U/W NAVIGATION

This activity is organized with fun in mind, and is often the object of a treasure hunt. Participants have to follow a route with specific destination points to find, and then reorient themselves to the next point along the course, and so on until the end of the diving route.

SEARCH & RECOVERY

The object of a search and recovery dive may be to find an object or a shipwreck. This type of dive requires very detailed planning, considerable organization and special techniques.

Divers use lift bags during a recovery operation.
Photo: U.S. Coast Guard

For the recreational diver, search and recovery dives are normally limited to small objects.

ICE DIVING

For many divers, winter is not an impediment to exploring frozen lakes. When properly trained and equipped with basic scuba equipment, a dry suit, and a regulator that is protected from freezing, divers are often treated with better-than-usual visibility and a stable dive platform. A dive light may also be useful. Preparing the dive requires special equipment such as a long-bladed chain saw to cut through the ice, fencing or other material to outline the hole, jute or other material to place around the ice hole to keep divers from sliding, special harnessing and a sturdy rope which is monitored at all times by a tendor at the surface.

Ice divers talk to their divemaster who is kneeling by the hole in the ice. Photo: J. Gallant / D.A.Y.

Ice diver Shawn Harper "stands" on the ice ceiling above him. Ice diving on this cruise is different from other types of diving as work is conducted on the ice close to the surface while thousands of meters of blue water unfold below. Photo: NOAA/OCEAN EXPLORER - *The Hidden Ocean*, Arctic 2005 Exploration

Whenever possible, a tent, hut, cabin or other heated place where divers are able to change and warm up after the dive should be available.

Ice diving, as all other diving activities, should be well planned and organized. The particularities associated with ice diving include very cold water temperature and the ice ceiling which forces the diver to exit the water from the same hole in which he entered. The diver wears a harness over the dry suit. This harness is tied to the tether rope controlled by the tendor at the surface. A "Y" connector tied to the single tether rope can also connect two divers. The length of the rope used by the divers is normally 50 to 75 ft (16 to 25 m). Each rope is held taut by the tendor at the surface. Communication between the tendor and divers is done through signals on the rope, or via an u/w comm system. For safety reasons, there is always a fully-suited diver at the surface ready to dive.

WRECK DIVING

Wreck diving is very interesting and impressive. It is thrilling to discover underwater relics from the past, some recent, some old. A recreational diver should never attempt to enter a shipwreck without the proper training for many reasons, among them, getting lost if the wreck is big, the dangers of the wreck caving in, or getting hooked or stuck inside the wreck. It is preferable to visit a wreck on the outside. Generally a wreck in sea water is covered with animals and plants. These wrecks, as well as wrecks in fresh water, provide a refuge for an abundance of fish.

A diver who discovers an unknown wreck while diving should advise the authorities. Taking objects from a wrecksite, be it part of the structure, its equipment or its cargo, is strictly prohibited in many countries.

Divers explore the wreck of the *Odyssey* off Anthony's Key Resort, Roatan. Photo: J. Gallant / D.A.Y.

NOTABLE SHIPWRECKS FROM AROUND THE WORLD

Some historical, some rated as the best. Most popular wrecks are also listed in the countries section.

AUSTRALIA

SS YONGALA
Passenger/freight ship: Great Barrier Reef Marine Park
Sank in 1911
Depth: 30m

BIKINI

USS SARATOGA
33,000 ton aircraft carrier; Bikini Atoll Lagoon
Sank in 1946
Depth: 54m

BRAZIL

V17 IPIRANGA
Navy corvette: Fernando de Noronha marine reserve
Sank in 1983
Depth: 63m

BRITISH VIRGIN IS-LANDS

RMS RHONE
2738 ton mail/passenger ship off Salt Island coast
Sank in 1867
Depth: 24m

CANADA

GEORGE C. MARSH
Schooner near Kingston Harbour ON
Sank in 1917
Depth: 26m

ALOHA
Schooner Barge: Nine Mile Point ON
Sank in 1917
Depth: 18m

EMPRESS OF IRELAND
Liner off Point-au-Pere QC
Sank in 1914
Depth: 45m
KOLKHOSNIK
Russian freight near Halifax

Sank in 1942
Depth: 42m

CHUUK (TRUK)

*SAN FRANCISCO MARU,
168*
Passenger/cargo ship:
Chuuk lagoon
Sank in 1944
Depth: 55m

CYPRUS

ZENOBIA
Ro-ro ferry off Larnaca
fishing harbour
Sank in 1980
Depth: 42m

EGYPT

SS THISTLEGORM
British cargo ship: Straits
of Gobal
Sank in 1941
Depth: 30m

FRANCE

KLEBER
French cruiser off Brittany
coast
Sank in 1917
Depth: 45m

TOGO
Cargo ship: Cavalaire
Bay
Sank in 1918
Depth: 56m

ESPINGOLE
Torpedo boat: Cavalaire
Bay
Sank in 1903
Depth: 38m

GIBRALTAR

SS EXCELLENT
1600 ton steel-hulled
schooner: Gibraltar har-
bour breakwater
Sank in 1880
Depth: 31m

GREECE

HMHS BRITANNIC
Hospital ship/liner: Kea
Channel off Athens
Sank in 1916
Depth: 120m

GRENADA

BIANCA C.
Liner: East coast of Gre-
nada
Sank in 1961
Depth: 50m

MALAYSIA

HMS REPULSE
32,000 ton battlecruiser
north of Tioman Island
Sank in 1941
Depth: 55m

NEW ZEALAND

MIKHAIL LERMONTOV
Soviet cruise ship: Port
Gore
Sank in 1986
Depth: 40m

PAPUA NEW GUINEA

B17 BLACK JACK
Bomber aircraft: Cape
Vogel
Sank in 1943
Depth: 48m

PHILIPPINES

USS NEW YORK
Battle cruiser: Subic Bay
Sank in 1941
Depth: 30m

SOLOMON ISLANDS

HIROKAWA MARU
Japanese transport west
of Honiara
Sank in 1942
Depth: 50m

SOUTH AFRICA

PRODUCE
Norwegian molasses
tanker off the Aliwal
Shoal
Sank in 1974
Depth: 33m

SPAIN

SIRIO
Italian passenger liner:
Spanish coast
Sank in 1906
Depth: 50m

WESTBURN
Steamer: North of Santa
Cruz
Sank in 1916
Depth: 30m

SRI LANKA

CONCH
Oil tanker: Hikkaduwa
Sank in 1903
Depth: 20m

SUDAN

SS UMBRIA
Passenger/cargo ship:
Port Sudan
Sank in 1940
Depth: 36m

SWEDEN

KRONAN
Battleship: Oland
Sank in 1676
Depth: 27m

THAILAND

KING CRUISER
3000 ton ferry: Anemone
Reef
Sank in 1997
Depth: 30m

HARDEEP
Indonesian freighter:
Channel near Koh
Chuang
Sank in 1942
Depth: 27m

TURKS & CAICOS

HMS *ENDYMION*
British Frigate off Sand
Cay
Sank in 1790
Depth: 9m

UNITED KINGDOM

KARLSRUHE
5400 ton cruiser: Orkney,
Scapa Flow
Sank in 1915
Depth: 27m

SMS *KRONPRINZ WILHELM*
26000 ton battleship:
Scapa Flow
Sank in
Depth: 37m

LUCY
Dutch coaster off Sko-
mer Island
Sank in 1967

Depth: 41m

LA SURVEILLANTE
French Frigate: Bantry
Bay Ireland
Sank in 1797
Depth: 34m

U.S.A.

R.M.S. *REPUBLIC*
Passenger liner off Nan-
tucket
Sank in 1909
Depth: 81m

HYDRO ATLANTIC
Sank in 1987
Depth: 51m

USS *MASSACHUSETTS*
Battleship SW of Pensa-
cola Pass
Sank in 1921
Depth: 14m

HMS *BEDFORDSHIRE*
British Trawler off Cape
Lookout, NC
Sank in 1942
Depth: 31m

SEA TIGER
Vessel off Waikiki
Sank in 1996
Depth: 30m

VANUATU

SS *PRESIDENT COOLIDGE*
22,000 ton liner off
Espiritu Santo
Sank in 1942
Depth: 65m

STAR OF RUSSIA
Sailing ship: Port Vila
Harbour
Sank in 1953
Depth: 33m

ARTIFICIAL REEFS

An artificial reef is a structure placed on the ocean floor to provide a hard substrate for sea life to colonize. Artificial reefs are constructed by sinking dense materials, such as old ships and barges, concrete ballasted tire units, concrete and steel demolition debris and dredge rock on the sea floor within designated reef sites

SOURCE: NOAA

AUSTRALIA

HMAS *Perth*
Destroyer sunk in 2001
Australia, Albany,

HMAS *Brisbane*
Warship sunk in 2005
Australia, Mooloolaba

BAHAMAS

Theo's Wreck
Cement hauler sunk in 1982
Off Freeport coast

CANADA

MV *G.B. Church*
Freighter sunk in 1991
British Columbia

HMCS *Chaudiere*
Destroyer Escort sunk in 1992
British Columbia

HMCS *Saguenay*
Navy Warship sunk in 1994
Lunenburg NS

HMCS *Mackenzie*
Destroyer Escort sunk in 1995
British Columbia

HMCS *Columbia*
Destroyer Escort sunk in 1996
British Columbia

HMCS *Saskatchewan*
Destroyer Escort sunk in 1997
British Columbia

HMCS *Yukon*
Destroyer Escort sunk in 2000
British Columbia

HMCS *Cape Breton*
WWII Victory Ship sunk 2001
British Columbia

HMCS *Nipigon*
Military Escort Ship sunk in 2003
St. Lawrence River QC

Boeing 737
Airframe sunk in 2006
British Columbia

CAYMAN ISLANDS

M/V *Captain Keith Tibbetts*
Russian warship sunk in 1996
Cayman Brac

MEXICO

C58 *General Anaya*
Navy minesweeper sunk in 2000
Cozumel

OMAN

Al Munnassir
3000 tonne vessel sunk in 2003
Bandar Khairan

NEW ZEALAND

HMNZS *Tui*
Research ship sunk in 1999
Tutukaka

HMNZS *Waikato*
Frigate sunk in 2000
Tutukaka

HMNZS *Wellington*
Frigate sunk in 2003
Wellington

TOBAGO

MV *Maverick (Scarlet Ibis)*
auto ferry sunk in 1997
Mt. Irvine

UNITED KINGDOM

HMS *Scylla*
Navy frigate sunk in 2004
Cornwall

USA - FL

USS *Oriskany*
Aircraft carrier sunk in 2006

USS *Spiegel Grove*
Landing Ship dock sunk in 2002

USAFS *Gen. Hoyt S. Vandenberg*
13,000 tonne War ship Project

USCG *Duane*
Cutter sunk in 1987

USCG *Bibb*
Coast Guard Vessel sunk in 1987

Eagle
Freighter sunk in 1985

USA - NJ

USS *Algol*
Cargo attack vessel sunk in 1991
New Jersey

USA - HI

Sea Tiger
168 ft. vessel sunk in 1996
Waikiki

YO257
Navy yard oiler sunk in 1989
Waikiki

ARTIFICIAL REEF DEVELOPMENT & CONSULTING

Artificial Reef Society of British Columbia
c/o Vancouver Maritime Museum
1905 Ogden Avenue
Vancouver BC V6J 1A3
Phone: (604) 836-1120
www.artificialreef.bc.ca

Canadian Artificial Reef Consulting
466 Kings Road East
North Vancouver, British Columbia V7M 2H9
CANADA
Tel: +1 (604) 984-3646
Fax: +1 (604) 984-8573
www.artificialreefs.net

California Artificial Reef Enhancement Program (CARE)
1008 Tenth Street #298
Sacramento, CA 95814
(800) 804-6002
www.calreefs.org

Reef Ball Foundation
890 Hill Street
Athens, GA 30606 USA
www.reefball.org

A diver explores the Speigel Grove artificial reef off Key Largo, Florida. Photo: Stephen Frink / Florida Keys TDC

ARCHEOLOGY

There are many regulations and restrictions governing underwater archaeology. Generally only experienced divers are asked to accompany archaeologists on these types of dives.

CAVE DIVING

Cave diving is similar to ice diving and night diving. It is probably the diving activity that requires the most preparation, the most experience and infallible equipment. The dive is in darkness with visibility often reduced and a ceiling above.

The fishing line is tied to the diver just before entering the cave and is unwound during the excursion in the cave. It is important to pay attention to the rock face, narrow passages, and the mud on the cave floor which is stirred up as you go by. Stay in constant contact with your partner. Avoid going too far inside the cave. Respect your air supply: 1/3 to go into the cave, 1/3 to exit the cave, and 1/3 for the unexpected. When returning, follow the line and rewind it as you go along.

DECOMPRESSION DIVING

Decompression diving involves diving beyond the standard, no decompression time/depth limits and requires one or more mandatory decompression stops during ascent. Failure to make the required in-water stops is a violation of the decompression tables and may result in decompression sickness (aka. "the bends"). The rationale for using decompression diving is to extend divers' bottom time. Decompression diving is a diving procedure and is not limited to a specific type of equipment (i.e., open circuit scuba and surface-supplied, semi-closed circuit, fully closed-circuit).

SOURCE: NOAA

TECHNICAL DIVING

Tech diver Rudi Asseer readies for deep wreck exploration in the St. Lawrence Seaway. Photo: J. Gallant / D.A.Y.

In the late 1970's, NOAA pioneered the use of nitrogen-oxygen breathing mixtures or NITROX, which allows the diver to spend considerably more time at depth, then when breathing compressed air. Each breathing gas has different properties and allows the diver to dive to certain maximum depths.

Nitrox scuba diving is now supported by most dive shops and academic dive lockers in the country, spurred primarily by NURP development activities.

SOURCE: NURP

Tech divers explore the wreck of a WWII German Dornier bomber in the Mediterranean Sea. Photo: Patrice Strazzera - www.sommeildesepaves.com

Tech divers explore the wreck of the *Togo* in the Mediterranean Sea. Photo: Patrice Strazzera / www.sommeildesepaves.com

(Above) Diver explores wreck of the Keystorm in Ontario, Canada. Photo: J. Gallant / D.A.Y.

(Left) Tech diver explores Mediterranean shipwreck. Photo: Patrice Strazzera - sommeildesepaves.com

Nitrox gas mixing system and recompression chamber. Photo: OAR/National Undersea Research Program (NURP); Univ. of North Carolina at Wilmington

PROFESSIONAL DIVING

Professional divers are paid to perform various work-related tasks underwater. The tasks require specialized training and equipment, and the work is subject to various government and industry-specific safety standards and procedures. Professional diving includes activities such as saturation diving on oil rigs, underwater inspection and underwater photography.

Diving within the aquarium itself requires the use of a specialised dive team including two divers and a surface tender using a safety line and communications system. If only one diver is in the water, the second diver must be suited and ready at the surface during the entire dive in case of an emergency.

TYPES OF PROFESSIONAL DIVING

Aquarium Diving
Commercial Diving
- HAZMAT[16] Diving
- Inland / Onshore Diving
- Nuclear Industry Diving
- Offshore Diving
- Saturation Diving
Fisheries Diving
Media Diving
Scientific Diving

AQUARIUM DIVING

Aquarium divers are largely regarded as scientific divers who work within a confined body of water in a large tank. The aquarium is run by a recognized institution that has implemented a scientific diving program and specific safety protocol. The main purpose of the aquarium can be to serve as a public exhibit or for research or husbandry. Diving operations – including specimen collecting – fall under scientific diving regulations.

AQUARIUM DIVER DUTIES

The duties of an aquarium diver are varied. Some tasks need to be done on a daily basis and others are accomplished on a regular schedule or when determined necessary by husbandry or technical staff.

**Chief Diver Paul Boissinot nearing the surface after brushing the acrylic tunnel at the Quebec Aquarium.
Photo: J. Gallant / D.A.Y.**

---

[16] HAZMAT: Hazardous materials

- Feeding specimens
- Adding/retrieving specimens
- Observing specimen behavior
- Observation habitat colonization
- Cleaning walls and tunnels
- Underwater vacuuming
- Live interpretation for the public
- Maintaining equipment
- Maintaining diving records
- Specimen collecting in the field
- Underwater photography

AQUARIUM DIVER TRAINING

Aquarium divers are normally certified as scientific divers. Training is often dispensed at the institution itself if it is a member of a recognized scientific association. Training is also offered by aquarium dive clubs where divers from the local community serve as volunteers. Some aquariums have a permanent staff of full-time divers while others have a diving coordinator who is manages a team of volunteer divers from the local community.

RELATED LINKS

➢ Florida Aquarium Dive Team (www.flaquarium.org)
➢ National Aquarium in Baltimore Volunteer Dive Program (aquadivers.org)
➢ New England Aquarium Dive Club (www.neadc.org)

COMMERCIAL DIVING

Commercial divers perform underwater activities related to construction, inspection, search, salvage, repair and photography. They are employed by commercial diving contractors, shipping and marine construction companies, and oil and gas companies with offshore operations.

The work is physically and mentally demanding in difficult conditions which include freezing water temperatures, dark-

ness, confined areas, and areas containing hazardous materials or waste.

Commercial divers perform some or all of the following duties:

- Perform offshore oil and gas exploration and extraction duties such as underwater surveys, nondestructive testing, blasting, construction, and repair and maintenance of drill rigs and platforms.

Yan Labrie on his way down at Les Escoumins, Quebec. Photo: J. Gallant / D.A.Y.

- Operate underwater video, sonar, recording and related equipment for scientific or exploratory purposes.
- Inspect vessels, buoyage systems, pipelines, sluice gates, plant intakes and outfalls and other materials, visually and by nondestructive testing.
- Perform construction duties such as welding and installing pilings for cofferdams or footings for piers, and maintain these and dry docks, breakwaters, marine ways and bridge foundations using

hand and power tools and pneumatic equipment.

- Operate winches, derricks or cranes to manipulate cables and chains to raise sunken objects.
- Set up and detonate explosives to remove obstructions and break up or refloat submerged objects.
- Participate in underwater search and rescue, salvage, recovery and clean up operations.
- Check and maintain diving equipment such as helmets, masks, air tanks, harnesses, gauges, air compressors, diving suits, underwater cutting torches and welding equipment.
- May supervise and train other divers.

SOURCE: Human Resources and Skills Development Canada, Commercial Divers., http://www23.hrdc-drhc.gc.ca/2001/e/groups/7382.shtml. Reproduced with the permission of the Minister of Public Works and Government Services Canada, 2006.

Albert Levesque, diver, weighs 200 lbs (91 kg) without his suit and tips the scales at 525 lbs (238 kg) fully clad. His job is to dive under the ice to locate rocks and other debris at the lower opening of the units where the water pours into the tailrace below the power house at the Shipshaw Power Development project. Photo: Ronny Jacques / Library and Archives Canada (1943)

EQUIPMENT USED

Diver uses a hammer and chisel to free deck plating from the historic wreck of USS *Monitor*. Staples and other U.S. Navy saturation divers worked around the clock with archaeologists from the National Oceanographic and Atmospheric Administration (NOAA) to salvage the main engine and other artifacts from the wreck to be preserved and later displayed at The Mariners Museum in Newport News. Photo: U.S. Navy Photographer's Mate 2nd Class Petty Officer Eric Lippmann.

Commercial divers typically use wear surface-supplied diving equipment, including a diving helmet. The choice of diving suit depends on environmental conditions and the planned duration of the dive. When diving in very cold water, a dry suit may be equipped with a warm water flow system to keep the diver comfortable.

Cables and hoses for surface-supplied air, communications, electricity, compressed air for tools, video or lighting cables, are wound together inside an umbilical to avoid tears or snags. The umbilical is supervised by a surface team at all times.

Diver works his way around the sunken vessel *Ehime Maru*. Photo: U.S. Navy Chief Photographer's Mate Andrew McKaskle.

Chief Hospital Corpsman Mitch Pearce makes adjustments to the saturation air system during a dive on the sunken Civil War ironclad, USS *Monitor*, which rests 240 ft (73 m) below the ocean's surface. Photo: U.S. Navy Chief Photographer's Mate Eric J. Tilford.

Diver adjusting his helmet before conducting a salvage operation on the cargo of a wreck in an eastern Canadian port. By repairing damaged ships and salvaging sunken cargo Dept. of Munitions and Supply saves important tonnage, thousands of dollars worth of war goods. Photo: Library and Archives Canada (1943)

Diver drills holes in the ocean floor to secure small boat moorings. Photo: U.S. Navy Photographer's Mate 2nd Class Andrew Mckaskle

Diver is thoroughly cleaned and sanitized after completing dive operations in contaminated water. Photo: U.S. Navy Photographer's Mate 3rd Class Kristopher Wilson

The Personnel Transfer Capsule (PTC) maintains the divers inside under pressure for days at a time so they may work without decompressing between dives. Photo: U.S. Navy Chief Photographer's Mate Andrew Mckaskle.

Divers breathe oxygen in a decompression chamber after returning from a 240 ft. (73 m) dive on the USS *Monitor*. Photo: U.S. Navy Photographer's Mate 1st Class Chadwick Vann.

FISHERIES DIVING

Thousands of divers around the world make a living fishing for species that are in high demand on the food market. Some of the most important fisheries include sea urchins, sea cucumbers, the geoduck and other molluscs. Although sport divers in certain countries may obtain a permit for personal consumption, commercial harvesting is strictly regulated and conducted only by licensed operators in an attempt to manage the fisheries and control stocks.

The Northern abalone export fishery began in British Columbia in 1975 and peaked in 1977-78. Despite setting a government quota in 1979, the fishery steadily declined and was eventually closed in 1990 to conserve stocks. The commercial fishery off California was closed in 1997 but is set to reopen in Southern California in 2006 to the dismay of conservationists. Divers in Northern California may obtain a permit to hunt for the more abundant Red abalone without the use of air tanks or other underwater breathing gear, thus safeguarding most specimens beyond the depth of 25 feet (7.6 m). Recreational divers are also forbidden to sell their catch. Similar recreational rules are also in effect in New Zealand. Divers caught poaching are exposed to heavy fines, equipment confiscation, and potential jail time.

Licensed professional divers and their bounty of red sea urchins (*Strongylocentrotus franciscanus*) off the coast of British Columbia. Photo courtesy Pacific Urchin Harvesting Association / www.puha.org

FISHERIES TRAINING

Training for underwater harvesting is normally dispensed by the licensed operator to experienced divers.

RELATED LINKS

➤ Pacific Urchin Harvesting Association www.puha.org
➤ Underwater Harvesters Association www.geoduck.org

MEDIA DIVING

Underwater photography and videography is a professional occupation for a lucky few. These are highly experienced divers that are hired to shoot images for high-profile magazines such as National Geographic or for documentary series or feature films. They work much in the same way as land-based photographers and cinematographers although they work underwater. Even for the best and most experienced of these people, contracts are often few and far between.

Chris Harvey-Clark, a professional cinematographer from British Columbia, assumes a stable position while filming a passing school of fish. Photo: J. Gallant / D.A.Y.

Other media divers make it on the big screen in a live format. They cater mainly to interpretation centers, aquariums and museums that present live broadcasts of divers underwater. Divers at Parks Canada's Marine Discovery Centre near the town of Les Escoumins, Quebec, broadcast lives images of St. Lawrence marine life to a small auditorium where visitors can watch and ask questions during the dive.

MEDIA TRAINING

Little training is available beyond basic photography and videography courses offered by most training agencies. Many successful divers have simply learned by trial and error. Media work for a live audience requires the added skills of public speaking and teaching.

Divers get ready for a live underwater presentation at Parks Canada's Marine Discovery Center at les Escoumins in the St. Lawrence Estuary. Photo: J. Gallant / D.A.Y.

RELATED LINKS

➢ Australian Diver Accreditation Scheme (www.adas.org.au)
➢ Canadian Association of Diving Contractors (www.cadc.ca)

➢ Defence Research and Development Canada (Formerly known as DCIEM)
➢ Diver Certification Board of Canada (www.divercertification.com)
➢ International Marine Contractors Association (www.imca-int.com) (www.toronto.drdc-rddc.gc.ca)

SCIENTIFIC DIVING

As the title implies, the scientific certification is designed for those individuals needing to perform dives to collect scientific data. Examples include: collecting (water, bottom samples, flora and fauna, etc.), observing and documenting (including the use of cameras), and measuring and counting. Another way to describe this classification is "limited." The tasks of a scientific diver are limited to observation and data gathering and are performed in advancement of science. If tools are used, they are limited to "light" hand tools (e.g., small hammers, pliers, screw drivers, chisels, pneumatic-power drills, etc.). Other ancillary equipment such as small lift bags (<50 lbs / lifting capacity) and small air lifts can also be used if associated with data collection. Tasks typically associated with commercial diving, such as lifting heavy objects, construction, use of heavy hand or power tools, ship husbandry tasks are not authorized under the scientific diver classification.

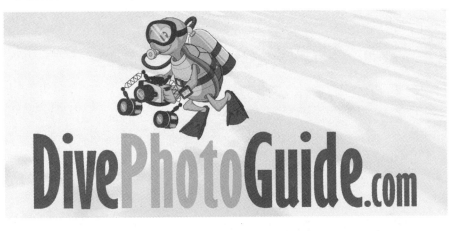

Dr. Chris Harvey-Clark of the University of British-Columbia (UBC) photo-identifies a Greenland shark (*Somniosus microcephalus*) in the St. Lawrence Estuary in Quebec, Canada (www.geerg.ca). Photo: J. Gallant / D.A.Y.

QUALIFICATION CRITERIA

In order to qualify scientific diver training, individuals must meet certain criteria which may vary slightly from one program to another. For example, to qualify for NOAA (National Oceanic and Atmospheric Administration) scientific diver certification, individuals must be previously certified scuba divers beyond the basic entry level (e.g., advanced open water, Divemaster, assistant instructor, instructor) by a recognized scuba diving certification agency (e.g., US Navy, NAUI, PADI, IANTD, SSI, TDI, YMCA, etc.). Candidates must also have completed a minimum of 25 dives; be current in CPR, First Aid, and oxygen administration training; pass a written examination (based on an advanced-level recreational scuba diving certification), a NOAA dive physical examination, and a swim test; and complete a checkout dive with a NOAA Unit Diving Supervisor, or their designee.

SOURCE: NOAA DIVING PROGRAM

Divers John Batt (Dalhousie University) and Paul Boissinot use a surface receiver to locate sharks tagged with underwater emitters prior to a dive. Photo: J. Gallant / D.A.Y.

SATURATION DIVING

Even scientific divers that use advanced diving techniques are still limited by diving depth, gas mixtures and supply, weather and decompression obligations. Saturation diving, a technique developed by the U.S. Navy in the 1950s, allows scientists to stay underwater for extended periods of time (i.e., days to weeks), thus extending their work time. Saturation diving works on the premise that if a diver's tissues are in equilibrium with the surrounding water, then the decompression time will not change for the length of time spent underwater. Undersea habitats (also known as undersea laboratories) take advantage of this principle by providing a dry living space on the ocean floor for small teams of divers, known as 'aquanauts.' Aquanauts conduct research dives in the ocean near the habitat during the day, and, instead of coming to the surface after diving, return to the undersea laboratory to eat, rest, and sleep.

SOURCE: NOAA Magazine

SCIENTIFIC vs. COMMERCIAL DIVING

According to the Code of Federal Regulations (*29CFR 1910.401(2)(iv)*, OSHA (the Federal Occupational Safety and Health Administration has determined that an organization may be exempt from the regulations that govern commercial diving activities provided it meets the following criteria: Defined as scientific diving and which is under the direction and control of a diving program containing at least the following elements:

A diving safety manual which includes at a minimum: Procedures covering all diving operations specific to the program; including procedures for emergency care, recompression and evacuation; and the criteria for diver training and certification.

Diving control (safety) board, with the majority of its members being active scientific divers, which shall at a minimum have the authority to: approve and monitor diving projects, review and revise the diving safety manual, assure compliance with the manual, certify the depths to which a diver has been trained, take disciplinary action for unsafe practices, and assure adherence to the buddy system (a diver is accompanied by and is in continuous contact with another diver in the water) for scuba diving.

Scientific divers at the Roatan Institute for Marine Science specialize in the study of tropical marine ecosystems and the bottlenose dolphin. Coral, fish and invertebrate populations, conditions on the reef such as salinity, turbidity and temperature are monitored over time in order to gauge reef health within the Sandy Bay Marine Reserve on the island of Roatan, Honduras. Photo: J. Gallant / D.A.Y.

Further guidelines for scientific diving appear in Appendix B to Subpart T:

The Diving Control Board consists of a majority of active scientific divers and has autonomous and absolute authority over the scientific diving program's operation. The purpose of the project using scientific diving is the advancement of science; therefore, information and data resulting from the project are non-proprietary. The tasks of a scientific diver are those of an observer and data gatherer. Construction and trouble-shooting tasks traditionally associated with commercial diving are not included within scientific diving.

Scientific divers, based on the nature of their activities, must use scientific expertise in studying the underwater environment and therefore, are scientists or scientists-in-training.

SOURCE: AAUS / www.aaus.org

The American Academy of Underwater Sciences

Organized in 1977, the AAUS was incorporated in the State of California in 1983. One of the primary contribution's of the AAUS to the Scientific Diving Community is the promulgation of *The AAUS Standards for Scientific Diving Certification and Operation of Scientific Diving Programs*. A consensual guideline for scientific diving programs, this document is currently the "Standard" of the scientific diving community. Followed by all AAUS Organizational members, these standards allow for reciprocity between institutions, and are widely used throughout the United States and in many foreign countries. Peer reviewed within the AAUS on a regular basis, they represent the consensus of the scientific diving community and state-of-the-art echnologies.

SOURCE: AAUS / www.aaus.org

NOAA Diving Program

The National Oceanic and Atmospheric Administration (NOAA) Diving Program, or NDP, is administered by NOAA and is headquartered at the NOAA Diving Center in Seattle, Wash. The NOAA Diving Program trains and certifies scientists, engineers and technicians to perform the variety of tasks carried out underwater to support NOAA's mission. With more than 300 divers, NOAA has the largest complement of divers of any civilian federal agency. In addition, NOAA's reputation as a leader in diving and safety training has led to frequent requests from other governmental agencies to participate in NOAA diver training courses.

SOURCE: NOAA

RELATED LINKS

➤ American Academy of Underwater Sciences (AAUS) (www.aaus.org)
➤ Australian Marine Sciences Association (www.amsa.asn.au/state/scidive.htm)
➤ Bamfield Marine Sciences Centre www.bms.bc.ca/research/diving
➤ Canadian Association for Underwater Science (www.caus.ca)
➤ NOAA Diving Program (www.ndc.noaa.gov)
➤ UK National Facility for Scientific Diving (NSFD) (www.sams.ac.uk/nfsd)
➤ The Underwater Science Group (USG) (www.usg.sut.org.uk)

RELATED READING

The NOAA Diving Manual was written for use by NOAA scientists/divers to assist them in conducting various operations. Significant contributions to the preparation of this manual were provided by experienced NOAA personnel. Noted to be the largest seller in the Government Printing Office, the manual is a comprehensive reference specifically designed for the diving professional. The manual is used by government agencies and commercial groups. The diversity of the manual ranges from polluted water diving procedures to saturation and underwater habitat diving. The NOAA Diving Manual contains USN Air Decompression Tables as well as USN, Royal Navy, and COMEX Recompression Treatment Tables.

NOAA Diving Manual
www.ntis.gov/product/noaadive.htm

Chapter 8

INFORMATION IN THIS SECTION
PROVIDED BY CAFA AND AIDA AND
ADAPTED BY D.A.Y.

FREEDIVING

RECREATIONAL FREEDIVING

In order to explore the aquatic universe, a diver has Professional divers are paid to perform various work-related tasks underwater. Recreational freediving runs the spectrum from snorkelling in shallow water to making deep dives to see things beyond the range of recreational scuba diving. The motivations and activities for recreational freediving are much the same as for recreational scuba.

Freediving on the Belize Barrier Reef. Photo: J. Gallant / D.A.Y.

The disadvantages are of course that your time on the bottom is limited. There are several advantages, however, to exploring the underwater world without tanks:

- Less equipment means you can get to more locations
- No bubbles means fish are less afraid of you

- No regulator noise so you can hear boat, fish and other sounds
- Movement along the bottom is effortless due to reduced drag
- You become more aware of planktonic and shallow water life

Along with the exploration of the underwater world comes the inner exploration of sensations and personal limits. Many people enjoy freediving for the feeling of sinking into the depths and floating back to the surface. Others enjoy the sensation of their heart slowing down as the diving reflex takes hold.

COMPETITIVE FREEDIVING

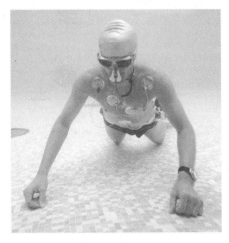

World-champion freediver Loïc Leferme (France) undergoing tests. Photo: Franck Seguin Deadline / Press Agency / www.deadline-press.com

Competitions provide a safe, fun and fair environment where freedivers have the chance to compete against others and challenge their personal limits. CAFA has a range of competition levels for freedivers of all abilities. Have a look at the CAFA Competition Program and Rules pages for more information.

Competitions involve testing a freediver's ability in time, distance and depth. To that end, all regional and national competitions in Canada have athletes competing in static apnea, dynamic apnea and constant ballast.

Other competitions may utilize a different mix of disciplines. Have a look at the Disciplines page to find a description of the recognized competitive styles of freediving.

Safety of the athletes, support and judging staff is of primary concern during competitions. Have a look at the Safety Protocols to see what measures are taken during competitions.

competitions by team, with Static apnea and Dynamic with fins.

World-champion freediver Loïc Leferme (France) during CWT dive. Photo: Franck Seguin Deadline / Press Agency / www.deadline-press.com

DISCIPLINES

AIDA only recognizes these 8 categories as official disciplines for world records and competitions; other kind of "similar" or "different" categories could only be considered as "demonstration disciplines", without any sanctioned world record. Men and women's records exist for each category. Links to the world records No other subdivision of these categories are considered (eg: lake/sea, altitude, under ice, 25/50 meter's pool, tandem-sled, etc).

CONSTANT WEIGHT (CWT)

The freediver descends and ascends using his fins/monofin and/or with the use of his arms without pulling on the rope or changing his ballast; only a single hold of the rope to stop the descent and start the ascent is allowed. Constant weight is the common sportive depth discipline of freediving, because of the specific fins or monofins used in it. Constant weight is one of the three disciplines considered for the international

CONSTANT WEIGHT WITHOUT FINS (CNF)

The freediver descends and ascends under water using only his own muscle strength, without the use of propulsion equipment and without pulling on the rope. Constant weight without fins is the most difficult sportive depth discipline, because of absolutely no propelling material to go down in the water. This category needs a perfect coordination between propelling movements, equalization, technique and buoyancy.

DYNAMIC WITHOUT FINS (DNF)

The freediver travels in a horizontal position under water attempting to cover the greatest possible distance. Any propulsion aids are prohibited. Dynamic without fins is the most natural of both disciplines measuring the distance for many freedivers, because it doesn't need any propelling material, but a very good technique. Performances also could only be recognized in pools with a minimum length of 25 meters, and are greatly appreciated from "old-swimmers".

DYNAMIC WITH FINS (DYN)

The freediver travels in a horizontal position under water attempting to cover the greatest possible distance. Any propulsion aids other than fins or a monofin and swimming movements with the arms are prohibited Dynamic with fins is the most typical of both disciplines measuring the distance in freediving, because of the specific means of propulsion : long fins or monofin. Performances could only be recognized in swimming-pools with a minimum length of 25 meters, and are sometimes considered in national or indoor's 'combiné', with the Static apnea.

STATIC APNEA (STA)

World-champion freediver Loïc Leferme (France) practices Static Apnea. Photo: Franck Seguin Deadline / Press Agency / www.deadline-press.com

The freediver holds his breath for as long as possible with his respiratory tracts immerged, his body either in the water or at the surface. Static apnea is the only discipline measuring the duration, and one of the three disciplines considered for the international competitions by team, with Constant weight and Dynamic with fins. Performances could be done and recognized in both pool and open water (sea, lake, river, etc).

FREE IMMERSION (FIM)

The freediver dives under water without the use of propulsion equipment, but only by pulling on the rope during descent and ascent. Free immersion is the sportive depth discipline with the purest sensations, because of the speed of the water in the body, and the power of each pull on the rope as only mean of propulsion. Performances could be done the head first during the descent, or the feet first, depending equalization facilities of each freedivers... Some of them also even use mixed solutions.

VARIABLE WEIGHT (VWT)

The freediver descends with the help of a ballast weight and ascends using his own strength: arms and/or legs, either by pulling or not pulling on the rope. Variable weight is the first of both depth disciplines using a sled to go down in the water. Old sleds was descending "head first", like presented in the famous Luc Besson's movie *Le Grand Bleu* (The Big Blue), but new sleds descending "feet first" are now generalized.

NO LIMIT (NLT)

The freediver descends with the help of a ballast weight and ascends via a method of his choice. No limit is the absolute depth discipline. Going down with a sled, and going back up with a balloon, a diving suit or a vest with inflatable compartments, or whatever other means.

(Above)
Video image of world-champion freediver Loïc Leferme (France) during No Limit record dive to 561 ft (171 m). Photo: Franck Seguin Deadline / Press Agency / www.deadline-press.com

(Left)
World-champion freediver Loïc Leferme (France) during No Limit dive. Photo: Franck Seguin Deadline / Press Agency / www.deadline-press.com

(Below)
World-champion freediver Loïc Leferme (France) during No Limit dive. Photo: Franck Seguin Deadline / Press Agency / www.deadline-press.com

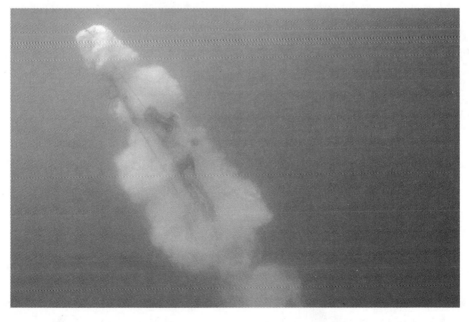

AIDA

HISTORY OF AIDA
By Claude Chapuis

It all started with Jacques Mayol, Enzo Maïorca and a few others. Then came *The Big Blue*. From 1985 to 1990, with still very few freedivers around the world, new performances and records were achieved. They were passionate about the sport... and were called the "lights of the Big Blue". A few years later, history would demonstrate that without them, modern freediving would have never come to be. This is how it all began; this is the history of the birth of AIDA... the International Association for Development of Apnea.

In 1990, Roland Specker, a freediver from Northeastern France, was training at a nearby lake with a replica of Jacques Mayol's weight ballast, which he had constructed. Roland Specker then met another Frenchman, Claude Chapuis, after having learned he had just achieved a world record in Static Apnea in Nice on the Côte d'Azur. They decided to organize clinics so that others could also discover the sport of freediving. The first clinic took place in Nice in May 1990.

Upon his return, Roland Specker thought he had more than enough time to create rules for records when in fact, many records were already being established. Roland traveled and met Umberto Pelizzari, German freedivers and many others attempting freediving records so he decided that it was important that an association be created in order to recognize these records.

On November 2, 1992, Roland Specker and a few friends created the International Association for the Development of Apnea with their head office in St. Louis, France, near Mulhouse. Roland was President, Thierry Meunier was Secretary and Claude Chapuis was the Technical Director. Two texts were drawn up: the rules and the recommendations for the recognition of records. Several records were recognized

very quickly by AIDA, which became the reference for freediving. The first AIDA journal was created in 1995 and during various assemblies, many freedivers, such as Umberto Pelizzari, Loïc Leferme, Olivier Heuleu, and Frédéric Buyle were officially recognized. Claude Chapuis also organized mini competitions between the freedivers attending the clinics held in Nice and the thought of organizing a world championship quickly grew in his mind as these competitions were fairly easy to organize.

Following a meeting in Nice attended by Umberto Pelizzari, Pierre Frolla and freedivers from Nice, and with the help of a few sports students at the University of Nice, the decision was made. The first competition rules were developed based on ski competition rules, as everyone would have to attempt performances that were not mastered. All of the freedivers agreed on one point right from the start... that performances would not be valid if the freediver experienced a blackout or a "samba", the first sign of the loss of motor control. Each freediver would present two events: Static Apnea and Constant Ballast. That way, a sea or pool specialist would not hold any advantage.

The first AIDA World Championship was held in Nice in October 1996. There were 25 participants in teams of 5 from Germany, Belgium, Colombia, Spain, France, Italy and a team representing the United Nations consisting of freedivers from different countries. Who could forget from this first World Championship the tears of Columbian Marlennedy, Claude Chapuis succeeding at leaving his country with 2 other fellow countrymen, the victory of the Italian team coached by Umberto, Jean Delmarre's 6 min. 5 sec. in Static, Jean-Michel Pradon's 174 ft (53 m) in Constant Ballast, and the incredible success of AIDA and the freedivers from Nice. Modern competitive freediving was born on that day and things could only get better. On departure day, Claude Chapuis shook Umberto Pelizzari's hand and said, "You won; now it's up to you to organize the second World Championship".

1997 was a year of transition and several freedivers created groups in their own countries. AIDA continued to certify records and 12 countries were linked thanks to AIDA. Since it was a year without a world rendez-vous, the French created the AIDA France World Cup, which is a circuit of individual competitions by team. The magnitude of the freediving phenomenon created the need to make a very important change. Each country was required to create an AIDA association. Thanks to Thierry Meunier, the AIDA website was created and Laurent Trougnou became the AIDA webmaster and Sébastien Nagel was now responsible for records. AIDA promoted the development of freediving over the Internet, which gave all freedivers the ability to stay in contact.

World-champion freediver Loïc Leferme (France) pauses prior to No Limit dive. Photo: Franck Seguin Deadline / Press Agency / www.deadline-press.com

Umberto Pelizzari never forgot his promise to Claude Chapuis and he organized the 2nd AIDA World Championship in Sardinia in 1998. Claude organized the European Trophy. This second world championship, supported by Club Med, demonstrated to all of the world's freediving federations that when sports activists get together and defend their interests, their sport advances by leaps and bounds. Twenty-eight countries attended and the presence of Jacques Mayol created an emotional atmosphere. France and Italy were neck and neck... it was just like a scene out of the Big Blue and the Mayol/Maïorca era, but it was Italy who reigned over France. AIDA France was created, which enabled AIDA to handle international challenges.

Egypt, January 1999: Magda Abdou had heard of AIDA and contacted Claude Chapuis to ask if he could organize a freediving competition in El Gouna, to the north of Hurgada, Egypt, and freedivers from around the world met in the Red Sea. Amidst all the coral and the dolphins, the competition program was somewhat insane. An individual competition was held at the start of the week, followed by a team competition. The idea was to test the realism of international individual competitions. France came second behind the Italians.

During the competition, just at the peak of suspense when the starter finished the countdown for a competitor, a spectator cried "dolphins!" In a fraction of a second, the entire group of competitors dove into the water to play with the dolphins, and the AIDA judges patiently waited with a smile to restart the competition. It was observed on that day, that competitive freedivers all shared the same passion... to feel the pleasure of being in the water and to marvel at all it has to offer.

In 1999, a very important change occurred. AIDA was dissolved so that AIDA International could emerge. On September 21, 1999, a Swiss, Sébastien Nagel, became the President of AIDA International, an executive board was created, and the assembly of delegates allowed each affili-

ated country to express itself via a vote procedure over the Internet. As of this date, and thanks to Sébastien Nagel, the media definitively recognized AIDA International. The new Swiss President was surrounded by freedivers from various countries on the executive board with Frédéric Buyle (Belgium), Dieter Baumann (Austria), Karoline Meyer Dal Toé (Brazil), Claude Chapuis (France), and Kirk Krack (Canada).

In 2000, an incredible effervescence existed throughout the world. AIDA assisted all new affiliate countries to create national associations. Notwithstanding the debut of competitions in 1996, national diving federations did not seem to take an interest in freediving. A new concept emerged while waiting for the next AIDA World Championship, which would take place in Ibiza, Spain: the World Cup. Several international competitions would take place throughout various countries in order to determine the winning team. Jean-Pol Francois in Belgium, Sébastien Nagel in Switzerland, Claude Chapuis and Pierre Frolla in France and Monaco, organized superb competitions among their friends and freedivers. Competitions for women were created, France arrived to battle with the Italians, and new nations such as Venezuela and Germany for men, and Canada and Switzerland for women emerged. Henceforth, AIDA competitions were organized in every country that had created a freediving association.

With the support of Club Med, Olivier Herrera, a young Spaniard, organized the 3rd AIDA World Championship in 2001, in Ibiza. Participating countries selected their best teams and the Italian men, under Umberto Pelizzari came first, France second, and Sweden third. For the women, in order, it was the Canadians with Mandy-Rae Cruickshank, the Americans with Tanya Streeter, and the Italians with Silvia Da Bone. Herbert Nitsch attained 282 ft (86 m) in Constant Ballast, which was a new world record. Since 1999 and the Red Sea Dive Off, Static Apnea and Constant Ballast records have been regularly broken in competition. Freedivers have become sports activists trained to go beyond human limits.

In 2002, USA AIDA Representative Glennon Gingo, organized a major international competition in Hawaii and world record holders were now regularly participating in competitions including Martin Stepanek (Czech Republic), Carlos Coste (Venezuela), Pierre Frolla (Monaco), Guillaume Nery and Stéphane Mifsud (France), Stig Severinsen (Denmark), Mandy-Rae Cruickshank (Canada) and Annabel Briseno (USA) and many others. AIDA had finally succeeded at uniting some of the best competitors in the world. Since 2000, new and old names would appear and disappear, which is the nature of the sport. It is only in competition that we discover who the best are.

Since 2000, freedivers have understood that if they want to be champions, they must confront each other. It is the challenge that Enzo offers to Jacques Mayol in "The Big Blue", and the challenge that AIDA proposes to freedivers. There will be those that will attempt the adventure... and then there are the others.

Cyprus was the world meeting place for freedivers in 2003. Englishman Howard Jones and creator of "Freediver" magazine had been following the AIDA adventure for a few years. His idea was to propose an individual match supported by AIDA. The celebration was monstrous and the performances were remarkable. Freediving had become a recognized sport and television around the world relayed the achievements of the "human dolphins." An international federation without freedivers attempted to organize a World Championship. Politicians and underwater hunters prepared strange competition rules, and as a result, the competition was canceled. The next AIDA competition was the 4th World Championship in Vancouver, Canada, in 2004.

Beyond the history of AIDA, freedivers around the world must unite in order to defend their sport and build the world of which they dream.

AIDA International wishes all freedivers around the world the very best of adventures...adventures that will build the future of freediving. Will you be among those who will continue the story?

FREEDIVING RECORDS

Go to the section on Diving Records and Aquatic Superlatives or see the very latest results on the AIDA website: www.aida-international.org

INTERNET LINKS

➢ AIDA International
  (www.aida-international.org)
➢ CAFA
  (www.freedivecanada.com)
➢ Performance Freediving
  (www.performancefreediving.com)

UNDERWATER HOCKEY

The British Navy invented underwater hockey in the 1950's to keep their divers fit and to improve their ability to move and work efficiently under water. The game came to Australia shortly after and has evolved into a fast dynamic sport played in more than 20 countries.

Underwater hockey. Photo : Olivier Mathieu / Cercle de Hockey Subaquatique de Pontoise-Cergy - http://chspc.free.fr

Underwater hockey is played in a 25m x 15m pool that is between 1.8 - 3 m deep. The game consists of 15 minutes halves and a three minutes half time. Each team is allowed one 60 seconds time out per half. The game clock stops for any infringements in the last 2 minutes of the game.

Each side has 12 players, 10 of who can play in any one game. During the game 6 players are in the pool with 4 interchange players on the side who can sub at any time. The players wear large fins, a diving mask and snorkel and a thick glove made from latex to protect the hand from the pool bottom and the puck. The top players can flick the puck well over 3m and it comes off the bottom enough to go over another player.

Underwater hockey players in action. Photo : Olivier Mathieu / Cercle de Hockey Subaquatique de Pontoise-Cergy - http://chspc.free.fr

The puck is made of lead and is coated with plastic, it weighs about 1.5 kg.

The teams start at each end of the pool with one hand on the wall. The puck is in the middle of the pool. When the referee souds the buzzer both teams race to get possession of the puck. There is a goal tray at each end of the playing area; it is 3m

long with a slope from the front into a shallow trough at the back wall. The puck must pass through the goal volume for a team to score the goal.

There are many team configurations but generally a team has 3 forwards; a strike and 2 wings and 3 backs; 2 half backs and a full back. The idea is to keep possession of the puck and outwit your opponents by using skill, speed, manoeuvrability and breathe hold.

Underwater hockey. Photo : Olivier Mathieu / Cercle de Hockey Subaquatique de Pontoise-Cergy - http://chspc.free.fr

The rules of Underwater Hockey are fairly simple. Basically it is a non contact sport; a player cannot interfere with another player with their free hand. There is no off side rule however shepherding and obstruction is not allowed. The puck must not rest on the glove or be carried on top of the bat or stopped deliberately by anything other than the bat.

Any infringement of the rules is judged by the 2 in-water referees who signal to the out of water prefer to sound the buzzer to stop play. Depending on the seriousness of the foul the Referees can award a free puck giving a 3m advantage to the disadvantaged team or can eject players for 1or 2 minutes or for the reminder of the game. If a foul has stopped a certain goal with 3m of the goal then the Referees can award a penalty 2 on 1, or just award a penalty goal.

Underwater hockey. Photo : Olivier Mathieu / Cercle de Hockey Subaquatique de Pontoise-Cergy - http://chspc.free.fr

The competitions in Underwater Hockey range for club to National to World titles. Every 2 years a World Championship is held around April or May. Every other year Australia, New Zealand and South Africa compete in a Tri - Nations cup. There are under 19 years teams, open men's and women's teams and masters teams (over 35 for men and over 32 for women).

Underwater hockey. Photo : Olivier Mathieu / Cercle de Hockey Subaquatique de Pontoise-Cergy - http://chspc.free.fr

Underwater Hockey is a great sport for all ages, shapes and sizes. Quite a few of us have been playing for well over 10 years. It is a sport that does not cause the injuries from running, stopping suddenly or being run into! Mets face it, you can't fall down. It is a sport that continues to grow and which keeps it players interested.

Each game is different; each player must overcome their opponent, moving in water, controlling the puck and the innate need to breathe. Teamwork and anticipation is essential and a lot of communication goes before and after the games.

The game is 3D, how you play is only limited by your imagination.

SOURCE: World Underwater Federation (CMAS) www.cmas2000.org

OTHER FREEDIVING ACTIVITIES

FINSWIMMING

Finswimming is an individual sport that uses a large "mono fin" to propel the swimmer through the water. The swimmer can reach high speeds, which makes these races faster and more exciting than conventional swimming races.

The history of finswimming goes back to 1927, where a Lt. Collier from France tried out a dolphin shaped fin to acheive higher swimming speeds. This fin was replaced in the early 70's by the current "mono fin", which is composed of fiberglass, or carbon-fibre. The swimmer also wears a mask.

Photo: Leaderfins - www.leaderfins.com

There are many disiplines involved in finswimming, some of which include surface swimming of distances from 25m to 1500m; apnea - where the swimmer is completely submerged and holding their breath, for distances from 25m to 50m; and immersion events of 100m, 400m & 800m, where the swimmer is submerged and has a pony bottle of air to breathe from.

Finswimming events take place in swimming pools and open water. CMAS, the World Diving Federation, is the organizing body for Finswimming. The sport is not as popular in North America, but has a large following in Europe, Asia, and South America.

Photo: Leaderfins - www.leaderfins.com

SOURCE: Canadian Underwater Games Association (CUGA) / www.cuga.org

SPEARFISHING

Activity that can be done snorkelling or with scuba

Essential requirements: Level 1 scuba diving course, knowledge on the use of the specific weapons used for this activity. Knowledge of the regulations in the area. Knowledge of the species to be fished.

Equipment: Snorkelling or scuba equipment, knife, spear gun

There are many varieties of spear guns. The spear gun generally has a trigger mechanism that holds the spear in place. The spear head can be a single, double or triple point. Rubber bands are used to launch the spear quickly and powerfully.

Each municipality, state, country will have its own laws on spear fishing. In many cases a permit will be required. In some areas, it is completely prohibited, in others, there are restrictions.

Spear fishing was very popular in Europe and North America, however, due it has lost favour because of abuse over the years.

SOURCE: CMAS Quebec / AMCQ

Freediving fin. Photo: Leaderfins - www.leaderfins.com

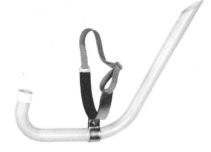

Photo: Leaderfins - www.leaderfins.com

UNDERWATER RUGBY

Underwater rugby is a team sport played at and below the surface of the water in a swimming pool, by two teams of 6 players, each wearing snorkeling gear (i.e.: mask, fins, snorkel). The object of the game is to put a negatively bouyant ball into the opposing team's goal. The goals are located at opposite ends of the pool on the bottom. The method of moving the ball is by carrying or passing below the surface. An opponent carrying the ball may be tackled below the neckline, but must be released once the ball is dropped or passed.

Goals are high baskets that the ball must be placed into, and defenders have many methods of ensuring that the ball does not go into the goal. The game is one of strategy, fitness, swimming/diving ability and breathholding. World Championships are held every 4 years.

SOURCE: Canadian Underwater Games Association (CUGA) / www.cuga.org

UNDERWATER ORIENTEERING

Underwater Orienteering is a sport where the swimmer uses modified scuba gear and navigates by use of compass, a course underwater at a depth of 1 to 10 ft (1 to 3 m). Competitions are held in lakes, with visibility sometimes nil.

Competitors are equipped with a mask, fins or a monofin, scuba tank held in front of the body, a regulator, flow meter, compass, and buoy with a 10-ft (3 m) rope to mark the participants' progress. A support person in a boat or kayak usually follows the swimmer's progress by using the buoy as a reference. The distances are pre-measured by the organizers ahead of the tournament and the competitors must take the instructions with them underwater. They are not allowed to orient themselves from the surface. Competitors follow a course that is written down on their forearm or attached to their compass.

There are 3 basic types of individual competition: M course- where a competitor has to round a series of 3 buoys, usually in an M shape in a certain amount of time; 5 points or finders: you have to find a series of 5 buoys in a certain order, usually by instigating a search pattern; and Star: a person has to round a buoy, or find one five times in a row. There are also team competitions of 2 or 4 competitors. At no time are competitors allowed to surface or have their

marker buoys go below the surface. There are points for accuracy & time.

World championships are held every 2 years with continental championships in the off year.

SOURCE: Canadian Underwater Games Association (CUGA) / www.cuga.org

UNDERWATER TARGET SHOOTING

Underwater target shooting is a sport that combines breathholding with shooting targets underwater. Competitors wear mask, fins and snorkel, a weighted belt, gloves and use a crossbow-type speargun. There are different events in target shooting which can include accuracy, biathlon, great biathlon, relay and combined ranking. There are points assigned based on how close the arrow is to the center of the target.

SOURCE: Canadian Underwater Games Association (CUGA) / www.cuga.org

FREEDIVING ASSOCIATIONS

Freediving associations, organizations, and websites not listed in the countries sections of the almanac.

AIDA International
Rue du Petit-Beaulieu 4
CH 1004 Lausanne - Switzerland
www.aida-international.org

Apnea Academy International
www.apnea-academy.com

Freediving Regulations & Education Entity
www.divingfree.com

NATIONAL ASSOCIATIONS

AUSTRIA
Freediving Austria
www.freediving.at

BELGIUM
AIDA Flanders
www.freediving.be

CANADA
Apnee Quebec
www.apneequebec.com

CAFA
101 - 9133 Capella Drive
Burnaby, BC,
Canada V3J 7K4
www.freedivecanada.com

Performance Freediving International
113 - 3075 Primrose Lane
Coquitlam, BC, Canada V3B 7S2
www.performancefreediving.com

CZECH REPUBLIC
Freediving Czech Republic
CSOB, a.s.
Kamenicka 26/599
170 00 Praha 7, Czech Republic
www.freediving.cz

DENMARK
Freediving Denmark
Timo Jattu
Bergsoe kollegiet
Skodsborgvej 190 - PBK404
2850 Naerum Denmark
www.freediving.dk

Hvidovre Freediving Club
Copenhagen Denmark
hfk.dk

FINLAND
Freediving team of Finland
www.freedivingfinland.net

JAPAN
Japan Apnea Society
1-9-17 tsuruma yamato
242-0004 Japan
www3u.kagoya.net/%7Ejas-apnea

MEXICO
Equipo Mexicano De Buceo Libre
Leibnitz 65, Anzures, DF, 11590
www.apneamx.com

NETHERLANDS
Apnea Netherlands
www.apnea.nl

POLAND

Freediving Poland
www.freediving.com.pl

Freediving Team Aland
www.freedivingteam.com

UNITED KINGDOM
British Finswimming Association
c/o Mr. A.B. Smith
Atherfield, Kent
United Kingdom TN12 6TJ
www.finswimming.co.uk

British Freediving Association
Marcus Sharp,
BFA Membership Officer,
12 Walker Close, Hampton,
Middlesex, TW12 3XT
www.britishfreediving.org

RELATED WEBSITES

Apnea Planet
www.apneaplanet.com

Apnea Magazine
www.apneamagazine.com

BlueWater Freedivers Publishing
www.freedive.net

World wide freediving spots
www.freedivingspots.net

Scott Cambell Photography
www.on1breath.com

Wolfgang Leander
Freediver and photographer
www.oceanicdreams.com

Chapter 9

MILITARY DIVING

Divers have been involved in military activities for thousands of years. Historical documents and drawings show divers performing underwater operations as far back as the 5th century BC.

Thanks to the advent of modern diving equipment such as scuba and rebreathers, today's military divers are deployed for a myriad of roles, from combat and covert missions, to rescue and recovery operations. Divers play a crucial role in the daily operations of navies all around the world.

U.S. NAVY

From their simple beginnings as swimmers disarming mines during the Civil War, divers have played critical roles in the Navy. In today's Navy, divers perform a number of essential tasks including: Underwater Reconnaissance, Demolition, Explosive Ordnance Disposal, Construction, Ship Maintenance, Search and Rescue, and Salvage operations.

Using the most modern diving equipment available, divers are taught how to operate in a variety of conditions — from clear, warm, tropical waters to frigid Arctic waters beneath icebergs to water so murky the work must be done by touch alone. From performing routine underwater maintenance of ships to salvaging a downed aircraft to surveying the Marianas Trench, Navy Divers are trained in a variety of specialties.

SCUBA Diver
These divers are trained and certified to perform underwater work projects, hull inspections and qualification dives using SCUBA gear. Navy Divers are assigned to Navy Dive Units (NDU), which are broken down by the type of tasks they execute. While some NDUs perform general duties, other units practice a dive subspecialty.

Second Class Diver
Second Class Divers are trained to perform underwater maintenance, including propeller changes and hull repair, on ships and submarines. Second Class Divers also participate in search and salvage of sunken vessels.

A search and rescue swimmer signals that he is ready to be hoisted back Photo: U.S. Navy Photographer's Mate Airman Kristopher Wilson

First Class Diver
A First Class Diver can perform operational planning for surface-supplied diving and act as a diving supervisor.

Master Diver
Obtaining Master Diver status is an enviable accomplishment in the dive community. A Master Diver is fully capable of acting as a supervisor in every type of dive application.

A deep sea diver from Mobile Diving and Salvage Unit One works his way around *Ehime Maru*. Photo: U.S. Navy Chief Photographer's Mate Andrew McKaskle.

Diving Officer
Diving Officers can perform SCUBA and surface-supplied-air dives.

Diving Medical Officer
Diving Medical Officers are U.S. Navy Doctors trained in diving and dive medicine. They are also qualified Navy Divers.

Medical Technician
Medical Technicians are Hospital Corpsmen who can perform operational surface-supplied air diving as a team member/diver.

Salvage, Construction, Demolition Diver
Salvage, Construction, Demolition Divers use munitions plus mechanical and chemical cutting equipment for salvage, battle damage repair and underwater construction projects.

Seabee Diver
Seabee Divers perform inspection, repair, removal and construction of in-water facilities in support of military operations.

Saturation Diver
Saturation Divers work at deep sea levels. First Class Divers, Medical Deep Sea Diving Technicians, Deep Sea Diving Officers and Diving Medical Officers can all become Saturation Divers.

Helium Oxygen Diver
This designation is assigned First Class Divers who have received training in all phases of surface-supplied mixed-gas diving (for deep sea diving).

Diver attaches an inert "Satchel Charge" to a training mine. Photo: U.S. Navy Chief Photographer's Mate Andrew McKaskle.

Explosive Ordnance Disposal (EOD):
EOD divers are capable of removing ordnance such as mines and other explosive devices, while utilizing SCUBA or surface-supplied-air diving systems. EOD teams are responsible for the detection, identification, neutralization and disposal of explosive ordnance and related devices. This includes foreign ordnance, chemical weapons, biological weapons, nuclear weap-

ons, clandestine improvised devices and any and all ordnance/devices that may be encountered underwater.

EOD/Marine Mammal:
Part of the Special Operations Community, the Marine Mammal Systems utilize specially trained bottlenose dolphins and sea lions to locate objects in the water.

The fleet marine mammal detachment is made up of dolphins and sea lions that can be deployed almost anywhere in the world to help with EOD.

Zak, a 375-pound California sea lion, shows his teeth during a training swim. Photo: U.S. Navy Photographer Mate First Class Brien Aho.

Deep Submergence Rescue Vehicle - DSRV
In the event of an underwater accident, a DSRV can be quickly deployed to rescue a submarine crew. A DSRV can be transported by truck, aircraft, ship or by a specially configured submarine. At the accident site, the DSRV, working with a "mother" ship or submarine, is sent down to conduct a sonar search and attach itself to the disabled submarine's hatch. A DSRV is capable of transporting 24 personnel to the "mother" vessel.

Navy Experimental Diving Unit (NEDU) scientists, engineers and divers have helped develop specialized underwater hydraulic tools and hull-scrubbing equipment for naval vessels as well as the various helmet designs used by Navy Divers. Today's NEDU provides equipment to help bolster the Navy's intelligence-gathering capabilities. The NEDU also has a rich history: Naval salvage diving; Submarine rescue and support; Inshore warfare; Acoustic coun-

termeasures; Mine and ordnance disposal and countermeasures; Navigation and amphibious operations.

Sailors assist in steadying the deep submergence rescue vehicle *Mystic* (DSRV-1) as it is lowered on to the fast-attack submarine *Dallas* (SSN-700). Photo: U.S. Navy / Journalist 1st Class Jason E. Miller

Consolidated Divers Unit (CDU):
The CDU is responsible for ships husbandry (ship cleaning and maintenance). With divers performing common operations like screw (propeller) changes and hull cleaning, the ship doesn't need to be taken out of the water and placed in dry dock.

Mobile Diving and Salvage Units (MDSU):
MDSU-1 services the Pacific Fleet, while MDSU-2 tends to the Atlantic Fleet. Both units have helped in recovery of boats, planes and even spacecraft. MDSUs provide: Mobile ship salvage; Towing; Battle damage repair; Deep ocean recovery; Harbor clearance; Underwater ship repair

Underwater Construction Teams (UCT):
The UCT, comprised of Seabees with specialized dive training, possess underwater repair and construction expertise, and are amphibious in nature. They are capable of constructing shallow and deep-water structures, mooring systems, underwater instrumentation, light salvage and precision blasting.

SOURCE: U.S. NAVY

U.S. NAVY SEALS

From 1962 when the first SEAL[17] teams were commissioned, to present day, Navy SEALs have distinguished themselves as an individually reliable, collectively disciplined and highly skilled maritime force. Because of the dangers inherent in NSW, prospective SEALs go through what is considered by many military experts to be the toughest training in the world.

Basic SEAL students take part in "Log PT." Photo: U.S. Navy / Robert Benson

The intense physical and mental conditioning it takes to become a SEAL begins at Basic Underwater Demolition/SEAL (BUD/S) training which is conducted at the Naval Special Warfare Center in San Diego, CA. Candidates must complete a mentally and physically demanding 6-month basic training course, 3 weeks of parachute training and a 15-week advanced training period

---

[17] SEAL: SEa Air and Land

prior to becoming a SEAL and earning the Trident--the warfare pin insignia of all SEAL operators.

Navy SEALs handle classified missions from the sea, air and land with razor-sharp precision, teamwork and cool-headedness. SEALs are considered the leading offensive force in the world. Their missions include reconnaissance, clandestine operations, and unconventional and counter-guerilla warfare.

U.S. Navy SEALs. Photo: U.S. Navy

All SEAL teams train in jungle, arctic, woodland, mountain, desert or urban terrain. Special tactics, techniques and equipment apply to each – from SEAL delivery vehicles and high – speed gunner boats to advanced SCUBA gear and other sophisticated equipment.

Today's Naval Special Warfare operators can trace their origins to the Scouts and Raiders, Naval Combat Demolition Units, Office of Strategic Services Operational Swimmers, Underwater Demolition Teams, and Motor Torpedo Boat Squadrons of World War II. While none of those early organizations have survived to present, their pioneering efforts in unconventional warfare are mirrored in the missions and professionalism of the present Naval Special Warfare warriors. Responding to President Kennedy's desire for the Services to develop an Unconveventional Warfare (UW) capability, the U.S. Navy established SEAL Teams ONE and TWO in January of 1962. Formed entirely with personnel from

Underwater Demolition Teams, the SEALs mission was to conduct counter guerilla warfare and clandestine operations in maritime and riverine environments. On May 1, 1983, all UDTs were redesignated as SEAL Teams or Swimmer Delivery Vehicle Teams (SDVT). SDVTs have since been re-designated SEAL Delivery Vehicle Teams.

SDVs are used to carry Navy SEALs from a submerged submarine to enemy targets while staying underwater and undetected. Photo: U.S. Navy / Chief Photographer's Mate Andrew McKaskle

SEAL MISSIONS

Special Operations is characterized by the use of small units with unique ability to conduct military actions that are beyond the capability of conventional military forces. SEALs are superbly trained in all environments, and are the master's of maritime Special Operations. SEALs are required to utilize a combination of specialized training, equipment, and tactics in completion of Special Operation missions worldwide.

A tactical force with strategic impact, NSW mission areas include unconventional warfare, direct action, combating terrorism, special reconnaissance, foreign internal defense, information warfare, security assistance, counter-drug operations, personnel recovery and hydrographic reconnaissance. Although NSW personnel comprise

less than one percent of U.S. Navy personnel, they offer big dividends on a small investment.

SEALs' proven ability to operate across the spectrum of conflict and in operations other than war in a controlled manner, and their ability to provide real time intelligence and eyes on target, offer decision makers immediate and virtually unlimited options in the face of rapidly changing crises around the world. The most important trait that distinguishes Navy SEALs from all other military forces is that SEALs are maritime special forces, as they strike from and return to the sea.

SOURCE: U.S. Navy SEALs

RESCUE SWIMMER

The mission of the Naval Aviation Rescue Swimmer is to execute search and rescue (SAR) operations from rotary wing aircraft.

Rescue swimmers conduct Search and Rescue (SAR) drills Photo: U.S. Navy Photographer's Mate Airman Sarah E. Ard

NAVY MARINE MAMMAL PROGRAM

Everyone is familiar with security patrol dogs. You may even know that because of their exceptionally keen sense of smell, dogs like beagles are also used to detect drugs and bombs, or land mines. But a dog would not be effective in finding a sea mine. Sea mines are sophisticated, expensive weapons that are designed to work in the ocean where they can sink ships, destroy landing craft, and kill or injure personnel.

Sea mines are made so that they cannot be set off easily by wave action or marine animals growing on or bumping into them. If undetected, sea mines can be deadly, destructive weapons. But just as the dog's keen sense of smell makes it ideal for detecting land mines, the U.S. Navy has found that the biological sonar of dolphins, called echolocation, makes them uniquely effective at locating sea mines so they can be avoided or removed.

Other marine mammals like the California sea lion also have demonstrated the ability to mark and retrieve objects for the Navy in the ocean. In fact, marine mammals are so important to the Navy that there is an entire program dedicated to studying, training, and deploying them. It is appropriately called the Navy Marine Mammal Program (NMMP)[18].

K-Dog, a Bottlenose Dolphin, leaps out of the water while training. Attached to the dolphin's pectoral fin is a "pinger" device that allows the handler to keep track of the dolphin when out of sight. Photo: U.S. Navy Photographer's Mate 1st Class Brien Aho.

SOURCE: U.S. Navy Marine Mammal Program

RELATED LINKS

- ➢ U.S. Navy (www.navy.com)
- ➢ United States Navy Seal (www.seal.navy.mil)
- ➢ Naval Special Warfare (www.sealchallenge.navy.mil)

[18] The Navy's Marine Mammal Program is an accredited member of the Alliance of Marine Mammal Parks and Aquariums, an international organization committed to the care and conservation of marine mammals. Accreditation by the Alliance means this facility meets or exceeds all the standards of excellence for marine mammal care, husbandry, conservation and education.

A sea lion recovers a MK 5 Marine Mammal System (MMS). Photo: U.S. Navy

➢ Naval Sea Cadet Corps
(www.seacadets.org)

NATIONAL UNITS

AUSTRALIA

Australian Clearance Diving Team One is one of two commissioned Clearance Diving Teams in the Royal Australian Navy. Clearance Diving Team was created 18 March 1966 at HMAS Penguin to support the Eastern based fleet. Australian Clearance Divers have always been the Australian Defence Forces' (ADF) specialist divers and have, since the inception of the Branch in 1951, operated all in-service diving equipment to the full extent of its operational capacity.

The primary focus of a Clearance Diver is to perform Explosive Ordnance Disposal (EOD) and are capable of locating and destroying or recovering underwater ordinance and Improvised explosive device disposal (IEDD). This role is conducted at sea in ships, in the oceans (particularly the vulnerable approaches to ports and anchorages), and onshore in port facilities, installations and the littoral environment associated with amphibious operations. The Australian Clearance Diving community represents the largest single ADF organization with a direct and primary interest in the conduct of EOD. The RAN Clearance Diving Branch's equipment has been state of the art and their techniques are regarded as world leading.

The **Clearance Diving Teams** of the Royal Australian Navy are similar to the United States Navy's former Underwater Demolition Teams (UDT) in terms of function and capabilities. Clearance Diving Team One consists of a headquarters element and three operational elements that specialize in Maritime Tactical Operations (MTO), Mine Counter-Measures (MCM) and Underwater Battle Damage Repair (UBDR). All elements are capable of performing IEDD and EOD operations and are capable of

being deployed independently or as a combined task unit.

All personnel joining the Diving Branch, including Officers, must undergo acceptance testing and complete the arduous requirements of the Clearance Diving qualification course. The clearance diving course spans 32 weeks for the basic clearance diver and 49 weeks for both advanced clearance divers and clearance diving officers. The demands placed on potential applicants to this category are not seen elsewhere in the ADF except with the Special Forces.

SOURCE: Royal Australian Navy, Australian Clearance Diving Team 1 - navy.gov.au/units/cdt1 - Copyright Commonwealth of Australia reproduced by permission.

RELATED LINKS

➢ Royal Australian Navy
(www.navy.gov.au/units/cdt1)

CANADA

There are three kinds of divers in the Canadian Navy. The first are clearance divers. "These are the Navy's elite professionals," explains LCdr Gwalchmai, "and for good reason, since they must carry out the riskiest assignments, often under difficult circumstances." These divers are trained to perform all kinds of underwater tasks, including repairs to ships and conducting salvage operations (such as the example in the opening section of this article). But one of their most important duties to which a diver must attend is mine countermeasures (MCM)—which is polite talk for "bomb disposal." Says LCdr Gwalchmai: "a clearance diver has to possess extraordinary physical and mental agility to handle this kind of work. Neutralizing a mine can be tasking enough, but add about 100 metres of water over your head, and it adds a whole new dimension of risk to the challenge."

Clearance divers are assisted in their work by the two other types of Navy divers: ship's-team, and naval reserve divers.

Ship's-team divers are found on every warship. They are trained in SCUBA and assist the clearance divers by checking waters around a vessel for previously unspotted ordinance. Since this group is the proving-ground from which clearance divers are selected, ship's-team divers sometimes provide direct assistance to clearance divers in a mission. Similarly, **naval reserve divers** participate in ordinance recognition and complementary clearance, performing underwater inspections of port and harbor facilities, search and rescue operations, and identification of surface and underwater ordinance.

While clearance divers are described as the elite group, a look at the cumulative total of divers (clearance, ship's-team and reserve combined) in the Canadian Navy suggests that all divers belong to a special group. There are a total of 450 divers currently in service in the Navy, of which 150 are clearance divers, 200 are ship's-team, and 100 are reservists.

A Search and Rescue swimmer practices personnel recovery operations with a Canadian SH-3. Photo: U.S. Navy Photographer's Mate 2nd Class Jimmy Lee

Training to become a diver is as rigorous as the job of being a diver. This is especially true of the program for clearance divers. Starting with a two-week preliminary course, out of a classroom of 30 candidates, only about a dozen will be selected. What follows after candidate selection is an eight to ten-month course with in-depth

training on the use and skills of SCUBA and rebreather apparatus, working with special underwater repair and construction tools. Divers learn precise skills about handling ordinance and defusing underwater mines. They also learn general seamanship skills, as well as diving physics and physiology. Hence the training requires that divers have a firm grasp of both the theoretical as well as the physical dynamics of working and swimming in deep water.

"Because we have so few people in the Navy," explains LCdr Gwalchmai, "it's important that every member's skills be used to the fullest." That's why all clearance divers are trained not only in bomb disposal, but in ship repair as well. "It takes a long time to dry-dock a ship," says the Lieutenant Commander. "Fixing a propeller underwater versus dry dock is a difference between days and weeks. In fact, I've seen a team of divers replace two propellers on a destroyer in about a weekend." Like all parts of the Canadian Forces, the Navy and its divers always stand ready to provide aid to civilian tragedies. One example was the Swissair 111 crash off the coast of Nova Scotia on September 2, 1998. To provide assistance and salvage support, the Navy provided 140 clearance divers—almost its entire staff—as well as the HMCS *Protecteur*, RHIBS and Zodiacs and various forms of support ashore.

Risk and adventure go hand-in-hand for Navy divers. Whether their mission is in Canada's coastal waters or at far away locations in the waters of the Persian Gulf or the Indian Ocean, these professionals can be counted on to deliver nothing short of excellence every time. That's just the way things are done in Canada's Navy.

SOURCE: Descent by LCdr R. Gwalchmai, www.navy.forces.gc.ca/navres/home/navres_welco me_e.asp. Reproduced with the permission of the Minister of Public Works and Government Services Canada, 2006.

Clearance Divers, Ship's-Team Divers, Naval Reserve Divers. www.navy.forces.gc.ca/navres/home/navres_welco me_e.asp. Reproduced with the permission of the Minister of Public Works and Government Services Canada, 2006.

Port Inspection Divers are responsible for conducting operations using compressed air breathing apparatus (CABA), performing underwater inspections of port and harbour facilities, participating in mine countermeasures (MCM) operations, performing underwater search and recovery operations, performing identification of surface and underwater ordnance, recognizing diving or pressure-related ailments, and neutralizing underwater anti-ship sabotage devices as well as providing assistance to civil authorities. They must also carry out several tasks in order to support diving activities such as driving inflated boats, preparing dive sites, and maintaining equipment. They must also carry out the instruction and administration of the Diving Branch.

SOURCE: Port Inspection Diver – What They Do., http://stage.multimediaservices.ca/v3/engraph/jobs/jobs.aspx?id=R345&bhcp=1. Reproduced with the permission of the Minister of Public Works and Government Services Canada, 2006.

French combat diver with assault rifle. Photo: Marine Nationale (French Navy)

FRANCE

The French diving commando unit bears the name of Lieutenant Augustin Hubert, killed on June 6, 1944, during the D-Day invasion of Normandy. The *Commando Hubert* is comprised of an operational company and a support company. The operational company is subdivided into 4 specialized sections: support, maritime counter-terrorism, underwater machines and reconnaissance. The unit gathers about fifty naval frogmen. Together, the four sections comprise about 50 combat divers.

The Clearance Diving Unit (GPD) based at the Toulon Naval Base was founded in 1955. Comprised of 27 divers, the group carries out actions such as mine clearance, neutralization of explosive devices as well as various missions of public service.

French Navy clearance diver recovering WWII ammunition in the Mediterranean. Photo © Marine Nationale

The GPD has taken part in several operational missions: mine clearance of the Suez Canal in 1974, in Lebanon in 1983 and 1984, during the Iran-Iraq conflict in 1987, during the Gulf War off the coast of Kuwait in 1991, during the conflict in ex-Yugoslavia (1992-1996). GPD divers also participate in reconnaissance missions to survey underground networks in urban areas.

Commando Hubert combat diver. Photo © Marine Nationale / Pascal Fournier

SOURCE: *MARINE NATIONALE*

UNITED KINGDOM

The Royal Navy's Special Boat Service (SBS) is the lesser-known sister unit of the British Army's Special Air Service (SAS) regiment. Based in Poole, Dorset, the SBS is a Special Forces unit which specializes in special operations at sea, along coastlines and on river networks. The SBS also have a team on standby for maritime counter terrorism (MCT) operations. Whilst the unit specializes in water-borne activities, they are also highly skilled on dry land. Previously known as the Special Boat Squadron and exclusively drawn from Royal Marine Commandos, the SBS is now open to members of other regiments and services.

The Special Boat Service is organized into 3 squadrons: C, M & Z. For reasons of security, the exact number of SBS ranks is not made public; however the number is speculated to be between 200 & 300.

The roles of the SBS include covert infiltration using canoes and small boats, maritime counter terrorism (MCT), assaulting ships at sea and attacking docked ships via mini-subs and swimmer delivery vehicles.

SOURCE: SPECIALBOATSERVICE.CO.UK

OTHER UK DIVER UNITS

British commando frogmen; Royal Engineers Specialist – Army Diver; Royal Navy Clearance Divers

OTHER NATIONAL UNITS

- **DENMARK:** Frømandskorpset (Danish Frogman Corps)
- **INDONESIA: Kopaska – TNI-AL / Indonesian Navy Underwater Combat Unit**
- **ITALY:** COMSUBIN – *Comando Raggruppamento Subacquei ed Incursori Teseo Tesei*
- **MALAYSIA:** Paskal Special Maritime Unit – *Pasukan Khas Laut*

- **NORWAY:** Froskemanskorpset – Part of (MJK) *Marinejegerkommandoen* commando unit
- **RUSSIA:** Водолаз разведчик / *Vodolaz razvedchik* (Combat diver) – Part of Naval Spetsnaz; Боевой Пловец / *Boyevoy plovets* (Combat swimmer) - Special purpose anti-sabotage diving unit.

EQUIPMENT

Since military diving units are supported by their respective governments, they have access to significant financial resources and the most specialized equipment available, some of which is not available to recreational divers.

DPVs

French combat divers and hydrojet propulsion vehicle. Photo: Marine Nationale (French Navy) / Reynald Boivin

NAVIGATION

Team of French commando divers navigate using a compass during a training exercise. Photo: Marine Nationale (French Navy) / Reynald Boivin

PARACHUTE

A Navy SEAL tries to steer clear of surrounding parachutes In the Gulf of Mexico Photo: U.S. Air Force Senior Airman Andy M. Kin.

CAMOUFLAGE

Rebreather-equipped French commando divers wearing camouflage. Photo: Marine Nationale / Reynald Boivin

TASKS

Since military diving units are financed and supported by their respective governments, they have access to significant resources and the most specialized equipment available, some of which is not available to recreational divers.

RECOVERY

Search and rescue swimmers retrieve an aerial drone following an air defense exercise. Photo: U.S. Navy Journalist 2nd Class Brian P. Biller

Search and rescue swimmer secures an exercise torpedo. Photo: U.S. Navy Photographer's Mate 2nd Class Brandon A. Teeples.

SHIP OPERATIONS

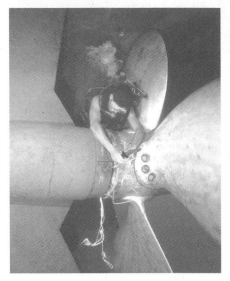

Navy Diver uses his dive knife to cut away heavy gauge fishing line to free a fouled propeller. Photo: U.S. Navy Petty Officer 1st Class Andrew McKaskle

RECONNAISSANCE

Two French commando divers defend their perimeter while another takes reconnaissance photos. Photo: Marine Nationale (French Navy) / Pascal Fournier

U.S. NAVY DEEP SUBMERGENCE UNIT (DSU)

Deep Submergence Unit (DSU) was established in 1989 and is home of the Navy's manned and unmanned deep diving submersibles. Located at Naval Air Station North Island (NASNI) in San Diego are Deep Submergence Rescue Vehicles (DSRV) *MYSTIC* and *AVALON*, a variety of unmanned Remotely Operated Vehicles (ROV), and Submarine Rescue Chambers (SRC).

AVALON (DSRV-2) - Maximum Depth: 5,000 ft (1,524 m); Weight: 76,000 lbs (34,473 kg); Displacement: 82,000 lbs (37,195 kg); Dimensions: 49 x 8 x 11 ft (15 x 2.4 x 3.4 m); Crew: 4, 24 rescues; Life support: 384 man hours; Speed: 4.1 knots/8 hours (max), 2.5 knots/14 hours (transit), 1.5 knots/18 hours (search); Max controlled ascent rate: 100 ft/min (30 m/min)

The U.S. Navy Los Angeles attack submarine USS *La Jolla* (SSN 701) with the deep submergence rescue vehicle Mystic (DSRV-1) attached, Mystic was specifically designed to fill the need for an improved means of rescuing the crew of a submarine immobilized on the ocean floor. It can operate independently of surface conditions or under ice for rapid response to an accident anywhere in the world. Photo: U.S. Navy Journalist 3rd Class Wes Eplen.

DSU features worldwide submarine rescue, deep ocean search and recovery and scientific research. DSU was originally chartered as Submarine Rescue Unit following the loss of USS *THRESHER* (SSN 593), and received DSRV-1 *MYSTIC* in August 1971 and DSRV-2 *AVALON* in July 1972, with a mandate to maintain the capability to locate a disabled submarine, accomplish reliable personnel escape and rescue and optimize survival possibilities in a bottomed submarine.

The primary mission of the DSRVs is to provide a quick reaction, worldwide, all-weather capability to rescue personnel from disabled submarines (DISSUB) at depths up to 2,000 ft. The maximum operating depth is approximately 5,000 ft.

AVALON and *MYSTIC* can be transported by truck, aircraft, surface ship, or on a mother submarine. For a rescue operation, *AVALON* can dive, locate the DISSUB, and attach itself to the DISSUB's rescue seat. After the DSRV is properly attached to the submarine, the DISSUB's access hatches are opened and submarine personnel can move directly into the DSRV. The DSRV then detaches from the submarine and transfers to rescued personnel to the support ship.

UNMANNED VEHICLES DETACHMENT

The UMV was initially organized in the mid-1970s from personnel in the various departments of Submarine Development Squadron 5 and Deep Submergence Unit.

UMV was first assigned a Side Looking Sonar (SILOS) system and a precision navigation system. These systems allowed UMV to begin search and survey operations, mostly in shallow water and near land.

As deep ocean ROV technology continued to develop, UMV continued as well. In August of 1987, the unit's recovery capability was further extended with the delivery of the *Super Scorpio Tethered Unmanned Work Vehicle System*. The Scorpio system, of which UMV has two vehicles, was an extremely advanced vehicle, capable of lifting far more payload than the RCV. UMV's final system was delivered in 1992, the Advanced Tethered Vehicle (ATV). ATV is similar in design to Scorpio, but has a tether for more efficient data transfer between the ROV and its surface operators greater depth capacity and a fiber optic.

TETHERED UNMANNED WORK VEHICLE SYSTEM (TUWVS) - Super Scorpio ROV - Maximum depth 5,000 ft (1,524 m); Weight: 4,500 lbs. (2,041 kg); Dimensions: 4 x 4 x 8 ft (1.22 x 1.22 x 2.44 m); Speed: 4 knots forward/AFT and 2 knots laterally; Fly away capable; 107-122kHz CTFM SONAR, 2000 ft (610 m) range, (EDO 250); Two black and white video cameras (OSPREY SL-90); Two HMI lights, Four 250W incandescent lights; 1 in. (2.54 cm) steel cable cutter; Two manipulators capable of lifting 250 lbs. (113 kg) each

In recent years, the ROVs of Unmanned Vehicles Detachment have been responsible for the recovery of over 100 million dollars worth of military and civilian hardware. Also, the unit has been instrumental in the successful completion of various research endeavors by the United States' scientific community. UMV remains a flexible and potent asset, continuing to evolve as equipment becomes available.

cue Exercise off the coast of Denmark. Photo: U.S. Navy Journalist 2nd Class Steve Vasquez.

The DSSD detachment is the one with the longest historical background. Well before the loss of the USS *Thresher* prompted the forming of the Deep Submergence Unit, Diving Systems Support Detachment's progenitors were saving submariners from unfortunate mishap. In the 1930s a Navy commander, A. E. McCann, helped build the McCann / Erickson rescue chamber, what is now known as the submarine rescue chamber (SRC). This was done in response to the loss of the USS *S-4* earlier in the decade. Work on the rescue chamber was completed just in time, too, because in 1939, USS *Squalus* went down. This time, however, the Navy was prepared. McCann and his Experimental Diving Unit were dispatched to rescue the Sailors and bring them home to safety. This is what he did and because of his innovations, 33 of the 53 Sailors aboard *Squalus* were saved. This is the history of the rescue chamber's current home, Diving Systems Support Detachment (DSSD).

The U.S. Remote Operated Vehicle (ROV) Super Scorpio is retrieved after live Submarine Search and Res-

Members of the U. S. Navy's Deep Submergence Unit Diving Systems Detachment secure the Submarine Rescue Chamber (SRC) aboard the MV *Kendrick* in preparation for "Exercise Pacific Reach." Photo: U.S. Navy Senior Chief Photographer's Mate Terry Cosgrove.

SUBMARINE RESCUE CHAMBER (SRC 21) - Maximum depth: 850 ft; Weight: 21,600 lbs. in air 50 lbs. - positive in water); Crew: 2, six rescues

The unit now operates out of the DSU compound on Naval Air Station North Island. They have three SRCs and little has changed since their initial development in the '30s. Also, DSSD operates as the underwater rigging experts for recovery operations. Working hand-in-hand with the other units within DSU, DSSD helps to rig objects for recovery by the underwater robots of Unmanned Vehicles Detachment.

SOURCE: U.S. Navy Deep Submergence Unit

RELATED LINKS

➢ U.S. Navy Deep Submergence Unit
www.csp.navy.mil/csds5/dsu/dsu.htm

POLICE DIVING

Police diving units provide underwater search and recovery operations such as the search for missing persons or stolen property, evidence of major crimes, and the disposal of explosives.

The Quebec Provincial Police Diving Unit prepares to launch a dive boat. Photo courtesy Sûreté du Québec

Police divers provide underwater security at major events; respond to aquatic disas-

ters, plane crashes and anti-terrorist activities. Police divers are also given the unenviable task of recovering bodies.

SOURCE: Ontario Provincial Police (OPP); Norfolk Constabulary Underwater Search and Recovery Unit

Under-ice recovery operation by the Quebec Provincial Police Diving Unit. Photo courtesy Sûreté du Québec

DIVE FEDERATIONS & ASSOCIATIONS

Chapter 10

ALGERIA
Fédération Algérienne De Sauvetage De Secourisme Et Des Activités Subaquatiques (FASSAS)
20, Avenue du 1er Novembre, Alger, Algeria
Tel.: 213 2 71 02 72
Fax : 213 2 71 02 71
Email: ctnfassas@yahoo.fr
www.fassas-dz.com

ANDORRA
Federació Andorrana d'Activitats Subaquàtiques (FADAS)
Avinguda C.P. De Gaulle nº 9,
Baixos - 1 Escaldes Engordany, Andorra
Tel.: 376 87 45 95
Email: ins@fadas.ad
www.fadas.ad

ARGENTINA
Federación Argentina de Actividades Subacuáticas (FAAS), Argentine Underwater Federation
Arribeños 1599, Piso 15º "B"
C 1426 BLG Capital Federal
Argentina
Tel. /Fax: 54 11 47 82 28 70
Email: faas@giga.com.ar
www.faas.org.ar

AUSTRALIA
Australian Underwater Federation
Apartment 183, Dockside Tower,
538-542, Little Lonsdale Street
3000 Melbourne Australia
Tel.: 61 41 815 1787
Fax: 61 39 670 4308
Email: secretary@auf.com.au
www.auf.com.au

AUSTRIA
Tauchsportverband Österreichs
Huettergasse 25c
Wien A-1140 Austria
Tel.: 43 66 42 53 45 66
www.tsvoe.or.at
Email: office@tsvoe.or.at

BAHAMAS
Bahamas Diving Association
P.O. Box 21707
Fort Lauderdale , FL 33335, USA
Tel.: 954 236 9292
Fax: 954 236 9282
Email: bda@clinegroup.net
www.bahamasdiving.com

BELARUS
Belarus Federation of Underwater Sport
7 Ignatenko St , P.O. Box 54
220035 Minsk Belarus
Tel./Fax : 375 172 23 25 52
Email: adm-blrf00@cmas.org

BELGIUM
Fédération Belge De Recherches Et D'activités Sous-marines (FEBRAS)
Rue Jules Broeren 38
1070 Bruxelles, Belgium
Tel.: 32 2 524 15 60
Fax: 32 15 29 04 86
Email: febras.belgium@skynet.be
www.befos-febras.be

Nederlandstalige Liga voor Onderwateronderzoek en -Sport
Brusselsesteenweg 313-315
2800 Mechelen
Tel.: 32 15 29 04 86
Fax: 32 15 20 61 58
Email: secretariaat@nelos.be
www.nelos.be

BOSNIA-HERZEGOVINA
Diving Association of Bosnia And Herzegovina
Hiseta bb
71000, Sarajevo
Tel.: 385 71 42 15 33
Fax: 385 71 66 44 48
Email: adm-bihf00@cmas.org

BRAZIL
Conf. Brasileanos de Pesca e Desportos Subaquaticos (CBPDS)
Rua Buenos Aires 93,
grupo 1203 / Centro,
Rio de Janeiro, Brazil
Tel/Fax : 55 /21/22 21 21 10
Email: cbpds@cbpds.com.br
www.cbpds.com.br

BULGARIA
Bulgarian National Association of Underwater Activity (BNAUA)
P.O. Box 152,
9000 Varna, Bulgaria
Tel.: 359 52 370487
Fax: 359 52 370483
Email: krastev@io-bas.bg

CANADA
ACUC International
379 West Street,
Brantford, ON N3R 3V9 Canada
Tel.: 519 750 5767
Fax: 519 750 5771
Email: info@acuc.ca
www.acuc.ca

Canadian Underwater Games Association Association Canadienne Des Jeux Subaquatiques (CUGA)
4010 Stanley Road SW
Calgary, Alberta, T2S 2P4, Canada
Tel.: 403 243 5467
Fax: 403 287 1607
Email : cugainfo@shaw.ca
www.cuga.org

Continental Sub-Aquatic Certification (CSAC) Certification Sub-Aquatique Continentale
297 Mayrand
Saint Jean sur Richelieu, Quebec
J3B 3L8, QUEBEC, Canada
Tel.: 450 346 5671
Fax: 450 346 5617
Email: lavigne.jrp@netc.net

Combat Diver Association of Canada
www.geocities.com/armyflipper/index2.htm

Alberta Underwater Council
Percy Page Centre, 11759 Groat Road
Edmonton, Alberta T5M 3K6 Canada
Tel.: 780 427 9125
Fax: 780 4278139
info@albertaunderwatercouncil.com
www.albertaunderwatercouncil.com

Fédération Québécoise des activités subaquatiques
4545, av. Pierre-De Coubertin
C.P. 1000, Succ. M
Montréal (Québec), H1V 3R2, Canada
Tel.: 514 252 3009
Fax: 514 254 1363
Toll free: 866 391 8835
Email: info@fqas.qc.ca
www.fqas.qc.ca

Manitoba Underwater Council
Box 711Winnipeg, Manitoba R3C 2K3
Canada
Email: info@manunderwater.com
www.manunderwater.com

Nova Scotia Underwater Council
6484 Young Street ,
Halifax, Nova Scotia, B3L 2A3, Canada
Tel.: 902 4547826
Email: rollylewis@hotmail.com
www.nsuc.net

Ontario Underwater Council
1185 Eglinton Ave.
E Suite 104,
North York, Ontario, M3C 3C6, Canada
Tel.: 416 426 7033
Fax: 416 426 7336
Email: ouc@underwatercouncil.com
www.underwatercouncil.com

P.E.I. Underwater Council
Sport P.E.I.
3 Queen St.
Charlottetown, PEI C1A 7K7, Canada
Tel.: 902 368 4110

Saskatchewan Underwater Council
Box 7651
Saskatoon, SK S7K 4R4 Canada
executive@saskuc.com
www.saskuc.com

Underwater Council of British Columbia (UCBC)
334 - 1367 W Broadway,
Vancouver BC, V6h 4A9, Canada
Tel.: 604 737 3058
Fax: 604 737 3666
Email: tbeasley@pop.intergate.ca

Yukon Underwater Diving Association
www.yukonweb.com/community/yuda

CHILI
Federacion Chilena De Deportes Submarinos (FCDS)
Almirante Simpson N°5
Providencia, Santiago de Chile
Tel.: 56 2 222 0365
Fax: 56 2 222 0385
Email: fedesub@entelchile.net
www.fedesub.cl

CHINA
Chinese Underwater Association (CUA)
9, Tiyu Guan Road,
Beijing, China
Tel.: 86 10 6711 3689, 6711 3247
Fax: 86 10 6711 2793
Email : diving@public.bta.net.cn
www.cmasasia.org

Chinese Taipei Underwater Federation (CTUF)
N° 10, Lane 68, Shinn Yie Road
Tzyguan county
Kaohsiung Hsien
Tel.: 886 07 617 11 26
Fax: 886 07 619 48 95
Email: cmas.dive@msa.hinet.net
www.cmasasia.org

Hong Kong Underwater Association
Room 1026, Olympic House,
1 Stadium Path, So Kon Po,
Causeway Bay, Hong Kong
Tel.: 852 2504 8154
Fax: 852 2577 5601
Email: enquiry@hkua.org.hk
www.hkua.org.hk

COLOMBIA
Federación Colombiana De Actividades Subacuáticas (FEDECAS)
Calle 9 Carrera 36
Piscinas Panamericanas - Hernando Botero O'Byrne
Cali, Colombia
Tel.: 57 2 514 64 29
Fax: 57 2 558 01 50
Email: fedecas@telesat.com.co
www.telesat.com.co/fedecas

CROATIA
Hrvatski Ronilacki Savez (HRS) / Croatian Diving Federation
Dalmatinska 12
10 000 Zagreb, Croatia
Tel.: 385 1 484 87 65
Fax: 385 1 484 91 19
Email: info@diving-hrs.hr
www.diving-hrs.hr

CUBA
Federación Cubana De Actividades Subacuaticas (FCAS)
Calle 7 entre 1 y 3 Santa Maria Playa
Ciudad de La Habana, Cuba
Tel.: 53 7 56 14 69
Email: adm-cubf00@cmas.org

CYPRUS
Cyprus Federation of Underwater Activities (CFUA)
P.O.Box: 21503,
1510 Lefkosia, Cyprus
Tel: 02 45 46 47
Email: adm-cypf00@cmas.org
www.kypros.org/PIO/cyprus/cto_guide/s/sports.htm

CZECH REPUBLIC
Svaz Ceskych Potapecu (SPCR)
Divers Association Of Czech Republic
Na Strzi, 9
140 00 Prague 4
Tel. /Fax: 420 2 41 44 58 03, 58 04
Email: diver@svazpotapecu.cz
www.svazpotapecu.cz

DENMARK
Dansk Sportsdykker Forbund (DSF)
Danish Sportdiver Federation
Idrœttens Hus
Brøndby Stadion 20
DK 2605 Brøndby
Tel.: 43 26 25 60
Fax: 43 26 25 61
Email: dsf@sportsdykning.dk
www.sportsdykning.dk

DOMINICA
Dominica Watersports Association
PO Box 635, Roseau,
Commonwealth of Dominica, WI
Tel.: 767 440 8181
Fax: 767 448 6088
Email: info@dominicawatersports.com
www.dominicawatersports.com

ECUADOR
Federacion Ecuatoriana De Buceo Y Actividades Subacuaticas
P.O. Box 09-06-2249,
Guayaquil, Guayas
Ecuador
Email: fedasub@coe.org.ec
www.fedasub.com

EGYPT
Egyptian Underwater & Lifesaving Federation (EULF)
18, Dr. Mostafa AL-dewani St.
Garden City, P.O. Box 115
11516 Cairo
Tel.: 20 2 794 08 93
Fax: 20 2 795 09 43
Email: uwf@access.com.eg
www.eulf.org

ESTONIA
Eesti Allveeliit (EAL)
Pirita tee 12,
10127 Tallinn, Estonia
Tel.: 37 25 14 30 06
Email: allveeliit@hot.ee

EUROPE
European Underwater Federation
Ch. des Rethieux, Frontenex
F-74210 Faverges, France
Tel. /Fax: 33 450 444 046
Mobile: 33 616 800 275
Email: info@euf.org.uk
www.euf.org.uk

FINLAND
Finnish Divers´ Federation
Radiokatu 20
FI-00093 SLU, Finland
Tel.: 358 9 3481 2258
Fax: 358 9 3481 2516
Email: office@sukeltaja.fi
www.sukeltaja.fi

FRANCE
Fédération Française d'Études et des Sports Sous-marins
24, Quai de Rive-Neuve
13284 Marseille, Cedex 07, France
Tel.: 33 0 4 91 33 99 31
Fax : 33 0 4 91 54 77 43
Email: secretariat@ffessm.fr
www.ffessm.fr

FRENCH POLYNESIA (FRANCE)
Fédération Tahitienne des Sports Subaquatiques de Compétition (FTSSC)
Fantaua Pirae B.P. 650
Papeete, French Polynesia
Tel.: 689 82 94 64
tahiti-ia@ifrance.com

GERMANY
Verband Deutscher Sporttaucher (VDST)
Berliner Str. 312

63067 Offenbach, Germany
Tel.: 069 981902 5
Fax: 069 981902 98
Email: vdst.ev@vdst.de
www.vdst.de

GREECE
Hellenic Federation for Underwater Activities Sportsfishing & Finswimming
Agios Kosmas,
West Terminal Post Office
Elliniko, Attikis 16604 Greece
Tel.: 01 9819961
Fax: 01 9817558
Email: Press@finswimming.org.gr
www.sportsnet.gr/main_en.html

GRENADA
Grenada Scuba Diving Association
Tel.: 473 444 1126
Fax: 473 444 1127
Email:
presdent@grenadascubadivingassociation.com
www.grenadascubadivingassociation.com

HOLLAND (See Netherlands)

HONG KONG (See China)

HUNGARY
Magyar Buvar Szauszovetseg / Hungarian Divers Federation
Dozsa Gyorgy Street 53
H-1134 Budapest, Hungary
Tel/Fax: 36 1 270 01 17
Email: mbsz@nextramail.hu
www.mbsz.net

Underwater Explorers' Federation (UEF)
H-1116 Budapest, Sopron út 64
Hungary
Tel.: 36 1 412 1755
Fax: 36 1 412 1756
Email: info@uef.hu
www.uef.hu

ICELAND
Sportkafarafélag Íslands / Icelandic Sport-diving Association
Brautarendi, Flugvallarvegi,
101 Reykjavik, Iceland
Tel.: 00354 551 1211
Email: kofun@kofun.is
www.kofun.is

INDIA
Underwater Federation of India (UFI)
Khaquan Manzil 103 Wazeer Ganj

Lucknow 18, India

INDONESIA
**Persatuan Olah Raga Selam Seluruh Indonesia (POSSI) / Pengurus Besra Hq
Indonesian Subaquatic Sport Association (ISSA)**
Stadion Renang Gelora
Bung Karno Senayan
Jakarta, Indonesia 10270
Tel.: 62 21 5790 0486
Fax: 62 21 5790 0487
Email: adm-inaf00@cmas.org

IRAN (Islamic Republic of)
Iran Scuba Divers Association
Kish Island - Iran
Tel.: 0098 934 769 3981
Email: mrbn56@yahoo.com
www.iranscubadiver.com

IRELAND
**The Irish Underwater Council (IUC) /
Comhairle Fo-Thuinn**
78A Patrick Street, Dun Laoghaire, Co. Dublin,
Ireland
Tel.: 353 01 2844601
Fax: 353 01 2844602
Email: hq@irishunderwatercouncil.com
www.irishunderwatercouncil.com

ISRAEL
The Israeli Diving Federation
PO Box 22421,
61223, Tel Aviv, Israel
Tel.: 972 3 5465760
Fax: 972 3 5465154
Email: adm-irsf00@cmas.org
www.diving.org.il

ITALY
**Federazione Italiana Pesca Sportiva E Attivita
Subacquee (FIPSAS)**
Viale Tiziano, 70
00196 Rome, Italy
Tel.: 39 06 36 85 82 38
Fax: 36 06 36 85 81 09
Email: nuotopinnato@fipsas.it
www.fipsas.it

**Federazione Italiana Sport Acquatici (FISASUB)
Italian WaterSport Federation**
Tel.: 39 06 451 1704
Fax: 39 06 451 1747
Email: info@fisasub.it
www.fisasub.it

JAPAN
Japan Underwater Sports Federation (JAFSA)
4-4 Pacific Building B-1
Kojimachi Chiyoda-ku
102-0083 Tokyo Japan
Tel.: 81 3 32 22 11 92
Fax: 81 3 32 88 03 93
Email: info@jusf.gr.jp
www.jusf.gr.jp

JORDAN
Royal Jordanian Marine Sports Federation (RJMSF)
PO Box 930
77110 Aqaba Jordan
Tel.: 962 3 201 43 57
Fax: 962 3 201 43 79
Email: adm-jorf00@cmas.org

KAZAKHSTAN
Kazakhstan Underwater Activities
Ul Djandosova 182, kv. 7
480051 Almaty Kazakhstan
Tel.: 7 3272 64 12 44
Fax: 7 3272 64 12 44
Email: adm_kazf00@cmas.org

LATVIA
**Akademiskais Daivinga klubs (Academic
Diving Club, CMAS Baltic)**
Zolitudes str 46/3-28
Riga, Latvia
Tel.: 371 928 2629
Email: letsgo@deepdive.info
www.deepdive.info/rus/kursi

LIBYA
LIBYAN DIVING ASSOCIATION (LDA)
P.O. Box 80679
Tripoli, Libya
Tel.: 218 21 333 56 06
Fax: 218 21 444 78 42
Email: adm-lbaf00@cmas.org

LIECHTENSTEIN
Liechtensteiner Tauchsport Verband
Postfach 579
9494 Schaan
Tel.: 41 81756 62 36
Email: info@bubbles.li
www.bubbles.li

LITHUANIA
**Lietuvos Povandeninio Sporto Federacija /
Lithuanian Underwater Sport Federation**
Pylimo 20-18
01118 Vilnius

Lithuania
Tel.: 370 5 212 0336
Email: adm-ltuf00@cmas.org

LUXEMBURG
Federation Luxembourgeoise Des Activites Et Sports Subaquatiques (FLASSA)
Boite Postale 53
L-2010 Luxembourg
Tel./Fax : 35 2 48 96 64
Email: fil@pt.lu
www.flassa.lu

MALAYSIA
Malayan Sub Aqua Club (MSAC)
73 Lorong Lai Tet Loke
54100 Kuala Lumpur
Tel.: 60 3 293 54 12
Fax: 60 3 232 19 19
Email: seongl@pc.jaring.my
www.cmasasia.org/auf_mem/malayan.htm

MALTA
Malta Federation of Underwater Activities
PO Box 29
Gzira, Malta
Email: fuam@digigate.net
www.fuam.org

MAURITIUS
Mauritius Scuba Diving Association (MSDA)
36 Bis, rue Meldrum
Beau Bassin, Mauritius
Tel.: 230 454 00 11
Fax: 230 454 00 11
Email: msda@.intnet.mu

MEXICO
Federacion Mexicana De Actividades Subacuaticas (FMAS)
Av. Rio Churubusco Puerta 9 s/n
Colonia Ciudad Deportiva, Magdalena Mix-huca, Del./Mun. Iztacalco
Mexico, D.F., C.P. 08010
Tel. / Fax: 52 5 5803 0172
Email: tmas@codeme.org.mx
www.fmas.org.mx

MOLDOVA
Federation of Underwater Activities of the Republic Of Moldova / Federatia De Activitati Subacvatice Din Republica Moldova
57, Petru Rares str.
Chisinau, MD-2005, Moldova
Tel.: 373 22 211464
Fax: 373 22 227106
Email: diving@acm.md

www.diving.md

MONACO
Federation Monegasque Des Activites Subaquatiques (FMAS)
Cale de halage du port de Fontvieille,
MC 98000 Monaco
Tel. /Fax: 377 97 98 11 55
Email: fmas@monte-carlo.mc
www.fmas-monaco.com

NAMIBIA
Namibian Underwater Federation (NUWF)
PO. Box 2600
9000 Windhoek, Namibia
Tel.: 26 61 26 74 01
Fax: 26 61 26 48 98
Cell: 264 81 124 8030
Email: pieterf@vectorlog.com

NETHERLANDS
Nederlandse Onderwatersport Bond (NOB) / Dutch Underwater Federation
Nassaustraat, 12
3583 XG Utrecht, NL
Tel.: 31 30 251 70 14
Fax: 31 30 251 07 73
Email: info@onderwatersport.org
www.onderwatersport.org

NEW ZEALAND
New Zealand Underwater Association (NZUA)
1/40 Mt Eden Rd, Mt Eden,
PO Box 875, Auckland, NZ
Tel.: 64 9 623 3252
Fax: 64 9 623 3523
Email: nzu@nzunderwater.org.nz
www.nzunderwater.org.nz

NORWAY
Norges Dykkeforbund (NDF) / Norwegian Diving Federation
Serviceboks 1 Ullevål Stadion
0840 Oslo, Norway
Tel.: 47 21 02 97 42
Fax: 47 21 02 97 41
Email: dykking@nif.idrett.no
www.ndf.no

PALESTINE
Palestinian Swimming Federation & Aquatic Sports
P.O. Box 54598,
97300 Jérusalem, Palestine
Tel.: 972 2 626 2539.
Fax: 972 2 627 1871

Email: palsf@jrol.com
www.palsport.com

PAPUA NEW GUINEA
Papua New Guinea Divers Association, Inc.
PO Box 1646
Port Moresby, NCD 121, New Guinea
Tel.: 675 321 3913
Fax: 675 321 5650
Email: pngdive@online.net.pg
www.pngdive.com

PERU
Federacion Peruana De Actividades Subacuaticas Subacuaticas (FEPASA)
Estadio Nacional Puerta 4, Second floor
Lima 1, Peru
Tel.: 51 14 424 3481
Email: fedesub@viaibcp.com

PHILIPPINES
Philippines CMAS Instructors Association (PCIA)
Robelle Mansion
877 J. P. Rizal Street
1200 Makati City, Philippines
Tel.: 63 2 899 73 88
Fax: 63 2 899 73 93
Email: cmas@divephil.com
www.divephil.com

POLAND
Polski Zwiazek Pletwonurkowania Sportowego (PZPNS)
Polish Underwatersports Federation
UL. M. Sklodowskiej-Curie 19/201
81-231 Gdynia
Poland
Tel.: 48 58 626 55 81
Fax: 48 58 626 55 72
Email: divepzpn@mw.mil.pl
www.pzp-n.pl

PORTUGAL
Federação Portuguesa De Actividades Subaquáticas / Portuguese Underwater Federation
Rua José Falcão, Nº 4, 2º
1170-193 Lisbon Portugal
Tel.: 218 166 547
Fax: 218 141 148
Email: fpas@fpas.pt
www.fpas.pt

Centro Português de Actividades Subaquáticas - CPAS
Rua Alto do Duque, N.º 45,

1400-009 Lisbon
Tel.: 21 301 69 61
Fax: 21 302 03 56
Email: cpas@cpas.pt
www.cpas.pt

ROMANIA
Asociatia nationala a scafandrilor profesionisti si salvamarilor din Romania
Str. Gheorghe Lazar, Nr. 1
Constanta, Romania
Tel. /Fax: 40 241 52 02 44
Email: adm-romf01@cmas.org

RUSSIA
Russian Underwater Federation / Confederation Russe Des Activites Subaquatiques (CRASA)
2/15, Marosseika Str.
101000 Moscow
Tel.: 70 95 928 12 81
Email: mail@diver.ru
www.diver.ru

SAN MARIN
Federazione Sammarinese Attivita Subacquee (FSAS)
Via Rancaglia, 30
47890 Serrevalle, San Marin
Tel.: 0549.88.56.00
Fax: 0549.88.56.52
Email: duiliomarcante@hotmail.com

SAUDI ARABIA
Saudi Divng Federation
PO. BOX 102723,
11685 Al-Riyad
Saudi Arabia
Tel.: 966 1 227 39 72
Fax: 966 1 228 65 45

SENEGAL
Federation Senegalaise Des Activites Subaquatiques (FSAS)
Océanium Centre de la Mer
Route de la Petite Corniche Est
BP 2224
Dakar, Senegal
Tel.: 221 8 22 24 41
Fax: 221 8 21 02 24
Email: adm-senf00@cmas.org

SERBIA AND MONTENEGRO
Savez Organizacija Podvodnih Aktivnosti Republike Srbije / Serbia And Montenegro Divers Association
Poštanski Fah 35-81

11020 Beograd 35
Serbia and Montenegro
Tel. /Fax: 381 11 32 222 32
Email: calypso@eunet.yu
www.sopas.org.yu

SINGAPORE
Singapore Underwater Federation (SUF)
C/o Queenstown Swimming Complex,
473 Stirling Road, Singapore 148948
Tel.: 65 6479 9001
Fax. 65 6479 9029
Email: sufnet@mbox3.singnet.com.sg
www.geocities.com/singaporeunderwaterfed
eration/index.html

SLOVAKIA
Zväz Potapacov Slovenska (ZPS)
Slovak Divers Association
Junácka 6,
832 80 Bratislava (Dom športu)
Slovakia
Tel. /Fax: 421 2 492 492 20
Email: zps@netax.sk
www.zps-diving.sk

SLOVENIA
Slovenska Potapljaska Zveza (SPZ)
Celovska c. 25
1000 Ljubljana, Slovenia
Tel.: 386 1 433 93 08
Email: mitja.slavinec@uni-mb.si
www.spz.si/portal

SOUTH AFRICA
South Africa Underwater Union (SAUU) / Zuid-Africaanse Onderwater Unie
PO Box 557
7499 Parow - Cape Town
Tel.: 27 21 930 65 49
Fax: 27 21 930 65 41
Email: adm-rsaf00@cmas.org
www.sa-underwater.org.za

SOUTH KOREA
Korea Underwater Association (KUA)
Rm 149 NO. 2
Gymnasium 88-2
Oryun-Dong Songpa - Ku
138-151 Seoul, South Korea
Tel.: 82 2 420 42 93
Fax: 82 2 421 88 98
Email: kua@kua.or.kr
www.kua.or.kr

SPAIN
Federacion Española De Actividades Subacuaticas (FEDAS)
C/Santaló,15 3°1ª
08021 Barcelona Spain
Tel.: 34 93 200 67 69
Fax: 34 93 241 16 80
Email: fedas@fedas.es
www.fedas.es

SPAIN CANARY ISLANDS
Federación Canaria de Actividades Subacuáticas (FEDECAS)
Puerta Canseco,49 2°2ª (Edificio Jamaica)
38003 Santa Cruz De Tenerife
Tel.: 922 240 041
Fax: 922 240 041
secretaria@fedecas.com
www.fedecas.com

SPAIN CATALANA
Federació Catalana d'Activitats Subaquàtiques
Rambla Guipúscoa 23-25,
5 D 08018, Barcelona, Spain
Tel.: 93 3304472
Fax: 93 4902054
Email: info@fecdas.org
www.fecdas.org

SWEDEN
Svenska Sportdykarförbundet (SSDF)
Drottshuset
123 87 Farsta, Sweden
Tel. : 08 605 88 02
Fax : 08 605 88 32
Email: sportdykning@ssdf.se
www.ssdf.se

SWITZERLAND
Fédération Suisse de Sports Subaquatiques (FSSS)
Secrétariat permanent
Pavillonweg 3
3012 Berne Switzerland
Tel.: 031 301 43 43
Fax: 031 301 43 93
Email: admin@fsss.ch
www.susv.ch

SYRIA
Syrian Underwater Sport Federation
P.O. Box 421
Damas, Syria
Tel.: 963 1311 213 10 16
Email: syroc@mail.sy

TAHITI (See French Polynesia)

THAILAND
TDA Diving Association (Thailand)
52 Moo 5, Thanon Thepkrasattri,
Ampher Thalang, Phuket 83110 Thailand
Tel.: 076 206514-5
Fax: 076 206094
Email: office@cmas-thailand.org
www.tda-cmas.org

TRINIDAD AND TOBAGO
Association of Tobago Dive Operators
P.O. Box 1105
Canaan/Bon Accord, Tobago
www.tobagoscubadiving.com

TUNISIA
Fédération des Activités Subaquatiques de Tunisie (FAST)
B.P. 46
1082 Cité Mahrajène, Tunis
Tel.: 216 71 28 11 40
Fax: 216 71 28 15 42
Email: president.fast@planet.tn

TURKEY
Türkiye Sualtý Federasyonu (SCSF) / Turkish Underwater Federation
Genclik ve Spor Genel Mudurlugu Ulus Is Hani ,
A Blok   Ulus,
ANKARA - Turkey
Tel.: 90 312 310 3960
Fax: 90 312 310 4136
Email: info@tssf.gov.tr
www.tssf.gov.tr

TURKS AND CAICOS
Watersports Association of the Turks and Caicos Island WATCI
Tel.: 649 946 5034

UKRAINE
Ukrainian Underwater Sports Federation (UUSF)
Teslyarska St. 4
03022 Kiev, Ukraine
Tel.: 38 044 259 87 64
Fax: 38 044 259 91 11
Email: president@ufua.org
www.ufua.org

UNITED ARAB EMIRATES
Emirates Diving Association EDA
Heritage & Diving Village,
Shindaga Area,
P.O.Box: 33220. Dubai, UAE
Tel.: 971 43 93 93 90
Fax: 971 43 93 93 91
Email: edadiver@emiratesdiving.com

www.emiratesdiving.com

UNITED KINGDOM
Sub-Aqua Association (SAA)
Space Solutions Business Centre,
Sefton Lane,
Maghull, Liverpool, L31 8BX, UK
Tel.: 0151 287 1001
Email: admin@saa.org.uk
www.saa.org.uk/old_site/index.html

U.K. SCOTLAND
The Scottish Federation of Sub Aqua Clubs (SCOTFED)
www.arcl.ed.ac.uk/scotfed

U.K. WALES
Welsh Association of Sub Aqua Clubs (WA-SAC)

U.K. NORTHERN IRELAND
Northern Ireland Federation of Sub-Aqua clubs (NIFED)

UNITED STATES OF AMERICA
Underwater Society of America
53C Appian Way,
South San Francisco CA 94080, USA
Tel.: 650 583-8492
Fax: 650 583-0614
Email: CROSEUSOA@aol.com
www.underwater-society.org

VANUATU
Vanuatu Scuba Operators Association
Email: sailaway@vanuatu.com.vu
http://www.vanuatutourism.com/dive

VENEZUELA
Federacion Venezolana De Actividades
Subacuaticas (FVAS) / Venezuelan Diving
Federation
Calle Cachaito,
Edif. DOS Piso 3, Ofic.: 3C
CP.: 1050, Chacaito
Bello Monte, Distrito Venezuela
Tel.: 58 212 816.24.20
Fax: 58 414 126.20.89
Email: info@fvas.com.ve
www.fvas.com.ve

VIETNAM
Hiep Hoi The Thao Duoi Nuoc Viet Nam (VASA) / Vietnam Aquatic Sports Association
36 Tran Phu Str.,
Hanoi, Vietnam
Tel.: 84 48 23 45 53.
Fax: 84 47 33 11 98

Email: vasa@fpt.vn
www.cmasasia.org/auf_mem/vietnam.htm

TRAINING AGENCIES & ASSOCIATIONS

AAUS American Academy of Underwater Sciences
101 Bienville Blvd.,
Dauphin Island, AL 36528 USA
Tel.: 251 861 7504
Fax: 251 8617540
Email: aaus@disl.org
www.aaus.org

ACUC Association of Canadian Underwater Councils
World Headquarters
379 West Street;
Brantford Ontario N3R 3V9, Canada
Tel: 1 519 750 5767
Fax:1 519 750 5771
Email: acuchq@acuc.ca
www.acuc.es

ACUC European Headquarters
C/ Añastro, 25
28033 Madrid, Spain
Tel: 34 91 766 84 12
Fax: 34 91 766 86 51
Email: acuc@acuc.es
www.acuc.es

ADAS Australian Diver Accreditation Scheme
526 Duncan Road
Dunoon NSW 2480
Australia
Tel: 02 66 89 5656
Fax: 02 6689 5657
(International) 61 2 66 89 5656
Email: paul.butler@adas.org.au
www.adas.org.au

ANDI American Nitrox Divers, Inc.
74 Woodcleft Avenue
Freeport, New York 11520-3342 USA
Tel.: 516 546 2026
Fax: 516 546 6010
Email: andi@andihq.com
www.andihq.com

ANMP Association nationale des moniteurs de plongée
Euro 92, bâtiment F
Z.I. les trois moulins, Rue des Cistes
06600 Antibes, France

Tel.: 33 493 332 200
Fax: 33 493 743 228
Email: anmpinfo@wanadoo.fr
www.anmp-plongee.com

BSAC British Sub Aqua Clubs
Telford's Quay, South Pier Road,
Ellesmere Port, Cheshire CH65 4FL, UK
Tel.: 0151 350 6200
Fax: 0151 350 6215
Email: postmaster@bsac.com
www.bsac.com

CADC Canadian Association of Diving Contractors
23 Abbotsford Road
North York, Ontario M2N 2P9 Canada
Tel.: 416 225 1753
Fax: 416 225 7643
www.cadc.ca

Canadian Working Divers Institute
4420 Hwy 507,
Buckhorn, ON Canada, K0L 1J0
Tel/Fax: 705 657 2766
Email: cwdi@trytel.net
www.canadianworkingdivers.com

CEDIP European Organisation for Professional Diving Instructors
62, Avenue des Pins du Cap
06160 ANTIBES-JUAN LES PINS
FRANCE
Tel: 33 4 93 614 545
Fax: 33 4 93 673 493
Email: cedip@cedip.com
www.cedip.com

CMAS, Confédération mondial des activités sub-aquatique (World Underwater Federation)
Viale Tiziano, 74
00196 - Roma - Italia
Tel.: 39 06 32 11 05 94
Fax: 39 06 32 11 05 95
Email: cmas@cmas.org
www.cmas.org

DAN Divers Alert Network
(See Chapter 4: Diving Medicine)

DDRC Diving Diseases Research Centre
The Hyperbaric Medical Centre
Tamar Science Park,
Research Way,
Plymouth, PL6 8BU
Tel.: 01752 209999
Fax: 01752 209115
Email: enquiries@ddrc.org

www.ddrc.org/docs

**DEMA (Diving Equipment &
Marketing Association)**
3750 Convoy St., Ste. 310
San Diego, CA 92111-3741 USA
Toll Free: 800 862-DIVE (3483)
Tel.: 858 616 6408
Fax: 858 616 6495
Email: info@dema.org
www.dema.org

DIA Dive International Agency
Email: diveagency@diveagency.org
www.diveagency.org

Diver Certification Board of Canada
Suite 503
5121 Sackville Street
Halifax, Nova Scotia B3J 1K1 Canada
Tel.: 902 465 3483
Fax: 902 465 1057
www.divercertification.com

DRI Dive Rescue International
201 North Link Lane
Fort Collins, Colorado
80524-2712 USA
Tel.: 800 248 3483 (toll free)
Tel.: 970 482 0887
Fax: 970 482 0893
www.diverescueintl.com

**ESA Worldwide
European Scuba Agency**
07026 Olbia (OT) Italy
Via Imperia Vicenza 123/2
Tel.: 39 078 964 1063
Fax: 39 078 964 1611
www.esaweb.net

GUE Global Underwater Explorers
15 South Main Street
High Springs, FL 32643 USA
Tel.: 386 454 0820
Tel.: 800 762- 3483
Fax: 386 454 0815
Email: info@gue.com
www.gue.com

HDS The Historical Diving Society
Little Gatton Lodge, 25 Gatton Road
Reigate RH2 0HD UK
www.thehds.com

HSA Handicapped Scuba Association International
1104 El Prado

San Clemente, CA 92672-4637 USA
Tel.: 949 498 4540
Fax: 949 498 6128
Email: hsa@hsascuba.com
www.hsascuba.com

**IADRS International Association of Dive Rescue
Specialists**
201 North Link Lane
Fort Collins, Co 80524 USA
Tel.: 800 423 7791
Fax: 970 482 0893
www.iadrs.org

IAHD International Association for Handicapped Divers
Hazelaarlaan 47
1775 EE Middenmeer , Netherlands
Tel.: 0031 22 750 3631
Fax : 0031 84 741 5861
Email: info@iahd.org
www.iahd.org

**IANTD International Association of Nitrox and
Technical Divers**
World Headquarters
Miami Shores, FL 33138-2665 USA
Temporary Phone: 305 754 1027
Fax: 509 355 1297
Email: iantd@iantd.com
www.iantd.com

IAST International Association of Scuba Technicians
4574 North Hiatus Road
Sunrise, Florida 33351 USA
Tel.: 954 748 4772
Fax: 954 748 0637
IASTus@aol.com
www.iast.us

IDD Instructor Dive Development
Nieuwpoortkade 16
1055 RX Amsterdam, Netherlands
Tel.: 31 0 20 6815148
Fax: 31 0 20 6880397
Email: pde@iddworld.com
www.iddworld.com

IDEA International Diving Educators Association / www.idea-scubadiving.com

IDEA North America
P.O. Box 8427
Jacksonville, FL 32239-8427 USA
Tel.: 904 744 5554
Fax: 904 743 5425
Email: ideahq@idea-scubadiving.com

IDEA Europe
L'Aquila, Italy
Tel.: 39 0862 318499
Fax: 39 0862 318542
Email: HQ@idea-europe.com
www.idea-europe.com

IDEST Inspectorate for Diving Equipment Servicing and Testing
29 Ravenswood Avenue,
West Wickham,
Kent BR4 0PN, UK
Tel.: 020 8777 6740
Email: pat@sita.org.uk
www.sita.org.uk

ITDA International Technical Diving Agency
www.itdagroup.com

ITDA Asia Pacific
Email: prodivin@singnet.com.sg

ITDA Egypt
Tel.: 002 012 585 1162
Email: egypt@itda.net
www.itdamidest.com

ITDA Germany
Email: egypt@itda.net
itdamidest.com

ITDA U.K.
Tel. /Fax: 44 01386 861 862

ITDA Spain
Tel/Fax: 44 01386 861 862
Email: info@itda.net

MAHS Maritime Archaeological and Historical Society
P.O. Box 44382 L'Enfant Plaza
Washington, DC 20026
(301) 419-8222
Email: SAnthony@mahsnet.org
www.mahsnet.org

NABS National Association of Black Scuba Divers, Inc.
P. O. Box 91630
Washington, D.C. 20090-1630
Tel.: 1 800 521 NABS
Fax: 202 526 2907
Email: secy@nabsdivers.org
www.nabsdivers.org

NACD National Association for Cave Diving
P.O. Box 14492
Gainesville, FL 32604

Tel.: 1 888 565 NACD (6223)
Fax: 1 888 565 NACD (6223)
Email: gm@safecavediving.com
www.safecavediving.com

NASDS National Association of Scuba Diving Schools (See SSI)

The Nautical Archaeology Society,
Nautical Archaeology Society
Fort Cumberland
Fort Cumberland Road
Portsmouth PO4 9LD UK
Tel/Fax: 44 0 23 9281 8419
www.nasportsmouth.org.uk

NAUI Worldwide Headquarters
National Association of Underwater Instructors
PO Box 89789
Tampa, FL 33689-0413 USA
Tel.: 813 628 6284
Fax: 813 628 8253
www.padi.com

NBDHMT National Board of Diving and Hyperbaric Medical Technology
1816 Industrial Blvd
Harvey, LA 70058 USA
Tel.: 1 504 328 8871
Fax: 1 504 3661029
Email: nbdhmt@bellsouth.net
www.nbdhmt.org

NOAA National Oceanographic and Atmospheric Administration
14th Street & Constitution Avenue, NW
Room 6217
Washington, DC 20230 USA
Tel.: 202 482 6090
Fax: 202 482 3154
Email: answers@noaa.gov
www.noaa.gov

PADI Americas
30151 Tomas Street
Rancho Santa Margarita, CA
USA 92688
Tel.: 1 949 858 7234
www.padi.com

PADI Canada
107 - 1680 Broadway Street
Port Coquitlam, B.C. V3C 2M8, Canada
Tel.: 1 604 552 5969
Fax: 1 604 552 5921
Toll Free: 800 565 8130 (Canada)
Email: valerie.walsh@padi.com
www.padi.com

PADI Europe
Oberwilerstrasse 3
Hettlingen
Switzerland CH-8442
41 52-3041414
www.padi.com

PADI International
Unit 7 St. Philips Central
Albert Road
Bristol, UK BS2 0XJ
44 117-300-7234
www.padi.com

PDIC International
Professional Diving Instructors Corporation
PO Box 3633, Scranton, PA 18505
Tel.: 570 342 1480
Fax: 570 342 6030
Email: info@pdic-intl.com
www.pdic-intl.com

PSA International Professional Scuba Association International
9425 NW 115th Avenue,
Ocala, Florida 34482 USA
Tel.: 352 861 7724
Fax: 352 694 7724
Email: psainternational@aol.com
www.mrscuba.com

SAA Sub Aqua Association
Space Solutions Business Centre,
Sefton Lane,
Maghull, Liverpool, L31 8BX, UK
Tel.: 0151 287 1001
Email: Admin@saa.org.uk
www.saa.org.uk

SDI Scuba Diving International
18 Elm Street,
Topsham, Maine 04086 USA
Tel.: 888 778-9073
Email: worldhq@tdisdi.com
www.tdisdi.com

SITA Scuba Industries Trade Association
29 Ravenswood Avenue,
West Wickham, Kent, UK
Email: pat@sita.org.uk
www.sita.org.uk

SSI Scuba Schools International
2619 Canton Court
Fort Collins, CO 80525-4498, USA
Tel.: 970 482 0883
Fax: 970 482 6157
Email: admin@ssiusa.com

www.ssiusa.com

TDI World Headquarters
18 Elm Street
Topsham, Maine, 04086 USA
Contact: Brian Carney
Tel.: 207 729 4201
Fax: 207 729 4453
Email: worldhq@tdisdi.com
www.tdisdi.com

YMCA of the USA
SCUBA Program
101 N. Wacker Drive
Chicago, IL 60606 USA
Tel.: 800 872 9622
Fax: 312 279 4492
Email: scuba@ymca.net
www.ymcascuba.org

UKSDMC UK Sport Diving Medical Committee
Dr Mike O'Kane
Cwmfelin Surgery
298 Carmarthen Road
Swansea SA1 1HW, UK
www.uksdmc.co.uk

TRADE SHOWS

NORTH AMERICA

Dive shows in North America typically take place just before and during the winter months from November to April.

BENEATH THE SEA
31st Annual Undersea Dive & Travel Exposition
Location: Secaucus, NJ
Date: March 23-25, 2007
Attendance: 14,000 (2005)
Number of exhibitors: 300
Seminars: 60
Workshops: 12
Phone: 800 536 EXPO or 914 664 4310
Fax: 914 664 4315
Email:info@BeneathTheSea.org
Web: www.beneaththesea.org

DEMA SHOW
Diving Equipment and Marketing Association
Location: Orlando, Florida
Date: November 8-11, 2006
Attendance: 10,000 (Industry professionals only)
Number of exhibitors: 600
Seminars: 40

Next show: Orlando FL, Oct. 31-Nov. 3, 2007
Phone: 858 616 6408 Toll Free: 800 687 7469
Email: cvonsteiger@ntpshow.com
Web: www.demashow.com

FLORIDA DIVE SHOW
2nd Annual Trade & Consumer Dive
Show
Location: West Palm Beach, FL
Date: December 2, 3, 2006
Attendance: General public
Tel.: 866 557 2822
Fax: 954 337 2223
Email: info@floridadiveshow.com
Web: www.floridadiveshow.com

GHOST SHIPS FESTIVAL
Great Lakes Ships Research Foundation
Location: Milwaukee, WI
Date: March 23-24, 2007
Attendance: 600+
Number of exhibitors: 36 (2006)
Seminars: 15
Workshops: 3
Email: info@ghost-ships.org
Web: www.ghost-ships.org

MEXICO UNDERWATER
Consumer & Trade Dive Show
Location: *Cozumel, Mexico.*
Attendance: General public
Tel.: 52 987 872 1444
Fax: 52 987 872 0004
Web: www.mexicounderwater.net

OCEAN FEST DIVE & ADVENTURE SPORTS EXPO
Consumer Ocean Festival, Dive & Adventure
Sport Show
Location: Fort Lauderdale, Florida
Date: April 20-22, 2007
Attendance: General public
Number of exhibitors: 200+
Seminars: 15+
Phone: 954 839 8516 Toll Free: 800 513 5902
Fax: 954 364 8342
Email: info@oceanfest.com
Web: www.oceanfest.com

OHIO SCUBAFEST 2007 AND 48TH ANNUAL
Location: Columbus, Ohio
Date: March 9-11, 2007
Attendance: General public
Number of exhibitors: 60 +
Seminars: 22
Tel.: 1 877 364 8344
Email: publicity@scubafest.org
Web: www.scubafest.org

OUR WORLD UNDERWATER XXXVII
37th Annual Consumer Dive and
Travel Exposition.
Location: Rosemont, IL.
Date: February 9-11, 2007
Attendance: General public
Tel.: 708 226 1614 Toll Free: 800 778 3483
Fax: 708 403 5447
Email: info@ourworldunderwater.com
Web: www.ourworldunderwater.com

SCUBASHOW 2007
Location: Long Beach, California
Date: June 2,3, 2007
Attendance: General public
Number of exhibitors: 350+
Years running: 18
Phone: 310 792 2333
FAX: 310 792 2336
Email: mail@saintbrendan.com
Web: www.saintbrendan.com

Seas Scuba Expo
Location: Durham, NC
Date: October 14, 15, 2006
Attendance: General public
Tel.: 919 341 4524
Fax: 919 341 5740
Email: seas@nc.rr.com
Web: www.seas-expo.com

SEASPACE
Location: Houston, Texas
Date: March 31 & April 1, 2007
Attendance: General public
Number of exhibitors: 200+
Years running: 38
Phone: 713 467 6675
Email: seaspace@seaspace.org
Website: www.seaspace.org

SURF EXPO
31st Annual Industry Trade Show
Location: Orlando, FL
Date: January 11-14, 2007, September 2007
Attendance: General public
Number of exhibitors: 950
Tel.: 800 947 SURF
Fax: 678-781 7920
Email: ahornby@surfexpo.com
Webs: www.surfexpo.com

THE BOSTON SEA ROVERS
52nd Annual International u/w Clinic
Location: Boston, MA
Date: March 2007
Attendance: General public
Tel.: 617 424 9899

Fax: 508 857 1182
Email: bsrover@aol.com
Web: www.bostonsearovers.com

UNDERWATER INTERVENTION

Underwater Intervention is an International Conference covering the Underwater Operations Industries, especially, Commercial Diving, ROVs, AUVs, Manned Submersibles, Military, Industrial, and Scientific applications for ROV and Commercial Diving Technology.
Location: New Orleans, LA
Date: January 30-February 1, 2007
Attendance: General public
Number of visitors (2006): 2,000
Number of exhibitors: 150+
Seminars: 100
Tel.: 800 316 2188.
Fax: 281 893 5118
Email: rroberts@adc-int.org
Web: www.UnderwaterIntervention.com

OCEANIA

OZTeK'07 - Diving Technologies Conference & Exhibition
Location: Sydney, Australia
Date: March 17-18, 2007
Attendance: Diving consumers
Number of exhibitors: 70
Events: Underwater Photographic Competition
Tel.: 61 29 300 6865
Fax: 61 29 300 6865
Email: mick@dive-expo.com
Web: www.diveoztek.com.au

ASIA

ASIA DIVE EXPO
Location: Bangkok
Date: April 27-29 2007
Attendance: 9,200
Number of exhibitors: 175
Tel.: 65 6825 2258
Web: www.asiadiveexpo.com

Malaysia International Dive Expo (MIDE)
Location: Kuala Lumpur
Date: July 6-8, 2007
Attendance: General public
Tel.: 603 9058 6033
Fax: 603 9058 9033
Email: asiaeven@streamyx.com
Web: www.mide.com.my

EUROPE

SALON DE LA PLONGÉE DE PARIS
Location: Paris, France
Date: January 12-15, 2007
Attendance: 35,000 (General public)
Number of exhibitors: 300+
Tel.: 00 33 0 1 43 74 72 89
Fax : 00 33 (0)1 43 65 81 73
Website: www.salondelaplongee.com

DIVE - THE INTERNATIONAL SUB-AQUA AND WATERSPORTS SHOW
Location: Birmingham, UK
Date: October 13, 4, 2007
Attendance: 17,000 (General public)
Number of exhibitors: 300+
Phone: 44 020 8943 4288
Website: www.diveshows.co.uk

THE LONDON INTERNATIONAL DIVE SHOW (LIDS)
Location: London
Date: March 10-11, 2007
Number of exhibitors: 260+

www.seesharks.com

Chapter 11

LOTTE HASS (1950)
Photo courtesy Hans-Hass-Institut

NOTABLE PERSONS
FROM THE DIVING COMMUNITY

The following list presents over 200 people that have made a significant contribution to the world diving community. Some of these dedicated and accomplished individuals have done a lot more than is described in their short bios.

Since this is the first edition of the Diving Almanac & Yearbook, many important people from all over the world have inadvertently been overlooked. If you know someone who should be listed in next year's edition, please send his/her name, nationality, year of birth/death, and contribution to diving to: **info@divingalmanac.com**

ALARY, Danielle, Canada (1956-). Award-winning underwater photographer; author; public speaker; chairman of the photo jury at the Antibes World Festival of Underwater Images; Diver of the Year (Beneath the Sea), Palme d'argent Award (Antibes); member of the Women Divers Hall of Fame (2001); www.sub-images.com

Danielle Alary. Photo courtesy Sub-Images

ALEXANDER, Steve, United States (NA). Research scientist; oceanographer; prolific writer, author and photographer (scientific and popular); www.worldoceans.com

ALLEN, Gerald, Ph.D., Australia (1942-). Former curator of fishes at the Western Australian Museum; Conservation International science team leader (Southeast Asia); prolific author and scientific writer

ANDERSON, Dick, United States (1932-2006). Underwater photographer and pioneer diver; writer; filmmaker; diving equipment engineer; trained the U.S. Navy underwater demolition team; dive technician for *20,000 Leagues under the Sea*; member of the International Scuba Diving Hall of Fame (2004)

ANTONIOU, Dr. Alex, United States (1957-). Shark researcher; Field Director Shark Research Institute; efforts led to government decree protecting whale sharks in Honduran territorial waters; www.sharks.org

AUERBACH, Paul M.D., M.S., United States (NA). Consultant on hazardous marine life to DAN, medical editor for Dive Training magazine, advisor to numerous medical, recreational and scientific organizations and recognized internationally as a leading expert on the clinical management of hazardous marine encounters

AUXIER, Jim, United States (NA). Co-founder of *Skin Diver Magazine* with Chuck Blakeslee.

AW, Michael, Australia (NA). Award-winning nature photographer / videographer; prolific writer and author; www.michaelaw.com

B

BALL, Mike, Australia (1948-). **Opened** the 'Dive School' in Townsville in 1969; Australia's first school to use cylinder pressure gauges and BCD's; invented the 'Stinger Suit', later known as 'diveskins;' pioneer of the diving liveaboard industry; member of the Internatioal Scuba Diving Hall of Fame (2004); www.mikeball.com

Mike Ball. Photo courtesy Mike Ball Dive Expeditions

BALLESTA, Laurent, France (1977-). Award-winning underwater photographer; biologist; professional diver; main contributor to Planète Mers; www.planete-mers.fr

BALLARD, Robert, United States (1942-). Underwater explorer; discoverer of the RMS *Titanic* and many other shipwrecks including German battleship *Bismarck*, the USS *Yorktown* and JFK's PT-109; National Geographic Society explorer-in-residence; president of the Institute for Exploration; www.ife.org

BARADA, Bill, United States (NA). Underwater photographer; founder of Los Angeles Neptunes (1940); author and script writer; designer of equipment including first dry suit, rubber snorkel and CO_2 speargun

BARSKY, Steven, United States (NA). Prolific author; award-winning photographer / videographer; consultant; co-founder of Hammerhead Press with his wife Kristine; www.hammerheadpress.com

BARTH, Bob, United States (NA). Author and navy diver; chief diver in the Sealab programs

BARTON, Otis, United States (1899-NA). Co-creator of the bathysphere with Dr. William Beebe; dove to 3,028 ft (923 m) off the coast of Bermuda in 1932

BASS, Dr. George, United States (1932-). Professor emeritus and pioneer in marine archaeology; author; directed the the first complete archaeological excavation of an ancient wreck on the sea bed off Cape Gelidonya, Turkey, in 1960

Laurent Ballesta. Photo courtesy *L'Œil d'Andromède*

BASSEMAYOUSSE, Frédéric, France (1967-). Award-winning underwater photographer; professional diver and photographer

BATT, John, Canada (1967-). Award-winning photographer; author; marine biologist; manager of the Aquatron Laboratory (Dalhousie University); www.marinelife-explorer.com

BEEBE, William, United States (1877-1962). Explorer, author, and inventor; co-invented the bathysphere with Otis Barton; made record descent to 3,028 ft (923 m) in 1934

BEHNKE, Albert R., United States (NA). Physician and captain in the United States Navy; research includes diving, decompression and diving physiology

BELLEFEUILLE, Michael G., Canada (1952-). World renowned gemstone sculptor; award-winning photographer; has contributed artwork to different charities and non-profit organizations such as the Shark Research Institute and The Women Divers Hall of Fame; has presented his work to diving legends such as actor Lloyd Bridges, astronaut Scott Carpenter, and filmmakers Jacques Y. Cousteau and Jean-Michel Cousteau; www.artmirage.ca

BELLEFEUILLE, Monique J., Canada (1952-). Prolific writer and public speaker; co-founder of the Ottawa chapter of Save Ontario Shipwrecks; has conducted extensive research and field studies on St. Lawrence Seaway marine archeology; founder of several national and international non-profit photo contests; member of the Women Divers Hall of Fame (2002)

BENCHLEY, Peter, United States (1941-2006). Author; conservationist; published *Jaws* in 1974

BENNETT, John, United Kingdom (1959-2004). First man to dive below 1,000 ft (1010 ft / 308 m) on open-circuit in 2001; died during a salvage dive in Korea

BENNETT, Dr. Peter, United States (1931-). Founder and president of DAN (Divers Alert Network) from 1980 to 2003; pioneer in dive safety

BERGMAN, Dewey, United States (NA-1993). Underwater photographer, founder of photographic equipment manufacturer See & Sea in 1965; successful dive travel operator; member of the International Scuba Diving Hall of Fame (2005)

BERT, Paul, France (1833-1886). French physiologist; research pioneer on decompression sickness (*La pression barométrique* - 1878)

BEUCHAT, Georges, France (1910- NA). Dive equipment manufacturing pioneer; founded the Beuchat Society in Marseilles in 1946

BIRD, Jonathan, USA (1968-). Emmy Award-winning cinematographer and producer; photographer; author; speaker; president of Oceanic Research Group; www.oceanicresearch.org

BLAKESLEE, Chuck, United States (NA). Co-founder of *Skin Diver Magazine*

BLESSINGTON, Mark, USA (NA). Chief diver for the Cousteau Society for over 15 years

BODNER, Alon, Israel (1956-). Israeli inventor and designer of underwater breathing apparatus that extracts dissolved air from water

Jonathan Bird. Photo courtesy Oceanic Research

BOISSINOT, Paul (1953-). Professional diver; co-founder of dive suit manufacturer Atlan; chief diver of the Quebec Aquarium; president of the Quebec Federation of Underwater Activities (FQAS); instructor; public speaker; www.debdive.com

BOND, George F., United States (NA). Pioneer in saturation diving and dive table development; developer of the of Sealab missions

BONIN, Dick, United States (NA). Founded equipment manufacturer Scubapro with Gustav Dalla Valle in 1963.

BORELLI, Giovanni, Italy (1608-1679). Physicist; designed a self-contained leather rebreather

BOREN, Lamar, United States (NA). Underwater photographer; stuntman; instructor; cinematographer: *The Old Man and the Sea* (1958), *Flipper* (1963), *Namu the Killer Whale* (1966)

BOUTAN, Louis, France (1859-1934). Inventor of the first underwater camera in 1892; used the first underwater flash bulb designed by Frenchman Chauffour in 1893; author of *La Photographie Sous-Marine*, a book on underwater photography

BRADNER, Dr. Hugh, United States (1916-). Developer of the neoprene wet suit in 1950[19]; took the first plunge in a neoprene wetsuit in the winter of 1950 at Lake Tahoe;

[19] RAINEY, Carolyn, *Wet Suit Pursuit: Hugh Bradner's Development of the First Wet Suit*, Scripps Institution of Oceanography, November 1998; EISENSTADT, David, *Surfing whodunit - Who created the neoprene wetsuit?*, The L.A. Times, October 11, 2005

UC Berkeley physics professor and Manhattan Project scientist

BRASHEAR, Carl Maxie, United States (1931-2006). First black diver in the U.S. Navy in 1953; leg partially amputated during recovery mission of an atomic bomb off Spain in 1966; first amputee to be restored to duty as a diver; became Master Diver in 1970; retired from the Navy in 1979 as a master chief petty officer; subject of the film "Men of Honor" in 2000.

BRIDGES, Lloyd, United States (1913-1998). Star of *Sea Hunt* TV series from 1957 to 1961; member of the International Scuba Diving Hall of Fame

BRITNELL, Jett, Canada (NA). Award-winning photographer; prolific writer; marine journalist

BROOKS II, Ernest, United States (1935-). Photographer; educator; member of the International Scuba Diving Hall of Fame (2005)

BUCHER, Raimondo, Italy (1912-). Set the first free-diving world record at 98 ft (30 m) in 1949

BUEHLMANN, Albert, Switzerland (NA). Scientist; specialist in lung function and blood circulation

BULL, Richard, United Kingdom (NA). Expert technical diver; commercial diver; instructor; writer

BUSH-ROMERO, Don Pablo, Mexico (NA). Founder of CEDAM (Conservation, Education, Diving, Awareness and Marine-research) in 1967; president of the Club de Exploraciones Mexico; Mexican underwater Archeological Society

BUSSOZ, Rene, United States (NA). First importer of the Cousteau Aqua-Lung to the U.S. in 1948

CALDWELL, Jim, United States (NA). Navy and commercial diver; advocate of diving safety

CALHOUN, Fred, United States (NA). Noted instructor, lecturer and author

CALOYIANIS, Nick, United States (NA). Award-winning cinematographer and photographer; Arctic explorer

CALYPSO, The, France (1941-). *BYMS-1 Class Motor Minesweeper*: Laid down 12 August 1941 as BYMS-26 by the Ballard Marine Railway Co., Inc., Seattle, WA; completed and transfered to Great Britain in August 1942 as J-826; converted to a car ferry and named Calypso in 1947; acquired by Loël Guinness in 1950 and offered to Jacques Cousteau who transformed it into a world-famous oceanographic vessel; struck by a barge 8 January 1996 and sank at Singapore; salvaged and towed to Marseille, France; sold to Carnival Cruise Lines for one Euro in 2005 to be restored and moored as an exhibit in the Bahamas

CAMERON, James, Canada (1954-). Award-winning screenwriter, director, and producer (*Titanic, Abyss, Aliens of the Deep, Ghosts of the Abyss, Expedition Bismarck, Terminator, Aliens*)

CAMERON, Mike, Canada (NA). Engineer; deep ROV; designer

CARDONE, Bonnie, United States (1942-). Editor/writer/photographer for Skin Diver Magazine for 22 years; author; Woman Diver of the Year (1999); member of the Women Divers Hall of Fame; www.bonniejcardone.com

Bonnie J. Cardone. Photo courtesy Bonnie J. Cardone

CARPENTER, Malcolm Scott, United States (1925-). Astronaut; aquanaut; explorer and scientist; participated in SEALAB II and III; consultant and designer in diving equipment and instruments

CASTRO, Dr. Jose, United States (1925-). World-renowned expert on sharks; Mote Marine Laboratory Senior Biologist; National Oceanic and Atmospheric Administration scientist; author of Sharks of North American Waters (1983)

Dr. Jose Castro. Photo: J. Gallant / D.A.Y.

CHARRIER, Éric, France (1964-1999). World champion freediver known as *L'homme otarie* (the Human Otter); held three freediving world records including the deepest freedive under ice (-70m) established at Lake Témiscouata (Québec), in March, 1997; ruptured both eardrums on a dive two months before committing suicide at his home in Corsica

CHATTERTON, John, United States (NA). Noted technical and wreck diver *Brittanic, Lusitania, Andrea Doria*; discovered the German submarine U-869 with Richie Kohler off New Jersey in 1991; host of *Deep Sea Detectives* on the History Channel

Eric Cheng. Photo courtesy www.echeng.com

CHENG, Eric, H., USA (1975-). Award-winning underwater photographer (2005 Nature's Best Photography Competition); digital imaging expert; author; public speaker; talented musician; Antibes Website of the Year 2003 (www.wetpixel.com)

CHISHOLM, John Wesley, Canada (1963-); Award-winning producer of ocean / diving-themed documentaries; series include *Oceans of Mystery, Sea Hunters, Marine Machines, Dreamwrecks* and *GO DEEP*; writer and accomplished musician; president of Arcadia Entertainment; commended by the US Navy for hazardous ordinance disposal in 1994; joined forces with NUMA (National Underwater Marine Agency) in 2005 to help protect the HMS *Fantome* wrecked near Halifax in 1814; www.arcadiatv.com

CHRISTIANSEN, Jim, United States (1926-1999). Co-founder of Scubapro and champion spearfisherman

CHURCH, Cathy, United States (1945-). Underwater photographer; author; member of the Women Divers Hall of Fame; www.cathychurch.com

CHURCH, Jim, United States (1932-2002). Pioneer underwater photographer; author; www.jimchurchphoto.com

CHURCH, Ron, United States (1934-1973). Pioneer underwater photographer; author; cinematographer; co-founder of the San Diego Underwater Photographic Society with Chuck Nicklin; founded Underwater Photographers of America

CLARK, Bob, United States (NA). Founder of SSI (Scuba Schools International) in 1970

CLARK, Dr. Eugenie, United States (1922-). Ichthyologist and world authority on sharks; founding member of the Beebe Project in 1983; a.k.a. the Shark Lady; author; member of the Women Divers Hall of Fame; www.sharklady.com

CONDERT, Charles, United States (NA - 1831). Developed a compressed air reservoir made of copper tube worn around the body in 1831; air was released into a hood over the head; Condert drowned while testing his invention

COLE, Brandon, United States (NA). Award-winning photographer; author; www.brandoncole.com

COLEMAN, Neville, Australia (NA); Award-winning photographer; prolific writer; educational author; public speaker; Honorary Fellow, Australian Institute of Professional Photography; Board Member, Project AWARE Asia/Pacific; member of the International Scuba Diving Hall of Fame (2007); www.nevillecoleman.com.au

Neville Coleman. Photo courtesy Neville Coleman

COLL, Raymond, France (NA). Longtime crewmember and diver aboard Jacques-Y. Cousteau's *Calypso*

COLLA, Phil, United States (1963-). Award-winning photographer and natural history writer; www.oceanlight.com

CONLAN, Kathy, Canada (1950-). Marine biologist with the Canadian Museum of Nature; author; public speaker

CONLIN, Mark, USA (1959-). Award-winning underwater photographer; author; www.markconlin.com

de CORLIEU, Louis, France (NA). Inventor of swim fins; received his first European patent for swimming propellers in 1933; designed a broadbladed fin in 1935

COUSTEAU, Alexandra, United States (1976-). Environmentalist; co-founder of EarthEcho International; author; lecturer; consultant; www.earthecho.org

COUSTEAU, Anne-Marie, France (NA). Photographer; wife of Jean-Michel Cousteau

COUSTEAU, Céline, France (NA). Daughter of Jean-Michel Cousteau; spokesperson for Oceans Futures; www.oceanfutures.org

COUSTEAU, Fabien, France (NA). Engineer; filmmaker; designed a shark-shaped submersible for great white shark documentary *Mind of a Demon*; son of Jean-Michel Cousteau; spokesperson for Oceans Futures; www.oceanfutures.org

COUSTEAU, Francine, France (NA). President of the Cousteau Society / Équipe Cousteau; second wife of Jacques-Yves Cousteau; mother of Diane and Pierre-Yves Cousteau; www.cousteau.org

COUSTEAU, Jacques-Yves, France (1910-1997). Diving pioneer; oceanographer; author; film-producer; environmentalist; co-inventor of the Aqualung; one of the three *Mousquemers* along with Frédéric Dumas and Philippe Taillez; co-founder of the *Groupement d'études et de recherches sous-marines* (GERS) in 1945; member of the International Scuba Diving Hall of Fame; inspired thousands to become divers; a.k.a. Captain Cousteau, Captain Planet, JYC; www.cousteau.org

COUSTEAU, Jean-Michel, France (1938-). Environmentalist; film-maker; explorer; educator; architect; son of Jacques Y. Cousteau and Simone Melchior; president of Ocean Futures; www.oceanfutures.org

COUSTEAU, Philippe, France (1940-1979). Environmentalist; explorer; film-producer; pilot; son of Jacques-Yves Cousteau and Simone Melchior

COUSTEAU, Philippe Jr., United States (1980-). Environmentalist; co-founder of EarthEcho International; president and founder of Thalassa Ventures Corporation; author; lecturer; film producer; www.earthecho.org

COUSTEAU, Simone Melchior, France (1919-1990). First woman scuba diver; wife and business partner of Jacques-Yves Cousteau; a.k.a. La Bergère (The Shepherdess)

CRABBE, Buster, United States (1908-1983). Olympic athlete; actor; NAUI instructor

CRAIG, John D., United States (NA). Adventurer; stunt diver; author; wrote *Danger is my Business* in 1938

CRILLEY, Frank W., United States (1883-1947). In 1915, while a Chief Gunner's Mate, he made dives to over 300 ft (91 m) during salvage operations on the sunken submarine *F-4* (SS-23) off Honolulu, Hawaii. On 17 April 1915 he rescued a fellow diver entangled at a depth of 250 ft (76 m); Medal of Honor in 1929; salvage of USS *S-51* (SS-162); recovery of USS *S-4* (SS-109); Navy Cross; salvage of USS *Squalus* (SS-192) in 1939. USS *Crilley* (YHLC-1) named in his honor

CRONIN, John, United States (1929-2003). Sport diving pioneer; co-founder and CEO of PADI (Professional Association of Diving Instructors), the largest dive training and certification organization in the world; member of the International Scuba Diving Hall of Fame (2002)

CROPP, Ben, Australia (NA). Filmmaker; champion spearfisherman in the 60s; 1964

World Underwater Photographer of the Year; member of the International Scuba Diving Hall of Fame; bencropp.com.au

CROSS, Ellis R., United States (1913-2000). Author; commercial diving instructor; owner of Sparling School of Deep Sea Diving; member of the International Scuba Diving Hall of Fame

CYR, Mario, Canada (1959-). Award-winning cinematographer from the Magdalen Islands (Québec); chief diver and underwater videographer on the SEDNA IV expeditions to the Arctic and Antarctica (National Film Board of Canada)

D

DALLA VALLE, Gustav, Italy (NA -1995). Pioneer manufacturer and diver; founded Scubapro with Dick Bonin in 1963; member of the International Scuba Diving Hall of Fame (2000)

DAVIDSON, Sam, United States (NA). Founder of DACOR in 1954

DAVIS, Ralph, United States (NA). Founded the International Underwater Spearfishing Association in 1950

DAVIS, Chuck, USA (NA). Underwater cinematographer; longtime crewmember and diver aboard Jacques-Y. Cousteau's *Calypso* and *Alcyone*; tidalflatsphoto.com

DAVIS, Dr. Jefferson C. Jr., United States (NA). Pioneer in the treatment of decompression sickness and air embolism in divers; member of the International Scuba Diving Hall of Fame

DAVIS, Sir Robert H., United Kingdom (NA). Creator of Davis False Lung (1911) and the first submersible decompression chamber (1912); Davis Submarine Escape Apparatus (DSEA)

D'AUGERVILLE, Lemaire, France (NA). Inventor of the first self-contained underwater breathing apparatus in 1828; the unit consisted of a low-pressure cylinder and a helmet connected to a valve-operated lung via a tube; the system also included a rudimentary buoyancy compensation device

DA VINCI, Leonardo, Italy (1452-1519). Devised a leather diving suit and cane hoses fixed together by leather joints for breathing, possibly the world's first snorkel device.

DELAUZE, Henri-Germain, France (1929-). Founded the *Compagnie maritime d'expertises* (COMEX) in 1963; pioneered deep saturation diving using synthetic breathing mixtures; first man to reach 360m on Helium mixture

DELEMOTTE, Bernard, France (NA). Longtime crewmember and diver aboard Jacques-Y. Cousteau's *Calypso* and *Alcyone*.

DENAYROUZE, August, France (1837-1883). Co-developer with of a self-contained breathing apparatus with Benoit Rouquayrol in 1864

DESMIER, Xavier, France (NA). Professional diver and underwater photographer; served aboard Cousteau's *Calypso* for three years

Bernard Delemotte. Photo: J. Gallant / D.A.Y.

Graham Dickson. Photo: Brian Dickson – Arctic Kingdom Marine Expeditions

DICKSON, Graham, Canada (1975-). Chief expedition leader for Arctic Kingdom Marine Expeditions; led the first sport diving expedition to Nunavut to dive with walrus in 1999; led the first ice climbing expedition to Nunavut to climb the icebergs of Pond

Inlet in the summer of 2000; founded the University of Pennsylvania Scuba Club in 1994; dive instructor; writer; photographer; www.arctickingdom.com

DOUBILET, David, United States (1946-). Possibly the best-known award-winning underwater photographer in the world; resident photographer for National Geographic Magazine; explorer; prolific author; recipient of several prestigious prizes including: The Sara Prize, The Explorers Club Lowell Thomas Award and the Lennart Nilsson Award in Photography; member of the Royal Photographic Society and the International Diving Hall of Fame (2002); began shooting underwater at the age of 12 using a Brownie Hawkeye camera in an improvised rubber housing; david-doubilet.com

David Doubilet. Photo courtesy Undersea Images Inc.

DROGIN, Steve, United States (NA). Award-winning underwater photographer; public speaker

DUMAS, Frédéric, France (1913-1991). Pioneer of diving and underwater exploration; cinematographer; scientist with the *Groupement d'études et de recherches sous-marines* (GERS) founded by Jacques Y. Cousteau and Philippe Taillez in 1945; one of the three *Mousquemers* along with Jacques Y. Cousteau and Philippe Taillez; chief diver of the *Calypso*; one of the three *Mousquemers* along with J-Y Cousteau and Philippe Taillez; co-publisher of Cousteau's *The Silent World*; a.k.a. Didi

DWYER, Terry Canada (1962-). Nova Scotia wreck hunter; dive entrepreneur; motion picture diving consultant; videographer; public speaker; member of the Explorers Club; author of *Wreck Hunter*; www.wreckhunter.ca

EARLE, Dr. Sylvia, U.S. (1935-). Scientist; author; multiple record holder; explorer-in-residence for the National Geographic Society; *Time* Magazine 'Hero for the Planet' in 1998; member of the International Scuba Diving Hall of Fame; member of the Women Divers Hall of Fame; a.k.a. Her Deepness

Dr. Sylvia Earle prepares to dive in a JIM suit. Photo: OAR/National Undersea Research Program (NURP)

EATON, Bernard, United Kingdom (NA). Co-founder of The Marine Conservation Society (MCS) an organization for the protection of the marine environment and its wildlife; member of the International Scuba Diving Hall of Fame

ELLIOTT, Ron, United States (NA). Commercial diver; only person to actively dive for urchins at the Farallon Islands (California); has had over 400 encounters with the great white shark, *Carcharodon carcharias*, without the protection of a cage.

EMPLETON, Bernie, United States (NA). Creator of the national YMCA program; author of *The New Science of Skin and SCUBA Diving* in 1957

ERICKSON, Ralph, United States (1922-2006). Co-founder of PADI, the largest dive training and certification organization in the world, with John Cronin in 1967; member of the International Scuba Diving Hall of Fame (2007)

EVANS, Bob, United States (1950-). Inventor; entrepreneur; manufacturer; revolutionary fin designer; founder of Bob Evans Designs in 1985; www.forcefin.com

EXLEY, Sheck, United States (1949-1994). Pioneer cave and deep diver; deep diving record holder; first to reach 1000 cave dives; did over 4000 cave dives in 29 years; died while attempting to dive below 1000 feet in Zacaton Cave, Mexico

F

FALCO, Albert, France (1927-). Longtime captain of Cousteau's flagship Calypso; expedition leader; world's first aquanaut with Claude Wesley (Diogenes, 1962); first diver to pilot Cousteau's mini-sub the *Soucoupe*; a.k.a. *Bébert*

FANE, CDR Douglas, United States (1909-2002). Member of the U.S. Navy Underwater Demolition Teams (UDT during WWII and the Korean War; led to advances of UDT; developed specialized diving equipment and combat techniques; influenced scientific and sport diving

FARR, Martyn, United Kingdom (1951-). Expert cave diver; prolific author; www.farrworld.co.uk

FEINBERG, Walter, United States (NA). Noted treasure hunter

FENZY, Maurice, France (NA). Patented the first commercially successful buoyancy compensator in 1961.

FERRERAS, Francisco 'Pipin,' United States / Cuba (1962-). World champion freediver; record dive to 558 ft (170 m) in 2003

FISHER, Mel, United States (1922-1998). Famed treasure hunter and discoverer of the Spanish galleon *Nuestra Senora de Atocha* in 1985; www.melfisher.com

FLEETHAM, David, Canada (1958-). Award-winning underwater photographer; www.davidfleetham.com

FLEUSS, Henry, United Kingdom (NA). Inventer of a self-contained oxygen rebreather successfully tested at a depth of 5.5m in 1879. He later died from Oxygen toxicity using the device beyond 10m.

FOX, Rodney, Australia (1940-). Great White Shark attack victim, film maker and expedition leader; World Authority on the Great White Shark; member of the International Scuba Diving Hall of Fame (2007); www.rodneyfox.com.au

FRASIER, Dottie, United States (1922-). First female scuba instructor in the U.S.; member of the Women Divers Hall of Fame

FRINK, Stephen, United States (1949-). Possibly the world's most frequently published underwater photographer; director of photography for Scuba Diving magazine; owner of WaterHouse Tours and Reservations dive travel company; North American and Caribbean distributor for the Austrian camera housing manufacturer Seacam; inventor and patent-holder of a unique diver safety device known as the Safety Observation Signal (SOS); www.stephenfrink.com

Stephen Frink. Photo courtesy Stephen Frink Photographic

G

GAFFNEY, John, United States (NA). Founder of NASDS in 1961; NOGI Award (1997); DEMA Hall of Fame (1998)

GAGNAN, Émile, France/Canada (1900-1984). Co-inventor of the Aqua-lung, or first demand-valve regulator with Jacques-Yves Cousteau in 1943

GALERNE, André, France (1926-). Founded SOGETRAM (*Société générale de travaux*

marins et fluviaux); founded the International Underwater Contractors (IUC) in Canada in 1959, then in the United States in 1962; founded IUC International in in 1970 and Deep Sea International in 1978; he has won several pretigious awards including the NOGI Award in 1988

GALLANT, Jeffrey J., Canada (1966-). Award-winning photographer / cinematographer; author; aquanaut (L.S.-1 Laboratory, Romania); former chief diver of the Quebec Aquarium; director of Greenland Shark and Elasmobranch Research Group; www.geerg.ca; www.aqualog.com

GENONI, Gianluca, Italy (1968-). World champion freediver; www.genoni.com

GENTILE, Gary, United States (NA). Prolific author (more than 40 books); lecturer; photographer; explorer; expert wreck-diver (discovered more than 40 shipwrecks); www.ggentile.com

Al Giddings. Photo courtesy Al Giddings Images

GIDDINGS, Al, United States (1937-). Award-winning cinematographer (4 Emmy Awards); films include *The Deep, For Your Eyes Only, The Abyss, Titanic*; member of the International Scuba Diving Hall of Fame; dove off a boat in an attempt to save a diver caught in the jaws of a 16-foot white shark off the Farallon Islands in 1962; www.algiddings.com

GILBERT, Michel, Canada (1955-). Award-winning underwater photographer; author; public speaker; past president of FQAS; Diver of the Year (Beneath the Sea), Palme

d'argent Award (Antibes); chairman of the photo jury at the Antibes World Festival of Underwater Images; www.sub-images.com

Michel Gilbert. Photo courtesy Sub-Images

GILLIAM, Bret, United States (NA). Founder of SDI/TDI, DiveSafe Insurance and Ocean Tech; author; publisher of Fathoms Magazine; underwater photographer / videographer; public speaker

GILPATRIC, Guy, United States (1896-1950). Freediving pioneer; developed the use of rubber goggles with glass lenses off the coast of Southern France; he and his group of friends were known as the *Serious Sinkers*; author of *The Compleat Goggler* in 1938; was said to have influenced the careers of Jacques Y. Cousteau and Hans Hass

GLOVER, Penny, UK (1963-2005). One of the British Sub Aqua Club's top instructors and one of the most experienced divers in the UK. Died while rebreather diving off the French island of Porquerolles.

GOLDING, Peter, Canada (NA). Author; editor of Diver Magazine (Canada)

GODDIO, Franck, France (NA). Marine archaeologist, founded the *Institut européen d'archéologie sous-marine* (IEASM); discovered ancient shipwrecks including Napoleon Bonaparte's flagship *L'Orient*; Royal Quarters in Alexandria; president of Franck Goddio Society; www.underwaterdiscovery.org

GOTERA, Gustavo G., Spain (NA). Underwater photographer and author

GRAVER, Dennis, United States (NA). Author; underwater photographer; instructor; former training director for NAUI and PADI; designed the PADI Modular Scuba Course and original dive tables; developing the Pocket Mask aquatic rescue breathing technique; designed the NAUI Dive Time Calculator

GREENBERG, Jerry, United States (NA). Pioneer of underwater photographer and founder of Seahawk Press; member of the International Scuba Diving Hall of Fame (2004)

GRENIER, Robert, Canada (NA). President of UNESCO's International Scientific Committee on Underwater Cultural Heritage; Manager of Parks Canada's Underwater Archaeology section; Officer of the Order of Canada; world leader in archaeology and underwater conservation; discovered North America's oldest heritage wreck off the coast of Labrador; worked on several films and projects including the protection of the *Titanic* and the *Empress of Ireland*.

GUGEN, Oscar, United Kingdom (NA). Co-founder of British Sub-Aqua Club with Peter Small in 1953; www.bsac.co.uk

HALDANE, John Scott, UK, (1860 - 1936). Established first dive tables in 1907

HALL, Howard (1949) **& Michele** (1951), United States. Possibly the best known underwater filmmaking duo in the world; multiple award-winning productions for both television and wide-screen (IMAX) formats; winners of seven Emmys and several other awards for wildlife films; prolific writers and authors; www.howardhall.com

Howard & Michele Hall. Photo © John Dunham - hhp@howardhall.com

HALLEY, Edmond, UK (1656-1742). Invented diving bell with weighted barrels containing renewable air supply.

HAMPTON, Trevor, UK (1912-2002). Ex-RAF bomber pilot and test pilot who opened the UK's first dive school in Warfleet Creek, Dartmouth, Devon, in 1953. His first 3-day diving course cost only £5 ($8.60 USD)

HANAUER, Eric, United States (NA). Photojournalist specializing in the underwater world; author; dive instructor; www.ehanauer.com

HANDLEMAN, Lad, United States (NA). Co-founder of Oceaneering International with Phil Nuytten

HANDON, Norma, United States (NA). Pioneer in commercial diving

HANNA, Nick, United Kingdom (1956). Prolific author of dive publications including *The Art of Diving*; www.nickhanna.co.uk

HARDY, Jon, United States (NA). Pioneer instructor, author

Dr. Chris Harvey-Clark. Photo: J. Gallant / D.A.Y.

HARVEY-CLARK, Dr. Chris, Canada (1960-). Award-winning cinematographer and photographer; veterinarian; marine biologist; director of Animal Care Centre (University of British Columbia); director of Greenland Shark and Elasmobranch Education and Research Group; www.geerg.ca

HASS, Hans, Germany (1919-). Scientist; diving and underwater photography pioneer; prolific author first published in 1941 with *Unter Korallen und Haien* (Diving to Adventure); member of the International Scuba Diving Hall of Fame (2000); made his first dive in the Mediterranean Sea in July 1937, where he met American Guy Gilpatric; he led several expeditions around the world aboard his vessel the *Xarifa*; www.hans-hass.de

Hans Hass. Photo courtesy Hans-Hass-Institut

HASS (BAIERL), Lotte, Germany (1928-), Diving and underwater photography pioneer; member of the International Scuba Diving Hall of Fame (2000); member of the Women Divers Hall of Fame; See *Hans Hass*

Lotte Hass. Photo courtesy Hans-Hass-Institut

HAWKES, Graham, United States (1947-). President of Hawkes Ocean Technologies (HOT), inventor; engineer; designer the Wasp and Mantis Atmospheric Diving Suits, the Deep Rover research submersibles, and the experimental Deep Flight series of winged submersibles; plans to take the next generation sub - Deep Flight II - to the deepest point on the planet, The Mariana Trench, which lies at 37,000 ft (11,278 m)

beneath the ocean's surface; currently world record holder for the deepest solo ocean dive – 3,000 ft (914 m) - achieved while test piloting his Deep Rover submersible; www.deepflight.com

HESS, Neal (NAUI #3), United States (NA), Co-founder of NAUI, the first international scuba diving certification agency in 1960

HIGH, Bill, United States (NA). Scientist; commercial diver; aquanaut; spent over 365 days underwater in undersea laboratories and deep submersibles

HORNSBY, Al, United States, (NA). Former publisher and editor of Skin Diver Magazine; award-winning photographer and writer; PADI executive for 20 years; Vice President, Legal Affairs for PADI Worldwide; DEMA President; Boards of Ocean Futures and the Earth Communications Office

HOWLAND, Garry, United States (NA). Engineer and dive instructor; sat on NAUI's first board of directors; inventor of long hose octopus for cave diving

HUGHES, Peter, United States (NA). Highly successful operator of a diving liveaboard fleet since 1986; www.peterhughes.com

HUMANN, Paul, United States, (1937-). Award-winning photographer and writer; author of 14 marine life books, captain/owner of the Caribbean's first liveaboard dive operation, co-founder of REEF (Reef Environmental Education Foundation); U.S. Coral Reef Task Force's Outstanding Public Awareness and Education Award (2006); DEMA Reaching Out Award (2006); member of the International Scuba Diving Hall of Fame (2007)

Paul Humann. Photo courtesy New World Publications

I

ICORN, Nick, United States (NA). Instructor; developed training programs and manuals; part of the first formal underwater instructors course; became PADI's first and only Executive Director in 1972, increasing their instructor base from 234 to over 12,000 worldwide; member of the NAUI Hall of Honor and NOGI Award recipient

J

JAMES, William, United Kingdom (NA). Inventor of first practical SCUBA in 1825; used a belt of compressed air tanks, a complete watertight suit and a copper helmet

JARRAT, Jim, United Kingdom (NA). Located the sunken Lusitania wearing the "Iron Man" armored suit in 1935. Modern Jim suits are named for him.

JEHLE, Charles, United States (1924-2005). Pioneer in the design and manufacture of buoyancy compensators; co-founder of DEMA; founder of Sea Quest (retired in 1983); served in the U.S. Navy Seabees during World War II

JOHNSON, Jim, Canada (1938-2001). Pioneer of diving in Nova Scotia; underwater photographer and videographer; artist; craftsman; explorer and historian

K

KAYLE, Dr Allan, South Africa (NA). Author of *Salvage of the Birkenhead, Safe Diving: A Medical Handbook for Scuba Divers and How to Manage Diving Problems*. He is the medical journalist for *Divestyle* magazine in South Africa, a past president of the Southern African Undersea and Hyperbaric Medical Association, and on the board of DAN Southern Africa.

KELLER, Hannes, Switzerland (NA). Scientist; tested deep breathing gases with Dr. Albert Buehlmann; emerged from a diving bell at a depth of 1,020 feet (310 m) off Catalina Island, California, with BSAC co-founder Peter Small in December, 1962; a series of mishaps led to the death of Small

and support diver Chris Whittaker while surfacing

KELLY, Mike, United States (NA). Co-founder of DEMA

KIRBY, Bob, United States (NA). Co-developer of commercial diving helmets with Bev Morgan in the 1960s; author

KLEIN, Jordan, United States (NA). Owner/operator of first Miami dive shop; founder of Mako underwater cameras & housings and Mako Air Compressors; film director and cameraman (Flipper, Thunderball); designer of underwater film props

KOBEH, Pascal, Lebanon (1960-). Award-winning underwater photographer; writer; www.scuba-photos.com

KOHLER, Richie, United States (1962-). Noted technical and wreck diver; discovered the German submarine U-869 with John Chatterton off New Jersey in 1991; host of *Deep Sea Detectives* on the History Channel

KOZMIK, Jim & Lorna, Canada (NA). Award-winning photographers and filmmakers; prolific writers; co-founders of Aqua Images and producers of *Sport Diver* television series

KRISTOFF, Emory, United States (1942-). National Geographic photographer; explorer; pioneer of deep underwater camera and ROV development; founding member of the Beebe Project in 1983

KULISEK, Capt. Gary, Canada (1954-). Technical and wreck diving expert; expedition leader and trainer; public speaker; consultant; resort operator in St. Vincent and the Grenadines; technicaldivingops.com

L

LABAN, André, France (NA). Underwater photographer and painter; musician; longtime crewmember and diver of the Cousteau Society; chemist; engineer; co-designer of Cousteau's mii-*sub the Soucoupe*; first pilot of the *Soucoupe*

LAMBERTSEN, Dr. Christian, United States (NA). Scientist; the term SCUBA was coined by Dr. Christian Lambertsen in 1939 who designed a Self-Contained Underwater Breathing Apparatus for the U.S. military, a closed-circuit oxygen rebreather known as the Lambertsen Amphibious Respiratory Unit (LAUR); Lifetime Achievement Award in 1999 for his many contributions to diving and diving equipment design (Beneath the Sea)

LAVANCHY, Jack, Switzerland (NA). President of PADI Europe; pioneer in the development of recreational diving member of the International Scuba Diving Hall of Fame

LECOCQ, Pascal, France (1958-). *The Painter of Blue*; doctorate in Art (U. of Paris); famous for his paintings of divers in surreal situations enveloped in remarkable blue vistas; www.pascal-lecocq.com

Pascal Lecocq. Photo courtesy www.pascal-lecocq.com

LECOCQ, Sam, United States (NA). Inventor of the single host regulator and first engineer for Aqua Lung

LEFERME, Loïc, France (1970-). World-champion freediver; first person to dive to beyond 500 ft (152.40 m) on one breath of air; www.loicleferme.fr

Loïc Leferme – Photo courtesy Loïc Leferme.

LE GUEN, Francis, France (1956-). Host of *Carnet de plongée*, a highly popular French television series on sport diving; record-setting cave diver since 1978; founder and chief editor of *Plongeurs International* (French diving magazine) from 1998 to 2001; www.carnetsdeplongee.net; www.francis-leguen.com

Francis Le Guen. Photo courtesy *Carnets de plongée*

LE PRIEUR, Yves, France (1885-1963). Modified the Rouquayrol-Denayrouse diving apparatus by combining a demand valve and high pressure air tank (1500 psi) thus eliminating all hoses and lines

LEE, Owen, United States (NA). Author of *The Skin Divers Bible*; crewmember and diver for the Cousteau Society in the 1960s; owner Las Gatas Beach Club; www.lasgatasbeachclub.com

LEVINE, Marie, United States (1945-). Executive director of the Shark Research Institute (SRI); former officer of the Natal Sharks Board; re-established the South African Shark Attack File; author of several scientific papers, childrens' books and magazine articles on sharks; www.sharks.org

L'HOUR, Michel, France (1954-). Noted underwater archaeologist with DRASM (*Direction des recherches archéologiques sous-marines*)

LILLAS, Mel, United States (NA). Pioneer diver; architect of the NOGI Award

LIMBAUGH, Conrad, United States (1925-1960). Scientific diving officer at Scripps Oceanographic Institution; developed the first SCUBA classes both for science and sport in 1951; author of scientific dive safety manuals and procedures; died while cave diving in France in 1960; west coast nudibranch *Cadlina limbaughorumn* named in his honor by Jim Lance in 1962.

LINK, Edwin, United States (1904-1981). Engineer; oceanologist; pilot; industrialist; invented flight simulators; led archaeological expeditions in the Mediterranean; designed submersible decompression chamber; designed the first submersible with an exit hatch for divers; designed HBOI's Sea Diver II submersible which was later renamed RV Edwin Link in honor of her builder

LONG, Dick, United States (NA). Designer; inventor; president of Diving Unlimited International (DUI); www.dui-online.com

LONGLEY, W.H., United States (NA). Ichthyologist, took the first ever underwater Autochromes (natural-color photo) of sea life off Florida's Dry Tortugas with Charles Martin for the January 1927 issue of National Geographic Magazine

LOW, Stephen, Canada (NA). Wide screen cinematographer specializing in deep sea productions; works include IMAX films *Titanica* and *Volcanoes of the Deep Sea*; www.stephenlow.com

M

MACINNIS, Dr. Joe, Canada (1937-). Pioneer in diving medicine; Arctic explorer; discovered wreck of HMS *Breadalbane*; first to dive and film under the North Pole; author; lecturer; dive instructor to Prince Charles, Walter Cronkite and Pierre Elliott Trudeau; founding member of the Beebe Project in 1983; www.drjoemacinnis.com

MAIORCA, Enzo, Italy (1931-). World champion freediver, held 13 No Limits records in the 60s and 70s; first man to freedive beyond 50 meters

MAIORCA, Rossana, Italy (1951-2005). World champion freediver; daughter or Enzo Maiorca

MARDEN, Luis, United States (1913-2003). Explorer; photographer; writer; filmmaker; pioneered many underwater color photography techniques; discovered the remains of the HMS *Bounty* at Pitcairn Island in the South Pacific in 1957; National Geographic Society resident shipwreck expert; Chief Foreign Editorial Staff

MARTIN, R. Aidan, Canada (1965-). Internationally recognized expert in shark biology and behavior; director of ReefQuest Centre for Shark Research; research associate; adjunct professor; author, illustrator; expedition leader; public speaker; www.elasmo-research.org

MARTIN, Charles, United States (NA). Took the first ever underwater Autochromes (natural-color photo) of sea life off Florida's Dry Tortugas with W.H. Longley for the January 1927 issue of National Geographic Magazine

MARTINEZ, Andrew, United States (1946,). Award-winning underwater photographer; prolific writer and author of popular natural history field guides; assignment photographer for the National Geographic Society; www.netevents.net/martinez

MARX, Robert F., United States (1938-). Pioneer in the field of underwater archaeology, authored over 800 scientific reports/articles and 59 books on history, archaeology, shipwrecks and exploration; co-founded the Advisory Council on Underwater Archaeology in 1959; reportedly discovered a 2nd Century BC Roman shipwreck off Brazil in 1981

Nell McDaniel. Photo: Tenny McDaniel

MAYOL, Jacques, France (1927-2001). World champion freediver; first freediver in the world to descend to 100 meters (330 feet) in 1976. Mayol was the inspiration for Luc Besson's cult film *The Big Blue* in 1988. Also known as the Human Dolphin, Mayol committed suicide at his villa on the island of Elba, Italy

McALLISTER, Jacques, United States (1923-). Professor of Ocean Engineering (Florida Atlantic U.); geologist; oceanographer; ocean engineer, prolific author and expedition leader

MCDANIEL, Neil, Canada (1949-). Award-winning writer, photographer and cinematographer (IMAX); Associate Producer of *The Blue Realm*; past editor of Diver Magazine (Canada); principal of Subsea Enterprises; www.neilmcdaniel.com

MCDONALD, Kendall, United Kingdom (NA). Prolific author and wreck enthusiast; public speaker; scriptwriter and presenter of the first British TV series about diving; past chairman of the BSAC; BSAC Vice-President; one of the first journalists to dive on the wreck of King Henry VIII's famous warship *Mary Rose*; member of the International Scuba Diving Hall of Fame (2004)

MCKENNEY, Jack, Canada (1938-1988). Award-Winning underwater cinematographer; founding member of Freeport Underwater Explorers Society; editor of Skin-Diver Magazine; member of the International Scuba Diving Hall of Fame

MEARNS David, United Kingdom (1958-). Undersea explorer; director of Blue Water Recoveries; lead the search for HMS *Hood* at a depth of 9,845 ft (3,000 m) in the Denmark Strait between Greenland and Iceland using sonar and ROVs in 2001; bluewater.uk.com

MEISTRELL, Bill, United States (1928-2006). Pioneer instructor; commercial diver; inventor; co-founder of Body Glove International with brother Bob; bodyglove.com

MEISTRELL, Bob, United States (1928-). Pioneer instructor; commercial diver; inventor; co-founder of Body Glove International with brother Bill

MESTRE, Ferreras, Audrey, France (1974-2002). World champion freediver married to Francisco 'Pipin' Ferreras; died in the Dominican Republic while attempting a No-Limits dive of 561ft (171m); inducted posthumously into the Women Divers Hall of Fame; subject of Pipin Ferreras book - *The Dive: A Story of Love and Obsession*

MIHAI, Constantin, Romania (NA). European record holder for longest habitat dive

(L.S.-1 Underwater Laboratory, Lake Bicaz, 2004); pioneer of diving in Romania

MILLER, Sam, United States (NA). Pioneer diver; director of numerous diving clubs; director of Recreational Diving for the Historical Diving Society

MILLINGTON, Dr. J. Thomas, United States (NA). Researcher in hyperbaric and diving medicine (DCI); public speaker

MILNE-EDWARDS, Henri, France (1800-1885). Biologist; led the first underwater studies of marine life in 1826

MIRON, Dr. Ionel, Romania (NA). Director of the SALMO Lacustris Dive Programme (A.I. Cuza University); Pioneer of scientific diving in Romania

MIRON, Dr. Liviu, Romania (NA). Director of the SALMO Lacustris Dive Programme (A.I. Cuza University); European record holder for longest habitat dive (L.S.-1 Underwater Laboratory, Lake Bicaz, 2004)

Dr. Ionel Miron emerging from the L.S.-1 Underwater Laboratory in Lake Bicaz, Romania. Photo: J. Gallant / D.A.Y.

MORGAN, Bev, United States (1932-). Manufacturer of the world's most famous diving helmets; commercial diver; dive equipment designer and manufacturer; www.kirbymorgan.com

MORGAN, Jane, United Kingdom (1965-). Award-winning photographer; writer; member of the British Society of Underwater Photographers; online editor of Dive Magazine; www.divemagazine.co.uk

MORRIS, Simon, Canada (1958-). Internationally-renowned sculptor; creator of nine-foot (2.75 m) tall bronze mermaid sculptures placed underwater as attractions for divers in Grand Cayman, BWI, & British Columbia, Canada; creator of other life size bronze memorials including Capt. Henry Larsen, Master of the RCMP Vessel *St. Roch*, the first vessel to cross the Northwest Passage from West to East; recipient of the Canadian National Diving Achievement Award; www.morrissculpture.com

Simon Morris. Photo courtesy Simon Morris Sculpture

MOTT, Blair, USA (NA). Professional diver; chief diver of Ocean Futures; www.oceanfutures.org

MURPHY, Larry, United States (NA). Chief of the Submerged Resources Center (SCRU) for the U.S. National Park Service

MURPHY, Dr. Richard C, USA (NA). Marine biologist; photographer; author; longtime chief scientist and expedition researcher for the Cousteau Society; Vice President of Science and Education for Ocean Futures Society; oceanfutures.org

MUSTARD, Dr. Alexander, U.K. (NA). Marine scientist; award-winning underwater photographer; founder of the Young Underwater Photographer's Group; digital officer for the British Society of Underwater Photographers; co-administrator of Wetpixel.com

NACHOUM, Amos, Israel (1954-). Award-winning marine and wildlife photographer; writer; author; public speaker; expedition leader for Big Animals Photography Expeditions; co-founded Marine National Park of Israel on the Red Sea; biganimals.com

NESBIT, John, United States (1954-2005). Diving entrepreneur; former manager of the PADI Retail Association; DEMA Reaching Out Award (2006)

NICKLIN, Chuck, United States (1927-). Pioneer underwater cinematographer and photographer; opened the Dive Locker in San Diego in 1959; www.chucknicklin.com

NICKLIN, Flip, United States (1948-). National Geographic photographer; author; freediver; son of Chuck Nicklin

NIXON, Ted, United States (NA). Introduced the American red and white *Diver Down* flag in 1956

NITSCH, Herbert, Austria (1973-). World-champion freediver; set AIDA No Limit record of of 564.3 ft (172 m) on October 2, 2005, off Zirje, Croatia. Reached depth of 656.17 ft (200 m) during a training dive. www.herbertnitsch.com

NOHL, Max, United States (NA-1960). Engineer and designer; dove to 420 feet (128 m) in Lake Michigan in 1937 using a helium-oxygen mixture

NOIROT, Didier, France (1957-). Underwater cinematographer; cameraman for the Cousteau Society from 1986 to 1998; www.didiernoirot.net

Herbert Nitsch. World-champion freediver Herbert Nitsch. Photo: Harald Lautner / www.freediving.at

NORTH, Wheeler J., United States (1922-2002). Professor of environmental science; pioneer of scientific diving; devised techniques for restoring and farming kelp forests purchased one of the first 10 Aqua-Lungs sold in the U.S.

NUYTTEN, Phil, Canada (1942-). Businessman, sub-sea engineer, diver, marine archaeologist, author, carver and native advocate; opened first dive shop in 1958; founded Can-Dive Service in 1966; designer of the Newt Suit; the Kwakwaka 'waka tribe have given him the name of Tlaxan, which means Red Snapper; NOGI Award (1997); Beneath the Sea Diver of the Year; Order of British Columbia (1992); owner/publisher of DIVER Magazine, Immersed Magazine and owner/president of Nuytco Research Ltd; www.nuytco.com; www.divermag.com

Phil Nuytten piloting his DeepWorker submersible.
Photo: Nate Johnson / Courtesy Nuytco Research Ltd

ORR, Dan, United States (NA). President and CEO of DAN (Divers Alert Network); best-known for establishing the DAN Training department and Oxygen for scuba diving courses

PACCALET, Yves, France (1945-). Prolific author; edited and co-authored several books by Jacques-Yves Cousteau; naturalist; poet; philosopher
PARKER, Torrance, United States (NA). Pioneer of the commercial diving industry;

author; founded Parker Diving Service in 1947; author of 20,000 Jobs Under the Sea; member of the Advisory Board of the Historical Diving Society; 2006 Commercial Diving Hall of Fame Award (ADCI)
PARRY, Zale, United States (NA). Underwater actress and stuntwoman (Sea Hunt, Kingdom of the Sea, Voyage to the Bottom of the Sea); first woman to descend below 200 ft (209 ft / 64 m - 1954); dive instructor; member of the International Scuba Diving Hall of Fame; member of the Women Divers Hall of Fame
PEDDIE, Clare, United Kingdom (NA). BSAC national diving officer; instructor trainer; expedition leader
PELIZZARI, Umberto, Italy (1965-). Champion freediver; founded Apnea Academy of freediving; umbertopelizzari.com
PERRINE, Doug, United States (1952-). Award-winning marine wildlife photographer; author; founder of SeaPics.com; BG Wildlife Photographer of the Year 2004; www.seapics.com

Doug Perrine and tiger shark. Photo © Brandon Cole - www.brandoncole.com

Christian Petron. Photo courtesy Cinémarine

PETRON, Christian, France (1944-). Clearance Diver in the French Navy; professional diver (COMEX); founder, producer and chief cameraman of Cinémarine; 70+ films to his credit including *The Big Blue, Atlantis,* and a documentary on the *Titanic;* www.cinemarine.net

PICCARD, Dr. Auguste, Switzerland (1884-1962). Professor of physics; designer of the bathyscaph *Trieste* with his son Jacques; before exploring the deep, Piccard designed a spherical, pressurized aluminum gondola for ballooning; he and Paul Kipfer reached a record altitude of 15,785 m (51,775 ft) in 1931

PICCARD, Jacques, Switzerland (1922-). Explorer; engineer; one of only two persons - along with Lt. Don Walsh - to have reached the deepest point on the earth's surface, the Challenger Deep (10,916m - 35,813ft), in the Mariana Trench on January 23, 1960 aboard the bathyscaph; built four submarines including the *Auguste Piccard,* the world's first passenger submarine; founder of the Foundation for the Study and Protection of Seas and Lakes

POTTS, Wallis (Wally), United States (1918-). Underwater weapons designer; co-founder of the Bottom Scratchers Dive Club (San Diego) in 1933, possibly the first dive club in the world

POWELL, David, United States (1927-). Pioneer in diving and aquarium operations; aquarist; director Life Exhibit Development at the Monterey Bay Aquarium until 1997; author of *A Fascination for Fish / Adventures of an Underwater Pioneer*

POZZOLI, Lionel, France (NA). Award-winning underwater photographer; organized CMAS underwater photographic world championships; president of the CMAS photo-film-video commission

PREZELIN, Louis, United States / France (1946). Longtime crewmember and diver of the Cousteau Society; cameraman; director of Pacific Visions; pacificvisionsinc.com

PRINCE ALBERT I OF MONACO, Monaco (1848-1942). Oceanographer; statesman; humanitarian; founded the Oceanographic Museum of Monaco; led several research expeditions in the Mediterranean Sea and North Atlantic between 1885 and 1915

Louis Prezelin. Photo courtesy Pacific Visions

PRODONOVICH, Jack, United States (1913-). Underwater weapons designer; co-founder of the Bottom Scratchers Dive Club (San Diego) in 1933, possibly the first dive club in the world

QUILICI, Folco, Italy (1930-). Award-winning cinematographer; author; founding member of the Historical Diving Society and of the Marevivo Environmentalist Association; president of the Central Institute for Applied Marine Research, (ICRAM); editor *Mondo Sommerso* from 1978 to 1982; www.folcoquilici.com

RANETKINS, Val, Canada, (NA). Pioneer in the development of underwater camera systems used by scientists, cinematographers and recreational divers; founder of Amphibico; www.amphibico.com

RAWLINS, Sir John, United Kingdom (1922-). Surgeon Vice Admiral; Director of Health and Research (Navy) 1975-1977; Medical Director General (Navy) 1977-1980; member of SEALAB program; developer of sea escape techniques for pilots of downed aircraft

REBIKOFF, Dimitri, France (1921-1997). Oceanographer and underwater surveyor; engineer; pioneer diver; underwater photographer; designed a revolutionary speargun; invented the portable electronic flash in 1947; developed the first underwater electronic flash, stereophoto and film cameras; developed the world´s first underwater scooter, *Torpille*, in 1952, which later became the world's first ROV, the *Poodle*; inventor of the *Pegasus*, an underwater vehicle for divers; www.rebikoff.org

RECHNITZER, Andreas B., United States (1924-2005). Masterminded bathyscaph record dive in the Marianas Trench; developed the first scuba-diver training program for ocean scientists with Connie Limbaugh and Jim Stewart; confirmed the discovery and location of the Civil War ironclad, the *Monitor* in 1974; founding president of the Orange County Marine Institute; prolific author; received Presidential Distinguished Citizen Service Award from President Eisenhower; member of the International Scuba Diving Hall of Fame (2005)

REED, Jeff, United Kingdom (NA). Head of the technical group (BSAC Diving Council); instructor; curriculum developer

RICARD, Paul, France (1909-1997). Founder of the Paul Ricard Oceanographic Institute on the French Mediterranean island of Embiez in 1966; founder of the *Société Ricard*, makers of the namesake Ricard anis and licorice-based appetizer (1932), a favorite of D.A.Y. editor J. Gallant

RICHARDS, Mose, United States (NA). Cinematographer; producer; longtime crewmember and cameraman for the Cousteau Society; author

RIEFENSTAHL, Leni, Germany (1902-2003). Riefenstahl became a diver at the age of 71. She released her first underwater documentary *Impressionen unter Wasser* (*Underwater Impressions*) on her 100th birthday in 2002; www.leni-riefenstahl.de

RIICHI, Watanabe, Japan (NA). Engineer, develops an underwater breathing device under the name of Ohgushi's Peerles Respirator in 1920; the system using air cylinders carried on a diver's back was adopted by the Japanese Navy

RINALDI, Roberto, Italy (1963-). Award-winning photographer; longtime crewmember and diver of the Cousteau Society; www.nautica.it/rinaldi

ROESSLER, Carl, USA (1933-). Prolific author and writer; award-winning underwater photographer; former president of See&Sea Travel; led the first diving expeditions to many of today's most famous remote diving sites; member of the International Scuba Diving Hall of Fame (2007); www.divexprt.com

Carl Roessler. Photo courtesy Carl Roessler

ROGERSON, Simon, U.K. (1970-). Prolific writer; underwater photographer; editor of Dive Magazine; www.divemagazine.co.uk

ROUGERIE, Jacques, France (1945-). Underwater architect; designed underwater habitations and various see-through vessels; plans to build a platform called the *Sea Orbiter*, that will drift across the oceans of the world with the aid of the currents and the wind in 2008; www.rougerie.com; www.seaorbiter.com

ROUQUAROL, Benoit, France (1826-1875). Co-developer with Lt. August Denayrouze of a breathing device with an automatic demand valve and an air reservoir.

ROUSE, Norine, United States (1925-2005). One of the world's first female diving instructors; active environmentalist involved in sea turtle and reef protection.

RUSSELL, Matthew A., United States (NA). Archeologist with the National Park Service's Submerged Resources Center; Project Director for the USS *Arizona* Preservation Project; Society for Historical Archaeology (SHA) UNESCO Committee; Advisory Council on Underwater Archaeology

SAGALEVITCH, Prof. Anatoly, Russia (NA). Oceanologist; chief scientist for Russian

"Mir" submersibles aboard the research vessel *Akademik Mstislav Keldysh*; has led expeditions to the *Titanic*, the *Bismarck*, and the crippled Russian submarine *Komsomolets*; member of the Explorers Club

SARANO, Dr. François, France (1954-). Oceanographer; longtime scientific adviser to the Cousteau Society; expedition leader; research director of Deep Ocean Odyssey; public speaker; president of Longitude 181 Nature; www.longitude181.com

François Sarano. Photo courtesy *Longitude 181 Nature*

SAWATZKY, Dr. David, Canada (NA). Consultant in Diving Medicine at DRDC (Defence Research and Development Canada) Toronto, Ontario (formerly DCIEM); IANTD Board of Advisors; medical columnist for DIVER Magazine (Canada); won the Star of Courage for rescuing a trapped diver in a Tobermory cave

SAWYER, Ty, United States, (NA). Editor-in-Chief of Sport Diver Magazine; editorial director of Islands Magazine; former editor of Skin Diver Magazine and Discover Diving; award-winning photographer and prolific writer; fellow national member of the Explorers Club

SCALLI, Frank, United States (1931-2004). Author of the first nationally adopted scuba instruction manual in 1954; in charge of business development for US Divers Co. for more than 30 years; part of the first dive expedition to the sunken Italian luxury liner *Andrea Doria*; founding member of the Boston Sea Rovers; member of the Diving Hall of Fame

SHANKS, Harry, United States (NA). Diving pioneer; established the Our World Underwater Scholarship Society and the Academy of Underwater Arts and Sciences (AUAS) which administers the NOGI Award, diving's oldest and best recognized award

SIEBE, August, Germany (1788-1872). Developed a diving helmet fitted to an airtight diving suit fed with air pumped from the surface

SIMONEAU, Clifford, United States (1959-2005). Educator; environmentalist; pioneer of the recreational rebreather industry; co-founder of Silent Diving Systems (SDS); officer of the Shark Research Institute (SRI)

SLATE, Capt. Spencer, United States (1947-). Started Capt. Slate's Atlantis Dive Center Inc. in 1978; founding member in 1983 and president for 15 years of the Keys Association of Dive Operators; co-founder in 1985 and president of the Florida Assn. of Dive Operators; instructor and instructor-trainer for several dive agencies; author of several dive training manuals; project manager the *Spiegel Grove* artificial reef project; member of the International Scuba Diving Hall of Fame (2004); captainslate.com

SMALL, Peter UK (NA-1962). Co-founder of British Sub-Aqua Club with Oscar Gugen in 1953; died at the surface after a record dive with Hannes Keller (survived) in which the latter exited a diving bell at a depth of 1,020 ft (311 m) off Catalina Island, California, in 1962

Marty Snyderman. Photo courtesy of Marty Snyderman

SNYDERMAN, Marty, United States (1949-). Emmy Award winning cinematographer; still photographer, film producer, author and public speaker specializing in the marine environment; martysnyderman.com

SOMERS, Dr. Lee, United States (NA). Pioneer in diving safety; Diving Safety Officer (University of Michigan); diving instructor; lecturer; author. During the 1970's, Dr. Somers and his team were respectfully known as the Michigan Mafia

SOTO, Bob, Cayman Islands (NA). Pioneer of diving in the Cayman Islands since 1957; member of the International Scuba Diving Hall of Fame (2000);

STEEL, John, United States (1921-1998). Diving's first underwater artist; underwater photographer; often illustrated the cover of Skin Diver Magazine

STÉNUIT, Robert, Belgium (1933-). Wreck hunter; explorer; experimented with a submersible decompression chamber in 1964; discovered the Armada warship *Girona* (1967), the *Slotter Hooge* (1974), and a treasure trove of rare Ming porcelain on the *Witte Leeuw* (1977); raised a rare bronze statue from a wreck site near island of Vele Orjule, Croatia (2000)

STEWART, Capt. Don, Bonaire (1925-). Diving and environmental protection pioneer; founder of Capt. Don's Habitat; member of the International Scuba Diving Hall of Fame (2005); a.k.a. the Father of Bonaire

STEWART, James, United States (NA). Diving pioneer; diving officer emeritus at Scripps Institution of Oceanography; consultant to NASA; developer of underwater training techniques for astronauts; NAUI Hall of Honor

STEWART, Richard H. IV, United States (NA). Ocean explorer, publisher and editor, photojournalist, television producer and founder of *Sport Diver, Ocean Realm, Dive Travel* and *Planet Ocean;* co-founder and travel editor of *Florida Diver* magazine (1976); founder of *Sport Diver* magazine in 1977; co-founder and executive producer of *OceanFest;* underwater video systems designer; founder and executive director of the B2B Dive Travel Association; executive producer of Dive Travel Conference; lecturer; marketing consultant; founder of Big Grouper Media; dive instructor; oceanrealmmedia.com

STONEMAN, John, Canada (1963-). Award-winning underwater cinematographer; president of Mako Films Ltd; producer of *The Ocean World of John Stoneman*

STRAZZERA, Patrice, France (1963-). Award-winning underwater photographer and author specializing in Mediterranean wrecks; www.sommeildesepaves.com

Patrice Strazzera. Photo courtesy *Le sommeil des épaves*

STREETER, Tanya, Cayman Islands (1973-). World champion freediver; has repeatedly beaten both men's and women's records including the No Limits in August 2002 (525 ft / 160 m in 3 min & 26 sec); called "The World's Most Perfect Athlete" by Sports Illustrated in 2002; redefineyourlimits.com

SUMIAN, Dominique, France (NA). Long-time crewmember and diver of the Cousteau Society; chief diver & expedition leader on the *Calypso;* cinematographer;

Richard Stewart. Photo courtesy Ocean Realm

commando marine and frogman in the French Navy; chief diver for the French Oceanographic Service; international sales for Aqua-Lung

TAILLIEZ, Philippe, France (1905-2002). Diving pioneer; author; introduced Jacques Y. Cousteau to the sport of goggle fishing in 1936; one of the three *Mousquemers* along with Jacques Y. Cousteau and Frédéric Dumas; first commanding officer of the *Groupe d'études et de recherches sous-marines* (GERS) in 1945; first military group to employ the Cousteau-Gagnan Aqua-Lung; a.k.a. The Father of Diving

TALBOT, Bob, United States (NA). Award-winning filmmaker in various formats including IMAX; has developed specialized aquatic filming techniques using camera rigs, boats, and underwater propulsion vehicles; award-winning photographer specializing in whale and dolphin photography; member of the Sea Shepherd Advisory Board; www.talbotcollection.com

TATEISHI, Akira, Japan (1930-). Publisher; underwater photographer; filmmaker; founder of diving magazine *Marine Diving*; member of the International Scuba Diving Hall of Fame (2004)

TAYLOR, Ron, Australia (1934-). Pioneer underwater explorer; award-winning underwater filmmaker and photographer; first to film the Great white shark, first to dive with the Great white shark without a cage; invented the chain-mail shark suit; ocean conservationist; helped get the Great white shark and the Grey nurse shark protected; member of the International Scuba Diving Hall of Fame (2000); Senior Australian of the Year 2006 Finalist

TAYLOR, Valerie, Australia (1936-). Pioneer underwater explorer; award-winning underwater filmmaker and photographer; first to film the Great white shark, first to dive with the Great white shark without a cage; invented the chain-mail shark suit; ocean conservationist; helped get the Great white shark and the Grey nurse shark protected; member of the International Scuba Diving Hall of Fame (2000); member of the

Women Divers Hall of Fame; Senior Australian of the Year 2006 Finalist

THOMPSON, William, United Kingdom (1822-1879). Naturalist; took the world's first underwater photo in February, 1856; exposure time was 10 minutes during which the camera flooded

TILLMAN, Albert (NAUI #1), United States (1928-2004). Co-founder of NAUI and the Los Angeles County instructor program with Bev Morgan; implemented the first instructor certification courses in the world; founded UNEXSO in Freeport, Grand Bahama Island, the world's first dedicated diving resort; member of the International Scuba Diving Hall of Fame

TUCKER, Teddy, Bermuda (1925-). Shipwreck hunter; historian; artist; lecturer; founding member of the Beebe Project in 1983; discovered the six-gill shark in Bermuda waters in the 1970's; Member of the Most Excellent Order of the British Empire Medal; www.teddytucker.com

TZIMOULIS, Paul, United States (1937-2003). Underwater photographer; author; former editor of Skin Diver Magazine; chairman of the Academy of Underwater Arts and Sciences

Masa Ushioda. Photo courtesy CoolWaterPhoto.com

USHIODA, Masa, United States (1969-). Award-winning underwater photographer; photographs have appeared nationally and internationally in hundreds of magazines, books, calendars, advertisements, and are also exhibited in many museums and aquariums around the world; www.coolwaterphoto.com

VAN DREBBEL, Cornelius, Netherlands (1572-1633). Inventor credited with building the first workable submarine in 1620; Drebbel Lunar Crater named in his honor.

VASSILOPOULOS, Peter, Canada (NA). Author; photographer; longtime owner / publisher of Diver Magazine (Canada)

WADSLEY, Jim, United States (NA). Treasure hunter and salvager; discovered and participated in the salvage of the *Brother Jonathan*, California's only known treasure wreck

WALSH, Dr. Don, United States (NA). Dove to the deepest point of the ocean (Challenger Deep - 35,798 feet / 10,911 m) with Swiss undersea explorer Jacques Piccard aboard the Bathyscaph in 1960; past dean of marine programs and professor of ocean engineering at the University of Southern California; founded International Maritime Incorporated in 1983; prolific author; public speaker; Honorary Life Member of the Explorers Club; Honorary Life Member of the Adventurers Club and a Fellow of the Royal Geographic Society

WATERMAN, Stan, United States (1923-). Pioneer underwater filmmaker and photographer; winner of five Emmys; prolific writer; president of the Shark research Institute (SRI); member of the International Scuba Diving Hall of Fame (2000); www.stanwaterman.com

WATSON, Neal, United States (NA). Pioneer of dive resort franchising; president of the Bahamas Diving Association; commercial diver; dive instructor; treasure salver; underwater stuntman; holds the Guinness World Record for underwater distance on scuba (66 miles non-stop underwater without surfacing); held the Guinness World Record for compressed-air diving depth (437 feet / 133 m) from 1968 to 1999; a.k.a. The Dive God; www.nealwatson.com

WATT, James, United States (1951-). Award-winning wildlife photographer; prolific writer; www.wattstock.com

Hal Watts. Photo courtesy PSA International

WATTS, Hal, United States (1935-). Founder of the Professional Scuba Association (PSA), originally known as the Florida State Skin Diving Schools in 1962; set a world depth record at 390 ft (119 m) on air (1967); set a world cave diving record at 415 ft (127 m) on air (2001); published the first manual for extended range deep diving for instructors in 1970; formed a specialty diving club known as the Forty Fathom Scubapros; a.k.a. Mr. Scuba; www.mrscuba.com

WESLEY, Claude, France (NA). Longtime crewmember and diver of the Cousteau Society; chief diver aboard the Calypso; world's first aquanaut with Albert Falco aboard the undersea habitat Diogenes, in 1962 (Conshelf I); also an aquanaut during Conshelf II; passionate public speaker

WHITE, Daniel, Canada (1959-). Wide screen cinematographer specializing in deep sea exploration; www.bigfilms.ca

WHITE, Frank, Canada (NA). Founded Whites Manufacturing in 1956, the first wet suit manufacturing company in Canada, and first drysuit manufacturing company in North America; owner/founder of Frank Whites Dive Stores; www.whitesdiving.com

WHITE, Ralph, United States (NA). Explorer, underwater cinematographer; photographer; deep submersible cameraman

WISEMAN, James, United States (NA). Award-winning underwater photographer; administrator of Wetpixel.com

WU, Norbert, United States (1961-). Award-winning photographer and filmmaker; prolific writer and author; awarded National Science Foundation (NSF) Artists and Writers Grants to document wildlife and research in Antarctica; awarded the Antarctica Service Medal of the United States of America for his contributions to exploration and science in the U.S. Antarctic Program; the only photographer to have been awarded a Pew Marine Conservation Fellowship; named Outstanding Photographer of the Year (2004) by the North American Nature Photographers Association (NANPA); www.norbertwu.com

Norbert Wu with Sony HDCAM housing. Photo © James Watt

ZISSOU, Steve, Unknown origin (NA). Fictitious character from the film *The Life Aquatic* (2004); a.k.a. Stevesy

INTERNATIONAL SCUBA DIVING HALL OF FAME

Every year, the Board of Directors of the International Scuba Diving Hall of Fame under the Chairmanship the Cayman Islands Minister for Tourism, Commerce, Transport & Works, selects a group of persons from around the globe, who have made a contribution to the development and/or promotion of recreational scuba diving. (**www.scubahalloffame.com**)

2007
COLEMAN, Neville
ERICKSON, Ralph
FOX, Rodney
HUMANN, Paul
ROESSLER, Carl

2005
BERGMAN, Dewey
BROOKS, Ernest, II
RECHNITZER, Andreas B., Ph.D.
STEWART, Don

Ministry of Tourism Award
HUBBELL, Tom
MILBURN, Peter

2004
ANDERSON, Dick
BALL, Mike
GREENBERG, Jerry
McDONALD, Kendall
SLATE, Captain Spencer
TATEISHA, Akira

2003
AUXIER, Jim
BLAKESLEE, Chuck
COUSTEAU, Jean-Michel
DUMAS, Frederic
KLEIN Sr., Jordan
SCALLI, Frank

2002
CRONIN, John J.
DOUBILET, David
HOLLIS, Bob
PARRY, Zale
TORS, Ivan
TZIMOULIS, Paul J.

2000 (Inaugural Inductees)
BRIDGES, Lloyd
COUSTEAU, Jacques-Yves
CROPP, Ben
CROSS, E.R.
DALLA VALLE, Gustav
DAVIS, Dr. Jefferson C. Jr.
EARLE, Sylvia, Ph.D.

EATON, Bernie
GAGNAN, Émile
GIDDINGS, Al
HASS, Hans
HASS, Lotte
LAVANCHY, Jack
MCKENNEY, Jack
SOTO, Bob
TAYLOR, Ron
TAYLOR, Valerie
TILLMAN, Al
WATERMAN, Stan

WOMEN DIVERS HALL OF FAME

The members of WDHOF are an elite group that includes the most notable women leaders and innovators in the diving community. It became the goal of its founders to recognize and honor, while raising public awareness of these women's exceptional contributions. WDHOF was founded and continues to be a collaborative effort on behalf of Beneath the Sea, Hillary Viders, Ph.D., the Underwater Society of America, The Women Scuba Association and Women Underwater Ezine.

For biographies of the members or to make a nomination, go to the WDHOF website: **www.wdhof.org**

2006
BRADLEY, Georgienne
KEGELES, Sharon Lee
OCHERT, Adina S.
RUNNALLS, Dr. Lesley A.
UGUCCIONI, Donna Marie
VAN HEEST, Valerie

2005
BUNKLEY-WILLIAMS, Lucy, Ph.D.
BUSH, CDR Bette
HUBBELL, Linda C.
STAYER, Pat
WIDDER, Edie, Ph.D.

2004
BINELLI, Carla
CASSANO, Capt. Victoria Anne, MD
GILLIGAN, M. Veronica (Ronni)

HERNANDEZ, CDR Rene S., Ph.D.
HODGES, Vallorie J.
PUGH, Michelle
TALGE, Helen K., Ph.D.

2003
APPLEGATE, Renee Steven
BALDWIN, Carole, Ph.D.
DUDZINKI, Kathleen, Ph.D.
HARDEN, CDR Gina
de MEYER, Kalli
MURRAY, Rusty
PITKIN, Linda
POMPONI, Shirley, Ph.D.
YOST, CDR Lori

2002
BELLEFEUILLE, Monique J
BODENSTEDT, Commander Debra
FOLLMER, Joan M.
GILKES, Martha Watkins
JOHNSON, Connie
MESTRE, Audrey
PASCAL-GUARINO, Carolyn
REED, Sherry A.
SAHLER, LCDR Erica
SAMMON, Susan
SERPIERI, Claudia
TEGNER, Mia Jean, PhD
TRUKKEN, Sue J.
WAHRMANN, Sally A.
WILMS, Birgitte
ZIEFLE, Julianne

2001
ALARY, Danielle
BONEM, Rena M., Ph.D.
BONNIN, Mary J.
CARRELL, Toni
CASTLE, Cathryn
CONNELLY, Cecelia A.
FLETCHER, Susie
GAAR, Frances
HANSON, Norma
HAYWARD, Joyce S.
JERMAN, Paula M.
KAYAR, Susan R., Ph.D.
KIESER, June M.
KOHANOWICH, Cdr Karen
LEVINE, Marie
MITCHELL, Lisa A.
MOORE, Valerie S.
MURPHY, Geri
PREKER, Marianne

RABER, Janice
ROTHSCHILD, Kathy
SEFTON, Nancy
SHECKLER, Kim Reed
STOCKERT, Andrea D.
TOBIAS, Donna M.
THOMAS, Bridget K., RN
TURNER, Ruth, Ph.D.
VERDIER, Eveline
WATTS, Scarlett D.
WILSON, Laurie J.
ZIGAHN, JoAnn

2000 (Inaugural Inductees)
BANGASSER, Susan, Ph.D
BIESER, Capt. Janet
BOOKSPAN, Dr. Jolie
BRADLEY, Jana
BROWN, Tamara
CARDONE, Bonnie J.
CARTER, Jennifer
CHURCH, Cathy
CLARK, Dr. Eugenie
COURTER, Cindi
CUSH, Cathie
DAVIS, Helen T.
DRAFAHL, Sue
DUDAS, Evelyn Bartram
EARLE, Dr. Sylvia
ECKHOFF, Mary Ellen
FERRIS-FISCHER, Mary Jo
FISHER, Dolores F.
FIFE, Dr. Caroline
FRAZIER, Dottie
FRANKLIN, Regina
FUNKHOUSER, Lynn
GIESECKE, Anne, Ph.D.
GRAY, Linda
GRIMM, Brigit K.
HALEY, Erika-Leigh
HASS, Lotte
HALL, Michele
HAUSER, Hillary
HEANEY-GRIER, Mehgan
HEINERTH, Jill
HOFFMAN, Edith D.
HULTS, Maria
KINAHAN, Lise
KING, Jennifer
KNAFELC, Capt. Marie, MD Ph.D
KRISTOVICH, Dr. Ann H
LANDER, Barb
LILLIS, Mary Edith (Mel)
LYNN, Capt. Diann Karin

MORGAN, Connie Lyn
MORGAN, Ella Jean
MORRA, Sue, Ph.D.
MORRISSETTE, Denise J.
MOUNT, Patti
NEAL, Jan
NEWELL-MORTARA, Patty
O'NEILL, Erin
ORR, Betty
PARRY, Zale
PECHTER, Alese O.
PRAGER, Ellen J., Ph.D.
RODUNER, Vreni
ROSE, Carol Taylor
ROUSE, Norine
ROYAL, Betsy
SADLER, Lorraine Bemis
SCARR, Dee
SCHOLLEY, Cdr. Bobbie
SLEEPER, Jeanne Bear
ST LEDGER-DOWSE, Marguerite
STREETER, Tanya
TAYLOR, Dr. Maida Beth
TAYLOR, Valerie
VAN HOESEN, Dr. Karen
VIDERS, Hillary, Ph.D.
WALTEN, Kay
WESTERFIELD, Renee
WEYDIG, Kathy A.
WINGERT, Frankie
YAGER, Jill, Ph.D.
ZAFERES, Andrea

DEMA HALL OF FAME

The Reaching Out Award was first presented in 1989. The original intent was to recognize individuals who have made a significant contribution to the sport of diving by "reaching out" in some special way to improve the sport for everyone (**www.dema.org**)

2006
HUMANN, Paul
NESBIT, John

2005
ICORN, Nick, Training Agencies
WATSON, Neal, Travel Destinations

2004
LONG, Dick, Manufacturer

RICHARDSON, Drew, Training Agencies

2003
CHURCH, Jim, Photographer/Educator
CHRISTINI, Ed, Training Agencies
GALLAGHER, Jean, Educator

2002
KIPP, Ron - Travel Destinations
JEHLE, Charlie - Manufacturer
HARDY, Jon - Educator
BENNETT, Dr. Peter B. - Educator

2001
BRIGHAM, Ike - Manufacturer
CAHILL, James - Retailer
TAYLOR, David - Environmental Award Recipient

2000
CHURCH, Cathy - Photographer
HOLLIS, Bob - Manufacturer
SHEARER, Gordon - Manufacturer

1999
CUSSLER, Clive - Author
GIDDINGS, Al - Photographer/Cinematographer
HALL, Howard - Photographer/Cinematographer
MERKER, Ron - Retailer/Educator

1998
GAFFNEY, John - Training Agencies
CLARK, Bob - Training Agencies
STEWART, Captain Don - Travel Destinations

1997
DORSEY, Joe - Retailer
HASS, Dr. Hans - Photography & Cinema
TZIMOULIS, Paul – Photojournalist

1996
McANIFF, John - Educator
MORGAN, Bev - Manufacturer
WEISS, Fred - Manufacturer

1995
GRAY, Robert - The DEMA Show

1994
AUXIER, Jim - Creator of Skin Diver Magazine

BLAKESLEE, Chuck - Creator of Skin Diver Magazine
BRIDGES, Lloyd - Actor
COUSTEAU, Jean-Michel - Environmentalist & Explorer

1993
CARPENTER, Scott - Explorer & Author
CLARK, Eugenie - Marine Biologist
PARRY, Zale – Actress

1992
BONIN, Dick - Manufacturer
ERICKSON, Ralph - Training Agencies
KEVORKIAN, Michael - Inventor, Educator & Retailer
SCALLI, Frank - Training Agencies

1991
CRONIN, John - Training Agencies
DAVISON, Sam Jr. - Manufacturer
EARLE, Dr. Sylvia - Marine Biologist
POST, Arnold - Retailer
STEWART, James - Scripps Institute of Oceanography

1990
CROSS, E.R. - Educator
MEISTRELL, Bill & Bob - Manufacturers
KELLY, T.A. "Mike" - Founder of DEMA
TILLMAN, Al - Training Agencies

1989
COUSTEAU, Jacques-Yves - Environmentalist, Explorer & Inventor
EGSTROM, Dr. Glen - Educator
McKENNEY, Jack - Photography & Cinema
WATERMAN, Stan - Photography & Cinema

AUAS NOGI AWARDS

The **Academy of Underwater Arts & Sciences** (AUAS) is one of the oldest and most prestigious organizations in the diving community worldwide. (**auas-nogi.org**)

The Academy of Underwater Arts and Sciences is dedicated to recognizing the pioneers and leaders who have made a global impact on the exploration, enjoyment, and preservation of the underwater world and to passing the stewardship of the sea on to future generations.

The NOGI New Orleans Grand Isle Award is the oldest award and most prestigious award in the diving industry, dating back to 1960. The NOGI Award was originally created by Jay Albanese and Louis Cuccia as sanctioned by the Underwater Society of America (USOA). Each NOGI is a 24" high statuette which resembles the Hollywood Oscar statuette, thus earning the title, "the Academy Award of Diving."

ARTS: Filmmakers, painters, photographers, sculptors and other artists who bring the majesty of the underwater world to people everywhere.

SCIENCE: Explorers, inventors, doctors and scientists whose work helps us understand, enjoy and protect our precious underwater realm.

SPORTS/EDUCATION: Outstanding athletes and teachers who make diving a safe, enjoyable and accessible activity for all who love the ocean.

DISTINGUISHED SERVICE: World-renowned as well as quiet achievers whose contributions keep the wheels of the diving industry and the global diving community turning.

ALBANESE, Joseph D. Jr. (DS, 1963) (D)
ANDERSON, Richard (Arts, 1970)
ASTURIAS, Oscar (DS, 1970)
AUXIER, Jim (Arts, 1960) (D)
BACHRACH, Arthur J., Ph.D. (Science, 1973)
BALLARD, Robert D., Ph.D. (Science, 1975)
BARADA, Bill (Arts, 1967) (D)
BASS, George, Ph.D. (Science, 1974)
BEHNKE, Albert, M.D. (Science, 1969) (D)
BENCHLEY, Peter (Art, 2004)
BENJAMIN, George, Ph.D. (DS, 1978) (D)
BENNETT, Peter B., Ph.D. (Science, 1980)
BERGMAN, Dewey (S & E, 1977) (D)
BLAKESLEE, Chuck (Arts, 1960)
BOND, Capt. George (Sicence, 1964) (D)
BONIN, Dick (DS, 1982)
BOREN, Lamar (Arts, 1974) (D)
BOVE, Alfred, M.D., Ph.D. (Science, 1994)
BRIDGES, Lloyd (S & E, 1982) (D)
BROOKS, Ernest H., II (Arts, 1975)
BROWN, Jim (S & E, 1979) (D)
BROWNING, Ricou (Arts, 1996)
BUSH ROMERO, Pablo (DS, 1965) (D)

CAHILL, Jim (Science, 2003)
CAMERON, James (Arts, 1999)
CARGILE, Edward C. (S & E, 2002)
CARPENTER, Scott (DS, 1995)
CHRISTIANSEN, Jim (Science, 1961) (D)
CHURCH, Cathy (Arts, 1985)
CHURCH, Jim (Arts, 1985) (D)
CHURCH, Ron (Arts, 1973) (D)
CLARK, Eugenie, Ph.D. (Arts, 1965 / Sci. 87)
CLARK, Robert (S & E, 1997)
COOK, Roger W. (Science, 1979)
COOPER, Richard A., Ph.D. (Science, 1982)
COUSTEAU, Capt. Jacques-Y. (DS, 1966) (D)
COUSTEAU, Jean-Michel (Science, 1993)
COUSTEAU, Philippe Pierre (Arts, 1977) (D)
CRAIG, Lt. Col. John D. (Arts, 1997) (D)
CRONIN, John (DS, 1985/S & E, 2001) (D)
CROSS, Ellis F.R. (S & E, 1975/ DS, 1992) (D)
CUCCIA, Louis R. (DS, 1967)
DALLA VALLE, Gustav (S & E, 1962) (D)
DAVIS, C. B. "Ben" (DS, 1961)
DAVIS, Helen Turcotte (S & E, 1983) DAVIS, Jefferson, M.D. (S & E, 1981) (D)
DAVIS, Ralph (S & E, 1967)
DAYTON, Paul, Ph.D. (Science, 2004)
DELAUZE, Henri G. (DS, 2004)
DILL, Robert, Ph.D. (Science, 1977) (D)
DOUBILET, David N. (Arts, 1978)
DRAKE, Harold (S & E, 1971)
DUGAN, James (Arts, 1962) (D)
DUMAS, Frederic (DS, 2000) (D)
EARLE, Sylvia A., Ph.D. (Science, 1976)
EDGERTON, Harold, Ph.D. (Sci., 1970) (D)
EGSTROM, Glen, Ph.D. (DS, 1969 / Sci. 1981)
EMPLETON, Bernard (S & E, 1973) (D)
ERNST, John (S & E, 1965)
EVANS, Bob (S & E, 2004)
FALCO, Albert (DS, 1999)
FAVER, Jack (Science, 1961) (D)
FEAD, Louis M. (S & E, 1980)
FEINBERG, Walter (DS, 1971) (D)
FENNELL, Frank (S & E, 1992)
FINE, John Christopher (S & E, 1993)
FINKLE, Elliott, Ph.D. (DS, 1983) (D)
FISHER, Melvin (S & E, 1978) (D)
FRESHEE, Rick (Arts, 1981) (D)
GAFFNEY, Jon (S & E, 1989) (D)
GAGNAN, Emile (DS, 2002) (D)
GALERNE, Andre (DS, 1988)
GEISZLER, John (S & E, 1981) (D)
GIDDINGS, Al (Arts, 1972)
GIMBLE, Peter (Arts, 1971) (D)
GRAVER, Dennis K. (S & E, 1990)
GRIFFIS, Nixon (DS, 1981) (D)

GRIGG, Richard W., Ph.D. (Science, 1999)
GROSVENOR, Melvin, Ph.D. (DS, 1975) (D)
HALL, Howard W. (Arts, 1993)
HAMILTON, R. W. Bill, Ph.D. (Science, 1995)
HARDY, Jon (S & E, 1988) (D)
HARVEY, Guy C., Ph.D. (Arts, 2004)
HASS, Hans, Ph.D. (Sci. 1998 / DS, 1998)
HAUBER, Carl H. (DS, 1960)
HENDRICK, Walt, Sr. (S & E, 1985)
HIGH, William (Bill) (S & E, 1964 / Sci. 1991)
HOLLIS, Bob (Science, 2001)
HURTADO, Genaro (Arts, 1982) (D)
ICORN, Nick (DS, 1974)
KILBRIDE, Bert (S & E, 1987)
KLEIN, Sr., Jordan (Arts, 1991)
KOBLICK, Ian G. (DS, 1990)
KRISTOF, Emory (Arts, 1987)
LAMBERTSEN, Christian J., M.D. (Sci. 1971)
LANPHIER, Edward, M.D. (Sci. 1963) (D)
LEANEY, Leslie (S & E, 2003)
LENTZ, Terry (S & E, 1968)
LILLIS, Mary Edith (S & E, 1963 / DS, 1994)
LIMBAUGH, Conrad (Science, 1978) (D)
LINK, Edwin (Science, 1965) (D)
LITTLEHALES, Bates (Arts, 1976)
LONG, Richard W. (S & E, 1991)
MACINNIS, Joseph, M.D. (Science, 1972)
MARDEN, Luis (Arts 1963) (D)
MARX, Robert F. (DS, 1976)
McANIFF, John J. (DS, 1962)
McKENNY, Jack (DS, 1977 / Arts, 1988) (D)
MILLER, James W., Ph.D. (Science, 1986)
MORGAN, Bev (Arts, 1990 / S & E, 1995)
MOUNT, Tom (S & E, 2000)
MURPHY, Geri (Arts, 2001)
MURPHY, Richard, Ph.D. (S & E, 1998)
NEWBERT, Chris (Arts, 2003)
NICHOLSON, Christopher (Science, 1992)
NICKLIN, Charles (S & E, 1975 / Arts, 1986)
NICKLIN, Flip (Arts, 1994)
NICHOLSON, Christopher (science, 1992)
NORTH, Wheeler, Ph.D. (S &E, 1974) (D)
NUYTTEN, Phil, Ph.D. (Science, 1997)
ORR, Dan, M.S. (S & E, 1996)
OSTERHOUT, Ralph (DS, 1984)
OWEN, David M. (Science, 1962)
PARRY, Zale (DS, 1973)
PAWLOWICZ, T. F. "Duke" (S & E, 1970)
PECHTER, Alese (DS, 2003)
PECHTER, Mort (DS, 2003)
PERRY, Jr., John H. (DS, 1986)
PETERSON, Mendel (Arts, 1983)
PHINIZY, Coles (Arts, 1964) (D)
PICCARD, Hon. Jacques, Ph.D. (Sci. 1967)

PYLE, Richard, Ph.D (Science, 2004)
RANDALL, John E., Ph.D. (Science, 2000)
RAWLINS, John, Surgeon V-Admiral (DS, '96)
REBIKOFF, Ada (Arts, 2000)
REBIKOFF, Dimitri (Arts, 1966) (D)
RECHNITZER, Andreas B., Ph.D. (Science,
1968 / DS, 1989 /S & E, 1999) (D)
RUGGIERI, George, Ph.D. (Science) (D)
SAGALEVITCH, Anatoly M., Ph.D. (Sci. 2002)
SAMMON, Richard M. (DS, 1987)
SCALLI, Frank (DS, 1972)
SEFTON, Nancy (Arts, 1984)
SELISKY, Lee (DS, 2004)
SHANKS, Harry (DS, 1980)
SHILLING, Charles, M.D. (DS, 1979) (D)
SHINN, Gene (Science, 1984)
SLATER, Richard A., Ph.D. (Science, 1988)
SOMERS, Lee H., Ph.D. (S & E, 1994)
STEWART, James R. (S & E, 1969)
STITH, David R. (DS, 1968)
STONEMAN, John (Arts, 2002)
SULLIVAN, Kathryn D., Ph.D. (Science, 1996)
TAILLIEZ, Capt. Philippe (DS, 1997) (D)
TALBOT, Bob (Arts, 1995)
TAYLOR, Ron (S & E, 1966)
TAYLOR, Valerie (Arts, 1980)
TEPLEY, Lee, Ph.D. (Arts, 1979)
TILLMAN, Albert (DS, 1964) (D)
TORS, Ivan (Arts, 1989) (D)
TUCKER, E. B. Teddy, M.B.E. (DS, 1991)
TZIMOULIS, Paul (Arts, 1969) (D)
VAN DER AUE, Otto, M.D. (Sci. 1983) (D)
ULLRICH, Arthur H. (S & E, 1976)
VEZZANI, Eugene J.D., Ph.D. (Science, 1960)
VIDERS, Hillary, Ph.D. (DS, 2001)
WALSH, Don, Ph.D. (Science, 1989)
WATERMAN, Stanton A. (Arts, 1968)
WEICKER, Gov. Lowell P., Ph.D. (DS, 1993)
WELLS, J. Morgan, Ph.D. (S & E, 1984)
WHITE, Ralph (Arts, 1992)
WICKLUND, Robert I. (Science, 1990)
WILMS, Birgitte (Arts, 2003)
WORKMAN, Robert M.D. (Sci. 1966) (D)
WYLAND (Arts, 1998)
YOUMANS, George (S & E, 1960) (D)
ZIGAHN, Armand (S & E, 2004)

Harry Shanks Award for Leadership in Diving

In 2005, the AUAS Board of Directors created the Harry Shanks Award for Leadership in Diving. The award was created to recognize outstanding young leaders in all sectors of the diving industry.

Any male or female diver aged 18 to 45, who has made an outstanding contribution to the world of diving, is eligible for this award. Candidates may be nominated or apply themselves. Applications should include the candidate's full name, contact information, biosketch, and two letters of recommendation. Applications are accepted throughout the year.

harryshanksaward@auas-nogi.org

SHANKS, Harry, 2005

BENEATH THE SEA DIVER OF THE YEAR

Diver of the Year is awarded annually to individuals that are highly respected for their accomplishments in areas affecting the diving community. Up to four recipients may be selected from the following categories:

- Arts
- Science – Environment
- Sports – Education
- Distinguished Service

Nominations must be sent prior to October 1st in the year preceding the awards ceremony. (**www.beneaththesea.org**)

2005
BOSTON SEA ROVERS - In memory of
SCALLI, Frank (Education)
CHATTERTON, John (Education)
ELLIS, Richard (Arts)
HOLLIS, Bob (Pioneer)
KOHLER, Richie (Education)

Beneath the Sea Honor Roll

ALARY, Danielle (Arts)
ALBRECHT, David (Arts)
ANDERSON, Dick (Arts)
BACHAND, Robert (Service)
BACKER, Terry (Environment)
BALLARD, Robert (Science)

BLANCO, Leandro (Arts)
THE BLUE PLANET (Arts)
BROOKS, Ernest II (Arts)
BERG, Dan (Arts)
BRIDGES, Lloyd (Lifetime Achievement)
BOWEN, Margaret (Service)
CARPENTER, Scott (Science)
CHOWDHURY, Bernie (Education)
COUSTEAU, Jean-Michel (Environment)
DOUBILET, David (Arts)
DRAFAHL, Jack & Sue (Arts)
EMMERMAN, Michael (Education)
FINE, John C. (Science)
FENNELL, Frank (Service)
FULLMER, Jack (Education)
GALERNE, Andre (Pioneer)
GIPSTEIN, Tod (Arts)
GILBERT, Michel (Arts)
GILLIAM, Bret (Education)
GIMBEL, Peter (Pioneer)
HASSON, Wayne (Environment)
HAMILTON, Bill (Science)
HAMMOND, Bill (Service)
HARDICK, Steve (Education)
HENDRICK, Walter Sr (Education)
HENDRICK, Walter III (Education)
HODGE, Bunky (Education)
HUGHES, Peter (Environment)
JAHR, Ray (Service)
JANULIS, Ted (Arts)
JERMAN, Paula (Service)
KRISTOF, Emory (Science)
LAMBERTSEN, Christian (Lifetime Achievement)
LEANEY, Leslie (Service)
LOEWY, Nita (Environment)
LONG, Dick (Service)
McANIFF, John (Service)
MARX, Sir Robert (Lifetime Achievement)
MOLINARI, Hon. Guy (Service)
MOUNT, Tom (Education)
MYERS, Roy (Science)
NAWROCKY, Pete (Arts)
NUYTTEN, Phil (Science)
PAKAN, Joe (Service)
PARRY, Zale (Arts)
PIERCE, Albert (Education)
POST, Arnold (Pioneer)
ORR, Dan (Education)
ROSE, Carol (Service)
SAMMON, Rick (Arts)
SCALLI, Frank (Service)
SCARR, Dee (Environment)

SEGARS, Herb (Arts)
SKILES, Wes (Education)
STANTON, Mark (Arts)
STEWART, Lance (Science)
STOLZENBERG, Ed (Service)
STRATTON, Charles (Science)
TUCKER, Ray Jr. (Service)
UNDERWATER SOCIETY OF AMERICA (Service)
VIDERS, Hillary (Environment)
WARD, Lee (Service)
WATERMAN, Stan (Arts)
WATTS, Hal (Education)
WHITE, Ralph (Science)
WYLAND (Arts)
ZAFERES, Andrea (Education)
ZARZYNSKI, Joseph (Education)
ZIELINSKI, Richard (Service)

ADCI COMMERCIAL DIVING HALL OF FAME

The Commercial Diving Hall of Fame was established in 2003 and officially inaugurated at Underwater Intervention 2005 with 25 inductees. This first class of inductees was previous recipients of the John B. Galletti and Tom Devine Awards. The purpose of the ADCI Commercial Diving Hall of Fame is to recognize and honor the lifetime achievement of those individuals whose dedication and accomplishments have significantly contributed to Commercial Diving. Persons are nominated by commercial diving industry peers and reviewed by a committee of previous Commercial Diving Hall of Fame recipients that have been selected by the ADCI Board of Directors. (**www.adc-int.org**)

2006
CRUZE, Rod
LONG, Dick
PARKER, Torrance
REEDY, Jack

2004
BARTH, Bob

The John B. Galletti Memorial Award

HOLLAND, R.H. (Dutchy), 2003
GRUBBS, Conway Whitey, 2002 (deceased)
SAXON, Ross, 2001
KIRBY, Bob, 2000
DORE, Bill, 1999
HELBURN, Steve, 1998
SAVOIE, Joe, 1997 (deceased)
CROSS, Ellis R., 1996 (deceased)
GALERNE, Andre, 1995
SMITH, Jack D., 1994
JOHNSON, John T., 1993
NEWBURY, Herbert G., 1992
MACINNIS, Dr. Joseph, 1991
HANDELMAN, Lad, 1990
BLACK, Murray, 1989 (deceased)
NUYTTEN, Phil, 1988
DELAUZE, Henri, 1987
JOINER, Jim, 1986
SAMPSON, George W., 1985 (deceased)
EVANS, Dick, 1984 (deceased)
HUGHES, D. Michael, 1983
MORGAN, Bev, 1982
WILSON, Hugh (Dan), 1981
LAMBERTSEN, Dr. Chris, 1980
WARNER, Cdr. Jackie, 1979 (deceased)
BOND, Capt. George, 1978 (deceased)
GALLETTI, John B.

Tom Devine Memorial Award

CALDWELL, Jim, 2002
HAZELBAKER, Jon, 2001
JAGER, Rick, 2000
AICHELE, Fred, 1999
MCGOVERN, Mike, 1997
CROFTON, Juan F., 1996
MCKENZIE, Ms. Bernice, 1995 (deceased)
DEVINE, Tom

DIVING QUOTES

BEEBE, William – Explorer, inventor (1877-1962)

I am not at home, nor near any city or people; I am far out in the Pacific on a desert island, sitting on the bottom of the ocean; I am deep down under the water in a place where no human being has ever been before; it is one of the greatest moments in my whole life; thousands of people would pay large sums, would forego much for five minutes of this!

I can only think of one experience which might exceed in interest a few hours spent under water, and that would be a journey to Mars.

BOUTAN, Louis – Pioneer underwater photographer (1859-1934)

Why did these first attempts furnish only mediocre pictures? Is water an unsuitable medium for getting good photographs?

BRIDGES, Lloyd – Actor, diver (1913-1988)

The pollution could ruin our oceans. I love the sea and I love diving.

COOPER, Robert - Professor of Old Testament

There is no dilemma compared with that of the deep-sea diver who hears the message from the ship above, "Come up at once. We are sinking."

COUSTEAU, Jacques-Yves (1910-1997)

A lot of people attack the sea, I make love to it.

Buoyed by water, he can fly in any direction-up, down, sideways-by merely flipping his hand. Under water, man becomes an archangel.

Farming as we do it is hunting, and in the sea we act like barbarians.

From birth, man carries the weight of gravity on his shoulders. He is bolted to earth. But man has only to sink beneath the surface and he is free.

However fragmented the world, however intense the national rivalries, it is an inexorable fact that we become more interdependent every day.

I am not a scientist. I am, rather, an impresario of scientists.
I believe that national sovereignties will shrink in the face of universal interdependence.

If we go on the way we have, the fault is our greed and if we are not willing to change, we will disappear from the face of the globe, to be replaced by the insect.
If we were logical, the future would be bleak, indeed. But we are more than logical. We are human beings, and we have faith, and we have hope, and we can work.

In order to stabilize world population, we must eliminate 350,000 per day.

It is certain that the study of human psychology, if it were undertaken exclusively in prisons, would also lead to misrepresentation and absurd generalizations.

It takes generosity to discover the whole through others. If you realize you are only a violin, you can open yourself up to the world by playing your role in the concert.

Man, of all the animals, is probably the only one to regard himself as a great delicacy.

Mankind has probably done more damage to the Earth in the 20th century than in all of previous human history.

No aquarium, no tank in a marine land, however spacious it may be, can begin to duplicate the conditions of the sea. And no dolphin that inhabits one of those aquariums or one of those marine lands can be considered normal.

No sooner does man discover intelligence than he tries to involve it in his own stupidity.

People protect what they love.

The awareness of our environment came progressively in all countries with different outlets.

The best way to observe a fish is to become a fish.
The biggest obstacle was mixing abortion with overpopulation. These are two things that have nothing to do with each other.

The happiness of the bee and the dolphin is to exist. For man it is to know that and to wonder at it.

The real cure for our environmental problems is to understand that our job is to salvage Mother Nature. We are facing a formidable enemy in this field. It is the hunters... and to convince them to leave their guns on the wall is going to be very difficult.

The road to the future leads us smack into the wall. We simply ricochet off the alternatives that destiny offers. Our survival is no more than a question of 25, 50 or perhaps 100 years.

The sea is the universal sewer.

The sea, once it casts its spell, holds on in its net of wonder forever.

The sea, the great unifier, is man's only hope. Now, as never before, the old phrase has a literal meaning: We are all in the same boat.

To yackety-yak about the past is for me time lost. Every morning I wake up saying, 'I'm still alive - a miracle.' And so I keep on pushing.

Wuler and air, the two essential fluids on which all life depends, have become global garbage cans.

We forget that the water cycle and the life cycle are one.

We must plant the sea and herd its animals using the sea as farmers instead of hunters. That is what civilization is all about - farming replacing hunting.

What is a scientist after all? It is a curious man looking through a keyhole, the keyhole of nature, trying to know what's going on.

When one man, for whatever reason, has the opportunity to lead an extraordinary life, he has no right to keep it to himself.

---

de BALZAC, Honoré

In diving to the bottom of pleasure we bring up more gravel than pearls.

DIOLÉ, Philippe – Author

A vivid sense of delight takes hold off one, when for the first time one penetrates the surface. After thousands of years of fear and effort Man has at last succeeded in getting beneath the top layer of the sea, winning a long battle against asphyxia and terror. A palace untouched by human hand, with its gardens of rock and water where living creatures play the part of flowers, is the goal of all our striving.

Between the air and the water a steel wave quivers. What people call the surface is also a ceiling. A looking glass above, watered silk below. Nothing is torn on the way through. Only a few bubbles mark the diver's channel and behind him the frontier soon closes. But once the threshold is crossed you can turn back slowly and look up: that dazzling screen is the border between two worlds, as clear to the one as to the other. Behind the looking glass the sky is made of water.

DRYDEN, John – Writer (1631-1700)

He who would search for pearls must dive.

EARLE, Sylvia – Diver, explorer

Going into the ocean is like diving into the history of life on Earth.

ELLSBERG, Edward – US Navy

Nothing that the ingenuity of man has permitted his to do is more unnatural than working as a diver in deep water.

ENZO – World champion freediver

Roberto! Mio palmo!

GILPATRIC, Guy – Pioneer freediver & spearfisher

As inward love breeds outward talk,
The hound some praise, and some the hawk;
Some, better pleased with private sport,
Use tennis; some a mistress court:
But these delights I neither wish,
Nor envy, while I freely fish.

KENNEDY, John F. – U.S. President

Knowledge of the oceans is more than a matter of curiosity. Our very survival may hinge on it.

MAYOL, Jacques – Pioneer world champion freediver

I'd rather lose myself in passion than lose my passion.

My life is inspired by dolphins.

One day babies of the future will be re-connected to the aquatic evolutionary past. They will be totally in harmony with the sea and diving and playing at great depth with their marine cousins, holding the breath for a long period of time and giving birth in the sea even in the presence of dolphins. Homo Delphinus is not just a concept.

The sea is my mistress. I make love to her when I dive.

Water - the ocean - is our most natural environment. We are born naked from the miniature ocean of the mother's womb.

MELVILLE, Herman

I love all men who dive. Any fish can swim near the surface, but it takes a great whale to go down stairs five miles or more; & if he doesn't attain the bottom, why, all the lead in Galena can't fashion the plummet that will.

MOTHER SHIPTON – Prophetess (1488-1561)

Underwater men will walk, will ride, will sleep, will talk.

SHAKESPEARE, William

Fishes live in the sea, as men do a-land; the great ones eat up the little ones.

SIMPSON, Abe[20]

Now, remember the plan Bart. If you run out of air, tug on the rope 63 times; 64 is if you found the treasure!

61... 62... 63... Oh no! 63! He's out of air! I've sent my only grandson to a watery gra... 64! He's found the treasure! I'm rich!

---

[20] The Simpsons (*The Curse of the Flying Hellfish*); Original Airdate: 28-Apr-96

STEINBECK, John

An ocean without its unnamed monsters would be like a completely dreamless sleep.

TAILLIEZ, Philippe – The Father of Diving (1905-2002)

How many men occupied by war, glory and power have passed by this indissociable and essential element: the Sea?

One must dive naked to understand the sea.

The water is welcoming for those who know it. It washes away our worries as it rids us of gravity.

VALÉRY, Paul – Poet (1871-1945)

A man alone is in bad company.[21]

When we think of the sea bed, abandoning ourselves to its fantasy, we become poets of childlike wonder. We roam around like divers in colored shadows overhung with liquid skies.

VERNE, Jules

How do you get to the great depths? How do return to the surface of the ocean? And how do you maintain yourselves in the requisite medium? Am I asking too much?

The sea is everything. It covers seven-tenths of the terrestrial globe. Its breath is pure and healthy. It is an immense desert where man is never alone for he feels life, quivering around him on every side. There is supreme tranquility. The sea does not belong to despots. On its surface iniquitous rights can still be exercised, men can fight there, devour each other there, and transport all terrestrial horrors there. But at thirty feet (9 m) below its level their power ceases, their influence dies out, their might disappears. Ah, sir, live in the bosom of the waters! There alone is independence. There I recognize no masters! There I am free.

ZISSOU, Steve – Ocean explorer & cinematographer

What about my dynamite?

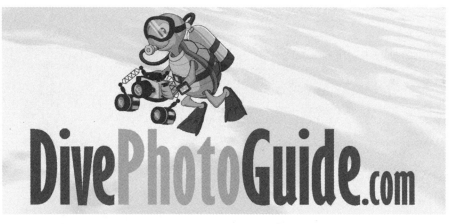

---

[21] Quoted by Jacques-Yves Cousteau to describe how he suddenly felt when the lights went out inside the wreck of the *Britannic* at a depth of 390 ft (119m) in the Aegean Sea.

Chapter 12

WORLD WITHOUT SUN (1964)
Award-winning film by Jacques-Yves
Cousteau and Louis Malle

ARTS &
ENTERTAINMENT

The following section presents a thorough listing of the many films, documentaries, dive magazines, e-zines, books and other publications which cater to the diving community.

Since this is the first edition of the Diving Almanac & Yearbook, some films, publications and websites have inadvertently been overlooked. If you know of any film or publication that should be listed in next year's edition, please send suggestions or relevant information to:
info@divingalmanac.com

DIVE MAGAZINES

Languages: (CZ) Czech, (DA) Danish, (DU) Dutch, (E) English, (F) French, (G) German, (GR) Greek, (I) Italian, (J) Japanese, (K) Korean, (N) Norwegian, (PL) Polish, (PT) Portuguese, (R) Russian, (SP) Spanish, (SW) Swedish, (T) Turkish

ARGENTINA

Tiempo de fondo (SP)
Circulation: 10,000
Frequency: Bi-monthly giveaway
Years in circulation: 3
webmaster@tiempodefondo.com.ar
www.tiempodefondo.com.ar

AUSTRALIA

DiveLog Australasia (E)
Circulation: 10,000
Frequency: monthly giveaway
Years in circulation: 17
MOT Publications PTY LTD
PO Box 355 Upper Beaconsfield,
Victoria, Australia 3808
Tel.: 61 3 5944 3774
Fax: 61 3 5944 4024
divelog@motpub.com.au
www.divetheblue.net

Intl Freediving & Spearfishing News (E)
Circulation: 7,000
Frequency: Quarterly
Years in circulation: 11

165 Quamby Road
Guys Hill VIC 3807 Australia
Tel.: 68 0 06 642 422
Fax: 61 3 59 444 024
freediving@motpub.com.au
www.diving-action.com/

Sportdiving Magazine (E)
Circulation: 15,000
Frequency: Bi-monthly
Years in circulation: 35
MOT Publications PTY LTD
PO Box 355, Upper Beaconsfield,
Victoria, Australia 3808
Tel.: 61 3 5944 3774
Fax: 61 3 5944 4024
divelog@motpub.com.au
www.divetheblue.net

AUSTRIA

Tauch Sport SeaStar (G)
www.tauchsport.net

BELGIUM

Fun plongée (F)
Frequency: 5 issues/year
Éditions Fun
Rue du Pinson, 32
1170 Bruxelles
Tel.: 02 660 02 95
Fax: 02 660 02 95
info@plongee.be
www.plongee.be

Hippocampe (F)
Circulation: 8,500/9,000
Frequency: quarterly
Years In circulation: 42
Revue officielle de la Ligue Francophone de Recherches et d'Activites Sous-Marines (LIFRAS)
Rue Jules Broeren, 38
B-1070 Bruxelles
Tel.: 02 521.70.21
Fax: 02 522.30.72
lifras@lifras.be
www.lifras.be/hippocampe

BRASIL

Deco Stop (PT)
Circulation: 5,000
Frequency: quarterly
Years in Circulation: 8
Rua João Batista Vieira, 855
Bairro Camargos
Cep: 30525-380 - Belo Horizonte - MG
Tel.: 31 3388-6463
www.decostop.com.br

Mergulho (PT)
Frequency: monthly
Grupo Um Editora
Av. Brig. Faria Lima, 3064,
10° andar, São Paulo
SP CEP 01451-000
Tel.: 11 2186 1000
www.mergulho.com.br

CANADA

Diver Magazine (E)
Circulation: 20,000
Frequency: 8 times/year
Years in Circulation: 35
241 East 1st Street
North Vancouver, BC
Canada V7L 1B4
Tel.: 604 948 9937
Toll-free 1 877 974 4333
Fax 604 948 9985
mail@divermag.com
www.divermag.com

En profondeur (F)
Circulation: 20,000
Frequency: bi-monthly
Fédération Québécoise des Activités Subaquatiques
4545, av. Pierre-De Coubertin
C.P. 1000, Succ. M
Montréal (Québec)

Canada H1V 3R2
Tel.: 514 252-3009
Toll Free: 1 866 391 8835
Fax: 514 254 1363
enprofondeur@fqas.qc.ca
www.fqas.qc.ca

CZECH REPUBLIC

Dobrá voda (CZ)
Frequency: Quarterly
Years in circulation: 9
Gnóm-Eisenmann Media, s. r. o.
Na Okraji 42
162 00 Praha 6
eisenmann.j@quick.cz
www.nova-vodni-revue.cz

Ocean(CZ)
Circulation: 8,200
Frequency: monthly
Years in Circulation: 7
Czech Press Group a.s.
Klíšská 1432/18
400 01 Ústí nad Labem
Tel.: 47 521 10 88 l. 124
Tel.: 47 521 16 66
predplatne@koktejl.cz
www.czech-press.cz

Potápění (CZ)
Circulation: 12,000
Frequency: monthly
In circulation: 7
Nedvědovo nám. 1164/14
147 00 Praha 4
Tel.: 420 244 466 682
Fax: 420 241 430 036
yacht@yacht-magazine.cz
www.yacht-magazine.cz/diving

DENMARK

DYK (DA)
Circulation: 76,000 (includes Sweden)
Frequency: 11 issues/year
Years in Circulation: 12
Diver Group Scandinavia ApS
Thoravej 13, 3
Copenhagen NV, DK-2400
Tel.: 45 7026 3015
Fax: 45 7026 9015
martin@dykmag.net
www.dykmag.net

Sportsdykkeren (DA)
Circulation: 9,000
Frequency: 8 issues/year

Years in circulation: 5
Sorgenfri Allé 19
5250 Odense SV
Tel.: 26 71 65 24
redaktionen@sportsdykkeren.dk
www.sportsdykkeren.dk

FRANCE

Apnea
Circulation: 35,000
Frequency: 10 issues/year
Years in circulation: 20
Groupe Sofimav (F)
Future Building II
1280 Avenue des Platanes
Boirargues - 34970 Lattes
Tel.: 04 67 20 06 82
Fax. 04 67 20 06 83
infos@sofimav.com
www.apnea.fr

Bio sous-marine (F)
27 rue Louls Braille
75012 Paris
Tel,: 01 49 80 39 25
Fax. 01 49 56 15 22
polvert@octopus-fr.com
www.octopus-fr.com

Océans (F)
Circulation: 35,000
Frequency: bi-monthly
Years in circulation: 36
Groupe Sofimav
Future Building II
1280 Avenue des Platanes
Boirargues - 34970 Lattes
Tel.: 04 67 15 03 98
Fax. 04 67 20 06 83
info@sofimav.com
www.oceans.fr

Partir plonger (F)
Circulation: 30,000-35,000
Frequency: bi-monthly
Years in circulation: 2
Groupe Sofimav
Future Building II
1280 Avenue des Platanes
Boirargues - 34970 Lattes
info@sofimav.com
www.partirplonger.com

Plongée magazine (F)
Circulation: 35,000
Frequency: bi-monthly
Years in circulation: 12

Groupe Sofimav
Future Building II
1280 Avenue des Platanes
Boirargues - 34970 Lattes
Tel.: 04 67 22 22 78
Fax. 04 67 20 06 83
infos@sofimav.com
www.plongee-mag.net

Plongeurs international (F)
Circulation: 45,000
Frequency: 9 issues/year
Years in circulation: 9
6, avenue de Toulon
13006 MARSEILLE - France
Tel.: 33 0 4 91 17 72 50
Fax: 33 0 4 91 79 69 15
info@plongeursinternational.com
wwwplongeursinternational.com

Spéléo Magazine (F)
Circulation: 1,500
Frequency: quarterly
Years in circulation: 16
8 avenue L'Cygula
F-38700 CORENC France
Tel/Fax: 33(0)476 271 711
publicite@speleomag.com
www.speleomag.com

Subaqua (F)
Circulation: 25,000
Frequency: bi-monthly
Years in circulation: 18
24 quai de Rive Neuve
13284 Marseille cedex 07
Tel.: 04 91 33 99 76
Fax. 04 91 54 77 43
subaqua.pub@ffessm.fr
www.ffessm.fr

GERMANY

Divemaster (G)
Circulation: 30,000
Frequency: quarterly
Years in circulation: 14
Senefelderstr.10
70178 Stuttgart
Germany
Tel.: 0711 618378
Fax: 0711 612323
www.divemaster.de

Tauchen (G)
Circulation : 47,235 copies
Frequency: bi-monthly

Redaktion *tauchen*
Jessenstraße 1
D-22767 Hamburg
Tel.: 49 0 40 389 06 191
Fax: 49 0 40 389 06 303
www.tauchen.de

Unterwasser (G)
Frequency: monthly
In circulation: 12 years
Olympia-Verlag
Badstr. 4-6
D-90402 Nuernberg
Germany
Tel.: 0911 216 22 22
Fax: 0911 216 22 30
www.unterwasser.de

GREECE

Thalassa (GR)
Σε διαταγή PLANET SEA - Εκδόσεις Ε.
Ευγενιτάκης -
Σοφιανού 7 - Αθήνα 117 41
Tel.: 210 9213120
Fax: 210 9213125
info@thalassamag.gr www.thalassamag.gr

Vythos (GR)
Tel.: 7223168, 7250981
Fax: 7258787
www.netplan.gr/hellas/vythos

IRELAND

Subsea Magazine
Circulation: 5,000
Frequency: quarterly
Years in circulation: 25
Irish Underwater Council
78A Patrick Street
Dun Laoghaire
Co. Dublin, Ireland
Tel.: 353 0 1 2844601
Fax: 353 0 1 2844602
hq@irishunderwatercouncil.com
www.irishunderwatercouncil.com

ITALY

Aqua Geographia,
Life Above and Below Water
Frequency: quarterly
Aquapress
Via G. Falcone, 11
I-27010 Miradolo Terme (PV) Italy
Tel.: 39 0382 754707
Fax: 0382 754129

aquapress@pmp.it
www.aquageo.com

Aqva (I)
Circulation: 30,000
Frequency: 11 issues/yr
Years in circulation: 20
El mensual AQVA
Via Carroccio, 12
20123 - Milán (Italia)
Tel.: 39 02 3656 9512
Fax: 39 02 3656 9550
redazione@aqva.com
www.aqva.com

Archeologo Subacqueo (I)
Circulation: 1,200
Frequency: 3 issues/year
Years in circulation: 11
Roma Via Tripolitania 195
Italia 00199
Tel.: 080 5333056
Fax: 080 5333057
edipugli@tin.it
www.edipuglia.it/riviste/archeologo.php

Fotosub (I)
Adventures Srl
Emilio Morosini 27/A
Milano, Italy
Tel.: 02 55188494, 025517425
Fax: 02 5464407
info@fotosub.org
www.fotosub.org

Mondo Sommerso (I)
Frequency: 11 issues/year
Gruppo Editoriale Olimpia Spa
v. E. Fermi, 24
loc. Osmannoro
50019 Sesto Fiorentino
Firenze, Italia
Tel.: 055 30321
Fax: 055 3032280
mondosommerso@edolimpia.it
www.mondosommerso-online.it

Pesca in apnea (I)
Frequency: Monthly
Distribuzione Media S.p.A.
via Cazzaniga 2
20132 Milano,
Tel.: 02 25821
Fax: 02 25825 302
redazione@subacqueo.it
ilsubacqueo.subacqueo.it

Pescasub (I)
Circulation: 34,000

Frequency: monthly
Adventures Srl
Via E. Morosini 27/a
20135 MILANO - MI
Tel.: 02 55188494
Fax: 02 5464407
redazione@adventuresub.it
www.adventuresub.it

Sub (I)
Circulation: 20,000
Frequency: monthly
Adventures Srl
Via E. Morosini 27/a
20135 MILANO - MI
Tel.: 02 55188494
Fax: 02 5464407
advsub@tin.it
www.adventuresub.it

Subacqueo (I)
Frequency: monthly
Distribuzione Media S.p.A.
via Cazzaniga 2
20132 Milano,
Tel.: 02 25821
Fax: 02 25825302
redazione@subacqueo.it
www.subacqueo.it

JAPAN

Diving World (J)
Tel.: 045 770 5462
Fax: 045 770 5469
divingworld@mpcy.co.jp
www.divingworld.tv/

I Love Diving (J)
Marine Art Center Co.
Tel.: 03 3222 0311
Fax: 03 3222 0310
md@marinediving.co.jp
marinediving.com

Marine Diving (J)
Marine Art Center Co.
Tel.: 03 3222 0311
Fax: 03 3222 0310
md@marinediving.co.jp
marinediving.com

Marine Photo (J)
Marine Art Center Co.
Tel.: 03 3222 0311
Fax: 03 3222 0310
md@marinediving.co.jp
marinediving.com

KOREA (See South Korea)

MEXICO

Espacio profundo (SP)
The official DAN magazine for Latin-America
Circulation: 11,000
Frequency: bi-monthly
Years in circulation: 11 years
Mar Célebes No. 12-1
Col. Popotla México, D.F.
C.P. 11400
Tel/ fax: 52 55 5396 9058
espacioprofundo@prodigy.net.mx
espacioprofundo.com

NETHERLANDS

Duiken Magazine (DU)
Circulation: 26,500
Frequency: monthly
Years in circulation: 20
Postbus 7272
4800 GG Breda
Nederland
Tel.: 076 572 25 36
Fax: 076 572 25 35
duiken@vipmedia.nl
www.duiken.nl

IDDive Magazine (DU)
Frequency: quarterly
Nieuwpoortkade 16
1055 RX Amsterdam
Nederland
Tel.: 0900-2.000.000
Tel.: 31 0 20 6815148
Fax: 31 0 20 6880397
pde@iddworld.com
www.iddworld.com

NEW ZEALAND

Dive New Zealand / Dive Pacific (E)
Circulation: 23,500
Frequency: bi-monthly
Years in circulation: 14
Dive New Zealand Magazine distributed nation-wide into New Zealand.
Dive Pacific Magazine distributed into Australia and the South Pacific regon.
PO Box 42-020
Orakei, Auckland
New Zealand
Tel.: 64 9 521 0684
Fax: 64 9 521 3675
divenz@divenewzealand.co.nz
www.divenewzealand.com

www.dive-pacific.com

NORWAY

Dykking (N)
Circulation: 20,000
Frequency: bi-monthly
Years in circulation: 22 years
Forlaget Dykking AS
Postboks 233
N-3081 Holmestrand
Norway
Tel.: 47 33 05 05 68
Fax: 47 33 05 05 98
info@dykking.no
www.dykking.no

PHILIPPINES

Scuba Globe Asia Pacific (E)
Samon Publishing Co. Ltd.
89/72 Moo 2 Green Lake
Bang Na Trat, Bang Phli
Samut Prakan 10540
Thailand
Tel.: 66 1334 7539
Fax: 66 2316 0106
diver@scubaglobe.com
www.diver.com.ph

The Philippine Diver
Circulation: 8,000
Frequency: quarterly giveaway
Years in circulation: 15
Samon Publishing Inc.
P.O. Box 1587,
Metro Manila, Philippines.
Fax: 63 2 713 8882
h@diver.com.ph
www.diver.com.ph

POLAND

Magazyn Nurkowanie (PL)
ul. Kolumba 86
70-035 Szczecin
Tel.: 091 489 22 83
Tel/fax 091 482 68 08
dana@nurkowanie.v.pl
www.nurkowanie.v.pl

Wielki Błękit (PL)
Wydawnictwo Manta
al. Niepodległości 107/109
02-626 Warszawa
Tel.: 022 254 40 02
Fax: 022 254 40 02
e-mail: redakcja@wielkiblekit.pl

www.wielkiblekit.pl

PORTUGAL

Mundo submerso (PT)
Circulation: 12,000
Frequency: Monthly
Calibre 12 Editores, S.A.
Av. de Berna, 13
5° Drt°
1050-036 Lisbon
Tel.: 21 780 38 10
Fax: 21 780 38 11
editora@calibre12.pt
www.calibre12.pt

RUSSIA

Neptune XXI - Нептун XXI ВЕК (R)
Years in circulation: 6
24, Building 3, Leningradsky Avenue,
125040, Moscow, Russia
info@neptun21.ru
www.neptun21.ru

Octopus (E, R)
Frequency: bi-monthly
Years in circulation: 7
8/10, of. 603
Onezhskaya str.
Moscow, 125438
RUSSIA
Tel.: 7 095 741 45 93
Fax: 7 916 686 61 67
pg@octopus.ru
www.octopus.ru

Spearfishing World – Mir Podvodnoj Okhoty (R)
Frequency: bi-monthly
MK-Periodica
Ul.Giliarovskogo, 39,
Moscow, 129110, Russia
Tel.: 7 495 684 50 08
Fax: 7 495 681 37 98
info@periodicals.ru
www.podvoh.ru

Underwater Club (R)
Circulation: 30,000
Frequency: monthly
119021 Москва,
Фрунзенская наб., д. 2/1, кв. 20
Подводный Мир
Tel./fax: 7 095 245 3993
info@dive-magazine.ru
www.dive-magazine.ru

SINGAPORE

Asian Diver (E)
Circulation: 40,000
Frequency: bi-monthly + annual
Years in circulation: 14
MediaCorp Publishing Pte Ltd,
Techpoint #01-06/08
10 Ang Mo Kio St 65
Singapore 569059
Tel.: 6483 1555
Fax: 6484 2512
sales@mediacorppublishing.com.sg
www.asiandiver.com

Fins (E)
Circulation:
Frequency: bi-monthly
Years in circulation:
Frequency: Bi-monthly
17A Cavan Road
Singapore 209850
Tel.: 65 6292 5778
Fax: 65 6292 0302
www.finsonline.com

SOUTH AFRICA

DiveStyle (K)
Circulation: 15,000
Frequency: bi-monthly
Years in circulation: 16
PO Box 1737
Saxonworld 2132
South Africa
editor@divestyle.co.za
www.divestyle.co.za

SOUTH KOREA

Scuba Diver (K)
Frequency: bi-monthly
Years in circulation:
Tel.: 02 568 2402
Fax: 02 558 1207
diver@scuba-diver.net
www.scuba-diver.net

Underwater World (K)
Frequency: bi-monthly
Tel.: 02 547 3267
Fax: 02 547 3268
uwworld@hanafos.com
www.uwworld.co.kr

SPAIN

Buceo XXI (SP)

Apart. 1.847- 20.080
San Sebastián, Spain
Tel.: 943 21 4584
buceo21@buceo21.com
www.buceo21.com

Diving a fondo (SP)
Ancora 40
28045 Madrid
España
Tel.: 91 347 01 00
diving@mpib.es
www.divingafondo.com

Inmersión (SP)
Grupo V
C/ Valportillo Primera, 11
28108 Alcobendas Madrid - España
Tel.: 91 662 21 37
Fax. 91 662 26 54
inmersion@editorialv.es
www.grupov.es

Revista Apnea
Calle Fastenrath, n° 12
08035 Barcelona
Tel.: 93 417 38 76
Fax: 93 212 26 10
iriera@revistaapnea.com
www.revistaapnea.net/

Revista Buceadores
Calle Fastenrath, n° 12
08035 Barcelona
Tel.: 93 417 38 76
Fax.: 93 212
redaccion@revistabuceadores.com2
www.revistabuceadores.net

SWEDEN

DYK (SW)
Circulation: 76,000 (includes Denmark)
Frequency: 11 issues/year
Years in circulation: 26
Diver Group Scandinavia AB
Trollsjövägen 36
132 46 Saltsjö-Boo

SWITZERLAND

Aquanaut (G)
Circulation: 14,000
Frequency: bi-monthly
Years in circulation: 28
TOP Special Verlag AG
Alte Landstrasse 19
8596 Scherzingen

Switzerland
Tel.: 0041 0 71 680 02 60
Fax: 0041 0 71 680 02 64
info@aquanaut.ch
www.aquanaut.ch
Nereus (F, G, I)
Frequency: bi-monthly
Federation Suisse de Sports Subaquatiques
(SUSV-FSSS)
Pavillonweg, 3
3012 Bern
Tel.: 031 301 43 43
Fax: 031 301 43 93
admin@fsss.ch
www.fsss.ch

Taucher Revue (G)
Ildikó Isabella Komáromi
Giacomettistrasse 115
7000 Chur
Tel.: P 081 353 52 67
Tel.: G 081 258 33 33
Fax G 081 258 33 77
ildiko.komaromi@casanova.ch
www.taucher-revue.ch

THAILAND

Scuba Globe Thai Diver (E)
89/400, Moo 2,
Green Lake,
Bang Na Trad, Bang Pi,
Samut Prakan, 10540, Thailand
Tel.: 66-2 316 4331
passana@thaidiver.net
www.diver.com.ph/thaidiver

TURKEY

Deniz magazin (T)
Deniz Magazin Dergisi
Gazeteciler Mah.
Zincirlidere Cad.
Kýlýç Apt. No:42/-3
Esentepe/Ýstanbul
Tel.: 0 212 288 28 21 274 98 09
Fax: 0 212 267 43 93
deniz@denizmagazin.com.tr
www.denizmagazin.com.tr

UNITED KINGDOM

Beyond the Blue (E)
Frequency: quarterly
Old St. Lawrence School,
Westminster Road,
Liverpool, L4 3TQ, UK

Tel.: 44 0 151 933 8282
info@beyondmagazine.co.uk
www.beyondmagazine.co.uk

Dive Magazine (E)
Circulation: 41,622
Frequency: monthly
2nd Floor,
83/84 George Street,
Richmond, Surrey,
TW9 1HE, England.
Tel.: 020 8332 2709
Fax: 020 8332 9307 simon@dive.uk.com
 www.divemagazine.co.uk

Diver (E)
Circulation: 35,000
Frequency: monthly
Years in circulation: 43
*(Originally Triton, from 1963-79)

55 High Street
Teddington, Middlesex
TW11 8HA England
Tel.: 44 0 208 943 4288
Fax: 44 0 208 943 4312
bernard@divermag.co.uk
www.divernet.com

Diving Trade International (E)
Circulation: 25,000
Frequency: monthly (10 issues/year)
Jan/Feb; July/Aug.
Years in circulation: 6
Temple House, 221-225 Station Road,
Harrow, Middlesex, HA1 2TH
United Kingdom
Tel/Fax: 44 0 208 861 4565
headoffice@divingtradeint.com
www.divingtradeint.com

H₂Ops Magazine
Frequency: bi-monthly
Years in circulation: 2
Davis Sharples Media Ltd
PO Box 452, Winchester, Hants, SO23 3AA, UK
Tel.: 44 0 1962 760601
www.cdimagazine.com

International Ocean Systems
Circulation: 10,000
Frequency: bi-monthly
Years in circulation: 27
(originally launched in 1979 as International
Underwater Systems Design; in 1997 the title
changed to International Ocean Systems
Design and in 2000 it became International
Ocean Systems.

55 High Street
TEDDINGTON
Middlesex
TW11 8HA UK
Tel.: 44 0 20 8943 4288
Fax: 44 0 20 8943 4312
astrid@divermag.co.uk
www.intoceansys.co.uk

Scottish Diver (E)
Frequency: quarterly
5 Craighall House
58a, High Craighall Road
Glasgow, G4 9UD
Tel.: 0141-425-1021
hq@scotsac.com
www.scotsac.com

Underwater Contractor Magazine (E)
Frequency: bi-monthly
Underwater World Publications Ltd.
55 High Street, Teddington
Middx., TW11 8HA, United Kingdom
Tel.: 44 0 20 8943 4288
Fax: 44 0 20 8943 4312
editor@under-water.co.uk
www.under-water.co.uk

USA

Advanced Diver Magazine (E)
Circulation: 20,000
Frequency: monthly
Advanced Diver Magazine
P.O. Box 21222
Bradenton, FL 34204-1222 USA
Tel.: 941 748 3483
AdvDvrMag@aol.com
www.advanceddivermagazine.com

Baja Life Magazine (E)
Circulation: 15,000
Frequency: quarterly
P.O. Box 4917
Laguna Beach, CA 92652
Tel.: 949 376 2252
Fax: 949 376 7575
admin@bajalife.com
www.bajalifemag.com

California Diving News (E)
Circulation: 25.000
Frequency: monthly
Years in circulation: 22
P.O. Box 11231
Torrance, CA
90510 USA
Tel.: 310 792 2333

Fax: 310 792 2336
mail@saintbrendan.com
www.saintbrendan.com

Dive Chronicles (E)
Frequency: quarterly
1323 SE 17th Street # 308
Fort Lauderdale, Florida 33316
Tel.: Toll Free 888 557-2822
International: 954 520 8888
Fax: 954 337 2223
Email: info@divechronicles.com
www.divechronicles.com

Dive Training (E)
Frequency: monthly
5215 Crooked Road
Parkville, MO 64152
USA
Tel.: 816 741 5151
Fax: 816 741 6458
divetraining@spc-mag.com
www.dtmag.com

Fathoms (E)
Frequency: quarterly
Years in circulation: 5
910 Echo Place.
Gatlinburg TN 37738
Tel.: 888 744 3182
Fax: 865 686 6287
admin@fathomspub.com
www.fathomspub.com

Hawaii Skin Diver (E)
Circulation: 12,000
Frequency: quarterly
Years in circulation: 10
1733 Dillingham Blvd
Honolulu, HI
USA 96819
Tel.: 808 843 8182
Fax: 808 848 5539
hanapaafishing@hawaii.rr.com
www.hawaiiskindiver.net

Historical Diver Magazine (E)
Circulation: 4,000 (39 countries)
Frequency: quarterly
Years in circulation: 14
Historical Diving Society USA
PO BOX 2837
Santa Maria
· CA 93457
Tel.: 805 934 1660
Fax: 805 938 0550
hds@hds/orgwww.hds.org

Northwest Dive News (E)
Circulation: 20,000
Frequency: monthly
PO Box 1494
Oak Harbor, WA 98277
Tel.: 360) 240-1874
Fax Number (360) 279-1814
nwdiver@nwdivenews.com
www.nwdivenews.com

Ocean News and Technology (E)
Circulation: 25,000
Frequency: 6 times/year
Years in circulation: 25
Technology Systems Corporation
P.O. Box 1096
Palm City, Florida 34991 USA
Tel.: 1 772 221 7720
Fax: 1 772 221 7715
techsystems@sprintmail.com
www.ocean-news.com

Ocean Realm Journal (E)
Circulation: 12,500
Frequency: quarterly
8802 E. Broadway, Suite #412
Tucson, AZ, USA 58710
Tel.: 352.817.5893
Fax: 801 697 4672
Info@OceanRealmMedia.com
www.oceanrealmjournal.com

Sea Technology
Circulation: 15,774
Frequency: monthly
Years in circulation: 46
1501 Wilson Blvd., Suite 1001
Arlington, VA 22209
Tel.: 703 524 3136
Fax: 703 841 0852
seatechorder@sea-technology.com
www.sea-technology.com

Scuba Diving (E)
Frequency: monthly
6600 Abercorn St., Suite 208
Savannah, GA 31405
Tel.: 912 351 0855
Fax: 912 351 0890
edit@scubadiving.com
www.scubadiving.com

Scuba News (Florida) (E)
Frequency: monthly
Years in circulation: 20
5395 Lenox Ave
Jacksonville, Florida
USA 32205
Tel.: 904 783 1610

Fax: 904 693 0474
godiving@scubanews.com
www.scubanews.com

Shark Diver Magazine (E)
Circulation: 10,000
Frequency: quarterly
Years in circulation: 3.5
P.O. Box 1179
1300 N. Alamo Rd
Alamo, TX 78516
Tel.: 956 782 7969
Fax: 956 782 8119
www.sharkdivermag.com

Spearfishing Magazine (E)
Frequency: quarterly
Enterprise Publications
649 U.S. Hwy. One, Suite 3
North Palm Beach, FL
USA 33408
Tel.: 561 622 8922
www.spearfishingmagazine.com

Sport Diver (E)
Frequency: quarterly
Years in circulation: 3
World Publications
460 North Orlando Ave
Suite 200
Winter Park, FL 32789
Tel.: 407 628 4802
Fax: 407 628 7061
carolyn.pascal@worldpub.net
www.sportdiver.com

Undercurrent (E)
Circulation: 15,000
Frequency: monthly
Years in circulation: 31
3120 Sausalito
Ca 94966
Fax: 415.289.0137
editor@undercurrent.org
www.undercurrent.org

DIVING WEBSITES

A listing of current websites from around the world: e-magazines, newsletters, directories, etc. The following links do not include the websites of print magazines. The name of the e-zine or website is followed with either the country of origin or the language of site. To suggest new links or to

report broken links, please contact us at:
info@divingalmanac.com

AcuSub **(Spain)**
www.acusub.net

Aqualog Magazine **(Canada)**
www.aqualog.com

Aquanet **(Spain)**
www.revista-aquanet.com

Bluworld **(Italy)**
www.bluworld.com

Buzos **(Argentina)**
www.buzosargentinos.org.ar

Bulles de rêves **(France)**
www.bulles-de-reves.com

Cousteau World **(French & English)**
www.cousteau.org/

Cyber Diver News Network **(U.S.A.)**
www.cdnn.info

DécomPresse **(Canada)**
http://decompresse.net

Deeper Blue **(U.K.)**
www.deeperblue.net

Dive Girls **(U.K.)**
http://users.aber.ac.uk/mdb2

Divernet **(U.K.)**
www.divernet.com

Dive News **(U.S.A.)**
www.divenews.com

Dive Site Directory **(U.K.)**
Online diving information
www.divesitedirectory.com

Diving history **(Denmark)**
www.dykkehistorisk.dk

Escafandra **(Spanish)**
www.escafandra.org

eScuba **(U.S.A.)**
www.escuba.com

Explore UnderWater **(U.S.A.)**
www.exploreuw.com

Fins Online **(Asia Pacific)**
www.finsonline.com

Girl Diver **(U.S.A.)**
www.girldiver.com

Historical Diving Times **(U.K.)**
www.thehds.com

Net Divers **(Argentina)**
http://netdivers.tripod.com.ar

Plongez Loisir **(France)**
www.aquanaute.com/PlongezLoisir

Quest **(U.S.A.)**
www.dirquest.com

Revista de buceo **(Mexico)**
www.scuba.com.mx

ScubaCore DVD **(U.S.A.)**
www.scubacore.com

Scuba Guide **(Canada)**
www.thescubaguide.com

ScubaWeb **(Italy)**
www.nautica.it/scubaweb

Skin Diver Online **(U.S.A.)**
www.skin-diver.com

Underwater Photography **(U.K.)**
www.uwpmag.com

Unterwasserfoto **(Germany)**
www.unterwasserfoto.com

UnterWasserWelt **(Germany)**
www.unterwasserwelt.de

Underwater Times **(U.S.A.)**
http://underwaterTimes.com

Verband Deutscher Tauchlehrer e.V
Newsletter **(Germany)**
www.vdtl.de

X-Ray Mag **(Denmark)**
www.xray-mag.com

BOOKS

To suggest new books, please contact us
at: **info@divingalmanac.com**

Title
Author
Publisher and year
Genre

2006

Best Dives of the Caribbean
Joyce Huber
Hunter Publishing (2006)
Destination

Deeper into Diving 2nd Edition
John Lippmann & Dr. Simon Mitchell
Aqua Quest Publications, Inc. (2006)

Dive in Style
Tim Simond
Thames & Hudson (2006)
Travel

Diver Travel Guide
Underwater World Publications (2006)
Travel

Diving the World
Beth Tierney, Shaun Tierney
Footprint Handbooks (2006)

Diving to a Deep-Sea Volcano:
Kenneth Mallory
Houghton Mifflin Company (2006)

First Dive to Shark Dive
Peter Lourie
Boyds Mills Pr (2006)
Diving (children)

For the Love of Scuba
David Huntrods
Weigl (2006)

Scuba Diving
Monty Hall
DK Publishing (2006)

The Art of Diving: Adventures in the Underwater World
Nick Hanna, Alex Mustard
Ultimate Sports Publications Ltd (2006)
Spiritual

World Atlas of Marine Fishes
Helmut Debelius, Rudie H. KuiterHollywood
Import & Export, Inc. (2006)
Atlas

FRENCH

La Saga des épaves de la Côte d'Albâtre - Tome 2
Yvon Chartier - Anthony Lalouelle - François Mathieu - Michel Torché
Éditions du G.R.I.E.M.E. (2006)

L'orientation sous-marine en plongée loisir
Alain Perrier
Éditeur Plaisancier (2006)

Manuel de plongée au Nitrox - 2eme Edition
Jean-Louis Blanchard - Jean-Yves Kersalé
Editions Gap (2006)

Plongée sans Frontières
Henri Eskanazi
Editions GAP (2006)

2005

A Diver's Guide to Underwater Malaysia – Macrolife
Andrea and Antonella Ferrari
Nautilus Publishing (2005)

Black Saturday
Alexander McKee
Aquapress (2005)
Historical

Cayman Cowboys
Eric Douglas
Publish America (2005)
Fiction

Collins Gem Sharks
Collins (2005)
Sea life

Complete Diving Manual
Jack Jackson
International Marine/Ragged Mountain Press (2005)
Manual

Coral Reefs: Nature's Wonders
Walter Deas, Jean Deas
Western Australia Museum (2005)
Sea life

Dangerous Depths
Kathy Brandt
Penguin Group (2005)
Fiction

Dark Descent: Diving and the Deadly Allure of the Empress of Ireland
Kevin McMurray
American Media International (2005)
Wreck diving

DDRC Underwater Diving Accident Manual
DDRC
Aquapress (2005)
Technical

Deep, Dark, and Dangerous: Adventures and Reflections on the Andrea Doria
Gary Gentile
Gary Gentile Productions (2005)
Historical

Digital Imaging for the Underwater Photographer
Jack and Sue Drafahl
Aquapress (2005)
Photography

Dive West Scotland
Lawson Wood
Underwater World Publications (2005)
Guide

Diver Down
Michael R. Ange
International Marine/Ragged Mountain Press (2005)
Dive stories

Diving Bermuda, Second Edition (Aqua Quest Diving Series)
Jesse Cancelmo, Mike Strohofer
Aqua Quest Publications, Inc. (2005)
Guide

Diving in Thailand
Colin Piprell and Ashley J Boyd
Times Editions (2005)
Guide
Diving the World's Coral Reefs
Editor Jack Jackson
New Holland Publishers (UK) (2005)
Sea life

Double Cross
Patrick Woodrow
Aquapress (2005)
Fiction

Extreme Diving
Kim Covert
Edge Books (2005)
Diving general

Great British Marine Animals: 2nd Edition
Paul Naylor
Sound Diving Publications (2005)
Sea life

Guide to Sea Anemones and Corals of Britain and Ireland
C. Wood
Marine Conservation Society (2005)
Sea life

How to Manage Diving Problems
Penguin Books (SA) (Pty) Ltd (2005)

Into the Abyss: Diving to Adventure in the Liquid World
Rod Macdonald
Mainstream Publishing (2005)
Diving general

Marine Life of the Pacific Northwest
Andy Lamb, Bernard P. Hanby
Harbour Publishing (2005)

Master Guide for Underwater Digital Photography
Jack Drafahl and Sue Drafahl
Amhert Media (2005)
Photography

No Safe Harbor : The Tragedy of the Dive Ship Wave Dancer
Joe Burnworth
Emmis Books (2005)
Historical

Nudibranch Behavior
David W. Behrens, Constantinos Petrinos
New World Publications (2005)
Sea life

Ocean Gladiator
Mark Ellyatt
Emily Eight Publications (2005)
Diving general

Oceans: Surviving in the Deep Sea (X-Treme Places)
Michael Sandler
Bearport Publishing (2005)
Ocean

Out of the Blue: A Journey Through the World's Oceans
By Paul Horsman
The MIT Press (2005)
Sea life

Scuba Diving (Extreme Sports)
Carol Ryback
Gareth Stevens Publishing (2005)
Technical

Sea Salt: Memories & Essays
Stan Waterman
New World Publications (2005)
Dive stories

Seamanship a guide for divers
BSAC
Aquapress (2005)
Guide

Seasearch Guide to Sea Anemones and Corals of Britain and Ireland
Chris Wood
Seasearch (2005)
Sea life

Sharks of the World
Leonard Compagno, Marc Dando & Sarah Fowler
Collins (2005)
Sea life

Sipadan, Mabul, Kapalai
Scubazoo, Co-author Simon Christopher
Natural History Publications (2005)
(Borneo)

Sylvia Earle
by Beth Baker (Author)
Lerner Publishing Group (2005)
Diving General Children

The Art Of Living Under Water
Marten Triewald
Historical Diving Society (2005)
Historical

The Art of Living Under Water
Marten Triewald
Historical Diving Society (2005)
Manual

The Devil's Teet : A True Story of Obsession and Survival Among America's Great White Sharks
Susan Casey
Henry Holt and Co. (2005)
The Essential Underwater Photography Manual
Larry and Denise Tackett
Aquapress (2005)
Photography

The Essential Underwater Photography Manual
Denise & Larry Tackett
RotoVision (2005)

Photography

The Essential Underwater Photography Manual
Denise Nielson Tackett and Larry Tackett
Rotovision (2005)
Photography

The Life and Death of the Liverpool Barque Dryad (1874-91)
Henry Alexander
Aunemouth Books (2005)
Wreck diving

The Red Sea - Underwater Paradise
A. Mojetta
Aquapress (2005)
Sea life

The Saltwater Wilderness
Glenn Vanstrum
Oxford University Press (2005)
Sea life

Under Antartic Ice: The Photographs of Norbert Wu
Norbert Wu and Jim Mastro
University of California Press (2005)
Photography

Under Water To Get Out Of The Rain
By Trevor Norton
Century (2005)
Diving general

Underwater Digital Video Made Easy
Steven Barsky, Lance Milbrand & Mark Thurlow.
Hammerhead Press (2005)
Photography

United States Navy Diver
Mark V. Lonsdale
Best Publishing Company (2005)
Historical

Warriors From The Deep
Eric Micheletti
Histoire and Collections (2005)
History

FRENCH

Apnée : De l'initiation à la performance
Umberto Pelizzari, Stefano Tovaglieri
Éditeur Amphora (2005)

100 belles plongées en Languedoc-Roussillon

Éric Dutrieux, Sébastien Thorin et Jean-Yves Jouvene
Éditions Gap

100 belles plongées à Marseille et dans sa région
Scorsonelli, Boghossian, Chauvez et Garrier
Éditions Gap

2004 & EARLIER

A Diver's Guide to Underwater Malaysia Macrolife
Andrea and Antonella Ferrari
Nautilus Publishing (2004)
Sea life

Adventures with Sharks
Jonathan Bird
Best Publishing (2004)
Sea life

Aliens of the Deep
James Cameron
Aquapress (2004)
Ocean

An Essential Guide to Digital Underwater Photography
Michael Aw
www.OceanNEnvironment.com (2004)
Photography

Bound For Australia
Edward J Bourke
Edward J Bourke (2004)
Wreck diving

Chariots of War
Robert W Hobson
Ulric Publishing (2004)
Underwater warfare

Cold Water Diving: A Guide to Ice Diving
John N. Heine
Best Publishing Company (2004)
Technical

Coral Reef Guide to the Red Sea
Robert Myers and Ewan Lieske
Collins (2004)
Sea life

Dark Water Dive: An Underwater Investigation
Kathy Brandt
Mass Market Paperback (2004)
Fiction

Deep Sea Odyssey
Yves Paccalet & Sophie de Wilde
Hachette (2004)
Photography

Descent into Darkness : Pearl Harbor, 1941: A Navy Diver's Memoir
Edward Raymer
Random House (2004)
Military

Dive: The Ultimate Guide To 60 Of The Worlds Top Dive Locations
Monty Halls
Firefly Books Ltd (2004)
Guide

Diving Cozumel, 2nd Edition
Steve Rosenberg
Aqua Quest Publications, Inc. (2004)
Guide

Diving in Darkness
Martin Farr
Aquapress (2004)
Cave diving

Diving in Thailand
Colin Piprell and Ashley J Boyd
Times Editions (2004)

Diving Science
Michael Strauss and Igor V. Aksenov
Human Kinetics Publishers (2004)
Manual

Encyclopedia of underwater archaeology
By Mare Nostrum
Periplus (2004)

End of Voyages
Michael Stammers
Tempus Publishing (2004)
Ships

Essential guide to Digital Underwater Photography
Michael Aw with Mathieu Meur
OceanNEnvironment (2004)
Photography

Hidden Splendors of the Yucatan
Lalo Fiorelli
Hidden Splendors Publishing (2004)
Cave diving

Into The Abyss – Diving To Adventure In The Liquid

By Rod Macdonald
Mainstream Publishing (2004)
Diving general

Last of the Blue Water Hunters
Carlos Eyles
Aqua Quest Publications (2004)
Dive stories

Lost On The Ocean Floor: Diving The World's Ghost Ships
John Christopher Fine
Naval Institute Press (2004)
Wreck diving

Manual of Freediving: Underwater on a Single Breath (Freediving)
Umberto Pelizzari, Stefano Tovaglieri
Idelson Gnocchi Pub (2004)
Freediving

Marine Fish & Invertebrates of Northern Europe
Frank Emil Moen, Erling Svensen
Aquapress (2004)
Sea life

Naval Forces under the Sea: A look Back, A Look Ahead
United States Navy (2004)
Diving Navy

NSS Cave Diving Manual - Revised Edition
C Mahaney & A W Mahaney
Aquapress (2004)
Cave diving

Raggie Sanctuary
Chano Montelongo and Jorge Keller
Deep Blue Video (2004)
Sea life

Reef Fish Identification: Baja to Panama
Paul Humann, Ned Deloach
New World Publications (2004)
Sea life

Scuba Bunnies
Christine Loomis, Ora Eitan
Grosset & Dunlap (2004)
Dive stories

Shadow Divers
Robert Kurson
Random House (2004)
Historical

Shipwrecks of the Cayman Islands - A diving guide to historic & modern shipwrecks
L. Wood

Aquapress (2004)
Wreck diving

Shipwrecks of the Isle of Man
Adrian Corkill
Tempus Publishing (2004)
Wreck diving

Silent World (NG Adventure Classics)
Jacques Cousteau
National Geographic (2004)
Ocean

Simple Guide to Commercial Diving
Steven M. Barsky and Robert W. Christensen
Hammerhead Press (2004)
Manual

Sunken Cities, Sacred Cenotes & Golden Sharks: Travels of a Water-Bound Adventurer
Bill Belleville
University of Georgia Press (2004)
Sea life

Svalbard and the Life in Polar Oceans
Aquapress (2004)
Sea life

Swimming with the Dead: An Underwater Investigation
Kathy Brandt
Mass Market Paperback (2004)
Fiction

Technical Diving From the Bottom Up
Kevin Gurr
Aquapress (2004)
Manual

The Certified Diver's Handbook: The Complete Guide to Your Own Underwater Adventures
Clay Coleman
International Marine/Ragged Mountain Press (2004)
Manual

The Comprehensive Guide to Shipwrecks of the East Coast, Volume 2 (1918-2003)
Ron Young
Tempus Publishing (2004)
Guide
The DAN Guide to Dive Medical FAQs
Divers Alert Network
Manual

The Dive - A Story of Love and Obsession
'Pipin' Ferreras
Aquapress (2004)
Free diving

The Essential Underwater Guide to North Wales, Vol 1
Chris Holden
Calgo Publications (2004)
Guide

The Jaws Of Death
Xavier Maniguet
Collins (2004)
Sea life

The Jaws of Turmoil
Neil Clift
Self-Publishing Network (2004)
Fiction

The Shipwrecks Off North East Norfolk
Ayer Tikus
Ayer Tikus Publications (2004)
Wreck diving

The Simple Guide to Commercial Diving
Steven M. Barsky
Hammerhead Press (2004)
Guide

The Treasure
Kathleen Harrison
Authorhouse (2004)
Fiction

The Universe Next Door: A Personal Odyssey
Judith Hemenway
Best Publishing Company (2004)
Diving general

Thirteenth Beach : Diving Adventures Around the World
Wade Hughes
iUniverse, Inc. (2004)
Dive stories

Titanic's Predecessor
Per Kristian Sebak
Seaward Publishing (2004)
Wreck diving

Underwater Caribbean
Kurt Amsler
Random House Inc (2004)
Guide

Underwater Video - A step by step guide
John Boyle
Circle Books (2004)
Photography

Whales & Dolphins of the World
Mark Simmonds
Aquapress (2004)
Sea life

Wreck Hunter - The Quest for Lost Shipwrecks
Terry Dwye
Aquapress (2004)
Wreck diving

Wrecks - The World's Best Dives
Egidio Trainito, editor
White Star S.p.A. (2004)
Wreck diving

Dive Atlas of the World: An Illustrated Reference to the Best Sites
Jack Jackson
New Holland Publishers (UK) (2003)
Guide

Diving in Darkness: Beneath Rock, Under Ice, into Wrecks
Martyn Farr, M. Farr, C. Howes
Wild Places Publishing (2003)
Wreck diving

Diving the World: Photography by Norbert Wu
Ken McAlpine, Norbert Wu
Hugh Lauter Levin Associates (2003)
Photography

Fatal Depth: Deep Sea Diving, China Fever, and the Wreck of the Andrea Doria
Joe Haberstroh
The Lyons Press (2003)
Historical

Fish Face
David Doubilet
Phaidon Press (2003)
Sea life

Great Lakes Shipwrecks: A Photographic Odyssey
Gary Gentile
Gary Gentile Productions (2003)
Wreck diving

Deep Descent : Adventure and Death Diving the Andrea Doria
Joe Haberstroh
Atria (2002)
Historical

Submerged: Adventures of America's Most Elite Underwater Archeology Team
Daniel F. Lenihan
Newmarket Press (2002)

Historical

Technical Diving in Depth
Bruce R. Wienke
Best Publishing Company (2002)
Manual

The Last Dive : A Father and Son's Fatal Descent into the Ocean's Depths
Bernie Chowdhury
Harper Paperbacks (2002)
Historical

In the Wake of Galleons
Robert F. Marx
Best Publishing Company (2001)
Wreck diving

The Salvage of the Century
Ric Wharton
Best Publishing Company (2001)
Wreck diving

Cousteau's Great White Shark
Jean-Michel Cousteau, Mose Richards , Harry
N. Abrams (2000)
Sea life

SS Yongala: Townsville's Titanic
Max Gleeson
Max Gleeson Publishing (2000)
Wreck Diving

Stars Beneath the Sea: The Pioneers of Diving
Trevor Norton
Arrow (2000)
Historical

Deep, Deeper, Deepest: Man's Exploration of the Sea
Robert F. Marx
Best Publishing Company (1999)
Historical

Diving in High-Risk Environments
Steven M. Barsky
Hammerhead Press (1999)
Manual

Diving Pioneers: History of Diving in America
Eric Hanauer
Watersport Publishing (1994)
History

The Ocean World
Jacques Cousteau
Harry N Abrams (1985)
Sea life

MOVIES & DOCUMENTARIES

To suggest new books, movies or documentaries, please contact us at:
info@divingalmanac.com

Title
Author and/or producer, year

2005

Aliens of the Deep
IMAX (Walt Disney) 2005

A World Below: Malta
H2Ocean Underwater Productions (2005)

British Sea Life
Anita Sherwood (2005)

California Marine Life Identification
Hammerhead Video (2005)

Deep Blue
BBC Productions (2005)

Discovery of Sacred Waters
Curt Bowen
ADM Productions (2005)

Dreams of "Admiral Nakhimov"
Russian Underwater Expeditions (2005)

Into the Blue
Sony Pictures (2005)

Jungle Blue
Sharkbay Films (2005)

Lost Submarines of the Royal Navy
Periscope Publishing (2005)

Marine Passions - submerge the senses
Planula Productions & GreenhouseFx (2005)
Memories of Salem Express
Russian Underwater Expeditions (2005)

Naturally Ningaloo
Wet & Dry Productions (2005)

Ocean Weirdo's
Sharkbay Films (2005)

Prisoners of Abu-Nukhas

Russian Underwater Expeditions (2005)

Rulers of the Ocean
IMAX (2005)

Submerged
Emmett/Furla Films Production Corporation (2005)

The cave
Screen Gems (2005)

The Jacques Cousteau Odyssey
Warner Brothers (2005)
1 The Nile
2 Calypso`s Search for Atlantis
3 Time Bomb at 50 Fanthoms
  Mediterranean: Cradle or Coffin?
4 Calypso`s Search for the Britannic
  Diving for Roman Plunder
5 Blind Prophets of Easter Island
  Clipperton: The Island Time Forgot
6 Lost Relics of the Sea
  The Warm-blooded Sea: Mammals of the Deep

The Lost Radeau
Lake George Documentary 1758 Warship (2005)

Totally Wrecked
Full Circle Expeditions (2005)

2004 & EARLIER

Australia's Great Barrier Reef
David Hannan Productions (2004)

Cave Diving Beneath the Ozark Mountains
Richard Dreher, Eric Parker Andersen
Expedition Divers (2004)

Diving Instructors: Roles, Responsibilities & Risk Assessments
HSE, 08701 545500, www.hse.gov.uk (2004)

Diving in Russia
Russian Underwater Expeditions (2004)

Email from a Shark
Sharkbay Films (2004)

Eye on the Reef
David Hannan Productions (2004)

Fathom 1
Ambrosia Productions (2004)

"Mikhail Lermontov". The last cruise.
Russian Underwater Expeditions (2004)

Night of the Sea - A Visual Meditation
Mach 1 Audio (2004)

Ningaloo
David Hannan Productions (2004)

Raptures, an Underwater Odyssey
David Hannan Productions (2004)

ScubaCore DVD Issues I, II, III
Core Group Ltd. (2004)

Sea Spies (2004)
Winstar (2004)

Sipadan - the Island of turtles
Russian Underwater Expeditions (2004)

The Big Wet
ABC Productions (2004)

The Blue Experience
Scuba Scenes (2004)

The dive into Antarctica
Russian Underwater Expeditions (2004)

The Life Aquatic with Steve Zissou
Miramax Home Entertainment (2004)

The Silent Wrecks of Truk Lagoon
MBH Productions (2004)

The Simple Guide to Boat and Wreck Diving
Hammerhead Video (2004)

The Simple Guide to Boat and Wreck Diving (DVD
Steve and Kristine Barsky (2004)

The Wreck Hunters: Dive to the Wreck of the USS Bass
NorLantique Video LLC (2004)

They
Russian Underwater Expeditions (2004)

Watery Creatures and Rocky Shores
David Hannan Productions (2004)

Wolves of the Sea
ABC Productions (2004)

Atlantis: Milo's Return

Walt Disney Home Studio (2003)

Atlantis (Sub) (2000)
Sony Pictures (2003)

Baby Genius: Underwater Adventures
Warner Home Video (2003)

California Lobster Diving
Hammerhead Video (2003)

Coral Reef Adventure (2003)
Greg MacGillivray
Image Entertainment
1 The making of and retrospective
2 Coral Reef Adventure

Drysuit Diving in Depth
Hammerhead Video (2003)

Open Water
Lions Gate Films (2003)

Into the Deep
IMAX (2002)

The Blue Planet (2002)
BBC/Discovery Channel Co-Production
Ocean World/Frozen Seas
Open Ocean/The Deep
Seasonal Seas/Coral Seas
Tidal Seas/Coasts

Atlantis: The Lost Empire
Disney Studios (2001)

Azure Dreams of Existence: A Visual Meditation
Mach 1 Audio (2001)

Diving Into Darkness: The Elements of Safe Night Diving
Robert N. Rossier (2001)

Journey Into Amazing Caves
Image Entertainment (2001)

U-234-Hitler's Last U-Boat
Andreas Gutzeit (2001)
Dolphins
Greg MacGillivray
Image Entertainment (2000)

Men of Honor
Twentieth Century-Fox (2000)

Nova - Hitler's Lost Sub
Wgbh Boston (2000)

Ocean Men
IMAX (2000)

Wonders of the Deep
Madacy Records (2000)

Into the Depths of the Ocean
IMAX (1993-1999)
The Great Barrier Reef
The Search for the Great Sharks
Hidden Hawaii
Whales: An Unforgettable Journey

Island of the Sharks
Image Entertainment (1999)

The Great Barrier Reef
CAV Distribution (1999)

The Search for the Great Sharks
CAV Distribution (1999)

Australia's Great Barrier Reef
National Geographic (1998)

Secrets of the Ocean Realm
PBS Home Video (1998)

Sphere
Warner Home Video (1998)

Wonders of the Deep: Australia/ Queensland
Madacy Records (1998)

Wonders of the Deep:Costa Rica Cocos Islands/Galapagos Islands
Madacy Records (1998)

Wonders of the Deep: Emerald Sea/British Columbia Shipwrecks
Madacy Records (1998)

Whales: An Unforgettable Journey
IMAX (1997)

Coral Sea Dreaming
DVD International (1996)

The Living Sea
Image Entertainment (1995)

Blue Planet
IMAX (1990)

Dead Calm
Warner Studios (1989)

Lords of the Deep
Concorde Productions (1989)

The Abyss
Twentieth Century-Fox (1989)

The Big Blue
Gaumont (1988)

For Your Eyes Only
MGM/Ua Studios (1981)
The Deep
Sony Pictures (1977)

Jaws
Universal (1975)

Thunderball
MGM/UA Studios (1965)

Voyage to the Bottom of the Sea
Twentieth Century-Fox (1961)

20,000 Leagues Under the Sea
Walt Disney Home Studio (1954)

Beneath the Twelve Mile Reef
Twentieth Century-Fox (1953)

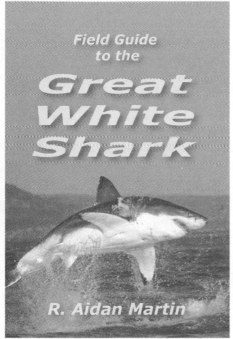

Field Guide to the Great White Shark

R. Aidan Martin

The Ultimate Guide to Great White Watching

The definitive, world-wide guide on when and where to watch Great White Sharks and how to interpret their behavior. Includes:

- Great White Shark "hot spots" around the globe
- A comprehensive illustrated catalogue of Great White Shark surface and social behaviors
- Guidelines for watching Great White Sharks
- Tips for cage diving
- Tips on photographing and filming Great White Sharks
- The world's best Great White watching sites, including when to go, what conditions to expect, and how to get there
- Safety tips for divers
- Interactive CD-ROM, featuring specially created computer animations, film clips of spectacular Great White behavior, and web-links to selected on-line resources

Chapter 13

U/W PHOTO & VIDEO

The underwater world is a fantastic and unique place for producing underwater imagery. Training and equipment is readily accessible to all levels of divers and budgets. Knowing how to use your camera equipment and applying proven techniques is the key to becoming a successful photographer or videographer.

ter imagery, modern and user-friendly camera systems make it possible for even beginners to bring back unforgettable souvenirs of their underwater explorations.

SOURCE: CMAS/AMCQ

FILMMAKING

We have all seen educational and entertainment films about the marine world. Underwater filmmakers create these wonderful films that you have seen. This is not an easy career to enter because filmmakers must work on their own with the hope that someone will want the films, but the job is very rewarding. A related career would be underwater videography in which a person takes videos for various fields like education, oil companies, or tourism.

SOURCE: NOAA

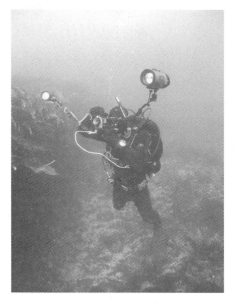

John Batt frames a shot using a Nikonos V in the North Atlantic. Photo: J. Gallant / D.A.Y.

In addition to applying safe diving practices, photographers must also pay attention to physical phenomena that affect image quality and composition such as refraction, absorption, diffusion, color disparity, field of view reduction, etc. Despite the many difficulties involved in underwa-

Underwater film session at Montreal's Olympic Stadium. Photo: J. Gallant / D.A.Y.

SCIENCE

Scientists also rely on photography and videography to conduct their work.

Underwater video footage can be collected in a variety of ways. Cameras can be vertically dropped from a ship, towed, hand-held by divers, or mounted on remotely operated vehicles (ROVs). All of these methods are subject to negative effects due to poor water clarity. The specific method employed is determined based on water depth, water clarity, size of survey area, purpose for survey, and costs of operating the equipment.

SOURCE: NOAA

Sea & Sea DX-D100 Housing and YS-90AUTO strobe.
Photo: www.seaandsea.com

EQUIPMENT

PHOTO

There are countless camera systems on the market for every budget. Modern photo systems typically include a digital camera, a waterproof housing and a lighting system made up of one or more strobe lights. Housings are usually made of aluminum or clear plastic with various pressure limitations.

Sea & Sea DX-D100 Housing and YS-90AUTO & YS-90DX (slave) strobes. Photo: www.seaandsea.com

VIDEO

The most popular video systems include DV (Digital Video) or HD (High Definition) cameras, a housing, video lights and a battery pack. Affordable HD systems allow even sport divers the opportunity to film TV quality images.

Amphibico HD Amphibicam
Photo courtesy Amphibico - amphibico.com

Amphibico DV housing system and ARC lamps. Photo courtesy Amphibico - amphibico.com

Amphibico *Phenom* Pro Digital Marine Housing and ARC lamps. Photo courtesy Amphibico – www.amphibico.com

INTERNET LINKS

- ➤ Digideep (www.digideep.com)
- ➤ DivePhotoGuide.com (www.divephotoguide.com)
- ➤ Dive Portal Video Magazine (www.diveportaldvd.com)
- ➤ The Underwater Photographer (www.theunderwaterphotographer.com)
- ➤ Underwater Photography (www.underwaterphotography.com)
- ➤ Underwater Photography Magazine (www.uwpmag.com)
- ➤ Wetpixel (www.wetpixel.com)

INTL FESTIVALS & COMPETITIONS

CZECH REPUBLIC

International Film Festival Voda, More, Oceany (Water, Seas, Oceans)
October 17-18, 2006
Host: University of Jan Evangelista Purkyně
IFF
Milady Horákové 107
Praha 6, 160 00
Czech Republic
Phone/Fax: +420 233 321 294
festival@vodamoreoceany.cz
www.vodamoreoceany.cz

FRANCE

Antibes World Festival of Underwater Pictures (32nd Edition)
Festival Mondial de l'Image Sous-marine
October 25-29, 2006
Host: Spondyle Club
FMISM
62, Av. des Pins du Cap
06160 Antibes
Juan-les-Pins, France
info@underwater-festival.com
www.underwater-festival.com

Challenge de photos sous-marines de Marseille (8th Edition)
Sept.30 Oct.1, 2006
Host: Association MERS
Contact: Blue Lagoon
45 Rue Montgrand
13006 MARSEILLE, France
brigitte.scorsonelli@wanadoo.fr
www.challenge-de-marseille.com

Fête de l'image sous-marine
March 16-18, 2007, Strasbourg
Host: Comité Inter-Régional Est & Comité
Départemental du Bas-Rhin (F.F.E.S.S.M.)
Societe Television et Technique
C/O Léo Barkate
30 rue de Rathsamhausen
F-67100 Strasbourg, France
fete.image.s.marine@free.fr
http://fete.image.s.marine.free.fr

RUSSIA

Moscow International Diving Festival - Golden Dolphin
February 15-18, 2007
Moscow International Diving Festival
127299 Kosmonavta Volkova St.,
10, 3th floor. ,
Moscow, Russia
org@mosfest.ru
http://english.mosfest.ru

SERBIA

International Underwater Film Festival
Host: Belgrade Diving Club
December 8-11, 2006
International Underwater Film Festival (Belgrade)
Pop Lukina br. 4
11000 Beograd, Serbia
dive.bgd@eunet.yu
www.kpa.co.yu

SEYCHELLES

SUBIOS – Seychelles Underwater Film and Image Festival
Host: Seychelles Tourism Board
(http://www.seychelles.com)
SUBIOS 2007 (March 19-25, 2007)
SUBIOS Organizing Committee,
Seychelles Tourism Board (STB)
PO Box 1262, Victoria
Mahé, Seychelles
info@seychelles.com
www.subios.sc

SINGAPORE

Celebrate the Sea Marine Imagery Festival
April 21-23, 2006
Celebrate the Sea
PO Box 2138, Carlingford Court
Carlingford, NSW
2118 AUSTRALIA
info@celebratethesea.com
www.celebratethesea.oneocean.com

SPAIN

FESTIVAL INTERNACIONAL DE IMAGEN
SUBACUATICA
Host: Serveis Integrals Subacuatics S.L
Sept. 23, 2006
Serveis Integrals Subacuatics S.L.
Apratato de Correos 9228
08080 Barcelona, Spain
info@videosub.org
www.videosub.org

TURKEY

Eastern Mediterranean International Underwater Photography and Film Festival
March 23-25, 2006
Host: Eastern Mediterranean University
Eastern Mediterranean University
Underwater Photography and Video Center
CMS 111, Famagusta
TRN Cyprus via Mersin 10, Turkey
hakan.oniz@emu.edu.tr
http://emu.edu.tr/underwaterfestival

International Kemer Underwater Days (IKUD)
May 2007
Host: Underwater Archeological Research Association (ASAD) & Foundation for the Promotion of Kemer (KETAV)
www.ketav.org

Marmara International Underwater Photo/Video Festival
Sept. 4-10, 2006, Istanbul-Turkey
Host: Caddebostan Scuba Diver's Sport Club
Contact: Balikadamlar Spor Kulubu
Iskele Cikmazi No: 69 Caddebostan 81070
Istanbul-Turkey
E-mail: info@marmarafestival.org
www.marmarafestival.org

USA

Beneath the Sea Worldwide Underwater Photo/Video Contest
Host: Beneath The Sea Dive Exposition
(March 23-25, 2007)
Beneath the Sea Photo
495 New Rochelle Road, Suite 2A,
Bronxville, NY
USA 10708
www.beneaththesea.org

Environmentally aware Photographic Image Competition
Host: EPIC
February 15, 2007
EPIC
17675 Riverbend Road

Salinas, CA, USA, 93908
scuba2me@msn.com
www.epicphotocontest.org

LAUPS 2005 - 43rd Annual International Competition

Host: Los Angeles Underwater Photographic Society
Deadline for Entries: Sept. 22, 2006
LAUPS International Competition
C/O TMO, 2075 Belgrave Ave.
Huntington Park, CA 90255
info@laups.org
www.laups.org

SEA2005 International Underwater Photo Competition

Host: Northern California Underwater Photographic Society (NCUPS)
October 13, 2006
NCUPS - Sea 2005
3871 Piedmont Ave., Box 19
Oakland, CA, 94611, USA

Sea2005@ncups.org
www.ncups.org/sea.html

Underwater Images

Host: Ohio Council of Skin & Scuba Divers
Scubafest 2006 will be March 10-12
March 9-11, 2007
Underwater Images Competition
10632 Cinderella Drive
Cincinnati, OH, USA, 45242
director@uwimages.org
www.uwimages.org

WORLD

CMAS Underwater Photo Championship

September 2006, Estartit, Spain
Host: CMAS (World Underwater Federation)
Contact: Lionel Pozzoli
E-mail: pozzl@cmas2000.org

Chapter 14

MARINE BIOLOGY

The ocean is essential to life on Earth. 97% of all the water on Earth, and 99% of the habitable space on this planet, is in the ocean.

Imagine that we are in space, about as far away as the Moon, looking back at the Earth. What does it look like? Like many astronauts, we would likely first notice that the Earth appears blue. The reason it looks blue is the oceans - about 70% of the Earth's surface consists of water. The oceans are a key element for the existence of life on Earth. 97% of all the water on Earth, and 99% of the habitable space on this planet, is in the ocean. The atmosphere we breathe, and which controls the weather and climate, is intimately connected to the oceans - half of the oxygen produced by plants is produced in the ocean, and the oceans are also responsible for absorbing 50% of the carbon dioxide humans have released into the atmosphere by burning fossil fuels for energy.

If we take a closer look, we would see that the ocean is actually painted in a palette of blue and green. The most important influence of its variations in color are the phytoplankton drifting at the ocean surface. Phytoplankton (commonly known as algae) are to the ocean what grass and bushes and trees are to the land - the biological foundation of life, due to their ability to convert sunlight into organic matter. Phytoplankton are single-celled organisms that contain chlorophyll which allows them to carry out photosynthesis. Phytoplankton, along with microbes, share the bottom rung of the oceanic food ladder. Bacteria and viruses prey on phytoplankton, returning their nutrients to the sea as part of a

very important microbial loop. At the same time, tiny animals graze on phytoplankton, and they are eaten by small fish or crustaceans, which are eaten by larger fish, whales, penguins, and everything else that swims in the ocean's salty waters. Were it not for phytoplankton, the world's largest animal, the blue whale, would not exist.

If we looked just a little closer, then we would notice the coastlines, the irregular boundaries between land and sea. There are about 372,000 miles (600,000 km) of coastline. Over one-third of the total human population, nearly 2.4 billion people, lives within 60 miles (100 km) of an oceanic coast, a fact emphasized by the devastating tsunami in the Indian Ocean in 2004. Many people are most familiar with the view of the ocean from the beach, and not from space. Yet because the human population is growing, and because more and more people are living close to the ocean, the human impact on the oceans, particularly the coastal zone, is increasing as well. Increasing population and their needs for home, shelter, and food lead to depletion of oceanic fisheries, deterioration of water quality, death of coral reefs, and beach erosion. The oceans are also vital to the world's economy through shipping, mineral resources and tourism.

SOURCE: NASA

MARINE BIOLOGY

Marine biology is the study of the living organisms of the world ocean, from microscopic plankton to the largest animal in the world, the blue whale.

Although many people today are familiar with the term "marine biologist," most don't realize that, in reality, the job title of marine biologist rarely exists. The term is actually used for many disciplines and jobs in the marine sciences which deal with the study of marine life, not just for those which deal with the physical properties of the sea, though many biologists study both. So a marine biologist might be a biological technician, ichthyologist, fishery biologist, marine mammalogist, microbiologist, systems analyst, or a mathematician.

Even economists and sociologists, who deal with living marine resource issues, are found within the so-called field of marine biology. In addition, other marine scientists concern themselves exclusively with the physical and chemical aspects of the sea, such as physicists, hydrologists, and physical oceanographers.

CAREERS IN MARINE BIOLOGY

The employment outlook in this field is not encouraging. The supply of marine scientists far exceeds the demand, and the number of government jobs (the federal and state governments are important employers) is decreasing. Other employers are local governments, aquaria/museums, colleges and universities, and private research laboratories or consulting firms.

In fishery science, where the study of fish and marine mammal population dynamics is in the most demand, a strong background in advanced mathematics and computer skills in addition to course work in the animal and aquatic sciences is recommended to get a competitive edge in the job market. Also, more universities are offering courses and programs in fisheries or wildlife management, another increasingly important aspect of the study of fishes, marine mammals, and sea turtles.

SOURCE: NOAA Fisheries

MARINE MAMMALS

CETACEANS

Approximately 78 species of whales, dolphins, and porpoises are included in the Order Cetacea. Cetaceans are broken into two Suborders, or main groups, *Mysticeti* (baleen whales) and *Odontoceti* (toothed whales). There are 11 species of baleen whales and 67 species of toothed whales. Cetaceans are relatively large, generally characterized by streamlined bodies that glide easily through the marine environment.

Orcas (a.k.a. killer whales). Photo: Captain Budd Christman / NOAA Corps

Cetaceans spend their whole lives in water and some live in family groups called "pods." Cetaceans are known for their seemingly playful behavior including "breaching," "spyhopping," or "tail slapping."

Baleen whales are very large, have paired blow holes, and characteristic baleen plates that they use to filter food.

Toothed whales have 1 to 65 teeth depending on the species and tend to be smaller than baleen whales. Toothed whales have a single blowhole and do not have baleen plates.

Nearly 90% of cetacean species are toothed whales. Most toothed whales are small dolphins and porpoise; however there are a few large toothed whales such as the killer whale and the mighty sperm whale, which grows to 60 feet (18.3 meters) in length. Toothed whales are believed to be some of the most intelligent animals on earth. Dolphins as well as beluga and killer whales have demonstrated their intelligence while in captivity, and sperm whales possess the largest brain of any creature alive. The presence of teeth and one external blowhole distinguishes toothed whales from baleen whales. Also, most toothed whales use echolocation to locate food and "see" their environment.

TOOTHED WHALES

There are several families of Odontoceti, or toothed whales, including sperm whales, pygmy sperm whales, beaked whales, river-dolphins (3 families) belugas and narwhals, dolphins and porpoises.

The sperm whale is the most famous of the Physeteridae family. It is also the largest of the toothed whales and may dive deeper than any other cetacean. Herman Melville made the sperm whale famous in his classic novel Moby Dick. A similar toothed whale family is the Kogiidae family which includes the pygmy sperm whale and dwarf sperm whale which are significantly smaller than the sperm whale but share characteristics such as the spermaceti organ, the blunt head, and the distinctive narrow lower jaw.

Beaked whales are members of the Ziphiidae family. The name Ziphiidae was derived from the Greek word "*xiphos*" meaning sword so beaked whales are the "sword-nosed whales." Beaked whales are the least well-known of all cetaceans. Some species have never been seen alive and have been studied only when dead animals wash ashore. Beaked whales may be rare or simply elusive but, generally, they live in deep water far from land and are rarely seen. It is believed that there are 20 living species of beaked whales, including the North Pacific bottlenose whale, Shepard's beaked whale, Sowerby's beaked whale, and Stejneger's beaked whale.

River-dolphins are considered to be "primitive" dolphins retaining the slender beaks with numerous teeth, flexible necks, pronounced forehead melons, and the undeveloped dorsal fins of early dolphins. River-dolphins live in muddy river estuaries and rely on their excellent echolocation skills in order to "see" the world they live in. The family taxonomy has not been agreed upon by the scientific community. Species considered to be river-dolphins are the Indian river-dolphin (Indus and Ganges river-dolphins), Amazon river-dolphin (boto), Yangtse river-dolphin (baiji), and the La Plata dolphin.

There are only two species in the Monodontidae family, the narwhal and the beluga (white whales). Both species lack dorsal fins, have blunt-shaped heads, are gray colored at birth, and whiten as they mature. Adult beluga whales are a brilliant white while narwhals have white bellies and mottled grayish-green backs and flanks (although old animals may be completely white). Belugas have 8-10 teeth in each jaw, while the narwhal is toothless except for two embedded teeth in the upper jaw: one of these teeth develops into a spiral tusk in males and some females.

The spiral tusk of the male narwhal (*Monodon monoceros*). Image: Historic NMFS Collection

Members of the dolphin, or Delphinidae family, usually have teeth in both jaws (the number and shape of the teeth vary by species), a melon-shaped head with a distinct beak, and a dorsal fin. A few of the 36 species in this family are the bottlenose dolphin, Risso's dolphin, false killer whale, Pacific whitesided dolphin, killer whale (orca), longfinned pilot whale, shortfinned pilot whale, and Irrawaddy dolphin.

Members of the porpoise, or the Phocoenidae family, have blunt heads and small spade-shaped teeth. Porpoises grow up to 7 ft (2.1 m) in length and lack the "beak" and melon-shaped foreheads of most dolphin species. Porpoise species include the Harbor porpoise, Gulf of California porpoise, Burmeister's porpoise, spectacled porpoise, finless porpoise, and Dall's porpoise.

Bottlenose dolphin (*Tursiops truncatus*) at Roatan, Honduras. Photo: J. Gallant / D.A.Y.

BALEEN WHALES

Baleen whales are the largest animals on earth, yet they feed on some of the smallest animals in the ocean. There are 12 baleen whale species divided into 4 families: right, pygmy right, gray and rorqual whales.

Right whales were called the "right" whales to catch by early hunters because they are large, swim slowly, have long baleen plates, contain lots of oil, and float when killed. Right whales do not have dorsal fins or throat grooves. The taxonomy of this family is rather confusing, but currently there are three species of right whales: the Northern right whale, Southern right whale, and Bowhead whale. The Pygmy right is in a separate family although it shares similar characteristics to right whales.

Gray whales have their own taxonomic family, genus, and species. They are the most coastal of the baleen whales and are

often found within a few miles of shore. Each year gray whales migrate between their summer feeding grounds in the Bering, Chukchi, and Beaufort Seas to their winter breeding grounds off Baja California, Mexico. This is one of the longest migrations by a mammal species.

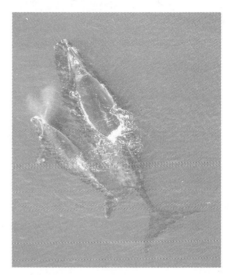

Northern right whale (*Eubalaena glacialis*) with calf. Photo: NOAA / Florida Fish and Wildlife Conservation Commission

Gray whale trapped in the ice in the Bering Sea. Joint American-Russian effort ultimately saved 2 out 3 trapped whales. Photo: NOAA Office of NOAA Corps Operations

Gray whales are gray in color and their skin is encrusted with barnacles and a unique species of small crustaceans known as "whale lice." They have 2-3 short throat grooves and instead of a dorsal fin they have a low dorsal hump followed by 6-12 "knuckles" or bumps. Whalers used to call gray whales "devil fish" because of their aggressive response to being hunted.

Rorqual whales are relatively streamlined in appearance and have pointed heads and small pointed fins. They can be distinguished from other whales by many (25-90) deep groves along their throats that expand when they feed. There are 8 species of rorqual whales: the humpback whale, fin whale, Bryde's whale, blue whale, northern minke, antarctic minke, Eden's ("small-type") whale, and sei whale.

Blue whales on the surface. Photo: NOAA Sanctuary Collection

ECHOLOCATION

Toothed whales (also known as odontocetes) have developed a special sense called echolocation that allows them to navigate and hunt in turbid-water and at depths where no light penetrates.

Water transmits sound extremely efficiently. Toothed whales have developed the capability of emitting sounds that travel from their melons (or foreheads) and reflect off objects. Like bats, odontocetes use this echolocation process to gather information in order to "see" the world around them.

Echolocation involves the emission of sound and reception of its echo. The sound is emitted in the head region and focused by the melon. The received echoes pass through special sound conducting tissue in the lower jawbone to the inner ear.

Scientists do not agree about where the sound comes from. Some scientists suggest that sound is emitted from a nasal plug and that the shape of the melon is altered by muscles to focus sound. Other scientists believe that the larynx emits sound and argue that echolocation focusing is achieved by bouncing sound off various parts of the skull.

A humpback whale sounds in the Gulf of the Farallones National Marine Sanctuary. Photo: NOAA Sanctuary Collection / Ken Balcomb

Whales use echolocation mainly for navigation and hunting. The cetacean environment is often dark and hard to see in. Echolocation provides whales a way to gather information about objects and prey around them including their range and configuration.

Echolocation is extremely sensitive. For example, dolphins in aquariums can distinguish between objects that are the size of a B-B pellet and a kernel of corn (each less than 1/2 in. (1.27 cm) in diameter) at about 50 ft (15.2 m) away. Echolocation is so sensitive that some cetaceans, like river-dolphins, may use echolocation in place of sight.

STATUS OF CETACEAN SPECIES

All marine mammals are protected under the Marine Mammal Protection Act (MMPA). There are also cetaceans listed as endangered and threatened under the Endangered Species Act (ESA), which receive extra protection due to their endangered or threatened status.

PINNIPEDS

The word pinnipedia translates from Latin as "feather or fin foot," referring to their often large fin-like flippers. All pinnipeds must come ashore to breed, give birth, and nurse their young. Seals, sea lions, and walruses are taxonomically related to other carnivores, including bears, dogs, raccoons, and weasels (including otters).

Sea otter (*Enhydra lutris*). Photo: NOAA's Ark Collection

Three families of living pinnipeds are recognized, Phocidae (earless seals or true seals), Otaridae (eared or fur seals and sea lions), and Odobenidae (walrus). **Phocid seals** include elephant seals, several ice seals, monk seals, and harbor seals. All of these seals have rear flippers that point backwards, and they move on land with a vertical undulating motion called "galluphing." They lack external ears and use their hind flippers for propulsion through the water. Typically, phocids have thin fur that does not trap air, therefore, they use blubber for insulation.

Spotted seal - *Phoca largha*. Photo: NOAA's Ark Collection

A harbor seal (*Phoca vitulina*) nibbles on a diver's toes near Vancouver, British Columbia. Photo: J. Gallant / D.A.Y.

Otariids, including fur seals and sea lions, have external ear flaps (hence the name "eared seals"). Sea lions and fur seals can rotate their hind feet forward and move with considerable speed. Otariids are also known for having dense fur that traps air to aid in insulation. They use large, fore flippers for locomotion in the marine environment.

Steller sea lions (*Eumetopias jubatus*) hauling out in the Gulf of Alaska. Photo: Captain Budd Christman, NOAA Corps

Walruses, the only member of the Odobenidae family, are currently found in both Pacific and Atlantic Arctic ice pack areas, but in colonial times they were found as far south as Sable Island off Nova Scotia. They move in a similar fashion to otariids.

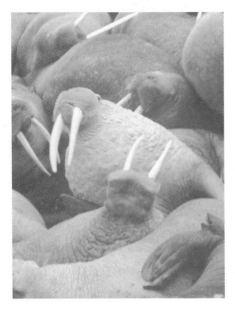

Walrus on Bering Sea Island. Photo: Captain Budd Christman / NOAA Corps

One of their most distinctive features is their tusks. They are also known for nearly hairless skin and thin blubber. Similar to phocids, walruses lack external ears. Similar to otariids, walruses can rotate their pelvis so that their hind limbs are under the body. In the water, walruses use either fore flippers (like otariids) or hind flippers (like phocids) for propulsion. The U.S. Fish and Wildlife Service (USFWS) has jurisdiction over walruses.

SOURCE: NOAA

FISH

The most often quoted estimate of the number of fish species in the world is 20,000. There may in fact be as many as 20,000 more yet unknown to science.

The most primitive fish-like animals are those with sucking mouths, such as lam-preys and *hagfishes*, whose evolution stopped short of the development of biting jaws. Mainly bottom-dwellers, these animals are of great interest to zoologists, for many parts of their bodies show forms and functions that help to explain some of the evolutionary steps leading from low to advanced life forms.

A pair of North Pacific wolfeels. Photo J. Gallant / D.A.Y.

The largest fish is the whale shark, which grows to more than 50 ft (15 m) in length and may weigh several tons; second largest is the basking shark, which may measure 35 ft to 40 ft (10 to 12 m) long. The smallest fish is the tiny goby, an inhabitant of fresh-to-brackish-water lakes in Luzon, Philippines. It seldom is longer than a 1/2 in. (1.27 cm) at adulthood, yet is so abundant it supports a fishery.

The most plentiful fish is any of the several species of Cyclothone, a deepwater fish sometimes called a "bristle mouth." Rarely visible at depths that man can readily reach, the fish is about the size of a small minnow. It is netted at 1,640 ft (500 m) or deeper all over the world.

FISH HABITATS

Freshwater fish live in lakes and rivers while marine fish live in oceans, seas and estuaries. Marine fish use many types of habitats including seagrass, salt marsh, coral reefs, kelp forests, and rocky intertidal areas among others.

An **anadromous** fish, born in fresh water, spends most of its life in the sea and returns to fresh water to spawn. Salmon, smelt, shad, striped bass, and sturgeon are common examples.

A **catadromous** fish does the opposite - lives in fresh water and enters salt water to spawn. Most of the eels are catadromous.

Amphidromous species move between estuaries and coastal rivers and streams, usually associated with the search for food and/or refuge rather than the need to reproduce. Amphidromous fish can spawn in either freshwater or in a marine environment.

FISH FACTS

Most fish are colorblind, despite the opinion of many sportfishermen. Fish can see color shadings, reflected light, shape, and movement, which probably accounts for the acceptance or rejection of artificial lures used by fishermen.

More than 240 species contain so little salt that doctors recommend them in salt-free diets. *Shark* meat is salty - as salty as the sea the shark lives in.

All puffer-like fish inflate by pumping water into special sacs when in their natural environment. Out of water, a puffer fills the sacs with air instead, and takes on a balloon-like appearance.

Long-spined porcupine fish - Diodon sp. Photo: NOAA Coral Kingdom Collection

For most species, truly fresh fish is almost odorless. Fish begin to smell "fishy" when deterioration sets in, often caused by incorrect storage practices that bring about the release of oxidized fats and acids through bacterial and enzymatic action.

Except for the rare abnormal specimen, two of the four flatfish families (tongue soles and turbots) are always sinistral (eyes on the left side); the other two (both flounders) are dextral (eyes on the right side).

The average discharge on an electric eel is more than 350 volts, but discharges as high as 650 volts have been measured. Voltage increase until the eel is about three feet (1 m) long, after which only amperage increases. Some South American eels measure 10 ft (3 m) in length.

DO FISH SLEEP?

The dictionary says that sleep is a period of rest in which the eyes are closed and there is little or no thought or movement. That is, sleeping means closing your eyes and resting. The first thing we notice is that most fish don't have eyelids (except for sharks). Also, while some deep ocean fish never stop moving a great many fishes live nearly motionless lives and many do so on a regular diurnal/nocturnal cycle, some active by day others by night. So we can't generalize and say that all fish sleep like we do. But most fish do rest. Usually they just blank their minds and do what we might call daydreaming. Some float in place, some wedge themselves into a spot in the mud or the coral, some even build themselves a nest while remaining alert for danger at all times.

SHARKS

Sharks are fish. They live in water, and use their gills to filter oxygen from the water. Sharks are a special type of fish because their body is made out of cartilage instead of bones like other fish. The name or classification of this type of fish is called "Elasmobranchs." This category also includes Rays, Sawfish, and Skates." Sharks have 8 unique senses. They are hearing, smell, lateral line, pit organs, vision, ampullae of Lorenzini, touch, and taste. The shark shares many sense that humans do such as taste and smell, but it has three senses that we do not have. The lateral line, pit organs and ampullae of Lorenzini play an important role in how the shark functions when swimming around. Most sharks have very good eyesight. In fact, sharks can see extremely well in dark lighted areas, have fantastic night vision, and can see colours. Avoid wearing bright colours in the water, such as oranges and 'yum yum' yellows, as sharks appear to be attracted to them.

Caribbean reef shark (*Carcharhinus perezi*). Photo J. Gallant / D.A.Y.

Sharks are omnivorous, which means they eat both meat and vegetation. Sharks will eat just about anything, and if there is not an abundant supply of meat in the area, they will resort to eating marine plants. The largest shark of them all, the Whale Shark is mainly a plankton feeder. It has been observed that sharks can go up to approximately 6 weeks without feeding, and the record for a shark fasting was observed with the Swell Shark, in which it did not eat for 15 months.

SOURCE: NOAA

REPTILES

MARINE TURTLES

Sea turtles, air-breathing reptiles with streamlined bodies and large flippers, are well adapted to life in the marine environment. They inhabit tropical and subtropical ocean waters throughout the world. Of the seven species of sea turtles, six are found in U.S. waters: green, hawksbill, Kemp's ridley, leatherback, loggerhead, and olive ridley. Although sea turtles live most of their lives in the ocean, adult females must return to beaches on land to lay their eggs. They often migrate long distances between foraging grounds and nesting beaches.

STATUS OF MARINE TURTLES

Hawksbill turtle (*Eretmochelys imbricata*). Photo: J. Gallant / D.A.Y.

All 7 species of marine turtles are listed under the Endangered Species Act (ESA); 6 of those species fall under the jurisdiction of the NOAA Fisheries Office of Protected Resources. Green turtles and olive ridley turtles have breeding populations that were listed separately under the ESA, and therefore, have more than one ESA status.

SOURCE: NOAA

INVERTEBRATES

CORALS

When corals are mentioned, most people immediately think about clear, warm tropical seas and fish-filled reefs. In fact, the stony, shallow-water corals—the kind that build reefs—are only one type of coral. There are also soft corals and deep water corals that live in dark cold waters.

Almost all corals are colonial organisms. This means that they are composed of hundreds to hundreds of thousands of individual animals, called polyps. Each polyp has a stomach that opens at only one end. This opening, called the mouth, is surrounded by a circle of tentacles. The polyp uses these tentacles for defense, to capture small animals for food, and to clear away debris. Food enters the stomach through the mouth. After the food is consumed, waste products are expelled through the same opening.

Elkhorn coral in the Caribbean. Photo by J. Gallant / D.A.Y.

Most corals feed at night. To capture their food, corals use stinging cells called nematocysts. These cells are located in the coral polyp's tentacles and outer tissues. If you've ever been "stung" by a jellyfish, you've encountered nematocysts.

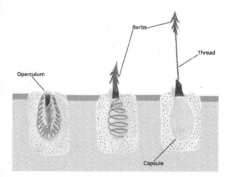

Image: NOAA

The preceding diagram shows the anatomy of a nematocyst cell and its "firing" sequence, from left to right. On the far left is a nematocyst inside its cellular capsule.

The cell's thread is coiled under pressure and wrapped around a stinging barb. When potential prey makes contact with the tentacles of a polyp, the nematocyst cell is stimulated. This causes a flap of tissue covering the nematocyst—the operculum—to fly open. The middle image shows the open operculum, the rapidly uncoiling thread and the emerging barb. On the far right is the fully extended cell. The barbs at the end of the nematocyst are designed to stick into the polyp's victim and inject a poisonous liquid. When subdued, the polyp's tentacles move the prey toward its mouth and the nematocysts recoil back into their capsules.

Nematocysts are capable of delivering powerful, often lethal, toxins, and are essential in capturing prey. A coral's prey ranges in size from nearly microscopic animals called zooplankton to small fish, depending on the size of the coral polyps. In addition to capturing zooplankton and larger animals with their tentacles, many corals also collect fine organic particles in mucous film and strands, which they then draw into their mouths.

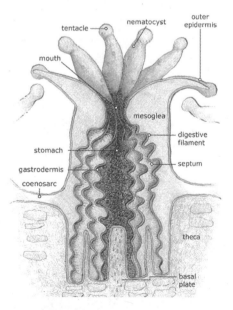

Image: NOAA

Most corals are made up of hundreds of thousands individual polyps like the one in the preceding illustration. Many stony coral polyps range in size from 0.04 in. to 0.12 in. (1-3 mm) in diameter.

Coral polyps. Photo: NOAA Sanctuary Collection / Brent Deuel

Anatomically simple organisms, much of the polyp's body is taken up by a stomach filled with digestive filaments. Open at only one end, the polyp takes in food and expels waste through its mouth. A ring of tentacles surrounding the mouth aids in capturing food, expelling waste and clearing away debris. Most food is captured with the help of special stinging cells called nematocysts which are inside the polyp' outer tissues, which is called the epidermis.

A fish uses coral for cover. Photo: J. Gallant / D.A.Y.

Calcium carbonate is secreted by reef-building polyps and forms a protective cup called a calyx within which the polyps sit. The base of the calyx upon which the polyp sits is called the basal plate. The walls surrounding the calyx are called the theca.

The coenosarc is a thin band of living tissue that connects individual polyps to one another and help make it a colonial organism.

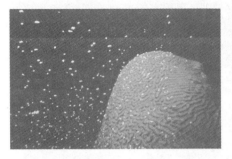

Brain Coral spawning. Photo: NOAA Sanctuary Collection / Emma Hickerson

25 THINGS YOU CAN DO TO SAVE CORAL REEFS

1. Support reef-friendly businesses. Ask what your dive shop, boating store, tour operators, hotel and other coastal businesses are doing to save the coral reefs. This is especially important in coastal areas with reefs. Let them know you are an informed consumer and care about reefs.

2. Don't use chemically enhanced pesticides and fertilizers. Although you may live thousands of miles from a coral reef ecosystem, these products end up in the watershed and may ultimately impact the waters that support coral.

3. Volunteer for a reef cleanup. You don't live near a coral reef? Then do what many people do with their vacation: visit a coral reef. Spend an afternoon enjoying the beauty of one of the world's treasures while helping to preserve it for future generations.

4. Learn more about coral reefs. How many different species live in reefs? What new medicines have been discovered in reef organisms? Participate in training or educational programs that focus on reef ecology. When you further your own education, you can help others understand the fragility and value of the world's coral reefs.

5. Become a member of your local aquarium or zoo. Ask what they are doing and what your donation can do toward saving the world's coral reefs. The answer may pleasantly surprise you.

6. When you visit a coral reef, help keep it healthy by respecting all local guidelines, regulations, recommendations, and customs. Ask local authorities or your dive shop hot to protect the reef.

7. Support conservation organizations. Many of them have coral reef programs, and your much-needed monetary support will make a big difference.

8. Spread the word. Remember your own excitement at learning how important the planet's coral reefs are to us and the intricate global ecosystem. Sharing this excitement gets everyone you speak with involved.

9. Be an informed consumer. Consider carefully the coral objects that you buy for your coffee table. Ask the store owner or manager from what country the coral is taken and whether or not that country has a management plan to insure that the harvest was legal and sustainable over time.

10. Don't pollute. Never put garbage or human waste in the water. Don't leave trash on the beach.

11. Recycle. This is the first step each of us can take to make a change. Recycle anything and everything. If your community doesn't have a program, do it anyway, and get one started.

12. Conserve water. The less water you use, the less runoff and wastewater that eventually finds its way back into our oceans.

13. Report dumping or other illegal activities. Environmental enforcement cannot

be everywhere, and your involvement can make a big difference.

14. Keep it clean. You may be in the habit of picking up your own trash. You may even participate in an organized cleanup. But have you considered carrying away the trash that others have left behind?

15. Only buy marine aquarium fish if you know they have been collected in an ecologically sound manner. In some areas, marine fish harvested for the pet trade, are stunned with sodium cyanide so that capturing them is easier.

Red soft coral (*Gersemia rubiformis*). North Atlantic. Photo: J. Gallant / D.A.Y.

16. Surf the net! Many different addresses exist to link you to information about coral reefs and what you can do to become involved. A good starting point is at http://www.noaa.gov/public-affairs/coral-reef.html

17. Don't start a live rock aquarium. Although this living rock is still harvested legally in some places, its collection is devastating to the reef organisms' habitat.

18. Hire local guides when visiting coral reef ecosystems. Not only do you learn about the local resources, but you will be protecting the future of the reef by supporting a non-consumptive economy around that reef.

19. Don't anchor on the reef. If you go boating near a coral reef, use mooring buoy systems when they are available.

20. If you dive, don't touch! Take only pictures and leave only bubbles! Keep your fins' gear, and hands away from the coral, as this contact can hurt you and will damage the delicate coral animals. Stay off the bottom because stirred-up sediment can settle on coral and smother it.

21. Participate in the Great American Fish Count. What better way to enjoy your vacation time than snorkeling or diving in America's coral reefs and helping scientists better understand reef fish populations?

22. Volunteer. Volunteer and community coral reef monitoring programs are very important. If you do not live near a coast, get involved in your local save the river (bay, lake, or other estuarine environment) program. Remember, all watersheds affect the oceans and eventually the coral reefs.

23. Support the creation and maintenance of marine parks and reserves. Encourage your friends to get involved with projects to protect special areas.

24. Be a wastewater crusader! Make sure that sewage from your boat, from others' boats, and from land is correctly treated. The nutrients from sewage feed growing algae that can smother and kill corals.

25. Inform yourself. Find out about existing and proposed laws, programs, and projects that could affect the world's coral reefs.

SOURCE: NOAA

MOLLUSKS

Mollusks (from the Latin word molluscus, meaning "soft") are a phylum of invertebrates with over 50,000 known species. The majority of mollusks (including abalone) are of the Class Gastropoda, whose name translates from Latin as "stomach foot." Mollusks are soft-bodied animals that may have a hard external shell (composed by secreting calcium carbonate), a hard internal shell, or no shell at all. Mollusks are taxonomically related to annelids (segmented worms) and pogonophora (deep-sea tube worms).

There are seven classes of mollusks:

Gastropoda (e.g., abalone and conch, such as black abalone, green abalone, pink abalone, pinto abalone, white abalone, and queen conch)
Bivalvia (e.g., oysters and clams)
Cephalopoda (e.g., octopus and squid)
Aplacophora (worm-like mollusks)
Monoplacophora (only mollusk with a segmented internal structure)
Polyplacophora (e.g., chitons)
Scaphopoda (e.g., tusk shells)

The invasive zebra mussel has practically wiped out larger indigenous species of freshwater mussels in the St. Lawrence Seaway. Photo: J. Gallant / D.A.Y.

BRACHIOPODS

Brachiopods are bottom-dwelling, filter-feeding invertebrates whose name translates from Latin as "arm feet." Brachiopods are sessile (stationary, attached), and were the first sessile animals to surround their bodies with a solid external shell. They appear similar to clams on the outside, but have a unique anatomy. Most brachiopods attach to substrate using a muscular stalk (or pedicle) and feed using an appendage called a lophophore. The brachiopoda phylum is common in the fossil record, and brachiopods were extremely abundant in the Paleozoic era. Their numbers were greatly reduced during the Permo-Triassic mass extinction approximately 250 million years ago, and today there are approximately 300 living species of brachiopods. Brachiopods are taxonomically related to bryozoans, or lace corals.

There are two main classes of brachiopod: **Inarticulata** (e.g., inarticulate brachiopod) and **Articulata**.

MARINE PLANTS

Mangroves provide habitats for wildlife including fish and crustaceans. Photo by J. Gallant / D.A.Y.

There are several categories of marine plants, including seagrasses, mangroves, and algae. Seagrasses, such as Johnson's sea grass, are true flowering plants that have adapted to life in the marine environment. Most seagrasses reproduce via pollination (similar to many terrestrial plants) and are found in coastal marine areas.

Mangroves are also true flowering plants and are found in coastal waters of varying salinities. Algae are not true flowering plants and range in size from microscopic phytoplankton to large seaweed species.

PORIFERA

Porifera - an animal phylum that contains the sponges. They are the most primitive of the multicellular animals. Sponges assume many sessile body forms, such as finger, branching, bushy, spherical, tubular, vase and tube-like, encrusting, amorphous and massive. Some bore into coral and mollusk shells. Many of the 5,000 species are colorful and prominent inhabitants of coral reefs.

A colony of breadcrumb sponge shares a boulder with other filter feeders in the Saguenay-St.-Lawrence Marine Park. Photo by J. Gallant / D.A.Y.

The sponge is a multicellular animal (metazoa) below the tissue grade of construction. Sponges belong to the phylum Porifera. There are approximately 5,000 living species classified in three distinct groups, the Hexactinellida (glass sponges), the Demospongia, and the Calcarea (calcareous sponges). They are important components of a coral reef ecosystem.

ECHINODERMS

Echinodermata - an animal phylum that contains starfishes, sea cucumbers, sand dollars, brittlestars, basket stars, sea lilies, feather stars, and sea urchins. Adults exhibit pentamerous radial symmetry, secondarily derived from a bilateral ancestor. They are not at all related to the other radiate phyla, such as the Cnidaria.

Red sea urchin from the northern Pacific. Photo by J. Gallant / D.A.Y.

CHORDATES

Chordata - an animal phylum that includes sea squirts (tunicates), lampreys and hagfishes, fishes, amphibians, reptiles, birds and mammals. Many species of marine chordates play prominent roles in the ecology of coral reef ecosystems

A sea lamprey (*Petromyzon marinus*) feeds on a Greenland shark[22]. Photo by J. Gallant / D.A.Y.

[22] Gallant, J., C. Harvey-Clark, R.A. Myers, and M.J.W. Stokesbury. 2005. Sea lamprey (Petromyzon marinus) attached to a Greenland shark (*Somniosus microcephalus*) in the St. Lawrence Estuary, Canada. Northeastern Naturalist. 2006 13(1):35–38

CNIDARIANS

A fish-eating anemone (*Urticina piscivora*). Photo by J. Gallant / D.A.Y.

The purple striped jellyfish (*Pelagia panopyra*) possesses very potent stingers. Photo: NOAA Sanctuary Collection / Kip Evans

Cnidarians are multicellular animals with a tissue grade of construction that contains the stony (hard) corals, anemones, sea fans, sea pens, hydroids, and jellyfish.

SOURCE: NOAA

TIPS FOR DIVERS & SNORKELERS

Before booking a reef trip, check out weather conditions; it's best not to go out in rough seas. Poor visibility, strong winds and waves reduce safe interaction at the reef.

Remember that even the lightest touch with hands or equipment can damage sensitive coral polyps.

Snorkelers should wear float coats — inflatable snorkel vests — to allow gear adjustment without standing on the coral. Never stand upon a coral reef!

To avoid contact with the ocean bottom, divers should only use the weight needed and practice proper buoyancy control. Areas that appear empty may support new growth if left undisturbed.

Avoid wearing gloves and touching or collecting marine life. Most tropical fish captured die within a year. Queen conch is a protected species, and cannot be taken.

Resist the temptation to feed fish, seabirds and marine mammals; it changes their natural behavior and diet.

Remember, it's illegal to harvest coral in Florida and buying it at local shops only depletes reefs elsewhere in the world.

Bring back any trash you find and recycle it, if possible.

Snorkel aware, dive with care!

SOURCE: Florida Keys National Marine Sanctuary

INTERNET LINKS

➢ National Oceanic & Atmospheric Administration - NOAA (www.noaa.gov)
➢ MarineBio.com (www.marinebio.com)

REFERENCES

o NASA (www.science.hq.nasa.gov)
o NOAA Fisheries' Office of Habitat Conservation (www.nmfs.noaa.gov/habitat/habitatprotection/index.htm)
o NOAA Fisheries Service - Office of Protected Resources (www.nmfs.noaa.gov)
o NOAA National Marine Fisheries Service Southwest Fisheries Science Center (http://swfsc.nmfs.noaa.gov)
o NOAA's National Marine Fisheries Service - Northeast Fisheries Science Center (www.nefsc.noaa.gov)
o NOAA National Marine Mammal Laboratory (http://nmml.afsc.noaa.gov)
o NOAA National Ocean Service (www.oceanservice.noaa.gov)
o NOAA Pacific Marine Environmental Laboratory (www.pmel.noaa.gov)
o NOAA West Coast & Alaska Tsunami Warning Center (wcatwc.arh.noaa.gov)

DIVING WITH SHARKS

By R. Aidan Martin
ReefQuest Centre for Shark Research

Encounters in the wild between humans and sharks are becoming commonplace. Increasing world demand for alternate sources of protein and recreation pushes us ever farther into their realms. As commercial fisheries expand, entire populations of sharks are threatened. At the same time, about five new species of sharks are discovered each year as exploration of life in the sea continues.

Deep-sea submersibles afford us glimpses into the lives of bizarre abyssal sharks we formerly knew only as lifeless specimens.

Sport anglers are turning their attentions to sharks, once considered the 'poor man's marlin', as challenging quarry with a new-found respectability. In some areas, tourists pay enterprising boat owners to go on escorted 'shark-watching' cruises. Yet the merest whisper of the word causes swimmers to scramble wildly out of the ocean in desperate fear.

Lemon shark (*Negaprion brevirostris*). Photo: Neil Hammerschlag - ReefQuest Centre for Shark Research

Advances in scuba technology and diver training have made exploration of the underwater world available to more people than ever before. These advances make possible new kinds of encounters between humans and sharks. For only on scuba can we encounter sharks on their own terms.

Sport divers and underwater photographers are beginning to seek out encounters with these fascinating creatures. But diving with sharks calls for preparation, experienced and competent companions, prudence, and more than a little fortitude. The rules are simple and straight-forward. Keep your diving skills current and never dive alone. Be aware of conditions that can bring trouble. The potential hazards increase with the size and number of sharks and their degree of stimulation. Don't stay in the water with very large sharks and never enter water where sharks are actively feeding. Don't grab or poke at sharks or block their paths in narrow confines. In short: the keys to remaining safe in the presence of sharks are knowledge, self-control, and common sense.

Caribbean reef shark (*Carcharhinus perezi*). Photo: J. Gallant / D.A.Y.

Incidents are rare, occurring in tropical latitudes more frequently than in temperate zones. This is not because tropical sharks are particularly ferocious, but simply because most people prefer to swim and dive in the warm, clear water of the tropics. In the Caribbean, the large and powerful Tiger Shark (*Galeocerdo cuvier*) has an almost overwhelmingly nasty reputation. But this may not be justified, as many less spectacular shark species are more common and much more aggressive than this infamous predator.

Blue shark (*Prionace glauca*). Photo: Chris Harvey-Clark / www.geerg.ca

Large reef sharks – such as the Bull (*Carcharhinus leucas*), Tiger, or Great Hammerhead (*Sphyrna mokarran*) – rarely charge, but will investigate a diver closely by circling slowly. The open-ocean Blue Shark (*Prionace glauca*) will rarely approach a diver directly unless drawn in by food, while the Oceanic Whitetip (*Carcharhinus longimanus*) and Silky (*Carcharhinus falciformis*) Sharks will swim straight toward a diver. It is therefore important to learn to be able to identify sharks underwater, to know what to expect of a given species' behaviour, and how to respond appropriately. Last but not least, the ability to recognize the kinds of sharks common where you dive and interpret their behaviour enhances your enjoyment of a close encounter with one.

Today, at least 450 species of shark have been described, representing an amazing diversity of forms and lifestyles. Sharks have undergone several major adaptive radiations since their earliest beginnings, the most recent concurrent with the mammalian radiation which eventually produced ourselves; there is nothing 'primitive' about today's sharks. Sharks, it turns out, are not merely an interesting sideline of fishy evolution. They are a fundamental lifeform, at least as distinct from bony fishes as amphibians are from mammals. What is more, sharks break or warp many rules of biological common sense, that one can take virtually nothing for granted about them. The more one learns about sharks, the more incredible they seem. With the advent of modern research equipment, sharks are beginning to yield some of the mysteries of their day-to-day lives.

Tiger shark (*Galeocerdo cuvier*). Photo: Neil Hammerschlag - ReefQuest Centre for Shark Research

Sharks have been swimming, feeding, breeding, and otherwise going about their own shark-business for some 425 millions years. Perhaps a few hundred years ago, a clever terrestrial primate discovered that it is great fun to play in the same aquatic

environment that sharks have been using for a long, long time. Once in a great while, a 'conflict of interest' occurred between a shark and one of the clever primates. So the clever primates branded all sharks as 'Bad Animals' and proceeded to wrest from the sea every shark they could hook, net, or spear. We clever primates have successfully vanquished all terrestrial challengers to our supremacy, but in the sea lurk shadows that still make us feel powerless and afraid.

As sociobiologist E. O. Wilson put it, "We are more than fascinated by predators; we are transfixed by them – prone to weave myths and legends about them." The more spectacular or successful the predator, the greater our admiration. Intellectually, most of us can appreciate that predators are a necessary part of the natural scheme of things. Yet we reserve our greatest fear and loathing for those few creatures that occasionally have the audacity to attack us. That such a predator seems to operate on principles beyond our control or understanding adds greatly to our fears. For many people, sharks are the epitome of the 'unpredictable killer'. Yet often it is we who kill with little or no warning.

Sixgill shark (*Hexanchus griseus*). Photo: Aidan R. Martin - ReefQuest Centre for Shark Research

Thermodynamically speaking, Life is an energy juggling act which ultimately fails. All animals need food to fuel their bodies' needs. Sharks are carnivores. Catching, killing, and eating other animals is the way sharks secure the fuel they need for self-maintenance. Within a shark's body, this fuel is 'burned' (combined with oxygen) to provide the energy enable it to carry out all the activities need to survive: locomotion, feeding, self-defense, growth, and reproduction. There is nothing 'evil' or 'cruel' about this way of life. To remain alive, sharks must kill. When we kill, we rarely have shark's pure and simple motives.

There is a wide-spread notion that sharks act as sea-going garbage disposals, scavenging the dead and culling the sick or injured. While it is true that sharks will avail themselves to such opportunities as they arise, their bodily needs to not allow them to wait for such easy feeding. There are very few 'free lunches' in Nature. The ocean is aflow with an astonishing diversity of plant and animal life. Among them, sharks prey upon virtually every kind of organism that occurs on or in the sea. But not all this life is available as prey to all sharks at all times. Distribution and abundance of potential prey animals vary with location and season. Some potential prey is camouflaged, others 'hide' in crevices, while still others are very large or well-armed. So sharks have evolved a variety of predatory strategies to enable them to carry out the business of survival.

Greenland shark (*Somniosus microcephalus*). Photo: J. Gallant / D.A.Y.

JAWS crystallized the popular image of sharks as large, spectacular 'super-predators'. Despite the decades of media hype which followed, most shark species are small – less than 4 ft (1.2 m) long at maturity. To an average shark, a human swimmer must seem a large, unfamiliar, noisy, and altogether frightening creature. If you had never seen an extraterrestrial ('extra-aquatical'?) before, would your first impulse be to try eating one? Of course not. You would probably investigate such an alien cautiously, from what you hope is a safe distance. This is basically how most sharks behave when confronted by an 'alien' from somewhere above their silvery liquid ceiling.

A nurse shark (*Ginglymostoma cirratum*) resting in a crevasse. Photo: J. Gallant / D.A.Y.

As a marine biologist specializing in the behaviour, ecology, and life history of sharks, I have had opportunity to spend a great deal of time in the water with sharks of many species and under a wide variety of diving conditions. I can attest that most sharks are very ware of people in the water and are extremely difficult to get close to in their natural habitats.

SHARK 'SMARTS'

When you enter the sea, your presence is perceived and interpreted by all manner of creatures – including sharks. Because of the intimate relationship that exists between aquatic animals and their environment, sharks are wholly immersed in their world – flowing with and responding to the ocean's rhythms. In the water, you impose a localized change in the sea's natural pulse, broadcasting your presence to every creature that lives there. No matter how good a swimmer you are in human terms, by the standards evolved over countless eons by life in the sea you are clumsy and awkward. Sharks have evolved a complex batter of sensory systems, and their perceptual universe in unimaginably rich. As a result, sharks are among the most sensitive and responsive creatures on our planet, fully attuned to the sights, sounds, vibrations, chemical and electrical signals of their liquid universe.

The intelligence of sharks has been much maligned. Sharks were traditionally thought of as fairly stupid animals, each little more than an appetite with fins, led around by a phenomenal sense of smell – a kind of 'swimming nose'. However, recent evidence suggests that sharks may make use of as many as 13 different sensory systems. This complex battery of integrated sensory systems does not – of itself- imply great intelligence on the part of sharks. However, sharks may legitimately be thought of as a kind of 'swimming computer'. For a shark to interpret and respond to a continuous stream of several types of sensory input and manage to function as an effective predator must require something akin to a computer for a brain.

Mako shark (*Isurus oxyrinchus*). Photo: Chris Harvey-Clark / www.geerg.ca

Sharks have largish, fairly complex brains. Shark brain weight to body weight ratios typically fall well within the range of those for birds and mammals. The cerebrum of many sharks is convoluted and asymmetrically developed, indicating some degree of specialization in this integratory region of the vertebrate brain. Further, it has been demonstrated experimentally that sharks can learn and remember as well as some mammals. This is consistent with their ecological niche. After all, a cow only has to be smart enough to outwit blades of grass. Sharks are opportunistic predators, often exploiting a very broad prey spectrum. Since their potential prey is strongly motivated to avoid being eaten, sharks are condemned to a life of perpetual ambush. But predatory behaviors that allow a shark

to successfully overpower and consume a stingray may not work for a school of fish; what works for capturing a sea turtle may not for a sea lion. Sharks must therefore draw on past experience to analyze the type of prey, choose a hunting strategy based on familiarity with that prey type, and modify their attack 'strategy' in response to opportune changes in 'tactical advantage'.

Part of the shark's success as predators is their ability to adapt, to exploit as broad a spectrum of food resources as possible. They are by nature curious, ready to investigate any unfamiliar signal which may lead to a potential meal. But curiosity is only half of the sharks' success equation. Their natural curiosity is balanced with a healthy measure of caution. Young sharks are often bolder in investigating divers than older members of the same species. It is as though less experienced sharks have not yet learned to be wary of divers, which may carry bait, cameras...or powerheads. A shark may spend many minutes circling a person in the water, carefully searching for any signs of weakness or vulnerability. This is not 'chinless cowardice' – as zoologist William Beebe once called it – but merely a sound strategy for staying alive and well.

Oceanic whitetip (*Carcharhinus longimanus*). Photo: Neil Hammerschlag - ReefQuest Centre for Shark Research

When faced with an unknown creature, it doesn't make sense for an animal to risk a tussle which could result in injury and thus interfere with its ability to feed or represent its genes in future generations. This is why so many animals posture and display to one another in competitive contexts – the idea is to bluff one's opponent into backing down without having to engage in actual fighting. If your swimming movements are strong and regular, 400 millions years' of instinct will usually prompt a shark to seek more familiar and less formidable-looking prey.

Given their enormous spectrum of prey types and feeding behaviors, it hardly seems surprising that occasionally an exceptionally large shark may extend its diet to include a person. But, I can assure you, it's nothing personal.

SHARK ATTACKS RELATED TO THE ACTIVITIES OF PEOPLE

Statistically, sharks are not particularly dangerous to us, but in truth some sharks under some conditions are. Certain offshore sharks are notoriously persistent in investigating divers. This may be because away from the continental shelves, the oceans are largely empty of life. When a large pelagic shark, such as the Oceanic Whitetip (*Carcharhinus longimanus*), encounters an unfamiliar animal, it tends to regard the creature as potential prey. The shark repeatedly tests the creature's defenses; eventually either the prey's defenses break down, or the shark gives up and moves on. But most swimmers and divers would not intentionally enter the offshore waters inhabited by open-ocean sharks.

Inshore sharks, having more abundant and varied prey, can afford to be picky. If you appear in control and seem capable of defending yourself, most inshore sharks will simply leave you alone.

Still, once in a great while a shark will attack a person who exhibits strong and regular swimming movements. Why? From an examination of case histories, the reasons are almost always obvious. For example, if the water is murky or the person is only partially submerged (as when entering or leaving the water), a shark may not be able to accurately assess just how large the swimmer is. If another predator is nearby, the shark may risk a grab at the unfamiliar swimmer before its competitor does. Usually the 'grab' is half-hearted and the shark lets go as soon as it realizes that the swimmer is much larger that it had bargained for. Unfortunately, the sharks' dental equipment is so frighteningly efficient, that the knowledge that "the fish simply made a mistake" is of little consolation to the victim.

Scuba divers, however, are rarely accidentally bitten by sharks. Fully submerged, a diver's true size is readily apparent (sharks have excellent eyesight), and the face mask increases a diver's changes of seeing an approaching shark. In my experience, sharks are basically "path-of-least-resistance types" given an opportunity for flight rather than fight, most will simply swim away. Avoiding conflict with sharks is often simply a matter of applying a few common-sense rules. On entering the water, it is safer to slip in quietly rather than jump in with tremendous splash; I have seen sharks react with great excitement to the commotion caused by a diver entering the water. Spearfishing is well-know to attract sharks. If you insist on participating in this 'sport', boat your catch as quickly as possible; if a shark seems intent on 'stealing' your catch – DON'T ARGUE! Underwater, a shark has every advantage over a clever primate. To grab, knife, or spear a shark – even a small and apparently harmless one – is to invite a defensive attack.

ON DIVERS AND THE GREAT WHITE SHARK

Great White Shark (*Carcharodon carcharias*). Illustration: R. Aidan Martin.

Despite the popular misconception that sharks are ravenous and indiscriminate feeders, many species eat infrequently and are very picky eaters.

Great white shark. Photo: Scott Davis
www.greatwhiteadventures.com

Sharks typically consume only 3 to 14% of their body weight in food per week and some can fast as long as 15 months without suffering serious debilitation; active species such as the Grey Reef Shark (*Carcharhinus amblyrhynchos*) typically feed on a six to twelve day cycle and individuals often go as much as six weeks without eating. In addition, many species have definite prey preferences. The Great Hammerhead (*Sphyrna mokarran*), for example, shows a clear predilection for stingrays; the Sicklefin Weasel Shark (*Hemigaleus microstoma*) is one of the most specialized feeders among sharks – fully 98% of its diet consists of cephalopods, principally octopuses.

Great white shark (*Carcharodon carcharias*). Photo: Aidan R. Martin - ReefQuest Centre for Shark Research

The infamous Great White Shark (*Carcharodon carcharias*) is a special case; adults of this species specialize in feeding on marine mammals. The implications for mankind are obvious and ominous: We're mammals too.
Divers who like to skin and scuba dive off pinniped rookeries should realize that, dressed in black neoprene and flippers, they look overwhelmingly like the seals and sea lions that large White Sharks feed upon. If a diver floats in a prone position on the surface, he or she not only has the size and shape of a pinniped, but also behaves like a seal or sea lion hyperventilating between dives – when they are at their most vulnerable. Even if we don't look "quite right" to a White Shark, it may bite out of curiosity.

UNDERSTANDING THE BEHAVIOR OF SHARKS

Scuba has proven itself to be a powerful tool for those of us wanting to understand sharks on their own terms, allowing us to observe them at close quarters in their natural habitats. It is becoming clear that sharks are far from the unpredictable and socially unsophisticated creatures we had long mistaken them for. From my own work on the behavioral ecology of Indo-Pacific reef sharks, I discovered that at least some sharks have a definite sense of "home turf" and of "personal space". I have learned that individual sharks have distinct 'personalities' and their daily and seasonal movements are highly regular, often strongly linked to local tidal fluctuations.

Repeated observations of many individuals of several species have indicated that a given shark will tend to stay within its own discrete area on the reef and will tolerate other sharks swimming – and even feeding – within its "home range". Thus sharks cannot be said to be territorial (that is, defending a specific geographical area for their exclusive use). My research has also revealed that individual sharks, like people, have a kinesphere (or 'personal space') with well-defined boundaries – a kind of 'moving territory' which they definitely will defend. This personal space is roughly spherical in shape and its limits are directly proportional to the size of the animal (about twice the body length) for most reef sharks. Just like people, larger sharks have larger kinespheres.

Sharks also display a complex and subtle form of 'body language'. When a diver persistently violates a shark's kinesphere, the animal may attempt to communicate that it is on the verge of either attacking or fleeing through a stereotyped behaviour called an "agonistic display". Shark agonistic displays seem to be ritualized, exaggerated swimming movements punctuated with other ritualized, exaggerated swimming movements punctuated with other behavioral elements used to communicate that the animal "feels" threatened. My research on whaler sharks (genus *Carcharhinus*) indicates that each species has it own characteristic agonistic display. However, the agonistic displays of all shark species studied so far share certain features: pectoral fins depressed, back hunched and/or snout raised, tail lowered, exaggerated swimming movements, and an over-all increase in muscular tension.

If a shark you are observing demonstrates any or all of these behaviors, your remaining there – even without any further attempts to approach the shark – could elicit a defensive attack. Make no mistake about it: you cannot defend yourself against the mind-stutteringly fast, slashing attack that may follow. Your most prudent course of action is to leave the water as quietly and efficiently as possible. Don't panic into surfacing immediately – unless your exit point is directly above you – a long surface swim is strenuous and leaves you vulnerable to attack from below. KEEPING YOUR EYE ON THE SHARK, swim slowly but powerfully to your pre-planned exit point (boat, dock, etc.). Remain close to the bottom until you are directly below your exit point, then – without altering your slow, powerful swimming movements – swim directly to the surface and exit the water.

ORGANIZED SHARK FEEDINGS[23]

Sharks are large, long-lived, and wide-ranging marine animals, combining curiosity and caution in a way that frustrates close observation. Further, sharks do not seem to like heavily-dived resort areas;

after a few months, most simply move away. For many sport divers, getting close to a shark – or better yet, getting a good picture on film – remains an unfulfilled desire.

Sharks and groupers wait for a diver to open a bucket full of chum. Photo: J. Gallant / D.A.Y.

Sharks and divers vie for position before the bucket is opened. Photo: J. Gallant / D.A.Y.

In recent years, many dive operators, hoping to cash in on the diving public's fascination with sharks, offer 'shark dives' by baiting in several mid-to-large-sized sharks. If the dive operator is highly experienced at coordinating excited divers, agitated sharks, and takes the proper precautions, a mob shark feeding is spectacular, photogenic, and reasonably safe.

[23] Publication of the section on shark feeding does not constitute endorsement of the activity by the D.A.Y. Shark feeding is illegal in the states of Florida and Hawaii, as well as in the Cayman Islands.

When choosing a diver operator to stage an organized shark feeding, be skeptical of those who assure complete safety. Seek out an operator who admits that there is a possibility you will be injured and stresses that to reduce your personal risk you must follow their safe guidelines. Most of these guidelines are fairly straightforward. ("Remain on the bottom where indicated. Do not touch or restrain any shark. Keep your hands either clasped in front of your waist or cross your arms and 'hide' them in your armpits.") If you stick to these rules, you'll more than likely surface healthy and whole, having experienced one of sport diving's most spectacular sights.

Observing sharks within the safety of a cage. Photo: J. Gallant / D.A.Y.

Some dive operators advocate the use of shark cages in baited situations. Diving inside a shark cage is safer than without, but near the surface water movement can cause the diver inside to collide with the cage bars, resulting in some nasty bruises. Still, it beats a shark bite any day.

For organized mob feedings of mid-sized tropical reef sharks, I prefer kneeling quietly on the bottom and observing the action from a respectful distance (about 20 feet

or 6 m.). When it comes to aggregations of large open-ocean sharks like the Blue Shark (*Prionace glauca*) or the solitary and so-bering massiveness of the Great White, shark cages are definitely the safest way to go.

GETTING CLOSE TO SHARKS IN THE WILD

The best way to get close to sharks under natural conditions is to let them come to you. You can increase your odds by taking advantage of the sharks' natural curiosity. Try clanging the blade of your dive knife against the butt of your tank – this simple trick is often effective in attracting sharks. Once it is within your range of vision, DO LOSE SIGHT OF THE SHARK. However, avoid looking directly at the shark; try watching 'from the corner of your eye'. In my experience, sharks are very aware of a diver's eyes and seem to dislike being stared at as much as you or I do.

Blue shark (*Prionace glauca*). Photo: Chris Harvey-Clark / www.geerg.ca

A diver who is vertically oriented often seems to inhibit the animal from investigating closely, possibly because an upright diver seems strange and frightening to a shark. Sharks, like other wild animals, seem to be more unnerved by height than length; this is probably because most swimming creatures are longest horizontally, in the direction of movement. You can reduce your strangeness by crouching down on sandy bottom near the outer face of a reef, of if the bottom lies in water too deep for scuba press yourself gently against the substrate or assume a back-to-back alignment with your buddy. Avoid touching the shark. DO NOT – under any circumstances – ATTEMPT TO HOLD OR RESTRAIN ANY SHARK, no matter how small or harmless it may seem.

To maximize your time underwater with a shark, it is import to maintain the animal's curiosity – otherwise, the shark will quickly become bored with you and swim away. Try humming a tune through your regulator; almost anything composed of relatively low notes and with a simple but not-too-regular rhythm works quite well ("Waltzing Matilda" has always worked a treat for me). Underwater photographers may want to try wearing brightly colored reef gloves to pique the shark's interest while taking pictures. But be warned: do not attempt to swim with or gesture with such gloves on – they may look edible to a shark. No matter how long you can keep the shark interested, you will remember the encounter long after the shark has forgotten you.

ADOPTING AN ENLIGHTENED ATTITUDE TOWARD SHARKS

Whale shark (*Rhincodon typus*). Photo: Aidan R. Martin - ReefQuest Centre for Shark Research

No doubt about it, sharks add special 'electricity' to any dive. The mere presence of a shark in your immediate vicinity should not be cause for alarm. A healthy respect for sharks' capabilities combined with an understanding of their behaviour is the only protection you really need. Accept sharks as a normal part of the underwater environment. Learn to recognize the shark species common where you dive

and find out what you can about their behaviour.

Because they are free to roam the depths and breadths of the world ocean, a close encounter with a shark in the wild is a rare and special event in a diver's life. But a clever primate must never lose sight of the fact that sharks are, after all, wild animals. Like the unicorn of the middle ages, sharks are the perfect mythological beast for our time; they seem the embodiment of all that is mysterious and untamable under the sea. Seen underwater in the context of their environment, sharks are among the most magnificent of living creatures. Many species are beautifully proportioned symphonies of grace and power in motion, exquisite examples of evolutionary perfection. Enjoy the beauty, forget the fear. Behold the true masters of their vast aquatic realm.

The serrated teeth of the Great white shark (*Carcharodon carcharias*). Photo: Scott Davis / greatwhiteadventures.com

The danger posed by sharks is greatly exaggerated and the hysteria surrounding each shark attack is grossly out of proportion to the actual risk. Taking into account the different population sizes and number of shark attacks (assuming all other factors to be the same), the chances in Australia are 50 to 1, in South Africa they are 600 to 1, and in the United States (including Hawaii) the chances are greater than 1000 to 1. The main reason that the risk of shark attack is relative high in Australia isn't that Australian sharks are more ferocious than South African or American sharks, but simply that Aussies play in the ocean far more frequently and intensely than most coastal people. There is thus a direct relationship between the number of people entering the sea and the incidence of shark attack.

Accurate records of shark attacks in the Caribbean region are available for the past 150 years or so. Over this considerable time span, fewer than 600 shark attacks have been recorded from the area bounded by the Gulf of Mexico, the Bahama Islands, and the Caribbean Sea. Shark attacks in this region have been increasing in frequency with increasing tourism and occur more-or-less evenly throughout the year. This increase and the lack of seasonal weighting is not surprising for a subtropical region with an ever-expanding, year-round tourist season. Almost half of Caribbean-region shark attacks have been fatal – a much higher proportion than the world average of about 30%. I suspect this, too, has more to do with the behaviour of people than the ferocity of Caribbean sharks.

Abundant and diverse alcoholic beverages are a large part of the Caribbean tourist experience. Most of us – at one time or another – have been known to say or do things 'under the influence' that we would otherwise not. Enthusiastic alcohol consumption not only causes loss of judgment but also complicates the treatment of any injuries one might incur. Due to the physiological nature of our sport, it is never a good idea to mix alcohol consumption and scuba diving. Regardless, the number of shark attacks recorded from the Caribbean region is really quite small compared with the millions of visitors to this region each year.

MOTIVATION OF SHARK ATTACKS

Motivation is the key to understanding shark attacks on humans. Aggression may be defined as any self-assertive behaviour, including charging, hitting, stabbing, or biting directed against a competitor. Compared with other vertebrates, most shark species do not seem to be very aggressive. This may seem surprising in view of the popular image of sharks as vicious predators, but aggression is usually considered to be distinct from predation. Most (96%) injuries sharks inflict on humans are single slashes, apparently made with the upper teeth only, suggesting that hunger is not usually the motivating force. Such wounds are more consistent with fighting than feeding. Whatever the motivation of shark attack, it is clear that very few sharks are aggressive toward people in the water.

A **Caribbean reef shark** (*Carcharhinus perezi*). Photo: J. Gallant / D.A.Y.

It has been suggested that sharks may become more aggressive at certain times of the year, such as when the water is warmest and/or during their mating season. Temperature is one of the most pervasive forces in biology, shaping everything from ecosystems to individuals. In general, the higher the temperature, the faster the rate of chemical reactions; with increasing temperature, the network of biochemical reactions which maintain life is also increased.

Sharks, with few exceptions, are ectothermic ("cold-blooded") creatures whose body temperatures fluctuate with the temperature of the environment. They are likely to become more active and thus feed more as water temperature increases. Some shark 'attacks' may actually be exploratory feeding; without benefit of hands, a shark often tests novel items with its teeth. Shark attacks are general more common during warmer parts of the year, but since the vast majority of attacks do not seem to be feeding-motivated, it is more likely that tis trend has more to do with the seasonal increase of people entering the water.

Recent research by L.E. 'Bets' Rasmussen on hormone levels in sharks off Bimini, Bahamas, indicates that levels of testosterone in the blood and urine of male and female sharks can reach astronomical levels during their mating season. In fact, one of the highest known blood testosterone concentrations of any animal is recorded from an adolescent male Caribbean Reef Shark (*Carcharhinus perezi*) from Bimini. Elevated levels of the sex hormone testosterone have been fuzzily linked to aggressive behaviour in several animal studies. But there is neither a simple nor a direct relationship between testosterone levels and aggressive behaviour. Shark mating in the Caribbean region generally occurs in the late sprig or early summer. However, incidence of shark attack against swimmers (one possible manifestation of shark aggression) seems independent of the sharks' presumed mating season. Occurrences of shark attacks seem to reflect seasonal patterns of beach patronage rather than any supposed shark biological rhythms. In the final analysis, patterns of shark attack tell us much more about human activity than the behaviour of sharks.

REDUCING THE RISK

First and foremost, it is important to bear in mind that a shark attack is an extremely rare phenomenon, despite media hyperbole to the contrary. Millions of people use the ocean every year without being attacked, and your chances of being bitten by a shark are much less than drowning. The sea itself is far more dangerous than any shark. Most people have heard that sharks are attracted to blood in the water. In truth, sharks may be curious about human blood, but are neither excited nor stimulated to attack by it. Most sharks are piscivores and may be stimulated to feed by fish blood but probably not by mammal blood, which is chemically different from fish blood. An obvious exception is the White Shark (*Carcharodon carcharias*) – adults of this species feed largely on marine mammals, and it is conceivable that human blood may be sufficiently similar to stimulate attack behaviour.

The following guidelines may reduce divers' risk of being attacked by a shark. These guidelines are based on the cumulative experience of myself, my diving colleagues, and the advice of authorities who specialize in the study of shark attacks, most notably Perry W. Gilbert, Victor Coppleson, David H. Davies, H. David Baldridge, Donald R. Nelson, Ralph Collier, Beulah Davis, Tim Wallett, George H. Burgess, and Electa Pace. These guidelines are relative straightforward and appeal to one's commonsense.

1. **Never dive alone.** A dive buddy team has a far better chance of sighting a nearby shark, and the very presence of your buddy may deter a shark. Also, if the shark were to attack you, your buddy would be close at hand to lend assistance.

2. **Do not provoke a shark** – even a small and apparently harmless one. Touching a shark, poking or spearing it, riding it, or holding its tail are all known to incite defensive attack. Sharks are amazingly powerful, and even a small shark can inflict serious, possible fatal, injuries to a human.

3. **Remove speared or wounded fish from the water immediately.**

4. **Do not spearfish for extended periods in the same waters.** Curious sharks may be drawn to your activities, the thrashing of

speared fish, or the blood and other body juices exuded by speared fish.

5. Leave the water as soon as possible after sighting a shark more than 5 ft (1.5 m) in length. While swimming toward the safety of a boat or the shore, remain submerged, keep the shark in sight, and use smooth swimming strokes. Do not count on the shark circling or making exploratory pass before it makes a direct charge.

6. Use discretion in choosing wetsuit colors. In general, low contrast is probably best to avoid attracting or exciting sharks. Avoid colors and patterns which might be mistaken for a large shark's natural prey of choice.

Greenland shark (*Somniosus microcephalus*) and divers. Photo: J. Gallant / D.A.Y.

7. Carry a stout prod ("shark billy") or plan to use the butt of a speargun to hold an over-attentive shark at bay until its interest in you wanes. Use the prod gingerly and only as a last resort. Do not attack the shark or attempt to injure it – the shark may respond aggressively.

8. Be aware of changes in the surrounding underwater environment. Take fullest advantage of your submerged vantage point, using central and peripheral vision to watch for movement at the limit of underwater visibility. Watch for changes in the behaviour of nearby marine life; if the largish fish suddenly disappear, look around very carefully: a big shark is probably hunting in the immediate area. Trust your 'diver instincts': if a shark seems tense or agitated

– or something doesn't 'feel right' – leave the water immediately. Shark attack case histories indicate that such vigilance has played a major role in lowering injury and mortality rates among diver-victims.

9. Do not maneuver a shark into a trapped position between yourself and any obstacle – such as the beach, a reef, the walls of an underwater cave, a sandbar, or possibly even a boat.

10. Do not wander away from an established group of other divers. Alone, you may give the appearance of easy prey.

11. Avoid diving at dawn and dusk, as many sharks hunt most intensively during these twilight hours.

WHAT TO DO IF THE WORST SHOULD HAPPEN

While one's chances of being bitten by a shark are extremely remote, that fact is of little consolation to the victim of a shark attack. There is, after all, a tremendous difference between potential and actual.

IF YOU ARE ATTACKED

The following advice is modified from H. David Baldridge's excellent book, *Shark Attack*, based on my own and others' experience with aggressive sharks.

1. Try to remain calm and keep the shark in sight in front of you, taking full advantage of any weapons available to you.

2. Use any object at hand to fend off the shark, but take care not to provoke it further. Keep fully in mind the limitations of such devices as spearguns, powerheads, gas-dart guns, et cetera and do not expect them to accomplish the impossible. Such weapons, if used improperly, may serve only to injure the user or further agitate the shark.

3. Use available spears and knives to fend off the shark, attempting to wound it only as a last resort.

4. Use discretion in making aggressive movements toward a shark. A shark which has not yet committed itself to attack might be incited by such movements if interpreted as a threat. Conversely, quick movements toward a shark at close quarters might produce a desirable startle response. If the shark's pectoral fins are depressed (held stiffly downward) and its movements seem quick and agitated, keep the animal in sight and try to increase the distance between you and it, noting its reaction. If the shark seems to relax somewhat, continue this tactic while heading toward your pre-planned exit site.

5. Once the shark has attacked – or attack seems imminent – fight the shark as best you can. Hit it with your bare hands only as a last resort. Probing the shark's eyes has often proved effective in causing the shark to abort its attack; probing the gills may produce a similar effect. Shouting underwater or blowing bubbles has sometimes produced startle responses in attacking sharks, which may buy valuable time. Do anything that comes to mind, for the seconds or minutes during which the shark might withdraw could be sufficient to allow you to escape or for others to effect your rescue.

6. Most shark attacks produce wounds that are readily survivable. Bleeding should be controlled as quickly as possible – even before you have been brought ashore; try using a strip cut from an undamaged portion of your wetsuit or the rubber sling from your speargun. Do not remove your mask; in the unlikely event the shark returns and launches a second attack, you will be better able to defend yourself if you can see clearly. Do not remove your wetsuit, as it may limit bleeding and help hold damaged tissue in place. Treatment by a physician is indicated even when the wounds seem relatively minor.

IF YOUR BUDDY IS ATTACKED

Beulah Davis, then Director of the Natal Sharks Board I South Africa, in collaboration with two physicians, has published detailed instructions for the treatment of shark attack victims. Their advice is summarized below and modified for diving situations.

Shark attack victims usually die from a combination of shock and blood loss. Therefore, the following actions should be taken as soon as possible:

1. Remove the victim from the water as quickly as possible and place victim on his or her left side, head-downward on the beach slope on an inclined surface on deck (Trendelenberg position). This serves to combat shock by increasing blood flow to the head. Administer oxygen if available, ideally at 100% concentration.

2. Control bleeding by pressing on pressure points, or by applying tourniquets. Efforts to stop bleeding should start while the victim is still in the water. Your inventiveness could dramatically improve the victim's prospects for recovery. Try using a strip cut from a wetsuit or Lycra dive skin, a neck seal, the rubber sling from a speargun, a mask strap, a towel, or any free hands available. Do not remove the victim's wetsuit, as it may limit bleeding and help hold damaged tissue in place. Locate the victim's I.D. and recent diving history. Secure the victim's gear, rinse and hold – but do NOT disassemble it.

3. Notify a physician, paramedic or hospital. State "This is a scuba diving emergency" to allow responding physicians to prepare equipment needed to treat any diving-related injuries (barotraumas) that may have occurred during the attack or rescue. Make only factual statements, DO NOT make value judgments or express opinions. If possible, take the victim's blood pressure and pulse rate for future reference by a physician or hospital.

4. DO NOT give the victim warm drinks or alcohol, only sips of fresh water or fruit juice. Protect the victim from cold by wrapping him or her in a blanket to minimize heat loss.

5. Bring aid to the victim rather than take the victim to the aid. This is because movement can increase shock. The victim should not be moved unless he or she has recovered from shock and a physician is present. Victims are better off left alone than moved unwisely or unnecessarily.

6. Untrained people should not try to help the victim in any way, other than by carrying out the steps outlined above – more harm than good can result from well-meant but incorrect attempts to render aid. Experts think that this is one of the most important factors in determining whether a victim recovers or not.

To assist research on the causes, etiology, treatment, and prevention of shark attacks, contact:

International Shark Attack File
Florida Museum of Natural History
University of Florida
Gainesville, FL 32611
United States of America
Phone: (904) 392-1721
FAX: (904) 392-8783

The Shark Attack File (SAF) will send you a standardized form for reporting the details of the attack in which you were involved. The SAF is maintained by the American Elasmobranch Society as a unique database for the collection and analysis of shark attack information on a world-wide basis. The SAF is staffed by highly skilled researchers and file access is restricted to physicians and shark biologists currently active in the scientific study of shark attacks. The SAF is non-profit and treats all correspondence regarding shark attack case histories in the strictest of confidence.

It is hoped that the reader never has cause to use the information presented in this section, but it you do, I hope it will prove helpful. More than likely, though, if you see a shark underwater it will be swimming away from you. If a shark does approach and investigate you, try to be a respectful and well-mannered visitor. As *National Geographic's* "Shark Lady", Eugenie Clark put it, "If you behave, they'll behave also". If you do your best to act on this last bit of advice, I'm sure that all your shark encounters will be pleasant ones.

- R. Aidan Martin

Up-dated by the author, from:

o Martin, R. 1995. *Shark Smart: the Divers Guide to Understanding Shark Behaviour*. Diving Naturalist Press, North Vancouver. 177 pp.

R. AIDAN MARTIN

R. Aidan Martin is the Director of the ReefQuest Centre for Shark Research, a Research Associate of the Zoology Department of the University of British Columbia, and an Adjunct Professor of the Oceanographic Center of Nova Southeastern University.

Aidan is internationally recognized as an expert on shark biology and behavior. He has studied elasmobranch fishes (sharks and rays) for over 30 years in some 40 countries or island states. Aidan is author or co-author of over 20 scientific papers in the primary literature, author of two books, *Shark Smart: the Divers' Guide to Understanding Shark Behaviour* (1995) and *Field Guide to the Great White Shark* (2003), and 130 popular articles on various aspects of marine ecology and conservation, which collectively have been published in eight languages; he is currently working on a scholarly book about shark behavior for Cambridge University Press.

INTERNET LINKS

> ➢ ReefQuest Centre for Shark Research
>   www.elasmo-research.org
> ➢ ReefQuest Marine Projects
>   www.reefquest.com
> ➢ Biology of Sharks and Rays (NSU)
>   nova.edu/ocean/sharksandrays.html

SHARK ANATOMY
BASED ON ILLUSTRATION BY R. AIDAN MARTIN

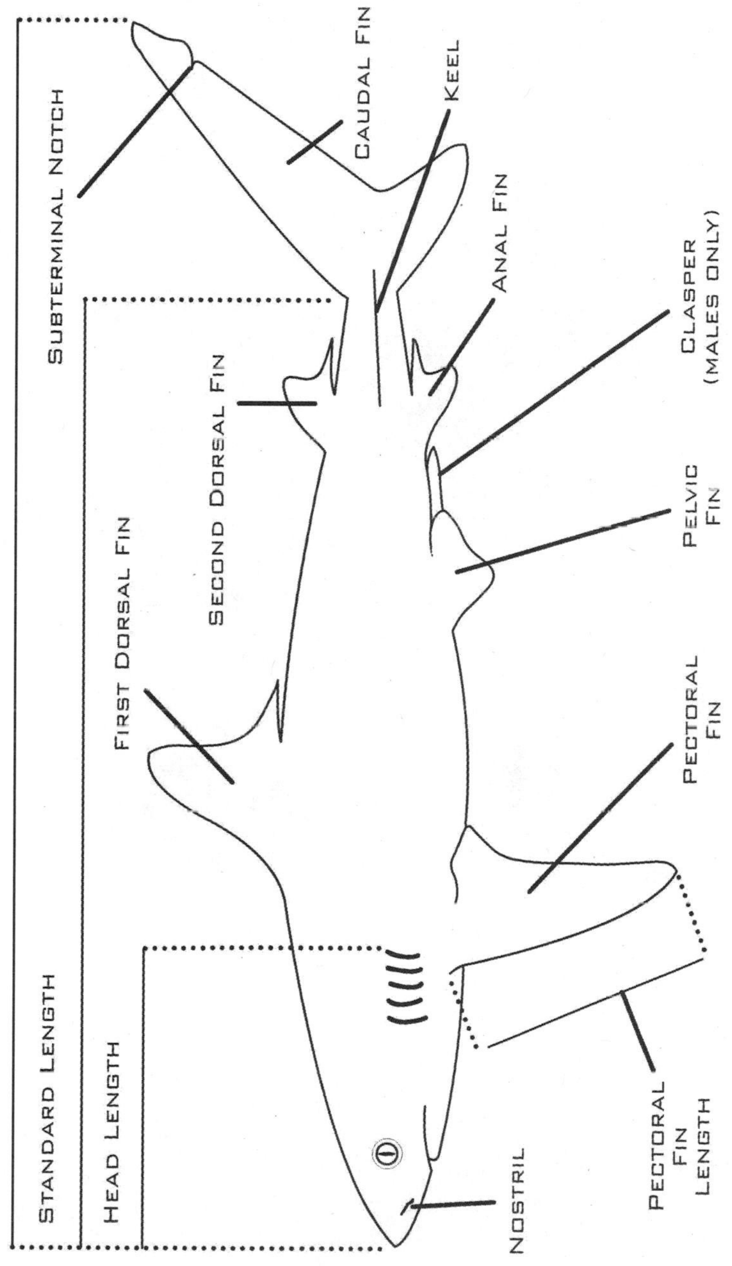

CAUDAL FIN

KEEL

ANAL FIN

CLASPER (MALES ONLY)

PELVIC FIN

PECTORAL FIN

PECTORAL FIN LENGTH

NOSTRIL

HEAD LENGTH

STANDARD LENGTH

TOTAL LENGTH

FIRST DORSAL FIN

SECOND DORSAL FIN

SUBTERMINAL NOTCH

www.seesharks.com

Navy diver during salvage of the
Ehime Maru off Honolulu, Hawaii
U.S. Navy Photo

Digital montage
Aquart Underwater Art Exhibit
Photo © Jeffrey Gallant
www.aquart.ca

Draeger Pionier Tauchergeraet (Circa 1925)
(Draeger Army Engineers Diving Apparatus)
Photos & equipment by David L. Dekker
www.pieds-lourds.com

Sphinx blenny
Black Sea, Romania
Photo © Jeffrey Gallant

SEAL Delivery Vehicle (SDV) the back of the Los Angeles-class attack submarine USS Philadelphia (SSN 690) U.S. Navy Photo

Loïc Leferme
Mediterranean Sea
Photo © Franck Seguin Deadline / Press Agency
www.deadline-press.com

Hardhat diver
Lac Saint-Pierre, Quebec
Photo © Jeffrey Gallant (Self-portrait)

Rubis submarine
Mediterranean Sea - 135 ft (41 m)
Photo © Patrice Strazzera
www.sommeildesepaves.com

Rubis submarine
Mediterranean Sea - 135 ft (41 m)
Photo © Patrice Strazzera
www.sommelidesepaves.com

Loïc Leferme
Mediterranean Sea
Photo © Franck Seguin Deadline / Press Agency
www.deadline-press.com

Hawksbill turtle
Roatan, Honduras
Photo © Jeffrey Gallant

1st Place, Macro Unrestricted
"Open Wide"
by Cor Bosman / Solomon Islands
www.underwatercompetition.com

1st Place, Compact Camera
"Hidden Treasures"
by John Johnson / Oahu, Hawai'i
www.underwatercompetition.com

1st Place, Environment/Conservation
'It all starts here'
by Martin Oernroth / Stockholm, Sweden
www.underwatercompetition.com

1st Place, Macro Traditional
"Seahorse"
by Noam Kortler / Eilat, Israel
www.underwatercompetition.com

1st Place, Wide-Angle Unrestricted
"Bat Fishes"
by Tibor Dombovari / Papua New Guinea
www.underwatercompetition.com

1st Place, Wide-Angle Traditional
"Shark in Motion"
by Christopher Guglielmo / Turks & Caicos Islands
www.underwatercompetition.com

underwater
competition.com

The 2nd Annual WetPixel.com and DivePhotoGuide.com
International Photo & Video Competition
...in association with Our World Underwater.

Over $35,000 in Prizes!

Wetpixel.com and DivePhotoGuide.com have teamed up again in association with Our World Underwater to celebrate the beauty and delicacy of the marine environment with their 2nd annual international underwater photography and video competition. The competition aims to become the "Superbowl" of international underwater photo competitions - with fantastic prizes, celebrity judges and the opportunity to have your images showcased to the world as some of the world's best.

A new website has launched to support the competition at www.underwatercompetition.com

Photographers will compete in six still image categories plus one video category, to win more than $35,000 in prizes, including premium dive travel, underwater photography equipment, and more! Dive packages include trips to some of the top photo destinations in the world: South Africa, Socoros Islands, Raja Empat, Komodo, Grand Cayman, the Galapagos Islands, Bora Bora, the Solomon Islands, Manado, Lembeh Strait, Yap, Cocos (Keeling) Island and the Bahamas! Other prizes include camera housings, strobes, lighting systems, and other valuable items. The competition includes a category for images that focus on conservation and the marine environment, and one specifically for entries taken by compact digital cameras.

Celebrity judges Stephen Frink, Dr. Alexander Mustard, and Eric Cheng will select winners after the Jan 7, 2007 deadline. Winners will be announced on stage at the 2007 Our World-Underwater film festival in Chicago, Illinois (February 9-11, 2007), and will be published by our supporting media partners worldwide.

15% of entry proceeds will be donated to marine conservation efforts.

For more information, please visit UnderwaterCompetition.com

2006 WINNERS

OCEANOGRAPHY

Oceanography (Ocean + Greek γράφειν = write) is a multidisciplinary science concerned with knowledge of the oceans and improvements in technology based on such knowledge. It incorporates many scientific fields that can be applied to the marine environment: physics, geology, chemistry, biology, meteorology, geography, and geodesy.

The physical oceanographer studies the physical properties of the ocean and the relationship between the sea and the atmosphere. The geological oceanographer studies the topographic features, rocks, sediments, and physical composition of the ocean floor.

SOURCE: Office of Naval Research

OCEANS & SEAS

Oceans and seas are very large bodies of sea water. They occupy 71% or 140 million mi² (361 million km²) of the surface of the earth and contain 317,000 mi³ (1,322 million km³) of water.

The planet's five oceans separate the continents and together for the World Ocean. Seas are smaller parts of the oceans which are surrounded to various degrees by land. Overall, seas are also shallower than oceans. There are three types of seas:

❖ continental seas are connected to oceans by straights;
❖ border seas form gulfs;
❖ closed seas are in fact large saltwater lakes.

ARCTIC OCEAN

The Arctic Ocean is the smallest of the world's five oceans (after the Pacific Ocean, Atlantic Ocean, Indian Ocean, and the recently delimited Southern Ocean). The Northwest Passage (US and Canada) and Northern Sea Route (Norway and Russia) are two important seasonal waterways. A sparse network of air, ocean, river, and land routes circumscribes the Arctic Ocean.

Area: 5.427 million mi² (14.056 million sq km)

Coastline: 28,203 mi. (45,389 km)

Climate: Polar climate characterized by persistent cold and relatively narrow annual temperature ranges; winters characterized by continuous darkness, cold and stable weather conditions, and clear skies; summers characterized by continuous daylight, damp and foggy weather, and weak cyclones with rain or snow.

The Royal Navy Trafalgar class attack submarine HMS Tireless sits on the surface of the North Pole. Photo: U.S. Navy Chief Journalist Kevin Elliott

Terrain: central surface covered by a perennial drifting polar icepack that, on average, is about 10 ft (3 m) thick, although pressure ridges may be three times that thickness; clockwise drift pattern in the Beaufort Gyral Stream, but nearly straight-line movement from the New Siberian Islands (Russia) to Denmark Strait (between Greenland and Iceland); the icepack is surrounded by open seas during the summer, but more than doubles in size during the winter and extends to the encircling landmasses; the ocean floor is about 50% continental shelf (highest percentage of any ocean) with the remainder a central basin interrupted by three submarine ridges (Alpha Cordillera, Nansen Cordillera, and Lomosonov Ridge).

Deepest point: Fram Basin 15,305 ft (4,665 m)

ATLANTIC OCEAN

The Atlantic Ocean is the second largest of the world's five oceans (after the Pacific Ocean, but larger than the Indian Ocean, Southern Ocean, and Arctic Ocean). The Kiel Canal (Germany), Oresund (Denmark-Sweden), Bosporus (Turkey), Strait of Gibraltar (Morocco-Spain), and the Saint Lawrence Seaway (Canada-US) are important strategic access waterways. The decision by the International Hydrographic Organization in the spring of 2000 to delimit a fifth world ocean, the Southern Ocean, removed the portion of the Atlantic Ocean south of 60 degrees south.

Area: 29.638 million mi² (76.762 million km²). Includes Baltic Sea, Black Sea, Caribbean Sea, Davis Strait, Denmark Strait, part of the Drake Passage, Gulf of Mexico, Labrador Sea, Mediterranean Sea, North Sea, Norwegian Sea, almost all of the Scotia Sea, and other tributary water bodies).

Coastline: 69,510 mi (111,866 km)

Climate: tropical cyclones (hurricanes) develop off the coast of Africa near Cape Verde and move westward into the Caribbean Sea; hurricanes can occur from May to December, but are most frequent from August to November.

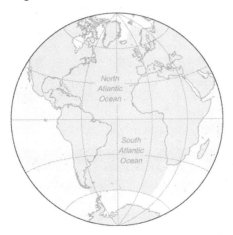

Terrain: surface usually covered with sea ice in Labrador Sea, Denmark Strait, and coastal portions of the Baltic Sea from October to June; clockwise warm-water gyre (broad, circular system of currents) in the northern Atlantic, counterclockwise warm-water gyre in the southern Atlantic; the ocean floor is dominated by the Mid-Atlantic Ridge, a rugged north-south centerline for the entire Atlantic basin.

Deepest point: Milwaukee Deep in the Puerto Rico Trench 28,232 ft (8,605 m)

INDIAN OCEAN

The Indian Ocean is the third largest of the world's five oceans (after the Pacific Ocean and Atlantic Ocean, but larger than the Southern Ocean and Arctic Ocean). Four critically important access waterways are the Suez Canal (Egypt), Bab el Mandeb (Djibouti-Yemen), Strait of Hormuz (Iran-Oman), and Strait of Malacca (Indonesia-Malaysia). The decision by the International Hydrographic Organization in the spring of 2000 to delimit a fifth ocean, the Southern Ocean, removed the portion of the Indian Ocean south of 60 degrees south.

Area: 26.470 million mi² (68.556 million km²). Includes Andaman Sea, Arabian Sea, Bay of Bengal, Flores Sea, Great Australian Bight, Gulf of Aden, Gulf of Oman, Java Sea, Mozambique Channel, Persian Gulf, Red Sea, Savu Sea, Strait of Malacca, Timor Sea, and other tributary water bodies.

Coastline: 41,337 mi. (66,526 km)

Climate: northeast monsoon (December to April), southwest monsoon (June to October); tropical cyclones occur during May/June and October/November in the northern Indian Ocean and January/February in the southern Indian Ocean.

Terrain: surface dominated by counter-clockwise gyre (broad, circular system of currents) in the southern Indian Ocean; unique reversal of surface currents in the northern Indian Ocean; low atmospheric pressure over southwest Asia from hot, rising, summer air results in the southwest monsoon and southwest-to-northeast winds and currents, while high pressure over northern Asia from cold, falling, winter air results in the northeast monsoon and northeast-to-southwest winds and currents; ocean floor is dominated by the Mid-Indian Ocean Ridge and subdivided by the Southeast Indian Ocean Ridge, Southwest Indian Ocean Ridge, and Ninetyeast Ridge.

Deepest point: Java Trench 23,812 ft (7,258 m)

PACIFIC OCEAN

The Pacific Ocean is the largest of the world's five oceans (followed by the Atlantic Ocean, Indian Ocean, Southern Ocean, and Arctic Ocean). Strategically important access waterways include the La Perouse, Tsugaru, Tsushima, Taiwan, Singapore, and Torres Straits. The decision by the International Hydrographic Organization in the spring of 2000 to delimit a fifth ocean, the Southern Ocean, removed the portion of the Pacific Ocean south of 60 degrees south.

Area: 60.061 million mi² (155.557 million km²). Includes Bali Sea, Bering Sea, Bering Strait, Coral Sea, East China Sea, Gulf of Alaska, Gulf of Tonkin, Philippine Sea, Sea of Japan, Sea of Okhotsk, South China Sea, Tasman Sea, and other tributary water bodies.

Coastline: 84,297 mi. (135,663 km)

Climate: planetary air pressure systems and resultant wind patterns exhibit remarkable uniformity in the south and east; trade winds and westerly winds are well-developed patterns, modified by seasonal fluctuations; tropical cyclones (hurricanes) may form south of Mexico from June to October and affect Mexico and Central America; continental influences cause climatic uniformity to be much less pronounced in the eastern and western regions at the same latitude in the North Pacific Ocean; the western Pacific is monsoonal - a rainy season occurs during the summer months, when moisture-laden winds blow from the ocean over the land, and a dry season during the winter months, when dry winds blow from the Asian landmass back to the ocean; tropical cyclones (typhoons) may strike southeast and east Asia from May to December.

Terrain: surface currents in the northern Pacific are dominated by a clockwise, warm-water gyre (broad circular system of currents) and in the southern Pacific by a counterclockwise, cool-water gyre; in the northern Pacific, sea ice forms in the Bering Sea and Sea of Okhotsk in winter; in the southern Pacific, sea ice from Antarctica reaches its northernmost extent in October; the ocean floor in the eastern Pacific is dominated by the East Pacific Rise, while the western Pacific is dissected by deep trenches, including the Mariana Trench, which is the world's deepest.

Deepest point: Challenger Deep in the Mariana Trench 35,798 ft (10,911 m)

SOUTHERN OCEAN

A decision by the International Hydrographic Organization in the spring of 2000 delimited a fifth world ocean - the Southern Ocean - from the southern portions of the Atlantic Ocean, Indian Ocean, and Pacific Ocean. The Southern Ocean extends from the coast of Antarctica north to 60 degrees south latitude, which coincides with the Antarctic Treaty Limit. The Southern Ocean is now the fourth largest of the world's five oceans (after the Pacific Ocean, Atlantic Ocean, and Indian Ocean, but larger than the Arctic Ocean).

Area: 7.848 million mi² (20.327 million km²). Includes Amundsen Sea, Bellingshausen Sea, part of the Drake Passage, Ross Sea, a small part of the Scotia Sea, Weddell Sea, and other tributary water bodies.

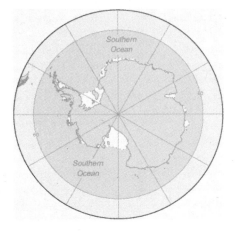

Coastline: 11,165 mi. (17,968 km)

Climate: sea temperatures vary from about 50F to 28F (10°C to -2°C); cyclonic storms travel eastward around the continent and frequently are intense because of the temperature contrast between ice and open ocean; the ocean area from about latitude 40 south to the Antarctic Circle has the strongest average winds found anywhere on Earth; in winter the ocean freezes outward to 65 degrees south latitude in the Pacific sector and 55 degrees south latitude in the Atlantic sector, lowering surface temperatures well below 32F (0°C); at some coastal points intense persistent drainage winds from the interior keep the shoreline ice-free throughout the winter.

Terrain: the Southern Ocean is deep, 13,123 ft to 16,404 ft (4,000 to 5,000 m) over most of its extent with only limited areas of shallow water; the Antarctic continental shelf is generally narrow and unusually deep, its edge lying at depths of 1,312 ft to 2,625 ft (400 to 800 m) (the global mean is 436 ft / 133 m); the Antarctic icepack grows from an average minimum of 1.004 million mi² (2.6 million km²) in March to about 7.3 million mi² (18.8 million km²) in September, better than a six fold increase in area; the Antarctic Circumpolar Current (13, 049 mi. / 21,000 km in length) moves perpetually eastward; it is the world's largest ocean current, transporting 31.189 mi³ (130 million km³) of water per second - 100 times the flow of all the world's rivers.

Deepest point: 23,737 ft (7,235 m) at the southern end of the South Sandwich Trench

SOURCE: CIA World Fact Book

ESTUARIES

An estuary is a partially enclosed body of water, and its surrounding coastal habitats, where saltwater from the ocean mixes with fresh water from rivers or streams. In fresh water the concentration of salts, or salinity, is nearly zero. The salinity of water in the ocean averages about 35 parts per thousand (ppt). The mixture of seawater and fresh water in estuaries is called brackish water and its salinity can range from 0.5 to 35 ppt. The salinity of estuarine water varies from estuary to estuary, and can change from one day to the next depending on the tides, weather, or other factors (Levinton, 1995.)

Estuaries are transitional areas that straddle the land and the sea, as well as freshwater and saltwater habitats. The daily tides (the regular rise and fall of the sea's surface) are a major influence on many of these dynamic environments. Most areas of the Earth experience two high and two low tides each day. Some areas, like the Gulf of Mexico, have only one high and one low tide each day.

The tidal pattern in an estuary depends on its geographic location, the shape of the coastline and ocean floor, the depth of the water, local winds, and any restrictions to water flow. For example, tides at the end of a long, narrow inlet might be amplified because a large volume of water is being forced into a very small space. However, the tides in wetlands composed of broad mud flats might appear to be rather small. With the variety of conditions across the Earth, each estuary displays a tidal pattern unique to its location (Nielsen 1982).

While strongly affected by tides and tidal cycles, many estuaries are protected from the full force of ocean waves, winds, and storms by reefs, barrier islands, or fingers of land, mud, or sand that surround them. The characteristics of each estuary depend upon the local climate, freshwater input, tidal patterns, and currents. Truly, no two estuaries are the same. Yet they are typically classified based on two characteristics: their geology and how saltwater and fresh water mix in them.

Whale-watching in the St. Lawrence Estuary, one of the richest marine environments in the world. Photo: J. Gallant / D.A.Y.

However, not all estuaries contain brackish waters. There are a small number of ecosystems classified as freshwater estuaries. These estuaries occur where massive freshwater systems, such as the Great Lakes in the United States, are diluted by river or stream waters draining from adjacent lands.

SOURCE: NOAA

LAKES

A lake is a body of water surrounded by land, usually stagnant water, soft water, lake bottoms can be rocks, sand and/or mud, can have a gentle slope or a cliff overhang, water can be clear or colored.

Lakes are interesting dive sites when you know where to dive. Look for rocky areas and where grass and aquatic plants grow. These sites will have soft water sponges and insect larvae and eggs which will attract fish. In short, a lake dive will be more interesting in areas where people do not usually swim due to mud, rocks, plants and grass. This is where the fish will be. Plants needing plenty of light and, not being able to tolerate pressure, will be found in shallow water. Dive to see both fish and lake vegetation.

Be attentive and move gently and slowly. There is a lot of life in a lake. Spawning grounds are easily observed in shallow water. Read up on the fish species to be found in the lakes. There is very little to see in the middle of a lake unless a wreck is located there. Most of what there is to see is close to the sides and near floating piers and docks. For that reason, snorkeling is ideal in a lake.

The water is generally clearer in the fall and winter seasons with fewer particles being suspended in cold water. Avoid disturbing the lake bottom, in particular if it is mud. Treat the flora as precious and fragile to protect the environment. When diving close to a cliff, be careful of rocks which can be set loose. As lakes are often used for fishing, be careful of hooks, fishing lines and nets. This is where a dive knife comes in handy.

When diving or snorkeling in algae or aquatic plants, palm slowly to avoid getting caught. Do not adventure into unknown caves or wrecks.

SOURCE: CMAS/AMCQ

Spawning smallmouth bass in Quebec's Eastern Townships. Photo: J. Gallant / D.A.Y.

CMAS QUÉBEC
www.cmasquebec.org

10 LARGEST LAKES OF THE WORLD

Name and location	Surface area mi^2	Surface area km^2	Volume mi^3 km^3	Max depth ft	Max depth m
Caspian Sea Azerbaijan, Iran, Kazakhstan, Russia, Turkmenistan	168,341	436,000	18,761 78,200	3,363	1,025
Superior Canada - U.S.A.	31,820	82,414	2,903 12,100	1,332	406
Victoria Tanzania-Uganda	26,828	69,485	662 2,760	269	82
Huron Canada - U.S.A.	23,010	59,596	849 3,540	751	229
Michigan U.S.A.	22,400	58,016	1,180 4,920	922	281
Tanganyika Congo - Tanzania	12,700	32,893	4,458 19,000	4,708	1,435
Baikal Russia	12,162	31,500	5,662 23,600	5,712	1,741
Great Bear Canada	12,000	31,080	550 2,292	269	82
Nyasa (Malawi) Malawi - Mozambique - Tanzania	11,600	30,044	1,865 7,775	2,316	706
Great Slave Canada	11,170	28,930	501 2,088	2,015	614

RIVERS

A river is a body of running water flowing into another body of water. The current is always present, can be strong or weak depending on the water level, and can be different from one area to another and from one season to another.

Visibility in a river will vary though rarely very good. It will depend on what is being carried in the water. When it is raining or has rained, or when ice has been thawing, visibility is greatly reduced.

Algae and aquatic plant life is generally abundant. The river bottom can be rocks, sand or mud. The water is generally shallow and rapids are found on many rivers.

Snorkeling down a river is a good diving activity. Scuba diving in a river is interesting and not too demanding. Divers will go into the water from a boat and simply follow the current to be picked up further down the river by the same boat. Fauna and flora are generally abundant and vary depending on factors such as the bottom of the river, the speed of the current, the water depth. Species will vary depending on the mouth of the river.

Rivers containing spawning grounds near the banks among the rocks, grasses and plant life. To fully observe and appreciate the life found in a river, a diver must understand that dives will be in shallow water and care must be taken not to scare away any species.

Another interesting aspect of river diving is finding traces of civilization: wrecks and archaeological finds are present in many rivers.

Avoid public docks as these are invariably dump sites, whether in rivers, lakes or at sea.

Always know the river that you plan to dive in and, if it is a first dive, be accompanied by divers who have already explored it.

Northern Crayfish (*Orconectes virilis***). Drummondville, Québec. Photo: J. Gallant / D.A.Y.**

SOURCE: CMAS/AMCQ

10 PRINCIPAL RIVERS OF THE WORLD

River	Outflow	Location	mi.	km
Nile	Mediterranean Sea	Egypt	4,180	6,690
Amazon	Atlantic Ocean	Brazil	4,080	6,570
Chang Jiang (Yangtze)	China Sea	China	3,720	5,980
Mississippi - Missouri - Red Rock	Gulf of Mexico	U.S.A.	3,710	5,970
Yenisei	Arctic Ocean	Russia	2,800	4,506
Heilong (Amur)	Tatar Strait	Russia	2,704	4,352
Ob	Gulf of Ob	Russia	3,459	5,567
Paraná	Río de la Plata	Argentina - Uruguay	2,795	4,498
Huang He (Yellow)	Gulf of Chihli	China	2,900	4,667
Zaire (Congo)	Atlantic Ocean	Angola - Zaire	2,716	4,371

OCEAN CURRENTS

Ocean and atmospheric circulation play an essential role in sustaining life by moderating climate over much of Earth's surface. An important part of the circulation of heat and freshwater and other sea water constituents are ocean surface currents. Their strength and variability play a role in weather and climate, impact environments for all life on Earth.

Global surface current patterns are driven by the wind, impacted by the barriers to flow provided by the land masses and the rotation of the earth, and ultimately derive their energy (like the wind) from the sun.

Two circulation patterns dominate the ocean: wind-driven currents in the upper ocean and the circulation in the deep ocean. Wind-driven currents are maintained by momentum transferred by the winds to the ocean surface. The ocean wind sets the surface waters in motion as a current, the Coriolis force[24], the density distribution of sea water, and the shape of the ocean basin modify the speed and direction of the current.

Western boundary currents such as the Gulf Stream are among the fastest surface currents in the ocean. Western boundary currents flow toward the poles, northward in the Northern Hemisphere and southward in the Southern Hemisphere along the western boundaries of the ocean basins. Water moving in these currents transport large quantities of heat from tropics to mid-latitudes.

Eastern Boundary currents, such as the California current are slower, shallower, and wider than the western boundary currents. Similar to the return flow in a household heating system, these currents transport colder waters into the tropics where they are heated and transported poleward in the western boundary currents.

Ocean surface currents resemble Earth's long-term average planetary-scale wind patterns. Surface currents form gyres[25] roughly centered in each ocean basin. Viewed from above, currents in these subtropical gyres flow in a clockwise direction in the Northern Hemisphere and a counterclockwise direction in the Southern Hemisphere.

SOURCE: NASA

TIDES

Tides are one of the most reliable phenomena in the world. As the sun rises in the east and the stars come out at night, we are confident that the ocean waters will regularly rise and fall along our shores. The following pages describe the tremendous forces that cause the world's tides, and why it is important for us to understand how they work.

Basically, tides are very long-period waves that move through the oceans in response to the forces exerted by the moon and sun. Tides originate in the oceans and progress toward the coastlines where they appear as the regular rise and fall of sea surface. When the highest part, or crest of the wave reaches a particular location, high tide occurs; low tide corresponds to the lowest part of the wave, or its trough. The difference in height between the high tide and the low tide is called the tidal range.

A horizontal movement of water often accompanies the rising and falling of the tide. This is called the tidal current. The incoming tide along the coast and into the bays and estuaries is called a flood current; the outgoing tide is called ebb current. The strongest flood and ebb currents usually occur before or near the time of the high and low tides. The weakest currents occur between the flood and ebb currents and are called slack tides. In the

---

[24] The deflection of moving objects (air and water currents) due to the rotation of the Earth--to the right in the northern hemisphere, and to the left in the southern.

[25] A great, circular motion of water in each of the major ocean basins centered on subtropical high-pressure region, with circulation clockwise in the northern hemisphere and counterclockwise in the southern hemisphere.

open ocean tidal currents are relatively weak. Near estuary entrances, narrow straits and inlets, the speed of tidal currents can reach up to several miles/kilometers per hour (Ross, D.A., 1995).

WHAT CAUSES TIDES?

Gravity is one major force that creates tides. In 1687, Sir Isaac Newton explained that ocean tides result from the gravitational attraction of the sun and moon on the oceans of the earth (Sumich, J.L., 1996). Newton's law of universal gravitation states that the gravitational attraction between two bodies is directly proportional to their masses, and inversely proportional to the square of the distance between the bodies (Sumich, J.L., 1996; Thurman, H.V., 1994). Therefore, the greater the mass of the objects and the closer they are to each other, the greater the gravitational attraction between them (Ross, D.A. 1995).

Tidal forces are based on the gravitational attractive force. With regard to tidal forces on the Earth, the distance between two objects usually is more critical than their masses. Tidal generating forces vary inversely as the cube of the distance from the tide generating object. Gravitational attractive forces only vary inversely to the square of the distance between the objects (Thurman, H.V., 1994). The effect of distance on tidal forces is seen in the relationship between the sun, the moon, and the Earth's waters.

Our sun is 27 million times larger than our moon. Based on its mass, the sun's gravitational attraction to the Earth is more than 177 times greater than that of the moon to the Earth. If tidal forces were based solely on comparative masses, the sun should have a tide-generating force that is 27 million times greater than that of the moon. However, the sun is 390 times further from the Earth than is the moon. Thus, its tide-generating force is reduced by 390^3, or about 59 million times less than the moon. Because of these conditions, the sun's tide-

generating force is about half that of the moon (Thurman, H.V., 1994).

Tide gauge at Knik Harbor, Alaska, showing 30-ft range of tide. Photo: NOAA/C&GS Season's Report Hand 1918-32

FREQUENCY OF TIDES

Most coastal areas, with some exceptions, experience two high tides and two low tides every lunar day (Ross, D.A., 1995). Almost everyone is familiar with the concept of a 24-hour solar day, which is the time that it takes for a specific site on the Earth to rotate from an exact point under the sun to the same point under the sun. Similarly, a lunar day is the time it takes for a specific site on the Earth to rotate from an exact point under the moon to the same point under the moon. Unlike a solar day, however, a lunar day is 24 hours and 50 minutes. The lunar day is 50 minutes longer than a solar day because the moon revolves around the Earth in the same direction that the Earth rotates around its axis. So, it takes the Earth an extra 50 minutes to "catch up" to the moon (Sumich, J.L., 1996; Thurman, H.V., 1994).

Because the Earth rotates through two tidal "bulges" every lunar day, coastal areas experience two high and two low tides every 24 hours and 50 minutes. High tides occur 12 hours and 25 minutes apart. It takes six hours and 12.5 minutes for the water at the shore to go from high to low, or from low to high.

TYPES AND CAUSES OF TIDAL CYCLES

If the Earth were a perfect sphere without large continents, all areas on the planet would experience two equally proportioned high and low tides every lunar day. The large continents on the planet, however, block the westward passage of the tidal bulges as the Earth rotates. Unable to move freely around the globe, these tides establish complex patterns within each ocean basin that often differ greatly from tidal patterns of adjacent ocean basins or other regions of the same ocean basin (Sumich, J.L., 1996).

Three basic tidal patterns occur along the Earth's major shorelines. In general, most areas have two high tides and two low tides each day. When the two highs and the two lows are about the same height, the patterns called a semi-daily or semidiurnal tide. If the high and low tides differ in height, the pattern is called a mixed semidiurnal tide. Some areas, such as the Gulf of Mexico, have only one high and one low tide each day. This is called a diurnal tide. The U.S. West Coast tends to have mixed semidiurnal tides, whereas a semidiurnal pattern is more typical of the East Coast (Sumich, J.L., 1996; Thurman, H.V., 1994; Ross, D.A., 1995).

WHAT ELSE AFFECTS TIDES?

The relative distances and positions of the sun, moon and Earth all affect the size and magnitude of the Earth's two tidal bulges. At a smaller scale, the magnitude of tides can be strongly influenced by the shape of the shoreline. When oceanic tidal bulges hit wide continental margins, the height of the tides can be magnified. Conversely, mid-oceanic islands not near continental margins typically experience very small tides of 3.28 ft (1 m) or less (Thurman, H.V., 1994).

The shape of bays and estuaries also can magnify the intensity of tides. Funnel-shaped bays in particular can dramatically alter tidal magnitude. The Bay of Fundy in Nova Scotia is the classic example of this effect, and has the highest tides in the world - over 49.21 ft (15 m) (Thurman, H.V., 1994). Narrow inlets and shallow water also tend to dissipate incoming tides. Inland bays such as Laguna Madre, Texas, and Pamlico Sound, North Carolina, have areas classified as non-tidal even though they have ocean inlets. In estuaries with strong tidal rivers, such as the Delaware River and Columbia River, powerful seasonal river flows in the spring can severely alter or mask the incoming tide.

Local wind and weather patterns also can affect tides. Strong offshore winds can move water away from coastlines, exaggerating low tide exposures. Onshore winds may act to pile up water onto the shoreline, virtually eliminating low tide exposures. High-pressure systems can depress sea levels, leading to clear sunny days with exceptionally low tides. Conversely, low-pressure systems that contribute to cloudy, rainy conditions typically are associated with tides than are much higher than predicted.

SOURCE: NOAA

DIVING & TIDES

The best time to dive is when the tide slackens, that is when it is reversing. This is when there is a period of stability, i.e. weak current or no current.

High tide: There is more water and it is clearer, however you have to dive deeper and there is a risk due to the stronger current with outgoing tides.

Low tide: Visibility is less, you may have to go over slippery rocks, but you will not have to dive as deep and the incoming tide can help you return when your dive is over.

SOURCE: CMAS/AMCQ

TSUNAMIS

The phenomenon we call a tsunami (soo-NAH-mee) is a series of waves of extremely long wave length and long period generated in a body of water by an impulsive disturbance that displaces the water. Tsunamis are primarily associated with earthquakes in oceanic and coastal regions. Landslides, volcanic eruptions, nuclear explosions, and even impacts of objects from outer space (such as meteorites, asteroids, and comets) can also generate tsunamis.

As the tsunami crosses the deep ocean, its length from crest to crest may be a hundred miles or more, and its height from crest to trough will only be a few feet or less. They can not be felt aboard ships nor can they be seen from the air in the open ocean. In the deepest oceans, the waves

will reach speeds exceeding 600 mph (966 km/h). When the tsunami enters the shoaling water of coastlines in its path, the velocity of its waves diminishes and the wave height increases. It is in these shallow waters that a large tsunami can crest to heights exceeding 100 ft (30 m) and strike with devastating force.

Tsunami damage at Kodiak at Kodiak, Alaska. following 1964 Good Friday Earthquake. Photo: NOAA Central Library

The term tsunami was adopted for general use in 1963 by an international scientific conference. Tsunami is a Japanese word represented by two characters: "tsu" and "nami". The character "tsu" means harbor, while the character "nami" means wave. In the past, tsunamis were often referred to as "tidal waves" by many English speaking people. The term "tidal wave" is a misnomer. Tides are the result of gravitational influences of the moon, sun, and planets. Tsunamis are not caused by the tides and are unrelated to the tides; although a tsunami striking a coastal area is influenced by the tide level at the time of impact. Also in the past, the scientific community referred to tsunamis as "seismic sea waves". "Seismic" implies an earthquake-related mechanism of generation. Although tsunamis are usually generated by earthquakes, tsunamis are less commonly caused by landslides, infrequently by volcanic eruptions, and very rarely by a large meteorite impact in the ocean.

Earthquakes generate tsunamis when the sea floor abruptly deforms and displaces the overlying water from its equilibrium position. Waves are formed as the displaced water mass, which acts under the influence of gravity, attempts to regain its equilibrium. The main factor which determines the initial size of a tsunami is the amount of vertical sea floor deformation. This is controlled by the earthquake's magnitude, depth, fault characteristics and coincident slumping of sediments or secondary faulting. Other features which influence the size of a tsunami along the coast are the shoreline and bathymetric configuration, the velocity of the sea floor deformation, the water depth near the earthquake source, and the efficiency which energy is transferred from the earth's crust to the water column.

A tsunami can be generated by any disturbance that displaces a large water mass from its equilibrium position. Submarine landslides, which often occur during a large earthquake, can also create a tsunami. During a submarine landslide, the equilibrium sea-level is altered by sediment moving along the sea-floor. Gravitational forces then propagate the tsunami given the initial perturbation of the sea-level. Similarly, a violent marine volcanic eruption can create an impulsive force that displaces the water column and generates a tsunami. Above water (subarial) landslides and space born objects can disturb the water from above the surface. The falling debris displaces the water from its equilibrium position and produces a tsunami. Unlike ocean-wide tsunamis caused by some earthquakes, tsunamis generated by non-seismic mechanisms usually dissipate quickly and rarely affect coastlines far from the source area.

Tsunamis are characterized as shallow-water waves. Shallow-water waves are different from wind-generated waves, the waves many of us have observed at the beach. Wind-generated waves usually have period (time between two sucessional waves) of five to twenty seconds and a wavelength (distance between two sucessional waves) of about 300 to 600 ft (100 to 200 m).

A tsunami can have a period in the range of ten minutes to two hours and a wavelength in excess of 300 mi. (500 km). It is because of their long wavelengths that tsunamis behave as shallow-water waves. A wave is characterized as a shallow-water wave when the ratio between the water depth and its wavelength gets very small. The speed of a shallow-water wave is equal to the square root of the product of the acceleration of gravity (32 ft/sec/sec or 980 cm/sec/sec) and the depth of the water. The rate at which a wave loses its energy is inversely related to its wavelength. Since a tsunami has a very large wave length, it will lose little energy as it propagates. Hence in very deep water, a tsunami will travel at high speeds and travel great transoceanic distances with limited energy loss. For example, when the ocean is 20,000 ft (6,100 m) deep, unnoticed tsunamis travel about 550 mph (890 km/h), the speed of a jet airplane. And they can move from one side of the Pacific Ocean to the other side in less than one day.

As a tsunami leaves the deep water of the open sea and propagates into the more shallow waters near the coast, it undergoes a transformation. Since the speed of the tsunami is related to the water depth, as the depth of the water decreases, the speed of the tsunami diminishes. The change of total energy of the tsunami remains constant. Therefore, the speed of the tsunami decreases as it enters shallower water, and the height of the wave grows. Because of this "shoaling" effect, a tsunami that was imperceptible in deep water may grow to be several feet/meters or more in height.

When a tsunami finally reaches the shore, it may appear as a rapidly rising or falling tide, a series of breaking waves, or even a bore. Reefs, bays, entrances to rivers, undersea features and the slope of the beach all help to modify the tsunami as it approaches the shore. Tsunamis rarely become great, towering breaking waves. Sometimes the tsunami may break far offshore. Or it may form into a bore: a step-like wave with a steep breaking front. A bore can happen if the tsunami moves from deep water into a shallow bay or river. The water level on shore can rise many feet. In extreme cases, water level can rise to more than 50 ft (15 m) for tsunamis of distant origin and over 100 ft (30 m) for tsunami generated near the earthquake's epicenter. The first wave may not be the largest in the series of waves. One coastal area may see no damaging wave activity while in another area destructive waves can be large and violent. The flooding of an area can extend inland by 1000 ft (305 m) or more, covering large expanses of land with water and debris. Flooding tsunami waves tend to carry loose objects and people out to sea when they retreat. Tsunamis may reach a maximum vertical height onshore above sea level, called a run-up height, of 30 m (98 ft). A notable exception is the landslide generated tsunami in Lituya Bay, Alaska in 1958 which produced a 1,722-ft (525 m) wave.

Fishing boat washed into town by tsunami at Kodiak, Alaska. Photo: NOAA Central Library

Since science cannot predict when earthquakes will occur, they cannot determine exactly when a tsunami will be generated. But, with the aid of historical records of tsunamis and numerical models, science can get an idea as to where they are most likely to be generated. Past tsunami height measurements and computer modeling

help to forecast future tsunami impact and flooding limits at specific coastal areas. There is an average of two destructive tsunamis per year in the Pacific basin. Pacific wide tsunamis are a rare phenomenon, occurring every 10 -12 years on the average.

TSUNAMI FAQs

What is a tsunami?

A tsunami is a series of waves with a long wavelength and period (time between crests) generated by a large, impulsive displacement of sea water.

Time between crests of the wave can vary from a few minutes to over an hour.

Tsunamis are often incorrectly called tidal waves; they have no relation to the daily ocean tides.

How are tsunamis generated?

Tsunamis are generated by any large, impulsive displacement of the sea level.

Tsunamis are also triggered by landslides into or under the water surface, and can be generated by volcanic activity and meteorite impacts.

How often do tsunamis occur?

On the average, two tsunamis occur per year throughout the world which inflict damage near the source.

Approximately every 15 years a destructive, ocean-wide tsunami occurs.

Can strike-slip (horizontal motion) earthquakes trigger tsunamis?

Yes, approximately 15% of all damaging tsunamis were triggered by strike-slip earthquakes.

This type of earthquake is less likely to trigger a tsunami than one with vertical motion.

The waves are likely generated by associated landslides or motion of a sloping bathymetric feature.

Tsunamis generated by strike-slip earthquakes normally affect regions near the source only.

What does the word "tsunami" mean?

Tsunami (soo-NAH-mee) is a Japanese word meaning harbor wave.

How fast do tsunamis travel?

Tsunami velocity depends on the depth of water through which it travels (velocity equals the square root of the product of the water depth times the acceleration of gravity).

Tsunamis travel approximately 475 mph (764 km/h) in 15,000 ft (4,572 m) of water. In 100 ft (30 m) of water the velocity drops to about 40 mph (64 km/h).

A tsunami travels from the central Aleutian Is. to Hawaii in about 5 hours and to California in about 6 hours or from the Portugal coast to North Carolina in about 8.5 hours.

How big is a tsunami?

Tsunamis range in size from inches to over a hundred feet (30.5 m).

In deep water (greater than 600 ft/183 m), tsunamis are rarely over 3 ft (0.9 m) and will not be noticed by ships due to their long period (time between crests).

As tsunamis propagate into shallow water, the wave height can increase by over 10 times.

Tsunami heights vary greatly along a coast. The waves can be amplified by shoreline and bathymetric (sea floor) features.

A large tsunami can flood low-lying coastal land over a mile from the coast.

What does a tsunami look like when it reaches shore?

Normally, a tsunami appears as a rapidly advancing or receding tide. In some cases a bore (wall of water) or series of breaking waves may form.

How is a tsunami different from a wind-generated wave?

Wind-generated waves usually have periods (time between crests) between 5 and 20 seconds. Tsunami periods normally range from 5 to 60 minutes. Wind-generated waves break as they shoal and lose energy offshore. Tsunamis act more like a flooding wave. A twenty-foot (6 m) tsunami is a twenty foot rise in sea level.

MOST DAMAGING TSUNAMIS WORLDWIDE

Deaths	Year	Location
283,100	2004	N. SUMATRA
40,000	1782	S. CHINA SEA
36,500	1883	S. JAVA SEA
30,000	1707	JAPAN
26,360	1896	JAPAN
25,674	1868	N. CHILE
15,030	1792	JAPAN
13,486	1771	RYUKYU
8,000	1976	PHILIPPINES
5,233	1703	JAPAN
5,000	1605	NANKAIDO, JAPAN
5,000	1611	SANRIKU, JAPAN
3,800	1746	LIMA, PERU
3,620	1899	INDONESIA
3,000	1692	JAMAICA
3,000	1854	NANKAIDO, JAPAN
3,000	1933	SANRIKU, JAPAN*
2,243	1674	INDONESIA
2,182	1998	PAPUA N.-GUINEA
2,144	1923	TOKAIDO, JAPAN
2,000	1570	CHILE
1,997	1946	NANKAIDO, JAPAN
1,700	1766	SANRIKU, JAPAN
1,000+	2006	S. JAVA SEA
119	1964	ALASKA, USA

SOURCE: NOAA

HURRICANES

A hurricane is a severe tropical storm that forms in the North Atlantic Ocean, the Northeast Pacific Ocean east of the dateline, or the South Pacific Ocean east of 160E. Hurricanes need warm tropical oceans, moisture and light winds above them. If the right conditions last long enough, a hurricane can produce violent winds, incredible waves, torrential rains and floods. In other regions of the world, these types of storms have different names.

Typhoon - (Northwest Pacific Ocean west of the dateline)

Severe Tropical Cyclone - (Southwest Pacific Ocean west of 160E or Southeast Indian Ocean east of 90E)

Severe Cyclonic Storm - (North Indian Ocean)

Tropical Cyclone - (Southwest Indian Ocean)

Typhoon Ewiniar is located south-southeast of Okinawa, Japan. Maximum sustained winds are at 125 knots, with gusts at 150 knots. Photo: NOAA

Hurricanes rotate in a counterclockwise direction around an "eye." A tropical storm becomes a hurricane when winds reach 74 mph (119 km/h). There are on average six Atlantic hurricanes each year; over a three-year period, approximately five hurricanes strike the United States coastline

from Texas to Maine. The Atlantic hurricane season begins June 1 and ends November 30. The East Pacific hurricane season runs from May 15 through November 30, with peak activity occurring during July through September. In a normal season, the East Pacific would expect 15 or 16 tropical storms. Nine of these would become hurricanes, of which four or five would be major hurricanes.

A hurricane makes landfall at Woods Hole Massachusetts in 1938. Photo: NOAA Photo Library

When hurricanes move onto land, the heavy rain, strong winds and heavy waves can damage buildings, trees and cars. The heavy waves are called a storm surge. Storm surge is very dangerous and a major reason why you MUST stay away from the ocean during a hurricane.

These are terms used to describe the progressive levels of organized disturbed weather in the tropics that are of less than hurricane status.

Hurricane *Katrina* over the Gulf of Mexico in August, 2005. Photo by NOAA

Tropical Disturbance
A discrete tropical weather system of apparently organized convection - generally

200 to 600 km (100 to 300 mi.) in diameter - originating in the tropics or subtropics, having a non-frontal migratory character, and maintaining its identity for 24 hours or more. It may or may not be associated with a detectable perturbation of the wind field. Disturbances associated with perturbations in the wind field and progressing through the tropics from east to west are also known as easterly waves.

Tropical Depression

A tropical cyclone in which the maximum sustained wind speed (using the U.S. 1 minute average standard) is 33 kt (38 mph, 61 km/h). Depressions have a closed circulation.

Tropical Storm

A tropical cyclone in which the maximum sustained surface wind speed (using the U.S. 1 minute average standard) ranges from 34 kt (39 mph / 63 km/h) to 63 kt (73 mph / 117 km/h). The convection in tropical storms is usually more concentrated near the center with outer rainfall organizing into distinct bands.

Hurricane

When winds in a tropical cyclone equal or exceed 64 kt (74 mph, 119 km/h) it is called a hurricane (in the Atlantic and eastern and central Pacific Oceans). Hurricanes are further designated by categories on the Saffir-Simpson scale. Hurricanes in categories 3, 4, 5 are known as Major Hurricanes or Intense Hurricanes. The wind speed mentioned here are for those measured or estimated as the top speed sustained for one minute at 33ft (10 m) above the surface. Peak gusts would be on the order of 10-25% higher.

Cape Verde-type hurricanes are those Atlantic basin tropical cyclones that develop into tropical storms fairly close (<600 mi. / 1000 km or so) of the Cape Verde Islands and then become hurricanes before reaching the Caribbean. Typically, this may occur in August and September, but in rare years (like 1995) there may be some in late July and/or early October. The numbers range from none up to around five per year - with an average of around 2.

Storm surge is the onshore rush of sea or lake water caused by the high winds associated with a landfalling cyclone and secondarily by the low pressure of the storm.

Tidal surge is often misused to describe storm surge, but storm surge is independent of the usual tidal ebb and flow. In some inlets, such as the Bay of Fundy, rapid changes in sea level due to the tides will cause a tidal bore or surge to move in to or out of the inlet. This surge occurs independent of the present weather.

WATCH vs. WARNING

A **HURRICANE WATCH** issued for your part of the coast indicates the possibility that you could experience hurricane conditions within 36 hours. This watch should trigger your family's disaster plan, and protective measures should be initiated, especially those actions that require extra time such as securing a boat, leaving a barrier island, etc.

A **HURRICANE WARNING** issued for your part of the coast indicates that sustained winds of at least 74 mph (119 km/h) are expected within 24 hours or less. Once this warning has been issued, your family should be in the process of completing protective actions and deciding the safest location to be during the storm.

STORM NAMING

Tropical cyclones are named to provide ease of communication between forecasters and the general public regarding forecasts, watches, and warnings. Since the storms can often last a week or longer and that more than one can be occurring in the same basin at the same time, names can reduce the confusion about what storm is being described.

According to *Dunn and Miller (1960)*, the first use of a proper name for a tropical cyclone was by an Australian forecaster early in the 20th century. He gave tropical cyclone names "after political figures whom he disliked. By properly naming a hurricane, the weatherman could publicly describe a politician (who perhaps was not too generous with weather-bureau appropriations) as 'causing great distress' or 'wandering aimlessly about the Pacific.'" (Perhaps this should be brought back into use ;-)

During World War II, tropical cyclones were informally given women's names by US Army Air Corp and Navy meteorologists (after their girlfriends or wives) who were monitoring and forecasting tropical cyclones over the Pacific. From 1950 to 1952, tropical cyclones of the North Atlantic Ocean were identified by the phonetic alphabet (Able-Baker-Charlie-etc.), but in 1953 the US Weather Bureau switched to women's names. In 1979, the WMO and the US National Weather Service (NWS) switched to a list of names that also included men's names.

SOURCE: NOAA

2007 TROPICAL CYCLONE NAMES

ATLANTIC
Andrea
Barry
Chantal
Dean
Erin
Felix
Gabrielle
Humberto
Ingrid
Jerry
Karen
Lorenzo
Melissa
Noel
Olga
Pablo
Rebekah
Sebastien
Tanya
Van
Wendy

EASTERN NORTH PACIFIC
Alvin
Barbara
Cosme
Dalila
Erick
Flossie
Gil
Henriette
Ivo
Juliette
Kiko
Lorena
Manuel
Narda
Octave
Priscilla
Raymond
Sonia
Tico
Velma
Wallis
Xina
York
Zelda

PHILIPPINE REGION
Amang
Bebeng
Chedeng
Dodong
Egay
Falcon
Goring
Hanna
Ineng
Juaning
Kabayan
Lando
Mina
Nonoy
Onyok
Pedring
Quiel
Ramon
Sendong
Tisoy
Ursula
Viring
Weng
Yoyoy
Zigzag

SOURCE: National Hurricane Center

SAFFIR-SIMPSON HURRICANE SCALE

The Saffir-Simpson Hurricane Scale is a 1-5 rating based on the hurricane's present intensity. This is used to give an estimate of the potential property damage and flooding expected along the coast from a hurricane landfall. Wind speed is the determining factor in the scale, as storm surge values are highly dependent on the slope of the continental shelf and the shape of the coastline, in the landfall region. Note that all winds are using the U.S. 1-minute average.

CATEGORY ONE HURRICANE

Winds 74-95 mph (64-82 kt or 119-153 km/h). Storm surge generally 4-5 ft (1.2-1.5 m) above normal. No real damage to building structures. Damage primarily to unanchored mobile homes, shrubbery, and trees. Some damage to poorly constructed signs. Also, some coastal road flooding and minor pier damage. Hurricane Lili of 2002 made landfall on the Louisiana coast as a Category One hurricane. Hurricane Gaston of 2004 was a Category One hurricane that made landfall along the central South Carolina coast.

CATEGORY TWO HURRICANE

Winds 96-110 mph (83-95 kt or 154-177 km/hr). Storm surge generally 6-8 ft (1.83-2.4 m) above normal. Some roofing material, door, and window damage of buildings. Considerable damage to shrubbery and trees with some trees blown down. Considerable damage to mobile homes, poorly constructed signs, and piers. Coastal and low-lying escape routes flood 2-4 hours before arrival of the hurricane center. Small craft in unprotected anchorages break moorings. Hurricane Frances of 2004 made landfall over the southern end of Hutchinson Island, Florida as a Category Two hurricane. Hurricane Isabel of 2003 made landfall near Drum Inlet on the Outer Banks of North Carolina as a Category 2 hurricane.

CATEGORY THREE HURRICANE

Winds 111-130 mph (96-113 kt or 178-209 km/h). Storm surge generally 9-12 ft (2.7-3.66 m) above normal. Some structural damage to small residences and utility buildings with a minor amount of curtain-wall failures. Damage to shrubbery and trees with foliage blown off trees and large trees blown down. Mobile homes and poorly constructed signs are destroyed. Low-lying escape routes are cut by rising water 3-5 hours before arrival of the center of the hurricane. Flooding near the coast destroys smaller structures with larger structures damaged by battering from floating debris. Terrain continuously lower than 5 ft (1.52 m) above mean sea level may be flooded inland 8 mi. (13 km) or more. Evacuation of low-lying residences with several blocks of the shoreline may be required. Hurricanes Jeanne and Ivan of 2004 were Category Three hurricanes when they made landfall in Florida and in Alabama, respectively.

CATEGORY FOUR HURRICANE

Winds 131-155 mph (114-135 kt or 210-249 km/h). Storm surge generally 13-18 ft (4-5.5 m) above normal. More extensive curtain-wall failures with some complete roof structure failures on small residences. Shrubs, trees, and all signs are blown down. Complete destruction of mobile homes. Extensive damage to doors and windows. Low-lying escape routes may be cut by rising water 3-5 hours before arrival of the center of the hurricane. Major damage to lower floors of structures near the shore. Terrain lower than 10 ft (3 m) above sea level may be flooded requiring massive evacuation of residential areas as far inland as 6 mi (9.7 km). Hurricane Charley of 2004 was a Category Four hurricane made landfall in Charlotte County, Florida with winds of 150 mph (241 km/h). Hurricane Dennis of 2005 struck the island of Cuba as a Category Four hurricane.

CATEGORY FIVE HURRICANE

Winds greater than 155 mph (135 kt or 249 km/h). Storm surge generally greater than

18 ft (5.5 m) above normal. Complete roof failure on many residences and industrial buildings. Some complete building failures with small utility buildings blown over or away. All shrubs, trees, and signs blown down. Complete destruction of mobile homes. Severe and extensive window and door damage. Low-lying escape routes are cut by rising water 3-5 hours before arrival of the center of the hurricane. Major damage to lower floors of all structures located less than 15 ft (4.6 m) above sea level and within 500 yards (457 m) of the shoreline. Massive evacuation of residential areas on low ground within 5-10 miles (8-16 km) of the shoreline may be required.

Only 3 Category Five Hurricanes have made landfall in the United States since records began: The Labor Day Hurricane of 1935, Hurricane Camille (1969), and Hurricane Andrew in August, 1992. The 1935 Labor Day Hurricane struck the Florida Keys with a minimum pressure of 892 mb – the lowest pressure ever observed in the United States. Hurricane Camille struck the Mississippi Gulf Coast causing a 25-ft (7.62 m) storm surge, which inundated Pass Christian.Hurricane Andrew of 1992 made landfall over southern Miami-Dade County, Florida causing 26.5 billion dollars in losses-- the costliest hurricane on record. In addition, Hurricane Gilbert of 1988 was a Category Five hurricane at peak intensity and is the strongest Atlantic tropical cyclone on record with a minimum pressure of 888 mb.

Ocean-going vessels left high and dry by Hurricane Camille in 1969. Photo: Historic NWS Collection

BEAUFORT WIND SCALE

#	Knots	mph	km/h	Wave Height (ft)	Wave Height (m)	WMO* Description	Effects on Water
0	< 1	< 1	< 1	0	0	Calm	Sea like mirror
1	1- 3	1 - 3	2 - 5	0.25	0.08	Light air	Ripples with appearance of scales; no foam crests
2	4 - 6	4 - 7	6 - 11	0.1 - 1	0.03 - 0.3	Light breeze	Small wavelets; crests of glassy appearance, not breaking
3	7 - 10	8 - 12	12 - 20	2 - 3	0.6 - 0.9	Gentle breeze	Large wavelets; crests begin to break; scattered whitecaps
4	11 - 16	13 - 18	21 - 29	3.5 - 5	1 - 1.5	Moderate breeze	Small waves, becoming longer; numerous whitecaps
5	17 - 21	19 - 24	30 - 39	6 - 8	1.8 - 2.4	Fresh breeze	Moderate waves, taking longer form; many whitecaps; some spray
6	22 - 27	25 - 31	40 - 50	9.5 - 13	3 - 4	Strong breeze	Larger waves forming; whitecaps everywhere; more spray
7	28 - 33	32 - 38	51 - 61	13.5 - 19	4 - 5.8	Near gale	Sea heaps up; white foam from breaking waves begins to be blown in streaks

8	34 - 40	39 - 46	62 - 74	18 - 25	5.5 - 7.6	Gale	Moderately high waves of greater length; edges of crests begin to break into spindrift; foam is blown in well-marked streaks
9	41 - 47	47 - 54	75 - 87	23 - 32	7 - 9.8	Strong gale	High waves; sea begins to roll; dense streaks of foam; spray may begin to reduce visibility
10	48 - 55	55 - 63	88 - 101	29 - 41	8.8 - 12.5	Storm	Very high waves with overhanging crests; sea takes white appearance as foam is blown in very dense streaks; rolling is heavy and visibility is reduced
11	56 - 63	64 - 72	102 - 116	37 - 52	11.3 - 15.8	Violent storm	Exceptionally high waves; sea covered with white foam patches; visibility further reduced
12	64 +	73 +	117 +	45 +	14 +	Hurri-cane	Air filled with foam; sea completely white with driving spray; visibility greatly reduced

SOURCE: World Meteorological Organization

EL NIÑO & LA NIÑA

El Niño is a disruption of the ocean-atmosphere system in the tropical Pacific having important consequences for weather around the globe. Among these consequences is increased rainfall across the southern tier of the US and in Peru, which has caused destructive flooding, and drought in the West Pacific, sometimes associated with devastating brush fires in Australia. Observations of conditions in the tropical Pacific are considered essential for the prediction of short term (a few months to 1 year) climate variations. To provide necessary data, NOAA operates a network of buoys which measure temperature, currents and winds in the equatorial band. These buoys daily transmit data which are available to researchers and forecasters around the world in real time.

In normal, non-El Niño conditions (top panel of schematic diagram), the trade winds blow towards the west across the tropical Pacific. These winds pile up warm surface water in the west Pacific, so that the sea surface is about 1.6 ft (0.5 m) higher at Indonesia than at Ecuador. The sea surface temperature is about 46F (8°C) higher in the west, with cool temperatures off South America, due to an upwelling of cold water from deeper levels. This cold water is nutrient-rich, supporting high levels of primary productivity, diverse marine ecosystems, and major fisheries. Rainfall is found in rising air over the warmest water, and the east Pacific is relatively dry. The observations at 110 W (left diagram of 110 W conditions) show that the cool water (below about 63F (17°C), the black band in these plots) is within 50m of the surface.

During El Niño (bottom panel of the schematic diagram), the trade winds relax in the central and western Pacific leading to a depression of the thermocline in the eastern Pacific, and an elevation of the thermocline in the west. The observations at 110W show, for example, that during 1982-1983, the 17-degree isotherm dropped to about 500 ft (150 m) depth. This reduced the efficiency of upwelling to cool the surface and cut off the supply of nutrient rich thermocline water to the euphotic zone. The result was a rise in sea surface temperature and a drastic decline in primary productivity, the latter of which adversely affected higher trophic levels of the food chain, including commercial fisheries in this region. The weakening of easterly trade winds during El Niño is evident in this figure as well. Rainfall follows the warm water eastward, with associated flooding in Peru and drought in Indonesia and Australia. The eastward displacement of the atmospheric heat source overlaying the warmest water results in large changes in the global atmospheric circulation, which in turn force changes in weather in regions far removed from the tropical Pacific.

LA NIÑA

La Niña is characterized by unusually cold ocean temperatures in the Equatorial Pacific, compared to El Niño, which is characterized by unusually warm ocean temperatures in the Equatorial Pacific. In the U.S., winter temperatures are warmer than normal in the Southeast, and cooler than normal in the Northwest.

LA NIÑA IMPACT ON THE GLOBAL CLIMATE

Global climate La Niña impacts tend to be opposite those of El Niño impacts. In the tropics, ocean temperature variations in La Niña tend to be opposite those of El Niño. At higher latitudes, El Niño and La Niña are among a number of factors that influence climate. However, the impacts of El Niño and La Niña at these latitudes are most clearly seen in wintertime. In the continental US, during El Niño years, temperatures in the winter are warmer than normal in the North Central States, and cooler than normal in the Southeast and the Southwest. During a La Niña year, winter temperatures are warmer than normal in the Southeast and cooler than normal in the Northwest. See U.S. La Niña impacts from the National Weather Service.

THE ORIGIN OF THE NAMES, LA NIÑA AND EL NIÑO

La Niña is sometimes referred to as El Viejo. El Niño was originally recognized by fisherman off the coast of South America as the appearance of unusually warm water in the Pacific Ocean, occurring near the beginning of the year. El Niño means The Little Boy or Christ child in Spanish. This name was used for the tendency of the phenomenon to arrive around Christmas. La Niña means The Little Girl. La Niña is sometimes called El Viejo, anti-El Niño, or simply "a cold event" or "a cold episode".

SOURCE: NOAA

ICE

Arctic sea ice covers significant portions of the northern hemisphere ocean, forming and persisting at temperatures below the freezing point of seawater. That freezing point is generally around 28.58F (-1.9°C) when the salinity is 33 parts per thousand, however, the freezing point changes with the concentration of salt in the seawater. As ice crystals grow in the water during the autumn season, small ice platelets begin to accumulate at the ocean surface, interlink, and form a porous structure of ice crystals filled with liquid, which is referred to as brine.

Canadian divers prepare for a dive at *Les Escoumins*, in the province of Quebec. Water temperature hovers just below 29F (-1.67°C) Photo: J. Gallant / D.A.Y.

Sea ice occupies about 7% of the area of the world ocean, and is of enormous importance climatically because it reflects most of the solar radiation that falls on it.

Thickest Ice
The greatest recorded thickness of ice is 2.97 mi. (4.78 km), measured by radio echo soundings from a US Antarctic research aircraft.

SOURCE: NOAA

ICE FORMATION

Water-fresh water, that is-freezes at a steady state of 32F (0°C). However, the freezing point of sea water is not only lower than 32F (0°C); it also varies depending on the degree of salinity. As salinity increases, the freezing point becomes lower.

Ice Divers Katrin Iken (left) and Shawn Harper (right) enter the water while Coast Guard Petty Officer Louis Bishop tends the line and Elisabeth Calvert stands by as the safety diver. Photo: NOAA/OCEAN EXPLORER - *The Hidden Ocean*, Arctic 2005 Exploration

Where Does Sea Ice Form First?
Ice will form first in shallow water, near the coast or over shoals or banks, and particularly in bays, inlets, and straits in which there are no currents, and in areas of low salinity (near the mouths of rivers, for instance). Shallow water is conducive to ice formation because of the relatively small depth of water that has to be cooled. The greater the depth of high-salinity water, the later the time of freezing. In fact, deep waters may never freeze over entirely, as not enough heat can be removed from the water during the course of a winter to bring this about.

Brine cells
As soon as the crystals form, the water in their immediate vicinity becomes a little

saltier because the salt in the solution does not become part of the initial crystals. This saltier water, being denser than before the crystals formed, immediately tends to sink. As more and more crystals form, they will eventually become frozen to one another in such a way that tiny spaces or pockets will remain between groups of crystals. Some of the residual brine will become trapped in those pockets, which are known as brine cells. If ice crystals form slowly on the water surface, most of the remaining brine is able to diffuse downward into the water underneath. Thus, when crystals freeze together, not as much brine is trapped and the ice will have lower salt content. However, when crystals freeze rapidly together, more brine is trapped in the brine cells before it can sink and mix with the water below.

Hence, ice which forms rapidly is initially saltier than ice which forms more slowly. Some of the brine which becomes trapped in cells in the ice remains liquid at very low temperatures. As the temperature within

the ice continues to fall, water is removed from the brine in the cells by the formation of ice crystals. Hence, the remaining brine becomes still saltier and the temperature must be lowered further before more ice crystals will form. There are various types of sea ice, according to its stage of development. Within each stage below, various sub-types also exist, depending on the internal structure of the ice. Please refer to the Glossary for more details.

An ice diver takes a picture of the view looking up at the surface through their dive entry hole with an underwater camera. A line tender and safety diver stand on the surface in front of the USCGC Healy, prepared to help in case of emergency. Photo: NOAA/OCEAN EXPLORER - *The Hidden Ocean*, Arctic 2005 Exploration.

SEA ICE TYPES

New Ice
Recently formed ice composed of ice crystals that are only weakly frozen together (if at all) and have a definite form only while they are afloat.

Nilas
A thin elastic crust of ice (up to 4 in. / 10 cm in thickness), easily bending on waves and swell and under pressure growing in a pattern of interlocking "fingers" (finger rafting).

Young Ice
Ice in the transition stage between nilas and first-year ice, 4-12 in. (10-30 cm) in thickness.

First-year Ice
Sea ice of not more than one winter's growth, developing from young ice, with a thickness of 12 in. (30 cm) or greater.

Old Ice
Sea ice that has survived at least one summer's melt. Its topographic features generally are smoother than first-year ice.

SOURCE: Sea Ice Types. http://ice-glaces.ec.gc.ca/App/WsvPageDsp.cfm?ID=181&Lang=eng. Reproduced with the permission of the Minister of Public Works and Government Services Canada, 2006.

SEA ICE FORMS

Ice can take on many forms, depending on external conditions and other physical considerations. Except in sheltered waters, an even sheet of ice seldom forms immediately:

The thickening slush breaks up into separate masses under wind and wave action, the masses taking on a characteristic pancake form due to the fragments colliding with each other.

The slush layer dampens down the waves, and if freezing continues, the pancakes will adhere together, forming a continuous sheet.

Pancake Ice
Circular pieces of ice 12 in. (30 cm) to 10 ft (3 m) in diameter, up to 4 in. (10 cm) in thickness, with raised rims due to the pieces striking against one another.

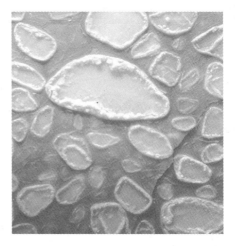

Largest pancake is approximately 4 ft (1.2 m) across.
Photo: NOAA Corps Collection / Michael Van Woert

Brash Ice
Accumulation of floating ice made up of fragments not more than 6.5 ft (2 m) across, the wreckage of other forms of ice.

Ice Cake
Any relatively flat piece of ice less than 66 ft (20 m) across.

Floe
Any relatively flat piece of ice 66 ft (20 m) or more across.

Fast Ice
Ice which forms and remains fast along the coast. Fast ice higher than 6.5 ft (2 m) above sea level is called an ice shelf.

SOURCE: Sea Ice Forms. http://ice-glaces.ec.gc.ca/App/WsvPageDsp.cfm?ID=10170&Lang=eng. Reproduced with the permission of the Minister of Public Works and Government Services Canada, 2006.

ICE THICKNESS VERSUS ICE STRENGTH

This table* provides the safe load for a given ice thickness of fresh ice (lake and river ice) and sea ice (Gulf of St. Lawrence, Arctic Ocean, etc.)

SOURCE: Table Ice Thickness Versus Ice Strength. http://ice-glaces.ec.gc.ca/App/WsvPageDsp.cfm?Lang=eng&l nid=10&ScndLvl=no&ID=10167. Reproduced with the permission of the Minister of Public Works and Government Services Canada, 2006.

SAFE LOAD	OPERATION	FRESH ICE	SEA ICE
One person	at rest	3 in. 8 cm	5 in. 13 cm
0.4 ton (Small car)	moving slowly	4 in. 10 cm	7 in. 18 cm
10-ton tracked vehicle	moving slowly	17 in. 43 cm	26 in. 66 cm
13-ton aircraft	parked	24 in. 61 cm	40 in. 102 cm

Heavy snowmobiles and a shark cage lie on the ice of Baie-Éternité in Canada's Saguenay Fjord during GEERG's (www.geerg.ca) Operation Skalugsuak II – *The Search for the Greenland Shark*. Photo: J. Gallant / D.A.Y

ICE TESTING

While there are many different types of ice, the two types of major concern are:

(a) clear ice - formed by the freezing of water;
(b) snow ice - formed when water-saturated snow freezes on top of ice, making an opaque white ice which is not as strong as clear ice.

Normand Piché cuts through 3 ft (1 m) of lake ice to prepare a site for diving. Photo: J. Gallant / D.A.Y.

ICE COLOR

The color of ice, which may range from blue to white to grey; provides an indication of its quality and strength:
(a) clear blue ice is generally the strongest;
(b) white opaque ice (snow ice) has a relatively high air content, and its strength depends on the density: the lower the density the weaker the ice; but high density white ice has a strength approaching that of blue ice;
(c) grey ice generally indicates the presence of water as a result of thawing, and must be considered highly suspect as a load-bearing surface.

ICE THICKNESS

The other major factor determining the bearing capability of ice is its thickness. Care must be taken when determining the thickness of ice covers to ensure that the readings are properly taken and are an accurate representation of the area under consideration.

Currents have a distinct bearing on the temperature required to form ice. Rivers and channels with strong currents may remain open all winter despite low air temperatures. Springs can cause currents, and also be the source of warmer water; currents can also cause variations in ice thickness without changing the uniform surface characteristics. Frequent checks of the ice thickness should be made in areas suspected of being affected by currents.

Ice under an insulating snow blanket thickens very slowly even in low temperatures. A heavy snow cover, before significant ice growth, may cause the ice to remain unsafe throughout the winter.

STAGE OF LAKE ICE DEVELOPMENT

Description	Thickness	Code
New Ice	< 2 in. < 5 cm	1
Thin Lake Ice	2-6 in. 5-15 cm	4
Medium Lake Ice	6-12 in. 15-30 cm	5
Thick Lake Ice	12-28 in. 30-70 cm	7
Very Thick Lake Ice	> 28 in. > 70 cm	1·
Undetermined/Unknown		X

SOURCE: Stages of Development of Lake Ice. http://ice-glaces.ec.gc.ca/App/WsvPageDsp.cfm?ID=11180&Lang=eng. Reproduced with the permission of the Minister of Public Works and Government Services Canada, 2006.

PARKED AND STATIONARY LOADS

Ice behaves elastically under moving loads; that is, the ice is depressed while loaded but recovers its original position after the load has passed.

With a stationary load the ice surface will sag continuously and may fail, depending on the strength of the ice cover. The safe bearing capability for stationary loads should be considered to be 50% less than that for moving loads.

A cut through 3 ft (1 m) of ice shows a pattern of successive layering with varying levels due to the effects of changing temperature and snowfall. Photo: J. Gallant / D.A.Y.

The sequence of failure for stationary loads is as follows:
(a) radiating cracks form at the bottom of the cover immediately beneath the load (and ultimately propagate through the cover);
(b) circular cracks form at the upper surface of the cover at some distance from the load (noticeable sagging of the ice may occur);

(c) the ice shears in a circle immediately adjacent to the loaded surface (failure may be imminent).

The initial radial cracks may not be of immediate concern if the load bearing capacity of the ice is substantially higher than the load. However, prolonged application of the load should cause concern about possible ice failure.

Stationary loads should be moved under any of the following conditions:
(a) when radial cracks develop;
(b) if noticeable sagging is observed;
(c) if the rate of sagging increases;
(d) if continuous cracking is heard or observed;
(e) if water appears on the surface of the cover.

Improper testing of ice strength can lead to serious consequences. Photo: J. Gallant / D.A.Y.

Work, travel, and parking on frozen bodies of water should be avoided whenever possible and be done only as a last resort. The ice must be tested before any workers or vehicles are allowed onto the surface. Loads that may safely travel on ice may not necessarily be left on ice for extended periods of time. This applies especially to parked vehicles. Before testing, learn as much as possible about ice conditions from local residents. Testing requires at least two persons on foot proceeding with caution.

Each person must wear an approved lifejacket or, preferably, an approved floatable survival suit that protects against hypothermia. For ice testing, a survival suit or lifejacket is required because a person falling into frigid water may lose consciousness and the suit or lifejacket will keep the person's face out of the water. Members of the ice-testing crew should stay about 30 ft (10 m) apart. The lead member must wear a safety harness attached to a polypropylene rescue rope 3/8 inch (9.5 mm) thick, at least 65 ft (20 m) long, and held by the trailing crew member.

Clear blue ice is the most desirable for strength. White or opaque ice forms from wet snow and has higher air content. It is less dense and therefore weaker than clear blue ice. Grey ice indicates the presence of water from thawing and should not be trusted as a load-bearing surface. The lead crew member should cut test holes every 25 ft (8 m) or so. If ice is less than 4 in. (10 cm) thick, the lead and trailing crew members should vacate the area immediately.

A diver seen through the ice of a frozen lake in Ontario, Canada. Photo: J. Gallant / D.A.Y.

The biggest uncertainty about the load-bearing capacity of ice is the natural variation in thickness and quality that can occur over a given area. Currents and springs can cause variations in thickness without changing the overall surface appearance of the ice. Considerable variation in ice thickness can occur where rivers have significant currents or high banks. Similar situations occur in lakes at the inlet and

outlet of rivers. Only the thickness of continuously frozen ice should be used to determine bearing capacity. The basis for capacity should be the minimum thickness measured. In addition to testing for thickness, crews should check ice for cracking.

SOURCE: Safety Guide for Operations over Ice. http://www.tbs-sct.gc.ca/pubs_pol/hrpubs/TBM_119/CHAP5_3-1_e.asp. Reproduced with the permission of the Minister of Public Works and Government Services Canada, 2006.

REFERENCES

o Canadian Ice Service (ice-glaces.ec.gc.ca)
o CIA World Factbook (www.cia.gov)
o CMAS (www.cmasquebec.org)
o NASA (www.science.hq.nasa.gov)
o National Hurricane Center (www.nhc.noaa.gov)
o National Research Council of Canada (www.nrc-cnrc.gc.ca)
o National Weather Service (www.nws.noaa.gov)
o NOAA National Ocean Service (www.oceanservice.noaa.gov)
o NOAA Pacific Marine Environmental Laboratory (www.pmel.noaa.gov)
o NOAA West Coast & Alaska Tsunami Warning Center (wcatwc.arh.noaa.gov)
o U.S. Navy (pao.cnmoc.navy.mil)
o World Meteorological Organization (www.wmo.ch)

OCEANOGRAPHIC ASSOCIATIONS

AFRICA

Western Indian OceanMarine Science Association (WIOMSA)
Mizingani Street, House No. 13644/10
P. O. Box 3298, Zanzibar,
United Republic of Tanzania,
Tel.: 255 24 223 3472; 223 4597
Fax: 255 24 223 3852
www.wiomsa.or

ARGENTINA

CIMA/CONICET-UBA
Intendente Guiraldes 2160

Ciudad Universitaria
Pabellón II - 2do. piso
(C1428EGA) Buenos Aires - Argentina
Tel.: 54 11 4787 2693
Fax: 54 11 4788 3572
www-cima.at.fcen.uba.ar

AUSTRALIA

Australian Institute of Marine Science
PMB 3, Townsville MC
Townsville 4810,
Queensland, Australia
Tel.: 07 4753 4444
Fax: 07 4772 5852
www.aims.gov.au

CSIRO Marine and Atmospheric Research
Castray Esplanade
HOBART TAS
7000 Australia
Tel.: 61 3 6232 5222
Fax: 61 3 6232 5000
www.cmar.csiro.au

National Tidal Centre
Australian Bureau of Meteorology
PO Box 421
Kent Town SA 5071
Tel.: 08 8366 2730
Fax: 08 8366 2651
www.bom.gov.au

BERMUDA

The Bermuda Biological Station for Research,
Inc.
17 Biological Lane
Ferry Reach
St. George's GE 01 Bermuda
Tel.: 441 297 1880
Fax: 441 297 8143
www.bbsr.edu

BELGIUM

Department of Astrophysics Geophysics and
Oceanography (AGO)
University of Liege,
Institut dePhysique (B5)
B-4000 Sart Tilman, Belgium
www.co2.ulg.ac.be

European Commission
B-1049 Brussels BELGIUM
ec.europa.eu/research/marine1.html

International Oceangraphic Dada and Infor-
mation Exchange (IODE)
Wandelaarkaai 7
B-8400 Oostende, Belgium
Tel.: 32 59 34 01 58
Fax: 32 59 34 21 32
www.iode.org

BRAZIL

Universidade de São Paulo
Instituto Oceanográfico
Praça do Oceanográfico, 191.
Cidade Universitária. São Paulo
SP - Cep: 05508-120 - Brasil –
Tel.: 11 3091 6501
www.io.usp.br

CANADA

Bamfield Marine Sciences Centre
100 Pachena Road
Bamfield, BC V0R 1B0
Tel.: 1 250 728-3301
Fax: 1 250 728-3452
www.bms.bc.ca

Geological Survey of Canada (Atlantic)
Bedford Institute of Oceanography
1 Challenger Drive
P.O. Box 1006
Dartmouth, Nova Scotia B2Y 4A2
Tel.: 902 426 3448
Fax: 902 426 1466
agcwww.bio.ns.ca

Partnership for Observation of the Global
Oceans - Bedford Institute of Oceanography
1 Challenger Drive
Dartmouth NS B2Y 4A2 , CANADA
Tel.: 902 426 8044
Fax: 902 426 9388
www.ocean-partners.org

Department of Earth and Ocean Sciences,
The University of British Columbia
6339 Stores Road,
Vancouver, British Columbia
Canada, V6T 1Z4
Tel.: 604 822 2449
Fax: 604 822 6088
www.eos.ubc.ca

Simon Fraser University
Centre for Coastal Studies
8888 University Drive
Burnaby, BC V5A 1S6
www.sfu.ca/coastalstudies

Dalhousie University
Department of Oceanography
1355 Oxford Street
Halifax, Nova Scotia
Canada, B3H 4J1
Tel.: 902 494 3557
Fax: 902 494 3877
www.oceanography.dal.ca

CHILE

Laboratorio de Procesos Oceanograficos y Clima - PROFC
Universidad de Concepcion
www.profc.udec.cl

CROATIA

Institute Of Oceanography And Fisheries
Setaliste Ivana Mestrovica 63,
21000 Split, Croatia
Tel.: 385 21 358688
Fax: 385 21358650
www.izor.hr/izor.html

Rudjer Boskovic Institute,
Center for Marine and Environmental Research,
POB 180, 10002
Zagreb, Croatia

DENMARK

International Council
for the Exploration of the Sea (ICES)
H. C. Andersens Boulevard 44-46
DK-1553
Copenhagen V Denmark
Tel.: 0045 3338 6700
Fax: 0045 3393 4215
www.ices.dk/indexfla.asp

FINLAND

Finnish Institute of Marine Research,
Erik Palménin aukio 1,
P.O. Box 2, FIN-00561 Helsinki,
Tel.: 358 9 613 941
Fax: 358 9 323 2970
www.fimr.fi/fi.html

FRANCE

Le Centre d'Océanologie de Marseille
Station marine d'Endoume
Rue Batterie-des-Lions
F-13007 MARSEILLE

Tel.: 33 04 91 04 16 00
Fax: 33 04 91 04 16 08
www.com.univ-mrs.fr

EUG at E.O.S.T.
5, rue René Descartes
Strasbourg Cedex 67084,
France
Tel.: 33 03 90 24 00 58
Fax: 33 03 88 60 38 87
eopg.u-strasbg.fr/EUG

French Research Institute
for Exploitation of the Sea
155, rue Jean-Jacques Rousseau
92138 Issy-les-Moulineaux Cedex
Tel.: 33 01 46 48 21 00
Fax: 33 01 46 48 21 21
www.ifremer.fr

Laboratoire d'Océanographie
Université Pierre et Marie Curie
Institut Pierre Simon Laplace
Tour 14-15 - 2ème étage –
Boîte 100 4, place Jussieu
75252 PARIS Cedex 05
Tel.: 33 0 1 44 27 32 48
Fax: 33 0 1 44 27 38 05
locean.lodyc.jussieu.fr

Intergovernmental Oceanographic
Commission (UNESCO)
1, rue Miollis
75015 Paris France
Tel: (33) 1 45 68 39 84
Fax: 33 1 45 68 58 12/10
ioc.unesco.org/iocweb/index.php

GREECE

The Hellenic Centre for Marine Research (HCMR)
P.O.Box 712
19013 Anavissos
Attika, Greece
Director's Office
Tel.: 302 2910 76466
Fax: 302 2910 76323
www.hcmr.gr

GERMANY

The Alfred Wegener Institute
Postfach 12 0161,
D-27515 Bremerhaven
Tel.:49 471 4831 0
www.awi-bremerhaven.de

Baltic Sea Research Institute Warnemunde
Institut für Ostseeforschung Warnemünde
Seestrasse 15
D-18119 Rostock
Tel.: 03 81 5197-0
www.io-warnemuende.de

Institut für Chemie und Biologie des Meeres (ICBM)
Carl von Ossietzky Universität Oldenburg
Carl-von-Ossietzky.Str. 9-11
Postfach 2503
26111 Oldenburg
Postleitzahl für Paketpost: 26129
Tel.: 49 0441 798 5342
Fax: 49 0441 798 3404
www.icbm.uni-oldenburg.de

Institute of Oceanography
Universität Hamburg
Zentrum für Meeres- und Klimaforschung
Institut für Meereskunde
Bundesstr. 53
D-20146 Hamburg
Germany
Tel.: 49 0 40 42838 5052
www.ifm.uni-hamburg.de

ICELAND

Icelandic Fisheries Laboratories
Skulagata 4
101 Reykjavik Iceland
Tel.: 354 530 8600
Fax: 354 530 8601
www.rfisk.is

Marine Research Institute (MRI)
Skulagata 4,
121 Reykjavik, Iceland
Tel.: 354 575 2000
Fax: 354 575 2001
www.hafro.is/

IRELAND

Marine Institute
Rinville Oranmore
Co. Galway, Ireland
Tel.: 353 0 91 387200
Fax: 353 0 91 387201
www.marine.ie

ITALY

NATO Undersea Research Centre
Viale San Bartolomeo 400,

19138 La Spezia (SP), Italy
Tel.: 39 0187 527 1
Fax: 39 0187 527 700
www.saclantc.nato.int

JAPAN

JOS/Mainichi Administrative Center for Academic Societies (MACAS
Floor 9, Palace-side Building,
1-1-1 Hitotsubashi, Chiyoda-ku,
Tokyo 100-0003, JAPAN
Fax: 81 3 3211 1413
www.soc.nii.ac.jp

MONACO

The Mediterranean Science Commission (CIESM)
Headquarters :Villa Girasole,
16 bd de Suisse, Monaco
www.ciesm.org

NETHERLANDS

Institute for Marine and Atmospheric research Utrecht (IMAU)
Princetonplein 5, 3584 CC Utrecht
PO box 80000, 3508 TA Utrecht
The Netherlands
Tel.: 31 30 253 3275
Fax: 31 30 254 3163
www.phys.uu.nl/-wwwimau

The National Oceanographic Data Committee (NODC)
The Rijks Instituut voor Kust en Zee (RIKZ
Attn: Dr W.T.B. van der Lee, NODC secretaris
Postbus 20907
2500 EX Den Haag, The Netherlands
www.nodc.nl

Royal Netherlands Institute for Sea Research
P.O.Box 59
NL-1790 AB Den Burg (Texel)
The Netherlands
Tel.: 31 0 222 369300
Fax: 31 0 222 319674
www.nioz.nl

Royal Netherlands Meteorological Institute (KNMI)
PO Box 201
NL-3730 AE De Bilt
Netherlands
Tel.: 3130 2206 911
Fax: 3130 2210 407

www.knmi.nl/research/oceanography

NEW ZEALAND

Cawthron Institute
98 Halifax Street East
Private Bag 2, Nelson
New Zealand
Tel.: 64 03 548 2319
Fax: 64 03 546 9464

NORWAY

Fugro OCEANOR
Pir-Senteret,
N-7462 Trondheim, Norway
Tel.: 47 73 54 5200
Fax: 47 73 54 5201
www.oceanor.no

Geofysisk Institutt,
Allégaten 70,
5007 Bergen
Tel.: 55 58 26 02
Fax: 55 58 98 83
www.gfi.uib.no

POLAND

**Institute of Oceanography
University of Gdańsk,**
Al. Marszałka Pitsudskiego 46,
81-378 Gdynia
Tel.: 48 58 660 1636
Fax: 48 58 660 1678; 48 58 620 2165
www2.ocean.univ.gda.pl

**Institure of Oceanology
Polish Academy of Sciences**
Powstancow Warszawy 55,
P.O. Box 68
81-712 Sopot, Poland,
Tel.: 48 58 551 72 81
Fax: 48 58 551 21 30
www.iopan.gda.pl

PORTUGAL

**Departamento de Oceanografia e Pescas,
Universidade dos Açores**
PT-9901-862 HORTA, Portugal
Tel.: 351 292 200 400
Fax: 351 292 20 0411
www.horta.uac.pt

**Instituto de Oceanografia,
Faculdade de Ciências da Universidade de
Lisboa,**

Campo Grande,
1749-016 Lisboa, PORTUGAL
Tel.: 21 750 01 48
Fax: 21 750 00 09
www.io.fc.ul.pt

RUSSIA

P.P.Shirshov Institute of Oceanology
36 Nakhimovsky Prospekt,
117997 Moscow, Russia
Tel.: 495 124 5996
Fax: 495 124 5983
www.sio.rssi.ru

SOUTH AFRICA

**The Southern African Data Centre for Ocean-
ography (SADCO)**
Dr. Marten Gründlingh, Manager, SADCO
P O Box 320
7599, Stellenbosch South Africa
Tel.: 27 21 888 2520
Fax: 27 21 888 2693
sadco.csir.co.za

**University of Cape Town
Department of Oceanography**
Private Bag X3
Rondebosch
Cape Town South Africa 7701
Tel.: 27 0 21 650-3277
Fax: 27 0 21 650-3979

SPAIN

Instituto Español de Oceanografía
Servicio de Coordinación y Publicaciones
Avda. de Brasil, 31
28020 Madrid, España
Tel.: 34 91 417 54 11
Fax: 34 91 597 47 70
www.ieo.es/inicial.htm

**Institute of Marine Sciences
Centre Mediterrani d'Investigacions Marines i**
Ambientals, CMIMA-CSIC
Passeig Marítim de la Barceloneta, 37- 49
E-08003 Barcelona, Spain
Tel.: 34 93 230 95 00
Fax: 34 93 230 95 55
www.icm.csic.es

SWEDEN

AB Hydroconsult
Drottninggatan 7
S-753 10 Uppsala

Sweden
Tel.: 018 14 88 00
Fax: 018 12 80 03
www.hydroconsult.se

Göteborgs universitets marina forskningscentrum (GMF)
Box 460, 405 30 Göteborg,
Tel.: 031 773 10 00,
Fax: 031 773 48 39
www.gmf.gu.se

SMHI Oceanography
Adress: Folkborgsvägen 1
SE-601 76 Norrköping
Tel.: 46 11 495 80 00
Fax: 46 11 495 80 01
www.smhi.se

Stockholm University
SE-106 91 Stockholm, Sweden
Tel.: 46 8 16 37 18
Fax: 46 8 16 16 20
www.smf.su.se/

Umeå Marine Sciences Centre
SE-910 20 Hörnefors, Sweden
Tel.: 46 0 90 786 79 74
Fax: 46 0 90 786 79 95
www.umf.umu.se

SWITZERLAND

WCRP Joint Planning Staff
c/o World Meteorological Organization
7 bis, Avenue de la Paix
Case Postale 2300
1211 Geneva 2, Switzerland
Tel.: 41 22 730 81 11
Fax: 41 22 730 80 36
www.wmo.ch

UKRAINE

Institute of Biology of the Southern Seas,
National Academy of Sciences of Ukraine,
2003.
2, Nakhimov av., Sevastopol,
99011, Crimea, Ukraine.
Tel.: 38 06 92 544110,
Fax: 38 06 92 557813
www.ibss.iuf.net

Marine Hydrophysical Institute
National Academy of Science of Ukraine
2, Kapitanskaya St., Sevastopol, 99011, Ukraine
Tel.: 38 06 92 540452
Fax: 38 06 92 554253

www.mhi.iuf.net

UNITED KINGDOM

Cefas Lowestoft Laboratory
Pakefield Road
Lowestoft, Suffolk NR33 0HT
Tel.: 44 0 1502 562244
Fax: 44 0 1502 513865
www.cefas.co.uk

The Challenger Sociery for Mariner Sciences
National Oceanography Centre Southampton,
University of Southampton,
Waterfront Campus,
Southampton SO14 3ZH
www.challenger-society.org.uk

European Society for Marine
Biotechnology
Dove Marine Laboratory
School of Marine Science & Technology
Cullercoats, North Shields
Tyne & Wear, NE30 4PZ U.K.
www.esmb.org

T.H.Huxley School of Environment, Earth Sciences and Engineering
Royal School of Mines Building,
(Rooms 1.24, 1.08A)
Prince Consort Road, London SW7 2BP
Tel.: 44 0 20 7594 7414
Fax: 44 0 20 7594 7444
www.huxlcy.ic.ac.uk

The Marine Biological Association of the
United Kingdom
The Laboratory
Citadel Hill
Plymouth, PL1 2PB
Devon UK
Tel.: 44 0 1752 633207
Fax: 44 0 1752 633102
www.mba.ac.uk

National Oceanography Centre,
University of Southampton Waterfront Campus,
European Way, Southampton, SO14 3ZH, UK,
Tel: +44 (0) 23 8059 6666
www.noc.soton.ac.uk

Proudman Oceanographic Laboratory
6 Brownlow Street Liverpool L3 5DA UK
Tel.: 0151 795 4800
Fax: 0151 795 4801
www.nbi.ac.uk

Satellite Observing Systems

15 Church Street
Godalming
Surrey GU7 1EL United Kingdom
Tel.: 44 0 1483 421213
Fax: 44 0 1483 428691
www.satobsys.co.uk

The Scottish Association for Marine Science
Dunstaffnage Marine Laboratory
Oban • Argyll • PA37 1QA • Scotland
Tel.: 44 0 1631 559000
Fax: 44 0 1631 559001
www.sams.ac.uk

Seasearch c/o Marine Conservation Society,
Unit 3 Wolf Business Park,
Alton Road,
Ross-on-Wye, Herefordshire, HR9 5NB.
Tel.: 07776 142096
www.seasearch.org.uk

Society for Underwater Technology (SUT)
80 Coleman Street
London
EC2R 5BJ UK
Tel.: 44 0 20 7382 2601
Fax: 44 0 20 7382 2684
www.sut.org.uk

University of Liverpool
Department of Earth and Ocean Sciences
Liverpool L69 3GP UK
Fax: 44 151 794 5196
www.liv.ac.uk/physocean

University of Wales Bangor,
School of Ocean Sciences,
Menai Bridge,
Anglesey,
LL59 5AB, UK
Tel.: 44 0 1248 382846
Fax: 44 0 1248 716367
www.sos.bangor.ac.uk

UNITED STATES

Atlantic Oceanographic and Meteorological
Laboratory
4301 Rickenbacker Causeway
Miami, FL 33149
Tel.: 305 361 4450
www.aoml.noaa.gov/

Florida State University
Dept. of Oceanography,
Tallahassee, FL 32306-4320,
Tel.: 850 644 6700
ocean.fsu.edu

Johns Hopkins University
Scientific Committee on Oceanic Research
(SCOR)
Department of Earth and Planetary Sciences
Baltimore, Maryland (USA).
www.jhu.edu/~scor

Joint Oceanographic Institutions (JOI)
1201 New York Ave, NW
Suite 400
Washington, DC 20005
Tel.: 202 232 3900
Fax: 202 265 4409
www.joiscience.org

Marine & Oceanographic
Technology Network
37 Teneycke Hill Rd.
P.O. Box 1950
N. Falmouth, MA 02556
Tel.: 508 548 3246
Fax. 508 548 8855
www.motn.org

Marine Technology Society,
5565 Sterrett Place, Suite 108,
Columbia, MD 21044
Tel.: 410 884 5330
Fax: 410 884 9060
www.mtsociety.org

The National Association of Marine Laborato-
ries (NAML)
www.mbl.edu/naml

National Center for Atmospheric Research
(NCAR)
P.O. Box 3000
Boulder, CO 80307-3000
Tel.: 1 303 497 1358
Fax: 1 303 497 1700
www.cgd.ucar.edu/oce/
National Geophysical Data Center
E/GC 325 Broadway
Boulder, Colorado USA 80305-3328
Tel.: 303 497 6826
Fax: 303 497 6513
www.ngdc.noaa.gov

National Oceanographic Data Center
NOAA/NESDIS E/OC1
SSMC3, 4th Floor
1315 East-West Highway
Silver Spring, MD 20910-3282
Tel.: 301 713 3277
Fax: 301 713 3302
www.nodc.noaa.gov/index.html

NSU Oceanographic Center
8000 North Ocean Drive
Dania Beach, FL 33004
Tel.: 800 39 OCEAN
Fax: 954 62 3600
www.nova.edu/ocean

The Oceanography Society,
P.O. Box 1931,
Rockville, MD 20849-1931 USA
Tel.: 1 301 251 7708
Fax: 1 301 251 7709
www.tos.org/

Old Dominion University
Center for Coastal Physical Oceanography
Norfolk, Virginia, 23529, USA
Tel.: 757 683 4945
www.odu.edu/sci/oceanography

Oregon State University
College of Oceanic and Atmospheric Sciences
104 COAS Admin Bldg
Corvallis, OR 97331-5503
Tel.: 541 737 3504
Fax: 541 737 2064
www.coas.oregonstate.edu

PACON International
2525 Correa Road, HIG 407A
Honolulu, HI 96822 USA
Tel.: 808 956 6163
Fax: 808 956 2580
www.hawaii.edu/pacon

The Physical Oceanography Distributed Active Archive Center (DAAC)
Tel.: 626 744 5508
Fax: 626 744 5506
podaac-www.jpl.nasa.gov/sst

Scripps Institution of Oceanography
9500 Gilman Drive, 0210
La Jolla, CA 92093-0210
Tel.: 858 534 3624
Fax: 858 534 5306
sio.ucsd.edu

Sea Grant National Media Relations Office
National Sea Grant College Program
1315 East-West Highway
SSMC3, #11460
Silver Spring, MD 20910
www.seagrantnews.org

Skidaway Institute of Oceanography
10 Ocean Science Circle
Savannah, GA 31411
Tel.: 912 598 2400
Fax: 912 598 2310
www.skio.peachnet.edu

University of Delaware
The Ocean Information Center
Graduate College of Marine Studies
700 Pilottown Road
Lewes, DE 19958
Tel.: 302 645 4225
Fax: 302 645 4007
diu.cms.udel.edu

University of Hawaii
Joint Institute for Marine and Atmospheric Research
1000 Pope Road
Marine Sciences Building,
Room 312
Honolulu, Hawaii 96822
Tel.: 808 956 8083
Fax: 808 956 4104
ilikai.soest.hawaii.edu/JIMAR

University of Miami
Rosenstiel School of Marine and Atmospheric Science
4600 Rickenbacker Causeway
Miami, FL 33149-1098
Tel.: 1 305 421 4000
www.rsmas.miami.edu

University of Rhode Island
Graduate School of Oceanography
Bay Campus Box 52
South Ferry Road
Narragansett, RI 02882-1197, USA
Tel.: 401 874 6222
Fax: 401-874-6889
www.gso.uri.edu

The University of Texas at Austin,
Marine Science Institute
750 Channel View Drive
Port Aransas, Texas 78373-5015
Tel.: 361 749 6711
Fax: 361 749 6777
wwwutmsi.zo.utexas.edu

Woods Hole Oceanographic Institution
Information Office
Co-op Building, MS #16
Woods Hole, MA 02543
Tel.: 508 548 1400
Fax: 508 457 2034
www.whoi.edu

WORLDWIDE ASSOCIATIONS

The International Association for the Physical Sciences of the Oceans (IAPSO)
www.olympus.net/IAPSO

International Society of Acoustic Remote Sensing of the Atmosphere and Oceans (ISARS)
www.boku.ac.at/imp/isars

RELATED LINKS

European Directory of the Ocean-observing System
www.edios.org

Oceanographers Net
www.oceanographers.net

INSTITUTES & SOCIETIES

AUSTRALIA

Australasian Institute for Maritime Archaeology Inc. (AIMA)
aima.iinet.net.au

The AWSANZ Project
ehlt.flinders.edu.au/archaeology/awsanz

CANADA

Great Lakes Institute for Marine Research
3219 Yonge Street Suite # 102
Toronto, Ontario M4N 3S1 Canada
Tel.: 416 917 7974
Fax: 416 484 4306
www.greatlakesinstitute.ca

The Underwater Archaeological Society of British Columbia
c/o Vancouver Maritime Museum
1905 Ogden Street
Vancouver, B.C., Canada V6J 1A3
www.uasbc.com

FRANCE

Centre Européen de Recherches et d'Etudes
Sous-marines
La Madeleine
50760 Montfarville, France
Tel.: 33 2 33 54 07 11
Fax: 33 2 33 54 02 07
www.ceresm.com

Groupe de Recherche en Archéologie Navale (GRAN)
Service historique de la Marine –
Passage de la Corderie
BP 45 - 83 800 Toulon Naval
Tel.: Toulon: 33 04 94 24 91 00
Tel.: Paris: 33 01 43 43 38 95
Fax: Paris: 33 01 43 43 32 75
archeonavale.org

Groupe de Recherches Archéologiques Subaquatiues (GRAS)
16 rue de Brunoy
91230 MONTGERON
archsubgras.free.fr

La Société d'Etudes en Archéologie Subaquatique – S.E.A.S. -
Centre Saint Exupery
20232 OLETTA
Tel.: 06 99 78 51 71
www.archeo-seas.org

Societe D'archeologie Maritime Du Morbihan
7 rue des Marronniers, 56480 Cléguerec
Tel.: 02 97 38 00 29
Fax: 02 97 38 10 08
membres.lycos.fr/sammorbihan

GERMANY

German Society for the Promotion of Underwater Archaeology (DEGUWA)
Hetzelsdorf 33
D-91362 Pretzfeld
Tel.: 49 9197 625889
Fax: 49 9197 1684
www.deguwa.org

Unterwasser- u. Feuchtbodenarchäologie,
Fischersteig 9,
78343 Gaienhofen
Hemmenhofen
Tel.: 07735 3001
Fax: 07735 1650
unterwasserarchaeologie.de/sonst/suwa.html

GREECE

Hellenic Institute of Marine Archaeology (HIMA)
4 Al Soutsou Str.,
10671 Athens
Tel.: 30 10 360 3662
Fax: 30 10 645 0033
www.culture.gr

INDIA

National Institute of Oceanography (NIO)
Dona Paula
403 004, Goa, India
Tel.: 91 0 832 - 2450450;
Fax: 91 0 832 - 2450602 & 2450603
www.nio.org

The Kyushi and Okinawa Society for Underwater Archaeology (KOSUWA)
Chisan Mansion Tenjin Chuo-ku,
Fukuoka City 810-0001 Japan
Tel. /Fax: 092 725 0171
www.h3.dion.ne.jp/~uwarchae

ITALY

Archeologia Subacquea Speleologia Organizzazione
Via Appia Pignatelli 235 - 00178 - ROMA (Italia)
– Tel. /Fax: 0039 6 7186919
www.assonet.org/asso/itasso.htm

NEW ZEALAND

The Maritime Archaeological Association of New Zealand MAANZ
c/o PO Box 893
Wellington, New Zealand.
www.maanz.wellington.net.nz

NORWAY

Institute for Archaeology and Religious Studies Norwegian University of Science and Technology
N-7491 Trondheim Norway
www.hf.ntnu.no/maritime

Nordic Underwater Archaelogy
www.subarch.com

SWITZERLAND

The Franck Goddio Society
3, Rue Bovy-Lysberg
CH-1204 Geneva, Switzerland
Fax: 1 509 479-3653
www.franckgoddio.org

TURKEY

Marmara Islands Underwater Archaeological Research
Tel.: 90 212 229 9329
Fax: 90 212 4737079

www.nautarch.org

UNITED KINGDOM

Anglo-Danish Maritime Archaeological Team
Penners Gardens, Langley Road, Surbiton.
Surrey. KT6 6JW. England.
Tel.: 44 0 20 8399 1284
www.admat.org.uk

The Centre for Maritime Archaeology University of Southampton
Highfield
Southampton GB: SO17 1BJ
www.cma.soton.ac.uk
The Nautical Archaeology Society
Fort Cumberland
Fort Cumberland Road
Portsmouth PO4 9LD UK
Tel./Fax: 44 0 23 9281 8419
www.nasportsmouth.org.uk

UNITED STATES

ARIZONA

National Underwater and Marine Agency
P.O. Box 5059
Scottsdale, AZ 85258
www.numa.net

CALIFORNIA

Project AWARE Foundation (Americas)
30151 Tomas Street, Suite 200
Rancho Santa Margarita
CA, 92688-2125 USA
Tel.: 1 866 80 AWARE (US and Canada)
Tel.: 1 949 858 7657
Fax: 1 949 858 7521
www.projectaware.org

DISTRICT OF COLUMBIA

The Maritime Archaeological and Historical Society (MAHS)
P.O. Box 44382,
L'Enfant Plaza,
Washington, D.C 20026,
Tel.: 301 419 8222
www.mahsnet.org

HAWAII

The Maritime Archaeology and History of the Hawaiian Islands Foundation (MAHHI)
PO Box 8807
Honolulu , HI 96830-0807

www.mahhi.org
FLORIDA

Archaeology Institute
The University of West Florida
11,000 University Parkway
Pensacola, Florida 32514
Tel.: 850 474 3015
Fax: 850 474 2764
www.uwf.edu

ILLINOIS

The Underwater Archaeological Society of Chicago
P.O. Box 11752
Chicago, IL 60611
Tel.: 708 636 5819
Fax: 708 636 5847
www.uaschicago.org

MARYLAND

Combined Caesarea Expeditions
Department of History
University of Maryland, College Park
College Park, MD 20742-7315
Tel.: 301 405 4353
Fax: 301 314 9399
www.digcaesarea.org
NOAA's National Ocean Service
SSMC4, Room 13632
1305 East-West Hwy
Silver Spring, Maryland 20910
Tel.: 301 713 3060
oceanservice.noaa.gov

MASSACHUSETTS

Archaeological Institute of America
Boston University
656 Beacon Street, 4th Floor
Boston, MA 02215-2006 USA
Tel.: 617 353 9361
www.archaeological.org

Deep Water Archaeology Research Group
Massachusetts Institute of Technology
77 Massachusetts Ave. Rm e51-194
Cambridge, MA 02139
web.mit.edu/deeparch

NEW MEXICO

Submerged Resources Center
National Park Service
P.O. Box 728
Santa Fe, New Mexico 87504

Tel.: 505 988 6750
Fax: 505 986 5236
www.nps.gov/applications/submerged

TEXAS

Institute of Nautical Archaeology
P.O. Drawer HG
College Station, TX 77841-5137 USA
Tel.: 979 845 6694
Fax: 979 847 9260
ina.tamu.edu

PROMARE
2800 Longmire Dr., #59
College Station, Texas 77845
USA
Tel.: 1 979 324 7081
www.promare.org

WISCONSIN

Wisconsin Underwater Archeology Association
PO Box 6081,
Madison, Wisconsin 53716
www.mailbag.com/users/wuaa

RELATED WEBSITES

Society for Historical Archaeology Underwater
www.sha.org/underwater.htm

Advisory Council on Underwater Archaeology
www.acuaonline.org

ENVIRONMENTAL ORGANIZATIONS

1 planet1ocean
P.O. Box 53090
Washington, DC
2009-9997 USA
Tel.: 309 216 5870
www.1planet1ocean.org

AfriOceans Conservation Alliance
PO BOX 22436
Fish Hoek 7974
South Africa
Tel.: 27 0 21 782 7590
www.aoca.org.za
Alaska Marine
Conservation Council
PO Box 101145
Anchorage, AK 99510
Tel.: 907 277 5357
Fax: 907 277 5975

www.akmarine.org

The Antarctic and Southern Ocean Coalition
1630 Connecticut Ave.,
NW Third Floor
Washington, D.C. 20009
Tel.: 202 234 2480
Fax: 202 387 4823
www.asoc.org

American Society of Limnology and Ocean-
ography (ASLO)
5400 Bosque Blvd.,
Suite 680
Waco, TX 76710
Tel.: 800 929-ASLO (USA, Canada, Mexico, and
the Caribbean)
Tel.: 254 399 9635
Fax.: 254 776 3767
www.aslo.org

Stichting ANEMOON
Postbus 29,
2120 AA Bennebroek.
The Netherlands
Tel.: 0252 531111
www.anemoon.org

**Andean Explorers Foundation & Ocean Sailing
Club**
P.O. Box 3279
Reno, NV 89505 USA
Tel.: 775 348 1818
Fax: 775 332 3086
www.aefosc.org

Association of Marine Scientists
Room B19,
New Academic Complex, University of Mauri-
tius,
Réduit, Mauritius
Tel.: 454 1041 ext 1409
Fax: 395 2005
pages.intnet.mu/ams/contact.htm

Australian Institute of Marine Science
PMB 3, Townsville MC
Townsville 4810,
Queensland, Australia
Tel: 07 4753 4444
Fax: 07 4772 5852
Tel: 617 4753 4444
Fax : 617 4772 5852
www.aims.gov.au

Australian Marine Conservation Society
PO Box 5136
Manly, QLD 4179 Australia

Tel.: 61 07 3393 5811
Toll free: 1 800 066 299
Fax: 61 07 3393 5833
www.amcs.org.au

**Australian Marine Sciences Association Inc.
(AMSA)**
PO Box 8
Kilkivan Qld 4600
Tel.: 61 7 5484 1179
Fax: 61 7 5484 1456
www.amsa.asn.au

B.C. Wild Killer Whale Adoption Program
Vancouver Aquarium Marine Science Centre
P.O. Box 3232
Vancouver, BC, Canada V6B 3X8
Tel.: 604 659 3430
www.killerwhale.org

British Marine Life Study Society
Glaucus House
14 Corbyn Crescent
Shoreham-By-Sea,
Sussex BN43 6PQ
www.glaucus.org.uk

**Centro Interdisciplinare di Bioacustica e
Ricerche Ambienta**
Via Taramelli 24,
27100 Pavia, Italy
Tel.: 39 0382 987874
www.unipv.it

Center for Coastal Physical Oceanography
Norfolk, Virginia, 23529
Tel.: 757 683 4945
Fax: 757 683 5550
www.ccpo.odu.edu

Cetacean Society International, P.O. Box 953,
Georgetown, CT 06829 U.S.A.
Tel.: 203 770 8615
Fax: 860 561 0187
csiwhalesalive.org

The Coastal Union (EUCC)
P.O. Box 11232,
2301 EE Leiden,
Netherlands
Tel.: 31 71 512 2900
Fax: 31 71 512 4069
www.eucc.nl

The Coral Reef Alliance
417 Montgomery Street, Suite 205
San Francisco, CA 94104 USA
Tel.: 415 834 0900

Fax: 415 834 0999
toll free 1-888-CORAL-REEF
www.coral.org

Conserve Our Ocean Legacy
1200 Eighteenth Street, N.W., Suite 500
Washington DC 20036
Tel.: 202 887 1350
Fax: 202 887 8889
www.oceanlegacy.org

CRESLI
Division of Natural Sciences and Mathematics
Kramer Science Center
Dowling College
Oakdale, NY 11769-1999
Tel.: 631 244 3352
www.cresli.org

Cousteau Society
710 Settlers Landing Road
Hampton, VA 23669, USA
Tel.: 757 722 9300
Tel.: 800 441 4395
Fax: 757 722 8185
www.cousteau.org

EarthEcho International
888 16th Street NW Suite 800
Washington, DC 20006
Tel.: 202.349.9828
Fax: 202.355.1399
www.earthecho.org

Ecology Action Centre
2705 Fern lane
Halifax, Nova Scotia
Canada B3K 4L3
Tel. 902 429 2202
www.ecologyaction.ca

European Cetacean Society
Brikkenwal 20
NL-2317 GT Leiden
The Netherlands
Tel.: 3171 521 20 76
www.europeancetaceansociety.eu

Florida Oceanographic Society
890 NE Ocean Boulevard,
Stuart, Florida 34996 USA
Tel.: 772 225 0505
www.floridaoceanographic.org

Global Coral Reef Alliance
37 Pleasant Street, Cambridge, Massachusetts
02139, USA
Tel.: 617 864 4226

www.globalcoral.org

Greenpeace International
Ottho Heldringstraat 5
1066 AZ Amsterdam
The Netherlands
Tel.: 31 20 718 2000
Fax: 31 20 514 8151
www.greenpeace.org/international

Harbor Branch Oceanographic
5600 US 1 North,
Ft. Pierce, Florida 34946
Tel.: 772 465 2400
Fax: 772 467 2061
www.hboi.edu

Hebridean Whale and Dolphin Trust
28 Main Street
Tobermory
Isle of Mull, PA75 6NU
Scotland
Tel.: 44 0 1688 302 620
Fax: 44 0 1688 302 728
www.whaledolphintrust.co.uk

Institute of Physics Marine Physics Group
Rainer Reuter University of Oldenburg
26111 Oldenburg, Germany
Tel.: 49 0 441 798 3522
Fax: 49 0 441 798 3340
las.physik.uni-oldenburg.de/projekte/earsel

Investigacion y Conservacion de Mamiferos
Marinos de Ensenada
Plácido Mata 2309 Depto D-5 Condominio Las
Fincas.
22830 Ensenada, Baja California, México.
Tel/Fax: 646178 7301
www.icmme.net

International Commission for the Scientific
Exploration of the Mediterranean Sea (CIESM)
Villa Girasole,
16 bd de Suisse,
MC 98000, Monaco
Tel.: 377 9330 3879
www.ciesm.org

International Marine Mammal Association Inc.
1474 Gordon St.
Guelph, Ontario
Canada N1L 1C8
Tel.: 519 767 1948
Fax: 519 7670284
www.imma.org

International Marinelife Alliance (IMA)
Hawaii Times Building Suite 307
928 Nuuanu Ave.
Honolulu, Hawaii 96817 (USA)
Tel.: 808 523 0144/0145
Fax: 808 523 0140
www.marine.org

International Maritime Organization
4 Albert Embankment
London
SE1 7SR
United Kingdom
Tel.: 44 0 20 7735 7611
Fax: 44 0 20 7587 3210
www.imo.org

International Ocean Institute
Headquarters
P.O. Box 3
Gzira GZR01, Malta
Tel.: 356 21 346529
Fax: 356 21 346502
www.ioinst.org

The International Whaling Commission
The Red House,
135 Station Road,
Impington,
Cambridge,
Cambridgeshire CB4 9NP, UK.
Tel.: 44 0 1223 233 971
Fax: 44 0 1223 232 876
www.iwcoffice.org

Marine Conservation Biology Institute (MCBI)
2122 112th Ave NE
Suite B-300
Bellevue WA 98004
Tel.: 425 274 1180
Fax: 425 274 1183
www.mcbi.org

Marine Conservation Society
Unit 3, Wolf Business park,
Alton Road, Ross-on-wye,
Herefordshire, HR9 5NB
Tel.: 01989 566017
Fax: 01989 567815
www.mcsuk.org

Marine Environmental Research Institute
(MERI)
55 Main Street
PO Box 1652
Blue Hill, ME 04614
Tel.: 207 374 2135
Fax: 207 374 2931

www.meriresearch.org

The Marine Technology Society
5565 Sterrett Place, Suite 108
Columbia, MD 21044
Tel.: 410 884 5330
www.mtsociety.org

Mundo Azul
www.peru.com/mundoazul

National Coalition for Marine Conservation
4 Royal Street SE, (NCMC)
Leesburg, VA 20175 USA
Tel.: 703 777 0037
Fax: 703 777 1107
www.savethefish.org

National Fish and Wildlife Foundation
1120 Connecticut Avenue, NW,
Suite 900
Washington, DC 20036 USA
Tel.: 202 857 0166
Fax: 202 857 0162
www.nfwf.org

National Oceanography Centre,
University of Southampton
Waterfront Campus, European Way, S
outhampton, SO14 3ZH, UK,
Tel.: 44 0 23 8059 6666
www.soc.soton.ac.uk

National Oceanic & Atmospheric Administra-
tion (NOAA)
14th Street & Constitution Avenue, NW
Room 6217
Washington, DC 20230
Tel.: 202 482 6090
Fax: 202 482 3154
www.noaa.gov

Natural Resources Defense Council
40 West 20th Street
New York, NY 10011
Tel.: 212 727 2700
Fax: 212 727 1773
www.nrdc.org

Northwest Straits Commission
10441 bayview-Edison Rd
Mt. Vernon, WA 98273
Tel.: 360 428 1084
Fax: 360 428 1491
www.nwstraits.org

Oceana
2501 M Street, NW

Suite 300
Washington, D.C. 20037-1311 USA
Tel.: 1 202 833 3900
Fax: 1 202 833 2070
www.oceana.org

The Ocean Alliance & The Whale Conservation Institute
191 Weston Rd.
Lincoln, MA 01773 USA
Tel.: 781 259 0423
Toll-free: 800 969 4253
www.oceanalliance.org

The Ocean Conservancy
2029 K Street, NW
Washington, DC 20006
Tel.: 202 429 5609
Toll-free: 800 519 1541
www.oceanconservancy.org

Ocean Conservation Society
P.O. Box 12860
Marina del Rey, California 90295
Tel.: 310 822 5205
Fax: 310 822 5729
www.oceanconservation.org

Ocean Defenders Alliance
19744 Beach Blvd.
Box #446
Huntington Beach, CA 92648
USA
Tel.: 714 875 5881
www.oceandefenders.org

Ocean Futures Society
325 Chapala Street
Santa Barbara, CA 93101
Tel.: (805) 899-8899
www.oceanfutures.org

Ocean Mammal Institute
P.O. Box 14422
Reading, PA 19612
Tel.: 610 670 7386
Fax: 800 226 8216
www.oceanmammalinst.org

Ocean Spirits Inc.
P.O. Box 1373
Grande Anse, St. George's
Grenada,West Indies
www.oceanspirits.org

Ocean Resource Foundation
1021-2000 Wellington Ave.
Suite 418

Winnipeg, Manitoba
Tel.: 204 480 8348
www.orf.org

Oceanic Society
Fort Mason Center
San Francisco, CA 94123
Tel.: 800 325 7491
www.oceanic-society.org

Pew Institute For Ocean Science Offices
126 East 56th Street,
New York, NY 10022
Tel.: 212 756 0042
Fax: 212 756 0045
www.pewoceanscience.org

Planktos
1151 Triton Dr. Suite C
Foster City, CA 94404
Tel.: 650 638 1975
Fax: 650 393 6184
www.planktos.com

PRETOMA (Programa Restauracion de Tortugas Marinas)
Tibas, San Jose
Costa Rica 1203-1100
Tel.: 506 241 52 27
Fax: 506 236 60 17
www.tortugamarina.org

Provincetown Center For Coastal Studies
115 Bradford Street
Provincetown, MA 02657
Tel.: 508 487 3622 ext. 101
Fax: 508 487 4495
www.coastalstudies.org

Project AWARE Foundation (Americas)
30151 Tomas Street, Suite 200
Rancho Santa Margarita
CA, 92688-2125 USA
Tel.: 1 866 80 AWARE (US and Canada)
Tel.: 1 949 858 7657
Fax: 1 949 858 7521
www.projectaware.org

REEF HQ
reefhq@reef.org
P.O. Box 246
Key Largo, FL 33037 USA
Tel.: 305 852 0030
Fax: 305 852 0301
www.reef.org

RiverOcean Research & Education
113 Queens Road

Brighton
BN1 3XG
England
Tel.: 01273 234032
Fax: 01273 234033
www.riverocean.org.uk

Save Our Seas Foundation
6 rue Bellot
1206 Geneva
Switzerland
www.saveourseas.com

Scripps Oceanographic Society
9500 Gilman Drive,
La Jolla, CA 92093-0207
Tel.: 858 534 5771
Fax: 858 534 6992
sos.ucsd.edu

SeaCare Inc.
C/-TIFC
P.O. Box 878
Sandy bay /004
Tasmania
www.seacare.org.au

Seas at Risk
Drieharingstraat 25
3511 BH Utrecht
The Netherlands
www.seas-at-risk.org

Sea Shepherd Conservation Society
International Headquarters
PO Box 2616
Friday Harbor WA 98250 USA
Tel.: 1 360 370 5650
Fax: 1 360 370 5651
www.seashepherd.org

Sea Watch Foundation
11 Jersey Road
Oxford OX4 4RT
United Kingdom
Telephone : +44 (0)1865 717276
Fax : +44 (0)1865 717276
www.seawatchfoundation.org.uk

SeaWeb
1731 Connecticut Ave., NW, 4th Floor
Washington, DC 20009
Tel.: 202 483 9570
Fax: 202 483 9354
www.seaweb.org

Shark Trust
4 Creykes Court

5 Craigie Drive
The Millfields
Plymouth
Devon PL1 3JB
Tel. UK: 0870 128 3045
Tel. Int'l: 44 0 870 128 3045
www.sharktrust.org

Society for Marine Mammalogy
Department of Biology,
SUNY Potsdam, Potsdam NY 13676. Tel.: 315 267 2290
Fax: 315 267 3170
www.marinemammalogy.org

Society of Marine Scientists
4th Floor,
30 Great Guildford Street,
London SE1 0HS
Tel.: 44 0 20 7928 9199
Fax: 44 0 20 7928 6599
www.maritimeindustries.org

UNESCO Intergovernmental Oceanographic Commission
1, rue Miollis
75015 Paris France
Tel.: 33 1 45 68 39 84
Fax: 33 1 45 68 58 12/10
ioc.unesco.org

Whales and Dolphins Conservation Society (WDCS)
Brookfield House
38 St Paul Street
Chippenham Wiltshire UK SN15 1LJ
Tel.: 0870 870 0027
Fax: 0870 870 0028
Tel (outside UK): 44 0 1249 449500
Fax (outside UK: 44 0 1249 449501
www.wdcs.org

WWF International Gland (CH)
Global Marine Programme
Av. du Mont-Blanc
1196 Gland Switzerland
Tel.: 41 22 364 91 11
Fax: 41 22 364 88 36
www.panda.org

AQUARIUMS & MUSEUMS

AFRICA

uShaka Marine World
1 Belle Street
Durban 4001 South Africa

www.ushakamarineworld.co.za/

AMERICAS

ARGENTINA

Acuario Municipal de Mendoza
Ituzaingó 1430
Ciudad de Mendoza, Argentina
www.intertournet.com.ar/mendoza/acuariom
za.htm

BERMUDA

The Bermuda Aquarium, Museum & Zoo
(BAMZ)
P. O. Box FL 145,
Flatts, FL BX, Bermuda
www.bamz.org

BRAZIL

Acqua Mundo
Avenida Miguel Stefano, 2001 Prala da
Enseada
Guaruja, SP, Brazil
www.aquarioguaruja.com.br

CANADA

The Huntsman Marine Science Centre
1 Lower Campus Road
St. Andrews, New Brunswick, E5B 2L7
www.huntsmanmarine.ca

Marine Museum of the Great Lakes
55 Ontario Street,
Kingston, Ontario K7L 2Y2
Tel.: 613 542 2261
Fax: 613 542 0043
www.marmuseum.ca

Parc Aquarium du Québec
1675, Des Hôtels Avenue
Québec (Sainte-Foy), Quebec
G1W 4S3
www.sepaq.com/aquarium

Vancouver Aquarium
P.O. Box 3232
Vancouver, British Columbia
Canada V6B 3X8
www.vanaqua.org

MEXICO

Acuario de Veracruz

Playón de Hornos s/n,
C.P. 91700, Veracruz, Ver, México
www.acuariodeveracruz.com

U.S.A.

ALASKA
Alaska SeaLife Center
301 Railway Avenue
P.O. Box 1329
Seward, AK 99664
www.alaskasealife.org

CALIFORNIA

Aquarium of the Pacific - CA
100 Aquarium Way,
Long Beach, CA 90802
www.aquariumofpacific.org

Aqua Tech Dive Center
1800 Logan Ave.
San Diego, CA. 92113
www.divecenter.com/index_museum.htm

Monterey Bay Aquarium
886 Cannery Row,
Monterey, CA 93940
www.mbayaq.org

DiscoverSea Shipwreck Museum
708 Ocean Highway
Fenwick Island, Delaware 19944
Tel.: 302 539 9366
Toll Free: 1 888 743 5524
www.discoversea.com

ILLINOIS

Lockwood Pioneer Scuba Diving Museum
7307 N. Alpine Road
Loves Park, IL 61111
Tel.: 815 633 6969
Fax: 815 633 3993
Toll Free: 800 541 1062
www.lockwoodmuseum.com

The Shedd Aquarium
1200 South Lake Shore Drive
Chicago, Illinois
www.sheddaquarium.org

FLORIDA

Clearwater Marine Aquarium
249 Windward Passage
Clearwater, Florida U.S.A.
www.cmaquarium.org

History of Diving Museum
P.O. 897
Islamorada, FL 33036
divingmuseum.com

Gulfarium
1010 Miracle Strip Parkway
Fort Walton Beach, FL 32548
www.gulfarium.com

Museum of Man-in-the-Sea
17314 Panama City Beach Parkway
Panama City Beach, Florida 32413
Tel.: 850 235 4101
museum-of-man-in-the-
sea.panamacitybeachfanatic.com

HAWAII

Maui Ocean Center
192 Ma'alaea Rd
Wailuku, HI 96793
www.mauioceancenter.com

LOUISIANA

Audubon Nature Institute
6500 Magazine Street
New Orleans, LA 70118

John W. Peck, Jr. Memorial Vintage Diving Museum
Dive Toledo Scuba Center
55 Perch Drive
Anacoco, La 71403

MASSACHUSETTS

New England Aquarium
Central Wharf
Boston, MA 02110
www.neaq.org

SOUTH CAROLINA

Ripley's™ Aquarium
1110 Celebrity Circle
Myrtle Beach, SC 29577
www.ripleysaquarium.com

TENNESSEE

Ripley's™ Aquarium of the Smokies
88 River Road
Gatlinburg, Tennessee 37738
(888) 240-1358 Toll Free
(865) 430-8818 FAX
www.ripleysaquarium.com

WASHINGTON

Naval Undersea Museum
Navy Region Northwest
1103 Hunley Road
Silverdale, WA 98315-1103
naval.undersea.museum

ASIA

BAHRAIN

Museum of Pearl Diving
Manamah, Bahrain

CHINA

Dalian Sun Asia Ocean World
www.ildalian.com/parkseaworld.asp

EGYPT

Underwater Museum of Sunken Monuments
Eastern Harbor
Anfoushy, Alexandria, Egypt
Tel./Fax: 00 203 483 2045
www.alexandra-dive.com

HONG KONG

Ocean Park
Aberdeen, Hong Kong
www.oceanpark.com.hk

JAPAN

Aquamarine Fukushima
50 Tatsumi-cho, Onahama-aza,
Iwaki-shi, Fukushima-ken
www.marine.fks.ed.jp

Okinawa Churaumi Aquarium
424 Ishikawa,
Motobu-cho, Kunigami-gun,
Okinawa Japan 905-0206
www.kaiyouhaku.com

ISRAEL

The Underwater Observatory Marine Park,
P.O. Box 829,
Eilat 88000, Israel
www.coralworld.com

KUWAIT

The Scientific Center of Kuwait
P.O. Box 3504, Salmiya,
22036 Kuwait
www.tsck.org.kw

SINGAPORE

Underwater World Singapore
80 Siloso Road
Sentosa , Singapore 098969
www.underwaterworld.com.sg

EUROPE

Sea Life Marine Park
www.sealifeeurope.com/
**Over 20 Sea life Centers in Europe

BELGIUM

Aquarium Of The University Of Liege
Institute of Zoology (bldg. I-1), 22, quay Van
Beneden,
B-4020 Liege Belgium
www.ulg.ac.be/aquarium

CROATIA

Aquarium Crikvenica
AQUARIUM
Vinodolska 8,
Crikvenica, Croatia
www.raviko.hr/aquarium

CZECH REPUBLIC

Giant Aquarium
Baarova ulice 1663 / 10
500 02 Hradec Kralove 2
Czech Republic
obriakvarium.cz/expwelc.htm

DENMARK

Danmarks Akvarium
Kavalergården
1, 2920 Charlottenlund
www.danmarksakvarium.dk

FRANCE

L'Aquarium de la rochelle
Oceanopolis
Ocearium du Croisic

Musée Frédéric Dumas

Sanary Sur Mer, France
www.sanarysurmer.com/Musee_Dumas.html

NAUSICAA
Centre National de la Mer
Boulevard Sainte Beuve
B.P. 189
62203 Boulogne-sur-Mer
Cedex, france
www.nausicaa.net

Roscoff Aquarium
Place Georges Teissier
29680 ROSCOFF, France
www.sb-roscoff.fr/Aquarium

GERMANY

Aquarium Kiel
Düsternbrooker Weg 20 . 24105 Kiel .
Deutschland
www.aquarium-kiel.de

GREECE

Aquaworld Aquarium
Filikis Etirias 7
Limani Hersonissou
Crete 70014 GREECE
www.aquaworld-crete.com

ITALY

Acquario di Genova
Piazza Caricamento
www.acquario.ge.it

Acquario Mediterraneo
Lungo Mare dei Navigatori,
44 - 48 58019 Porto S.Stefano Grosseto
www.acquarioargentario.com

NETHERLANDS (Dutch Antilles)

Curacao Sea Aquarium
Bapor Kibra z/n
P.O. Box 3102, Curaçao, Dutch Antilles
www.curacao-sea-aquarium.com

NORWAY

Atlanterhavsparken (Atlantic Sea Park)
Tueneset, Pb. 2090
Skarbøvik, N-6028
Ålesund Norway
www.atlanterhavsparken.no

PORTUGAL

Aquário Vasco da Gama
Rua Direita do Dafundo 1495 –
718 Cruz Quebrada –
Dafundo, Portugal
www.aquariovgama.pt

SPAIN

L'Aquàrium de Barcelona Moll d'Espanya del Port Vell,
s/n – 08039 BARCELONA
www.aquariumbcn.com

SWEDEN

Aquaria Water Museum
Djurgården
Falkenbergsgatan 2
115 21 Stockholm
www.aquaria.se

UNITED KINGDOM

Blue Planet Aquarium
Junction 10 of the M53
Kinsey Road, CH65 9LF
www.blueplanetaquarium.com

Blue Reef Aquariums
Newquay, Portsmouth, and
Tynemouth UK
www.bluereefaquarium.co.uk

Deep Sea World
Battery Quarry
North Queensferry
Fife KY11 1JR Scotland
www.deepseaworld.com

London Aquarium
County Hall
Westminster Bridge Road
London SE1 7PB
www.londonaquarium.co.uk

The Scottish Crannog Centre
Kenmore, Loch Tay, Aberfeldy,
Perthshire, PH15 2HY,
Scotland.
Tel.: 01887 830583
Fax: 01887 830876
www.crannog.co.uk

OCEANIA

AUSTRALIA

Reef HQ
2-68 Flinders Street
P.O. Box 1379
Townsville. Qld.
4810 AUSTRALIA
www.reefhq.com.au

Sydney Aquarium
Aquarium Pier
Darling Harbour
Australia NSW 2000
www.sydneyaquarium.com.au

Parkyn Parade,
Mooloolaba,
Sunshine Coast,
QLD Australia
www.underwaterworld.com.au

NEW ZEALAND

Kelly Tarlton's Antarctic Encounter & Underwater World
23 Tamaki Drive,
Orakei, Auckland
www.kellytarltons.co.nz

Otago Museum and Discovery World
419 Great King Street
PO Box 6202
Dunedin New Zealand
Tel.: 64 0 3 474 7474
Fax: 64 0 3 477 5993
www.otagomuseum.govt.nz

RELATED SITES

Diving Heritage
Virtual Diving Museum
www.divingheritage.com

The Historical Diving Society Worldwide
www.thehds.com

The Sea.Org
www.thesea.org

20,000 Leagues under the Sea
www.ofcn.org

BATHYSCAPH *TRIESTE*
DEEPEST DIVE IN HISTORY
35,798 ft (10,911 m) - 16,000 PSI (1,089 ATM)
23/01/1960 - CHALLENGER DEEP, GUAM

DIVING RECORDS
& AQUATIC SUPERLATIVES

Chapter **16**

Record verification: Although every attempt is made to verify the following records and world firsts, some information may be incorrect. If you can demonstrate that any of the following information is false or outdated, please contact us at: records@divingalmanac.com

New or unlisted record: If you have claim to a diving or underwater record/first, or if you know of a record not listed here, write to us to get your record published in the 2008 edition of the Diving Almanac and Yearbook: records@divingalmanac.com

AS OF OCTOBER 2, 2006

SCUBA DIVING AND SWIMMING

1. Deepest altitude dive (Men)
2. Deepest altitude dive (Women)
3. Deepest cave dive (Men)
4. Deepest cave dive (Women)
5. Deepest cave dive on air
6. Deepest dive in one-atmosphere suit
7. Deepest dive on air (Men)
8. Deepest dive on air (Women)
9. Deepest dive on scuba (Men)
10. Deepest dive on scuba (Women)
11. Deepest open-circuit dive in the Great Lakes
12. Deepest rebreather dive
13. Deepest wreck dive
14. Fastest drift dives
15. Fastest ice water swim
16. First dive in Antarctica
17. First person to complete long-distance swims in all five oceans of the world
18. First person to dive across the English Channel
19. First scuba dive at the North Pole
20. First undersea live video chat
21. First underwater radio show
22. Highest altitude dives
23. Largest underwater press conference
24. Largest underwater wedding
25. Longest continuous immersion on scuba (controlled environment)
26. Longest continuous immersion on scuba (natural environment)
27. Longest ice water swim
28. Longest ocean swim
29. Longest underwater distance without surfacing
30. Longest u/w distance w/out surfacing (Europe)
31. Longest immersion on scuba
32. Most couples married underwater
33. Most people breathing on a single first stage
34. Most people scuba diving simultaneously
35. Oldest active diver
36. Underwater cycling (Competition)
37. Underwater cycling (Deepest)
38. Underwater cycling (Distance)
39. Underwater juggling
40. Underwater mailbox
41. Underwater rope jumping
42. Underwater violinist

FREEDIVING

43. Constant Weight AIDA (Men)
44. Constant Weight AIDA (Women)
45. Constant Weight without fins AIDA (Men)
46. Constant Weight without fins AIDA (Women)
47. Dynamic Apnea without fins AIDA (Men)
48. Dynamic Apnea without fins AIDA (Women)
49. Dynamic Apnea with fins AIDA (Men)

50. Dynamic Apnea with fins AIDA (Women)
51. Free Immersion AIDA (Men)
52. Free Immersion AIDA (Women)
53. No Limits (Men)
54. No Limits AIDA (Men)
55. No Limits (Women)
56. No Limits AIDA (Women)
57. Static Apnea AIDA (Men)
58. Static Apnea AIDA (Women)
59. Under ice
60. Variable Weight AIDA (Men)
61. Variable Weight AIDA (Women)

DIVING EQUIPMENT

62. First Aqualung dive
63. First underwater electric lights

UNDERWATER IMAGING

64. First commercially-available camera
65. First underwater film
66. First underwater flash bulb
67. First underwater photo
68. Largest underwater camera system
69. Most powerful underwater lighting

COMMERCIAL DIVING

70. Deepest salvage operation (diver-assisted)
71. Deepest salvage operation (ROV)
72. Deepest saturation dive (experimental)
73. Deepest saturation dive (open sea)

DIVING BELLS & SUBMERSIBLES

74. Deepest diving submersible (in service)
75. Deepest submersible dive
76. Deepest submersible dive (solo)
77. First maneuverable research submersible
78. First dive on the Titanic
79. First submersible jamboree
80. First underwater vessel to operate from an underwater base
81. Highest altitude dive in a submersible
82. Most active research submersible

SUBMARINES

83. Fastest human-propelled submarine (Men)
84. Fastest human-propelled submarine (Women)
85. Fastest submarine
86. Fastest torpedo
87. Largest submarine

SHIPS

88. Deepest anchorage
89. Fastest vessel / World Water Speed Record
90. Largest cruise ship
91. Largest merchant ship
92. Largest warship
93. Oldest commissioned warship

UNDERWATER HABITATS

94. Deepest underwater habitat
95. First habitat to habitat communication
96. First manned underwater habitat
97. First self-sustaining underwater habitat
98. First underwater colony
99. First underwater hotel
100. Largest underwater hotel
101. Longest stays in an underwater habitat
102. Longest serving underwater habitat
103. Underwater habitats in service (2006)

ARCHAEOLOGY

104. Deepest ancient shipwreck ever found
105. Deepest shipwreck ever found
106. Deepest shipwreck salvage
107. First live Internet shipwreck exploration
108. Most valuable shipwreck recovery
109. Oldest intact war wreck in N. America
110. Oldest shipwreck ever found

BIOLOGY

111. Coldest fish
112. Deadliest jellyfish
113. Deadliest octopus
114. Deadliest shark

115. Deepest bird (flying)
116. Deepest bird (non-flying)
117. Deepest crinoid
118. Deepest fish (collected)
119. Deepest fish (observed)
120. Deepest frog
121. Deepest mammal
122. Deepest sea cucumber
123. Deepest sea star
124. Deepest sea urchin
125. Deepest turtle
126. Fastest bird (swimming)
127. Fastest fish
128. Fastest growing seaweed
129. Fastest mammal
130. Fastest pinniped
131. Fastest sea star
132. Fastest snail
133. Heaviest clam
134. Heaviest crustacean
135. Heaviest invertebrate
136. Highest leaping shark
137. Largest animal
138. Largest biomass for single species
139. Largest clam
140. Largest crinoid
141. Largest crocodile
142. Largest crustacean
143. Largest eye
144. Largest fish (bony)
145. Largest fish (carnivorous)
146. Largest fish (deep sea)
147. Largest fish (freshwater)
148. Largest fish (marine)
149. Largest frog (aquatic)
150. Largest gastropod
151. Largest jellyfish
152. Largest octopus
153. Largest pinniped
154. Largest sea cucumber
155. Largest sea star
156. Largest sea urchin
157. Largest sponge
158. Largest squid
159. Largest squid observed on a dive
160. Largest turtle (marine)
161. Longest bony fish
162. Longest distance flown by fish
163. Longest dive by bird
164. Longest dive by mammal
165. Longest gestation period
166. Longest invertebrate
167. Longest leaping salmon
168. Longest migration (mammal)

169. Longest migration (sea turtle)
170. Longest period of captivity for white shark
171. Longest seaweed
172. Longest walrus teeth
173. Loudest animal in the ocean
174. Most giant squid washed ashore
175. Most poisonous fish
176. Most poisonous reptile (aquatic)
177. Most poisonous snail
178. Most sensitive tooth
179. Most teeth (mammal)
180. Most teeth (fish)
181. Most valuable fish
182. Oldest crustacean (form)
183. Oldest lobster
184. Oldest marine vertebrate
185. Oldest pinniped
186. Rarest seal
187. Slowest fish
188. Smallest crab
189. Smallest crinoid
190. Smallest fish (freshwater)
191. Smallest fish (marine)
192. Smallest pinniped
193. Smallest sea cucumber
194. Smallest sea star
195. Smallest sea urchin

OCEANOGRAPHY

196. Clearest water
197. Coldest water
198. Deepest lake
199. Deepest point in the ocean
200. Deepest ray of light
201. Deepest recorded Secchi depth
202. Deepest sea cave
203. Fastest localized current
204. First oceanographic vessel
205. Greatest oceanic current
206. Greatest river flow
207. Highest lake
208. Highest tides
209. Highest wave (recorded)
210. Highest wave (wind-generated)
211. Hottest water
212. Largest atoll
213. Largest island
214. Largest ocean
215. Largest lake (saltwater)
216. Largest lake (freshwater - surface area)
217. Largest lake (freshwater - volume)

218. Largest lake (underground)
219. Largest polynya
220. Largest river basin
221. Largest tidal bore
222. Longest coral reef
223. Longest river
224. Longest waves
225. Most famous oceanographic vessel
226. Most people ever killed by a single wave
227. Most powerful tidal power plant
228. Most powerful tsunami
229. Most radioactive dive site
230. Saltiest body of water
231. Smallest ocean
232. Tallest iceberg
233. Thickest land ice
234. Thickest sea ice

AQUATIC ODDITIES

235. Deepest underwater concert

SCUBA DIVING AND SWIMMING

1. Deepest altitude dive (Men)
927 ft (282.6 m) - Nuno Gomez (South Africa), Bushmansgat, South Africa, August, 1996. Altitude: 4,921 ft (1,500 m) (Corrected depth: 1,106 ft / 337 m). Total dive time: 12 hours.

2. Deepest altitude dive (Women)
725 ft (221 m) - Verna van Schaik (South Africa), Bushmansgat, South Africa, October 25, 2004. Altitude: 4,921 ft (1,500 m) (Corrected depth: 856 ft / 261 m). Time to descend: 12 min. Total decompression time: 5 hours, 27 min. The record dive required 40 decompression stops.

3. Deepest cave dive (Men)
927 ft (282.6 m) - Nuno Gomez (South Africa), Bushmansgat, South Africa, August, 1996. Altitude: 4,921 ft (1,500 m) (Corrected depth: 1,106 ft / 337 m). Total dive time: 12 hours.

4. Deepest cave dive (Women)
725 ft (221 m) - Verna van Schaik (South Africa), Bushmansgat, South Africa, October

ber 25, 2004. Altitude: 4,921 ft (1,500 m) (Corrected depth: 856 ft / 261 m). Time to descend: 12 min. Total decompression time: 5 hours, 27 min. The record dive required 40 decompression stops.

5. Deepest cave dive on air
415 ft (127 m) - Hal Watts, January 2001.

6. Deepest dive in one-atmosphere suit
2,000 ft (610 m) - U.S. Navy Chief Diver Daniel P. Jackson using the Atmospheric Diving System (ADS), off the coast of La Jolla, Calif., on Aug. 1, 2006.

Chief Navy Diver Mark Schleef says hello to topside personnel as he takes the Atmospheric Diving System (ADS) suit for a dive 2,000 feet (610 m) underwater. Photo: U.S. Navy Mass Communication Specialist 3rd Class Mark G. Logico

Atmospheric Diving System (ADS) a.k.a. Hardsuit 2000. Photo: U.S. Navy Mass Communication Specialist Seaman Chelsea Kennedy

7. Deepest dive on air (Men)
519 ft (158 m) - Mark Andrews (UK), July 1999.

8. Deepest dive on air (Women)
425 ft (129 m) - Scarlett Watts (UK), 1999.

9. Deepest dive on scuba (Men)
1,083 ft (330 m) - Pascal Bernabé (France), Corsica, France, July 5, 2005. Time to descend: less than 10 min. Total decompression time: 529 min. Bernabé completed the open-circuit dive breathing Trimix carried in seven cylinders. Twenty cylinders were also placed on three decompression lines at depths of 1,148 ft (350 m), 197 ft (60 m) and 66 ft (20 m). The record involved 12 support divers.

10. Deepest dive on scuba (Women)
725 ft (221 m) - Verna van Schaik (South Africa), Bushmansgat, South Africa, October 25, 2004. Altitude: 4,921 ft (1,500 m) (Corrected depth: 856 ft / 261 m). Time to descend: 12 min. Total decompression time: 5 hours, 27 min. The record dive required 40 decompression stops.

11. Deepest open-circuit dive in the Great Lakes
530 ft (161.54 m) - Terrence Tysall and Mike Zee, Wreck of the Edmund Fitzgerald, Sept 1, 1995. Tysall and Zee carried nearly 500 ft³ (14.16 m³) of tri-mix. Bottom time: 12 min.

12. Deepest rebreather dive
889 ft (271 m) - David Shaw, Bushmansgat, South Africa, October 28, 2004. Total decompression time: 7 hours, 30 min. At 889 ft (271 m), Shaw found the body of Deon Dreyer who died on December 17, 1994. He attached a line to the body for recovery.

13. Deepest wreck dive
633 ft (193 m) - Lead diver Rob Lalumiere, (Nine-man technical diving team), Ormoc Bay, Philippines, May 29, 2005. Wreck: USS Cooper (Sunk by torpedo December 3, 1944). Time to descend: 7 min. Total dive time including decompression: 5 hours, 30 min.

14. Fastest drift dive

16.1 knots (18.4 mph / 29.6 km/h): Sechelt Rapids (Skookumchuck Narrows), British Columbia, Canada. It is estimated that for a 12-foot (3.6 m) tide, 200 billion gallons (757 billion liters) of seawater flow through the Sechelt Rapids in 6 hours. Several charter operators offer dives at the site during slack tide.

15. Fastest ice water swim
Lewis Gordon Pugh (UK) swam 1,640 ft (500 m) in 7 min. and 2 sec. at the World Winter Swimming Championships in Finland in March, 2006. Organizers of the event had to cut 8 swimming lanes in the frozen Oulu River. Ice thickness was 3 ft (1 m). www.lewispugh.com

16. First dive in Antarctica
Willy Heinrich (Germany), 1902 - German National Antarctic Expedition 1901-03. Using a surface-supplied Siebe diving helmet, Heinrich conducted repairs on the ship and also dove under ice.

17. First person to complete long-distance swims in all five oceans of the world
Lewis Gordon Pugh (UK) became the first person to complete long-distance swims in the Atlantic, Arctic, Southern, Indian and Pacific oceans after enduring a six-hour, 9-mile (15 km) swim from Manly north of Sydney to the Sydney Opera House in January 2006. Pugh (36) began his quest in 1992 by swimming across the English Channel in the Atlantic Ocean. He swam in the Arctic Ocean in 2003, the Southern Ocean in 2005, followed by the Indian and Pacific oceans in 2006. www.lewispugh.com

18. First person to dive across the English Channel
1962 - Fred Baldasare (USA). Baldasare covered total distance of 42 miles (67.59 km) in 19 hours and one minute using scuba equipment.

19. First scuba dive at the North Pole
Dr. Joseph MacInnis (Canada) - LOREX Expedition, 1979. Although several recent expeditions have laid claim to being the first to dive under the North Pole, the first dives at the top of the world were conducted during the Lomosonov Ridge Ex-

pedition in the spring of 1979. Also present were Al Giddings and the editor of National Geographic, Gilbert Grosvenor. The research station drifted on ice in the Arctic Ocean 13,000 feet (3,962 m) above the Lomosonov Ridge, 450 miles (724 km) north of Ellesmere Island. The surface temperature was 31°F (-0.56°C) with the water at 29°F (-1.67°C). Ice thickness was 6 feet (183 cm).

20. First undersea live video chat
On Earth Day (April 22) 1997, Jean-Michel Cousteau led the first undersea live video chat on Microsoft Internet, from the coral reefs of Fiji, celebrating the International Year of the Reef and answering questions from participants around the world.

21. First underwater radio show
Feb. 23, 1940 – Marineland (St. Augustine, Florida), Robert Ripley of *Ripley's Believe it or Not!* fame, hosts a radio show while diving with sharks and dolphins using a microphone-equipped hardhat. The show was broadcast coast to coast for an estimated audience of one million listeners.

Robert Ripley divingwith dolphins during underwater radio broadcast. Photo courtesy Ripley Entertainment www.ripleys.com

22. Highest altitude dives
19,000 ft (5,791 m) - Crater Lake, Licancabur Volcano (Chile / Bolivia). Team led by Johan Reinhard (1982) made 11 dives. Max depth: 20 ft (6.10 m)

23. Largest underwater press conference

12 Spanish journalists - El Hierro, Canary Islands, June 20, 1997. Depth 53 ft (16 m). Time: 20 min. Event: Book launch of *Champion's Secrets* (underwater photo manual) by Carlos Virgili Ribé. Participants communicated via two-way radios.

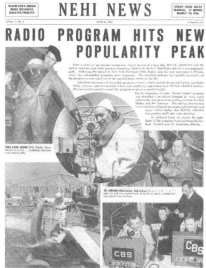

Photo courtesy Ripley Entertainment www.ripleys.com

24. Largest underwater wedding
105 divers - Rainbow Beach, St Croix, Virgin Islands, USA, September 13, 2003. Married couple: Toni Wilson and John Santino. Depth: 10 ft (3 m)

25. Longest continuous immersion on scuba (controlled environment)
220 hours (9.17 days) - Khoo Swee Chiow (Singapore), December 16 to 26, 2005. Khoo dove in a special mineral water tank for the entire duration, enduring dehydration, nausea and hunger. Khoo was on a 100% liquid diet. Toilet breaks had to be taken underwater in a private cubicle out of sight of the shoppers at a Singapore mall. The previous record was 212 hours and 30 min. set by British diver Michael Steven in a Royal Navy tank in Birmingham, England in 1986.

26. Longest continuous immersion on scuba (natural environment)

120 hours (5 days) - Jerry Hall (USA), Hampton, Tennessee, September 3, 2004.

27. Longest ice water swim

Lewis Gordon Pugh (UK) swam 0.75 miles (1.2 km) in a Norwegian fjord on May 12, 2006. The waters beneath the *Jostedalsbreen* glacier were still mostly covered with ice. It took him 23 min. and 50 sec. to complete the distance wearing only swim trunks, a cap and goggles. After 15 min. Pugh had lost sensation in his hands and feet. www.lewispugh.com

28. Longest ocean swim

Susie Maroney (Australia) swam 123 miles (198 km) from Mexico to Cuba without fins. She arrived in Cuba on June 1, 1998, after swimming for 38 hours and 33 minutes to complete the swim. She swam inside a shark-proof cage towed behind a boat. She also wore a skinsuit for protection against jellyfish stings.

29. Longest underwater distance without surfacing

66 miles (106 km) - Neil Watson (United States); swam from Freeport (Bahamas) to the Florida coast

30. Longest u/w distance w/out surfacing (Europe)

34.2 miles (55 km) - Jens Hilbert (Germany), October 15-16, 1994; total kicking time: 19.36 hours; resting periods (in water): 4 hours and 24 min.

31. Longest immersion in diving gear (no tank)

10 days (240 hours) - Progetto Abissi 2005 (The House at the Bottom of the Sea) - Stefano Barbaresi, Stefania Mensa (Italy), Ponza, Italy, September 17, 2005. Maximum depth: 26.4 ft (8 m). Total decompression time: 6 hours and 40. The two divers spent 240 hours on a platform anchored to the sea floor equipped with beds, exercise machines, a television, and a table and chairs. Every 5 to 6 hours, the divers were allowed to enter a dive bell where they could change, eat or use the toilet.

32. Most couples married underwater

34 couples from 22 countries simultaneously exchanged wedding vows. Location: Kradan Island, Thailand, February 14, 2001. Depth: 33 ft (10 m). Couples had to be certified divers.

33. Most people breathing from a single 1st stage

75 divers breathed simultaneously from one 1st stage regulator in Pretoria, South Africa, on August 31, 2002. Seventy-five Scubapro R190 octos were rigged up through an elaborate hose and manifold system and connected to a single Scubapro Mk25 1st stage. The entire regulator system was fed by a 50-liter, 300 bar cylinder. The participants had to synchronize their breathing so that everyone was inhaling and exhaling at exactly the same instant. Due to the extremely high flow, ice formed all over the cylinder valve, 1st stage and even on the low pressure hoses. The air supply was depleted in 10 min. 9 sec.

34. Most people scuba diving simultaneously

979 - Sunlight Thila, North Male' Atoll, February 25, 2006. Divers were aged between 10 and 73 and consisted of tourists, Maldivians and expatriates from 37 resorts, 9 dive centres, the Coast Guard and 14 safari vessels.

35. Oldest active diver

Leni Riefenstahl, Germany (1902-2003); Riefenstahl became a diver at the age of 71. She released her first underwater documentary *Impressionen unter Wasser* (*Underwater Impressions*) on her 100th birthday in 2002. www.leni-riefenstahl.de

36. Underwater cycling (competition)

Piero Gros (Italy) and Claudius Chiappucci (Italy) rode mountain bikes underwater over a distance of 1,969 ft (600 m) while using diving equipment in the communal swimming pool of La Spezia on June 24, 2001.

37. Underwater cycling (deepest)

Vittorio Innocente (Italy) pedaled to the depth of 172 ft (52.5 m) off the Park of Portofino on July 23, 2002. Innocente had to pedal 820 ft (250 m) to reach the record depth.

38. Underwater cycling (distance)
Vittorio Innocente (Italy) cycled 3,937 ft (1.2 km) in 23 min. 54 sec. in a swimming pool in Chiavera (Italy) on April 12, 2000.

39. Underwater juggling
Ashrita Furman juggled three balls while diving for 48 min. 36 sec. at Kelly Tarlton aquarium in Auckland (New Zealand) in 2002. Furman's attempt at breaking his own record in February 2006 was disrupted by a nurse shark nicknamed Guinness at the Aquatheatre Aquaria in Malaysia after 37 min. and 45 sec. www.ashrita.com

40. Underwater Mailbox
32.8 ft (10 m) - Susami Bay, Japan. Divers can use a mailbox to send waterproof postcards anywhere in the world. The mailbox is serviced by the Susami Post Office.

41. Underwater rope jumping
Ashrita Furman skipped 900 times in an hour in Bali in August, 2001.

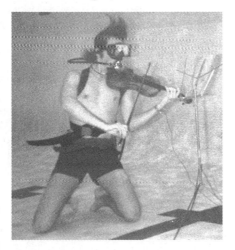

Mark Gottlieb performs underwater. Photo: Lois Gottlieb

42. Underwater violinist
Mark Gottlieb (USA) performed Handel's Water Music underwater at Evergreen State College in Olympia (Washington) in 1976. The music was played by speakers at the surface in the pool. He later played the Jaws theme underwater in the Shark Tank at Marine World in Northern California. An underwater violin is known as an aqualin.

FREEDIVING

Freediving records change frequently. Go to the Diving Almanac and Yearbook website (www.divingalmanac.com) for updates or go to: www.aida-international.org

43. Constant Weight[26] AIDA[27] (Men)
357.61 ft (109 m) – Guillaume Néry (France), Nice, France, September 6, 2006

44. Constant Weight AIDA (Women)
282 ft (86 m) - Natalia Molchanova (Russia), Nice, France, September 3, 2005

45. Constant Weight without fins[28] AIDA (Men)
263 ft (80 m) - Martin Stepanek (Czech Republic), Grand Cayman, Cayman Islands, April 9, 2005. Time: 3 min. 13 sec.

46. Constant Weight without fins AIDA (Women)
180 ft (55 m) - Natalia Molchanova (Russia), Dahab, Egypt, November 11, 2005

47. Dynamic Apnea without fins[29] AIDA (Men)
600.39 ft (183 m) - Tom Sietas (Germany), Tokyo, Japan, August 27, 2006.

---

[26] **Constant Weight (CWT):** Freediver descends and ascends using his fins/monofin and/or with the use of his arms without pulling on the rope or changing his ballast; only a single hold of the rope to stop the descent and start the ascent is allowed. (ref.: AIDA)

[27] **AIDA:** Association internationale pour le développement de l'apnée

[28] **Constant Weight without fins (CNF):** freediver descends and ascends under water using only his own muscle strenght, without the use of propulsion equipment and without pulling on the rope. (ref.: AIDA)

[29] **Dynamic Apnea without fins (DNF):** Freediver travels in a horizontal position under water attempting to cover the greatest possible distance. Any propulsion aids are prohibited. (ref.: AIDA)

48. Dynamic Apnea without fins AIDA (Women)
430 (131 m) - Natalia Molchanova (Russia), Tokyo, Japan, December 20, 2005

49. Dynamic Apnea with fins[30] AIDA (Men)
731.63 ft (223 m) - Tom Sietas (Germany), Tokyo, Japan, 28 August, 2006.

50. Dynamic Apnea with fins AIDA (Women)
656.17 ft (200 m) - Natalia Molchanova (Russia), Moscow, Russia, April 23, 2006

51. Free Immersion[31] AIDA (Men)
347.77 ft (106 m) - Martin Stepanek (Czech Republic), Grand Cayman, Cayman Islands, April 3, 2006

52. Free Immersion AIDA (Women)
262.47 ft (80 m) - Natalia Molchanova (Russia), Dahab, Egypt, June 6, 2006

53. No Limit[32] (Men)
688 ft (209.6 m) - Patrick Musimu (Belgium), Hurghada, Egypt, June 30, 2005. Musimu floods his sinuses and Eustachian tubes during descent. This allows him to dive so deep without having to equalize ear pressure at depths where it is impossible to equalize with the lungs.

54. No Limit AIDA (Men)
600.39 ft (183 m) - Herbert Nitsch (Austria), Zirje, Croatia, August 28, 2006

55. No Limit (Women)
545 ft (166 m) - Audrey Mestre (France), Bayahibe, Dominican Republic, October 4, 2002

56. No Limit AIDA (Women)
525 ft (160 m) - Tanya Streeter (USA), Providenciales, Turks & Caicos, August 17, 2002

57. Static Apnea[33] AIDA (Men)
9 min. 0 sec. - Tom Sietas (Germany), Tokyo, Japan, August 30, 2006

58. Static Apnea AIDA (Women)
7 min. 30 sec. - Natalia Molchanova (Russia), Moscow, Russia, April 22, 2006

59. Under ice
230 ft (70 m) - Éric Chapuis (France), Lake Témiscouata, Québec, Canada, March 28, 1997. Total dive time: 1 min. 59 sec. (1964-1999)

60. Variable Weight[34] AIDA (Men)
459.32 ft (140 m) - Carlos Coste (Venezuela), Sharm, Egypt, May 9, 2006

61. Variable Weight AIDA (Women)
400 ft (122 m) - Tanya Streeter (USA), Providenciales, Turks & Caicos, July 19, 2003

DIVING EQUIPMENT

62. First Aqualung dive
January 1943 - Cousteau tests the first Cousteau/Gagnan scuba unit the cold Marne River near Paris.

63. First underwater electric lights
French engineer Ernest Bazin developed the first underwater electric lights in 1864.

UNDERWATER IMAGING

64. First commercially-available underwater camera
1961 - The CalypsoPhot was the first waterproof 35 mm camera. It was developed by

---

[30] **Dynamic Apnea with fins (DYN):** Freediver travels in a horizontal position under water attempting to cover the greatest possible distance. Any propulsion aids other than fins or a monofin and swimming movements with the arms are prohibited. (ref.: AIDA)

[31] **Free Immersion (FIM):** freediver dives under water without the use of propulsion equipment, but only by pulling on the rope during descent and ascent. (ref.: AIDA)

[32] **No Limit (NLT):** Freediver descends with the help of a ballast weight and ascends via a method of his choice. No Limit is the absolute depth discipline. (Ref.: AIDA)

[33] **Static Apnea (STA):** Freediver holds his breath for as long as possible with his respiratory tracts immerged, his body either in the water or at the surface. (ref.: AIDA)

[34] **Variable Weight (VWT):** freediver descends with the help of a ballast weight and ascends using his own strength: arms and/or legs, either by pulling or not pulling on the rope. (ref.: AIDA)

Belgian Jean de Wouters in 1957. Nikon further developed the camera and produced the Nikonos I in 1963.

65. First underwater film
Kodak Ektachrome Underwater film appeared on the market in 1993. Production lasted only two years terminating in September, 1995.

Kodak Ektachrome Underwater film. Photo by D.A.Y.

66. First underwater flash bulb
The first ever flash bulb was designed by Frenchman Chauffour in 1893 for underwater photographer Louis Boutan. The glass bulb contained pressurized oxygen and magnesium which was ignited by a wire carrying an electrical discharge.

Boutan's method for using a magnesium flashlight under water. Photo: NOAA Ship Collection - Archival Photography by Steve Nicklas, NOS, NGS

67. First underwater photo
1856 - Photo taken by Englishman William Thompson. Total exposure time was 10 min. during which the camera flooded. The plate was removed and rinsed in freshwater. The plate still produced a weak underwater photo of the bay of Weymouth. No other attempts were made until Frenchman Louis Boutan in 1893.

68. Largest underwater camera systems
Howard Hall Productions designed and built an underwater housing for the Mark II IMAX® camera (2D), and consulted on the housing design for the Imax 3D Soledo camera. These camera systems have been used in the production of several large format films, including *Island of the Sharks* (2D), *Coral Reef Adventure* (2D), *Into the Deep* (3D), and *Deep Sea 3D* (3D). While both systems are neutrally buoyant in the water, on the surface the Mark II system weighs 250 lbs (114 kg) and the Solido 3D system weighs around 1,300 lbs (590kg). During the filming of *Coral Reef Adventure*, divers took the Mark II system to 373 ft (114 m): the deepest a diver has ever taken an IMAX camera. www.howardhall.com

69. Most powerful underwater lighting
The 20,000-feet (6,000 m) depth capable *Medusa*, built by Phoenix International, Inc., is a Remotely Operated Vehicle (ROV) that carries 10 high-powered, independently movable and controllable, HMI lights. *Medusa* can produce a total of 12,000 watts of illumination. It was suspended over the wreck of the RMS *Titanic* for the making of James Cameron's *Ghosts of the Abyss* in 2001.

COMMERCIAL DIVING

70. Deepest salvage operation (Diver-assisted)
803 ft (245 m) - Wreck of HMS *Edinburgh* (sunk during World War II), Barents Sea, Norway, 1981. British dive team recovered 431 gold ingots.

71. Deepest salvage operation (ROV[35])

17,300 ft (5,273 m) - Recovery of a U.S. Navy Helicopter (CH-46 Sea Knight), Wake Island, 1992. ROV: CURV III (U.S. Navy). Weight of ROV: 12,600 lbs (5,715 kg). Max. operating depth: 20,000 ft (6,096 m)

72. Deepest saturation[36] dive (Experimental)

2,300 ft (701 m) - Comex Hydra 10, Hyperbaric Experimental Centre, Marseille, France, 1992. Breathing gas mixture of hydrogen, helium and oxygen.

73. Deepest saturation dive (Open sea)

1,752 ft (534 m) - Comex Hydra 8, Hyperbaric Experimental Centre, Marseille, France, 1988. Breathing gas mixture of hydrogen, helium and oxygen.

SUBMERSIBLES

74. Deepest diving submersible (in service)

Research submarine *Shinkai 6500* (Japan). Maximum depth reached (1989): 21,411 ft (6,526 m), Japan Trench, Sanriku, Japan. Operated by: Japan Marine Science & Technology Centre (JAMSTEC). Crew: 3. Length: 31.16 ft (9.5 m). Width: 9.9 ft (2.7 m) Height: 10.5 ft (3.2 m).

SHINKAI 2000 operated by JAMSTEC. Photo: OAR/National Undersea Research Program (NURP); JAMSTEC

Russia's *Mir I* and *Mir II* submersibles have a maximum operating depth of 20,000 ft (6,000 m).

Both of the Mir submersibles have made several dives to the wreck of the RMS *Titanic*. Photo: OAR / National Undersea Research Program (NURP)

France's *Nautile* also has a maximum operating depth of 20,000 ft, (6,000 m).

Bathyscaph Trieste is hoisted out of the water, circa 1958-59. Photo: U.S. Naval Historical Center Photograph

75. Deepest submersible dive

35,798 ft (10,911 m) - Bathyscaph *Trieste* (Project Nekton) - 23 January 1960, Challenger Deep (Mariana Trench), Guam (Deepest known point on earth). Hydrostatic pressure: 16,000 PSI[37] (1,089 ATM[38]). Occupants: Dr Jacques Piccard (Switzerland), Lt. Donald Walsh, USN

---

[35] **ROV:** Remotely Operated Vehicle
[36] **Saturation:** Diver's tissues have reached the maximum partial pressure of gas possible for a given depth attained after prolonged exposure.

[37] PSI: Pounds per square inch
[38] ATM: Unit of pressure roughly equal to the average atmospheric pressure at sea level on Earth.

Close-up of Trieste's pressure sphere where the two passengers spend the entire dive. Photo: U.S. Naval Historical Center Photograph

76. Deepest submersible dive (Solo)
3000 ft (914 m) - Graham Hawkes (United States). Achieved while test piloting the Deep Rover submersible.

77. First maneuverable research submersible
The Diving Saucer DS-1 (*Soucoupe SP-300*) - Jacques-Yves Cousteau began designing small, maneuverable submersibles capable of being launched from the deck of a ship in the 1950s. His two-man DS-1 was first tested (unmanned) to a depth of 1,968 ft (600 m) in the Mediterranean Sea in 1957. It was lost when its tether snapped during ascent. A second saucer DS-2 (a.k.a. *Denise* in honor of the wife of engineer Jean Mollard), launched in 1959, was used on countless missions aboard Cousteau's research vessel *Calypso*. Unlike current submersible designs, the DS-2 was propelled by water jets. Its maximum operating depth was 1,000 ft (300 m).

78. First dive on the Titanic
Robert Ballard - Alvin submersible (Woods Hole Oceanographic Institution), July 13, 1986 - Depth: 12,600 ft (3,840 m)

79. First submersible jamboree
Catalina Island (California) – 7 submersibles: Cousteau Sea Fleas, Star II, Deep Quest, Nekton, Beaver and Dowb. During the dive, the combined fleet discovered a shipwreck and was surrounded by a mass of squid.

80. First underwater vessel to operate from an underwater base
Cousteau Society DS-2 (1963) - Conshelf[39] II Expedition (France). Eight divers lived in Conshelf II habitat in the Red Sea for one month under the supervision of Jacques-Yves Cousteau. The DS-1 Diving Saucer operated from an underwater hangar.

81. Highest altitude dive in a submersible
Albert Falco and Raymond Coll explored the depths of Lake Titicaca (Bolivia) aboard two Cousteau Sea Fleas (Puce de mer) at an altitude of 12,536 ft (3821 m) above sea level in 1968. They observed prints made by frogs at a depth of 394 ft (120 m). The Sea Fleas could attain deeper depths than Cousteau's Soucoupe.

Cousteau Society Sea Flea. Photo: J. Gallant / D.A.Y.

82. Most active submersible in service
Alvin - Woods Hole Oceanographic Institution (WHOI). Commissioned: June 5, 1964

Statistics as of Jan. 01, 2005: Total dives: 4,074; Total depth: 27,821,886 ft (8,480,111 m); Avg. depth: 6,831 ft (2,082 m); Total time submerged: 28,120 hours; Avg. time submerged: 6.90 hours; Total persons carried: 12,215; Speeds: Cruising - 0.5 knot (0.5

---

[39] CONSHELF: Continental Shelf Station

mph / 0.8 km/h), Full - 2 knots (2.11 mph / 3.4 km/h); Gross weight: 35,200 lbs (17 metric tons); Crew: One pilot and two scientific observers; *Alvin*'s most famous exploits: locating a hydrogen bomb in the Mediterranean Sea (1966); deep-sea hydrothermal vents (1980s); Wreck of the *Titanic* (1986)

The 35,200-lb (17 metric tons) *Alvin* is hoisted onto its support vessel. - Photo: OAR/NURP

Alvin (1978) - Photo: OAR/NURP

SUBMARINES

83. Fastest human-propelled submarine (Men)
Omer 5 - 7.061 knots (8.126 mph / 13.08 km/h) (July 2005). Two-person submersible designed and built by the *École de technologie supérieure* (ETS) *Université du Québec à Montréal.* Crew : 2

84. Fastest human-propelled submarine (Women)
Omer 5 - 5.885 knots (6.772 mph / 10.9 km/h) (July 2005). Two-person submersible designed and built by the *École de technologie supérieure* (ETS) *Université du Québec à Montréal.* Crew : 2

85. Fastest submarine
Alpha class nuclear-powered submarine (Russia). Reported maximum speed: 40 knots (46 mph / 74 km/h) Maximum operational depth: 2,500 ft (760 m)

86. Fastest torpedo
260 knots (300 mph / 483 km/h) - *Shkval* (squall) supercavitating rocket-propelled torpedo (Russia). The fastest NATO torpedo is the Spearfish (UK) at 75 knots (86 mph / 138 km/h). The Shkval produces an envelope of supercavitating bubbles preventing the surface of the torpedo from coming into contact with water thus reducing drag and friction. Maximum launch depth: 328 ft (100 m). In March 2006, the Islamic Republic of Iran reported that it had tested a Shkval-like torpedo called Hoot (whale), capable of speeds reaching 225 mph (360 km/h).

87. Largest submarine
Typhoon class (Russia)
Length: Approx. 574 ft (175 m); Beam: 75 ft (23 m); Draft: 38 ft (12 m); Displacement: 33,800 tons; Propulsion: 2 pressurized-water nuclear reactors driving 2 propellers; Crew: 150; Armament: 6 torpedo tubes, 20 ballistic missiles; First Sub Commissioned: December 12, 1981; Maximum Speed: Approx. 27 knots (31 mph / 50 km/h).

SHIPS

88. Deepest anchorage

24,928 ft (7,600 m) - Jacques-Yves Cousteau's *Calypso* is anchored over the Romanche Gap off the west coast of Africa using a 700-lb (318 kg) anchor, 100 ft (30 m) of heavy chain, a 550-lb (250 kg) pig iron, a 200-ft (61 m) steel cable and a quarter-inch braided nylon line 32,800 feet (9997 m) long.

89. Fastest vessel / World Water Speed Record

Spirit of Australia - 317.60 mph (511.11km/h), Blowering Dam, NSW Australia, October 1978. Pilot: Ken Warby.

90. Largest cruise ship

Freedom of the Seas (Royal Caribbean) - 160,000 tons / 1,112ft (339m). The vessel has 1,800 rooms for up to 4,375 passengers and a crew of 1,360. *Freedom of the Seas* was christened on May 12, 2006.

91. Largest merchant ship

Knock Nevis (Norway). The supertanker formerly known as *Seawise Giant*, *Happy Giant*, and *Jahre Viking* measures 1504 ft (458 m) in length and 226 ft (69 m) in width. *Knock Nevis* has a dead weight of 564,763 t and displaces 647,955 t (24.6 m draft) when fully laden with nearly 4.1 million barrels (650,000 m³) of crude oil.

92. Largest warship

Nimitz class aircraft carrier – Displacement: 97,000 tons; Length: 333 m (1092 ft) overall; Flight deck width: 76.8 m (252 ft); Aircraft: 85; Crew: Ship's Company: 3,200 - Air Wing: 2,480

Sailors man the rail aboard the Nimitz-class aircraft carrier USS *George Washington* as the ship returns to her homeport in Norfolk. U.S. Navy photo by Photographers Mate 3rd Class Christopher Stephens

93. Oldest commissioned warship

USS *Constitution* (a.k.a. *Old Ironsides*). The three-masted frigate was launched and christened in Boston on October 21, 1797. She is still listed in active service.

USS *Constitution* (*Old Ironsides*) the oldest commissioned warship afloat. Photo: U.S. Navy / Joe Burgess.

UNDERWATER HABITATS

HYDROLAB - Grand Bahama Island (1966). Photo: OAR/National Undersea Research Program (NURP)

During the 1960s, more than 60 underwater habitats were constructed around the world. The research to gain a permanent human foothold on the seafloor paralleled the American and Soviet efforts to put men on the moon. By the 1970s, interest and funding for habitat research and development had mostly dissipated.

94. Deepest underwater habitat

610 ft (185 m) - SeaLab III, February, 1969, San Clemente Island, California (USA). The SeaLab program was terminated after a man was killed while making repairs to a leak during an early test dive. No new habitats were built by the U.S. Navy. In fact, the main purpose of SeaLab III was to develop technology that would permit divers to operate at extreme depths after exiting a submarine.

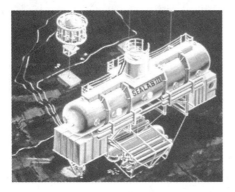

SeaLab III. Photo: OAR/National Undersea Research Program (NURP); U.S. Navy

Some of the experiments conducted during SeaLab remained classified till 2002 when it was revealed that in 1971, divers using SeaLab techniques successfully retrieved Soviet test missiles. The divers were deployed from a submarine carrying a pressure chamber welded to its deck, the USS *Halibut*, in the Sea of Okhotsk. They also tapped several underwater communications cables (Operation Ivy Bells) that ran from the Soviet submarine base at Petropavlovsk to Fleet headquarters near Vladivostok.

95. First habitat to habitat communication

André Laban in Jacques-Yves Cousteau's *Conshelf II* (Depth of 328 ft (100 m) off Saint-Jean-Cap-Ferrat, France) spoke for several minutes with Scott Carpenter in SEALAB II at depth of 203 ft (62 m) off California in September, 1965.

96. First manned underwater habitat

1962 - Conshelf 1 (France). In September, 1962, Albert Falco and Claude Wesly became the world's first aquanauts by spending seven days in the *Diogenes* habitat at a depth of 33 ft (10 m). The experiment was supervised by Jacques Y. Cousteau in the Mediterranean Sea near Marseilles. Falco and Wesly spent an average 19 hours inside the habitat and 5 hours on scuba conducting various experiments. The breathing gas was air.

97. First self-sustaining underwater habitat

BioSUB (Albury, Australia). In 2007, the BioSUB Project will see Australian marine scientist and diver Lloyd Godson survive in the world's first self-sufficient, self-sustaining underwater habitat. Located in a flooded quarry near Albury, the BioSUB Project will compare life underwater to life inside a closed ecological system. It requires the same specially-designed regenerative or recycling technology needed for any long-term manned mission to Mars. Lloyd must generate oxygen, grow food, obtain fresh water and deal with his waste. www.biosub.com.au

98. First underwater colony

Conshelf II (France). Seven divers lived underwater off Sha'ab Rumi (Sudan) in the Red Sea for one month under the supervision of Jacques-Yves Cousteau. The colony consisted of four manned habitats including a hangar for the DS-1 Diving Saucer and a tool shed. Eight additional structures including shark cages completed the colony. The main habitat called Starfish House was located at 33 ft (10 m) while the smaller Deep Cabin was located at 85 ft (26 m).

99. First underwater hotel

Jules Undersea Lodge - Key Largo Undersea Park. Launched as the research habitat La Chalupa off Puerto Rico in 1971, it was moved to Florida and transformed into an underwater hotel in 1986. The habitat can accommodate up to 6 guests at a depth of 21 ft (6.4 m). www.jul.com

100. Largest underwater hotel
The **Hydropolis Hotel** is planned to open off Jebel Ali, Dubai, in 2006. Construction of the hotel is estimated at $500 million USD. The 220-suite hotel will be constructed of a combination of concrete, steel and Plexiglas, at a maximum depth of 66 ft (60 m). The hotel will be linked to a land station by a 1,700-foot (515 m) transparent train tunnel. The security system includes anti-missile radar and watertight doors to seal off all section in case of attack. The cost for a day's lodging will reach up to $5,500 USD. www.hydropolis.com

Currently in the final design stages, the **Poseidon Undersea Resort** is also vying to become the world's first seafloor luxury resort complex. The resort will be a unique, intimate and exclusive, five-star destination providing the highest possible levels of luxury and service. The earliest anticipated opening date would be late 2007; www.poseidonresorts.com

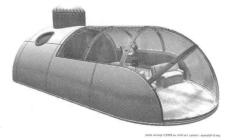

Room of the Poseidon Undersea Resort. Image: Chris Huf / www.huf.org

Longest stays in an underwater habitat
1969 - **Tektite I** / Man-in-the-Sea Project (USA). Four aquanaut-scientists of the U.S. Department of the Interior spent 60 consecutive days at 52 ft (16 m) in Lameshur Bay (U.S. Virgin Islands).

1994 - **Lacustris Programme** (Romania). Aquanauts Liviu Miron & Constantin Mihai

set the European record of 36 consecutive days living inside L.S.-1 Underwater Laboratory at variable depths.

Aquanauts Liviu Miron and Constantin Mihaï emerge through the hatch of the L.S.-1 Underwater Laboratory on Lake Bicaz, Romania. Photo: J. Gallant / D.A.Y.

1963 - **Conshelf II** (France). Conshelf II (France). Seven divers lived in Conshelf II colony off Sha'ab Rumi (Sudan) in the Red Sea for one month under the supervision of Jacques-Yves Cousteau. The colony consisted of four manned habitats including a hangar for the DS-1 Diving Saucer and a tool shed. Eight additional structures including shark cages completed the colony. The main habitat called Starfish House was located at 33 ft (10 m) while the smaller Deep Cabin (manned for one week) was located at 85 ft (26 m). Divers working from Deep Cabin dove to depths reaching 361 ft (110 m).

1965 - **Conshelf II** (France). A team of six Cousteau divers spent one month at 328 ft (100 m) in the Mediterranean Sea off the coast of southern France (Île du Levant). The spherical habitat weighed 140 tons and had a diameter of 20 ft (6 m). The divers breathed a gas mixture of 98% helium and 2% oxygen for the duration.

101. Longest serving underwater habitat
L.S.-1 Underwater Laboratory (Romania). Launch date: 1967 (still in service). Location: Lake Bicaz, Potoci, Romania. Operated by: Salmo Ecological Diver Association (APES), A.I. Cuza University. Crew: 2. Depth: Variable (mobile platform). Main purpose: Study of fish behaviour in aquaculture.

L.S.-1 Underwater Laboratory (1967) Photo: A.P.E.S. Salmo

102. Longest-running operational habitat

MarineLab Undersea Laboratory is the longest-running continuously operational habitat in the world, having been submerged since 1985. It was originally called the MEDUSA (Midshipmen Engineered and Designed Underwater Studies Apparatus). Depth: 27 ft (8.23m); www.mrdf.org

103. Underwater habitats in service (2006)

Aquarius (USA)
Launch date: 1986; Operated by: National Undersea Research Center (NURC), National Oceanographic and Atmospheric Administration (NOAA), University of North Carolina at Wilmington (UNCW); Crew: 6; Maximum operating depth: 120 ft (36.58 m); Location (2005): Florida; Average daily operating cost: $10,000 USD per day; www.uncw.edu/aquarius

L.S.-1 Underwater Laboratory (Romania)
Launch date: 1967; Operated by: SALMO Ecological Divers Association – A.I. Cuza University, Iasi; Location: Lake Bicaz; Depth: Variable (Fixed on mobile platform)

MarineLab Undersea Laboratory (USA)
Launch date: 1984; Operated by: Marine Resources Development Foundation; Location: Key Largo, Florida; Depth: 27 ft (8.23 m); www.mrdf.org

Jules Undersea Lodge (USA)
Launch date: 1971 (La Chalupa Habitat); Operated by: Marine Resources Development Foundation; Location: Key Largo Undersea Park; Depth: 21 ft (6.4 m)

AQUARIUS - NASA scientists gather around viewing port (2003). Photo: NASA JSC

ARCHAEOLOGY

104. Deepest ancient wreck ever found
10,000 ft (3,048 m) - Unknown shipwreck, Eastern Mediterranean, 1999. While searching for the lost Israeli submarine *Dakar* in the Eastern Mediterranean, the Nauticos Corporation discovered an ancient shipwreck which had been resting on the seabed for more than 2,000 years. The discovery of the wreck between the trading ports of Rhodes and Alexandria demonstrated for the first time that not all navigation of the period was done along the coastline as was previously believed.

105. Deepest shipwreck ever found
18,904 ft (5762 m) - SS *Rio Grande*, South Atlantic. The Rio Grande was a German blockade runner sunk by US naval ships 55 miles (89 km) off Northeast Brazil in 1944. It was discovered in 1996 by UK-based Bluewater Recoveries Ltd.

106. Deepest shipwreck salvage
2,591 m (8,500 ft) - SS *Central America*. The ship carrying an estimated one billion dollars in gold coins and bullion sank off the Carolina coast in 1857. The Columbus America Discovery Group began the search and salvage of the wreck in 1986.

107. First live Internet shipwreck exploration

HMS *Hood* Expedition - Depth: 9,843 ft (3,000 m). Location: Denmark Strait (Between Greenland and Iceland). The wreck was discovered by undersea explorer David Mearns of UK-based Bluewater Recoveries Ltd using sonar and ROVs. The expedition was funded by Channel Four Television.

108. Most valuable shipwreck recovery

HMS *Sussex* sank in a storm off the Straits of Gibraltar in 1694. When the 80-gun warship went down it took all but two of the 500-man crew and the equivalent of nine tons of gold coins, worth $4.54 billion USD (£2.6bn) in 2006. The wreck lies at a depth of almost half a mile in waters hotly contested by the UK and Spain. The hull of the vessel was discovered in 1998, but only identified in 2002. Salvage operations by Florida-based Odyssey Marine Exploration are currently underway; shipwreck.net

Nuestra Señora de Atocha - Key West, Florida. The *Atocha* was discovered by Mel Fisher (USA) in 1985 at a depth of 55 ft (17 m). *Atocha* was carrying 35 tons of silver (901 ingots and 255,000 coins) and 161 pieces of gold and 70 lb (32 kg) of emeralds, when it sank in a hurricane in 1622. A single jewel was valued at $2,000,000. Only five - three sailors and two slaves - of the 265 people aboard the *Atocha* survived the sinking. The discovery of the shipwreck took 16 years of planning, costing 10 million dollars and the lives of three people. Fisher also had to go through 10 years of litigation with the United States Government and the State of Florida over ownership of the wreck and its contents. Many artifacts from *Atocha* are on display at the Mel Fisher Maritime Museum in Key West, Florida. For more go to: www.melfisher.org

109. Oldest intact war wreck in N. America

The *Land Tortoise* – was sunk in Lake George, New York, during the French and Indian War in October 1758. The floating battery known as a radeau was 52 ft (16 m) long. It was discovered in 1990 using side-scan sonar and has since been made a National Historic Landmark.

www.thelostradeau.com

110. Oldest shipwreck ever found

14th or 13th century B.C. - Uluburun, Turkey. The wreck was discovered by a Turkish sponge diver Mehmet Cakir at a depth of 150 ft (46 m) in 1982. It is believed to be Levantine or Cypriot in origin. The shipwreck was thoroughly explored by George Bass of the Institute of Nautical Archaeology (Texas, USA) during 11 years. The cargo included gold, ivory, tin, copper, glass, ebony, ostrich eggshells, opercula, tortoise carapaces, and resin for burning incense.

BIOLOGY

111. Coldest fish

Fishes of the family Nototheniidae including Arctic and Antarctic cod are adapted to living in the coldest water on Earth. Their blood contains proteins called antifreeze glycoproteins (AFGPs) that keep them from freezing. The proteins affect crystal growth and allow blood to flow freely thus keeping the fish alive.

Arctic cod (*Boreogadus saida*) underneath the ice surface which supports an abundant and diverse assemblage of organisms. Photo: NOAA/OCEAN EXPLORER - *The Hidden Ocean*, Arctic 2005 Exploration

112. Deadliest jellyfish

The dreaded box jellyfish (Chironex fleckeri) of northern Australia contains one of the most potent animal venoms known to man. A sting from one of these creatures can induce death in minutes from cessation of breathing, abnormal heart rhythms and profound low blood pressure (shock)[40]. The Irukandji jellyfish (*Carukua barnesi*) is a smaller relative of the Sea wasp measuring only 0.6 in. (1.5 cm) to 1 in. (2.5 cm) across with four 20-inch (50 cm) tentacles. Irukandji has killed around 70 people in the past 50 years. *Chironex fleckeri* has killed around 100 people in the past 100 years.

113. Deadliest octopus
Blue-ringed octopus (genus *Hapalochlaena*). This small cephalopod measuring 0.8 in. to 8 in. (2 cm to 20 cm) and weighing 0.35 oz to 3.5 oz (10 g to 100 g) bites when attacked or threatened and injects tetrodotoxin contained in its saliva and for which there is no cure. This causes paralysis, respiratory arrest, and possibly cardiac arrest.

114. Deadliest shark
The Great white shark (*Carcharodon carcharias*) has killed more people than any other shark species. According to the International Shark Attack File[41] (ISAF), the Great white was the aggressor in 394 attacks on humans between 1580 and 2004.

115. Deepest bird (Flying)
656 ft (200 m) - Thick-billed Murre (*Uria lomvia*). It can remain underwater for over 3 min.

116. Deepest bird (Non-flying)
1,854 ft (565 m) - Emperor penguin (*Aptenodytes forsteri*), Ross Sea (Antarctica). Swimming speed is 3.7 to 5.6 mph (6 to 9 km/h).

117. Deepest crinoid
26,936 ft (8,210 m) - Unidentified species, Kermadec Trench (New Zealand), 1951.

118. Deepest fish (collected)
27,461 ft (8,370 m) - Cuskeel (*Abyssobrotula galatheae*). The specimen was collected in the Puerto Rican Trench.

119. Deepest fish (observed)

During his record dive aboard the bathyscaph on January 23, 1960, Jacques Piccard reported seeing a fish on the seafloor at the deepest known spot in the world, the Challenger Deep 35,798 ft (10,911 m). *"Lying on the bottom just beneath us was some type of flatfish, resembling a sole, about 1 ft (30 cm) long and 6 in. (15 cm) across. Even as I saw him, his two round eyes on top of his head... here apparently, was a true, bony teleost fish, not a primitive ray or elasmobranch... slowly, this flatfish swam away."*[42]

120. Deepest frog
Titicaca frog (*Telmatobius culeus*) as observed by Cousteau divers Albert Falco and Raymond Coll aboard two *Sea Flea* manned submersibles at a depth of 394 ft (120 m) in 1968. *Telmatobius coleus* is Latin for 'aquatic scrotum.'

121. Deepest mammal[43]
6,562 ft (2,000 m) - Bull sperm whale (*Physeter macrocephalus*), Dominica (Caribbean), 1991. Recorded by Woods Hole Oceanographic Institute Dive duration: 1 hour and 13 min. The sperm whale is the largest toothed creature to ever inhabit the earth. It also has the largest brain 20 lbs (9 kg) and the thickest skin of any living creature 14 in. (36 cm). The sperm whale was named after the milky-white substance called spermaceti found in its head which was mistaken for sperm.

122. Deepest sea cucumber
33,431 ft (10,190 m) - Unidentified species, Philippine Trench (Philippines), 1951.

123. Deepest sea star
25,033 ft (7,630 m) - *Eremicaster tenebrarius*

124. Deepest sea urchin
23,786 ft (7,250 m) - Unidentified species, Indonesia, 1951.

125. Deepest turtle

---

[40] SOURCE: DAN
[41] ISAF: www.flmnh.ufl.edu/fish

[42] *Seven Miles Down*: The Story of the Bathyscaph Trieste (1961) by J. Piccard and R. S. Dietz. pp. 172-174. Published by the Putnam, New York.
[43] **Marine mammal**: Ocean and/or coastal-dwelling animal that is warm-blooded, fur-bearing (or has rudimentary hairs), and nurses its offspring. All marine mammal species give birth to live young.

3,937 ft (1,200 m) - Leatherback turtle (*Dermochelys coriacea*), Virgin Islands (West Indies), May 1987.

126. Fastest bird (Swimming)
Gentoo Penguin (*Pygoscelis papua*) - 22 mph (36 km/h)

127. Fastest fish (Burst speed)
Sailfish (*Istiophorus platypterus*): 68 mph (109 km/h); Wahoo (*Acanthocybium solandri*): 60mph (96 km/h); Mako Shark (*Isurus oxyrinchus*): 60 mph (96 km/h); Bluefin Tuna (*Thunnus thynnus*): 50 mph (80 km/h); Marlin (*Tetrapturus sp.*): 50 mph (80 km/h); Blue Shark (*Prionace glauca*): 43mph (69 km/h); Swordfish (*Xiphius gladius*): 40 mph (64 km/h); White shark (*Carcharodon carcharias*): 35mph (56 kph); Flying fish: 35 mph (gliding); Salmon (leaping): 10.2 mph (16.5 km/h)

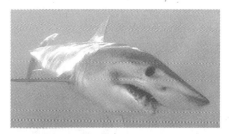

Mako shark (*Isurus oxyrinchus*) off Halifax, Nova Scotia (Canada). Photo: Chris Harvey-Clark / www.geerg.ca

128. Fastest growing seaweed
Giant Kelp (*Macrocystis pyrifera*) - 24 in. (61 cm) per day, northeastern Pacific. Although giant kelp plants are perennial, each frond survives for about 6-9 months.

Giant kelp forest. Photo: NOAA Sanctuary Collection

Bull kelp (*Nereocystis leutkeana*) - 6 in. (15 cm) per day, northeastern Pacific.

Caulerpa taxifolia, a.k.a. Killer weed - 3 in. (8 cm) per day, Côte d'Azur (France). Due to its fast-growing nature, *C. taxifolia* is very popular with aquarists. Accidental discharges of *C. taxifolia* in the Mediterranean Sea have led to the infestation of tens of thousands of acres. *C. taxifolia* was recently found in coastal areas in southern California.

129. Fastest mammal
Orca (*Orcinus orca*) - 35 mph (56 km/h), northeastern Pacific, 1957. The Dall's porpoise (*Phocoenoides dalli*) has also been clocked at 35 mph (56 km/h). In comparison, the Common dolphin (*Delphinus delphis*) can reach 37 mph (60 km/h) while riding a ship's bow wave and 28 mph (45 km/h) in open water.

Orca (*Orcinus orca*) spy-hopping in the ice - Photo: NOAA

Sea lions hauling out at Pier 39 in San Francisco, California. Photo courtesy of Tom Anderson

130. Fastest pinniped

California sea lion (_Zalophus californianus_) - 25 mph (40 km/h)

Sunflower star (**_Pycnopodia helianthoides_** in Howe Sound, British Columbia (Canada) Photo: J. Gallant / D.A.Y.

131. Fastest sea star:

Sunflower star (_Pycnopodia helianthoides_) - 3.3 ft/min (1 m/min.). The Sunflower star uses over 15,000 tube feet (4572 m) to reach such a high speed for an animal thought to be extremely slow.

132. Fastest snail

The Finger plough snail (_Bullia digitalis_) may be the fastest snail in the world. It extends its foot underwater and uses it like a sail to catch waves which carry it to shore. Once on the sandy beach, it uses its foot to crawl in the direction of its prey at over 1 in./sec. (2.5 cm/sec.), which it tears apart with its rasping and ripping teeth.

133. Heaviest clam

Giant clam (_Tridacna gigas_). Up to 750 lbs (340 kg)

Atlantic lobster (**_Homarus americanus_**) Photo: OAR/National Undersea Research Program (NURP)

134. Heaviest crustacean

Atlantic lobster (_Homarus americanus_) - 44 lbs 7oz (20.14 kg), caught in Nova Scotia (Canada) in 1977

135. Heaviest invertebrate (and mollusk)

Giant squid (_Architeuthis dux_). A tentacle of specimen captured in 1878 measured 35 ft (10.7 m) long. It is estimated that the animal could have weighed as much as 4,000 lbs (1,814 kg).

136. Highest leaping shark

Shortfin mako (_Isurus oxyrinchus_) 20 feet (6.1 m)

137. Largest animal

Blue whale (_Balaenoptera musculus_). This marine mammal is believed to be the largest animal ever to have lived. A specimen captured near the South Shetland Islands in 1926 measured 110 ft (33.27 m) and weighed an estimated 190 tons. The blue whale has one of the slowest heartbeats of any mammal at 4 to 8 beats per minute.

138. Largest biomass for single species

Antarctic krill (_Euphausia superba_). At 125 to 725 million tonnes, this is the world's largest known biomass for a single species.

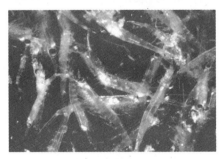

Mass of krill. Photo: NOAA Sanctuary Collection

139. Largest clam

Giant clam (_Tridacna gigas_). A specimen at the American Museum of Natural History measures close to 55 in. (140 cm). Another was found off Okinawa, Japan (1956) measuring 45.25 in. (115 cm) and weighing 734 lbs. (333 kg).

140. Largest crinoid
Helimoetra glacialis - 90 cm (35 in.) in diameter, Northeast Pacific.

141. Largest crocodile
Saltwater Crocodile *(Crocodylus porosus)* The saltwater crocodile is the largest crocodilian and the largest living reptile. Males can reach lengths of 23 ft (7 m). Females are smaller at over 10 ft (3 m). It is found in northern Australia and throughout South-east Asia. Salties, as they are known in Australia, are territorial and killed at least 3 divers in 2005.

142. Largest crustacean
Giant spider crab or Takashigani *(Macrocheira kaempferi)* - 12-14 in. (36 cm) body width. Claw span: 8-9 ft (2.7 m). One of these crabs weighed 41 lbs (18.6 kg) and had a span of 12 ft (3.7 m) between its outstretched claws.

143. Largest eye
Scientists have extrapolated that the giant squid *(Architeuthis dux)* has the largest eyeballs of any living creature today at up to 10 in. (25 cm) in diameter. It is reported that the eyes of a squid washed up in Newfoundland, Canada, measured 15.75 in. (40 cm).

Ocean sunfish off the Farallon Islands. Photo: NOAA Sanctuary Collection

144. Largest fish (Bony)
Ocean sunfish *(Mola mola)*. Length: 10 ft (3 m). Height: 14 ft (4.3 m). Weight: Up to 5,000 lbs (2,268 kg)

145. Largest fish (Carnivorous)
Great white shark *(Carcharodon carcharias)* - Up to 23 ft (7 m), 5,070 lbs (2,300 kg). Average 14 - 15ft (4.3 - 4.6 m), 1,150 - 1,700 lbs (520 - 770 kg). The great white shark inhabits sub-tropical waters around the world. It has up to 3,000 teeth. Its coloration enables it to attack its prey without being seen.

Numerous claims around the world have been made about the largest Great white ever captured. All have been contested due to lack of evidence such as photos or proper measuring. Some sizes were also estimated based on recovered body parts. A 23-ft (7m) specimen was reported captured off Malta (Mediterranean Sea) in 1987 but the measurement was later discredited. The length of a shark taken off Kangaroo Island (South Australia) in 1987 was estimated to be at least 23 ft (7 m) based on the size of its head and fins; all that was brought into port by the fisherman. A long-standing record holder was a 21-ft (6.4 m) Great white captured off Cuba in 1945. However, careful analysis of its photo would appear to reduce that estimate by at least 3 ft (0.9 m).

One of the largest specimens measured with any reliability was a 17.3-ft (5.26 m) great white captured off Prince Edward Island (Canada) in August 1983. Such large specimens are reported to be relatively common off the Farallon Islands (California).

146. Largest fish (Deep sea)
Greenland shark *(Somniosus microcephalus)*. Can grow to a length of 23 ft (7 m) and has been observed at a depth of 7,218 ft (2,200 m). The Greenland shark uses the entire water column and can also be observed swimming at the surface. It is also known as the sleeper shark due to its lethargic behaviour.

147. Largest fish (freshwater)

Mekong giant catfish (*Pangasianodon gigas*) - Up to 10 ft (3m) and 660 lbs (300kg). The giant stingray (*Himantura chaophraya*) found in northern Cambodia is believed by some to reach 16.4 ft (5 m) and 1,100 lbs (500 kg).

148. Largest fish (Marine)

Whale shark (*Rhincodon typus*) - Up to 41.5 ft (12.65 m) in length. A specimen captured in Thailand in 1919 was reported to measure 59 ft (18 m). Warm water shark found in the Atlantic, Pacific, and Indian Oceans. Despite its impressive size, the whale shark feeds only on plankton and is not a threat to people.

Whale shark (*Rhincodon typus*). Photo: Aidan R. Martin - ReefQuest Centre for Shark Research

149. Largest frog (Aquatic)

The Titicaca frog (*Telmatobius coleus*) is the largest, saggiest-skinned aquatic frog in the world. In 1968, a Cousteau team reported frogs up to 20 in. (50 cm) long in Lake Titicaca (Bolivia), with specimens commonly weighing 2.2 lbs (1 kg). *Telmatobius coleus* is Latin for 'aquatic scrotum.'

150. Largest gastropod

Australian trumpet conch, a.k.a. Baler conch (*Syrinx aruanus*), In 1979, a specimen weighing 40 lbs (18 kg) was found off the coast of Australia. Its shell had a length of 30.4 in. (77 cm) and a girth of 39.75 in. (101 cm). Shell lengths up to 3.3 ft (1 m) have been reported.

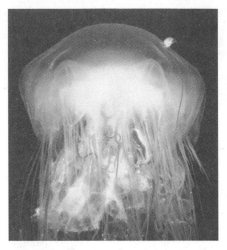

Despite its potent arsenal, the lion's mane (seen here in Lunenburg Bay, Nova Scotia) only feeds on plankton and fish. And although its body is made up of 95% water, it is the main food item of the Leatherback turtle. Scientists know this because the parasite amphipod *Hyperia medusarum*, such as the one seen riding piggyback on the photographed specimen, is often found in the stomach of the leatherback. Photo: J. Gallant / D.A.Y.

151. Largest jellyfish

Lion's mane (*Cyanea arctica*) - The largest specimens have a bell diameter of 7.5 ft (2.3 m) with tentacles reaching lengths of 120 ft (37 m). Its lifespan is only one year. It inhabits the cold waters of the Arctic, northern Atlantic and northern Pacific where much smaller specimens are often encountered by divers. Its stings are painful and can cause severe burns. Divers wearing full-body dive suits can still be stung around the lips.

152. Largest octopus

Giant octopus (*Enteroctopus dofleini*) weighs up to 600 lbs (272 kg) and can reach lengths up to 24 ft (7.3 m) from opposing arm tips. Average weight is 50 - 88 lbs (23 - 40 kg). *Enteroctopus dofleini* only lives 3-5 years. Mature female *E. dofleini* have 2240 suckers (280 per arm). The giant octopus is frequently observed in shallow water by divers in British Columbia. When left unmolested, it poses no risk. There are approximately 300 different octopus species.

Giant octopus in British Columbia. Photo: Neil McDaniel / www.neilmcdaniel.com

153. Largest pinniped
A Southern elephant seal (*Mirounga leonine*) measuring 21.3 ft (6.5 m) was caught on South Georgia Island (South Atlantic) in 1913. The largest Northern elephant seal (*Mirounga angustirostris*) was recorded off Santa Barbara (California), measuring 18 ft (5.5 m) and weighing 6,000 lbs (2,722 kg).

154. Largest sea cucumber
Genus *Stichopus* - Up to 40 in. (102 cm) in length, 8 in. (20 cm) in diameter.

155. Largest sea star
Evasterias echinosomo, 37.79 in. (96 cm) in diameter. Weight: 11 lbs (5 kg), North Pacific.

156. Largest sea urchin
Sperosoma giganteum - Test[44] diameter of 15 in. (38 cm)

Barrel sponge on the Belize Barrier Reef. Photo: J. Gallant / D.A.Y.

157. Largest sponge

Barrel sponge (*Xestospongia muta*). Specimens in the Caribbean measure up to 8 ft (2.4 m) tall and 8 ft (2.4 m) across.

158. Largest squid
Colossal Squid (*Mesonychoteuthis hamiltoni*), a.k.a. Antarctic cranch squid. A complete specimen was caught by fishermen in the Ross Sea (Antarctica) in 2003. The immature female measured 20 ft (6 m) with a mantle[45] length of 8.2 ft (2.5 m) and weighed 330 lbs (150 kg). It is believed the Colossal Squid can reach a length of 65 ft (20 m). Its eyes are over 12 in. (30.5 cm) in diameter. It swims to depths of 6,562 ft (2,000 m) in the Southern Ocean from Antarctica to South America, South Africa, and New Zealand. It feeds on fish and other squid species. Large specimens of colossal squid are themselves preyed upon by the sperm whale and the sleeper shark.

Giant squid are represented by at least eight species of the genus *Architeuthis*. They are believed to reach a length of 33 ft (10 m) for males and 43 ft (13 m) for females, including the two tentacles. A 56-ft (17 m) giant squid was reported washed ashore in Glover's Harbour, Newfoundland, on November 2, 1878. There are unverified reports of specimens measuring up to 66 ft (20 m). In September 2005, Japanese researchers produced the first images ever recorded of a live giant squid in its natural habitat.

Giant squid - Wellington, New Zealand, 20 February 1999. Photo: NASA

159. Largest squid observed on a dive
Humboldt Squid (*Dosidicus gigas*), a.k.a. Jumbo Squid or Jumbo Flying Squid. Grow to 6 ft (2 m) and weigh 100 lbs (45 kg) dur-

---

[44] **Test:** Urchin body without spines.

[45] **Mantle:** The mantle is the main swimming organ of a squid. It appears like a cylinder around the head and is measured from the posterior end of the body to the base without the tentacles.

ing their one-year lifespan. Although they are normally found at depths between 650 ft and 2300 ft (200 - 700 m) along the Eastern Pacific, they jet to the surface at night to feed. They are aggressive predators hunting in groups of over 1,000 individuals and there are several reports of attacks on divers and fishermen. Divers have suffered lacerations from the squids' hooked tentacles while others have been dragged to deeper water before being let go. Mexican fishermen call them *Diablos rojos* (red devils). Nonetheless, some researchers consider the Humboldt squid harmless to humans. William Gilly, a biology professor at Stanford University in Palo Alto, has studied the squid for more than two decades. He has repeatedly snorkeled at the surface at night in the presence of large squid and he has never been attacked.

Juvenile leatherback turtle. Photo: J. Gallant / D.A.Y.

160. Largest sea turtle
Leatherback turtle (*Dermochelys coriacea*) - In September 1988, a Leatherback turtle estimated to be 100 years old was found washed ashore in Gwynedd (UK). Length: 9 ft (2.74 m). Weight: 2,015 lbs (914 kg). Despite its amazing size, the leatherback feeds almost exclusively on jellyfish. A single leatherback may be able to eat the equivalent of its own bodyweight in jellyfish and other plankton every 3 days.

161. Longest bony fish
Oarfish (*Regalecus glesne*) - Up to 50 ft (15.2 m). Often mistaken for a sea-serpent.

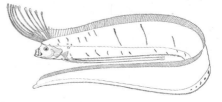

Oarfish - King of herrings (*Regalecus glesne*) NOAA/Goode and Bean, 1895

162. Longest dive by a bird
18 min. - Emperor penguin (*Aptenodytes forsteri*), Cape Crozier, (Antarctica), 1969.

163. Longest dive by a mammal
80 min. - The Elephant seal (*Mirounga angustirostris*) can hold its breath longer than any other mammal when it dives as deep as 5,015 ft (1,530 m) in the search for food.

164. Longest distance flown by fish
Flying fish of the family Exocoetidae can glide over distances of 325 ft (100 m) at a speed of 35 mph (56 km/h).

California flying-fish (*Exocoetus californiensis*) Image: NOAA Historic NMFS Collection

Basking shark (*Cetorhinus maximus*) - Photo: Chris Gotschalk, Marine Science Institute, University of California Santa Barbara

165. Longest gestation period

The basking shark (*Cetorhinus maximus*) has the longest gestation period for any animal, including terrestrial animals, at over 3 years. It is also the second largest fish in the world measuring up to 50 ft (15.2 m). The Basking shark is found in all temperate oceans.

166. Longest invertebrate
Siphonophore (*Praya dubia*) may be the world's longest animal growing to a length of 160 ft (50 m) or more. This drifting colonial cnidarian[46] delivers a powerful sting and is bioluminescent.

167. Longest leap by salmon
The Atlantic salmon (*Salmo salar*) can leap up to 12 ft (3.67 m) to traverse an obstacle such as a waterfall.

168. Longest migration (Mammal)
The Pacific gray whale (*Eschrichtius robustus*) makes the longest migration of any land or marine mammal traveling up to 14,000 miles (22.530 km), round-trip, from the Arctic Baja, California.

169. Longest migration (Sea turtle)
The Leatherback turtle (*Dermochelys coriacea*) has been found more than 3,107 miles (5,000 km) from its nesting sites.

Great white shark (*Carcharodon carcharias*) at the Monterey Bay Aquarium. Photo: Monterey Bay Aquarium - www.mbayaq.org

170. Longest period of captivity for white shark
198 days – The Monterey Bay Aquarium received a juvenile white shark in August 2004 after it was accidentally caught in a commercial fishing net. It was held in an ocean pen for 25 days where the shark remained healthy and ate frequently. It was transported to Monterey and placed in the Outer Bay exhibit where it remained for 198 days in the million-gallon Outer Bay exhibit. During that period, the shark grew from a length of 5 ft (1.52 m) and a weight of 62 lbs (28.12 kg) to a length at release of 6.4 ft (1.95 m) and a weight of 162 lbs (73.5 kg).

171. Longest seaweed
Giant kelp (*Macrocystis pyrifera*). Species of brown algae measuring up to 200 ft (60 m) of the Pacific coast of North America. The Giant kelp life cycle is believed to last 12 to 14 months.

172. Longest walrus teeth
The longest walrus tusk ever recorded measured 37 in. (94 cm) and had a diameter of 11 in. (27 cm). Its weight was over 5 kg (11 lbs).

Walrus - Photo: Captain Budd Christman, NOAA Corps

173. Loudest animal in the ocean
The Sperm whale (*Physeter macrocephalus*) produces focalized clicks that reach levels up to 230 decibels underwater. The whistle of the Blue whale (*Balaenoptera musculus*) can reach up to 188 decibels and can be heard for hundreds of miles underwater.

174. Most giant squid washed ashore
Up to 65 specimens of giant squid have been found on the shores of Newfoundland, Canada; one-fifth of all the giant squid ever found in the world. Several more have been caught or observed alive by fishermen and sailors, and there are verified records of giant squid attacking people in small boats close to shore. No diver

---

[46] **Cnidarian (Stinging creature):** Cnidarians include anemones, corals, hydroids, and jellyfish. The phylum *Cnidaria* contains approximately 9,000 living species worldwide. All cnidarians have tentacles with stinging cells.

has ever reported seeing a live giant squid underwater.

175. Most poisonous fish
The stonefish (*Synanceia verrucosa*), a.k.a. the reef stonefish or dornorn, is a shallow benthic fish with venomous spines that lies in wait camouflaged as a rock. It feeds on small fish and crustaceans. Its dorsal area is lined with spines that release a venomous toxin. Its venom can cause severe pain, shock, paralysis, and tissue death which can be fatal to humans. *Synanceia verrucosa* is found in the Pacific and Indian oceans.

176. Most poisonous aquatic reptile
All sea snakes (± 50 species) are venomous. The venom of some species is up to 10 times more potent than that of a rattlesnake. They are mostly found in the Indian and western Pacific Ocean. They do not normally seek contact with divers and do not bite unless molested.

Sea snake - Photo: OAR/National Undersea Research Program (NURP)

177. Most poisonous snail
Cone snails (*Conidae*) may reach lengths up to 9 in. (23 cm). They prey on invertebrates and small fish by injecting a neurotoxin with a venomous harpoon. The venom of some 20 species is potent enough to kill a person. Warm water neoprene dive suits offer little protection to divers as they are easily penetrated by the harpoon. The Geographic Cone (*Conus geographus*) is known also known as the "cigarette snail," as it is believed that a person injected with its neurotoxin has the time to smoke only one cigarette before dying. There is no known antivenom.

178. Most sensitive tooth
The narwhal's single spiral tusk is really an overgrown tooth. It has been recently discovered[47] that there are up to 10 million nerves extending from the surface of the tusk to its central core and ultimately to the Narwhal's brain. This enables it to detect changes in its environment such as pressure, temperature, salinity, and particle layering.

179. Most teeth (Fish)
Sharks may have over 3,000 at one time. The teeth are aligned in many rows and are not all used at once. When one tooth is lost, it is replaced by another. A shark may shed as many as 50,000 teeth in its lifetime thus making shark teeth one of the most commonly found fossils in the world.

180. Most teeth (Mammal)
Spinner dolphin (*Stenella longirostris*), formerly known as Long-snouted spinner dolphin - as many as 260 conical teeth spread evenly along it two jaws.

181. Most valuable fish
Beluga sturgeon (*Huso huso*) - In 1924, a single sturgeon weighing 2,706 lbs (1,227 kg) from the Tikhaya Sosna River produced 540 lbs (245 kg) of caviar. In 2005, the price for beluga caviar could fetch $3,000 a kilogram, putting the value of the 1924 fish at over $700,000.

The Bluefin tuna (*Thynnus thynnus*) can measure up to 10 ft (3 m) in length weigh more than 1,400 lbs (635 kg). In January 2001, a single bluefin sold for $173,600 at Tsukiji Central Fish Market in Tokyo. The previous year, a 441-lb (200 kg) bluefin was sold at the same market for 20 million yens ($200,000).

The value of the bluefin tuna is so high that U.N. experts believe that Italian and Russian organized crime are now involved in the fish trade.

---

[47] Dr. Martin Nweeia, Harvard School of Dental Medicine. 16th Biennial Conference on the Biology of Marine Mammals (Dec. 2005). Sponsored in part by the National Geographic Society's Expeditions Council

182. Oldest crustacean (Form)
The Horseshoe crab has existed in its current form for the past 135 million years.

183. Oldest lobster
Based on observations made by fishers during the colonization of New England, lobsters of that period may have lived up to 150 years. The oldest age on record is 100 years old (43 lbs / 20 kg).

184. Oldest marine vertebrate
Leatherback turtle (*Dermochelys coriacea*) - In September 1988, a leatherback was found washed ashore in Gwynedd (UK). It was estimated to be 100 years old.

The only recorded growth rate of the Greenland shark (*Somniosus microcephalus*) to date is approximately 0.4 in (1 cm) per year. At birth, it measures only 15 in (38 cm). Since the Greenland shark is known to reach lengths of over 22 ft (7 m), it is believed that a very large specimen could live over 200 years in the cold waters of the Arctic Ocean.

Greenland shark (*Somniosus microcephalus*). Photo: J. Gallant / D.A.Y.

185. Oldest pinniped
Ringed Seal (*Phoca hispida*) - 43 years, Baffin Island (Canada); Grey Seal (*Halichoerus grypus*) - 42 years. A specimen was kept in captivity in Sweden from 1901-1942.

186. Rarest seal
Mediterranean monk seal (*Monachus monachus*) - Less than 400. Its closest relative, the Caribbean monk seal, is already extinct.

187. Slowest fish
Dwarf sea horse (*Hippocampus zosterae*) - 0.001 mph (0.016 km/h). Size: 1.7 in (4.2 cm)

Seahorse (*Hippocampus sp.*) Image: NOAA - Historic NMFS Collection

188. Smallest crab
Pea crab (Family *Pinnotheridae*). Shell length of 0.25 in. (0.64 cm). The Pea crab is so small that it lives inside marine bivalve mollusks such as mussels & oysters.

189. Smallest crinoid
Unidentified species. Diameter: 1.18 in. (3 cm)

190. Smallest fish (Freshwater)
Pygmy goby (*Pandaka pygmaea*). Average length of male is 0.28 in (0.71 cm). It is found in streams near Luzon (Philippines).

Mature females of *Paedocypris progenetica*, a member of the carp family discovered in an acidic peat swamp in Indonesia in 2006, only grow to 0.31 in. (0.79 cm).

191. Smallest fish (Marine)
Dwarf goby (*Trimmatom nanus*). Average length of male is 0.34 in (8.6 mm). It inhabits the Indo-Pacific. It is also the shortest known vertebrate.

192. Smallest pinniped
Baikal Seal (*Pusa sibirica*). The adult of this freshwater species of seal attains a maximum size of 4.5 ft (1.37 m). Weight is about 140 lbs (64 kg)

193. Smallest sea cucumber
Rhabdomolgus ruber, Length: 0.39 in. (1 cm). Found in the North Sea.

194. Smallest sea star
Leptychaster propinquus. Diameter: 0.72 in. (1.83 cm)

195. Smallest sea urchin
Echinocyamus scabe. Test diameter (without spines): 0.21 in. (0.53 cm)

OCEANOGRAPHY

196. Clearest water
262 ft (80 m) - Weddell Sea (Antarctica), 1986

197. Coldest water
Sea water with an average salinity of 35 ppt (parts per thousand) freezes at 28.5°F (-1.94°C)

198. Deepest lake
5,712 ft (1,741 m) - Lake Baikal (Siberia).

199. Deepest point in the ocean
35,798 ft (10,911 m) - Challenger Deep (Mariana Trench), 250 miles (400 km) southwest of Guam in the Pacific Ocean.

200. Deepest ray of light
The deepest a ray of solar light can be perceived by the human eye is 1,600 ft (488 m).

201. Deepest recorded Secchi[48] depths

262 ft (80 m) - Weddell Sea (Antarctica), 1986.
217 ft (66 m) - Sargasso Sea, 1972.
174 ft (53 m) - Eastern Mediterranean, 1985.

The theoretical maximum value for a Secchi disk immersed in pure water is 262 ft (80 m).

Secchi disk pattern

202. Deepest sea cave
Dean's Blue Hole (Bahamas) - 663 ft (202 m). Depth of opening: 18 ft (5.5 m). Diameter of the upper ledge: 60 ft (18.3 m). Average diameter of cave: 250 ft (76 m). Estimated volume: 1.5 million yd² (1.25 million m²). The first diver to reach the bottom was Jim King (USA) in 1992. King took 11 min. to descend to the bottom on TRIMIX. After spending 3 min. on the bottom, his ascent back to the surface required nearly five hours of decompression.

203. Fastest localized current
16.1 knots (18.4 mph / 29.6 km/h): Sechelt Rapids (Skookumchuck Narrows), British Columbia, Canada. It is estimated that for a 12-foot (3.6 m) tide, 200 billion gallons (757 billion liters) of seawater flow through the Sechelt Rapids in 6 hours.

204. First oceanographic vessel
HMS *Challenger* (1872). In December 1872, Challenger sailed from Portsmouth (England) on a 3.5-year global oceanic expedition. The ship's mission was exclusively scientific and was lead by the academicians of the British Royal Society. Its objectives were to circumnavigate the globe, to take soundings at regular intervals, and to

---

[48] **Secchi disk:** 8-inch (20 cm) disk with alternating black and white quadrants lowered into a body of water until it can be no longer be observed from the surface. This method of measuring water transparency is known as the Secchi depth.

measure the physical and biological characteristics of the ocean, taking biological samples from the surface to the bottom using nets and dredges. The ship traveled 68,890 nautical miles (79.328 miles / 127,666 km) through every ocean except the Arctic charting 140 million miles^2 (363 million km^2) and collecting 4,417 new species of marine plants and animals. The findings of the Challenger science team would influence the world of biology and earth sciences for the next century. The oceanographic vessel was the namesake of the ill-fated space shuttle Challenger lost in 1986.

HMS *Challenger* under sail (1874). Photo: NOAA Ship Collection

205. Greatest oceanic current
Antarctic Circumpolar Current - 34 billion gallons (130 million m^3) of water per second. The wind-driven current moving eastward measures 13,049 miles (21,000 km) in length and reaches depths up to 13,123 ft (4,000 m). In comparison, the maximum flow rate of the Gulf Stream is 2.8 billion ft^3 (80 million m^3) per second.

206. Greatest river flow
The Amazon River – Average 200,000 m^3/sec (7,100,000 ft^3/sec) and 300,000 m^3/sec (10 million ft^3/sec) during floods. The Amazon Basin holds two-thirds of all the flowing freshwater water in the world. It is fed by more than 1,000 tributary rivers from Colombia, Bolivia, Brazil, Ecuador, Peru, Paraguay and Venezuela.

207. Highest lake
19,000 ft (5,791 m) - Crater Lake, Licancabur Volcano (Chile / Bolivia). In 1982, a

team led by Johan Reinhard made 11 dives. Max depth 20 ft (6.1 m)

208. Highest tides
Minas Basin, Bay of Fundy (Canada): 56-ft (17 m) tidal range. Record tide: 71 ft (21.6 m), on Oct. 4-5, 1869.
Leaf Basin, Ungava Bay (Canada): 55-ft (16.8 m) tidal range.

209. Highest wave (Recorded)
1,720 ft (525 m) - Lituya Bay (Alaska), July 9, 1958. Wave was caused by a massive landslide in an enclosed inlet.

210. Highest wave (Wind-generated)
112 ft. (34 m) - The wave was measured by the USS Ramapo in the Pacific Ocean on February 6, 1933. Wind force was measured at 68 knots (78 mph / 126 km/h)

The southernmost atoll of Diego Garcia in the Chagos Archipelago. Image courtesy of Earth Sciences and Image Analysis Laboratory, NASA Johnson Space Center

211. Hottest water
Seawater shooting out of hydrothermal vents[49] can reach temperatures up to 752°F (400°C), hot enough to melt lead.

---

[49] **Hydrothermal vent:** Hydrothermal vents form over mid-ocean ridges when the sea floor splits open due to the constant shifting of tectonic plates. Water fills the cracks where it is heated by magma before it rises back to the sea floor.

The extreme pressure at depth prevents the water from boiling. The temperature of the superheated water almost immediately drops to 35.6°F (2°C), the ambient temperature of the deep ocean.

212. Largest atoll[50]
Great Chagos Bank (Indian Ocean) - 5,019 mile² (13,000 km²). The atoll is mostly submerged. The total land area of the atoll is only 2.32 mile² (6 km²).

213. Largest island
Greenland (Denmark) - 840,000 miles² (2,175,600 km²). Australia is regarded as a continental land mass.

214. Largest ocean
The Pacific Ocean encompasses a almost one third of the Earth's surface, more than the total land area of the world, with a surface area of 60.061 million mi² (155.557 million km²)

215. Largest lake (Saltwater)
The Caspian Sea has a surface area of 168,341 mi² (436,000 km²). It is bordered by Azerbaijan, Iran, Kazakhstan, Turkmenistan and Russia.

216. Largest lake (freshwater by surface area)
Lake Superior (USA, Canada) has a surface area of 31,820 miles² (82,414 km²).

217. Largest lake (freshwater by volume)
Lake Baikal (Russia) has a volume of 5,662 miles³ (23,600 km³) which is equivalent to 20% of the world's fresh surface water or the combined volume of all five North American Great Lakes. It is also the deepest lake in the world at 5,712 ft (1,741 m).

218. Largest lake (Underground)
Dragon's Breath Cave (Namibia). When discovered in 1986 by the South African Speleological Association, its surface area was 6.4 acres (2.6 ha). Its greatest depth was 292 ft (89 m).

219. Largest polynya[51]
The Weddell Polynya in the Southern Ocean had a record surface area of 350,000 km² during the austral winters from 1974 to 1976.

Located in the Arctic Ocean (Canada), the polynya known as the North Water has a surface area reaching up to 19,305 mile² (50 000 km²) in July.

220. Largest river basin
Amazon River (South America) - 2,720,000 miles² 7,045,000 km²).

221. Largest tidal bore
Qiantang River (China) Up to 30 ft (9 m) at speeds up 25 mph (40 km/h).

The tidal bore in Turnagain Inlet, Alaska. (Up to 6 ft / 2 m and 12 mph / 20 km/h) Photo: NOAA America's Coastlines Collection

The Amazon River tidal bore is known as the Pororoca. It reaches up to 12 ft (3.7 m) high and speeds up to 15 mph (24 km/h).

222. Longest coral reefs
Great Barrier Reef (Australia) - Over 1,243 miles (2,000 km). The Great Barrier Reef is made up of over 900 islands and 3,400 reefs and it is so large that it can be seen from space. It is the largest structure on the planet built by living organisms. The Great Barrier Reef is home to more than 1,500 species of fish, 400 species of coral, 4,000 types of mollusks and more than 200 spe-

---

[50] **Atoll:** Group of low-lying coral islands surrounding a shallow lagoon. An atoll is usually the result of a subsided oceanic volcano eroded by sea and wind action. The surrounding coral belt continues to grow and eventually forms a ring of coral islands.

---

[51] Polynya: Area of open water surrounded by sea ice. They are kept ice-free due to upwellings, currents, tides, and winds.

cies of birdlife. It is a very popular destination for scuba divers.

The New Caledonia Barrier Reef is the world's second-largest coral reef. It surrounds Grand Terre, Île des Pins, and several smaller islands. Its total length is 932 miles (1,500 km) and it surrounds a lagoon of 9,266 mile^2 (24,000 km^2), with an average depth of 82 ft (25 m).

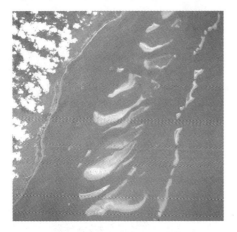

Great Barrier Reef, Queensland, Australia August 1992. Image courtesy of Earth Sciences and Image Analysis Laboratory, NASA Johnson Space Center

The Belize Barrier Reef (Caribbean Sea) is the longest in the western hemisphere with a length of approximately 162 miles (260 km). The barrier reef comprises three non-volcanic atolls - Lighthouse Reef, Turneffe Atoll and Glovers Reef - which are uncommon in the Caribbean. The Belize Barrier reef is estimated to contain at least 65 coral species and over 300 species of fish.

223. Longest river
The Nile - 4,180 mi. (6,727 km). Source: Lake Victoria (east central Africa), streams in Burundi.

224. Longest waves
Lunar tides travel across the oceans over periods of 12 to 24 hours.

The world's second largest barrier reef encircles Grande Terre. Image courtesy of Earth Sciences and Image Analysis Laboratory, NASA Johnson Space Center

225. Most famous oceanographic vessel
The *Calypso* (1951). The *Calypso* was a retired American minesweeper converted to an oceanographic vessel by Jacques-Yves Cousteau in 1951. Cousteau and his team pioneered the world of underwater exploration sailed all over the world aboard *Calypso* for more than 35 years. The *Calypso* sank in Singapore after being hit by a barge in 1996. She was raised and eventually towed back to La Rochelle where she now lies in an advanced state of decay awaiting her ultimate fate.

226. Most people ever killed by a single wave
300,000 to 500,000. East Pakistan (Bangladesh), 1970

227. Most powerful tidal power plant
La Rance (France) stretches 2,297 ft (700 m) across the La Rance Estuary near Saint-Malo, in Brittany. Its 24 reversible turbines generate 500 million kWh every year.

228. Most powerful tsunami
The largest tsunami ever recorded reached 210 ft (64 m) above sea level when it slammed into the Kamchatka Peninsula (Russia) in 1737.

229. Most radioactive dive site
Bikini Atoll (Marshall Islands). The most radioactive dive site accessible to recreational divers was opened in 1996, 50 years

after the site was blasted with 22 atomic bombs. At the time, the assembled American and enemy ships used in the atomic tests was the world's forth largest fleet. The ships sunk by the nuclear tests in 1946 now belong to the people of Bikini. Diving at Bikini is administered by the Bikini Atoll Council, under the name of Bikini Atoll Divers: www.bikiniatoll.com

230. Saltiest body of water
671 ppt - Don Juan Pond, Antarctica. Don Juan Pond is approximately 20 times saltier than sea water (35 ppt). Although its average depth is less than 1 ft (30 cm) and the surface temperature can reach -63.4°F (-53°C), the pond never freezes.

Iceberg in Melville Bay (1957) - Photo: U.S. Coast Guard

The salinity of the Dead Sea can reach up to 400 ppt in the top 115 ft (35 m). Below this level, the water is saturated with salt, which precipitates out of solution and sinks to the sea floor.

21-kiloton underwater blast codenamed 'Baker' - July 29, 1946. Photo: U.S. Department of Defense

231. Smallest ocean
The Arctic Ocean is the smallest of the world's five oceans with a surface area of 5.427 million mi² (14.056 million sq km).

232. Tallest iceberg
550 ft (167 m) - Melville Bay (Greenland), 1957

233. Thickest land ice
15,670 ft (4,776 m) / 2.97 mi. (4.78 km) - Antarctica polar ice cap. At its thickest, the Greenland ice cap is 11,483 ft (3,500 m) deep.

234. Thickest sea ice
Multi-year ice in the Arctic Ocean can reach more than 13 ft (4 m) thick with ridges up to 66 ft (20 m) thick.

AQUATIC ODDITIES

235. Deepest underwater concert
994 ft (303 m) - Katie Melua, the UK's biggest-selling female artist, performed a concert for staff of the *Statoil Troll* A gas rig (North Sea) on October 2, 2006. The concert which took place at the bottom of one of the rig's legs was to celebrate the 10th anniversary of the Norwegian gas production company.

Are You Prepared?

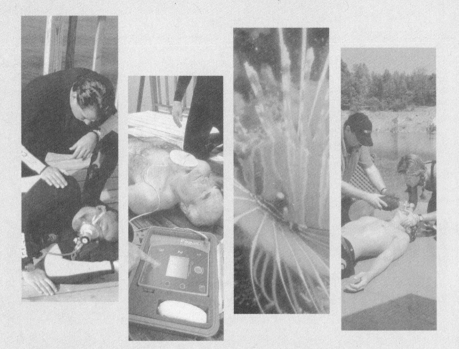

DAN Training Programs
Designed specifically with divers in mind.

www.DiversAlertNetwork.org
1-800-446-2671

The statistics shown are meant to present a comparison between the various nations that have a substantial diving community or that are dive destinations. Information is given on demographics, geography and the dive industry. All data is taken from the latest available sources. Information on diving was researched independently by D.A.Y. through direct contact with the federations and travel authorities of each country.

Other sources used for information include: CIA World Fact Book 2005 & 2006, the World Health Organization (WHO), the World Meteorological Organization (WMO), the World Ocean Atlas, the National Oceanographic Data Center, the Ocean Climate Laboratory, as well as various dive publications from around the world.

Note: At this time, only three countries - Burma, Liberia, and the US - have not adopted the International System of Units (SI, or metric system) as their official system of weights and measures. Although use of the metric system has been sanctioned by law in the US since 1866, it has been slow in displacing the American adaptation of the British Imperial System known as the US Customary System. The US is the only industrialized nation that does not mainly use the metric system in its commercial and standards activities, but there is increasing acceptance in science, medicine, government, and many sectors of industry.

Units used in this section of the Diving Almanac & Yearbook – except for water temperatures – are metric.

HEALTH INFORMATION

Reference on vaccination requirements and malaria situation is the World Health Organization (WHO) – International Health and Travel 2005.

Yellow fever vaccination is carried out for two different purposes:

1. To protect individual travellers who may be exposed to yellow fever infection. Vaccination in these cases is recommended but not mandatory. As yellow fever is frequently fatal for those who have not been vaccinated, vaccination is recommended for all travellers intending to visit areas where there may be a risk of exposure to yellow fever.

2. To protect countries from the risk of importing yellow fever virus. This is mandatory vaccination and is a requirement for entry into the countries concerned.

It is recommended that all travellers are fully vaccinated with the appropriate routine vaccines; schedules for booster doses should be followed at the recommended time intervals.

Cholera. No country requires a certificate of vaccination against cholera as a condition for entry.

Smallpox. Since the global eradication of smallpox was certified in 1980, WHO does not recommend smallpox vaccination for travellers.

Hepatitis A. Vaccination against hepatitis A is recommended for all travellers to developing countries and to countries with economies in transition.

Malaria. The recommended prevention for each country is decided on the basis of the following factors: the risk of contracting malaria; the prevailing species of malaria parasites in the area; the level and spread of drug resistance reported from the coun-

try; and the possible risk of serious side-effects resulting from the use of the various prophylactic drugs. Where *P. falciparum* and *P. vivax* both occur, prevention of falciparum malaria takes priority.

The numbers I, II, III and IV refer to the type of prevention based on the table below.

	MALARIA RISK	TYPE OF PREVENTION
Type I	Very limited risk of malaria transmission	Mosquito bite prevention only
Type II	Risk of P. vivax or fully chloroquine-sensitive P. falciparum only	Mosquito bite prevention plus chloroquine chemoprophylaxis
Type III	Risk of malaria transmission and emerging chloroquine resistance	Mosquito bite prevention plus chloroquine+proguanil chemoprophylaxis
Type IV	High risk of falciparum malaria plus drug resistance, or moderate/low risk falciparum malaria but high drug resistance	Mosquito bite prevention plus either mefloquine, doxycycline or atovaquone/proguanil (take one that no resistance is reported for in the specific areas to be visited)

SOURCE: World Health Organization (WHO)

WORLD

▶ PHYSICAL WORLD

Age: the world is now thought to be about 4.55 billion years old, just about one-third of the 13-billion-year age estimated for the universe
Area: *total:* 510.072 million sq km
land: 148.94 million sq km
water: 361.132 million sq km
note: 70.8% of the world's surface is water, 29.2% is land
Coastline: 356,000 km

98 nations and other entities are islands that border no other countries, they include: American Samoa, Anguilla, Antigua and Barbuda, Aruba, Ashmore and Cartier Islands, The Bahamas, Bahrain, Baker Island, Barbados, Bassas da India, Bermuda, Bouvet Island, British Indian Ocean Territory, British Virgin Islands, Cape Verde, Cayman Islands, Christmas Island, Clipperton Island, Cocos (Keeling) Islands, Comoros, Cook Islands, Coral Sea Islands, Cuba, Cyprus, Dominica, Europa Island, Falkland Islands (Islas Malvinas), Faroe Islands, Fiji, French Polynesia, French Southern and Antarctic Lands, Glorioso Islands, Greenland, Grenada, Guam, Guernsey, Heard Island and McDonald Islands, Howland Island,

Iceland, Jamaica, Jan Mayen, Japan, Jarvis Island, Jersey, Johnston Atoll, Juan de Nova Island, Kingman Reef, Kiribati, Madagascar, Maldives, Malta, Isle of Man, Marshall Islands, Martinique, Mauritius, Mayotte, Federated States of Micronesia, Midway Islands, Montserrat, Nauru, Navassa Island, New Caledonia, New Zealand, Niue, Norfolk Island, Northern Mariana Islands, Palau, Palmyra Atoll, Paracel Islands, Philippines, Pitcairn Islands, Puerto Rico, Reunion, Saint Helena, Saint Kitts and Nevis, Saint Lucia, Saint Pierre and Miquelon, Saint Vincent and the Grenadines, Samoa, Sao Tome and Principe, Seychelles, Singapore, Solomon Islands, South Georgia and the South Sandwich Islands, Spratly Islands, Sri Lanka, Svalbard, Tokelau, Tonga, Trinidad and Tobago, Tromelin Island, Turks and Caicos Islands, Tuvalu, Vanuatu, Virgin Islands, Wake Island, Wallis and Futuna, Taiwan

Maritime claims: a variety of situations exist, but in general, most countries make the following claims measured from the mean low-tide baseline as described in the 1982 UN Convention on the Law of the Sea: territorial sea - 12 nm, contiguous zone - 24 nm, and exclusive economic zone - 200 nm; additional zones provide for exploitation of continental shelf resources and an exclusive fishing zone; boundary situations with neighboring states prevent many countries from extending their fishing or economic zones to a full 200 nm

Elevation extremes: *lowest point:* Bentley Subglacial Trench -2,540 m
note: in the oceanic realm, Challenger Deep in the Mariana Trench is the lowest point, lying -10,924 m below the surface of the Pacific Ocean
highest point: Mount Everest 8,850 m

Average ocean temperature: Ocean surface waters: 17 degrees Celsius (62.6 degrees Fahrenheit). Ocean deep waters: 0-3 degrees Celsius (32-37.5 degrees Fahrenheit). The polar seas are the coldest reaching as low as -1.94 degrees Celsius (28.5 degrees Fahrenheit). The Persian Gulf is the warmest reaching temperatures as high as 36 degrees Celsius (96.8 degrees Fahrenheit).

▶ **HUMAN WORLD**

Countries: 272 nations, dependent areas, and other entities
Languages: Chinese, Mandarin 13.69%, Spanish 5.05%, English 4.84%, Hindi 2.82%, Portuguese 2.77%, Bengali 2.68%, Russian 2.27%, Japanese 1.99%, German, Standard 1.49%, Chinese, Wu 1.21% (2004 est.) *note:* percents are for "first language" speakers only
Population: 6,525,170,264 (July 2006 est.)
Religions: Christians 32.84% (of which Roman Catholics 17.34%, Protestants 5.78%, Orthodox 3.44%, Anglicans 1.27%), Muslims 19.9%, Hindus 13.29%, Buddhists 5.92%, Sikhs 0.39%, Jews 0.23%, other religions 12.63%, non-religious 12.44%, atheists 2.36% (2003 est.)
GDP per capita: $8,800 (2004 est.)

COUNTRIES

ALGERIA

▶ **GENERAL**

Capital: Algiers
Government: republic
Population: 32,531,853 (July 2005 est.)
Ethnic groups: Arab-Berber 99%, European less than 1%
Language(s): Arabic (official), French, Berber dialects
Religion(s): Sunni Muslim (state religion) 99%, Christian and Jewish 1%
GDP per capita: $6,600 (2004 est.)
Currency: Algerian dinar (DZD)
Time: GMT + 1
Electricity: 220V, 50Hz, European 2-pin plug
National holiday: Revolution Day, 1 November (1954)

▶ **GEOGRAPHY**

Location: Northern Africa, bordering the Mediterranean Sea, between Morocco and Tunisia
Border countries: Libya 982 km, Mali 1,376 km, Mauritania 463 km, Morocco 1,559 km, Niger 956 km, Tunisia 965 km, Western Sahara 42 km
Area: 2,381,740 sq km
Coastline: 998 km
Climate: arid to semiarid; mild, wet winters with hot, dry summers along coast; drier with cold winters and hot summers on high plateau; sirocco is a hot, dust/sand-laden wind especially common in summer

Terrain: mostly high plateau and desert; some mountains; narrow, discontinuous coastal plain
lowest point: Chott Melrhir -40 m
highest point: Tahat 3,003 m
Natural hazards: mountainous areas subject to severe earthquakes; mudslides and floods in rainy season
Vaccination(s): Yellow fever: A yellow fever vaccination certificate is required from travellers over 1 year of age coming from infected areas. **Malaria:** Malaria risk is limited. One small focus (P. vivax) has been reported in Ihrir (Illizi Department), but this is isolated and access is difficult. Recommended prevention: I

▶ DIVING

Number of certified divers: 2,500*
Dive federation(s): Federation Algerienne de sauvetage de secourisme et des activites subaquatiques (FASSAS)
Dive regulations: Diver Certification
Freediving federation(s): None*
Major bodies of water: Mediterranean Sea
Dive season: year-round*
Water temperature: 14°C/57F (Jan-Mar), 26°C/79F (July-Sept)
Hyperbaric chambers:
City: Firestations in BORDJ el KIFFAN, HAMIS, Oran
Popular dive sites: Alger : sidi fredj -la madrague-tigzirt-tipaza, Skikda, Annaba, Oran, Jijel*
Tourism information: Algerian Tourism (www.algeriantourism.com)
* SOURCE: FASSAS (Dec. 2005)

ANGUILLA

► GENERAL

Capital: The Valley
Government: overseas territory of the UK
Population: 13,254 (July 2005 est.)

Ethnic groups: black (predominant) 90.1%, mixed, mulatto 4.6%, white 3.7%, other 1.6% (2001 Census)
Language(s): English (official)
Religion(s): Anglican 29%, Methodist 23.9%, other Protestant 30.2%, Roman Catholic 5.7%, other Christian 1.7%, other 5.2%, none or unspecified 4.3% (2001 Census)
GDP per capita: $7,500 (2002 est.)
Currency: East Caribbean dollar (XCD)
Time: GMT -4
Electricity: 110/220V
National holiday: Anguilla Day, 30 May

▶ GEOGRAPHY

Location: Caribbean, islands between the Caribbean Sea and North Atlantic Ocean, east of Puerto Rico
Border countries: None
Area: 102 sq km
Coastline: 61 km
Climate: tropical; moderated by northeast trade winds
Terrain: flat and low-lying island of coral and limestone
Lowest point: Caribbean Sea 0 m
Highest point: Crocus Hill 65 m
Natural hazards: frequent hurricanes and other tropical storms (July to October)
Vaccination(s): Yellow fever: A yellow fever vaccination certificate is required from travellers over 1 year of age coming from infected areas.

▶ DIVING

Number of certified divers: Mainly tourists
Dive federation(s): None
Dive regulations: Diver certification
Freediving federation(s): None
Major bodies of water: Caribbean Sea, Atlantic Ocean
Dive season: year-round
Water temperature: 24°C/75F (Jan-Mar), 27°C/81F (July-Sept)
Hyperbaric chambers:
Closest: Saba (Netherlands Antilles)
Popular dive sites: Wreck of the Sarah and many others, Authors Deep, Stoney Ground Marine Park, Prickley Pear, Sandy Island, Frenchman's Reef
Tourism information: Anguilla Tourist Board (www.anguilla-vacation.com)

ANTIGUA & BARBUDA

► GENERAL

Capital: Saint John's (Antigua)
Government: constitutional monarchy with UK-style parliament
Population: 68,722 (July 2005 est.)

Ethnic groups: black, British, Portuguese, Lebanese, Syrian
Language(s): English (official), local dialects
Religion(s): Christian, (predominantly Anglican with other Protestant, and some Roman Catholic)
GDP per capita: $11,000 (2002 est.)
Currency: East Caribbean dollar (XCD)
Time: GMT -4
Electricity: 110/220V
National holiday: Independence Day (National Day), 1 November (1981)

▶ GEOGRAPHY

Location: Caribbean, islands between the Caribbean Sea and the North Atlantic Ocean, east-southeast of Puerto Rico
Border countries: None
Area: 442.6 sq km (Antigua 280 sq km; Barbuda 161 sq km)
Coastline: 153 km
Climate: tropical maritime; little seasonal temperature variation
Terrain: mostly low-lying limestone and coral islands, with some higher volcanic areas
lowest point: Caribbean Sea 0 m
highest point: Boggy Peak 402 m
Natural hazards: hurricanes and tropical storms (July to October)
Vaccination(s): Yellow fever: A yellow fever vaccination certificate is required from travellers over 1 year of age coming from infected areas.

▶ DIVING

Number of certified divers: Mainly tourists
Dive federation(s): None*
Dive regulations: Diver certification
Freediving federation(s): None*
Major bodies of water: Caribbean Sea
Dive season: year-round

Water temperature: 24°C/72.2F (Jan-Mar), 27°C/80.6F (July-Sept)
Hyperbaric chambers:
Closest: Saba and Guadeloupe*
Popular dive sites: Cades Reef, Pillars of Hercules, English Harbour, Sunken Rock, English Harbour, Sandy Island, Monkshead*
Tourism information: Antigua and Barbuda Department of Tourism
(www.geographia.com/antigua-barbuda)
*SOURCE: Indigo Divers (2006)

ARGENTINA

▶ GENERAL

Capital: Buenos Aires
Government: republic
Population: 39,537,943 (July 2005 est.)
Ethnic groups: white (mostly Spanish and Italian) 97%, mestizo (mixed white and Amerindian ancestry), Amerindian, or other non-white groups 3%
Language(s): Spanish (official), English, Italian, German, French
Religion(s): nominally Roman Catholic 92% (less than 20% practicing), Protestant 2%, Jewish 2%, other 4%
GDP per capita: $12,400 (2004 est.)
Currency: Argentine peso (ARS)
Time: GMT -3 (Western Province: GMT -4)
Electricity: 220V, 50Hz
National holiday: Revolution Day, 25 May (1810)

► **GEOGRAPHY**

Location: Southern South America, bordering the South Atlantic Ocean, between Chile and Uruguay
Border countries: Bolivia 832 km, Brazil 1,224 km, Chile 5,150 km, Paraguay 1,880 km, Uruguay 579 km
Area: 2,766,890 sq km
Coastline: 4,989 km
Climate: mostly temperate; arid in southeast; subantarctic in southwest
Terrain: rich plains of the Pampas in northern half, flat to rolling plateau of Patagonia in south, rugged Andes along western border
lowest point: Laguna del Carbon -105 m
highest point: Cerro Aconcagua 6,960 m
Natural hazards: San Miguel de Tucuman and Mendoza areas in the Andes subject to earthquakes; pamperos are violent windstorms that can strike the pampas and northeast; heavy flooding
Vaccination(s): No vaccination requirements for any international traveller. **Malaria:** Malaria risk - exclusively due to P. vivax - is low and is confined to rural areas along the borders with Bolivia (lowlands of Jujuy and Salta provinces) and with Paraguay (lowlands of Corrientes and Misiones provinces). Recommended prevention in risk areas: II

► **DIVING**

Number of certified divers: 3,200*
Dive federation(s): Federacion De Actividades Subacuaticas De Castilla-La Mancha Fcmas (Fc-Mas)
Dive regulations: Diver certification
Freediving federation(s): AIDA
Major bodies of water: South Atlantic Ocean
Dive season: year-round
Water temperature: 23°C/73.4F (Jan-Mar), 20°C/68F (July-Sept)
Hyperbaric chambers:
City: Formosa, Centro de Medicina Hiperbárica
Telephone: 03717432659
City: Naval Hospital of Buenos Aires
Telephone: 54(11)4863-4085
Popular dive sites: Puerto Madryn, Puerto Pirámides, Las Grutas, Bariloche, Cordoba*
Tourism information: Secretariat of Tourism (www.turismo.gov.ar)
* SOURCE: Buenos Aires Buceo (2006)

ARUBA

► **GENERAL**

Capital: Oranjestad
Government: Parliamentary democracy. Part of the Kingdom of the Netherlands; full autonomy in internal affairs obtained in 1986 upon separation from the Netherlands Antilles; Dutch Government responsible for defense and foreign affairs.

Population: 71,566 (July 2005 est.)
Ethnic groups: mixed white/Caribbean Amerindian 80%
Language(s): Dutch (official), Papiamento (a Spanish, Portuguese, Dutch, English dialect), English (widely spoken), Spanish
Religion(s): Roman Catholic 82%, Protestant 8%, Hindu, Muslim, Confucian, Jewish
GDP per capita: $28,000 (2002 est.)
Currency: Aruban guilder/florin (AWG)
Time: GMT -4
Electricity: 110AC, 60Hz
National holiday: Flag Day, 18 March

►**GEOGRAPHY**

Location: Caribbean, island in the Caribbean Sea, north of Venezuela
Border countries: None
Area: 193 sq km
Coastline: 68.5 km
Climate: tropical marine; little seasonal temperature variation
Terrain: flat with a few hills; scant vegetation
lowest point: Caribbean Sea 0 m
highest point: Mount Jamanota 188 m
Natural hazards: lies outside the Caribbean hurricane belt
Vaccination(s): Yellow fever: A yellow fever vaccination certificate is required from travellers over 6 months of age coming from infected area

► **DIVING**

Number of certified divers: Mainly tourists
Dive federation(s): None*
Dive regulations: Diver certification; No spear fishing, no removal of corals or sea shells*
Freediving federation(s): None
Major bodies of water: Caribbean Sea
Dive season: year-round

Water temperature: 26°C/78.8F (Jan-Mar), 28°C/82.4F (July-Sept)
Hyperbaric chambers:
Closest: Curacao, St. Elizabeth Hospital
Popular dive sites: Antilla Wreck, Jane Sea Wreck, Pedernales Wreck, Plonco Reef, Barcadera Reef*
Tourism information: Aruba Tourism Authority (www.aruba.com)
*SOURCE: Aruba Tourism Authority (2006)

AUSTRALIA

▶ **GENERAL**

Capital: Canberra
Government: democratic, federal-state system recognizing the British monarch as sovereign
Population: 20,090,437 (July 2005 est.)
Ethnic groups: Caucasian 92%, Asian 7%, aboriginal and other 1%
Language(s): English 79.1%, Chinese 2.1%, Italian 1.9%, other 11.1%, unspecified 5.8% (2001 Census)
Religion(s): Catholic 26.4%, Anglican 20.5%, other Christian 20.5%, Buddhist 1.9%, Muslim 1.5%, other 1.2%, unspecified 12.7%, none 15.3% (2001 Census)
GDP per capita: $30,700 (2004 est.)
Currency: Australian dollar (AUD)
Time: GMT + 9.5 to 10.5; Western GMT + 8
Electricity: 240/250V, 50Hz, 3-pin outlet
National holiday: Australia Day, 26 January (1788)

▶ **GEOGRAPHY**

Location: Oceania, continent between the Indian Ocean and the South Pacific Ocean
Border countries: None
Area: 7,686,850 sq km
Coastline: 25,760 km
Climate: generally arid to semiarid; temperate in south and east; tropical in north

Terrain: mostly low plateau with deserts; fertile plain in southeast
lowest point: Lake Eyre -15 m
highest point: Mount Kosciuszko 2,229 m
Natural hazards: cyclones along the coast; severe droughts; forest fires
Vaccination(s): Yellow fever: A yellow fever vaccination certificate is required from travellers over 1 year of age entering Australia within 6 days of having stayed overnight or longer in an infected country, as listed in the Weekly epidemiological record.

▶ **DIVING**

No. of certified divers: 34,600 **
Dive federation(s): Australian Underwater Federation (AUF**)**
Dive regulations: Diver certification; Australian Government Standards
Freediving federation(s): AUF (AIDA)
Major bodies of water: Indian Ocean, Coral Sea, Tasman Sea
Dive season: year-round in different parts of the country*
Water temperature:
North: 28°C/82.4F (Jan-Mar), 25°C/77F (July-Sept); East & West: 25°C/77F (Jan-Mar), 20°C/68F (July-Sept); South: 18°C/64.4F (Jan-Mar), 15°C/59F (July-Sept)
Hyperbaric chambers:
City: Melbourne Hyperbaric Service - The Alfred Hospital
Telephone: (03) 9276 2269
City: Prince of Wales Hospital, Sydney
Telephone: (02) 9382 3880 *
Popular dive sites: Great Barrier reef, Cairns, Ningaloo Reef Western Australia, Kangaroo Island South Australia, Kelp Forrest, Bicheno, Tasmania*
Tourism information: Australian Tourist Commission (www.australia.com)
* SOURCE: AUF (Dec. 2005)
** Study by ausport.gov (2000)

AUSTRIA

▶ **GENERAL**

Capital: Vienna
Government: federal republic
Population: 8,184,691 (July 2005 est.)
Ethnic groups: Austrians 91.1%, former Yugoslavs 4% (includes Croatians, Slovenes, Serbs, and Bosniaks), Turks 1.6%, German 0.9%, other or unspecified 2.4% (2001 census)
Language(s): German (official nationwide), Slovene (official in Carinthia), Croatian (official in Burgenland), Hungarian (official in Burgenland)
Religion(s): Roman Catholic 73.6%, Protestant 4.7%, Muslim 4.2%, other 3.5%, unspecified 2%, none 12% (2001 census)
GDP per capita: $31,300 (2004 est.)
Currency: euro (EUR)

Time: GMT + 1
Electricity: 220V. 50 Hz, 2-pin plug
National holiday: National Day, 26 October (1955)

▶ **GEOGRAPHY**

Location: Central Europe, north of Italy and Slovenia
Border countries: Czech Republic 362 km, Germany 784 km, Hungary 366 km, Italy 430 km, Liechtenstein 35 km, Slovakia 91 km, Slovenia 330 km, Switzerland 164 km
Area: 83,870 sq km
Coastline: 0 km (landlocked); major river is the Danube
Climate: temperate; continental, cloudy; cold winters with frequent rain and some snow in lowlands and snow in mountains; moderate summers with occasional showers
Terrain: in the west and south mostly mountains (Alps); along the eastern and northern margins mostly flat or gently sloping
lowest point: Neusiedler See 115 m
highest point: Grossglockner 3,798 m
Natural hazards: landslides; avalanches; earthquakes
Vaccination(s): No vaccination requirements for any international traveller.

▶ **DIVING**

Number of certified divers: N/A *
Dive federation(s): Tauchsportverband Österreichs (AIDA)
Dive regulations: Diver certification
Freediving federation(s): AIDA
Major bodies of water: Danube River,
Dive season: April-Oct; ice diving in winter*
Water temperature: 2°C /35.6F (Jan-Mar), 26°C/78.8F (July-Sept)
Hyperbaric chambers:

City: Graz: University Medical School of Graz
Telephone: +43 316 385-2803
City: Medical University of Vienna
Telephone: +43-1-40400/1001
Popular dive sites: Lake Traunsee, Lake Attersee, Lake Wiestalstausee, Salzkammergut, Samaranger See
Tourism information: Austrian Tourist Board (www.austria.info)

BAHAMAS (The)

▶ **GENERAL**

Capital: Nassau
Government: constitutional parliamentary democracy
Population: 301,790
Ethnic groups: black 85%, white 12%, Asian and Hispanic 3%
Language(s): English (official), Creole (among Haitian immigrants)
Religion(s): Baptist 35.4%, Anglican 15.1%, Roman Catholic 13.5%, Pentecostal 8.1%, Church of God 4.8%, Methodist 4.2%, other Christian 15.2%, none or unspecified 2.9%, other 0.8% (2000 census)
GDP per capita: $17,700 (2004 est.)
Currency: Bahamian dollar (BSD) - Bahamian dollars per US dollar - 1 (2004)
Time: GMT – 5
Electricity: 120V, 60Hz
National holiday: Independence Day, 10 July (1973)

▶ **GEOGRAPHY**

Location: Caribbean, chain of islands (30 inhabited) in the North Atlantic Ocean, southeast of Florida, northeast of Cuba
Border countries: None
Area: 13,940 km²

Coastline: 2,201 miles (3,542 km)
Climate: tropical marine; moderated by warm waters of Gulf Stream
Terrain: long, flat coral formations with some low rounded hills
lowest point: Atlantic Ocean 0 m
highest point: Mount Alvernia, on Cat Island 63 m
Natural hazards: hurricanes and other tropical storms cause extensive flood and wind damage
Vaccination(s): Yellow fever: A yellow fever vaccination certificate is required from travellers over 1 year of age coming from infected areas.

▶ **DIVING**

Number of certified divers: Mainly tourists
Dive federation(s): Bahamas Diving Association*
Dive regulations: Diver certification; total ban on harvesting any marine resource*
Freediving federation(s): None*
Major bodies of water: Atlantic Ocean
Dive season: year-round
Water temperature: 24°C/75.2F (Jan-Mar), 30°C/86F (July-Sept)
Hyperbaric chambers:
City: Nassau, Bahamas Hyperbaric Centre Ltd.
Telephone: 242-362-4025
Florida closer*
Popular dive sites: Many islands, many destinations. Grand Bahama Island sites: Theo's Wreck, Shark Junction;* Barracuda Shoals, Current Cut, Devil's Backbone
Tourism information: Ministry of Tourism (www.bahamas.com)
* SOURCE: Grand Bahama Scuba (2006)

BAHRAIN

▶ **GENERAL**

Capital: Manama
Government: constitutional hereditary monarchy
Population: 688,345 – incl. 235,108 non nationals (July 2005 est.)
Ethnic groups: Bahraini 62.4%, non-Bahraini 37.6% (2001 census)
Language(s): Arabic, English, Farsi, Urdu
Religion(s): Muslim (Shi'a and Sunni) 81.2%, Christian 9%, other 9.8% (2001 census)
GDP per capita: $19,200 (2004 est.)
Currency: Bahraini dinar (BHD) - Bahraini dinars per US dollar - 0.376 (2004)
Time: GMT + 3
Electricity: 220V. 60 Hz
National holiday: National Day, 16 December (1971)

▶ **GEOGRAPHY**

Location: Middle East, archipelago (33 islands) in the Persian Gulf, east of Saudi Arabia
Border countries: None
Area: 665 sq km
Coastline: 161 km

Climate: arid; mild, pleasant winters; very hot, humid summers
Terrain: mostly low desert plain rising gently to low central escarpment
lowest point: Persian Gulf 0 m
highest point: Jabal ad Dukhan 122 m
Natural hazards: periodic droughts; dust storms
Vaccination(s): No vaccination requirements for any international traveller.

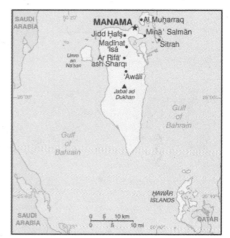

▶ **DIVING**

Number of certified divers: N/A
Dive federation(s): Bahrain Diving Committee (BDC)
Dive regulations: Diver certification
Freediving federation(s): None
Major bodies of water: Persian Gulf, Gulf of Bahrain
Dive season: year-round
Water temperature: 27°C/80.6F (Jan-Mar), 28°C /82.4F (July-Sept)
Hyperbaric chambers:
Closest: Saudi Arabia
Popular dive sites: Reef And Wreck Diving: Fifi Wreck, Caisson Wreck, Abu Thalma, Fasht Najwah
Tourism information: Bahrain Tourism (www.bahraintourism.com)

BARBADOS

▶ **GENERAL**

Capital: Bridgetown
Government: parliamentary democracy; independent sovereign state within the Commonwealth
Population: 279,254 (July 2005 est.)
Ethnic groups: black 90%, white 4%, Asian and mixed 6%
Language(s): English

Religion(s): Protestant 67% (Anglican 40%, Pentecostal 8%, Methodist 7%, other 12%), Roman Catholic 4%, none 17%, other 12%
GDP per capita: $16,400 (2004 est.)
Currency: Barbadian dollar (BBD) - Barbadian dollars per US dollar - 2 (2004)
Time: GMT - 4
Electricity: 110V, 50 Hz
National holiday: Independence Day, 30 November (1966)

► **GEOGRAPHY**

Location: Caribbean, island in the North Atlantic Ocean northeast of Venezuela (Easternmost Caribbean island)
Border countries: None
Area: 431 sq km
Coastline: 97 km
Climate: tropical; rainy season (June to October)
Terrain: relatively flat; rises gently to central highland region
lowest point: Atlantic Ocean 0 m
highest point: Mount Hillaby 336 m
Natural hazards: infrequent hurricanes; periodic landslides
Vaccination(s): Yellow fever: A yellow fever vaccination certificate is required from travellers over 1 year of age coming from infected areas.

► **DIVING**

Number of certified divers: 500*
Dive federation(s): Eastern Caribbean Safe Diving Association (E.C.S.D.A.); Barbados Professional Association of Dive Operators (B.P.A.D.O.) **
Dive regulations: Diver certification
Freediving federation(s): None*
Major bodies of water: Atlantic Ocean, Caribbean Sea
Dive season: year-round

Water temperature: 24°C/75.2F (Jan-Mar), 27°C/80.6F (July-Sept)
Hyperbaric chambers:
City: Bridgetown
Telephone: (246) 4366185 Ext.: 2155
St. Michael: Barbados Defence Force Headquarters
Telephone: 246 4365483**
Popular dive sites: Carlisle Bay marine Park, Stavronikita, Asta, Dottins, Pamir*
Tourism information: Barbados Tourism Authority (www.barbados.org)
* SOURCE: Eco Dive Barbados (2006)
** SOURCE: Hightide Watersports (2006)

BELGIUM

► **GENERAL**

Capital: Brussels
Government: federal parliamentary democracy under a constitutional monarch
Population: 10,364,388 (July 2005 est.)
Ethnic groups: Fleming 58%, Walloon 31%, mixed or other 11%
Language(s): Dutch (official) 60%, French (official) 40%, German (official) less than 1%, legally bilingual (Dutch and French)
Religion(s): Roman Catholic 75%, Protestant or other 25%
GDP per capita: $30,600 (2004 est.)
Currency: euro (EUR) - euros per US dollar - 0.8054 (2004)
Time: GMT + 1
Electricity: 220V, 50 Hz, 2-pin plug
National holiday: 21 July (1831)

▶ **GEOGRAPHY**

Location: Western Europe, bordering the North Sea, between France and the Netherlands
Border countries: France 620 km, Germany 167 km, Luxembourg 148 km, Netherlands 450 km
Area: 30,528 sq km
Coastline: 66.5 km
Climate: temperate; mild winters, cool summers; rainy, humid, cloudy
Terrain: flat coastal plains in northwest, central rolling hills, rugged mountains of Ardennes Forest in southeast
lowest point: North Sea 0 m
highest point: Signal de Botrange 694 m
Natural hazards: flooding is a threat along rivers and in areas of reclaimed coastal land, protected from the sea by concrete dikes
Vaccination(s): No vaccination requirements for any international traveller.

▶ **DIVING**

Number of certified divers: 21,500*
Dive federation(s): Federation Belge de recherches et d'activites sous-marines (FEBRAS)
Dive regulations: Diver certification
Freediving federation(s): Befos – sportcommissie j.j. falise, * AIDA
Major bodies of water: Atlantic Ocean
Dive season: year-round *
Water temperature: 10°C/50F (Jan-Mar), 14°C/57.2F (July-Sept)
Hyperbaric chambers:
City: Neder-over-Heembeek
Telephone: 0800/12382
City: Brugge
Telephone: 050 55 87 13*
Popular dive sites: Vodelée, Barrage de l'eau d'heure, De Nekker, Put van Ekeren, Noordzee*
Tourism information: Belgian Tourist Office (www.visitbelgium.com)
* SOURCE: FEBRAS (2005)

BELIZE

▶ **GENERAL**

Capital: Belmopan
Government: parliamentary democracy
Population: 279,457 (July 2005 est.)
Ethnic groups: mestizo 48.7%, Creole 24.9%, Maya 10.6%, Garifuna 6.1%, other 9.7%
Language(s): English (official), Spanish, Mayan, Garifuna (Carib), Creole
Religion(s): Roman Catholic 49.6%, Protestant 27% (Pentecostal 7.4%, Anglican 5.3%, Seventh-Day Adventist 5.2%, Mennonite 4.1%, Methodist 3.5%, Jehovah's Witnesses 1.5%), other 14%, none 9.4% (2000)
GDP per capita: $6,500 (2004 est.)
Currency: Belizean dollar (BZD) - Belizean dollars per US dollar - 2 (2004)
Time: GMT - 6

Electricity: 110V. 2 and 3-pin sockets
National holiday: Independence Day, 21 September (1981)

▶ **GEOGRAPHY**

Location: Central America, bordering the Caribbean Sea, between Guatemala and Mexico
Border countries: Guatemala 266 km, Mexico 250 km
Area: 22,966 sq km
Coastline: 386 km
Climate: tropical; very hot and humid; rainy season (May to November); dry season (February to May)
Terrain: flat, swampy coastal plain; low mountains in south
lowest point: Caribbean Sea 0 m
highest point: Victoria Peak 1,160 m
Natural hazards: frequent, devastating hurricanes (June to November) and coastal flooding (especially in south)
Vaccination(s): Yellow fever: A yellow fever vaccination certificate is required from travellers coming from infected areas. **Malaria:** Malaria risk—almost exclusively due to P. vivax—exists in all districts but varies within regions. Risk is highest in the southern region. No resistant P. falciparum strains reported. Recommended prevention in risk areas: II

▶ **DIVING**

Number of certified divers: Mainly tourists
Dive federation(s): None
Dive regulations: Diver certification
Freediving federation(s): None
Major bodies of water: Caribbean Sea, Gulf of Honduras
Dive season: year-round
Water temperature: 26°C/78.8F (Jan-Mar), 29°C/84.2F (July-Sept)

Hyperbaric chambers:
City: San Pedro, Sub Aquatic Services of Belize
Telephone: 011-501-226-2851 or 2852
Popular dive sites: The Blue Hole, Shark Ray Alley, Half Moon Caye, Lighthouse Reef, Victoria Canyon, Barrier Reef
Tourism information: Belize Tourism Board (www.belizetourism.org)

BERMUDA

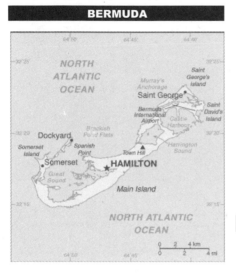

▶ **GENERAL**

Capital: Hamilton
Government: parliamentary British overseas territory with internal self-government
Population: 65,365 (July 2005 est.)
Ethnic groups: black 54.8%, white 34.1%, mixed 6.4%, other races 4.3%, unspecified 0.4% (2000 census)
Language(s): English (official), Portuguese
Religion(s): Anglican 23%, Roman Catholic 15%, African Methodist Episcopal 11%, other Protestant 18%, other 12%, unaffiliated 6%, unspecified 1%, none 14% (2000 census)
GDP per capita: $36,000 (2003 est.)
Currency: Bermudian dollar (BMD) - Bermudian dollar per US dollar - 1 (fixed rate pegged to the US dollar)
Time: GMT -4
Electricity: 110V, 60 Hz
National holiday: Bermuda Day, 24 May

▶ **GEOGRAPHY**

Location: North America, group of islands in the North Atlantic Ocean, east of South Carolina (US)
Border countries: None
Area: 53.3 sq km
Coastline: 103 km

Climate: subtropical; mild, humid; gales, strong winds common in winter
Terrain: low hills separated by fertile depressions
lowest point: Atlantic Ocean 0 m
highest point: Town Hill 76 m
Natural hazards: hurricanes (June to November)
Vaccination(s): No vaccination requirements for any international traveller.

▶ **DIVING**

Number of certified divers: Mainly tourists
Dive federation(s): None
Dive regulations: Diver certification
Freediving federation(s): None
Major bodies of water: North Atlantic Ocean
Dive season: year-round
Water temperature: 19°C/66.2F (Jan-Mar), 26°C/78.8 (July-Sept)
Hyperbaric chambers:
City: Hamilton, Hyperbaric and Wound Care Department
Telephone: (441) 236-2345 ext 1896
Popular dive sites: Wrecks: The Constellation, The Cristóbal Colón, The Marie Celeste and others; South West Breaker, Tarpon Hole
Tourism information: Bermuda Department of Tourism (www.bermudatourism.com)

BONAIRE (See Netherlands Antilles)

BOSNIA AND HERZEGOVINA

▶ **GENERAL**

Capital: Sarajevo
Government: emerging federal democratic republic
Population: 4,025,476 (July 2005 est.)
Ethnic groups: Serb 37.1%, Bosniak 48%, Croat 14.3%, other 0.6% (2000); *note:* Bosniak has replaced Muslim as an ethnic term in part to avoid confusion with the religious term Muslim - an adherent of Islam
Language(s): Bosnian, Croatian, Serbian
Religion(s): Muslim 40%, Orthodox 31%, Roman Catholic 15%, other 14%
GDP per capita: $6,500 (2004 est.)
Currency: marka (BAM) - marka per US dollar - 1.58 (2004)
note: the marka is pegged to the euro
Time: GMT + 1
Electricity: 220V, 50 Hz
National holiday: National Day, 25 November (1943)

▶ **GEOGRAPHY**

Location: Southeastern Europe, bordering the Adriatic Sea and Croatia
Border countries: Croatia 932 km, Montenegro 225 km, Serbia 302 km

Area: 51,129 sq km
Coastline: 20 km
Climate: hot summers and cold winters; areas of high elevation have short, cool summers and long, severe winters; mild, rainy winters along coast
Terrain: mountains and valleys
lowest point: Adriatic Sea 0 m
highest point: Maglic 2,386 m
Natural hazards: earthquakes
Vaccination(s): No vaccination requirements for any international traveller.

▶ **DIVING**

Number of certified divers: 143**
Dive federation(s): Diving Association of B&H *
Dive regulations: Diver certification; CMAS & IAHD Adriatic's standards and regulations*
Freediving federation(s): PSS and IAHD Adriatc (for handicapped divers), AIDA*
Major bodies of water: Adriatic Sea
Dive season: May to October; Ice diving: November to March *
Water temperature: 15°C/59F (Jan-Mar), 24°C/75.2F (July-Sept)
Hyperbaric chambers:
Closest: Croatia Republic 300 km from Sarajevo *
Popular dive sites: Una River, Cave on Buna River, Black Spring, Neretva River, Neum *
Tourism information: Tourism Association of the Federation of Bosnia and Herzegovina (www.bhtourism.ba)
* SOURCE: Scuba.co.ba (2006)
** SOURCE: Diving club "PANTERI" (2006)

BRAZIL

▶ **GENERAL**

Capital: Brasilia

Government: federative republic
Population: 186,112,794
Ethnic groups: white 53.7%, mulatto (mixed white and black) 38.5%, black 6.2%, other (includes Japanese, Arab, Amerindian) 0.9%, unspecified 0.7% (2000 census)
Language(s): Portuguese (official), Spanish, English, French
Religion(s): Roman Catholic (nominal) 73.6%, Protestant 15.4%, Spriritualist 1.3%, Bantu/voodoo 0.3%, other 1.8%, unspecified 0.2%, none 7.4% (2000 census)
GDP per capita: purchasing power parity - $8,100 (2004 est.)
Currency: real (BRL) - reals per US dollar - 2.9251 (2004)
Time: GMT -3 & -4; Atlantic Islands GMT - 1
Electricity: 110/120V, 60 Hz
National holiday: Independence Day, 7 September (1822)

▶ **GEOGRAPHY**

Location: Eastern South America, bordering the Atlantic Ocean
Border countries: Argentina 1,224 km, Bolivia 3,400 km, Colombia 1,643 km, French Guiana 673 km, Guyana 1,119 km, Paraguay 1,290 km, Peru 1,560 km, Suriname 597 km, Uruguay 985 km, Venezuela 2,200 km
Area: 8,511,965 sq km
Coastline: 7,491 km
Climate: mostly tropical, but temperate in south
Terrain: mostly flat to rolling lowlands in north; some plains, hills, mountains, and narrow coastal belt
lowest point: Atlantic Ocean 0 m
highest point: Pico da Neblina 3,014 m
Natural hazards: recurring droughts in northeast; floods and occasional frost in south

Vaccination(s): Yellow fever: A yellow fever vaccination certificate is required from travellers over 9 months of age coming from infected areas, unless they are in possession of a waiver stating that immunization is contraindicated on medical grounds.

Vaccination is recommended for travellers to endemic areas, including rural areas in the states of Acre, Amapá, Amazonas, Goiás, Maranhão, Mato Grosso, Mato Grosso do Sul, Pará, Rondônia, Roraima and Tocantins, and to others states areas where transmission risk exists including all the state of Minas Gerais and specific areas of Espírito Santo, Piauí, Bahia, São Paulo, Paraná, Santa Catarina and Rio Grande do Sul. The complete list of municipalities is available at: www.saude.gov.br/svs

Malaria: Malaria risk—P. vivax (78%), P. falciparum (22%)—is present in most forested areas below 900 m within the nine states of the "Legal Amazonia" region (Acre, Amapá, Amazonas, Maranhão (western part), Mato Grosso (northern part), Pará (except Belém City), Rondônia, Roraima and Tocantins). Transmission intensity varies from municipality to municipality, but is higher in jungle areas of mining, lumbering and agricultural settlements less than 5 years old, than in the urban areas, including in large cities such as Pôrto Velho, Boa Vista, Macapá, Manaus, Santarém, Rio Branco and Maraba, where the transmission occurs on the periphery of these cities. In the states outside "Legal Amazonia", malaria transmission risk is negligible or nonexistent. Multidrug-resistant P. falciparum reported. Recommended prevention in risk areas: IV.

▶ **DIVING**

Number of certified divers: 190,000*
Dive federation(s): CBPDS - Confederação Brasileira De Pesca E Desportos Subaquáticos
Dive regulations: Diver certification*
Freediving federation(s): Clube Barracuda de Desportos, AIDA
Major bodies of water: South Atlantic Ocean, South Atlantic Ocean, Amazon River
Dive season: year-round
Water temperature: 78.8F/26°C (Jan-Mar), 73.4F*/23°C (July-Sept)
Hyperbaric chambers:
Hospital da Beneficencia Portuguesa do Rio de Janeiro
Telephone: (0xx21) 222-2320
City: Campinas University Hyperbaric Center
Telephone: (55) 19 2341951*
Popular dive sites: Arraial do Cabo - Estado do Rio de Janeiro, Angra dos Reis - Estado do Rio de Janeiro, Recife - Estado de Pernambuco, Florianopolis - Estado de Santa Catarina, Ilhabela - Estado de São Paulo*
Tourism information: Brazil Tourism Office (www.braziltourism.org)
* SOURCE: CPBDS (2006)

BRITISH VIRGIN ISLANDS

▶ **GENERAL**

Capital: Road Town
Government: overseas territory of the UK; internal self-governing
Population: 22,643 (July 2005 est.)
Ethnic groups: black 83%, white, Indian, Asian and mixed
Language(s): English (official)
Religion(s): Protestant 86% (Methodist 33%, Anglican 17%, Church of God 9%, Seventh-Day Adventist 6%, Baptist 4%, Jehovah's Witnesses 2%, other 15%), Roman Catholic 10%, none 2%, other 2% (1991)
GDP per capita: $38,500 (2004 est.)
Currency: US dollar (USD)
Time: GMT -4
National holiday: Territory Day, 1 July
▶ **GEOGRAPHY**

Location: Caribbean, between the Caribbean Sea and the North Atlantic Ocean, east of Puerto Rico
Border countries: None
Area: 153 sq km (16 inhabited and more than 20 uninhabited islands)
Coastline: 80 km
Climate: subtropical; humid; temperatures moderated by trade winds
Terrain: coral islands relatively flat; volcanic islands steep, hilly
lowest point: Caribbean Sea 0 m
highest point: Mount Sage 521 m
Natural hazards: hurricanes and tropical storms (July to October)
Vaccination(s): No vaccination requirements for any international traveller.

▶ **DIVING**

Number of certified divers: Mainly tourists
Dive federation(s): None
Dive regulations: Diver certification; no spearfishing or removal of fauna or flora*
Freediving federation(s): AIDA
Major bodies of water: Caribbean Sea
Dive season: year-round
Water temperature: 24°C/75.2F (Jan-Mar), 27°C/80.6F (July-Sept)
Hyperbaric chambers:
City: St Thomas, USVI*
Popular dive sites: Wreck Of the RMS Rhone, The Indians, Rainbow Canyons, Blonde Rock, Painted Walls*
Tourism information: BVI Tourist Board (www.bvitourism.com)
* SOURCE: Blue Water Divers (2006)

BRUNEI

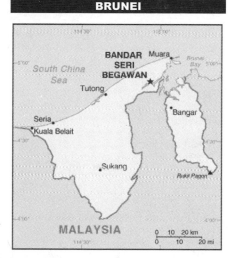

▶ **GENERAL**

Capital: Bandar Seri Begawan
Government: constitutional sultanate
Population: 7,450,349 (July 2005 est.)
Ethnic groups: Malay 67%, Chinese 15%, indigenous 6%, other 12%
Language(s): Malay (official), English, Chinese
Religion(s): Muslim (official) 67%, Buddhist 13%, Christian 10%, indigenous beliefs and other 10%
GDP per capita: $23,600 (2003 est.)
Currency: Bruneian dollar (BND) - Bruneian dollars per US dollar - 1.6902 (2004)
Time: GMT + 8
Electricity:
National holiday: National Day, 23 February (1984)

▶ **GEOGRAPHY**

Location: Southeastern Asia, bordering the South China Sea and Malaysia
Border countries: Malaysia 381 km
Area: 5,770 sq km
Coastline: 161 km
Climate: tropical; hot, humid, rainy
Terrain: flat coastal plain rises to mountains in east; hilly lowland in west
lowest point: South China Sea 0 m
highest point: Bukit Pagon 1,850 m
Natural hazards: typhoons, earthquakes, and severe flooding are rare
Vaccination(s): Yellow fever: A yellow fever vaccination certificate is required from travellers over 1 year of age coming from infected areas or having passed through partly or wholly endemic areas within the preceding 6 days. The countries and areas included in the endemic zones are considered as infected areas.

▶ **DIVING**

Number of certified divers: N/A
Dive federation(s): None
Dive regulations: Diver certification
Freediving federation(s): None
Major bodies of water: South China Sea, Brunei Bay
Dive season: year-round, best: March -November
Water temperature: 82.4F (28°C) (Jan-Mar), 84.2F (29°C) (July-Sept)
Hyperbaric chambers:
The Royal Brunei Navy (RBN)
Popular dive sites: Reefs, Oil Rigs and Wrecks: The Australian, American and Cement Wrecks. Brunei Patches, Pete's Reef, Abana Reef, Pelong Rock
Tourism information: Brunei Tourism (www.tourismbrunei.com)

BULGARIA

▶ **GENERAL**

Capital: Sofia
Government: parliamentary democracy
Population: 372,361 (July 2005 est.)
Ethnic groups: Bulgarian 83.9%, Turk 9.4%, Roma 4.7%, other 2% (including Macedonian, Armenian, Tatar, Circassian) (2001 census)
Language(s): Bulgarian 84.5%, Turkish 9.6%, Roma 4.1%, other and unspecified 1.8% (2001 census)
Religion(s): Bulgarian Orthodox 82.6%, Muslim 12.2%, other Christian 1.2%, other 4% (2001 census)
GDP per capita: $8,200 (2004 est.)
Currency: lev (BGL) - leva per US dollar - 1.5751 (2004)
Time: GMT + 2
Electricity:
National holiday: Liberation Day, 3 March (1878)

► **GEOGRAPHY**

Location: Southeastern Europe, bordering the Black Sea, between Romania and Turkey
Border countries: Greece 494 km, Macedonia 148 km, Romania 608 km, Serbia and Montenegro 318 km, Turkey 240 km
Area: 110,910 sq km
Coastline: 354 km
Climate: temperate; cold, damp winters; hot, dry summers
Terrain: mostly mountains with lowlands in north and southeast
lowest point: Black Sea 0 m
highest point: Musala 2,925 m
Natural hazards: earthquakes, landslides
Vaccination(s): No vaccination requirements for any international traveller.

► **DIVING**

Number of certified divers: 87*
Dive federation(s): Bulgarian National Association of Underwater Activity (BNAUA)
Dive regulations: Diver certification
Freediving federation(s): Bulgarian Underwater Spearfishing Federation*
Major bodies of water: Black Sea
Dive season: June to October*
Water temperature: 28°C/82.4F (Jan-Mar), 28°C/82.4F (July-Sept)
Hyperbaric chambers:
City Varna: Institute of Oceanology
Telephone: 359/52/370487
City Varna: Baromedic Medical Center
Telephone: 359/52/356703
City Varna: Navy Hospital
Telephone: 359/52/386210*
  Popular dive sites: Rusalka resort village, Middle ages shipwrecks near Shabla coast, Sunken Second World War Russian submarines near Varna's Bay, Remains of ancient petrified forest sub-

merged near the City of Sozopol, Caves near Kaliakra Cape*
Tourism information: National Tourism Information Center (www.bulgariatravel.org)
* SOURCE: BNAUA (Dec. 2005)

CAMBODIA

► **GENERAL**

Capital: Phnom Penh
Government: multiparty democracy under a constitutional monarchy established in September 1993
Population: 13,607,069
Ethnic groups: Khmer 90%, Vietnamese 5%, Chinese 1%, other 4%
Language(s): Khmer (official) 95%, French, English
Religion(s): Theravada Buddhist 95%, other 5%
GDP per capita: $2,000 (2004 est.)
Currency: riel (KHR) - riels per US dollar - 4,016.25 (2004)
Time: GMT + 7
Electricity:
National holiday: Independence Day, 9 November (1953)

► **GEOGRAPHY**

Location: Southeastern Asia, bordering the Gulf of Thailand, between Thailand, Vietnam, and Laos
Border countries: Laos 541 km, Thailand 803 km, Vietnam 1,228 km
Area: 181,040 sq km
Coastline: 443 km
Climate: tropical; rainy, monsoon season (May to November); dry season (December to April); little seasonal temperature variation
Terrain: mostly low, flat plains; mountains in southwest and north
lowest point: Gulf of Thailand 0 m

highest point: Phnum Aoral 1,810 m
Natural hazards: monsoonal rains (June to November); flooding; occasional droughts
Vaccination(s): Yellow fever: A yellow fever vaccination certificate is required from travellers coming from infected areas. **Malaria:** Malaria risk—predominantly due to P. falciparum—exists throughout the year in the whole country except in the Phnom Penh area and close around Tonle Sap. Malaria does, however, occur in the tourist area of Angkor Wat. P. falciparum resistant to chloroquine and sulfadoxine–pyrimethamine reported. Resistance to mefloquine reported in western provinces near the Thai border.

▶ **DIVING**

Number of certified divers: 40*
Dive federation(s): None

Dive regulations: Diver certification
Freediving federation(s): None
Major bodies of water: Gulf of Thailand
Dive season: Year round, best in the dry season*
Water temperature: 28°C/82.4F(Jan-Mar), 29°C/84.2F (July-Sept)
Hyperbaric chambers:
City: Bangkok
City: Koh Sumui*
Popular dive sites: Corner Bar, Sponge Factory, First Tree, Statutes, Giraffes*
Tourism information: Tourism of Cambodia (www.tourismcambodia.com)

* SOURCE: Dive Cambodia, EcoSea (2006)

CANADA

▶ **GENERAL**

Capital: Ottawa
Government: a constitutional monarchy that is also a parliamentary democracy and a federation.
Population: 32,805,041 (July 2005 est.); approximately 90% of the population is concentrated within 160 km of the US border
Ethnic groups: British Isles origin 28%, French origin 23%, other European 15%, Amerindian 2%, other,

mostly Asian, African, Arab 6%, mixed background**Language(s):** English (official) 59.3%, French (official) 23.2%, other 17.5%
Religion(s): Roman Catholic 42.6%, Protestant 23.3% (including United Church 9.5%, Anglican 6.8%, Baptist 2.4%, Lutheran 2%), other Christian 4.4%, Muslim 1.9%, other and unspecified 11.8%, none 16% (2001 census)
GDP per capita: $31,500 (2004 est.)
Currency: Canadian dollar (CAD), Canadian dollars per US dollar - 1.301 (2004)
Time: GMT + 3.5 (Newfoundland), GMT + 3 (Halifax), GMT + 5 (Toronto), GMT + 8 (Vancouver),

Electricity: 110V, 60Hz, twin parallel flat blade socket
National holiday: Canada Day, 1 July (1867

▶ **GEOGRAPHY**

Location: Northern North America, bordering the North Atlantic Ocean on the east, North Pacific Ocean on the west, and the Arctic Ocean on the north, north of the conterminous US
Border countries: US 8,893 km (includes 2,477 km with Alaska)
Area: 9,984,670 sq km
Coastline: 202,080 km
Climate: varies from temperate in south to subarctic and arctic in north
Terrain: mostly plains with mountains in west and lowlands in southeast
lowest point: Atlantic Ocean 0 m
highest point: Mount Logan 5,959 m
Natural hazards: continuous permafrost in north is a serious obstacle to development; cyclonic storms form east of the Rocky Mountains, a result of the mixing of air masses from the Arctic, Pacific, and North American interior, and produce most of the country's rain and snow east of the mountains
Vaccination(s): No vaccination requirements for any international traveller.

▶ **DIVING**

Number of certified divers: See Provinces
Dive federation(s): See provinces
Dive regulations: See provinces
Freediving federation(s): CAFA Canada AIDA, See provinces
Major bodies of water: Atlantic Ocean, Pacific Ocean, Arctic Ocean, St. Lawrence Seaway, Great Lakes
Dive season: year-round except Arctic
Water temperature: See provinces
Hyperbaric chambers: See provinces
Popular dive sites: See provinces
Tourism information: Canadian Tourism information (www.travelcanada.ca)

ALBERTA

Number of certified divers: 2,000-3,000*
Dive federation(s): Alberta Underwater Council
Dive regulations: Diver certification
Freediving federation(s): Canadian Assoc. Of Free Diving & Apenea, Burnaby, BC*
Major bodies of water: Lakes
Dive season: May-Oct, with some ice diving*
Water temperature: 1°C/33.8F(Jan-Mar), 17°C/62.6F (July-Sept)
Hyperbaric chambers:
City: Edmonton: Misericordia Hospital, Telephone: 780-930-5768
City: Calgary – HBOT Clinic, Telephone: 403-509-4740*

Popular dive sites: Jasper, five fresh water mountain lakes, Banff, two fresh water mountain lakes, one with 1912 submerged original dam site, Waterton Lake, Cold Lake, Twin Lakes*
* Source: Alberta Underwater Council (Dec. 2005)

BRITISH COLUMBIA

Number of certified divers: 115,000 PADI certified scuba divers*
Dive federation(s):
Dive regulations: Diver certification; All tidal waters within the Pacific Rim National Park Reserve are closed to scuba and skin dive fishing for all species, all year. Spear fishing is fishing by means of a spear propelled by a spring, an elastic band, compressed air, a bow or by hand. Spear fishing for salmon, trout, char, sturgeon and most species of shellfish is prohibited.*
Freediving federation(s): Canadian Association of Free Diving & Apenea, Burnaby, BC*
Major bodies of water: Pacific Ocean
Dive season: year round
Water temperature: 4°C /39.2F(Jan-Mar), 11°C/51.8F (July-Sept)
Hyperbaric chambers:
City: Burnaby, Simon Fraser University
Telephone: 604 291-3782
City: Burnaby, Baromedical Research Center
Telephone: 604 777-7055
Popular dive sites: The HMCS Saskatchewan, Hornby Island, Ten Mile Point, Francis Peninsula, Tyler Rock
* Source: Fisheries and Oceans Canada - Pacific Region

NEWFOUNDLAND & LABRADOR

Number of certified divers:
Dive federation(s):
Dive regulations: Diver certification
Freediving federation(s):
Major bodies of water: Atlantic Ocean
Dive season: May-Oct
Water temperature: 1°C/33.8F (Jan-Mar), 10°C/50F (July-Sept)
Hyperbaric chambers:
St. John's Health Sciences Centre
Popular dive sites: Bell Island wrecks, Conception Bay; Gros Morne National Park, Abraham's Cove, Sheaves Cove, Ship Cove Island

---

NOVA SCOTIA

Number of certified divers: 15,000**
Dive federation(s): Nova Scotia Underwater Council
Dive regulations: Diver certification
Freediving federation(s): None*
Major bodies of water: Atlantic Ocean
Dive season: year-round

Water temperature: 3°C/37.4F (Jan-Mar), 8°C/46.4F (July-Sept)
Hyperbaric chambers:
QE II Health Center, Halifax*
Popular dive sites: Halifax Harbour, Paddies Head, Train Bridge, Iona CB, Scatteri Island CB Arrow Wreck CB (Cape Breton)*
* SOURCE: NSUC (2005)
** N.S. Marine Tourism Study

ONTARIO

Number of certified divers: 300,000*
Dive federation(s):
Dive regulations: Diver certification
Freediving federation(s):
www.performancefreediving.com*
Major bodies of water: Great lakes, Georgian Bay, St. Lawrence River
Dive season: May-Oct, winter: some ice diving*
Water temperature: 0°C/32F (Jan-Mar), 18°C/64.4F (July-Sept)
Hyperbaric chambers:
City: Toronto,
Telephone: 911*
Popular dive sites: Tobermory (Georgian Bay), Kingston area (St Lawrence River), Lake Simcoe (Central Ontario) Port Colbourne (Lake Erie), thousands of inland lakes & quarries (Muskoka Lake, Kirkfield Quarry)*
* SOURCE: Scuba 2000.com (2006)

PRINCE EDWARD ISLAND

Number of certified divers: NA
Dive federation(s):
Dive regulations: Diver certification
Freediving federation(s):
Major bodies of water: Gulf of the St. Lawrence
Dive season: May-Oct
Water temperature: 0°C/32F (Jan-Mar), 20°C/68F (July-Sept)

QUEBEC

Number of certified divers: 101,000*
Dive federation(s): Fédération québécoise des activités subaquatiques (FQAS)
Dive regulations: Diver certification
Freediving federation(s): Club apnée sportive de montréal (see FQAS site)*
Major bodies of water: Gulf of the St. Lawrence, St. Lawrence Estuary and Seaway, Atlantic Ocean
Dive season: May-Oct; year-round for some*
Water temperature: 0°C/32F (Jan-Mar), 16°C/60.8F (July-Sept)
Hyperbaric chambers:
Ville : Centre de médécine Hyperbare de Lévis
Téléphone: 1-888-835-7121*

Popular dive sites: Escoumins, Cap Gaspé, Percé,Havre Saint-Pierre,Rimouski (Empress of Ireland)*
* SOURCE: FQAS (Dec. 2005)

CAYMAN ISLANDS

▶ **GENERAL**

Capital: George Town
Government: British crown colony
Population: 44,270 (July 2005 est.)
Ethnic groups: mixed 40%, white 20%, black 20%, expatriates of various ethnic groups 20%
Language(s): English
Religion(s): United Church (Presbyterian and Congregational), Anglican, Baptist, Church of God, other Protestant, Roman Catholic
GDP per capita: $32,300 (2004 est.)
Currency: Caymanian dollar (KYD) - Caymanian dollars per US dollar - 0.82 (29 October 2001)
Time: GMT - 5
Electricity: 110V, 60Hz
National holiday: Constitution Day, first Monday in July

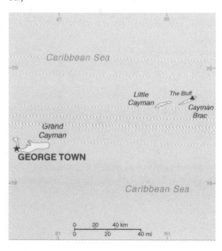

▶ **GEOGRAPHY**

Location: Caribbean, island group in Caribbean Sea, nearly one-half of the way from Cuba to Honduras
Border countries: None
Area: 262 sq km
Coastline: 160 km
Climate: tropical marine; warm, rainy summers (May to October) and cool, relatively dry winters (November to April)
Terrain: low-lying limestone base surrounded by coral reefs
lowest point: Caribbean Sea 0 m
highest point: The Bluff 43 m

Natural hazards: hurricanes (July to November)
Vaccination(s): No vaccination requirements for any international traveller.

▶ **DIVING**

Number of certified divers: Mainly tourists
Dive federation(s): None
Dive regulations: Diver certification
Freediving federation(s): AIDA
Major bodies of water: Caribbean Sea
Dive season: year-round
Water temperature: 26°C78.8F (Jan-Mar), 30°C86F (July-Sept)
Hyperbaric chambers:
City: Grand Cayman Hyperbaric Services
Telephone: (345) 949-2989
City: Georgetown Hospital
Telephone: (345) 949-8600
Popular dive sites: Anchor Wall, Bloody Bay Wall, Tarpon Alley, Trinity Caves, Greenhouse Reef, the Mermaid
Tourism information: Cayman Islands Department of Tourism (www.divecayman.ky)

CHILE

▶ **GENERAL**

Capital: Santiago
Government: republic
Population: 15,980,912 (July 2005 est.)
Ethnic groups: white and white-Amerindian 95%, Amerindian 3%, other 2%
Language(s): Spanish
Religion(s): Roman Catholic 89%, Protestant 11%, Jewish NEGL%
GDP per capita: $10,700 (2004 est.)
Currency: Chilean peso (CLP) - Chilean pesos per US dollar - 609.37 (2004)
Time: GMT - 4
Electricity: 220V, 50Hz, 2-pin plug
National holiday: Independence Day, 18 September (1810)

▶ **GEOGRAPHY**

Location: Southern South America, bordering the South Pacific Ocean, between Argentina and Peru
Border countries: Argentina 5,150 km, Bolivia 861 km, Peru 160 km
Area: 756,950 sq km
Coastline: 6,435 km
Climate: temperate; desert in north; Mediterranean in central region; cool and damp in south
Terrain: low coastal mountains; fertile central valley; rugged Andes in east
lowest point: Pacific Ocean 0 m
highest point: Nevado Ojos del Salado 6,880 m
Natural hazards: severe earthquakes; active volcanism; tsunamis
Vaccination(s): Yellow fever: A yellow fever vaccination certificate is required from travellers

coming from endemic areas and travelling to Easter Island.

▶ **DIVING**

Number of certified divers: Mainly tourists
Dive federation(s): FEDESUB (Federación Chilena de Deportes Submarinos)
Dive regulations: Diver certification
Freediving federation(s): Federacion De Buceo De Chile, AIDA*
Major bodies of water: South Pacific Ocean
Dive season: year-round
Water temperature: 21°C/69.8F (Jan-Mar), 15°C/60.8F (July-Sept)
Hyperbaric chambers:
Santiago Hospital del Trabajador Ramon
Telephone: (56) 2 2225533x2723
Hospital Naval de Viña del Mar
Telephone: (56)-32-686758
Popular dive sites: Quintay, Pichidangui, Zapallar, Isla De Pascua, Archipielago Juan Fernandez*
Tourism information: Chilean Tourism Promotion Corporation (www.visit-chile.org)

*SOURCE: Prodivers Chile (2006)

CHINA

▶ **GENERAL**

Capital: Beijing
Government: Communist state
Population: 1,306,313,812 (July 2005 est.)
Ethnic groups: Han Chinese 91.9%, Zhuang, Uygur, Hui, Yi, Tibetan, Miao, Manchu, Mongol, Buyi, Korean, and other nationalities 8.1%
Language(s): Standard Chinese or Mandarin (Putonghua, based on the Beijing dialect), Yue (Cantonese), Wu (Shanghaiese), Minbei (Fuzhou), Minnan (Hokkien-Taiwanese), Xiang, Gan, Hakka dialects, minority languages
Religion(s): Daoist (Taoist), Buddhist, Muslim 1%-2%, Christian 3%-4% *note:* officially atheist (2002 est.)
GDP per capita: $5,600 (2004 est.)
Currency: yuan (CNY) also referred to as the Renminbi (RMB) - yuan per US dollar - 8.2768 (2004)
Time: GMT + 8
Electricity: 220V, 50Hz
National holiday: Anniversary of the Founding of the People's Republic of China, 1 October (1949)

▶ **GEOGRAPHY**

Location: Eastern Asia, bordering the East China Sea, Korea Bay, Yellow Sea, and South China Sea, between North Korea and Vietnam
Border countries: Afghanistan 76 km, Bhutan 470 km, Burma 2,185 km, India 3,380 km, Kazakhstan 1,533 km, North Korea 1,416 km, Kyrgyzstan 858 km, Laos 423 km, Mongolia 4,677 km, Nepal 1,236 km, Pakistan 523 km, Russia (northeast) 3,605 km, Russia (northwest) 40 km, Tajikistan 414 km, Vietnam 1,281 km; *regional borders:* Hong Kong 30 km, Macau 0.34 km
Area: 9,596,960 sq km
Coastline: 14,500 km
Climate: extremely diverse; tropical in south to subarctic in north
Terrain: mostly mountains, high plateaus, deserts in west; plains, deltas, and hills in east

lowest point: Turpan Pendi -154 m
highest point: Mount Everest 8,850 m
Natural hazards: frequent typhoons (about five per year along southern and eastern coasts); damaging floods; tsunamis; earthquakes; droughts; land subsidence
Vaccination(s): Yellow fever: A yellow fever vaccination certificate is required from travellers coming from infected areas. **Malaria:** Malaria risk—including *P. falciparum* malaria—occurs in Hainan and Yunnan. Chloroquine and sulfadoxine-pyrimethamine resistant *P. falciparum* reported. Risk of *P. vivax* malaria exists in Fujian, Guangdong, Guangxi, Guizhou, Hainan, Sichuan, Xizang (only along the valley of the Zangbo river in the extreme south-east) and Yunnan. Very low malaria risk (*P. vivax* only) exists in Anhui, Hubei, Hunan, Jiangsu, Jiangxi and Shandong. The risk may be higher in areas of focal outbreaks. Where transmission exists, it occurs only in remote rural communities below 1500 m: from July to November north of latitude 33½N, from May to December between 33½N and 25½N, and throughout the year south of 25½N. There is no malaria risk in urban areas nor in the densely populated plain areas. In general, tourists do not need to take malaria prophylaxis unless they plan to stay in remote rural areas in the provinces listed above. Recommended prevention in risk areas: II; in Hainan and Yunnan, IV

▶ **DIVING**

Number of certified divers: 8,000*
Dive federation(s): Chinese Underwater Association (CUA)
Dive regulations: Diver certification
Freediving federation(s): AIDA
Major bodies of water: Yellow Sea, East China Sea, South China Sea
Dive season: year-round*
Water temperature: 24°C/75.2F (Jan-Mar), 28°C/84.2F (July-Sept)
Hyperbaric chambers:
City: Shanghai, Second Military Medical University
Telephone: (+86 21) 6549 2382
City: Guangzhou, Guangzhou Salvage
Telephone: (+86 20) 3406 2269
Popular dive sites: Sanya, Weizhou island, Dalian, Qingdao, Yantai*
Tourism information: China National Tourist Office (www.cnto.org)
* SOURCE: CUA (Dec. 2005)

COCOS (KEELING) ISLANDS

▶ **GENERAL**

Capital: West Island
Government: territory of Australia; administered from Canberra by the Australian Department of Transport and Regional Services
Population: 628 (July 2005 est.)

Ethnic groups: Europeans, Cocos Malays
Language(s): Malay (Cocos dialect), English
Religion(s): Sunni Muslim 80%, other 20% (2002 est.)
GDP per capita: NA
Currency: Australian dollar (AUD) - Australian dollars per US dollar - 1.3598 (2004)
Time: GMT + 6.5
Electricity: 240V, 50Hz
National holiday: Australia Day, 26 January (1788)

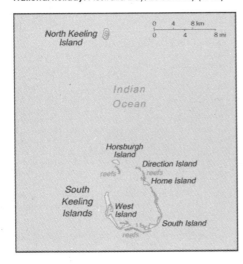

Closest: Fremantle Western Australia *
Contact via DAN, freecall: 1800 088 200
Popular dive sites: Cabbage Patch, Cologne Gardens, Garden of Eden, Spanish Eyes, Manta Beach*
Tourism information: Cocos (Keeling) Islands Tourism Association (www.cocos-tourism.cc)
* SOURCE: Cocos (Keeling) Islands Tourism Association (2006)

COLOMBIA

▶ GEOGRAPHY

Location: Southeastern Asia, group of islands in the Indian Ocean, southwest of Indonesia, about halfway from Australia to Sri Lanka
Border countries: None
Area: 14 sq km
Coastline: 26 km
Climate: tropical with high humidity, moderated by the southeast trade winds for about nine months of the year
Terrain: flat, low-lying coral atolls
lowest point: Indian Ocean 0 m
highest point: unnamed location 5 m
Natural hazards: cyclone season is October to April
Vaccination(s): NA

▶ DIVING

Number of certified divers: Mainly tourists
Dive federation(s): Australian Underwater Federation (AUF)
Dive regulations: Diver certification
Freediving federation(s): None
Major bodies of water: Indian Ocean
Dive season: year-round
Water temperature: 28.5°C83F (Jan-Mar), 26°C78.8F (July-Sept)
Hyperbaric chambers:

▶ GENERAL

Capital: Bogotá
Government: republic; executive branch dominates government structure
Population: 42,954,279 (July 2005 est.)
Ethnic groups: mestizo 58%, white 20%, mulatto 14%, black 4%, mixed black-Amerindian 3%, Amerindian 1%
Language(s): Spanish
Religion(s): Roman Catholic 90%, other 10%
GDP per capita: $6,600 (2004 est.)
Currency: Colombian peso (COP) - Colombian pesos per US dollar - 2,628.61 (2004)
Time: GMT - 5
Electricity: 110V, 60Hz
National holiday: Independence Day, 20 July (1810)

▶ GEOGRAPHY

Location: Northern South America, bordering the Caribbean Sea, between Panama and Venezuela, and bordering the North Pacific Ocean, between Ecuador and Panama
Border countries: Brazil 1,643 km, Ecuador 590 km, Panama 225 km, Peru 1,496 km (est.), Venezuela 2,050 km
Area: 1,138,910 sq km

Coastline: 3,208 km (Caribbean Sea 1,760 km, North Pacific Ocean 1,448 km)
Climate: tropical along coast and eastern plains; cooler in highlands
Terrain: flat coastal lowlands, central highlands, high Andes Mountains, eastern lowland plains
lowest point: Pacific Ocean 0 m
highest point: Pico Cristobal Colon 5,775 m
Natural hazards: highlands subject to volcanic eruptions; occasional earthquakes; periodic droughts
Vaccination(s): Yellow fever: Vaccination is recommended for travellers who may visit the following areas considered to be endemic for yellow fever: middle valley of the Magdalena River, eastern and western foothills of the Cordillera Oriental from the frontier with Ecuador to that with Venezuela, Urabá, foothills of the Sierra Nevada, eastern plains (Orinoquia) and Amazonia.
Malaria: Malaria risk—*P. falciparum* (42%), *P. vivax* (58%)—is high throughout the year in rural/jungle areas below 800 m, especially in municipalities of the regions of Amazonia, Orinoquía, Pacífico and Urabá-Bajo Cauca. Transmission intensity varies from department to department, with the highest risk in Amazonas, Chocó, Córdoba, Guainía, Guaviare, Putumayo and Vichada. Chloroquine-resistant *P. falciparum* exists in Amazonia, Pacífico and Urabá-Bajo Cauca. Resistance to sulfadoxine–pyrimethamine reported. Recommended prevention in risk areas: III; in Amazonia, Pacífico and Urabá-Bajo Cauca, IV

▶ **DIVING**

Number of certified divers: N/A
Dive federation(s): Federacion Colombiana De Actividades Subacuaticas
Dive regulations: Diver certification
Freediving federation(s): AIDA
Major bodies of water: Caribbean Sea, North Pacific Ocean
Dive season: year-round
Water temperature: 26°C/78.8F (Jan-Mar), 26°C/78.8F (July-Sept)
Hyperbaric chambers:
City: Cartagena, Navy Headquarters
Málaga, Navy Headquarters, Pacific
Popular dive sites: Providencia Island, Palancar Caves, Paradise Reefs, Adar Pass, Punta Sur
Tourism information: Fondo de Promoción Turística de Colombia (www.turismocolombia.com)

COMOROS

▶ **GENERAL**

Capital: Moroni
Government: independent republic
Population: 671,247 (July 2005 est.)
Ethnic groups: Antalote, Cafre, Makoa, Oimatsaha, Sakalava

Language(s): Arabic (official), French (official), Shikomoro (a blend of Swahili and Arabic)
Religion(s): Sunni Muslim 98%, Roman Catholic 2%
GDP per capita: $700 (2002 est.)
Currency: Comoran franc (KMF) - Comoran francs (KMF) per US dollar - 396.21 (2004)
Time: GMT + 3
Electricity: 220V, 50Hz
National holiday: Independence Day, 6 July (1975)

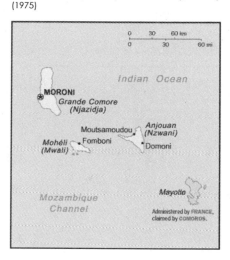

▶ **GEOGRAPHY**

Location: Southern Africa, group of islands at the northern mouth of the Mozambique Channel, about two-thirds of the way between northern Madagascar and northern Mozambique
Border countries: None
Area: 2,170 sq km
Coastline: 340 km
Climate: tropical marine; rainy season (November to May)
Terrain: volcanic islands, interiors vary from steep mountains to low hills
lowest point: Indian Ocean 0 m
highest point: Le Kartala 2,360 m
Natural hazards: cyclones possible during rainy season (December to April); Le Kartala on Grand Comore is an active volcano
Vaccination(s): No vaccination requirements for any international traveller. **Malaria:** Malaria risk—predominantly due to *P. falciparum*—exists throughout the year in the whole country. Resistance to chloroquine reported. Recommended prevention: IV

▶ **DIVING**

Number of certified divers: Mainly tourists
Dive federation(s): None
Dive regulations: Diver certification
Freediving federation(s): None

Major bodies of water: Indian Ocean, Mozambique Channel
Dive season: year-round
Water temperature: 29°C/84.2F (Jan-Mar), 25°C/77F (July-Sept)
Hyperbaric chambers: N/A
Closest: Réunion
Popular dive sites: Grande Comore area, Hahaya Wall, Black Coral Cave, Coelacanth, Banc Vailheu Sea mount
Tourism information: Comoros Portal (www.comores-online.com)

COOK ISLANDS

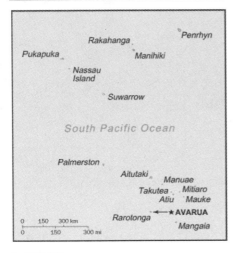

► **GENERAL**

Capital: Avarua
Government: self-governing parliamentary democracy in free association with New Zealand
Population: 21,388 (July 2005 est.)
Ethnic groups: Cook Island Maori (Polynesian) 87.7%, part Cook Island Maori 5.8%, other 6.5% (2001 census)
Language(s): English (official), Maori
Religion(s): Cook Islands Christian Church 55.9%, Roman Catholic 16.8%, Seventh-Day Adventists 7.9%, Church of Latter Day Saints 3.8%, other Protestant 5.8%, other 4.2%, unspecified 2.6%, none 3% (2001 census)
GDP per capita: $5,000 (2001 est.)
Currency: New Zealand dollar (NZD) - New Zealand dollars per US dollar - 1.5087 (2004)
Time: GMT -10
Electricity: 220V, 50Hz
National holiday: Constitution Day, first Monday in August (1965)

► **GEOGRAPHY**

Location: Oceania, group of islands in the South Pacific Ocean, about one-half of the way from Hawaii to New Zealand
Border countries: None
Area: 240 sq km
Coastline: 120 km
Climate: tropical; moderated by trade winds
Terrain: low coral atolls in north; volcanic, hilly islands in south
lowest point: Pacific Ocean 0 m
highest point: Te Manga 652 m
Natural hazards: typhoons (November to March)
Vaccination(s): No vaccination requirements for any international traveller.

► **DIVING**

Number of certified divers: 500*
Dive federation(s): None
Dive regulations: Diver certification
Freediving federation(s): None
Major bodies of water: Caribbean Sea, North Pacific Ocean
Dive season: year-round
Water temperature: 28.5°C83F (Jan-Mar), 25°C/77F (July-Sept)
Hyperbaric chambers: N/A
Rarotonga hospital
Aitutaki hospital
Popular dive sites: Avavaroa Passage, Papua Passage, Pinnacles, Manarangi's, Arorangi Rock Wall*
Tourism information: Cook Islands Tourism Corporation (www.cook-islands.com)
* SOURCE: Cook Islands Divers (2006)

COSTA RICA

► **GENERAL**

Capital: San Jose
Government: democratic republic
Population: 4,016,173 (July 2005 est.)
Ethnic groups: white (including mestizo) 94%, black 3%, Amerindian 1%, Chinese 1%, other 1%
Language(s): Spanish (official), English
Religion(s): Roman Catholic 76.3%, Evangelical 13.7%, Jehovah's Witnesses 1.3%, other Protestant 0.7%, other 4.8%, none 3.2%
GDP per capita: $9,600 (2004 est.)
Currency: Costa Rican colon (CRC) - Costa Rican colones per US dollar - 437.91 (2004)
Time: GMT -6
Electricity: 120V, 60Hz, 2-pin plug
National holiday: Independence Day, 15 September (1821)

► **GEOGRAPHY**

Location: Central America, bordering both the Caribbean Sea and the North Pacific Ocean, between Nicaragua and Panama
Border countries: Nicaragua 309 km, Panama 330 km
Area: 51,100 sq km
Coastline: 1,290 km
Climate: tropical and subtropical; dry season (December to April); rainy season (May to November); cooler in highlands
Terrain: coastal plains separated by rugged mountains including over 100 volcanic cones, of which several are major volcanoes
lowest point: Pacific Ocean 0 m
highest point: Cerro Chirripo 3,810 m
Natural hazards: occasional earthquakes, hurricanes along Atlantic coast; frequent flooding of lowlands at onset of rainy season and landslides; active volcanoes
Vaccination(s): No vaccination requirements for any international traveller. **Malaria:** Malaria risk—almost exclusively due to P. vivax—is moderate throughout the year in the cantons of Los Chiles (Alajuela Province) and Matina and Talamanca (Limón Province). Lower transmission risk exists in cantons in the provinces of Alajuela, Guanacaste and Heredia, and in other cantons in Limón Province. Negligible or no risk of malaria transmission exists in the other cantons of the country. Recommended prevention in risk areas: II

► **DIVING**

Number of certified divers: Mainly tourists
Dive federation(s): None
Dive regulations: Diver certification
Freediving federation(s): None
Major bodies of water: Caribbean Sea, North Pacific Ocean
Dive season: year-round

Water temperature: 27°C/80.6F (Jan-Mar), 28°C/82.4F (July-Sept)
Hyperbaric chambers: N/A
Closest: Panama
Popular dive sites: Caño Island, Drake Bay, Manuel Antonio Quepos, Bat and Catalina Islands
Tourism information: Costa Rica Tourism and Travel Bureau (www.costaricabureau.com); Costa Rican Tourist Board (www.visitcostarica.com)

CROATIA

► **GENERAL**

Capital: Zagreb
Government: Presidential/parliamentary democracy
Population: 4,495,904 (July 2005 est.)
Ethnic groups: Croat 89.6%, Serb 4.5%, other 5.9% (including Bosniak, Hungarian, Slovene, Czech, and Roma) (2001 census)
Language(s): Croatian 96.1%, Serbian 1%, other and undesignated 2.9% (including Italian, Hungarian, Czech, Slovak, and German) (2001 census)
Religion(s): Roman Catholic 87.8%, Orthodox 4.4%, other Christian 0.4%, Muslim 1.3%, other and unspecified 0.9%, none 5.2% (2001 census)
GDP per capita: $11,200 (2004 est.)
Currency: kuna (HRK) - kuna per US dollar - 6.0358 (2004)
Time: GMT + 1
Electricity: 230V, 50Hz
National holiday: Independence Day, 8 October (1991)

► **GEOGRAPHY**

Location: Southeastern Europe, bordering the Adriatic Sea, between Bosnia and Herzegovina and Slovenia
Border countries: Bosnia and Herzegovina 932 km, Hungary 329 km, Serbia and Montenegro (north) 241 km, Serbia and Montenegro (south) 25 km, Slovenia 670 km
Area: 56,542 sq km
Coastline: 5,835 km (mainland 1,777 km, islands 4,058 km)
Climate: Mediterranean and continental; continental climate predominant with hot summers and cold winters; mild winters, dry summers along coast
Terrain: geographically diverse; flat plains along Hungarian border, low mountains and highlands near Adriatic coastline and islands
lowest point: Adriatic Sea 0 m
highest point: Dinara 1,830 m
Natural hazards: destructive earthquakes
Vaccination(s): No vaccination requirements for any international traveller.

▶ DIVING

Number of certified divers: N/A
Dive federation(s): Croation Diving Federation
Dive regulations: Diver certification; certain areas restricted to diving
Freediving federation(s): AIDA
Major bodies of water: Adriatic Sea
Dive season: year-round
Water temperature: 13°C/55.4F (Jan-Mar), 23°C/73.4F (July-Sept)
Hyperbaric chambers:
City: Zagreb, Oxy Baromedical
Telephone: 01-290-3718
City: Osijek, Clinical Hospital Osijek
Telephone: 031-511-530
Popular dive sites: Kornati, Rasip, Susac, Te Vega, Bisevo, Modra Spilja; wrecks: Susak, Peljesac S 57, Dubrovnik, Taranto and others
Tourism information: Croatian National Tourist Board (www.croatia.hr)

CUBA

▶ GENERAL

Capital: Havana
Government: Communist state
Population: 11,346,670 (July 2005 est.)
Ethnic groups: mulatto 51%, white 37%, black 11%, Chinese 1%
Language(s): Spanish
Religion(s): nominally 85% Roman Catholic prior to CASTRO assuming power; Protestants, Jehovah's Witnesses, Jews, and Santeria are also represented
GDP per capita: $3,000 (2004 est.)
Currency: Cuban peso (CUP) and Convertible peso (CUC) - Convertible pesos per US dollar - 0.93; The US dollar is being withdrawn from circulation.

Time: GMT - 5
Electricity: 110V, 60Hz and 220V
National holiday: Independence Day, 10 December (1898)

▶ GEOGRAPHY

Location: Caribbean, island between the Caribbean Sea and the North Atlantic Ocean, 150 km south of Key West, Florida
Border countries: US Naval Base at Guantanamo Bay 29 km; *note:* Guantanamo Naval Base is leased by the US and thus remains part of Cuba
Area: 110,860 sq km
Coastline: 3,735 km
Climate: tropical; moderated by trade winds; dry season (November to April); rainy season (May to October)
Terrain: mostly flat to rolling plains, with rugged hills and mountains in the southeast
lowest point: Caribbean Sea 0 m
highest point: Pico Turquino 2,005 m
Natural hazards: the east coast is subject to hurricanes from August to November (in general, the country averages about one hurricane every other year); droughts are common
Vaccination(s): No vaccination requirements for any international traveller.

▶ DIVING

Number of certified divers: Mainly tourists
Dive federation(s): Federación Cubana De Actividades Subacuaticas
Dive regulations: Diver certification
Freediving federation(s): AIDA
Major bodies of water: Caribbean Sea, North Atlantic Ocean, Gulf of Mexico
Dive season: year-round
Water temperature: 24°C/75.2F (Jan-Mar), 28°C/82.4F (July-Sept)
Hyperbaric chambers:
City: Guantanamo Bay, Naval Station Guatanamo Bay
Telephone: 011-5399-3200City: Havana, La Habana Hyperbaric Medical Center
Telephone: (537) 97 3266
Popular dive sites: Jardines de la Reina, Cayo Largo, Isla de la Juventud, Maria la Gorda, Playa Giron*
Tourism information: Ministry of Tourism (www.cubatravel.cu)
* SOURCE: Cuba Diving (2006)

CURACAO (See Netherlands Antilles)

CYPRUS

▶ **GENERAL**

Capital: Nicosia
Government: republic; *note:* a separation of the two ethnic communities inhabiting the island began following the outbreak of communal strife in 1963; this separation was further solidified after the Turkish intervention in July 1974 that followed a Greek junta-supported coup attempt gave the Turkish Cypriots de facto control in the north; Greek Cypriots control the only internationally recognized government; on 15 November 1983 Turkish Cypriot "President" Rauf DENKTASH declared independence and the formation of a "Turkish Republic of Northern Cyprus" (TRNC), recognized only by Turkey

Population: 780,133 (July 2005 est.)
Ethnic groups: Greek 77%, Turkish 18%, other 5% (2001)
Language(s): Greek, Turkish, English
Religion(s): Greek Orthodox 78%, Muslim 18%, Maronite, Armenian Apostolic, and other 4%
GDP per capita: Republic of Cyprus: $20,300 (2004 est.); North Cyprus: $7,135 (2004 est.)
Currency: Greek Cypriot area: Cypriot pound (CYP); Turkish Cypriot area: Turkish lira (TRL) - Cypriot pounds per US dollar - 0.4686 (2004); Turkish lira per US dollar 1.426 million (2004)
Time: GMT +2
Electricity: 240V, 50Hz
National holiday: Independence Day, 1 October (1960); note - Turkish Cypriots celebrate 15 November (1983) as Independence Day

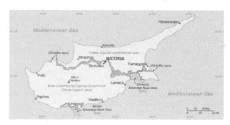

▶ **GEOGRAPHY**

Location: Middle East, island in the Mediterranean Sea, south of Turkey
Border countries: US Naval Base at Guantanamo Bay 29 km; *note:* Guantanamo Naval Base is leased by the US and thus remains part of Cuba
Area: 9,250 sq km (of which 3,355 sq km are in north Cyprus)
Coastline: 648 km

Climate: temperate; Mediterranean with hot, dry summers and cool winters
Terrain: central plain with mountains to north and south; scattered but significant plains along southern coast
lowest point: Mediterranean Sea 0 m
highest point: Mount Olympus 1,951 m
Natural hazards: moderate earthquake activity; droughts
Vaccination(s): No vaccination requirements for any international traveller.

▶ **DIVING**

Number of certified divers: Mainly tourists
Dive federation(s): Cyprus Federation Of Underwater Activities (CMAS)*
Dive regulations: Diver certification; forbidden to remove antiquities & sponges from seabed.
Freediving federation(s): AIDA
Major bodies of water: Mediterranean Sea
Dive season: year-round, best conditions April to December*
Water temperature: 17°C/62.6F (Jan-Mar), 26°C/78.8F (July-Sept)
Hyperbaric chambers:
City: Larnaka, Larnaka MakareionGeneral Hospital
Telephone: 00357-4-630300
Popular dive sites: Wrecks: Zenobia, Limassol, Tunnels and Caves, Canyon, Cape Awkward, Greenbay*
Tourism information: Cyprus Tourism Organization (www.visitcyprus.org.cy)
*SOURCE: Sea Eye Diving Centre 2006

CZECH REPUBLIC

▶ **GENERAL**

Capital: Prague
Government: parliamentary democracy
Population: 10,241,138 (July 2005 est.)
Ethnic groups: Czech 90.4%, Moravian 3.7%, Slovak 1.9%, other 4% (2001 census)
Language(s): Czech
Religion(s): Roman Catholic 26.8%, Protestant 2.1%, other 3.3%, unspecified 8.8%, unaffiliated 59% (2001 census)
GDP per capita: $16,800 (2004 est.)
Currency: Czech koruna (CZK) - koruny per US dollar - 25.7 (2004)
Time: GMT + 1
Electricity: 230V, 50Hz, 2-pin plug
National holiday: Czech Founding Day, 28 October (1918)

▶ **GEOGRAPHY**

Location: Central Europe, southeast of Germany
Border countries: Austria 362 km, Germany 646 km, Poland 658 km, Slovakia 215 km
Area: 78,866 sq km

Coastline: 0 km (landlocked)
Climate: temperate; cool summers; cold, cloudy, humid winters
Terrain: Bohemia in the west consists of rolling plains, hills, and plateaus surrounded by low mountains; Moravia in the east consists of very hilly country
lowest point: Elbe River 115 m
highest point: Snezka 1,602 m
Natural hazards: flooding
Vaccination(s): No vaccination requirements for any international traveller.

▶ **DIVING**

Number of certified divers: N/A*
Dive federation(s): Divers Association of Czech Republic
Dive regulations: Diver certification
Freediving federation(s): AIDA
Major bodies of water: Elbe River
Dive season: summer: May to October; dry suit: year-round*
Air temperature: 5°C (Jan-Mar), 20°C (July-Sept)
Hyperbaric chambers:
City: Kladno
Telephone: +420-312606146
City: Prague, Institute of Aviation Medicine Prague
Telephone: +420 973 212 450
Popular dive sites: Slapy lake: Nova Zivohost, bay of wreck, old villages; quarry Rumchapla, quarry Lestinka*
Tourism information: Czech Tourism (www.czechtourism.com)
* SOURCE: Kapr Divers (2006)

DENMARK

▶ **GENERAL**

Capital: Copenhagen
Government: constitutional monarchy

Population: 5,432,335 (July 2005 est.)
Ethnic groups: Scandinavian, Inuit, Faroese, German, Turkish, Iranian, Somali
Language(s): Danish, Faroese, Greenlandic (an Inuit dialect), German (small minority); *note:* English is the predominant second language
Religion(s): Evangelical Lutheran 95%, other Protestant and Roman Catholic 3%, Muslim 2%
GDP per capita: $32,200 (2004 est.)
Currency: Danish krone (DKK) - Danish kroner per US dollar - 5.9911 (2004)
Time: GMT + 1
Electricity: 220V, 50Hz
National holiday: Constitution Day, 5 June (1849) is generally viewed as the National Day

▶ **GEOGRAPHY**

Location: Northern Europe, bordering the Baltic Sea and the North Sea, on a peninsula north of Germany (Jutland); also includes two major islands (Sjaelland and Fyn)
Border countries: Germany 68 km
Area: 43,094 sq km (excludes the Faroe Islands and Greenland)
Coastline: 7,314 km (excludes the Faroe Islands and Greenland)
Climate: temperate; humid and overcast; mild, windy winters and cool summers
Terrain: low and flat to gently rolling plains
lowest point: Lammefjord -7 m
highest point: Yding Skovhoej 173 m
Natural hazards: flooding is a threat in some areas of the country (e.g., parts of Jutland, along the southern coast of the island of Lolland) that are protected from the sea by a system of dikes
Vaccination(s): No vaccination requirements for any international traveller.

▶ **DIVING**

Number of certified divers: N/A

Dive federation(s): Danish Sportdiver Federation
Dive regulations: Diver certification
Freediving federation(s): Danish Freediving Association (AIDA)
Major bodies of water: North Sea, Baltic Sea, Skagerrak, Kattegat
Dive season: Best: April through October*
Water temperature: 3°C /37.4F (Jan-Mar), 15°C/59F (July-Sept)
Hyperbaric chambers:
City: Copenhagen The Panum Institute
Telephone: (45) 35327509
Popular dive sites: Knud Rasmussen, S/S Otto, (wreck in waters between Denmark and Sweden), Bornholm Island*
Tourism information: Danish Tourist Board (www.visitdenmark.com)
* SOURCE: Marinadykker Center (2006)

DJIBOUTI

▶ **GENERAL**

Capital: Djibouti
Government: republic
Population: 476,703 (July 2005 est.)
Ethnic groups: Somali 60%, Afar 35%, French, Arab, Ethiopian, and Italian 5%
Language(s): French (official), Arabic (official), Somali, Afar
Religion(s): Muslim 94%, Christian 6%
GDP per capita: $1,300 (2002 est.)
Currency: Djiboutian franc (DJF) - Djiboutian francs per US dollar - 177.72 (2004)
Time: GMT + 3
Electricity: 220V, 50Hz
National holiday: Independence Day, 27 June (1977)

▶ **GEOGRAPHY**

Location: Eastern Africa, bordering the Gulf of Aden and the Red Sea, between Eritrea and Somalia
Border countries: Eritrea 109 km, Ethiopia 349 km, Somalia 58 km
Area: 23,000 sq km
Coastline: 314 km
Climate: desert; torrid, dry
Terrain: coastal plain and plateau separated by central mountains
lowest point: Lac Assal -155 m
highest point: Moussa Ali 2,028 m
Natural hazards: earthquakes; droughts; occasional cyclonic disturbances from the Indian Ocean bring heavy rains and flash floods
Vaccination(s): Yellow fever: A yellow fever vaccination certificate is required from travellers over 1 year of age coming from infected areas. **Malaria:** Malaria risk—predominantly due to *P. falciparum*—exists throughout the year in the whole country. Chloroquine-resistant *P. falciparum* reported. Recommended prevention: IV

▶ **BACKGROUND**

The French Territory of the Afars and the Issas became Djibouti in 1977. Hassan Gouled APII-DON installed an authoritarian one-party state and proceeded to serve as president until 1999. Unrest among the Afars minority during the 1990s led to a civil war that ended in 2001 following the conclusion of a peace accord between Afar rebels and the Issa-dominated government. Djibouti's first multi-party presidential elections in 1999 resulted in the election of Ismail Omar GUEL-LEH. Djibouti occupies a very strategic geographic location at the mouth of the Red Sea and serves as an important transhipment location for goods entering and leaving the east African highlands. The present leadership favors close ties to France, which maintains a significant military presence in the country, but has also developed increasingly stronger ties with the United States in recent years. Djibouti currently hosts the only United States military base in sub-Saharan Africa and is a front-line state in the global war on terrorism.

▶ **DIVING**

Number of certified divers: 250*
Dive federation(s): None*
Dive regulations: Diver certification
Freediving federation(s): None*
Major bodies of water: Gulf of Tadjoura, Gulf of Aden
Dive season: year-round, low season mid-June to end of August*
Water temperature: 25°C/77F (Jan-Mar), 29°C/84.2F (July-Sept)
Hyperbaric chambers:

City: Djibouti, within the Military Hospital
Telephone: (253) 351 351
Popular dive sites: Goubet al Kharab, Seven Brothers Archipelago, The Dome, Red Sand, Wreck of the Arcon Raphael* Arta, Obock, Wreck of Musha
Big animals: whale shark
Tourism information: Office national du tourisme de Djibouti (www.office-tourisme.dj)
* SOURCE: Dolphins Excursions (2006)

DOMINICA

▶ **GENERAL**

Capital: Roseau
Government: parliamentary democracy; republic within the Commonwealth
Population: 69,029 (July 2005 est.)
Ethnic groups: black, mixed black and European, European, Syrian, Carib Amerindian
Language(s): English (official), French patois
Religion(s): Roman Catholic 77%, Protestant 15% (Methodist 5%, Pentecostal 3%, Seventh-Day Adventist 3%, Baptist 2%, other 2%), other 6%, none 2%
GDP per capita: $5,500 (2003 est.)
Currency: East Caribbean dollar (XCD) - East Caribbean dollars per US dollar - 2.7 (2004)
Time: GMT - 4
Electricity: 220/240V, 50Hz
National holiday: Independence Day, 3 November (1978)

▶ **GEOGRAPHY**

Location: Caribbean, island between the Caribbean Sea and the North Atlantic Ocean, about one-half of the way from Puerto Rico to Trinidad and Tobago
Border countries: None

Area: 754 sq km
Coastline: 148 km
Climate: tropical; moderated by northeast trade winds; heavy rainfall
Terrain: rugged mountains of volcanic origin
lowest point: Caribbean Sea 0 m
highest point: Morne Diablatins 1,447 m
Natural hazards: flash floods are a constant threat; destructive hurricanes can be expected during the late summer months
Vaccination(s): Yellow fever: A yellow fever vaccination certificate is required from travellers over 1 year of age coming from infected areas.

▶ **DIVING**

Number of certified divers: 70
Dive federation(s): Dominica Watersports Association
Dive regulations: Diver certification
Freediving federation(s): None
Major bodies of water: Caribbean Sea, North Atlantic
Dive season: year-round
Water temperature: 24°C/75.2F (Jan-Mar), 27°C/80.6F (July-Sept)
Hyperbaric chambers:
The Princess Margaret Hospital*
Popular dive sites: L'Abym, Danglebens Pinnacles, Champagne, Nose reef, Toucarie*
Tourism information: Official Website of Dominica (www.dominica.dm)
* SOURCE: Dominica Watersports Association (2006)

DOMINICAN REPUBLIC

▶ **GENERAL**

Capital: Santo Domingo
Government: representative democracy
Population: 8,950,034 (July 2005 est.)
Ethnic groups: white 16%, black 11%, mixed 73%
Language(s): Spanish
Religion(s): Roman Catholic 95%
GDP per capita: $6,300 (2004 est.)
Currency: Dominican peso (DOP) - Dominican pesos per US dollar - 42.12 (2004)
Time: GMT - 4
Electricity: 110V, 60 Hz, 2-pin plug
National holiday: Independence Day, 27 February (1844)

▶ **GEOGRAPHY**

Location: Caribbean, eastern two-thirds of the island of Hispaniola, between the Caribbean Sea and the North Atlantic Ocean, east of Haiti
Border countries: Haiti 360 km
Area: 48,730 sq km
Coastline: 1,288 km
Climate: tropical maritime; little seasonal temperature variation; seasonal variation in rainfall

Terrain: rugged highlands and mountains with fertile valleys interspersed
lowest point: Lago Enriquillo -46 m
highest point: Pico Duarte 3,175 m
Natural hazards: lies in the middle of the hurricane belt and subject to severe storms from June to October; occasional flooding; periodic droughts
Vaccination(s): No vaccination requirements for any international traveller. **Malaria:** Low malaria risk—exclusively due to *P. falciparum*—exists throughout the year, especially in rural areas of the western provinces such as Castañuelas, Hondo Valle and Pepillo Salcedo. There is no evidence of *P. falciparum* resistance to any anti-malarial drug. Recommended prevention in risk areas: II

▶ **DIVING**

Number of certified divers: Mainly tourists
Dive federation(s): None
Dive regulations: Diver certification
Freediving federation(s): None
Major bodies of water: Caribbean Sea
Dive season: year-round
Water temperature: 25°C/77F (Jan-Mar), 28°C/82.4F (July-Sept)
Hyperbaric chambers:
City: Santo Domingo, Saint Souci Base
Telephone: (809) 592 3409,
City: Puerto Plata, Ricardo Limardo Hospital
Telephone: (809) 586 2210
Popular dive sites: The Limon, The San Jorge, Catalina Island, Three Rocks, Las Ballenas
Tourism information: Tourist Board of the Dominican Republic
(www.dominicanrepublic.com/Tourism)

EAST TIMOR (Timor-Leste)

▶ **GENERAL**

Capital: Dili
Government: Republic
Population: 1,040,880 (July 2005 est.)
Ethnic groups: Austronesian (Malayo-Polynesian), Papuan, small Chinese minority
Language(s): Tetum (official), Portuguese (official), Indonesian, English; *note:* there are about 16 indigenous languages; Tetum, Galole, Mambae, and Kemak are spoken by significant numbers of people
Religion(s): Roman Catholic 90%, Muslim 4%, Protestant 3%, Hindu 0.5%, Buddhist, Animist (1992 est.)
GDP per capita: $400 (2004 est.)
Currency: US dollar (USD)
Time: GMT + 9
Electricity: 220V, 50 Hz
National holiday: Independence Day, 28 November (1975)

▶ **GEOGRAPHY**

Location: Southeastern Asia, northwest of Australia in the Lesser Sunda Islands at the eastern end of the Indonesian archipelago; note - East Timor includes the eastern half of the island of Timor, the Oecussi (Ambeno) region on the northwest portion of the island of Timor, and the islands of Pulau Atauro and Pulau Jaco
Border countries: Indonesia 228 km
Area: 15,007 sq km
Coastline: 706 km
Climate: tropical; hot, humid; distinct rainy and dry seasons
Terrain: mountainous
lowest point: Timor Sea, Savu Sea, and Banda Sea 0 m

highest point: Foho Tatamailau 2,963 m
Natural hazards: floods and landslides are common; earthquakes, tsunamis, tropical cyclones
Vaccination(s): No vaccination requirements for any international traveller. **Malaria:** Malaria risk - Predominantly due to *P. falciparum*—exists throughout the year in the whole territory. *P. falciparum* resistant to chloroquine and sulfadoxine–pyrimethamine reported. Recommended prevention: IV

▶ **DIVING**

Number of certified divers: 250*
Dive federation(s): None
Dive regulations: Diver certification; no spear fishing on scuba. No taking of coral or protected species.*
Freediving federation(s): None*
Major bodies of water: Timor Sea, Savu Sea, Banda Sea
Dive season: March –December*
Water temperature: 29°C/84.2F (Jan-Mar), 26°C/78.8F (July-Sept)
Hyperbaric chambers:
Closest: Indonesia
Popular dive sites: K41, Dili Rock, Bob's Rock, Atauro, Com*
Tourism information: Turismo de Timor-Leste (www.turismotimorleste.com)
* SOURCE: FreeFlow (2006)

ECUADOR

▶ **GENERAL**

Capital: Quito
Government: Republic
Population: 13,363,593 (July 2005 est.)
Ethnic groups: mestizo (mixed Amerindian and white) 65%, Amerindian 25%, Spanish and others 7%, black 3%
Language(s): Spanish (official), Amerindian languages (especially Quechua)
Religion(s): Roman Catholic 95%, other 5%
GDP per capita: $3,700 (2004 est.)
Currency: US dollar (USD)
Time: GMT - 5
Electricity: 110V, 60Hz
National holiday: Independence Day (independence of Quito), 10 August (1809)

▶ **GEOGRAPHY**

Location: Western South America, bordering the Pacific Ocean at the Equator, between Colombia and Peru
Border countries: Colombia 590 km, Peru 1,420 km
Area: 283,560 sq km
Coastline: 2,237 km
Climate: tropical along coast, becoming cooler inland at higher elevations; tropical in Amazonian jungle lowlands

Terrain: coastal plain (costa), inter-Andean central highlands (sierra), and flat to rolling eastern jungle (oriente)
lowest point: Pacific Ocean 0 m
highest point: Chimborazo 6,267 m
Natural hazards: frequent earthquakes, landslides, volcanic activity; floods; periodic droughts
Vaccination(s): Yellow fever: A yellow fever vaccination certificate is required from travellers over 1 year of age coming from infected areas. Nationals and residents of Ecuador are required to possess certificates of vaccination on their departure to an infected area. **Malaria:** Malaria risk - *P. falciparum* (21%), *P. vivax* (79%) - exists throughout the year below 1500 m, with some risk in Cotopaxi, Loja and Los Rios. Higher transmission risk is found in El Oro, Esmeraldas and Manabi. There is no risk in Guayaquil or Quito. P.falciparum resistance to chloroquine and sulfadoxine-pyrimethamine reported. Recommended prevention in risk areas: IV

▶ **DIVING** (Incl. **Galapagos Islands**)

Number of certified divers: Mainly tourists
Dive federation(s): Federación Ecuatoriana De Buceo Y Actividades Subacuaticas
Dive regulations: Diver certification
Freediving federation(s): AIDA
Major bodies of water: Pacific Ocean
Dive season: year-round
Water temperature: 29°C/84.2F (Jan-Mar), 26°C/78.8F (July-Sept)
Hyperbaric chambers:
City: Santa Cruz island - Puerto Ayora, Hyperbaric Medical
Telephone: (593) 5-526-911
Popular dive sites: Galapagos, Darwin Island, Wolf Island

Tourism information: Ecuador Ministry of Tourism (www.vivecuador.com)

EGYPT

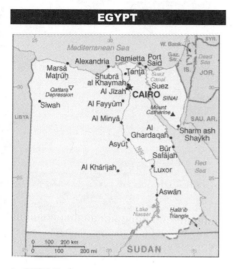

► **GENERAL**

Capital: Cairo
Government: Republic
Population: 77,505,756 (July 2005 est.)
Ethnic groups: Eastern Hamitic stock (Egyptians, Bedouins, and Berbers) 99%, Greek, Nubian, Armenian, other European (primarily Italian and French) 1%
Language(s): Arabic (official), English and French widely understood by educated classes
Religion(s): Muslim (mostly Sunni) 94%, Coptic Christian and other 6%
GDP per capita: $4,200 (2004 est.)
Currency: Egyptian pound (EGP) - Egyptian pounds per US dollar - 6.1963 (2004)
Time: GMT + 2
Electricity: 220V, 50 Hz
National holiday: Revolution Day, 23 July (1952)

► **GEOGRAPHY**

Location: Northern Africa, bordering the Mediterranean Sea, between Libya and the Gaza Strip, and the Red Sea north of Sudan, and includes the Asian Sinai Peninsula
Border countries: Gaza Strip 11 km, Israel 266 km, Libya 1,115 km, Sudan 1,273 km
Area: 1,001,450 sq km
Coastline: 2,450 km
Climate: desert; hot, dry summers with moderate winters
Terrain: vast desert plateau interrupted by Nile valley and delta
lowest point: Qattara Depression -133 m
highest point: Mount Catherine 2,629 m

Natural hazards: periodic droughts; frequent earthquakes, flash floods, landslides; hot, driving windstorm called khamsin occurs in spring; dust storms, sandstorms
Vaccination(s): Yellow fever: Yellow fever: A yellow fever vaccination certificate is required from travellers over 1 year of age coming from infected areas. **Malaria:** Very limited *P. falciparum* and *P. vivax* malaria risk may exist from June through October in El Faiyûm governorate (no indigenous cases reported since 1998). Recommended prevention: none

► **DIVING**

Number of certified divers: N/A
Dive federation(s): Egyptian Underwater & Lifesaving Federation
Dive regulations: Diver certification
Freediving federation(s): AIDA
Major bodies of water: Red Sea, Mediterranean Sea
Dive season: year-round
Water temperature: 20°C/68F (Jan-Mar), 27°C/80.6F (July-Sept)
Hyperbaric chambers:
Hyperbaric Medical Center
Phone +20 (69) 660 922/-3
Popular dive sites: Sharm El-Sheikh, Ras Mohamed, Dahab, Hurghada, Safaga, Qseir, Marsa Alam, Rocky and Daedelus
Tourism information: Egyptian Tourist Authority (www.egypttourism.org)

EL SALVADOR

► **GENERAL**

Capital: San Salvador
Government: Republic
Population: 6,704,932 (July 2005 est.)
Ethnic groups: mestizo 90%, white 9%, Amerindian 1%
Language(s): Spanish, Nahua (among some Amerindians)
Religion(s): Roman Catholic 83%, other 17%
GDP per capita: $4,900 (2004 est.)
Currency: US dollar (USD)
Time: GMT - 6
Electricity: 110V, 60 Hz
National holiday: Independence Day, 15 September (1821)

▶ **GEOGRAPHY**

Location: Central America, bordering the North Pacific Ocean, between Guatemala and Honduras

Border countries: Guatemala 203 km, Honduras 342 km

Area: 21,040 sq km

Coastline: 307 km

Climate: tropical; rainy season (May to October); dry season (November to April); tropical on coast; temperate in uplands

Terrain: mostly mountains with narrow coastal belt and central plateau

lowest point: Pacific Ocean 0 m

highest point: Cerro El Pital 2,730 m

Natural hazards: known as the Land of Volcanoes; frequent and sometimes very destructive earthquakes and volcanic activity; extremely susceptible to hurricanes

Vaccination(s): Yellow fever: A yellow fever vaccination certificate is required from travellers over 6 months of age coming from infected areas.

Malaria: Very low malaria risk—almost exclusively due to *P. vivax*—exists throughout the year in Santa Ana Province, in rural areas of migratory influence from Guatemala. Recommended prevention in risk areas: II

▶ **DIVING**

Number of certified divers: Mainly tourists

Dive federation(s): None

Dive regulations: Diver certification

Freediving federation(s): None

Major bodies of water: North Pacific Ocean

Dive season: year-round

Water temperature: 27°C/80.6F (Jan-Mar), 28°C/82.4F (July-Sept)

Hyperbaric chambers:

City: San Pedro

Popular dive sites: Los Cobanos, Coatepeque Lake, Ilopango Lake

Tourism information: Ministerio de Turismo (www.elsalvadorturismo.gob.sv)

ESTONIA

▶ **GENERAL**

Capital: Tallinn

Government: parliamentary republic

Population: 1,332,893 (July 2005 est.)

Ethnic groups: Estonian 67.9%, Russian 25.6%, Ukrainian 2.1%, Belarusian 1.3%, Finn 0.9%, other 2.2% (2000 census)

Language(s): Estonian (official) 67.3%, Russian 29.7%, other 2.3%, unknown 0.7% (2000 census)

Religion(s): Evangelical Lutheran 13.6%, Orthodox 12.8%, other Christian (including Methodist, Seventh-Day Adventist, Roman Catholic, Pentecostal) 1.4%, unaffiliated 34.1%, other and unspecified 32%, none 6.1% (2000 census)

GDP per capita: $14,300 (2004 est.)

Currency: Estonian kroon (EEK) - krooni per US dollar - 12.596 (2004)

Time: GMT +2

Electricity: 220V, 50 Hz, European 2-pin plug

National holiday: Independence Day, 24 February (1918)

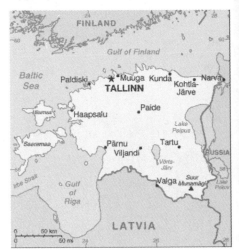

▶ **GEOGRAPHY**

Location: Eastern Europe, bordering the Baltic Sea and Gulf of Finland, between Latvia and Russia

Border countries: Latvia 339 km, Russia 294 km

Area: 45,226 sq km

Coastline: 3,794 km

Climate: maritime, wet, moderate winters, cool summers

Terrain: marshy, lowlands; flat in the north, hilly in the south

lowest point: Baltic Sea 0 m

highest point: Suur Munamagi 318 m

Natural hazards: sometimes flooding occurs in the spring

Vaccination(s): No vaccination requirements for any international traveller.

▶ **DIVING**

Number of certified divers: N/A

Dive federation(s): Eesti Allveeliit (EAL)

Dive regulations: Diver certification

Freediving federation(s): None*

Major bodies of water: Baltic Sea, Gulf of Finland, Gulf of Riga

Dive season: year-round

Water temperature: 3°C/37.4F (Jan-Mar), 14°C/57.2F (July-Sept)

Hyperbaric chambers: None

Popular dive sites: Lake Viljandi, Saadjärv*, wreck of the Polaris, wreck of the Jaen Täer, the Citadel, wreck of the Stalin **

Tourism information: Estonia Tourism (www.visitestonia.com)
*SOURCE: EAL
**SOURCE: Estonia Tourism (2006)

FIJI

▶ GENERAL

Capital: Suva (Viti Levu)
Government: republic
Population: 893,354 (July 2005 est.)
Ethnic groups: Fijian 51% (predominantly Melanesian with a Polynesian admixture), Indian 44%, European, other Pacific Islanders, overseas Chinese, and other 5% (1998 est.)
Language(s): English (official), Fijian, Hindustani
Religion(s): Christian 52% (Methodist 37%, Roman Catholic 9%), Hindu 38%, Muslim 8%, other 2% (1986)
GDP per capita: $5,900 (2004 est.)
Currency: Fijian dollar (FJD) - Fijian dollars per US dollar - 1.7331 (2004)
Time: GMT + 12
Electricity: 240V, 50 Hz
National holiday: Independence Day, second Monday of October (1970)

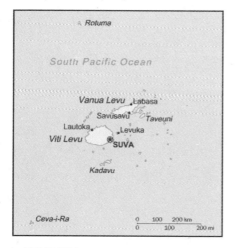

▶ GEOGRAPHY

Location: Oceania, island group in the South Pacific Ocean, about two-thirds of the way from Hawaii to New Zealand
Border countries: None
Area: 18,270 sq km
Coastline: 1,129 km
Climate: tropical marine; only slight seasonal temperature variation
Terrain: mostly mountains of volcanic origin
lowest point: Pacific Ocean *highest point:* Tomanivi 1,324 m

Natural hazards: cyclonic storms can occur from November to January
Vaccination(s): Yellow fever: A yellow fever vaccination certificate is required from travellers over 1 year of age entering Fiji within 10 days of having stayed overnight or longer in infected areas.

▶ DIVING

Number of certified divers: Mainly tourists
Dive federation(s): None
Dive regulations: Diver certification
Freediving federation(s): AIDA
Major bodies of water: South Pacific Ocean
Dive season: year-round
Water temperature: 27°C/80.6F (Jan-Mar), 22°C/71.6F (July-Sept)
Hyperbaric chambers:
City: Suva
Telephone: (679) 302 073
Popular dive sites: Chimneys, Yellow Wall, Great White Wall, Rainbow Reef, Bull Shark Dive, E-6
Tourism information: Fiji Visitors Bureau (www.bulafiji.com)

FINLAND

▶ GENERAL

Capital: Helsinki
Government: republic
Population: 5,223,442 (July 2005 est.)
Ethnic groups: Finn 93.4%, Swede 5.7%, Russian 0.4%, Estonian 0.2%, Roma 0.2%, Sami 0.1%
Language(s): Finnish 92% (official), Swedish 5.6% (official), other 2.4% (small Sami- and Russian-speaking minorities) (2003)
Religion(s): Lutheran National Church 84.2%, Greek Orthodox in Finland 1.1%, other Christian 1.1%, other 0.1%, none 13.5% (2003)
GDP per capita: $29,000 (2004 est.)
Currency: euro (EUR)
Time: GMT + 2
Electricity: 220V, 50Hz, European 2-pin plug
National holiday: Independence Day, 6 December (1917)

▶ GEOGAPHY

Location: Northern Europe, bordering the Baltic Sea, Gulf of Bothnia, and Gulf of Finland, between Sweden and Russia
Border countries: Norway 727 km, Sweden 614 km, Russia 1,340 km
Area: 338,145 sq km
Coastline: 1,250 km
Climate: cold temperate; potentially subarctic but comparatively mild because of moderating influence of the North Atlantic Current, Baltic Sea, and more than 60,000 lakes
Terrain: mostly low, flat to rolling plains interspersed with lakes and low hills
lowest point: Baltic Sea 0 m

highest point: Haltiatunturi 1,328 m
Natural hazards: NA
Vaccination(s): No vaccination requirements for any international traveller.

▶ **DIVING**

Number of certified divers: 50,000*
Dive federation(s): Finnish Divers' Federation
Dive regulations: Diver certification
Freediving federation(s): AIDA
Major bodies of water: South Pacific Ocean
Dive season: Year-round, ice diving in winter
Water temperature: 4°C/39.2F (Jan-Mar), 18°C/64.4F (July-Sept)
Hyperbaric chambers:
City: Turku University Hospital.
Telephone: (358) 2 2611212
City: Helsinki, Medioxygen
Telephone: +358 (0)9 454 0544

Popular dive sites: The Lehtojärvi Find, Lapuri Wreck, Vrouw Maria., Dive In Mines, Caves And Under Ice
Tourism information: Finnish Tourist Board (www.visitfinland.com)
* SOURCE: Live & Let Dive

FRANCE

▶ **GENERAL**

Capital: Paris
Government: republic
Population: 60,656,178 (July 2005 est.)
Ethnic groups: Celtic and Latin with Teutonic, Slavic, North African, Indochinese, Basque minorities
Language(s): French 100%, rapidly declining regional dialects and languages (Provencal, Breton, Alsatian, Corsican, Catalan, Basque, Flemish)
Religion(s): Roman Catholic 83%-88%, Protestant 2%, Jewish 1%, Muslim 5%-10%, unaffiliated 4%
GDP per capita: $28,700 (2004 est.)
Currency: euros per US dollar - 0.8054 (2004)
Time: GMT + 1
Electricity: 220 V, 50Hz, European 2-pin plug
National holiday: Bastille Day, 14 July (1789)

▶ **GEOGRAPHY**

Location: Western Europe, bordering the Bay of Biscay and English Channel, between Belgium and Spain, southeast of the UK; bordering the Mediterranean Sea, between Italy and Spain
Border countries: Andorra 56.6 km, Belgium 620 km, Germany 451 km, Italy 488 km, Luxembourg 73 km, Monaco 4.4 km, Spain 623 km, Switzerland 573 km
Area: 547,030 sq km
Coastline: 3,427 km

Climate: generally cool winters and mild summers, but mild winters and hot summers along the Mediterranean; occasional strong, cold, dry, north-to-northwesterly wind known as mistral
Terrain: mostly flat plains or gently rolling hills in north and west; remainder is mountainous, especially Pyrenees in south, Alps in east
lowest point: Rhone River delta -2 m
highest point: Mont Blanc 4,807 m
Natural hazards: flooding; avalanches; midwinter windstorms; drought; forest fires in south near the Mediterranean
Vaccination(s): No vaccination requirements for any international traveller.

▶ DIVING

Number of certified divers: Licensed under FFESSM 148,514*, total number: 340,000**
Dive federation(s): Fédération Française d'Études et de Sports Sous-Marins
Dive regulations: Diver certification
Freediving federation(s): Fédération Française d'Études et de Sports Sous-Marins* (AIDA)
Major bodies of water: Mediterranean Sea, North Atlantic Ocean, English Channel, Bay of Biscay
Dive season: year-round
Water temperature:
Atlantic: 13°C/55.4F (Jan-Mar), 18°C/64.4F (July-Sept). Mediterranean: 14°C/57.2F (Jan-Mar), 24°C/75.2F (July-Sept)
Hyperbaric chambers:
City: Le Havre, Hôpital J Monod
Telephone : 02.32.73.32.06
City : Bordeaux, Centre Hospitalier Pellegrin-Tripode
Telephone : 05.56.79.56.79
Popular dive sites: D-Day Wrecks, The Ussa, The Togo, Ile De Hyeres, The Dordogne/Lot Area
Tourism information: French Tourist Office (www.francetourism.com)
* SOURCE: FFESSM / Fédération française d'études et de sports sous-marins (2005)
** Study by the Ministère de la jeunesse, des sports et de la vie associative (Dec. 2005)

FRENCH POLYNESIA

▶ GENERAL

Capital: Papeete
Government: overseas lands of France; overseas territory of France from 1946-2004
Population: 270,485 (July 2005 est.)
Ethnic groups: Polynesian 78%, Chinese 12%, local French 6%, metropolitan French 4%
Language(s): French 61.1% (official), Polynesian 31.4% (official), Asian languages 1.2%, other 0.3%, unspecified 6% (2002 census)
Religion(s): Protestant 54%, Roman Catholic 30%, other 10%, no religion 6%
GDP per capita: $17,500 (2003 est.)

Currency: Comptoirs Français du Pacifique franc (XPF) - Comptoirs Français du Pacifique francs (XPF) per US dollar - 96.04 (2004)
Time: GMT - 10
Electricity: 220V, 60Hz, 2-pin plug
National holiday: Bastille Day, 14 July (1789)

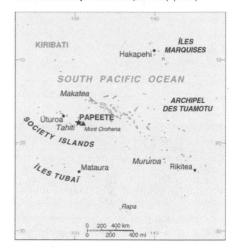

▶ GEOGRAPHY

Location: Oceania, archipelagoes in the South Pacific Ocean, about one-half of the way from South America to Australia
Border countries: None
Area: 4,167 sq km (118 islands and atolls)
Coastline: 2,525 km
Climate: tropical, but moderate
Terrain: mixture of rugged high islands and low islands with reefs
lowest point: Pacific Ocean 0 m
highest point: Mont Orohena 2,241 m
Natural hazards: flooding; avalanches; midwinter windstorms; drought; forest fires in south near the Mediterranean
Vaccination(s): Yellow fever: A yellow fever vaccination certificate is required from travellers over 1 year of age coming from infected areas.

▶ DIVING

Number of certified divers: 7,000*
Dive federation(s): Federation Tahitienne Des Sports Subaquatiques De Competition
Dive regulations: Diver certification
Freediving federation(s): None *
Major bodies of water: South Pacific Ocean
Dive season: year-round
Water temperature: 27°C/80.6F (Jan-Mar), 24°C/75.2F (July-Sept)
Hyperbaric chambers:
City: Papeete *

Popular dive sites: Tahiti, Moorea. Bora Bora, Rangiroa, Fakarava*
Tourism information: Tahiti Tourism (www.tahiti-tourisme.com)
* SOURCE: Topdive (2006)

GERMANY

▶ GENERAL

Capital: Berlin
Government: federal republic
Population: 82,431,390 (July 2005 est.)
Ethnic groups: German 91.5%, Turkish 2.4%, other 6.1% (made up largely of Greek, Italian, Polish, Russian, Serbo-Croatian, Spanish)
Language(s): German
Religion(s): Protestant 34%, Roman Catholic 34%, Muslim 3.7%, unaffiliated or other 28.3%
GDP per capita: $28,700 (2004 est.)
Currency: euro (EUR) - euros per US dollar - 0.8054 (2004)
Time: GMT + 1
Electricity: 230V, 50 Hz
National holiday: Unity Day, 3 October (1990)

▶ GEOGRAPHY

Location: Central Europe, bordering the Baltic Sea and the North Sea, between the Netherlands and Poland, south of Denmark
Border countries: Austria 784 km, Belgium 167 km, Czech Republic 646 km, Denmark 68 km, France 451 km, Luxembourg 138 km, Netherlands 577 km, Poland 456 km, Switzerland 334 km
Area: 357,021 sq km
Coastline: 2,389 km
Climate: temperate and marine; cool, cloudy, wet winters and summers; occasional warm mountain (foehn) wind

Terrain: lowlands in north, uplands in center, Bavarian Alps in south
lowest point: Neuendorf bei Wilster -3.54 m
highest point: Zugspitze 2,963 m
Natural hazards: flooding
Vaccination(s): No vaccination requirements for any international traveller.

▶ DIVING

Number of certified divers: N/A
Dive federation(s): Verband Deutscher Sporttaucher E.V.
Dive regulations: Diver certification
Freediving federation(s): AIDA
Major bodies of water: North Sea, Baltic Sea
Dive season: year-round, winter ice diving
Water temperature: 2°C/35.6F (Jan-Mar), 15°C/59F (July-Sept)
Hyperbaric chambers:
City: Berlin, HBOSAN, Institute for HBO -T
Tel: +49 - 30 - 4551708
City: Stuttgart, HBO-Zentrum-Stuttgart,
Tel: +49 711 5094453
Popular dive sites: Lake Constance, Lake Bodensee, Wreck diving and cave diving in the Baltic, Eckenforde Bucht, Fehman Peninsula
Tourism information: German Tourist Board (www.germany-tourism.de)

GIBRALTAR

▶ GENERAL

Capital: Gibraltar
Government: overseas territory of the UK
Population: 27,884 (July 2005 est.)
Ethnic groups: Spanish, Italian, English, Maltese, Portuguese, German, North Africans
Language(s): English (used in schools and for official purposes), Spanish, Italian, Portuguese

Religion(s): Roman Catholic 78.1%, Church of England 7%, other Christian 3.2%, Muslim 4%, Jewish 2.1%, Hindu 1.8%, other or unspecified 0.9%, none 2.9% (2001 census)
GDP per capita: $27,900 (2000 est.)
Currency: Gibraltar pound (GIP) - Gibraltar pounds per US dollar - 0.5462 (2004)
Time: GMT + 1
Electricity: 240V, 50Hz, round 2-pin plug
National holiday: National Day, 10 September (1967)

► GEOGRAPHY

Location: Southwestern Europe, bordering the Strait of Gibraltar, which links the Mediterranean Sea and the North Atlantic Ocean, on the southern coast of Spain
Border countries: Spain 1.2 km
Area: 6.5 sq km
Coastline: 12 km
Climate: Mediterranean with mild winters and warm summers
Terrain: a narrow coastal lowland borders the Rock of Gibraltar
lowest point: Mediterranean Sea 0 m
highest point: Rock of Gibraltar 426 m
Natural hazards: NA
Vaccination(s): No vaccination requirements for any international traveller.

► DIVING

Number of certified divers: Mainly tourists
Dive federation(s): None
Dive regulations: Diver certification
Freediving federation(s): None
Major bodies of water: Mediterranean Sea, North Atlantic Ocean
Dive season: year-round
Water temperature: 17°C/62.6F (Jan-Mar), 21°C/69.8F (July-Sept)
Hyperbaric chambers:
Closest: Spain
Popular dive sites: Bottle Site, Eastern Reef, Wrecks: The Helen, the SS Excellent and many others
Tourism information: Gibraltar Tourism (www.gibraltar.gov.gi)

GREECE

► GENERAL

Capital: Athens
Government: parliamentary republic; monarchy rejected by referendum 8 December 1974
Population: 10,668,354 (July 2005 est.)
Ethnic groups: Greek 98%, other 2%
Language(s): Greek 99% (official), English, French
Religion(s): Greek Orthodox 98%, Muslim 1.3%, other 0.7%
GDP per capita: $21,300 (2004 est.)

Currency: euro (EUR) - euros per US dollar - 0.8054 (2004)
Time: GMT + 2
Electricity: 220V, 50Hz
National holiday: Independence Day, 25 March (1821)

► GEOGRAPHY

Location: Southern Europe, bordering the Aegean Sea, Ionian Sea, and the Mediterranean Sea, between Albania and Turkey
Border countries: Albania 282 km, Bulgaria 494 km, Turkey 206 km, Macedonia 246 km
Area: 131,940 sq km
Coastline: 13,676 km
Climate: temperate; mild, wet winters; hot, dry summers
Terrain: mostly mountains with ranges extending into the sea as peninsulas or chains of islands
lowest point: Mediterranean Sea 0 m
highest point: Mount Olympus 2,917 m
Natural hazards: severe earthquakes
Vaccination(s): No vaccination requirements for any international traveller.

► DIVING

Number of certified divers: 600,000*
Dive federation(s): Hellenic Federation for Underwater Activities and Sportfishing, Finswimming
Dive regulations: Diver certification; not allowed to dive in the antiquities, not allowed to use a harpoon while scuba *
Freediving federation(s): AIDA
Major bodies of water: Mediterranean Sea, Aegean Sea, Ionian Sea
Dive season: May – October and year-round *
Water temperature: 16°C/60.8F (Jan-Mar), 28°C/82.4F (July-Sept)
Hyperbaric chambers:

City: Athens, Naval Hospital
Telephone: +302107216166
City: Athens, Hyperbaric Medicine Center
Telephone: +302103453982*
Popular dive sites: Santorini Island, Mykonos Island, Crete Island, Vouliagmeni – Athens, Zakynthos Island*
Tourism information: Greek National Tourism Organization (www.gnto.gr)
* SOURCE: IANTD Eastern Mediterranean (2006)

GRENADA

▶ GENERAL

Capital: Saint George's
Government: constitutional monarchy with Westminster-style parliament
Population: 89,502 (July 2005 est.)
Ethnic groups: black 82%, mixed black and European 13%, European and East Indian 5%, and trace of Arawak/Carib Amerindian
Language(s): English (official), French patois
Religion(s): Roman Catholic 53%, Anglican 13.8%, other Protestant 33.2%
GDP per capita: $5,000 (2002 est.)
Currency: East Caribbean dollar (XCD) - East Caribbean dollars per US dollar - 2.7 (2004)
Time: GMT - 4
Electricity: 220V, 50 Hz
National holiday: Independence Day, 7 February (1974)

▶ GEOGRAPHY

Location: Caribbean, island between the Caribbean Sea and Atlantic Ocean north of Trinidad and Tobago
Border countries: None
Area: 344 sq km
Coastline: 121 km

Climate: tropical; tempered by northeast trade winds
Terrain: volcanic in origin with central mountains
lowest point: Caribbean Sea 0 m
highest point: Mount Saint Catherine 840 m
Natural hazards: lies on edge of hurricane belt; hurricane season lasts from June to November
Vaccination(s): Yellow fever: A yellow fever vaccination certificate is required from travellers over 1 year of age coming from infected areas.

▶ DIVING

Number of certified divers: Mainly tourists
Dive federation(s): Grenada Scuba Diving Association
Dive regulations: Diver certification; no spear fishing on scuba, no removal of artefacts from wrecks*
Freediving federation(s): None
Major bodies of water: Caribbean Sea, North Atlantic Ocean
Dive season: year-round
Water temperature: 26°C78.8F (Jan-Mar), 28°C/82.4F (July-Sept)
Hyperbaric chambers: *
City: Barbados
Telephone: 1246-436-6185
City: Trinidad
Telephone: 1868-660-4000
Popular dive sites: Carriacou: Magic Garden, Barracuda Point, The Deep Blue, Westsider Wreck, Sharky's Hideaway. Grenada: Bianca C Wreck, Shark Reef, Shakem Wreck, Boss Reef, Flamingo Bay*
Tourism information: Grenada Board of Tourism (www.grenadagrenadines.com)
* SOURCE: Aquanauts Grenada; Grenada Scuba Diving Association (2006)

GUADELOUPE

▶ GENERAL

Capital: Basse-Terre
Government: overseas department of France
Population: 448,713 (July 2005 est.)
Ethnic groups: black or mulatto 90%, white 5%, East Indian, Lebanese, Chinese less than 5%
Language(s): French (official) 99%, Creole patois
Religion(s): Roman Catholic 95%, Hindu and pagan African 4%, Protestant 1%
GDP per capita: $7,900 (2003 est.)
Currency: euro (EUR) - euros per US dollar - 0.8054 (2004)
Time: GMT - 6
Electricity: 220V, 50Hz
National holiday: Bastille Day, 14 July (1789)

▶ GEOGRAPHY

Location: Caribbean, islands between the Caribbean Sea and the North Atlantic Ocean, southeast of Puerto Rico

Border countries: Netherlands Antilles (Sint Maarten) 10.2 km
Area: 1,780 sq km
Coastline: 306 km
Climate: subtropical tempered by trade winds; moderately high humidity
Terrain: Basse-Terre is volcanic in origin with interior mountains; Grande-Terre is low limestone formation; most of the seven other islands are volcanic in origin
lowest point: Caribbean Sea 0 m
highest point: Soufriere 1,484 m
Natural hazards: hurricanes (June to October); Soufriere de Guadeloupe is an active volcano
Vaccination(s): Yellow fever: A yellow fever vaccination certificate is required from travellers over 1 year of age coming from infected areas.

▶ **DIVING**

Number of certified divers: Mainly tourists
Dive federation(s): SNEPL guadeloupe, FFESSM
Dive regulations: Diver certification
Freediving federation(s): Commission d'apnée du corégua nicolas DIAZ
Major bodies of water: North Atlantic Ocean, Arctic Ocean
Dive season: year-round*
Water temperature: 26°C/78.8F (Jan-Mar), 27°C/80.6F (July-Sept)
Hyperbaric chambers:
City : au CHRU d'ABYMES - Pointe à pitre
Telephone: 05 90 89 11 22*
Popular dive sites: Ilets pigeon, Sec paté, Saintes, Saint Barthélémy, Saint Martin*
Tourism information: Comité du tourisme des îles de la Guadeloupe
(www.lesilesdeguadeloupe.com)

* SOURCE: Comité du tourisme des îles de Guadeloupe (2006)

GUAM

▶ **GENERAL**

Capital: Hagatna (Agana)
Government: organized, unincorporated territory of the US with policy relations between Guam and the US under the jurisdiction of the Office of Insular Affairs, US Department of the Interior
Population: 168,564 (July 2005 est.)
Ethnic groups: Chamorro 37.1%, Filipino 26.3%, other Pacific islander 11.3%, white 6.9%, other Asian 6.3%, other ethnic origin or race 2.3%, mixed 9.8% (2000 census)
Language(s): English 38.3%, Chamorro 22.2%, Philippine languages 22.2%, other Pacific island languages 6.8%, Asian languages 7%, other languages 3.5% (2000 census)
Religion(s): Roman Catholic 85%, other 15% (1999 est.)
GDP per capita: $21,000 (2000 est.)
Currency: US dollar (USD)
Time: GMT + 10
Electricity: 110V, 60Hz
National holiday: Discovery Day, first Monday in March (1521)

▶ **GEOGRAPHY**

Location: Oceania, island in the North Pacific Ocean, about three-quarters of the way from Hawaii to the Philippines
Border countries: None
Area: 549 sq km
Coastline: 125.5 km
Climate: tropical marine; generally warm and humid, moderated by northeast trade winds; dry

season from January to June, rainy season from July to December; little seasonal temperature variation
Terrain: volcanic origin, surrounded by coral reefs; relatively flat coralline limestone plateau (source of most fresh water), with steep coastal cliffs and narrow coastal plains in north, low hills in center, mountains in south
lowest point: Pacific Ocean 0 m
highest point: Mount Lamlam 406 m
Natural hazards: frequent squalls during rainy season; relatively rare, but potentially very destructive typhoons (June - December)
Vaccination(s): No vaccination requirements for any international traveller.

► **DIVING**

Number of certified divers: Mainly tourists
Dive federation(s): Guam Diving Industry Association*
Dive regulations: Diver certification; no decompression or overhead diving allowed without proper certification.**
Freediving federation(s): None **
Major bodies of water: North Pacific Ocean
Dive season: year-round **
Water temperature: 28°C/82.4F (Jan-Mar), 29°C/84.2F (July-Sept)
Hyperbaric chambers:
Harmon Doctors' Clinic
Telephone: 671 637 1777
Popular dive sites: Blue Hole, Crevice, Tokai Maru, Gab Gab 2, American Tanker **
Tourism information: Guam Visitors Bureau (www.visitguam.org)
* SOURCE: Guam Visitors Bureau
** SOURCE: Guam Tropical Dive Station

GUATEMALA

► **GENERAL**

Capital: Guatemala
Government: constitutional democratic republic
Population: 14,655,189 (July 2005 est.)
Ethnic groups: Mestizo (mixed Amerindian-Spanish - in local Spanish called Ladino) and European 59.4%, K'iche 9.1%, Kaqchikel 8.4%, Mam 7.9%, Q'eqchi 6.3%, other Mayan 8.6%, indigenous non-Mayan 0.2%, other 0.1% (2001 census)
Language(s): Spanish 60%, Amerindian languages 40% (23 officially recognized Amerindian languages, including Quiche, Cakchiquel, Kekchi, Mam, Garifuna, and Xinca)
Religion(s): Roman Catholic, Protestant, indigenous Mayan beliefs
GDP per capita: $4,200 (2004 est.)
Currency: quetzal (GTQ), US dollar (USD), others allowed - quetzales per US dollar - 7.9465 (2004)
Time: GMT - 6
Electricity: 115/125V, 60Hz

National holiday: Independence Day, 15 September (1821)

► **GEOGRAPHY**

Location: Central America, bordering the North Pacific Ocean, between El Salvador and Mexico, and bordering the Gulf of Honduras (Caribbean Sea) between Honduras and Belize
Border countries: Belize 266 km, El Salvador 203 km, Honduras 256 km, Mexico 962 km
Area: 108,890 sq km
Coastline: 400 km
Climate: tropical; hot, humid in lowlands; cooler in highlands
Terrain: mostly mountains with narrow coastal plains and rolling limestone plateau (Peten)
lowest point: Pacific Ocean 0 m
highest point: Volcan Tajumulco 4,211 m
Natural hazards: numerous volcanoes in mountains, with occasional violent earthquakes; Caribbean coast extremely susceptible to hurricanes and other tropical storms
Vaccination(s): Yellow fever: A yellow fever vaccination certificate is required from travellers over 1 year of age coming from countries with infected areas. **Malaria:** Malaria risk—predominantly due to *P. vivax*—exists throughout the year below 1500 m. There is high risk in the departments of Alta Verapaz, Baja Verapaz, Petén and San Marcos, and moderate risk in the departments of Escuintla, Huehuetenango, Izabal, Quiché, Retalhuleu, Suchitepéquez and Zacapa. Recommended prevention in risk areas: II

► **DIVING**

Number of certified divers: 12,300*
Dive federation(s): None
Dive regulations: Diver certification
Freediving federation(s): None

Major bodies of water: North Pacific Ocean, Caribbean Sea
Dive season: year-round
Water temperature: 26°C/78.8F (Jan-Mar), 28°C/82.4F (July-Sept)
Hyperbaric chambers:
City: Guatemala city*
Popular dive sites: Cabo Tres Puntas, Bahia de Amatique, Cayos de Belice, Cayo Limon, Lago Atitlan, Pacifico*
Tourism information: Turismo Guatemala (www.guatemala.travel.com.gt)
* SOURCE: Scuba World (2006)

HAITI

▶ **GENERAL**

Capital: Port-au-Prince
Government: elected government
Population: 8,121,622 (July 2005 est.)
Ethnic groups: black 95%, mulatto and white 5%
Language(s): French (official), Creole (official)
Religion(s): Roman Catholic 80%, Protestant 16% (Baptist 10%, Pentecostal 4%, Adventist 1%, other 1%), none 1%, other 3% (1982); *note:* roughly half of the population practices Voodoo
GDP per capita: $1,500 (2004 est.)
Currency: gourde (HTG) - gourdes per US dollar - 38.352 (2004)
Time: GMT - 5
Electricity: 110V, 60Hz
National holiday: Independence Day, 1 January (1804)

▶ **GEOGRAPHY**

Location: Caribbean, western one-third of the island of Hispaniola, between the Caribbean Sea and the North Atlantic Ocean, west of the Dominican Republic

Border countries: Dominican Republic 360 km
Area: 27,750 sq km
Coastline: 1,771 km
Climate: tropical; semiarid where mountains in east cut off trade winds
Terrain: mostly rough and mountainous
lowest point: Caribbean Sea 0 m
highest point: Chaine de la Selle 2,680 m
Natural hazards: lies in the middle of the hurricane belt and subject to severe storms from June to October; occasional flooding and earthquakes; periodic droughts
Vaccination(s): Yellow fever: A yellow fever vaccination certificate is required from travellers coming from infected areas. **Malaria:** Malaria risk—exclusively due to *P. falciparum*—exists throughout the year in certain forest areas in Chantal, Gros Morne, Hinche, Jacmel and Maissade. In the other cantons, risk is estimated to be low. No *P. falciparum* resistance to chloroquine reported. Recommended prevention in risk areas: II

▶ **DIVING**

Number of certified divers: 100*
Dive federation(s): None
Dive regulations: Diver certification
Freediving federation(s): La Cooperative des Pecheurs de LULY
Major bodies of water: Caribbean Sea
Dive season: year-round
Water temperature: 26°C/78.8F (Jan-Mar), 28°C/82.4F (July-Sept)
Hyperbaric chambers:
Closest: Naval Base 27 Febrero San Souci Santo Domingo RD, (809) 592-3409 (Day time Medical Corp) (809) 592-3412 (EmergencyService direct Naval Base: Guantanamo Bay CUBA*
Popular dive sites: Le tombant de La Gonave, Les Arcadins, Tina D Wreck, Eva's, L'ile de la Tortue*
Tourism information: Secrétairerie d'Etat au Tourisme (www.haititourisme.org)
* SOURCE: Pegasus Diving & Service (2006)

HONDURAS

▶ **GENERAL**

Capital: Tegucigalpa
Government: democratic constitutional republic
Population: 6,975,204
Ethnic groups: mestizo (mixed Amerindian and European) 90%, Amerindian 7%, black 2%, white 1%
Language(s): Spanish, Amerindian dialects
Religion(s): Roman Catholic 97%, Protestant 3%
GDP per capita: $2,800 (2004 est.)
Currency: lempira (HNL) - lempiras per US dollar - 18.206 (2004)
Time: GMT - 6
Electricity: 110V, 60Hz, 220V

National holiday: Independence Day, 15 September (1821)

► **GEOGRAPHY**

Location: Central America, bordering the Caribbean Sea, between Guatemala and Nicaragua and bordering the Gulf of Fonseca (North Pacific Ocean), between El Salvador and Nicaragua
Border countries: Guatemala 256 km, El Salvador 342 km, Nicaragua 922 km
Area: 112,090 sq km
Coastline: 820 km
Climate: subtropical in lowlands, temperate in mountains
Terrain: mostly mountains in interior, narrow coastal plains
lowest point: Caribbean Sea 0 m
highest point: Cerro Las Minas 2,870 m
Natural hazards: frequent, but generally mild, earthquakes; extremely susceptible to damaging hurricanes and floods along the Caribbean coast
Vaccination(s): Yellow fever: A yellow fever vaccination certificate is required from travellers coming from infected areas. **Malaria:** Malaria risk—predominantly due to *P. vivax*—is high throughout the year in 223 municipalities. Transmission risk is low in the other 71 municipalities, including San Pedro Sula and the city of Tegucigalpa. *P. falciparum* risk is the highest in Sanitary Region VI, including in the Islas de la Bahía. Recommended prevention: II

► **DIVING**

Number of certified divers: Mainly tourists
Dive federation(s): None
Dive regulations: Diver certification
Freediving federation(s): None
Major bodies of water: Caribbean Sea
Dive season: year-round: best: sept. - June

Water temperature: 26°C78.8F (Jan-Mar), 28°C/82.4F (July-Sept)
Hyperbaric chambers:
City: Roatan, Anthony's Key Resort
Telephone: (504) 45-10-49
Popular dive sites: Roatan: West End Wall, Enchanted Forest, The Bay Islands, El Aquila, The Odyssey; Tthe Prince Albert
Tourism information: Official Online Travel Guide of Honduras (www.letsgohonduras.com)

HONG KONG

► **GENERAL**

Capital: NA
Government: special administrative region of China
Population: 6,898,686 (July 2005 est.)
Ethnic groups: Chinese 95%, other 5%
Language(s): Chinese (Cantonese), English; both are official
Religion(s): eclectic mixture of local religions 90%, Christian 10%
GDP per capita: $34,200 (2004 est.)
Currency: Hong Kong dollar (HKD) - Hong Kong dollars per US dollar - 7.788 (2004)
Time: GMT + 8
Electricity: 220V, 50Hz
National holiday: National Day (Anniversary of the Founding of the People's Republic of China), 1 October (1949); note - 1 July 1997 is celebrated as Hong Kong Special Administrative Region Establishment Day

► **GEOGRAPHY**

Location: Eastern Asia, bordering the South China Sea and China
Border countries: China 30 km
Area: 1,092 sq km

Coastline: 820 km
Climate: tropical monsoon; cool and humid in winter, hot and rainy from spring through summer, warm and sunny in fall
Terrain: hilly to mountainous with steep slopes; lowlands in north
lowest point: South China Sea 0 m
highest point: Tai Mo Shan 958 m
Natural hazards: occasional typhoons
Vaccination(s): No vaccination requirements for any international traveller.

▶ **DIVING**

Number of certified divers: 20,000*
Dive federation(s): Hong Kong Underwater Association Limited
Dive regulations: Diver certification
Freediving federation(s): None
Major bodies of water: South China Sea
Dive season: year-round
Water temperature: 26°C/78.8F (Jan-Mar), 28°C/82.4F (July-Sept)
Hyperbaric chambers:
Hong Kong Diving and Hyperbaric Center
Telephone: 852) 2422-7733
Popular dive sites: Breaker Reef, Aberdeen, Sharp Island, The Ramp, Big Wave Bay
Tourism information: Hong Kong Tourism Board (www.discoverhongkong.com)
*Source: scubanet.hk

HUNGARY

▶ **GENERAL**

Capital: Budapest
Government: parliamentary democracy
Population: 10,006,835 (July 2005 est.)
Ethnic groups: Hungarian 92.3%, Roma 1.9%, other or unknown 5.8% (2001 census)
Language(s): Hungarian 93.6%, other or unspecified 6.4% (2001 census)
Religion(s): Roman Catholic 51.9%, Calvinist 15.9%, Lutheran 3%, Greek Catholic 2.6%, other Christian 1%, other or unspecified 11.1%, unaffiliated 14.5% (2001 census)
GDP per capita: $14,900 (2004 est.)
Currency: forint (HUF) - forints per US dollar - 202.75 (2004)
Time: GMT + 1
Electricity: 230V, 50Hz

National holiday: Saint Stephen's Day, 20 August

▶ **GEOGRAPHY**

Location: Central Europe, northwest of Romania
Border countries: Austria 366 km, Croatia 329 km, Romania 443 km, Serbia and Montenegro 151 km, Slovakia 677 km, Slovenia 102 km, Ukraine 103 km
Area: 93,030 sq km
Coastline: None
Climate: temperate; cold, cloudy, humid winters; warm summers
Terrain: mostly flat to rolling plains; hills and low mountains on the Slovakian border
lowest point: Tisza River 78 m
highest point: Kekes 1,014 m
Natural hazards: occasional typhoons
Vaccination(s): No vaccination requirements for any international traveller.

▶ **DIVING**

Number of certified divers: N/A
Dive federation(s): Hungarian Divers Federation; AMPHORA Búvár Klub
Dive regulations: Diver certification
Freediving federation(s): AIDA
Major bodies of water: Lake Balaton
Dive season: year-round possible,
Water temperature: 29°C (Jan-Mar), 35°C (July-Sept)
Hyperbaric chambers: N/A
Closest: Germany
Popular dive sites: Lake Heviz (thermal lake: 25-29C year-round), Lake Cave Tapolca,
Tourism information: Hungarian National Tourist Office (www.hungarytourism.hu)

ICELAND

▶ **GENERAL**

Capital: Reykjavik
Government: constitutional republic
Population: 296,737 (July 2005 est.)
Ethnic groups: homogeneous mixture of descendants of Norse and Celts 94%, population of foreign origin 6%
Language(s): Icelandic, English, Nordic languages, German widely spoken
Religion(s): Lutheran Church of Iceland 85.5%, Reykjavik Free Church 2.1%, Roman Catholic Church 2%, Hafnarfjorour Free Church 1.5%, other Christian 2.7%, other or unspecified 3.8%, unaffiliated 2.4% (2004)
GDP per capita: $31,900 (2004 est.)
Currency: Icelandic krona (ISK) - Icelandic kronur per US dollar - 70.192 (2004)
Time: GMT +0
Electricity: 220V, 50Hz, European 2-pin plug
National holiday: Independence Day, 17 June (1944)

▶ **GEOGRAPHY**

Location: Northern Europe, island between the Greenland Sea and the North Atlantic Ocean, northwest of the UK
Border countries: None
Area: 103,000 sq km
Coastline: 4,988 km
Climate: temperate; moderated by North Atlantic Current; mild, windy winters; damp, cool summers
Terrain: mostly plateau interspersed with mountain peaks, icefields; coast deeply indented by bays and fiords
lowest point: Atlantic Ocean 0 m
highest point: Hvannadalshnukur 2,119 m (at Vatnajokull glacier)
Natural hazards: earthquakes and volcanic activity
Vaccination(s): No vaccination requirements for any international traveller.

▶ **DIVING**

Number of certified divers: 1,400*
Dive federation(s): Sportkafarafélag Íslands / Icelandic Sportdiving Association*
Dive regulations: Diver certification
Freediving federation(s): None
Major bodies of water: North Atlantic Ocean, Greenland Sea
Dive season: year-round
Water temperature: 5°C/41F (Jan-Mar), 12°C/53.6F (July-Sept)
Hyperbaric chambers:
Landspitali Fossvogi
Telephone: (354) 543-1007
Popular dive sites: Silfra, Thingvellir. Strytan, Eyjafjafjordur, El Grillo, Seidisfjordur, Davidsgja, Thingvellir, Hindisvik, Hunavatnssysla*
Tourism information: Icelandic Tourist Board (www.icetourist.is)

* SOURCE: Kofun (2006)

INDIA

▶ **GENERAL**

Capital: New Delhi
Government: federal republic
Population: 1,080,264,388 (July 2005 est.)
Ethnic groups: Indo-Aryan 72%, Dravidian 25%, Mongoloid and other 3% (2000)
Language(s): English enjoys associate status but is the most important language for national, political, and commercial communication; Hindi is the national language and primary tongue of 30% of the people; there are 14 other official languages: Bengali, Telugu, Marathi, Tamil, Urdu, Gujarati, Malayalam, Kannada, Oriya, Punjabi, Assamese, Kashmiri, Sindhi, and Sanskrit; Hindustani is a popular variant of Hindi/Urdu spoken widely throughout northern India but is not an official language
Religion(s): Hindu 80.5%, Muslim 13.4%, Christian 2.3%, Sikh 1.9%, other 1.8%, unspecified 0.1% (2001 census)
GDP per capita: $3,100 (2004 est.)
Currency: Indian rupee (INR) - Indian rupees per US dollar - 45.317 (2004)
Time: GMT +5.5
Electricity: 220V, 50Hz
National holiday: Republic Day, 26 January (1950)

▶ **GEOGRAPHY**

Location: Southern Asia, bordering the Arabian Sea and the Bay of Bengal, between Burma and Pakistan
Border countries: Bangladesh 4,053 km, Bhutan 605 km, Burma 1,463 km, China 3,380 km, Nepal 1,690 km, Pakistan 2,912 km
Area: 3,287,590 sq km
Coastline: 7,000 km
Climate: varies from tropical monsoon in south to temperate in north
Terrain: upland plain (Deccan Plateau) in south, flat to rolling plain along the Ganges, deserts in west, Himalayas in north
lowest point: Indian Ocean 0 m
highest point: Kanchenjunga 8,598 m
Natural hazards: droughts; flash floods, as well as widespread and destructive flooding from monsoonal rains; severe thunderstorms; earthquakes
Vaccination(s): Yellow fever: Anyone (except infants up to the age of 6 months) arriving by air or sea without a certificate is detained in isolation for up to 6 days if that person (i) arrives within 6 days of departure from an infected area, or (ii) has been in such an area in transit (excepting those passengers and members of the crew who, while in transit through an airport situated in an infected area, remained within the airport premises during the period of their entire stay and the Health Officer agrees to such exemption), or (iii)

has come on a ship that started from or touched at any port in a yellow fever infected area up to 30 days before its arrival in India, unless such a ship has been disinfected in accordance with the procedure laid down by WHO, or (iv) has come by an aircraft which has been in an infected area and has not been disinsected in accordance with the provisions laid down in the Indian Aircraft Public Health Rules, 1954, or those recommended by WHO. **Malaria:** Malaria risk exists throughout the year in the whole country below 2000 m, with 40% to 50% of cases due to *P. falciparum*. There is no transmission in parts of the states of Himachal Pradesh, Jammu and Kashmir, and Sikkim. *P. falciparum* resistance to chloroquine and sulfadoxine–pyrimethamine reported. Recommended prophylaxis in risk areas: III. In Assam: IV

▶ DIVING

Number of certified divers: N/A
Dive federation(s): None
Dive regulations: Diver certification
Freediving federation(s): None
Major bodies of water: Indian Ocean, Arabian Sea, Bay of Bengal
Dive season: year-round: best: Nov.-May
Water temperature: 27°C/80.6F (Jan-Mar), 28.5°C/83F (July-Sept)
Hyperbaric chambers:
City: New Delhi Apollo Hospital Sarita Vihar
Telephone: -6925721
Popular dive sites: The Andamans, Lakswadweep Islands, Agatti Island, Nicobar Islands
Tourism information: Ministry of Tourism (www.tourisminindia.com)

INDONESIA

▶ GENERAL

Capital: Jakarta
Government: republic
Population: 241,973,879 (July 2005 est.)
Ethnic groups: Javanese 45%, Sundanese 14%, Madurese 7.5%, coastal Malays 7.5%, other 26%
Language(s): Bahasa Indonesia (official, modified form of Malay), English, Dutch, local dialects, the most widely spoken of which is Javanese
Religion(s): Muslim 88%, Protestant 5%, Roman Catholic 3%, Hindu 2%, Buddhist 1%, other 1% (1998)
GDP per capita: $3,500 (2004 est.)
Currency: Indonesian rupiah (IDR) - Indonesian rupiahs per US dollar - 8,938.9 (2004)
Time: GMT +7, +8, +9
Electricity: 220V, 50Hz, Round 2-pin plug
National holiday: Independence Day, 17 August (1945)

▶ GEOGRAPHY

Location: Southeastern Asia, archipelago between the Indian Ocean and the Pacific Ocean
Border countries: East Timor 228 km, Malaysia 1,782 km, Papua New Guinea 820 km
Area: 1,919,440 sq km
Coastline: 54,716 km
Climate: tropical; hot, humid; more moderate in highlands
Terrain: mostly coastal lowlands; larger islands have interior mountains
lowest point: Indian Ocean 0 m
highest point: Puncak Jaya 5,030 m
Natural hazards: occasional floods, severe droughts, tsunamis, earthquakes, volcanoes, forest fires
Vaccination(s): Yellow fever: A yellow fever vaccination certificate is required from travellers coming from infected areas. The countries and areas included in the endemic zones are considered by Indonesia as infected areas. **Malaria:** Malaria risk exists throughout the year in the whole country except in Jakarta Municipality, big cities, and within the areas of the tourist resorts of Bali and Java. *P. falciparum* resistant to chloroquine and sulfadoxine–pyrimethamine reported.

P. vivax resistant to chloroquine reported. Recommended prevention in risk areas: IV

▶ **DIVING**

Number of certified divers: 2,000*
Dive federation(s): Indonesian Subaquatic Sport Association (ISSA)
Dive regulations: Diver certification
Freediving federation(s): AIDA
Major bodies of water: Indian Ocean, South Pacific Ocean
Dive season: April to October
Water temperature: 27°C/80.6F (Jan-Mar), 27°C/80.6F (July-Sept)
Hyperbaric chambers:
City: Jakarta
City: Surabaya*
Popular dive sites: Manado , North Sulawesi, Bali, Lombok, Thousand Islands, Derawan, Kalimantan*
Tourism information: Indonesia Culture and Tourism Ministry (www.budpar.go.id); Indonesia Tourism (www.indonesiatourism.com); Indonesia and Bali Tourism (www.indonesia-tourism.com)
* SOURCE: POSSI (Dec. 2005)

IRAN

▶ **GENERAL**

Capital: Tehran
Government: theocratic republic
Population: 68,017,860 (July 2005 est.)
Ethnic groups: Persian 51%, Azeri 24%, Gilaki and Mazandarani 8%, Kurd 7%, Arab 3%, Lur 2%, Baloch 2%, Turkmen 2%, other 1%
Language(s): Persian and Persian dialects 58%, Turkic and Turkic dialects 26%, Kurdish 9%, Luri 2%, Balochi 1%, Arabic 1%, Turkish 1%, other 2%
Religion(s): Shi'a Muslim 89%, Sunni Muslim 9%, Zoroastrian, Jewish, Christian, and Baha'i 2%
GDP per capita: $7,700 (2004 est.)
Currency: Iranian rial (IRR) - rials per US dollar - 8,614 (2004)
Time: GMT + 3.5
Electricity: 220V, 50Hz
National holiday: Republic Day, 1 April (1979)

▶ **GEOGRAPHY**

Location: Middle East, bordering the Gulf of Oman, the Persian Gulf, and the Caspian Sea, between Iraq and Pakistan
Border countries: Afghanistan 936 km, Armenia 35 km, Azerbaijan-proper 432 km, Azerbaijan-Naxcivan exclave 179 km, Iraq 1,458 km, Pakistan 909 km, Turkey 499 km, Turkmenistan 992 km
Area: 1.648 million sq km
Coastline: 2,440 km; note - Iran also borders the Caspian Sea (740 km)
Climate: mostly arid or semiarid, subtropical along Caspian coast

Terrain: rugged, mountainous rim; high, central basin with deserts, mountains; small, discontinuous plains along both coasts
lowest point: Caspian Sea -28 m
highest point: Kuh-e Damavand 5,671 m

Natural hazards: periodic droughts, floods; dust storms, sandstorms; earthquakes
Vaccination(s): No vaccination requirements for any international traveller. **Malaria:** Limited risk—exclusively due to *P. vivax*—exists during the summer months in Ardebil and East Azerbijan provinces north of the Zagros mountains. Malaria risk due to *P. falciparum* exists from March through November in rural areas of the provinces of Hormozgan, Kerman (tropical part) and the southern part of Sistan–Baluchestan. P. falciparum resistant to chloroquine and sulfadoxine–pyrimethamine reported. Recommended prevention: II in *P. vivax* risk areas; IV in *P. falciparum* risk areas.

▶ **DIVING**

Number of certified divers: 3,200*
Dive federation(s): Islamic Republic Of Iran Lifesaving Federation
Dive regulations: Diver certification
Freediving federation(s): None*
Major bodies of water: Persian Gulf, Gulf of Oman, Caspian Sea
Dive season: year-round*
Water temperature: 19°C/66.2F (Jan-Mar), 26°C/78.8F (July-Sept)
Hyperbaric chambers:
City: Bandar abbas
City: Bushehr*
Popular dive sites: Hendorabi, Kish Island sites: Big Coral, Jurassic park, Southern reef, Oyster bank*
Tourism information: Iran Tourism & Touring organisation (http://itto.org)
* SOURCE: Iran Scuba Diver (2006)

IRELAND

▶ GENERAL

Capital: Dublin
Government: republic
Population: 4,015,676 (July 2005 est.)
Ethnic groups: Celtic, English
Language(s): English (official) is the language generally used, Irish (official) (Gaelic or Gaeilge) spoken mainly in areas located along the western seaboard
Religion(s): Roman Catholic 88.4%, Church of Ireland 3%, other Christian 1.6%, other 1.5%, unspecified 2%, none 3.5% (2002 census)
GDP per capita: $31,900 (2004 est.)
Currency: euro (EUR) - euros per US dollar - 0.8054 (2004)
Time: GMT + 0
Electricity: 220V, 50Hz
National holiday: Saint Patrick's Day, 17 March

▶ GEOGRAPHY

Location: Western Europe, occupying five-sixths of the island of Ireland in the North Atlantic Ocean, west of Great Britain
Border countries: UK 360 km
Area: 70,280 sq km
Coastline: 1,448 km
Climate: temperate maritime; modified by North Atlantic Current; mild winters, cool summers; consistently humid; overcast about half the time
Terrain: mostly level to rolling interior plain surrounded by rugged hills and low mountains; sea cliffs on west coast
lowest point: Atlantic Ocean 0 m
highest point: Carrauntoohil 1,041 m
Natural hazards: NA

Vaccination(s): No vaccination requirements for any international traveller.

▶ DIVING

Number of certified divers: N/A
Dive federation(s): The Irish Underwater Council (IUC)
Dive regulations: Diver certification
Freediving federation(s): British Freediving Association
Major bodies of water: North Atlantic Ocean, Irish Sea, Celtic Sea
Dive season: year-round
Water temperature: 7°C/44.6F (Jan-Mar), 15°C/59F (July-Sept)
Hyperbaric chambers:
City: Dublin, National Hyperbaric Centre
Telephone: 00 353 87 972 9366
City: Galway, Galway Regional Hospital.
Telephone: 00 353 91 24???
Popular dive sites: Skerries Cavern Inistrahull Island,.Shamrock Pinnacle, Wrecks: Girona, Hms Drake
Tourism information: Ireland Tourist Board (www.ireland.ie); Tourism Ireland (www.shamrock.org);
Official Guide (www.tourismireland.com)

ISRAEL

▶ GENERAL

Capital: Jerusalem; note - Israel proclaimed Jerusalem as its capital in 1950, but the US, like nearly all other countries, maintains its Embassy in Tel Aviv
Government: parliamentary democracy
Population: 6,276,883 (July 2005 est.)
Ethnic groups: Jewish 80.1% (Europe/America-born 32.1%, Israel-born 20.8%, Africa-born 14.6%, Asia-born 12.6%), non-Jewish 19.9% (mostly Arab) (1996 est.)
Language(s): Hebrew (official), Arabic used officially for Arab minority, English most commonly used foreign language
Religion(s): Jewish 76.5%, Muslim 15.9%, Arab Christians 1.7%, other Christian 0.4%, Druze 1.6%, unspecified 3.9% (2003)
GDP per capita: $20,800 (2004 est.)
Currency: new Israeli shekel (ILS) - new Israeli shekels per US dollar - 4.482 (2004)
Time: GMT + 2
Electricity: 220V, 50Hz
National holiday: Independence Day, 14 May (1948)

▶ GEOGRAPHY

Location: Middle East, bordering the Mediterranean Sea, between Egypt and Lebanon

Border countries: Egypt 266 km, Gaza Strip 51 km, Jordan 238 km, Lebanon 79 km, Syria 76 km, West Bank 307 km
Area: 20,770 sq km
Coastline: 273 km
Climate: temperate; hot and dry in southern and eastern desert areas
Terrain: Negev desert in the south; low coastal plain; central mountains; Jordan Rift Valley
lowest point: Dead Sea -408 m
highest point: Har Meron 1,208 m
Natural hazards: sandstorms may occur during spring and summer; droughts; periodic earthquakes
Vaccination(s): No vaccination requirements for any international traveler.

▶ **DIVING**

Number of certified divers: 120,000*
Dive federation(s): Israeli Diving Federation**
Dive regulations: Diver certification, personal dive insurance**
Freediving federation(s): Free Diving Israel (AIDA)

Major bodies of water: Mediterranean Sea, Gulf of Aqaba (Red Sea)
Dive season: year-round*
Water temperature: Eilat: 21°C/70F Haifa: 12°C/53.6F (Jan-Mar), Eilat: 27°C/80.6F Haifa: 27°C/80.6F (July-Sept)
Hyperbaric chambers:
City: Haifa, Assaf Ha Rofe Hospital
City: Rambam, Hospital*
City: Eilat, Yoseftal Hospital
Telephone: + 972 8 635011**
Popular dive sites: Eilat - Japanese Gardens, Eilat- Coral Beach, Eilat- Satil Wreck, Eilat - South Beach, Eilat- University* ; Japanese Gardens, Moses Rock, The Caves, Satil (Wreck), Aqua Sport Coral Beach**
Tourism information: Israel Ministry of Tourism (www.goisrael.com)
* SOURCE: Manta Diving Center (2006)
** SOURCE: Aqua-Sport Int. (2006)

ITALY

▶ **GENERAL**

Capital: Rome
Government: republic
Population: 58,103,033 (July 2005 est.)
Ethnic groups: Italian (includes small clusters of German-, French-, and Slovene-Italians in the north and Albanian-Italians and Greek-Italians in the south)
Language(s): Italian (official), German (parts of Trentino-Alto Adige region are predominantly German speaking), French (small French-speaking minority in Valle d'Aosta region), Slovene (Slovene-speaking minority in the Trieste-Gorizia area)
Religion(s): predominately Roman Catholic with mature Protestant and Jewish communities and a growing Muslim immigrant community

GDP per capita: $27,700 (2004 est.)
Currency: euro (EUR) - euros per US dollar - 0.8054 (2004)
Time: GMT + 1
Electricity: 220V, 50Hz
National holiday: Republic Day, 2 June (1946)

▶ GEOGRAPHY

Location: Southern Europe, a peninsula extending into the central Mediterranean Sea, northeast of Tunisia
Border countries: Austria 430 km, France 488 km, Holy See (Vatican City) 3.2 km, San Marino 39 km, Slovenia 232 km, Switzerland 740 km
Area: 301,230 sq km
Coastline: 7,600 km
Climate: predominantly Mediterranean; Alpine in far north; hot, dry in south
Terrain: mostly rugged and mountainous; some plains, coastal lowlands
lowest point: Mediterranean Sea 0 m
highest point: Mont Blanc (Monte Bianco) de Courmayeur 4,748 m (a secondary peak of Mont Blanc)
Natural hazards: regional risks include landslides, mudflows, avalanches, earthquakes, volcanic eruptions, flooding; land subsidence in Venice
Vaccination(s): No vaccination requirements for any international traveller.

▶ DIVING

Number of certified divers: N/A
Dive federation(s): Federation Italienne De La Peche Sportive Et Des Activites Subaquatiques (FISASUB); European Scuba Agency
Dive regulations: Diver certification
Freediving federation(s): AIDA
Major bodies of water: Mediterranean Sea, Adriatic Sea, Ionian Sea, Tyrrhenian Sea
Dive season: year-round, best: april – Oct.
Water temperature: 15°C/59F (Jan-Mar), 24°C/75.2F (July-Sept)
Hyperbaric chambers:
City: Rome, University La Sapienza
Telepone: (24h) +39 06 49970424
City: Siracusa, Azienda Ospedaliera Umberto I°
Telephone +390931724172
Popular dive sites: Costa Paradiso, Sardinia, Minahasa Lagoon , Tremeti Islands, The Grottoes of Giusti, Lake Fibreno
Tourism information: Italian Government Tourist Board (www.italiantourism.com)

JAMAICA

▶ GENERAL

Capital: Kingston
Government: constitutional parliamentary democracy
Population: 2,731,832 (July 2005 est.)

Ethnic groups: black 90.9%, East Indian 1.3%, white 0.2%, Chinese 0.2%, mixed 7.3%, other 0.1%
Language(s): English, patois English
Religion(s): Protestant 61.3% (Church of God 21.2%, Baptist 8.8%, Anglican 5.5%, Seventh-Day Adventist 9%, Pentecostal 7.6%, Methodist 2.7%, United Church 2.7%, Brethren 1.1%, Jehovah's Witness 1.6%, Moravian 1.1%), Roman Catholic 4%, other including some spiritual cults 34.7%
GDP per capita: $4,100 (2004 est.)
Currency: Jamaican dollar (JMD) - Jamaican dollars per US dollar - 61.197 (2004)
Time: GMT + 5
Electricity: 110V, 50Hz
National holiday: Independence Day, 6 August (1962)

▶ GEOGRAPHY

Location: Caribbean, island in the Caribbean Sea, south of Cuba
Border countries: None
Area: 10,991 sq km
Coastline: 1,022 km
Climate: tropical; hot, humid; temperate interior
Terrain: mostly mountains, with narrow, discontinuous coastal plain
lowest point: Caribbean Sea 0 m
highest point: Blue Mountain Peak 2,256 m
Natural hazards: hurricanes (especially July to November)
Vaccination(s): Yellow fever: A yellow fever vaccination certificate is required from travellers over 1 year of age coming from infected areas.

▶ DIVING

Number of certified divers: Mainly tourists
Dive federation(s): None
Dive regulations: Diver certification
Freediving federation(s): None
Major bodies of water: Caribbean Sea
Dive season: year-round
Water temperature: 26°C/78.8F (Jan-Mar), 28°C/82.4F (July-Sept)
Hyperbaric chambers:
City: Discovery Bay Marine Lab Chamber.
Telephone: 876 973-2241
Popular dive sites: The Pit, The Arches (Buoy #24), Middle Shoal Reef (Buoy #21), Frenchman Hole, Blue Castle Shipwreck, Throne Room (Buoy #3)
Tourism information: Visit Jamaica

(www.visitjamaica.com); Jamaica's Visitor Website (www.jam-boree.com)

JAPAN

► **GENERAL**

Capital: Tokyo
Government: constitutional monarchy with a parliamentary government
Population: 127,417,244 (July 2005 est.)
Ethnic groups: Japanese 99%, others 1% (Korean 511,262, Chinese 244,241, Brazilian 182,232, Filipino 89,851, other 237,914)
Language(s): Japanese
Religion(s): observe both Shinto and Buddhist 84%, other 16% (including Christian 0.7%)
GDP per capita: $29,400 (2004 est.)
Currency: yen (JPY) - yen per US dollar - 108.19 (2004)
Time: GMT + 9
Electricity: 100V, 50Hz
National holiday: Birthday of Emperor AKIHITO, 23 December (1933)

► **GEOGRAPHY**

Location: Eastern Asia, island chain between the North Pacific Ocean and the Sea of Japan, east of the Korean Peninsula
Border countries: None
Area: 377,835 sq km
Coastline: 29,751 km
Climate: varies from tropical in south to cool temperate in north
Terrain: mostly rugged and mountainous
lowest point: Hachiro-gata -4 m
highest point: Mount Fuji 3,776 m
Natural hazards: many dormant and some active volcanoes; about 1,500 seismic occurrences (mostly tremors) every year; tsunamis; typhoons

Vaccination(s): Yellow fever: A yellow fever vaccination certificate is required from travellers over 1 year of age coming from infected areas.

► **DIVING**

Number of certified divers: 1,000,000*
Dive federation(s): Japan Underwater Sports Federation
Dive regulations: Diver certification, not allowed to catch any fish during diving, Not allowed to fill scuba tanks without a license, Oxygen and other gases are very difficult to obtain for the purpose of technical diving*
Freediving federation(s): Japan Apnea Society* (AIDA)
Major bodies of water: North Pacific Ocean, Philippine Sea, East China Sea, Sea of Japan
Dive season: All year around, peak season August through November*
Water temperature: 17°C/62.6F (Jan-Mar), 25°C/78.8F (July-Sept)
Hyperbaric chambers: Many more than listed*
City: Hokkaido
Telephone: 011-716-1161
City: Kanto
Telephone: 0298-51-3511
City: Okinawa
Telephone: 098-854-5511
Popular dive sites: Osezaki - Izu Peninsula, Kerama Islands, Okinawa, Ishigaki Island, Mikomoto Island, Kumomi *
Tourism information: Japan National Tourist Organization (www.jnto.go.jp)
* SOURCE: PADI Japan, TokyoScuba.com (2006)

JORDAN

► **GENERAL**

Capital: Amman
Government: constitutional monarchy
Population: 5,759,732 (July 2005 est.)
Ethnic groups: Arab 98%, Circassian 1%, Armenian 1%
Language(s): Arabic (official), English widely understood among upper and middle classes
Religion(s): Sunni Muslim 92%, Christian 6% (majority Greek Orthodox, but some Greek and Roman Catholics, Syrian Orthodox, Coptic Orthodox, Armenian Orthodox, and Protestant denominations), other 2% (several small Shi'a Muslim and Druze populations) (2001 est.)
GDP per capita: $4,500 (2004 est.)
Currency: Jordanian dinar (JOD) - Jordanian dinars per US dollar - 0.709 (2004)
Time: GMT + 2
Electricity: 220V, 50Hz
National holiday: Independence Day, 25 May (1946)

► GEOGRAPHY

Location: Middle East, northwest of Saudi Arabia
Border countries: Iraq 181 km, Israel 238 km, Saudi Arabia 744 km, Syria 375 km, West Bank 97 km
Area: 92,300 sq km
Coastline: 26 km
Climate: mostly arid desert; rainy season in west (November to April)
Terrain: mostly desert plateau in east, highland area in west; Great Rift Valley separates East and West Banks of the Jordan River
lowest point: Dead Sea -408 m
highest point: Jabal Ram 1,734 m
Natural hazards: droughts; periodic earthquakes
Vaccination(s): Yellow fever: A yellow fever vaccination certificate is required from travellers over 1 year of age coming from infected areas.

► DIVING

Number of certified divers: 500*
Dive federation(s): Royal Jordanian Marine Sports Federation
Dive regulations: Diver certification
Freediving federation(s): Yes
Major bodies of water: Gulf of Aqaba (Red Sea)
Dive season: April to November *
Water temperature: 19°C/66.2F (Jan-Mar), 26°C/78.8F (July-Sept)
Hyperbaric chambers:
City: Aqaba...
Telephone: 96232014117*
Popular dive sites: Cedar Pride-Wreck, Saudi Porder, New Canyon-Tank, Japanese Garden, Gorgon1-2*
Tourism information: Jordan Tourism Board (www.see-jordan.com)
* SOURCE: Aqaba Gulf Dive Center (2006)

KENYA

► GENERAL

Capital: Nairobi
Government: republic
Population: 33,829,590 (July 2005 est.)
Ethnic groups: Kikuyu 22%, Luhya 14%, Luo 13%, Kalenjin 12%, Kamba 11%, Kisii 6%, Meru 6%, other African 15%, non-African (Asian, European, and Arab) 1%
Language(s): English (official), Kiswahili (official), numerous indigenous languages
Religion(s): Protestant 45%, Roman Catholic 33%, indigenous beliefs 10%, Muslim 10%, other 2%
GDP per capita: $1,100 (2004 est.)
Currency: Kenyan shilling (KES) - Kenyan shillings per US dollar - 79.174 (2004)
Time: GMT + 3
Electricity: 220/240V, 50Hz, square 3-pin plug
National holiday: Independence Day, 12 December (1963)

► GEOGRAPHY

Location: Eastern Africa, bordering the Indian Ocean, between Somalia and Tanzania
Border countries: Ethiopia 861 km, Somalia 682 km, Sudan 232 km, Tanzania 769 km, Uganda 933 km
Area: 582,650 sq km
Coastline: 536 km
Climate: varies from tropical along coast to arid in interior
Terrain: low plains rise to central highlands bisected by Great Rift Valley; fertile plateau in west
lowest point: Indian Ocean
highest point: Mount Kenya 5,199 m
Natural hazards: recurring drought; flooding during rainy seasons

Vaccination(s): Yellow fever: A yellow fever vaccination certificate is required from travellers over 1 year of age coming from infected areas. **Malaria:** Malaria risk—predominantly due to *P. falciparum*—exists throughout the year in the whole country. There is normally little risk in the city of Nairobi and in the highlands (above 2500 m) of Central, Eastern, Nyanza, Rift Valley and Western provinces. *P. falciparum* resistant to chloroquine and sulfadoxine–pyrimethamine reported. Recommended prevention: IV

▶ **DIVING**

Number of certified divers: Mainly tourists
Dive federation(s): None*
Dive regulations: Diver certification
Freediving federation(s): None*
Major bodies of water: Indian Ocean
Dive season: Best period November - end of March*
Water temperature: 28°C/82.4F (Jan-Mar), 25°C/77F (July-Sept)
Hyperbaric chambers:
City: Mombasa
Telephone: DIVECON Ltd or KENYA NAVY*
Popular dive sites: Watamu: Canyon, Moray Place, Black Coral, Deep Place, The Wreck"Shakwe"*
Tourism information: Kenya Tourist Board (www.magicalkenya.com)
* SOURCE: Scuba Diving Watamu Ltd (2006)

KIRIBATI

▶ **GENERAL**

Capital: Tarawa
Government: republic
Population: 103,092 (July 2005 est.)

Ethnic groups: Micronesian 98.8%, other 1.2% (2000 census)
Language(s): I-Kiribati, English (official)
Religion(s): Roman Catholic 52%, Protestant (Congregational) 40%, some Seventh-Day Adventist, Muslim, Baha'i, Latter-day Saints, and Church of God (1999)
GDP per capita: $800 (2001 est.)
Currency: Australian dollar (AUD) - Australian dollars per US dollar - 1.3598 (2004)
Time: GMT + 12
Electricity: 240V, 50Hz
National holiday: Independence Day, 12 July (1979)

▶ **GEOGRAPHY**

Location: Oceania, group of 33 coral atolls in the Pacific Ocean, straddling the equator; the capital Tarawa is about one-half of the way from Hawaii to Australia
Border countries: None
Area: 811 sq km (includes three island groups - Gilbert Islands, Line Islands, Phoenix Islands)
Coastline: 1,143 km
Climate: tropical; marine, hot and humid, moderated by trade winds
Terrain: mostly low-lying coral atolls surrounded by extensive reefs
lowest point: Pacific Ocean 0 m
highest point: unnamed location on Banaba 81 m
Natural hazards: typhoons can occur any time, but usually November to March; occasional tornadoes; low level of some of the islands make them very sensitive to changes in sea level
Vaccination(s): Yellow fever: A yellow fever vaccination certificate is required from travellers over 1 year of age coming from infected areas.

▶ **DIVING**

Number of certified divers: Mainly tourists
Dive federation(s): None
Dive regulations: Diver certification
Freediving federation(s): None
Major bodies of water: North Pacific Ocean
Dive season: year-round
Water temperature: 28.5°C/83F (Jan-Mar), 28.5°C/83F (July-Sept)
Hyperbaric chambers: N/A
Closest: Solomon Islands
Popular dive sites: South Tarawa, WWII plane wrecks at Butaritari, Christmas Island
Tourism information: Kiribati Visitor Bureau (www.kiritours.com)

KOREA (South)

▶ **GENERAL**

Capital: Seoul
Government: republic
Population: 48,422,644 (July 2005 est.)

Ethnic groups: homogeneous (except for about 20,000 Chinese)
Language(s): Korean, English widely taught in junior high and high school
Religion(s): no affiliation 46%, Christian 26%, Buddhist 26%, Confucianist 1%, other 1%
GDP per capita: $19,200 (2004 est.)
Currency: South Korean won (KRW) - South Korean won per US dollar - 1,145.3 (2004)
Time: GMT + 9
Electricity: 220V, 60Hz, 110V
National holiday: Liberation Day, 15 August (1945)

▶ GEOGRAPHY

Location: Eastern Asia, southern half of the Korean Peninsula bordering the Sea of Japan and the Yellow Sea
Border countries: North Korea 238 km
Area: 98,480 sq km
Coastline: 2,413 km
Climate: temperate, with rainfall heavier in summer than winter
Terrain: mostly hills and mountains; wide coastal plains in west and south
lowest point: Sea of Japan 0 m
highest point: Halla-san 1,950 m
Natural hazards: occasional typhoons bring high winds and floods; low-level seismic activity common in southwest
Vaccination(s): No vaccination requirements for any international traveller. **Malaria:** Limited malaria risk—exclusively due to *P. vivax*—exists mainly in the northern areas of Kyunggi Do and Gangwon Do Provinces. Recommended prevention: I

▶ DIVING

Number of certified divers: N/A
Dive federation(s): Korea Underwater Association
Dive regulations: Diver certification

Freediving federation(s): None
Major bodies of water: Sea of Japan, Yellow Sea
Dive season: year-round
Water temperature: 9°C/48.2F (Jan-Mar), 20°C/68F (July-Sept)
Hyperbaric chambers:
City: Seoul, Seoul Natl Univ. Col of Med.
Telephone: (82) 2 740 8323
Popular dive sites: Yang-Yang, Gangnam-Do, Pohang, Little Munsom Big Wall, Seopsom Reef
Tourism information: Korea National Tourism Organization (www.knto.or.kr)

KUWAIT

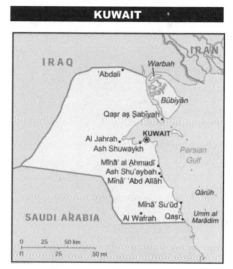

▶ GENERAL

Capital: Kuwait
Government: nominal constitutional monarchy
Population: 2,335,648; *note:* includes 1,291,354 non-nationals (July 2005 est.)
Ethnic groups: Kuwaiti 45%, other Arab 35%, South Asian 9%, Iranian 4%, other 7%
Language(s): Arabic (official), English widely spoken
Religion(s): Muslim 85% (Sunni 70%, Shi'a 30%), Christian, Hindu, Parsi, and other 15%
GDP per capita: $21,300 (2004 est.)
Currency: Kuwaiti dinar (KD) - Kuwaiti dinars per US dollar - 0.2947 (2004)
Time: GMT + 3
Electricity: 220/240V, 50Hz
National holiday: National Day, 25 February (1950)

▶ GEOGRAPHY

Location: Middle East, bordering the Persian Gulf, between Iraq and Saudi Arabia

Border countries: Iraq 240 km, Saudi Arabia 222 km
Area: 17,820 sq km
Coastline: 499 km
Climate: dry desert; intensely hot summers; short, cool winters
Terrain: flat to slightly undulating desert plain
lowest point: Persian Gulf 0 m
highest point: unnamed location 306 m
Natural hazards: sudden cloudbursts are common from October to April and bring heavy rain, which can damage roads and houses; sandstorms and dust storms occur throughout the year, but are most common between March and August
Vaccination(s): No vaccination requirements for any international traveller.

▶ DIVING

Number of certified divers: N/A
Dive federation(s): Underwater Sports Federation of Koweit
Dive regulations: Diver certification
Freediving federation(s): None
Major bodies of water: Sea of Japan, Yellow Sea
Dive season: year-round
Water temperature: 23°C/73.4F (Jan-Mar), 28°C/82.4F (July-Sept)
Hyperbaric chambers: N/A
Closest: Saudi Arabia
Popular dive sites: Benaider reefs, Garoh Island, Kubbar, Umm Al Maradam, Mudayrah Reef, Taylor's Rock
Tourism information: Kuwait Tourism (www.kuwaittourism.com)

LATVIA

▶ GENERAL

Capital: Riga
Government: parliamentary democracy
Population: 2,290,237 (July 2005 est.)
Ethnic groups: Latvian 57.7%, Russian 29.6%, Belarusian 4.1%, Ukrainian 2.7%, Polish 2.5%, Lithuanian 1.4%, other 2% (2002)
Language(s): Latvian (official) 58.2%, Russian 37.5%, Lithuanian and other 4.3% (2000 census)
Religion(s): Lutheran, Roman Catholic, Russian Orthodox
GDP per capita: $11,500 (2004 est.)
Currency: Latvian lat (LVL)

Time: GMT + 2
Electricity: 220V, 50Hz
National holiday: Independence Day, 18 November

▶ GEOGRAPHY

Location: Eastern Europe, bordering the Baltic Sea, between Estonia and Lithuania
Border countries: Belarus 141 km, Estonia 339 km, Lithuania 453 km, Russia 217 km
Area: 64,589 sq. km
Coastline: 531 km
Climate: maritime; wet, moderate winters
Terrain: low plain
lowest point: Baltic Sea 0 m
highest point: Gaizinkalns 312 m
Natural hazards: NA
Vaccination(s): No vaccination requirements for any international traveller.

▶ DIVING

Number of certified divers:. 70*
Dive federation(s): CMAS Baltic (Bund Staatlich Anerkanner Tauchlehrer)
Dive regulations: Diver certification
Freediving federation(s): None*
Major bodies of water: Baltic Sea, Gulf of Riga
Dive season: year-round (winter conditions require drysuit)*
Water temperature: 3°C/37.4F (Jan-Mar), 15°C59F (July-Sept)
Hyperbaric chambers:
Riga (Clinique Bikirnieki) - +371-7038123*
Popular dive sites: Sloka & Sloka-2 Lakes (important certification site), Pavilosta (wreck diving), Irbene (wreck diving), Dridzis Lake (deepest lake in Latvia at over 60m – great visibility), Birzhu Lake (flooded quarry – good certification site)*
Tourism information: Latvia Tourism (http://latviatourism.lv)
* SOURCE: CMAS Baltic (2005)

LEBANON

▶ GENERAL

Capital: Beirut
Government: republic
Population: 3,826,018 (July 2005 est.)
Ethnic groups: Arab 95%, Armenian 4%, other 1%
Language(s): Arabic (official), French, English, Armenian
Religion(s): Muslim 59.7% (Shi'a, Sunni, Druze, Isma'ilite, Alawite or Nusayri), Christian 39% (Maronite Catholic, Greek Orthodox, Melkite Catholic, Armenian Orthodox, Syrian Catholic, Armenian Catholic, Syrian Orthodox, Roman Catholic, Chaldean, Assyrian, Copt, Protestant), other 1.3%;
note: seventeen religious sects recognized
GDP per capita: $5,000 (2004 est.)

Currency: Lebanese pound (LBP) - Lebanese pounds per US dollar - 1,507.5 (2004)
Time: GMT + 2
Electricity: 110V, 220V, 50Hz
National holiday: Independence Day, 22 November (1943)

▶ **GEOGRAPHY**

Location: Middle East, bordering the Mediterranean Sea, between Israel and Syria
Border countries: Israel 79 km, Syria 375 km
Area: 10,400 sq km
Coastline: 225 km
Climate: Mediterranean; mild to cool, wet winters with hot, dry summers; Lebanon mountains experience heavy winter snows
Terrain: narrow coastal plain; El Beqaa (Bekaa Valley) separates Lebanon and Anti-Lebanon Mountains
lowest point: Mediterranean Sea 0 m
highest point: Qurnat as Sawda' 3,088 m
Natural hazards: dust storms, sandstorms
Vaccination(s): Yellow fever: A yellow fever vaccination certificate is required from travellers coming from infected areas.

▶ **DIVING**

Number of certified divers: 7,000*
Dive federation(s): CMAS Lebanese Diving Federation
Dive regulations: Diver certification
Freediving federation(s): None*
Major bodies of water: Mediterranean Sea
Dive season: May-October*
Water temperature: 17°C/62.6F (Jan-Mar), 26°C/78.8F (July-Sept)
Hyperbaric chambers:
City:Jounieh, Notre Dame du liban Hospital
Telephone: +961 9 831730*

Popular dive sites: Le souffleur (khaldé), Alice B (Jounieh), Sea Shell (Jounieh), The Etria (Jounieh), The caves (Bwar)*
Tourism information: Ministry of Tourism (www.lebanon-tourism.gov.lb)
* SOURCE: Atlantic Diving College (2006)

LIBYA

▶ **GENERAL**

Capital: Tripoli
Government: Jamahiriya (a state of the masses) in theory, governed by the populace through local councils; In fact, a military dictatorship
Population: 5,765,563 (July 2005 est.)
Ethnic groups: Berber and Arab 97%, Greeks, Maltese, Italians, Egyptians, Pakistanis, Turks, Indians, Tunisians
Language(s): Arabic, Italian, English, all are widely understood in the major cities
Religion(s): Sunni Muslim 97%
GDP per capita: $6,700 (2004 est.)
Currency: Libyan dinar (LYD) - Libyan dinars per US dollar - 1.305 (2004)
Time: GMT + 3
Electricity: 127/230V, 50Hz,
National holiday: Revolution Day, 1 September (1969)

▶ **GEOGRAPHY**

Location: Northern Africa, bordering the Mediterranean Sea, between Egypt and Tunisia
Border countries: Algeria 982 km, Chad 1,055 km, Egypt 1,115 km, Niger 354 km, Sudan 383 km, Tunisia 459 km
Area: 1,759,540 sq km
Coastline: 1,770 km
Climate: Mediterranean along coast; dry, extreme desert interior

Terrain: mostly barren, flat to undulating plains, plateaus, depressions
lowest point: Sabkhat Ghuzayyil -47 m
highest point: Bikku Bitti 2,267 m
Natural hazards: hot, dry, dust-laden ghibli is a southern wind lasting one to four days in spring and fall; dust storms, sandstorms
Vaccination(s): Yellow fever: A yellow fever vaccination certificate is required from travellers coming from infected areas.

▶ **DIVING**

Number of certified divers: N/A
Dive federation(s): None
Dive regulations: Diver certification
Freediving federation(s): None
Major bodies of water: Mediterranean Sea
Dive season: year-round
Water temperature: 17°C/62.6F (Jan-Mar), 26°C/78.8F (July-Sept)
Hyperbaric chambers: N/A
Popular dive sites: Many wrecks, Garabully, Lake Gabroun, Ain Al Dibana
Tourism information: Libya Online (www.libyaonline.com)

LITHUANIA

▶ **GENERAL**

Capital: Vilnius
Government: parliamentary democracy
Population: 3,596,617 (July 2005 est.)
Ethnic groups: Lithuanian 83.4%, Polish 6.7%, Russian 6.3%, other or unspecified 3.6% (2001 census)
Language(s): Lithuanian (official) 82%, Russian 8%, Polish 5.6%, other and unspecified 4.4% (2001 census)
Religion(s): Roman Catholic 79%, Russian Orthodox 4.1%, Protestant (including Lutheran and Evangelical Christian Baptist) 1.9%, other or unspecified 5.5%, none 9.5% (2001 census)
GDP per capita: $12,500 (2004 est.)
Currency: litas (LTL) - litai per US dollar - 2.7806 (2004)
Time: GMT + 2
Electricity: 220V, 50Hz
National holiday: Independence Day, 16 February (1918)

▶ **GEOGRAPHY**

Location: Eastern Europe, bordering the Baltic Sea, between Latvia and Russia
Border countries: Belarus 502 km, Latvia 453 km, Poland 91 km, Russia (Kaliningrad) 227 km
Area: 65,200 sq km
Coastline: 99 km
Climate: transitional, between maritime and continental; wet, moderate winters and summers
Terrain: lowland, many scattered small lakes, fertile soil

lowest point: Baltic Sea 0 m
highest point: Juozapines/Kalnas 292 m
Natural hazards: NA
Vaccination(s): No vaccination requirements for any international traveller.

▶ **DIVING**

Number of certified divers: 2,250*
Dive federation(s): Lithuanian Underwater Sport Federation
Dive regulations: Diver certification
Freediving federation(s): Lithuanian Freediving and Spearfishing association*
Major bodies of water: Baltic Sea
Dive season: year-round (winter conditions require drysuit)
Water temperature: 3°C/37.4F (Jan-Mar), 14°C/57.2F (July-Sept)
Hyperbaric chambers:
City: Klaipeda, Lithuanian NAVY decochamber for 4 divers up to 11.5Bar
Telephone: +37046391448*
Popular dive sites: Trakai area lakes, Alausas lake, Luokesa lake, Luokesaitis lake. Antalieptes marios (August - December), Baltic sea coastal area (difficult conditions - poor visibility, currents, low temperatures - but many wrecks)*
Tourism information: Lithuanian State Department of Tourism (www.tourism.lt)
* SOURCE: Diugonis (2006)

LUXEMBOURG

▶ **GENERAL**

Capital: Luxembourg
Government: constitutional monarchy
Population: 468,571 (July 2005 est.)
Ethnic groups: Celtic base (with French and German blend), Portuguese, Italian, Slavs (from Mon-

tenegro, Albania, and Kosovo) and European (guest and resident workers)
Language(s): Luxembourgish (national language), German (administrative language), French (administrative language)
Religion(s): 87% Roman Catholic, 13% Protestants, Jews, and Muslims (2000)
GDP per capita: $58,900 (2004 est.)
Currency: euro (EUR) - euros per US dollar - 0.8054 (2004)
Time: GMT + 1
Electricity: 220V, 50Hz
National holiday: National Day (Birthday of Grand Duchess Charlotte) 23 June

► **GEOGRAPHY**

Location: Western Europe, between France and Germany
Border countries: Belgium 148 km, France 73 km, Germany 138 km
Area: 2,586 sq km
Coastline: 0 km (landlocked)
Climate: modified continental with mild winters, cool summers
Terrain: mostly gently rolling uplands with broad, shallow valleys; uplands to slightly mountainous in the north; steep slope down to Moselle flood plain in the southeast
lowest point: Moselle River 133 m
highest point: Buurgplaatz 559 m
Natural hazards: NA
Vaccination(s): No vaccination requirements for any international traveller.

► **DIVING**

Number of certified divers: 700*
Dive federation(s): Fédération Luxembourgeoise des Activités et Sports Sub-Aquatiques
Dive regulations: Diver certification

Freediving federation(s): None
Major bodies of water: None
Dive season: Whole year diving, visibility is best in the "Lake of Haute Sûre" from May to July*
Water temperature: N/A
Hyperbaric chambers:
City: Esch-sur-Alzette
Telephone: +352 5711-22331 (emergency: +352 5711-1)*
Popular dive sites: Lake of Haute Sûre: Lultzhausen. Bonnal, Insenborn and Liefrange *
Tourism information: Luxembourg National Tourist Office in the United States (www.visitluxembourg.com); Luxembourg Tourist Office in London (www.luxembourg.co.uk)
* SOURCE: scuba.lu (2006)

MADAGASCAR

► **GENERAL**

Capital: Antananarivo
Government: republic
Population: 18,040,341 (July 2005 est.)
Ethnic groups: Malayo-Indonesian (Merina and related Betsileo), Cotiers (mixed African, Malayo-Indonesian, and Arab ancestry - Betsimisaraka, Tsimihety, Antaisaka, Sakalava), French, Indian, Creole, Comoran
Language(s): French (official), Malagasy (official)
Religion(s): indigenous beliefs 52%, Christian 41%, Muslim 7%
GDP per capita: $800 (2004 est.)
Currency: Madagascar ariary (MGA) - Malagasy francs per US dollar - 1,868.9 (2004)
Time: GMT + 3
Electricity: 220V, 50Hz
National holiday: Independence Day, 26 June (1960)

► **GEOGRAPHY**

Location: Southern Africa, island in the Indian Ocean, east of Mozambique
Border countries: None
Area: 587,040 sq km
Coastline: 4,828 km
Climate: tropical along coast, temperate inland, arid in south
Terrain: narrow coastal plain, high plateau and mountains in center
lowest point: Indian Ocean *highest point:* Maromokotro 2,876 m
Natural hazards: periodic cyclones, drought, and locust infestation
Vaccination(s): **Malaria:** Malaria risk—predominantly due to *P. falciparum*—exists throughout the year in the whole country, with the highest risk in the coastal areas. Resistance to chloroquine reported. Recommended prevention: IV

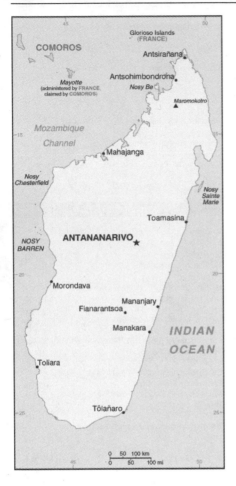

▶ DIVING

Number of certified divers: Mainly tourists
Dive federation(s): None*
Dive regulations: Diver certification
Freediving federation(s): None*
Major bodies of water: Indian Ocean, Mozambique Channel
Dive season: year-round
Water temperature: 28.5°C/83F (Jan-Mar), 25°C/77F (July-Sept)
Hyperbaric chambers:
City : Saint Denis de la Réunion*
Popular dive sites: Corail Noir, Epave, Les Arches, Tanikely, Sakatia*
Tourism information: Office Maison du Tourisme de Madagascar (www.madagascar-tourisme.com)
* SOURCE: Madaplouf SARL (2006)

▶ GENERAL

Capital: Kuala Lumpur
Government: constitutional monarchy
Population: 23,953,136 (July 2005 est.)
Ethnic groups: Malay 50.4%, Chinese 23.7%, Indigenous 11%, Indian 7.1%, others 7.8% (2004 est.)
Language(s): Bahasa Melayu (official), English, Chinese dialects (Cantonese, Mandarin, Hokkien, Hakka, Hainan, Foochow), Tamil, Telugu, Malayalam, Panjabi, Thai; *note:* in addition, in East Malaysia several indigenous languages are spoken, the largest are Iban and Kadazan
Religion(s): Muslim, Buddhist, Daoist, Hindu, Christian, Sikh; note - in addition, Shamanism is practiced in East Malaysia
GDP per capita: $9,700 (2004 est.)
Currency: ringgit (MYR) - ringgits per US dollar - 3.8 (2004)
Time: GMT + 8
Electricity: 240V, 50Hz
National holiday: Independence Day/Malaysia Day, 31 August (1957)

▶ GEOGRAPHY

Location: Southeastern Asia, peninsula bordering Thailand and northern one-third of the island of Borneo, bordering Indonesia, Brunei, and the South China Sea, south of Vietnam
Border countries: Brunei 381 km, Indonesia 1,782 km, Thailand 506 km
Area: 329,750 sq km
Coastline: 4,675 km (Peninsular Malaysia 2,068 km, East Malaysia 2,607 km)
Climate: tropical; annual southwest (April to October) and northeast (October to February) monsoons
Terrain: coastal plains rising to hills and mountains
lowest point: Indian Ocean 0 m
highest point: Gunung Kinabalu 4,100 m
Natural hazards: flooding, landslides, forest fires
Vaccination(s): Malaria: Yellow fever: A yellow fever vaccination certificate is required from travellers over 1 year of age arriving within 6 days from yellow fever endemic areas. The countries and areas included in the endemic zones are considered as infected areas. **Malaria:** Malaria risk exists only in limited foci in the deep hinterland. Urban and coastal areas are free from

malaria. *P. falciparum* throughout the year. *P. falciparum* resistant to chloroquine and sulfadoxine-pyrimethamine reported. Recommended prevention in risk areas: IV

▶ **DIVING**

Number of certified divers: Mainly tourists
Dive federation(s): Malayan Sub Aqua Club
Dive regulations: Diver certification
Freediving federation(s): None
Major bodies of water: South China Sea, Sulu Sea
Dive season: year-round, best: Nov.-June
Water temperature: 27°C/80.6F (Jan-Mar), 29°C/84.2F (July-Sept)
Hyperbaric chambers:
City: Perak, Armed Forces Hospital
Popular dive sites: Batu Layar, Tanjung Besi, Karang Nibong Laut, Terumbu Kuning (Yellow Reef), Tanjung Tokong
Tourism information: Malaysia Tourism Promotion Board (www.tourism.gov.my)

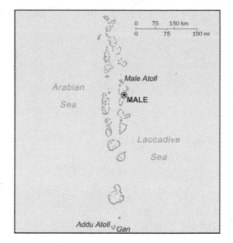

MALDIVES

▶ **GENERAL**

Capital: Male
Government: republic
Population: 349,106 (July 2005 est.)
Ethnic groups: South Indians, Sinhalese, Arabs
Language(s): Maldivian Dhivehi (dialect of Sinhala, script derived from Arabic), English spoken by most government officials
Religion(s): Sunni Muslim
GDP per capita: $3,900 (2002 est.)
Currency: rufiyaa (MVR) - rufiyaa per US dollar - 12.8 (2004)
Time: GMT + 5
Electricity: 230/240B, 50Hz
National holiday: Independence Day, 26 July (1965)

▶ **GEOGRAPHY**
Location: Southern Asia, group of atolls in the Indian Ocean, south-southwest of India
Border countries: None
Area: 300 sq km
Coastline: 644 km
Climate: tropical; hot, humid; dry, northeast monsoon (November to March); rainy, southwest monsoon (June to August)
Terrain: flat, with white sandy beaches
lowest point: Indian Ocean 0 m
highest point: unnamed location on Wilingili island in the Addu Atoll 2.4 m
Natural hazards: low level of islands makes them very sensitive to sea level rise
Vaccination(s): Yellow fever: A yellow fever vaccination certificate is required from travellers coming from infected areas.

▶ **DIVING**

Number of certified divers: 600*
Dive federation(s): None*
Dive regulations: Diver certification, no decompression diving, maximum dive depth for recreational diving 30 meters, no spear fishing*
Freediving federation(s): AIDA
Major bodies of water: Arabian Sea, Laccadive Sea
Dive season: year-round*
Water temperature: 29°C/84.2F (Jan-Mar), 25°C/77F (July-Sept)
Hyperbaric chambers:
City: Bandos Island Resort
City: Kuramathi Island Resort*
Popular dive sites: Banana Reef, Maya Thila, Fotheyo, Emboodhoo Express, MAldives Victory Wreck*
Tourism information: Ministry of Tourism (www.visitmaldives.com)
* SOURCE: Sea Explorers Dive School (2006)

MALTA

▶ **GENERAL**

Capital: Valletta
Government: republic
Population: 398,534 (July 2005 est.)
Ethnic groups: Maltese (descendants of ancient Carthaginians and Phoenicians, with strong elements of Italian and other Mediterranean stock)
Language(s): Maltese (official), English (official)
Religion(s): Roman Catholic 98%
GDP per capita: $18,200 (2004 est.)
Currency: Maltese lira (MTL) - Maltese liri per US dollar - 0.3444 (2004)
Time: GMT + 1
Electricity: 240V, 50Hz

National holiday: Independence Day, 21 September (1964)

► **GEOGRAPHY**

Location: Southern Europe, islands in the Mediterranean Sea, south of Sicily (Italy)
Border countries: None
Area: 316 sq km
Coastline: 196.8 km (does not include 56.01 km for the island of Gozo)
Climate: Mediterranean with mild, rainy winters and hot, dry summers
Terrain: mostly low, rocky, flat to dissected plains; many coastal cliffs
lowest point: Mediterranean Sea 0 m
highest point: Ta'Dmejrek 253 m (near Dingli)
Natural hazards: NA
Vaccination(s): Yellow fever: A yellow fever vaccination certificate is required from travellers over 9 months of age coming from infected areas. If indicated on epidemiological grounds, infants under 9 months of age are subject to isolation or surveillance if coming from an infected area.

► **DIVING**

Number of certified divers: 2,500*
Dive federation(s): Malta Federation of Underwater Activities
Dive regulations: Diver certification
Freediving federation(s): None (One club affiliated to FUAM)*
Major bodies of water: Mediterranean Sea
Dive season: year-round, best June-Sept.*
Water temperature: 15°C/59F (Jan-Mar), 24°C/75.2F (July-Sept)
Hyperbaric chambers: St Luke's Hospital, Pieta
Tel.: 25951549 or 112*

Popular dive sites: Blue Hole, Dwejra Gozo, Rozi wreck, (Cirkewwa), Umm el Farroud wreck, (Wied iz-zurrieq), Reqqa Point (Gozo), Ghar Lapsi*
Tourism information: Malta Tourism Authority (www.visitmalta.com)
* SOURCE: Malta Federation of Underwater Activities (2005)

MARIANAS (See Northern Marianas)

MARSHALL ISLANDS

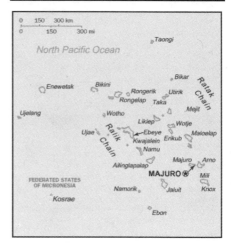

► **GENERAL**

Capital: Majuro
Government: constitutional government in free association with the US
Population: 59,071 (July 2005 est.)
Ethnic groups: Micronesian
Language(s): Marshallese 98.2%, other languages 1.8% (1999 census); note: English widely spoken as a second language; both Marshallese and English are official languages
Religion(s): Protestant 54.8%, Assembly of God 25.8%, Roman Catholic 8.4%, Bukot nan Jesus 2.8%, Mormon 2.1%, other Christian 3.6%, other 1%, none 1.5% (1999 census)
GDP per capita: $1,600 (2001 est.)
Currency: US dollar (USD)
Time: GMT + 12
Electricity: 110V, 60Hz
National holiday: Constitution Day, 1 May (1979)

► **GEOGRAPHY**

Location: Oceania, group of atolls and reefs in the North Pacific Ocean, about one-half of the way from Hawaii to Australia
Border countries: None

Area: 181.3 sq km. Two archipelagic island chains of 30 atolls and 1,152 islands; Bikini and Enewetak are former US nuclear test sites; Kwajalein, the famous World War II battleground, is now used as a US missile test range
Coastline: 370.4 km
Climate: tropical; hot and humid; wet season from May to November; islands border typhoon belt
Terrain: low coral limestone and sand islands
lowest point: Pacific Ocean 0 m
highest point: unnamed location on Likiep 10 m
Natural hazards: infrequent typhoons
Vaccination(s): No vaccination requirements for any international traveller.

▶ DIVING

Number of certified divers: Mainly tourists
Dive federation(s): None
Dive regulations: Diver certification
Freediving federation(s): None
Major bodies of water: North Pacific Ocean
Dive season: year-round
Water temperature: 27°C/80.6F (Jan-Mar), 28°C/80.6F (July-Sept)
Hyperbaric chambers: N/A
Closest: Guam
Popular dive sites: Majuro Lagoon, Arno Atolls, Kalalen Pass, Shark Chute, The Aquarium, The Kitsugawa Maru
Tourism information: Marshall Islands Visitor Authority (www.visitmarshallislands.com)

MARTINIQUE

▶ GENERAL

Capital: Fort-de-France
Government: overseas department of France
Population: 432,900 (July 2005 est.)
Ethnic groups: African and African-white-Indian mixture 90%, white 5%, East Indian, Chinese less than 5%
Language(s): French, Creole patois
Religion(s): Roman Catholic 85%, Protestant 10.5%, Muslim 0.5%, Hindu 0.5%, other 3.5% (1997)
GDP per capita: $14,400 (2003 est.)
Currency: euro (EUR) - euros per US dollar - 0.8054 (2004)
Time: GMT - 4
Electricity: 220V, 50Hz
National holiday: Bastille Day, 14 July (1789)

▶ GEOGRAPHY

Location: Caribbean, island between the Caribbean Sea and North Atlantic Ocean, north of Trinidad and Tobago
Border countries: None
Area: 1,100 sq km
Coastline: 350 km
Climate: tropical; moderated by trade winds; rainy season (June to October); vulnerable to

devastating cyclones (hurricanes) every eight years on average; average temperature 17.3 degrees C; humid
Terrain: mountainous with indented coastline; dormant volcano
lowest point: Caribbean Sea 0 m
highest point: Mont Pélée 1,397 m
Natural hazards: hurricanes, flooding, and volcanic activity (an average of one major natural disaster every five years)
Vaccination(s): No vaccination requirements for any international traveller.

▶ DIVING

Number of certified divers: Mainly tourists
Dive federation(s): None
Dive regulations: Diver certification
Freediving federation(s): None
Major bodies of water: North Atlantic Ocean, Caribbean Sea
Dive season: year-round
Water temperature: 25°C/77F (Jan-Mar), 28°C/82.4F (July-Sept)
Hyperbaric chambers: N/A
Closest: Barbados
Popular dive sites: Wreck of the Roraïma, Diamond Rock, Neptune Garden, The Nahoon, The Solomon Cave
Tourism information: Comité Martiniquais du Tourisme (www.touristmartinique.com)

MAURITIUS

▶ GENERAL

Capital: Port Louis
Government: parliamentary democracy
Population: 1,230,602 (July 2005 est.)
Ethnic groups: Indo-Mauritian 68%, Creole 27%, Sino-Mauritian 3%, Franco-Mauritian 2%

Language(s): Creole 80.5%, Bhojpuri 12.1%, French 3.4% (official), other 3.7%, unspecified 0.3% (2000 census)
Religion(s): Hindu 48%, Roman Catholic 23.6%, other Christian 8.6%, Muslim 16.6%, other 2.5%, unspecified 0.3%, none 0.4% (2000 census)
GDP per capita: $12,800 (2004 est.)
Currency: Mauritian rupee (MUR) - Mauritian rupees per US dollar - 27.499 (2004)
Time: GMT + 4
Electricity: 230V, 50Hz
National holiday: Independence Day, 12 March (1968)

► GEOGRAPHY

Location: Southern Africa, island in the Indian Ocean, east of Madagascar
Border countries: None
Area: 2,040 sq km; *note:* includes Agalega Islands, Cargados Carajos Shoals (Saint Brandon), and Rodrigues
Coastline: 177 km
Climate: tropical, modified by southeast trade winds; warm, dry winter (May to November); hot, wet, humid summer (November to May)
Terrain: small coastal plain rising to discontinuous mountains encircling central plateau
lowest point: Indian Ocean 0 m
highest point: Mont Piton 828 m
Natural hazards: cyclones (November to April); almost completely surrounded by reefs that may pose maritime hazards
Vaccination(s): Yellow fever: A yellow fever vaccination certificate is required from travellers over 1 year of age coming from infected areas. The countries and areas included in the endemic zones are considered as infected areas. **Malaria:** Malaria risk—exclusively due to *P. vivax*—may exist in certain rural areas (no indigenous cases reported since 1998).There is no risk on Rodrigues Island. Recommended prevention: none

► DIVING

Number of certified divers: Mainly tourists
Dive federation(s): Mauritius Scuba Diving Association
Dive regulations: Diver certification
Freediving federation(s): None
Major bodies of water: Indian Ocean
Dive season: year-round
Water temperature: 27°C/80.6F (Jan-Mar), 23°C/73.4F(July-Sept)
Hyperbaric chambers: N/A
Closest: Réunion
Popular dive sites: Japanese Gardens, Whale Rock, Stella Maru, Water Lilly, wreck: Le Sirius
Tourism information: Mauritius Tourism Promotion Authority (www.mauritius.net)

MAYOTTE

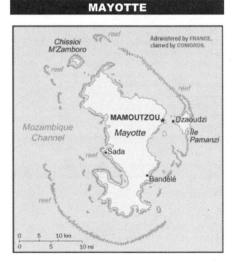

► GENERAL

Capital: Mamoutzou
Government: territorial collectivity of France
Mayotte has a number of fringing reefs and is almost completely encircled by its barrier reef. Image courtesy of Earth Sciences and Image Analysis Laboratory, NASA Johnson Space Center

Population: 193,633 (July 2005 est.)
Ethnic groups: NA
Language(s): Mahorian (a Swahili dialect), French (official language) spoken by 35% of the population
Religion(s): Muslim 97%, Christian (mostly Roman Catholic)
GDP per capita: $2,600 (2003 est.)
Currency: euro (EUR) - euros per US dollar - 0.8054 (2004)
Time: GMT + 3

Electricity: 220V, 50Hz
National holiday: Bastille Day, 14 July (1789)

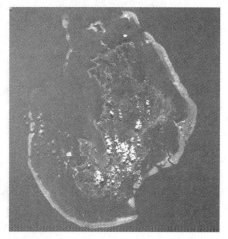

Photo: NASA

▶ **GEOGRAPHY**

Location: Southern Africa, island in the Mozambique Channel, about one-half of the way from northern Madagascar to northern Mozambique
Border countries: None
Area: 374 sq km
Coastline: 185.2 km
Climate: tropical; marine; hot, humid, rainy season during northeastern monsoon (November to May); dry season is cooler (May to November)
Terrain: generally undulating, with deep ravines and ancient volcanic peaks
lowest point: Indian Ocean 0 m
highest point: Benara 660 m
Natural hazards: cyclones during rainy season
Vaccination(s): No vaccination requirements for any international traveller. **Malaria:** Malaria risk—predominantly due to *P. falciparum*—exists throughout the year. Resistance to chloroquine and sulfadoxine-pyrimethamine reported. Recommended prevention: IV

▶ **DIVING**

Number of certified divers: Mainly tourists
Dive federation(s): Mayotte n'est pas rattachée à un comité régional de la **FFESSM**, mais dépend directement du comité directeur national.
Dive regulations: Diver certification
Freediving federation(s): None
Major bodies of water: Mozambique Channel
Dive season: year-round
Water temperature: 30°C/86F (Jan-Mar), 29°C/84.2F (July-Sept)
Hyperbaric chambers: N/A
Closest: Réunion

Popular dive sites: Mamoutzou, KaniKelli, Dzaoudzi
Tourism information: Comité du Tourisme de Mayotte (www.mayotte-tourisme.com)

MEXICO

▶ **GENERAL**

Capital: Mexico
Government: federal republic
Population: 106,202,903 (July 2005 est.)
Ethnic groups: mestizo (Amerindian-Spanish) 60%, Amerindian or predominantly Amerindian 30%, white 9%, other 1%
Language(s): Spanish, various Mayan, Nahuatl, and other regional indigenous languages
Religion(s): nominally Roman Catholic 89%, Protestant 6%, other 5%
GDP per capita: $9,600 (2004 est.)
Currency: Mexican peso (MXN) - Mexican pesos per US dollar - 11.286 (2004)
Time: GMT -8, -7, -6
Electricity: 127V, 60Hz
National holiday: Independence Day, 16 September (1810)

▶ **GEOGRAPHY**

Location: Middle America, bordering the Caribbean Sea and the Gulf of Mexico, between Belize and the US and bordering the North Pacific Ocean between Guatemala and the US
Border countries: Belize 250 km, Guatemala 962 km, US 3,141 km
Area: 1,972,550 sq km
Coastline: 9,330 km
Climate: varies from tropical to desert
Terrain: high, rugged mountains; low coastal plains; high plateaus; desert
lowest point: Laguna Salada -10 m
highest point: Volcan Pico de Orizaba 5,700 m
Natural hazards: tsunamis along the Pacific coast, volcanoes and destructive earthquakes in the center and south, and hurricanes on the Pacific, Gulf of Mexico, and Caribbean coasts
Vaccination(s): Yellow fever: No vaccination requirements for any international traveller. **Malaria:** Malaria risk—almost exclusively due to *P. vivax*—exists throughout the year in some rural areas that are not often visited by tourists. There is high risk of transmission in some localities in the

states of Chiapas, Quintana Roo, Sinaloa and Tabasco; moderate risk in the states of Chihuahua, Durango, Nayarit, Oaxaca and Sonora; and low risk in Campeche, Guerrero, Michoacán and Jalisco. Recommended prevention in risk areas: II

▶ **DIVING**

Number of certified divers: N/A
Dive federation(s): Federacion Mexicana De Actividades Subacuaticas A.C.
Dive regulations: Diver certification
Freediving federation(s): AIDA
Major bodies of water: Gulf of Mexico, Caribbean Sea, North Pacific Ocean
Dive season: year-round
Water temperature: 24°C/75.2F (Jan-Mar), 29°C/84.2F (July-Sept)
Hyperbaric chambers:
Camara Hiperbarica (Hiperbaric Chamber)
Telephone: (744) 484 02 07
Base Naval Icacos (Mexican Navi Base)
Telephone :(744) 484-00-20
Popular dive sites: Palacar Caves, Tormentos, Santa Rosa Wall, Taj Maha cenote, Paso del Cedral
Tourism information: Mexico Tourism Board (www.visitmexico.com)

MICRONESIA

▶ **GENERAL**

Capital: Palikir
Government: constitutional government in free association with the US
Population: 108,105 (July 2005 est.)
Ethnic groups: nine ethnic Micronesian and Polynesian groups
Language(s): English (official and common language), Trukese, Pohnpeian, Yapese, Kosrean, Ulithian, Woleaian, Nukuoro, Kapingamarangi
Religion(s): Roman Catholic 50%, Protestant 47%
GDP per capita: $2,000 (2002 est.)
Currency: US dollar (USD)
Time: GMT +11, +12
Electricity: 120V, 60Hz
National holiday: Constitution Day, 10 May (1979)

▶ **GEOGRAPHY**

Location: Oceania, island group in the North Pacific Ocean, about three-quarters of the way from Hawaii to Indonesia
Border countries: None
Area: 702 sq km; includes Pohnpei (Ponape), Chuuk (Truk) Islands, Yap Islands, and Kosrae (Kosaie)
Coastline: 6,112 km
Climate: tropical; heavy year-round rainfall, especially in the eastern islands; located on southern edge of the typhoon belt with occasionally severe damage

Terrain: islands vary geologically from high mountainous islands to low, coral atolls; volcanic outcroppings on Pohnpei, Kosrae, and Chuuk
lowest point: Pacific Ocean 0 m
highest point: Dolohmwar (Totolom) 791 m
Natural hazards: typhoons (June to December)
Vaccination(s): No vaccination requirements for any international traveller

▶ **DIVING**

Number of certified divers: 250*
Dive federation(s): None*
Dive regulations: Diver certification
Freediving federation(s): None*
Major bodies of water: North Pacific Ocean
Dive season: Year-round
Water temperature: 28°C/82.4F (Jan-Mar), 29°C/84.2F (July-Sept)
Hyperbaric chambers:
City: Yap
Telephone: (691) 350-3446*
Popular dive sites: Truk Lagoon, Miil Channel, Yap Caverns, Valley of the Rays, Rainbow Reef, Vertigo *
Tourism information: FSM Visitors Board (www.visitfsm.org)
* SOURCE: Beyond the Reef (2006)

MOLDOVA

▶ **GENERAL**

Capital: Chisinau
Government: republic
Population: 4,455,421 (July 2005 est.)
Ethnic groups: Moldovan/Romanian 78.2%, Ukrainian 8.4%, Russian 5.8%, Gagauz 4.4%, Bulgarian 1.9%, other 1.3% (2004 census)

Language(s): Moldovan (official, virtually the same as the Romanian language), Russian, Gagauz (a Turkish dialect)
Religion(s): Eastern Orthodox 98%, Jewish 1.5%, Baptist and other 0.5% (2000)
GDP per capita: $1,900 (2004 est.)
Currency: Moldovan leu (MDL) - lei per US dollar - 12.33 (2004)
Time: GMT + 2
Electricity: 220V, 50Hz
National holiday: Independence Day, 27 August (1991)

► **GEOGRAPHY**

Location: Eastern Europe, northeast of Romania
Border countries: Romania 450 km, Ukraine 939 km
Area: 33,843 sq km
Coastline: 0 km (landlocked)
Climate: moderate winters, warm summers
Terrain: rolling steppe, gradual slope south to Black Sea
lowest point: Dniester River 2 m
highest point: Dealul Balanesti 430 m
Natural hazards: landslides (57 cases in 1998)
Vaccination(s): No vaccination requirements for any international traveller.

► **DIVING**

Number of certified divers: 58*
Dive federation(s): Federatia De Activitati Subacvatice Din Republica Moldova

Dive regulations: Diver certification
Freediving federation(s): None
Major bodies of water: Dniester River
Dive season: May to November*
Water temperature: 0°C/32F (Jan-Mar), 20°C/68F (July-Sept)
Hyperbaric chambers:
Closest: Odessa, Ukraine (180 km)*
Popular dive sites: Dubasari*
Tourism information: UNDP Moldova (www.turism.md)
* SOURCE: Federatia De Activitati Subacvatice Din Republica Moldova (Dec. 2005)

MONACO

► **GENERAL**

Capital: Monaco
Government: constitutional monarchy
Population: 32,409 (July 2005 est.)
Ethnic groups: French 47%, Monegasque 16%, Italian 16%, other 21%
Language(s): French (official), English, Italian, Monegasque
Religion(s): Roman Catholic 90%
GDP per capita: $27,000 (2000 est.)
Currency: euro (EUR) - euros per US dollar - 0.8054 (2004)
Time: GMT + 1
Electricity: 127/220V, 50Hz
National holiday: National Day (Prince of Monaco Holiday), 19 November

► **GEOGRAPHY**

Location: Western Europe, bordering the Mediterranean Sea on the southern coast of France, near the border with Italy
Border countries: France 4.4 km

Area: 1.95 sq km
Coastline: 4.1 km
Climate: Mediterranean with mild, wet winters and hot, dry summers
Terrain: hilly, rugged, rocky
lowest point: Mediterranean Sea 0 m
highest point: Mont Agel 140 m
Natural hazards: NA
Vaccination(s): No vaccination requirements for any international traveller.

▶ **DIVING**

Number of certified divers: 250*
Dive federation(s): Federation Monegasque Des Activites Subaquatiques (FMAS)
Dive regulations: Diver certification
Freediving federation(s): LAPALM
Major bodies of water: Mediterranean Sea
Dive season: April to October*
Water temperature: 12°C/53.6F (Jan-Mar), 14°C/57.2F (July-Sept)
Hyperbaric chambers:
City: Nice - CH Pasteur*
Popular dive sites: Cap Estel, Mala, Cap Martin, St Nicolas, Tombant du Loews*
Tourism information: Monaco Tourism (www.visitmonaco.com)
* SOURCE: F.M.A.S. (2006)

MONTENEGRO

▶ **GENERAL**

Capital: Podgorica (administrative capital); Cetinje (capital city)
Government: republic
Population: 630,548 (2004)
Ethnic groups: Montenegrin 43%, Serbian 32%, Bosniak 8%, Albanian 5%, other (Muslims, Croats, Roma) 12%
Language(s): Serbian (Ijekavian dialect - official)
Religion(s): Orthodox, Muslim, Roman Catholic
GDP per capita: $3,800 (2005 est.)
Currency: euro (EUR)
Time: GMT + 1
Electricity: 220V, 50Hz
National holiday: National Day, 13 July

▶ **GEOGRAPHY**

Location: Southeastern Europe, between the Adriatic Sea and Serbia
Border countries: Albania 172 km, Bosnia and Herzegovina 225 km, Croatia 25 km, Serbia 203 km
Area: 14,026 sq km
Coastline: 293.5 km
Climate: Mediterranean climate, hot dry summers and autumns and relatively cold winters with heavy snowfalls inland

Terrain: highly indented coastline with narrow coastal plain backed by rugged high limestone mountains and plateaus
lowest point: Adriatic Sea 0 m
highest point: Bobotov Kuk 2,522 m
Natural hazards: destructive earthquakes
Vaccination(s): Yellow fever: No vaccination requirements for any international traveller.

▶ **DIVING**

Number of certified divers: 15,000 (includes Serbia)
Dive federation(s): Serbia and Montenegro Divers Association*
Dive regulations: Diver certification, very restrictive*
Freediving federation(s): AIDA*
Major bodies of water: Adriatic Sea*
Dive season: All year in Adriatic Sea*
Water temperature: 15°C/59F (Jan-Mar), 24°C/75.2F (July-Sept)
Hyperbaric chambers:
Popular dive sites: Cattaro submarine wrecks UC-24, U-72*
Tourism information: Montenegro Official Tourist Site (www.visit-montenegro.com

* SOURCE: Sea Wolf Diving School (2006)

MONTSERRAT

▶ **GENERAL**

Capital: Plymouth (abandoned in 1997 due to volcanic activity; interim government buildings have been built at Brades Estate, in the Carr's Bay/Little Bay vicinity at the northwest end of Montserrat)
Government: overseas territory of the UK

Population: 9,341; *note:* an estimated 8,000 refugees left the island following the resumption of volcanic activity in July 1995; some have returned (July 2005 est.)
Ethnic groups: black, white
Language(s): English
Religion(s): Anglican, Methodist, Roman Catholic, Pentecostal, Seventh-Day Adventist, other Christian denominations
GDP per capita: $3,400 (2002 est.)
Currency: East Caribbean dollar (XCD) - East Caribbean dollars per US dollar - 2.7 (2004)
Time: GMT - 4
Electricity: 110/220V, 60Hz
National holiday: Birthday of Queen ELIZABETH II, second Saturday in June (1926)

▶ **GEOGRAPHY**

Location: Caribbean, island in the Caribbean Sea, southeast of Puerto Rico
Border countries: None
Area: 102 sq km
Coastline: 40 km
Climate: tropical; little daily or seasonal temperature variation
Terrain: volcanic island, mostly mountainous, with small coastal lowland
lowest point: Caribbean Sea 0 m
highest point: Chances Peak (in the Soufriere Hills volcanic complex) 914 m
Natural hazards: severe hurricanes (June to November); volcanic eruptions (Soufriere Hills volcano has erupted continuously since 1995)
Vaccination(s): Yellow fever: A yellow fever vaccination certificate is required from travellers over 1 year of age coming from infected areas.

▶ **DIVING**

Number of certified divers: 110*

Dive federation(s): None*
Dive regulations: Diver certification
Freediving federation(s): None*
Major bodies of water: Caribbean Sea
Dive season: year-round*
Water temperature: 24°C/75.2F (Jan-Mar), 27°C/80.6F (July-Sept)
Hyperbaric chambers:
City: Guadeloupe*
Popular dive sites: Sea Studio, Little Rodanda, Aquarium, Pot of Gold, Bat Caves*
Tourism information: Montserrat Tourist Board (www.visitmontserrat.com)
* SOURCE: Sea Wolf Diving School (2006)

MOROCCO

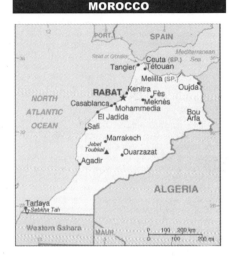

▶ **GENERAL**

Capital: Plymouth Rabat
Government: constitutional monarchy
Population: 32,725,847 (July 2005 est.)
Ethnic groups: Arab-Berber 99.1%, other 0.7%, Jewish 0.2%
Language(s): Arabic (official), Berber dialects, French often the language of business, government, and diplomacy
Religion(s): Muslim 98.7%, Christian 1.1%, Jewish 0.2%
GDP per capita: $4,200 (2004 est.)
Currency: Moroccan dirham (MAD) - Moroccan dirhams per US dollar - 8:868 (2004)
Time: GMT + 0
Electricity: 110/220V, 50Hz
National holiday: Throne Day (accession of King MOHAMED VI to the throne), 30 July (1999)

▶ **GEOGRAPHY**

Location: Northern Africa, bordering the North Atlantic Ocean and the Mediterranean Sea, between Algeria and Western Sahara
Border countries: Algeria 1,559 km, Western Sahara 443 km, Spain (Ceuta) 6.3 km, Spain (Melilla) 9.6 km
Area: 446,550 sq km
Coastline: 1,835 km
Climate: Mediterranean, becoming more extreme in the interior
Terrain: northern coast and interior are mountainous with large areas of bordering plateaus, intermontane valleys, and rich coastal plains
lowest point: Sebkha Tah -55 m
highest point: Jebel Toubkal 4,165 m
Natural hazards: northern mountains geologically unstable and subject to earthquakes; periodic droughts
Vaccination(s): No vaccination requirements for any international traveller. **Malaria:** Very limited malaria risk—exclusively due to *P. vivax*—may exist from May to October in certain rural areas of Chefchaouen Province. Recommended prevention: I

► **DIVING**

Number of certified divers: N/A
Dive federation(s): None
Dive regulations: Diver certification
Freediving federation(s): AIDA
Major bodies of water: North Atlantic Ocean, Mediterranean Sea
Dive season: year-round
Water temperature: 17°C/62.6F (Jan-Mar), 23°C/73.4F (July-Sept)
Hyperbaric chambers: N/A
Closest: Spain
Popular dive sites: Submarine wrecks, Agadir and Essaouira
Tourism information: Office national du tourisme marocain (www.tourisme-marocain.com); Tourism in Morocco (www.tourism-in-morocco.com)

MOZAMBIQUE

► **GENERAL**

Capital: Maputo
Government: republic
Population: 19,406,703
Ethnic groups: indigenous tribal groups 99.66% (Makhuwa, Tsonga, Lomwe, Sena, and others), Europeans 0.06%, Euro-Africans 0.2%, Indians 0.08%
Language(s): Emakhuwa 26.1%, Xichangana 11.3%, Portuguese 8.8% (official; spoken by 27% of population as a second language), Elomwe 7.6%, Cisena 6.8%, Echuwabo 5.8%, other Mozambican languages 32%, other foreign languages 0.3%, unspecified 1.3% (1997 census)

Religion(s): Catholic 23.8%, Zionist Christian 17.5%, Muslim 17.8%, other 17.8%, none 23.1% (1997 census)
GDP per capita: $1,200 (2004 est.)
Currency: metical (MZM) - meticais per US dollar - 22,581 (2004)
Time: GMT + 2
Electricity: 220V, 50Hz
National holiday: Independence Day, 25 June (1975)

► **GEOGRAPHY**

Location: South-eastern Africa, bordering the Mozambique Channel, between South Africa and Tanzania
Border countries: Malawi 1,569 km, South Africa 491 km, Swaziland 105 km, Tanzania 756 km, Zambia 419 km, Zimbabwe 1,231 km
Area: 801,590 sq km

Coastline: 2,470 km
Climate: tropical to subtropical
Terrain: mostly coastal lowlands, uplands in center, high plateaus in northwest, mountains in west
lowest point: Indian Ocean 0 m
highest point: Monte Binga 2,436 m
Natural hazards: severe droughts; devastating cyclones and floods in central and southern provinces
Vaccination(s): Yellow fever: A yellow fever vaccination certificate is required from travellers over 1 year of age coming from infected areas. **Malaria:**Malaria risk—predominantly due to *P, falciparum*—exists throughout the year in the whole country. *P. falciparum* resistant to chloroquine and sulfadoxine–pyrimethamine reported. Recommended prevention: IV

► **DIVING**

Number of certified divers: Mainly tourists
Dive federation(s): None
Dive regulations: Diver certification
Freediving federation(s): None
Major bodies of water: Indian Ocean, Mozambique Channel
Dive season: year-round
Water temperature: 26°C/78.8ᴼF (Jan Mar), 24°C/75.2F (July-Sept)
Hyperbaric chambers: N/A
Closest: South Africa
Popular dive sites: Bazaruto Archipelago, Inhaca Island, Quilálea, Ponta Mamoli, Sodwana
Tourism information: Mozambique Tourism (www.mozambiquetourism.co.za)

MYANMAR (Burma)

► **GENERAL**

Capital: Rangoon (government refers to the capital as Yangon)
Government: military junta
Population: 42,909,464 (July 2005 est.)
Ethnic groups: Burman 68%, Shan 9%, Karen 7%, Rakhine 4%, Chinese 3%, Indian 2%, Mon 2%, other 5%
Language(s): Burmese, minority ethnic groups have their own languages
Religion(s): Buddhist 89%, Christian 4% (Baptist 3%, Roman Catholic 1%), Muslim 4%, animist 1%, other 2%
GDP per capita: $1,700 (2004 est.)
Currency: kyat (MMK) - kyats per US dollar - 5.7459 (2004)
Time: GMT + 6.5
Electricity: 230V, 50Hz
National holiday: Independence Day, 4 January (1948); Union Day, 12 February (1947)

► **GEOGRAPHY**

Location: Southeastern Asia, bordering the Andaman Sea and the Bay of Bengal, between Bangladesh and Thailand
Border countries: Bangladesh 193 km, China 2,185 km, India 1,463 km, Laos 235 km, Thailand 1,800 km
Area: 678,500 sq km
Coastline: 1,930 km
Climate: tropical monsoon; cloudy, rainy, hot, humid summers (southwest monsoon, June to September); less cloudy, scant rainfall, mild temperatures, lower humidity during winter (northeast monsoon, December to April)
Terrain: central lowlands ringed by steep, rugged highlands
lowest point: Andaman Sea 0 m
highest point: Hkakabo Razi 5,881 m
Natural hazards: destructive earthquakes and cyclones; flooding and landslides common during rainy season (June to September); periodic droughts
Vaccination(s): Yellow fever: A yellow fever vaccination certificate is required from travellers

coming from infected areas. Nationals and residents of Myanmar are required to possess certificates of vaccination on their departure to an infected area. **Malaria:** Malaria risk—predominantly due to P. falciparum—exists throughout the year at altitudes below 1000 m, excluding the main urban areas of Yangon and Mandalay. Risk is highest in remote rural, hilly and forest areas. P. falciparum resistant to chloroquine and sulfadoxinepyrimethamine reported. Mefloquine resistance reported in Kayin state and the eastern part of Shan state. P. vivax with reduced sensitivity to chloroquine reported. Recommended prevention: **IV**

▶ **DIVING**

Number of certified divers: Mainly tourists
Dive federation(s): None
Dive regulations: Diver certification
Freediving federation(s): None
Major bodies of water: Bay of Bengal, Andaman Sea
Dive season: year-round
Water temperature: 27°C/80.6F (Jan-Mar), 28°C/82.4F (July-Sept)
Hyperbaric chambers: N/A
Closest: Thailand
Popular dive sites: Mergui Archipelago, Burma Banks, South Twin Island, Shark Cave, Tower Rock
Tourism information: Myanmar Tourism Promotion Board (www.myanmar-tourism.com)

NAMIBIA

▶ **GENERAL**

Capital: Windhoek
Government: republic
Population: 2,030,692
Ethnic groups: black 87.5%, white 6%, mixed 6.5%
Language(s): English 7% (official), Afrikaans common language of most of the population and about 60% of the white population, German 32%, indigenous languages: Oshivambo, Herero, Nama
Religion(s): Christian 80% to 90% (Lutheran 50% at least), indigenous beliefs 10% to 20%
GDP per capita: $7,300 (2004 est.)
Currency: Namibian dollar (NAD); South African rand (ZAR) - Namibian dollars per US dollar - 6.4597 (2004)
Time: GMT + 1
Electricity: 220V, 50Hz
National holiday: Independence Day, 21 March (1990)

▶ **GEOGRAPHY**

Location: Southern Africa, bordering the South Atlantic Ocean, between Angola and South Africa
Border countries: Angola 1,376 km, Botswana 1,360 km, South Africa 967 km, Zambia 233 km

Area: 825,418 sq km
Coastline: 1,572 km
Climate: desert; hot, dry; rainfall sparse and erratic
Terrain: mostly high plateau; Namib Desert along coast; Kalahari Desert in east
lowest point: Atlantic Ocean 0 m
highest point: Konigstein 2,606 m
Natural hazards: prolonged periods of drought

Vaccination(s): Yellow fever: A yellow fever vaccination certificate is required from travellers coming from infected areas. The countries, or parts of countries, included in the endemic zones in Africa and South America are regarded as infected,
Travellers on scheduled flights that originated outside the areas regarded as infected, but who have been in transit through these areas, are not required to possess a certificate provided that they remained at the scheduled airport or in the adjacent town during transit. All passengers whose flights originated in infected areas or who have been in transit through these areas on unscheduled flights are required to possess a certificate. The certificate is not insisted upon in the case of children under 1 year of age, but such infants may be subject to surveillance. **Malaria:** Malaria risk—predominantly due to P. falciparum—exists from November to June in the following regions: Oshana, Oshikoto, Omusati, Omaheke, Ohangwena and Otjozondjupa. Risk throughout the year exists along the Kunene river and in Kavango and Caprivi regions. Resistance to chloroquine and sulfadoxine-pyrimethamine reported. Recommended prevention in risk areas: IV

▶ **DIVING**

Number of certified divers: 50*
Dive federation(s): Namibiam Underwater Federation (NUF)
Dive regulations: Diver certification
Freediving federation(s): None*
Major bodies of water: South Atlantic Ocean
Dive season: year-round*
Water temperature:24C (Jan-Mar), 21°C (July-Sept)
Hyperbaric chambers:
City: Walvis Bay, Welwitschia Hospital
Telephone: 264 - (0)64 - 218 914
Popular dive sites: Lake Otjikoto, Dragon's Breath subterranean lake, Harasib Cave and Lake*; Friedenau Dam, Pelican Point, Von Bach Dam, Oanob Dam
Tourism information: Namibia Tourism Board (www.namibiatourism.com.na)

* SOURCE: NUF (2005)

NAURU

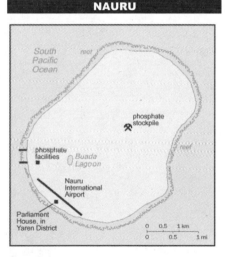

▶ **GENERAL**

Capital: no official capital; government offices in Yaren District
Government: republic
Population: 13,048 (July 2005 est.)
Ethnic groups: Nauruan 58%, other Pacific Islander 26%, Chinese 8%, European 8%
Language(s): Nauruan (official, a distinct Pacific Island language), English widely understood, spoken, and used for most government and commercial purposes
Religion(s): Christian (two-thirds Protestant, one-third Roman Catholic)
GDP per capita: $5,000 (2001 est.)

Currency: Australian dollar (AUD) - Australian dollars per US dollar - 1.3598 (2004)
Time: GMT + 12
Electricity: 110/240V, 50 Hz
National holiday: Independence Day, 31 January (1968)

▶ **GEOGRAPHY**

Location: Oceania, island in the South Pacific Ocean, south of the Marshall Islands
Border countries: None
Area: 21 sq km
Coastline: 30 km
Climate: tropical with a monsoonal pattern; rainy season (November to February)
Terrain: sandy beach rises to fertile ring around raised coral reefs with phosphate plateau in center
lowest point: Pacific Ocean 0 m
highest point: unnamed location along plateau rim 61 m
Natural hazards: periodic droughts
Vaccination(s): Yellow fever: A yellow fever vaccination certificate is required from travellers over 1 year of age coming from infected areas.

▶ **DIVING**

Number of certified divers: Mainly tourists
Dive federation(s): None
Dive regulations: Diver certification
Freediving federation(s): None
Major bodies of water: South Pacific Ocean
Dive season: year-round (rainy season Nov.-Feb.)
Water temperature: 28.5°C/83F (Jan-Mar), 28.5°C/83F (July-Sept)
Hyperbaric chambers: N/A
Closest: Solomon Islands
Popular dive sites: WWII wrecks and coral reef
Tourism information: Republic of Nauru (www.un.int/nauru/tourism.html)

NETHERLANDS (The)

▶ **GENERAL**

Capital: Amsterdam
Government: constitutional monarchy
Population: 16,407,491 (July 2005 est.)
Ethnic groups: Dutch 83%, other 17% (of which 9% are non-Western origin mainly Turks, Moroccans, Antilleans, Surinamese, and Indonesians) (1999 est.)
Language(s): Dutch (official), Frisian (official)
Religion(s): Roman Catholic 31%, Dutch Reformed 13%, Calvinist 7%, Muslim 5.5%, other 2.5%, none 41% (2002)
GDP per capita: $29,500 (2004 est.)
Currency: euro (EUR)
Time: GMT + 1
Electricity: 230V, 50Hz
National holiday: Queen's Day, 30 April

▶ GEOGRAPHY

Location: Western Europe, bordering the North Sea, between Belgium and Germany
Border countries: Belgium 450 km, Germany 577 km
Area: 41,526 sq. km
Coastline: 451 km
Climate: temperate; marine; cool summers and mild winters
Terrain: mostly coastal lowland and reclaimed land (polders); some hills in southeast
lowest point: Zuidplaspolder -7 m
highest point: Vaalserberg 322 m
Natural hazards: flooding
Vaccination(s): No vaccination requirements for any international traveller.

▶ DIVING

Number of certified divers: 20,000*
Dive federation(s): Nederlandse Onderwatersport Bond (NOB) – Dutch Underwater federation
Dive regulations: Diver certification
Freediving federation(s): NFDB – Dutch Free Diving Dereration (AIDA)
Major bodies of water: North Sea
Dive season: year-round*
Water temperature: 2°C/35.6F (Jan-Mar), 15°C/59F (July-Sept)
Hyperbaric chambers:
Den Helder: 022-3653076 / 022-3658220
Antwerpen (Belgium): 0032-38213055*
Popular dive sites:, Oosterschelde, Grevelingen*
North Sea, the Wadden Sea
Tourism information: Netherlands Board of Tourism (www.holland.com)
* Source: NOB (2005)

NETHERLANDS ANTILLES

▶ GENERAL

Capital: Willemstad (located on Curacao)
Government: an autonomous parliamentary country within the Kingdom of the Netherlands; full autonomy in internal affairs granted in 1954; Dutch Government responsible for defense and foreign affairs
Population: 219,958 (July 2005 est.)
Ethnic groups: mixed black 85%, Carib Amerindian, white, East Asian
Language(s): Papiamento 65.4% (a Spanish-Portuguese-Dutch-English dialect), English 15.9% (widely spoken), Dutch 7.3% (official), Spanish 6.1%, Creole 1.6%, other 1.9%, unspecified 1.8% (2001 census)
Religion(s): Roman Catholic 72%, Pentecostal 4.9%, Protestant 3.5%, Seventh-Day Adventist 3.1%, Methodist 2.9%, Jehovah's Witnesses 1.7%, other Christian 4.2%, Jewish 1.3%, other or unspecified 1.2%, none 5.2% (2001 census)
GDP per capita: $11,400 (2003 est.)
Currency: Netherlands Antillean guilder (ANG) - Netherlands Antillean guilders per US dollar - 1.79 (2004)
Time: GMT - 4
Electricity: 110/220V, 50 Hz
National holiday: Queen's Day, 30 April

▶ GEOGRAPHY

Location: Caribbean, two island groups in the Caribbean Sea - composed of five islands, Curacao and Bonaire located off the coast of Venezuela, and St. Maarten, Saba, and St. Eustatius lie east of the US Virgin Islands
Border countries: Guadeloupe (Saint-Martin) 10.2 km

Area: 960 sq km (includes Bonaire, Curacao, Saba, Sint Eustatius, and Sint Maarten)
Coastline: 364 km
Climate: tropical; improved by northeast trade winds
Terrain: generally hilly, volcanic interiors
lowest point: Caribbean Sea 0 m
highest point: Mount Scenery 862 m
Natural hazards: Curacao and Bonaire are south of Caribbean hurricane belt and are rarely threatened; Sint Maarten, Saba, and Sint Eustatius are subject to hurricanes from July to October
Vaccination(s): Yellow fever: A yellow fever vaccination certificate is required from travellers over 6 months of age coming from infected area.

▶ **DIVING**

Number of certified divers: (See Netherlands)
Dive federation(s): Nederlandse Onderwatersport Bond (NOB) – Dutch Underwater federation (www.onderwatersport.org)
Dive regulations: Diver certification
Freediving federation(s): AIDA
Major bodies of water: Caribbean Sea
Dive season: year-round*
Water temperature: 26°C/78.8F (Jan-Mar), 28°C/82.4F (July Sept)
Hyperbaric chambers:
City: Willemstad, Tel. 991*
Popular dive sites: Sea Aquarium Reef, Porto Mari, Wata Mula, Blue Bay, Tugboat*, The Hilma Hooker, Bari Reef
Tourism information: Bonaire Tourism Corporation (www.infobonaire.com); Curaçao Tourist Board (www.curacao-tourism.com); Saba Tourist Office (www.sabatourism.com); St. Eustatius (Statia) Tourist Office (www.statiatourism.com); St. Maarten Tourist Bureau (www.st-maarten.com)

* SOURCE: Tourism Curacao (2005)

NEW CALEDONIA

▶ **GENERAL**

Capital: Noumea
Government: overseas territory of France since 1956
Population: 216,494 (July 2005 est.)
Ethnic groups: Melanesian 42.5%, European 37.1%, Wallisian 8.4%, Polynesian 3.8%, Indonesian 3.6%, Vietnamese 1.6%, other 3%
Language(s): French (official), 33 Melanesian-Polynesian dialects
Religion(s): Roman Catholic 60%, Protestant 30%, other 10%
GDP per capita: $15,000 (2003 est.)
Currency: Comptoirs Francais du Pacifique franc (XPF) - Comptoirs Francais du Pacifique francs (XPF) per US dollar - 96.04 (2004)
Time: GMT + 11
Electricity: 220V, 50Hz

National holiday: Bastille Day, 14 July (1789)

▶ **GEOGRAPHY**

Location: Oceania, islands in the South Pacific Ocean, east of Australia
Border countries: None
Area: 19,060 sq km
Coastline: 2,254 km
Climate: tropical; modified by southeast trade winds; hot, humid
Terrain: coastal plains with interior mountains
lowest point: Pacific Ocean 0 m
highest point: Mont Panie 1,628 m
Natural hazards: periodic droughts
Vaccination(s): Cholera: Vaccination against cholera is not required. Travellers coming from an infected area are not given chemoprophylaxis, but are required to complete a form for use by the Health Service. **Yellow fever:** A yellow fever vaccination certificate is required from travellers over 1 year of age coming from infected areas. Note. In the event of an epidemic threat to the territory, a specific vaccination certificate may be required.

▶ **DIVING**

Number of certified divers: Mainly tourists
Dive federation(s): Nouvelle Caledonie Plongee
Dive regulations: Diver certification, underwater hunting with scuba diving equipment or surface supplied air is strictly prohibited.*
Freediving federation(s): Immersion (Amedee Diving Center)*
Major bodies of water: South Pacific Ocean, Coral Sea
Dive season: year-round
Water temperature: 27°C/80.6F (Jan-Mar), 22°C/71.6F (July-Sept)
Hyperbaric chambers:

City: Noumea
Telephone: (687) 769200*
Popular dive sites: Drift dives in the passages of the outer reef, drop-offs on the barrier reef, wreck dives, marine parks, grottos*
Tourism information: New Caledonia Tourism (www.visitnewcaledonia.com)
* SOURCE: Nouvelle Calédonie Plongée (2006)

NEW ZEALAND

▶ **GENERAL**

Capital: Wellington
Government: parliamentary democracy
Population: 4,035,461 (July 2005 est.)
Ethnic groups: European 69.8%, Maori 7.9%, Asian 5.7%, Pacific islander 4.4%, other 0.5%, mixed 7.8%, unspecified 3.8% (2001 census)
Language(s): English (official), Maori (official)
Religion(s): Anglican 14.9%, Roman Catholic 12.4%, Presbyterian 10.9%, Methodist 2.9%, Pentecostal 1.7%, Baptist 1.3%, other Christian 9.4%, other 3.3%, unspecified 17.2%, none 26% (2001 census)
GDP per capita: $23,200 (2004 est.)
Currency: New Zealand dollar (NZD) - New Zealand dollars per US dollar - 1.5087 (2004)
Time: GMT + 12
Electricity: 230/240V, 50Hz
National holiday: Waitangi Day, 6 February (1840)

▶ **GEOGRAPHY**

Location: Oceania, islands in the South Pacific Ocean, southeast of Australia
Border countries: None
Area: 268,680 sq km; *note:* includes Antipodes Islands, Auckland Islands, Bounty Islands, Campbell Island, Chatham Islands, and Kermadec Islands
Coastline: 15,134 km
Climate: temperate with sharp regional contrasts
Terrain: predominately mountainous with some large coastal plains
lowest point: Pacific Ocean 0 m
highest point: Aoraki-Mount Cook 3,754 m
Natural hazards: earthquakes are common, though usually not severe; volcanic activity
Vaccination(s): No vaccination requirements for any international traveller.

▶ **DIVING**

Number of certified divers: 320,000*
Dive federation(s): New Zealand Underwater Association (NZUA)
Dive regulations: Diver cerfitication
Freediving federation(s): CMAS (NZUA)*
Major bodies of water: South Pacific Ocean, Tazman Sea
Dive season: year-round, high season October – May*
Water temperature:
North: 21°C/69.8F (Jan-Mar), 15°C/59F (July-Sept)
South: 15°C/15F (Jan-Mar), 11°C/51.8F (July-Sept)
Hyperbaric chambers:
City: Auckland
Phone number (NZ) 0800 4 337 111
City: Christchurch
Phone number: 03 364 0045*
Popular dive sites: Poor Knights Islands, Goat Island, Milford Sound, Aldermen Islands, Marlborough Sounds* **Tourism information:** Tourism New Zealand (www.newzealand.com)
* SOURCE: NZUA (Dec. 2005)

NICARAGUA

▶ **GENERAL**

Capital: Managua
Government: republic
Population: 5,465,100 (July 2005 est.)
Ethnic groups: mestizo (mixed Amerindian and white) 69%, white 17%, black 9%, Amerindian 5%
Language(s): Spanish 97.5% (official), Miskito 1.7%, other 0.8% (1995 census)
note: English and indigenous languages on Atlantic coast
Religion(s): Roman Catholic 72.9%, Evangelical 15.1%, Moravian 1.5%, Episcopal 0.1%, other 1.9%, none 8.5% (1995 census)

GDP per capita: $2,300 (2004 est.)
Currency: gold cordoba (NIO) - gold cordobas per US dollar - 15.937 (2004)
Time: GMT - 6
Electricity: 110V, 60Hz; 220V
National holiday: Independence Day, 15 September (1821)

▶ **GEOGRAPHY**

Location: Central America, bordering both the Caribbean Sea and the North Pacific Ocean, between Costa Rica and Honduras
Border countries: Costa Rica 309 km, Honduras 922 km
Area: 129,494 sq km
Coastline: 910 km
Climate: tropical in lowlands, cooler in highlands
Terrain: extensive Atlantic coastal plains rising to central interior mountains; narrow Pacific coastal plain interrupted by volcanoes
lowest point: Pacific Ocean 0 m
highest point: Mogoton 2,438 m
Natural hazards: destructive earthquakes, volcanoes, landslides; extremely susceptible to hurricanes
Vaccination(s): Yellow fever: A yellow fever vaccination certificate is required from travellers over 1 year of age coming from infected areas. **Malaria:** Malaria risk—predominantly due to *P. vivax*—is high throughout the year in 119 municipalities, with the highest risk in Chinandega, Jinotega, Nueva Segovía, RAAN, RAAS and Rio San Juan. In the other 26 municipalities, in the departments of Carazo, Madriz and Masaya, transmission risk is low or negligible. No chloroquine-resistant *P. falciparum* reported. Recommended prevention in risk areas: II

▶ **DIVING**

Number of certified divers: 200*
Dive federation(s): None*

Dive regulations: Diver certification
Freediving federation(s): None*
Major bodies of water: Caribbean Sea, North Pacific
Dive season: year-round
Water temperature: 26°C/78.8F (Jan-Mar), 28°C/82.4F (July-Sept)
Hyperbaric chambers:
City: Puerto Cabeza*
Popular dive sites: Grant's Cave, Blowing Rock, Shark Hole, White Hole, Tarpon Channel*
Tourism information: Nicaraguan Tourism Institute (www.intur.gob.ni)
* SOURCE: Dive Little Corn (2006)

NORTHERN MARIANAS

▶ **GENERAL**

Capital: Saipan
Government: commonwealth in political union with the US
Population: 80,362 (July 2005 est.)
Ethnic groups: Asian 56.3%, Pacific islander 36.3%, Caucasian 1.8%, other 0.8%, mixed 4.8% (2000 census)
Language(s): Philippine languages 24.4%, Chinese 23.4%, Chamorro 22.4%, English 10.8%, other Pacific island languages 9.5%, other 9.6% (2000 census)
Religion(s): Christian (Roman Catholic majority, although traditional beliefs and taboos may still be found)
GDP per capita: $12,500 (2000 est.)
Currency: US dollar (USD)
Time: GMT + 10
Electricity: 110V, 60Hz
National holiday: Commonwealth Day, 8 January (1978)

▶ **GEOGRAPHY**

Location: Oceania, islands in the North Pacific Ocean, about three-quarters of the way from Hawaii to the Philippines
Border countries: None
Area: 477 sq km
Coastline: 1,482 km
Climate: tropical marine; moderated by northeast trade winds, little seasonal temperature variation; dry season December to June, rainy season July to October
Terrain: southern islands are limestone with level terraces and fringing coral reefs; northern islands are volcanic
lowest point: Pacific Ocean 0 m
highest point: unnamed location on Agrihan 965 m
Natural hazards: active volcanoes on Pagan and Agrihan; typhoons (especially August to November)
Vaccination(s): No vaccination requirements for any international traveller.

▶ **DIVING**

Number of certified divers: Mainly tourists
Dive federation(s): None
Dive regulations: Diver certification
Freediving federation(s): None
Major bodies of water: North Pacific Ocean, Philippine Sea
Dive season: year-round
Water temperature: 25°C/77F (Jan-Mar), 28°C/82.4F (July-Sept)
Hyperbaric chambers: N/A
Closest: Guam
Popular dive sites: The Grotto, Wing Beach, The Mushroom City dive, Hobbit House, Rota
Tourism information: Marianas Visitors Authority (www.mymarianas.com)

NORWAY

▶ **GENERAL**

Capital: Oslo
Government: constitutional monarchy
Population: 4,593,041 (July 2005 est.)
Ethnic groups: Norwegian, Sami 20,000
Language(s): Bokmal Norwegian (official), Nynorsk Norwegian (official), small Sami- and Finnish-speaking minorities
Religion(s): Church of Norway 85.7%, Pentecostal 1%, Roman Catholic 1%, other Christian 2.4%, Muslim 1.8%, other 8.1% (2004)
GDP per capita: $40,000 (2004 est.)
Currency: Norwegian krone (NOK) - Norwegian kroner per US dollar - 6.7408 (2004)
Time: GMT + 1
Electricity: 220V, 50Hz
National holiday: Commonwealth Day, 8 January (1978)

▶ **GEOGRAPHY**

Location: Northern Europe, bordering the North Sea and the North Atlantic Ocean, west of Sweden
Border countries: Finland 727 km, Sweden 1,619 km, Russia 196 km
Area: 324,220 sq km
Coastline: 25,148 km
Climate: temperate along coast, modified by North Atlantic Current; colder interior with increased precipitation and colder summers; rainy year-round on west coast
Terrain: glaciated; mostly high plateaus and rugged mountains broken by fertile valleys; small, scattered plains; coastline deeply indented by fjords; arctic tundra in north
lowest point: Norwegian Sea 0 m
highest point: Galdhopiggen 2,469 m
Natural hazards: rockslides, avalanches
Vaccination(s): No vaccination requirements for any international traveller.

▶ **DIVING**

Number of certified divers: N/A
Dive federation(s): Norwegian Diving Federation
Dive regulations: Diver certification
Freediving federation(s): None
Major bodies of water: North Sea, Norwegian Sea
Dive season: year-round
Water temperature: 6°C/42.8F (Jan-Mar), 11°C/51.8F (July-Sept)
Hyperbaric chambers:
City: Haukeland, Haukeland Hospital
Telephone: (47)55 97 39 75
Popular dive sites: Sandsfjord, Haaholmen Island, Runde Island, Hitra

Tourism information: Norwegian Tourist Board (www.visitnorway.com)

OMAN

▶ **GENERAL**

Capital: Muscat
Government: monarchy
Population: 3,001,583; *note:* includes 577,293 non-nationals (July 2005 est.)
Ethnic groups: Arab, Baluchi, South Asian (Indian, Pakistani, Sri Lankan, Bangladeshi), African
Language(s): Arabic (official), English, Baluchi, Urdu, Indian dialects
Religion(s): Ibadhi Muslim 75%, Sunni Muslim, Shi'a Muslim, Hindu
GDP per capita: $13,100 (2004 est.)
Currency: Omani rial (OMR) - Omani rials per US dollar - 0.3845 (2004)
Time: GMT + 4
Electricity: 220/240V, 50Hz
National holiday: Birthday of Sultan QABOOS, 18 November (1940)

▶ **GEOGRAPHY**

Location: Middle East, bordering the Arabian Sea, Gulf of Oman, and Persian Gulf, between Yemen and UAE
Border countries: Saudi Arabia 676 km, UAE 410 km, Yemen 288 km
Area: 212,460 sq km
Coastline: 2,092 km
Climate: dry desert; hot, humid along coast; hot, dry interior; strong southwest summer monsoon (May to September) in far south
Terrain: central desert plain, rugged mountains in north and south
lowest point: Arabian Sea 0 m
highest point: Jabal Shams 2,980 m

Natural hazards: summer winds often raise large sandstorms and dust storms in interior; periodic droughts
Vaccination(s): Yellow fever: A yellow fever vaccination certificate is required from travellers coming from infected areas. **Malaria:** Very limited malaria risk—including *P. falciparum*—may exist in remote areas of Musandam Province. No indigenous cases reported since 2001. Recommended prevention : none

▶ **DIVING**

Number of certified divers: 3,500*
Dive federation(s): Underwater Sports Federation of Oman
Dive regulations: Diver certification, no spearfishing, no removal from sea*
Freediving federation(s): None
Major bodies of water: Gulf of Oman, Arabian Sea
Dive season: year-round
Water temperature: 24°C/75.2F (Jan-Mar), 28°C/82.4F (July-Sept)
Hyperbaric chambers:
City: Muscat
Telephone: + 968 – 26346804*
Popular dive sites: Fahal Island, Bander Khiran, Daymanyat Islands, Al manassir Wrick, Ras Abu Dawood*
Tourism information: Oman Ministry of Tourism (www.omantourism.gov.om)
* SOURCE: Moonlight Dive (2006)

PAKISTAN

▶ **GENERAL**

Capital: Islamabad
Government: federal republic
Population: 162,419,946 (July 2005 est.)
Ethnic groups: Punjabi, Sindhi, Pashtun (Pathan), Baloch, Muhajir (immigrants from India at the time of partition and their descendants)
Language(s): Punjabi 48%, Sindhi 12%, Siraiki (a Punjabi variant) 10%, Pashtu 8%, Urdu (official) 8%, Balochi 3%, Hindko 2%, Brahui 1%, English (official and lingua franca of Pakistani elite and most government ministries), Burushaski, and other 8%
Religion(s): Muslim 97% (Sunni 77%, Shi'a 20%), Christian, Hindu, and other 3%
GDP per capita: $2,200 (2004 est.)
Currency: Pakistani rupee (PKR) - Pakistani rupees per US dollar - 58.258 (2004)
Time: GMT + 5
Electricity: 230V, 50Hz, round 2-3 pin plug
National holiday: Republic Day, 23 March (1956)

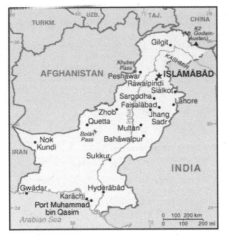

► GEOGRAPHY

Location: Southern Asia, bordering the Arabian Sea, between India on the east and Iran and Afghanistan on the west and China in the north
Border countries: Afghanistan 2,430 km, China 523 km, India 2,912 km, Iran 909 km
Area: 803,940 sq km
Coastline: 1,046 km
Climate: mostly hot, dry desert; temperate in northwest; arctic in north
Terrain: flat Indus plain in east; mountains in north and northwest; Balochistan plateau in west
lowest point: Indian Ocean 0 m
highest point: K2 (Mt. Godwin-Austen) 8,611 m
Natural hazards: frequent earthquakes, occasionally severe especially in north and west; flooding along the Indus after heavy rains (July and August)
Vaccination(s): Yellow fever: A yellow fever vaccination certificate is required from travellers coming from any part of a country in which yellow fever is endemic; infants under 6 months of age are exempt if the mother's vaccination certificate shows that she was vaccinated before the birth of the child. The countries and areas included in the endemic zones are considered as infected areas. **Malaria:** Malaria risk exists throughout the year in the whole country below 2000 m. *P. falciparum* resistant to chloroquine and sulfadoxine–pyrimethamine reported. Recommended prevention: IV

► DIVING

Number of certified divers: N/A
Dive federation(s): None
Dive regulations: Diver certification
Freediving federation(s): None
Major bodies of water: Arabian Sea
Dive season: year-round
Water temperature: 25°C/77F (Jan-Mar), 27°C/80.6F (July-Sept)

Hyperbaric chambers:
City: Karachi, Diving & Hyperbaric Medicine Department
Telephone: 56636505
Popular dive sites: Oyster Rock, Paradise Point, Churna Rock
Tourism information: Ministry of Tourism (www.tourism.gov.pk)

PALAU

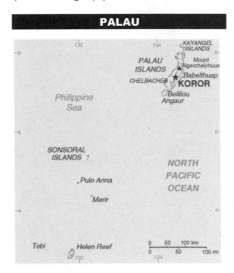

► GENERAL

Capital: Koror; note - a new capital is being built about 20 km northeast of Koror
Government: constitutional government in free association with the US
Population: 20,303 (July 2005 est.)
Ethnic groups: Palauan (Micronesian with Malayan and Melanesian admixtures) 69.9%, Carolinian 1.4%, other Micronesian 1.1%, Filipino 15.3%, Chinese 4.9%, other Asian 2.4%, white 1.9%, other or unspecified 3.2% (2000 census)
Language(s): Palauan 64.7% official in all islands except Sonsoral (Sonsoralese and English are official), Tobi (Tobi and English are official), and Angaur (Angaur, Japanese, and English are official), Filipino 13.5%, English 9.4%, Chinese 5.7%, Carolinian 1.5%, Japanese 1.5%, other Asian 2.3%, other languages 1.5% (2000 census)
Religion(s): Roman Catholic 41.6%, Protestant 23.3%, Modekngei 8.8% (indigenous to Palau), Seventh-Day Adventist 5.3%, Jehovah's Witness 0.9%, Latter-Day Saints 0.6%, other religion 3.1%, unspecified or none 16.4% (2000 census)
GDP per capita: $9,000 (2001 est.)
Currency: US dollar (USD)
Time: GMT + 9
Electricity: 115/230V, 60Hz
National holiday: Constitution Day, 9 July (1979)

► **GEOGRAPHY**

Location: Oceania, group of islands in the North Pacific Ocean, southeast of the Philippines
Border countries: None
Area: 458 sq km
Coastline: 1,519 km
Climate: tropical; hot and humid; wet season May to November
Terrain: varying geologically from the high, mountainous main island of Babelthuap to low, coral islands usually fringed by large barrier reefs
lowest point: Pacific Ocean 0 m
highest point: Mount Ngerchelchuus 242 m
Natural hazards: typhoons (June to December)
Vaccination(s): Yellow fever: A yellow fever vaccination certificate is required from all travelers over 1 year of age coming from infected areas or from countries in any part of which yellow fever is endemic.

► **DIVING**

Number of certified divers: Mainly tourists
Dive federation(s): None
Dive regulations: Diver certification
Freediving federation(s): None
Major bodies of water: North Pacific Ocean, Philippine Sea
Dive season: year-round
Water temperature: 28.5°C83F (Jan-Mar), 29°C/84.2F (July-Sept)
Hyperbaric chambers:
City: Koror, Belau National Hospital.
Popular dive sites: Big Drop Off, Blue Corner, Shark City, Ngemelis Wall, Turtle Cove
Tourism information: Palau Visitors Authority (www.visit-palau.com)

PALESTINE

► **GENERAL**

Capital: Administrative capital: Ramalla
Government: PNA, Palestine National Authority
Population: 1996 census predicts 3,900,000 by 2005
Ethnic groups: Arabic, Jewish
Language(s): Arabic, Hebrew, English
Religion(s): Muslim, Judaism, Christian, and others
GDP per capita: N/A
Currency: Jordanian Dinar, Israeli Shekel
Time: GMT+2
Electricity: 220V, 50Hz

► **GEOGRAPHY**

Location: Middle East bordering the Mediterranean Sea
Border countries: Jordan, Lebanon
Area: 10,435 square miles
Climate: Temperate sea climate, mild to cool
Terrain: Four distinct regions: coastal plain, mountains, valley, and plateau. South: Negev Desert

Natural hazards: dust storms and sandstorms
Vaccination(s): None

► **DIVING**

Number of certified divers: 60*
Dive federation(s): Palestine Swimming Federation & Aquatic Sports *
Dive regulations: Diver certification, max depth with air...40m, technical (>40m): preliminary registration at local police station, diving is prohibited in harbor area and in areas which are specially marked.
Freediving federation(s): None
Major bodies of water: Mediterranean Sea
Dive season: year-round
Water temperature: 12°C/53.6F (Jan-Mar), 27°C/80.6F (July-Sept)
Hyperbaric chambers:
City: Ljubljana
Telephone: +386 41 696 558
Telephone: +386 1 543 75 37*
Popular dive sites: Piran, Fiesa, Bled, Krka, Bohinj*
Tourism information:
* SOURCE: Palestine Swimming Federation & Aquatic Sports (Nov. 2005)

PANAMA

► **GENERAL**

Capital: Panama
Government: constitutional democracy
Population: 3,039,150 (July 2005 est.)
Ethnic groups: mestizo (mixed Amerindian and white) 70%, Amerindian and mixed (West Indian) 14%, white 10%, Amerindian 6%
Language(s): Spanish (official), English 14%; note - many Panamanians bilingual
Religion(s): Roman Catholic 85%, Protestant 15%
GDP per capita: $6,900 (2004 est.)
Currency: balboa (PAB); US dollar (USD) - balboas per US dollar - 1 (2004)
Time: GMT - 5
Electricity: 110V, 60Hz, 220V
National holiday: Independence Day, 3 November (1903)

► **GEOGRAPHY**

Location: Central America, bordering both the Caribbean Sea and the North Pacific Ocean, between Colombia and Costa Rica

Border countries: Colombia 225 km, Costa Rica 330 km
Area: 78,200 sq km
Coastline: 2,490 km
Climate: tropical maritime; hot, humid, cloudy; prolonged rainy season (May to January), short dry season (January to May)
Terrain: interior mostly steep, rugged mountains and dissected, upland plains; coastal areas largely plains and rolling hills
lowest point: Pacific Ocean 0 m
highest point: Volcan de Chiriqui 3,475 m
Natural hazards: typhoons (June to December)
Vaccination(s): Yellow fever: Yellow fever: A yellow fever vaccination certificate is recommended for all travellers going to Chepo, Darién and San Blas. **Malaria:** Low malaria risk—predominantly due to *P. vivax*—occurs throughout the year in three provinces: Bocas del Toro in the west and Darién and San Blas in the east. In the other provinces there is no or negligible risk of transmission. Chloroquine-resistant *P. falciparum* has been reported in Darién and San Blas provinces. Recommended prevention in risk areas: II; in eastern endemic areas, IV

▶ **DIVING**

Number of certified divers: 7000*
Dive federation(s): El Instituto Panameño de Turismo*
Dive regulations: Diver certification
Freediving federation(s): None*
Major bodies of water: North Pacific Ocean, Caribbean Sea
Dive season: year-round and May to December on Atlantic side at Isla Grande*
Water temperature: 28°C/82.4F (Jan-Mar), 29°C/84.2F (July-Sept)
Hyperbaric chambers:
City: Colón* ACP (Autoridad del Canal de Panama
Popular dive sites: Isla Coiba (Pacífico), Isla Grande (Atlántico), Portobelo (Atlántico), Bocas del Toro (Atlántico)*
Tourism information: Ministry of Tourism (www.visitpanama.com)
* SOURCE: Explora Tour (2006)

PAPUA NEW GUINEA

▶ **GENERAL**

Capital: Port Moresby
Government: constitutional monarchy with parliamentary democracy
Population: 5,545,268 (July 2005 est.)
Ethnic groups: Melanesian, Papuan, Negrito, Micronesian, Polynesian
Language(s): Melanesian Pidgin serves as the lingua franca, English spoken by 1%-2%, Motu spoken in Papua region; *note:* 715 indigenous languages - many unrelated

Religion(s): Roman Catholic 22%, Lutheran 16%, Presbyterian/Methodist/London Missionary Society 8%, Anglican 5%, Evangelical Alliance 4%, Seventh-Day Adventist 1%, other Protestant 10%, indigenous beliefs 34%
GDP per capita: $2,200 (2004 est.)
Currency: kina (PGK) - kina per US dollar - 3.2225 (2004)
Time: GMT + 10
Electricity: 240V, 50Hz
National holiday: Independence Day, 16 September (1975)

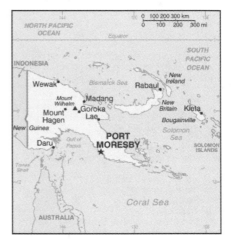

▶ **GEOGRAPHY**

Location: Oceania, group of islands including the eastern half of the island of New Guinea between the Coral Sea and the South Pacific Ocean, east of Indonesia
Border countries: Indonesia 820 km
Area: 462,840 sq km
Coastline: 5,152 km
Climate: tropical; northwest monsoon (December to March), southeast monsoon (May to October); slight seasonal temperature variation
Terrain: mostly mountains with coastal lowlands and rolling foothills
lowest point: Pacific Ocean 0 m
highest point: Mount Wilhelm 4,509 m
Natural hazards: active volcanism; situated along the Pacific "Ring of Fire"; the country is subject to frequent and sometimes severe earthquakes; mud slides; tsunamis
Vaccination(s): Yellow fever: A yellow fever vaccination certificate is required from all travellers over 1 year of age coming from infected areas.
Malaria: Malaria risk—predominantly due to *P. falciparum*—exists throughout the year in the whole country below 1800 m. *P. falciparum* resistant to chloroquine and sulfadoxine–pyrimethamine reported. *P. vivax* resistant to

chloroquine reported. Recommended prevention: IV

► **DIVING**

Number of certified divers: Mainly tourists
Dive federation(s): PNG Divers Association (represents dive tourism business)
Dive regulations: Diver certification
Freediving federation(s): None*
Major bodies of water: South Pacific Ocean, Coral Sea
Dive season: year-round; optimal seasons: mid-April to mid-June; mid Sept to mid-Dec *
Water temperature: 29°C/84.2F (Jan-Mar), 27°C/80.6F (July-Sept)
Hyperbaric chambers:
Port Moresby Medical Services (675) 325 6633 or 683 4444; Chamber Manager, (675) 323 1355 or 683 1200*
Popular dive sites: Kimbe Bay, Madang, The Duke of York Islands, Kavieng
Tourism information: Papua New Guinea Tourism Promotion Authority (www.pngtourism.org.pg)
* SOURCE: PNG Divers Association (2005)

PERU

► **GENERAL**

Capital: Lima
Government: constitutional republic
Population: 27,925,628 (July 2005 est.)
Ethnic groups: Amerindian 45%, mestizo (mixed Amerindian and white) 37%, white 15%, black, Japanese, Chinese, and other 3%
Language(s): Spanish (official), Quechua (official), Aymara, and a large number of minor Amazonian languages

Religion(s): Roman Catholic 81%, Seventh Day Adventist 1.4%, other Christian 0.7%, other 0.6%, unspecified or none 16.3% (2003 est.)
GDP per capita: $5,600 (2004 est.)
Currency: nuevo sol (PEN) - nuevo sol per US dollar - 3.4132 (2004)
Time: GMT - 5
Electricity: 220V, 60Hz
National holiday: Independence Day, 28 July (1821)

► **GEOGRAPHY**

Location: Western South America, bordering the South Pacific Ocean, between Chile and Ecuador
Border countries: Bolivia 900 km, Brazil 1,560 km, Chile 160 km, Colombia 1,496 km (est.), Ecuador 1,420 km
Area: 1,285,220 sq km
Coastline: 2,414 km
Climate: varies from tropical in east to dry desert in west; temperate to frigid in Andes
Terrain: western coastal plain (costa), high and rugged Andes in center (sierra), eastern lowland jungle of Amazon Basin (selva)
lowest point: Pacific Ocean 0 m
highest point: Nevado Huascaran 6,768 m
Natural hazards: earthquakes, tsunamis, flooding, landslides, mild volcanic activity
Vaccination(s): Yellow fever: Yellow fever vaccination is required from travellers over 6 months of age coming from infected areas and is recommended for those who intend to visit jungle areas of the country below 2300 m. **Malaria:** Malaria risk—*P. vivax* (78%), *P. falciparum* (22%)—is high in 21 of the 33 sanitary regions, including Ayacucho, Cajamarca, Cerro de Pasco, Chachapoyas, Chanca-Andahuaylas, Cutervo, Cusco, Huancavelica, Jaen, Junín, La Libertad, Lambayeque, Loreto, Madre de Dios, Piura, San Martín, Tumbes and Ucayali. *P. falciparum* transmission reported in Jaen, Lambayeque, Loreto, Luciano Castillo, Piura, San Martín, Tumbes and Ucayali. Resistance to chloroquine and sulfadoxine–pyrimethamine reported. Recommended prevention: II in *P. vivax* risk areas; IV in *P. falciparum* risk areas.

► **DIVING**

Number of certified divers: N/A
Dive federation(s): Federacion Peruana De Actividades Subacuaticas Subacuaticas
Dive regulations: Diver certification
Freediving federation(s): AIDA
Major bodies of water: South Pacific Ocean
Dive season: year-round
Water temperature: 24°C/75.2F (Jan-Mar), 20°C/68F (July-Sept)
Hyperbaric chambers:
City: Talara, E-med private medical services
Telephone: 51-074383159
Popular dive sites: Máncora, Organos; Lagunillas, Mendieta, Tortugas

Tourism information: Peru Tourism (www.peru.info)

PHILIPPINES

▶ **GENERAL**

Capital: Manila
Government: republic
Population: 87,857,473 (July 2005 est.)
Ethnic groups: Tagalog 28.1%, Cebuano 13.1%, Llocano 9%, Bisaya/Binisaya 7.6%, Hiligaynon Ilonggo 7.5%, Bikol 6%, Waray 3.4%, other 25.3% (2000 census)
Language(s): two official languages - Filipino (based on Tagalog) and English; eight major dialects - Tagalog, Cebuano, Ilocano, Hiligaynon or Ilonggo, Bicol, Waray, Pampango, and Pangasinan
Religion(s): Roman Catholic 80.9%, Evangelical 2.8%, Iglesia ni Kristo 2.3%, Aglipayan 2%, other Christian 4.5%, Muslim 5%, other 1.8%, unspecified 0.6%, none 0.1% (2000 census)
GDP per capita: $5,000 (2004 est.)
Currency: Philippine peso (PHP) - Philippine pesos per US dollar - 56.04 (2004)
Time: GMT + 8
Electricity: 220V, 60Hz
National holiday: Independence Day, 12 June (1898)

▶ **GEOGRAPHY**

Location: Southeastern Asia, archipelago between the Philippine Sea and the South China Sea, east of Vietnam

Border countries: None
Area: 300,000 sq km
Coastline: 36,289 km
Climate: tropical marine; northeast monsoon (November to April); southwest monsoon (May to October)
Terrain: mostly mountains with narrow to extensive coastal lowlands
lowest point: Philippine Sea 0 m
highest point: Mount Apo 2,954 m
Natural hazards: astride typhoon belt, usually affected by 15 and struck by five to six cyclonic storms per year; landslides; active volcanoes; destructive earthquakes; tsunamis
Vaccination(s): Yellow fever: A yellow fever vaccination certificate is required from travellers over 1 year of age coming from infected areas. **Malaria:** Malaria risk exists throughout the year in areas below 600 m, except in the provinces of Aklan, Bilaran, Bohol, Camiguin, Capiz, Catanduanes, Cebu, Guimaras, Iloilo, Leyte, Masbate, northern Samar, Sequijor and metropolitan Manila. No risk is considered to exist in urban areas or in the plains. *P. falciparum* resistant to chloroquine and sulfadoxine–pyrimethamine reported. Recommended prevention in risk areas: IV

▶ **DIVING**

Number of certified divers: N/A
Dive federation(s): Philippine Federation of Cmas Underwater Federation
Dive regulations: Diver certification
Freediving federation(s): None
Major bodies of water: South Pacific Ocean, Philippines Sea, Sulu Sea
Dive season: year-round
Water temperature: 26°C/78.8F (Jan-Mar), 29°C/84.2F(July-Sept)
Hyperbaric chambers: Many
City: Quezon City Manila
Armed Forces of the Philippines (AFP) Medical Center
Telephone: +(632) 920 7183 / 426 2701 to 14 ext. 6445 / 6245
City: Batangas , St. Patrick's Hospital Medical Center
Telephone: +(63-43) 723 7089 (Chamber)
Popular dive sites: Anilao, Puerto Galera, Cabilao Island, Balicasag Island, Apo Island, Malapascua, Tubbataha Reef National Park, Sarangani Bay, Mactan Island, Olango Island
Tourism information: Philippines Tourism (www.tourism.gov.ph)

POLAND

▶ **GENERAL**

Capital: Warsaw
Government: republic
Population: 38,635,144 (July 2005 est.)

Ethnic groups: Polish 96.7%, German 0.4%, Belarusian 0.1%, Ukrainian 0.1%, other and unspecified 2.7% (2002 census)
Language(s): Polish 97.8%, other and unspecified 2.2% (2002 census)
Religion(s): Roman Catholic 89.8% (about 75% practicing), Eastern Orthodox 1.3%, Protestant 0.3%, other 0.3%, unspecified 8.3% (2002)
GDP per capita: $12,000 (2004 est.)
Currency: zloty (PLN) - zlotych per US dollar - 3.6576 (2004)
Time: GMT + 1
Electricity: 230V, 50Hz
National holiday: Constitution Day, 3 May (1791)

► GEOGRAPHY

Location: Central Europe, east of Germany
Border countries: Belarus 407 km, Czech Republic 658 km, Germany 456 km, Lithuania 91 km, Russia (Kaliningrad Oblast) 206 km, Slovakia 444 km, Ukraine 526 km
Area: 312,685 sq km
Coastline: 491 km
Climate: temperate with cold, cloudy, moderately severe winters with frequent precipitation; mild summers with frequent showers and thundershowers
Terrain: mostly flat plain; mountains along southern border
lowest point: near Raczki Elblaskie -2 m
highest point: Rysy 2,499 m
Natural hazards: flooding
Vaccination(s): No vaccination requirements for any international traveller.

► DIVING

Number of certified divers: N/A
Dive federation(s): Polish Underwatersports Frderation
Dive regulations: Diver certification

Freediving federation(s): Freediving Poland (AIDA)
Major bodies of water: Baltic Sea
Dive season: year-round, ice diving in winter
Water temperature: 2°C/35.6F (Jan-Mar), 15°C/59F (July-Sept)
Hyperbaric chambers:
City: Gdynia, National Center of Hyperbaric Medicine
Telephone: (+48) 58 622 51 63
City: Lodz, Piotr Siermontowski, M.D.
Telephone: (48) 42 32 51 45
Popular dive sites: Hancza Lake
Tourism information: Polish National Tourist Office (www.polandtour.org)

PORTUGAL

► GENERAL

Capital: Lisbon
Government: parliamentary democracy
Population: 10,566,212 (July 2005 est.)
Ethnic groups: homogeneous Mediterranean stock; citizens of black African descent who immigrated to mainland during decolonization

number less than 100,000; since 1990 East Europeans have entered Portugal
Language(s): Portuguese (official), Mirandese (official - but locally used)
Religion(s): Roman Catholic 94%, Protestant (1995)
GDP per capita: $17,900 (2004 est.)
Currency: euro (EUR) - euros per US dollar - 0.8054 (2004)
Time: GMT + 1
Electricity: 220V, 50Hz
National holiday: Portugal Day, 10 June (1580); note - also called Camoes Day, the day that revered national poet Luis de Camoes (1524-80) died

▶ **GEOGRAPHY**

Location: Southwestern Europe, bordering the North Atlantic Ocean, west of Spain
Border countries: Spain 1,214 km
Area: 92,391 sq km; *note:* includes Azores and Madeira Islands
Coastline: 1,793 km
Climate: maritime temperate; cool and rainy in north, warmer and drier in south
Terrain: mountainous north of the Tagus River, rolling plains in south
lowest point: Atlantic Ocean 0 m
highest point: Ponta do Pico (Pico or Pico Alto) on Ilha do Pico in the Azores 2,351 m
Natural hazards: Azores subject to severe earthquakes
Vaccination(s): Yellow fever: A yellow fever vaccination certificate is required from travellers over 1 year of age coming from infected areas. The requirement applies only to travellers arriving in or bound for the Azores and Madeira. However, no certificate is required from passengers in transit at Funchal, Porto Santo and Santa Maria.

▶ **DIVING**

Number of certified divers: N/A
Dive federation(s): Portuguese Underwater Federation
Dive regulations: Diver certification
Freediving federation(s): AIDA
Major bodies of water: North Atlantic Ocean
Dive season: year-round
Water temperature: 13°C/55.4F (Jan-Mar), 20°C/68F (July-Sept)
Hyperbaric chambers:
City: Lisboa, Centro De Medicina Hiperbárica
Telephone: (+351-) 21 884 0821/2
City: Açores, Hospital Da Horta
Telephone: (+351-)292 200 100
Popular dive sites: Wreck Hildebrandt, Pedras Atlas, Olu, Boca Das Caldeirinhas, Navio Do Norte
Tourism information: Trade and Tourism of Portugal (www.portugal.org)

PUERTO RICO

▶ **GENERAL**

Capital: San Juan
Government: commonwealth associated with the US
Population: 3,916,632 (July 2005 est.)
Ethnic groups: white (mostly Spanish origin) 80.5%, black 8%, Amerindian 0.4%, Asian 0.2%, mixed and other 10.9%
Language(s): Spanish, English
Religion(s): Roman Catholic 85%, Protestant and other 15%
GDP per capita: $17,700 (2004 est.)
Currency: US dollar (USD)
Time: GMT - 4
Electricity: 110V, 60Hz
National holiday: US Independence Day, 4 July (1776); Puerto Rico Constitution Day, 25 July (1952)

▶ **GEOGRAPHY**

Location: Caribbean, island between the Caribbean Sea and the North Atlantic Ocean, east of the Dominican Republic
Border countries: None
Area: 9,104 sq km
Coastline: 501 km
Climate: tropical marine, mild; little seasonal temperature variation
Terrain: mostly mountains with coastal plain belt in north; mountains precipitous to sea on west coast; sandy beaches along most coastal areas
lowest point: Caribbean Sea 0 m
highest point: Cerro de Punta 1,338 m
Natural hazards: periodic droughts; hurricanes
Vaccination(s): No vaccination requirements for any international traveller.

▶ **DIVING**

Number of certified divers: N/A
Dive federation(s): None
Dive regulations: Diver certification
Freediving federation(s): None
Major bodies of water: North Atlantic Ocean, Caribbean Sea
Dive season: year-round
Water temperature: 24°C/75.2F (Jan-Mar), 28°C/82.4F (July-Sept)
Hyperbaric chambers:

City: San Juan, Puerto Rico Medical Center
Telephone: 787-777-3535 x 6475 / 6476
Popular dive sites: South Coast: from Guánica to
Cabo Rojo - 22 miles long black coral wall, West
Coast: Mona & Desecheo Islands, North Coast:
Isabela - Cave Diving, East Coast , Vieques &
Culebra Islands; East Coast, Fajardo*
Tourism information: Puerto Rico Tourism Com-
pany (www.gotopuertorico.com)

QATAR

► **GENERAL**

Capital: Doha
Government: traditional monarchy
Population: 863,051 (July 2005 est.)
Ethnic groups: Arab 40%, Pakistani 18%, Indian
18%, Iranian 10%, other 14%
Language(s): Arabic (official), English commonly
used as a second language
Religion(s): Muslim 95%
GDP per capita: $23,200 (2004 est.)
Currency: Qatari rial (QAR) - Qatari rials per US
dollar - 3.64 (2004)
Time: GMT + 3

Electricity: 240V, 50Hz
National holiday: Independence Day, 3 September (1971)

► **GEOGRAPHY**

Location: Middle East, peninsula bordering the
Persian Gulf and Saudi Arabia
Border countries: Saudi Arabia 60 km
Area: 11,437 sq km
Coastline: 563 km
Climate: arid; mild, pleasant winters; very hot,
humid summers
Terrain: mostly flat and barren desert covered
with loose sand and gravel
lowest point: Persian Gulf 0 m
highest point: Qurayn Abu al Bawl 103 m
Natural hazards: haze, dust storms, sandstorms
common
Vaccination(s): No vaccination requirements for
any International traveller.

► **DIVING**

Number of certified divers: N/A
Dive federation(s): None
Dive regulations: Diver certification
Freediving federation(s): None
Major bodies of water: Persian Gulf
Dive season: year-round
Water temperature: 22°C/71.6F (Jan-Mar),
26°C/78.8F (July-Sept)
Hyperbaric chambers: N/A
Popular dive sites: Old Club Reef and artificial
reefs
Tourism information: Qatar Tourism Authority
(www.experienceqatar.com)

RÉUNION

► **GENERAL**

Capital: Saint-Denis
Government: overseas department of France
Population: 776,948 (July 2005 est.)
Ethnic groups: French, African, Malagasy, Chi-
nese, Pakistani, Indian
Language(s): French (official), Creole widely used
Religion(s): Roman Catholic 86%, Hindu, Muslim,
Buddhist (1995)
GDP per capita: $6,000 (2004 est.)
Currency: euro (EUR) - euros per US dollar - 0.8054
(2004)
Time: GMT + 4
Electricity: 220V, 50Hz
National holiday: Bastille Day, 14 July (1789)

► **GEOGRAPHY**

Location: Southern Africa, island in the Indian
Ocean, east of Madagascar
Border countries: None
Area: 2,517 sq km
Coastline: 207 km

Climate: tropical, but temperature moderates with elevation; cool and dry from May to November, hot and rainy from November to April
Terrain: mostly rugged and mountainous; fertile lowlands along coast
lowest point: Indian Ocean 0 m
highest point: Piton des Neiges 3,069 m
Natural hazards: periodic, devastating cyclones (December to April); Piton de la Fournaise on the southeastern coast is an active volcano
Vaccination(s): Yellow fever: A yellow fever vaccination certificate is required from travellers over 1 year of age coming from infected areas.

▶ **DIVING**

Number of certified divers: Mainly tourists
Dive federation(s): None
Dive regulations: Diver certification
Freediving federation(s): None
Major bodies of water: Indian Ocean
Dive season: year-round
Water temperature: 27°C/80.6F (Jan-Mar), 23°C/73.4F(July-Sept)
Hyperbaric chambers:
City: Saint Denis, Felix Guyon Hospital
Popular dive sites: Trois Failles, Pain de Sucre, Roches merveilleuses, Wrecks: Navarra Langoustie, Hai Siang
Tourism information: Comité du Tourisme de La Réunion (www.la-reunion-tourisme.com)

ROMANIA

▶ **GENERAL**

Capital: Bucharest
Government: republic
Population: 22,329,977 (July 2005 est.)

Ethnic groups: Romanian 89.5%, Hungarian 6.6%, Roma 2.5%, Ukrainian 0.3%, German 0.3%, Russian 0.2%, Turkish 0.2%, other 0.4% (2002 census)
Language(s): Romanian (official), Hungarian, German
Religion(s): Eastern Orthodox (including all sub-denominations) 86.8%, Protestant (various denominations including Reformate and Pentecostal) 7.5%, Roman Catholic 4.7%, other (mostly Muslim) and unspecified 0.9%, none 0.1% (2002 census)
GDP per capita: $7,700 (2004 est.)
Currency: leu (ROL) - lei per US dollar - 32,637 (2004)
Time: GMT + 2
Electricity: 220V, 50Hz
National holiday: Unification Day (of Romania and Transylvania), 1 December (1918)

▶ **GEOGRAPHY**

Location: Southeastern Europe, bordering the Black Sea, between Bulgaria and Ukraine
Border countries: Bulgaria 608 km, Hungary 443 km, Moldova 450 km, Serbia and Montenegro 476 km, Ukraine (north) 362 km, Ukraine (east) 169 km
Area: 237,500 sq km
Coastline: 225 km
Climate: temperate; cold, cloudy winters with frequent snow and fog; sunny summers with frequent showers and thunderstorms
Terrain: central Transylvanian Basin is separated from the Plain of Moldavia on the east by the Carpathian Mountains and separated from the Walachian Plain on the south by the Transylvanian Alps
lowest point: Black Sea 0 m
highest point: Moldoveanu 2,544 m
Natural hazards: earthquakes, most severe in south and southwest; geologic structure and climate promote landslides

Vaccination(s): No vaccination requirements for any international traveller.

▶ **DIVING**

Number of certified divers: 2,300*
Dive federation(s): Asociatia Nationala A Scafandrilor Profesionisti Si Salvamarilor Din Romania
Dive regulations: Diver certification
Freediving federation(s): None*
Major bodies of water: Black Sea, Danube River
Dive season: 8 months (some 12 months)*
Water temperature: 2°C/30.2F (Jan-Mar), 26°C/78.8F (July-Sept)
Hyperbaric chambers:
City: Centrul de Scafandri Constanta - Constanta
City: Întreprinderea Electrocentrale - Râmnicu-Vâlcea
Popular dive sites: Paris and You Xiu wrecks Constanta - Black sea, Cap Turcului Eforie Sud - Black sea, Cazino - Constanta - Black sea, Caves – Isverna, Belis mountain lake (church partially - underwater)*
Tourism information: Romanian Tourist Office (www.romaniatourism.com)
* SOURCE: Aquarius Dive Centre (2006)

RUSSIA

▶ **GENERAL**

Capital: Moscow
Government: federation
Population: 143,420,309 (July 2005 est.)
Ethnic groups: Russian 79.8%, Tatar 3.8%, Ukrainian 2%, Bashkir 1.2%, Chuvash 1 1%, other or unspecified 12.1% (2002 census)
Language(s): Russian, many minority languages
Religion(s): Russian Orthodox, Muslim, other
GDP per capita: $9,800 (2004 est.)

▶ **DIVING**

Number of certified divers: 3,250 *
Dive federation(s): Confederation Russe des activites subaquatiques (CRASA)
Dive regulations: Diver certification
Freediving federation(s): AIDA
Major bodies of water: North Pacific Ocean, Sea of Japan, Arctic Ocean, Black Sea, Caspian Sea, Baltic Sea
Dive season: year-round including ice-diving*

Currency: Russian ruble (RUR) - Russian rubles per US dollar - 28.814 (2004)
Time: GMT +2 to +11
Electricity: 220V, 50Hz
National holiday: Russia Day, 12 June (1990)

▶ **GEOGRAPHY**

Location: Northern Asia (that part west of the Urals is included with Europe), bordering the Arctic Ocean, between Europe and the North Pacific Ocean
Border countries: Azerbaijan 284 km, Belarus 959 km, China (southeast) 3,605 km, China (south) 40 km, Estonia 294 km, Finland 1,340 km, Georgia 723 km, Kazakhstan 6,846 km, North Korea 19 km, Latvia 217 km, Lithuania (Kaliningrad Oblast) 227 km, Mongolia 3,485 km, Norway 196 km, Poland (Kaliningrad Oblast) 206 km, Ukraine 1,576 km
Area: 17,075,200 sq km
Coastline: 37,653 km
Climate: ranges from steppes in the south through humid continental in much of European Russia; subarctic in Siberia to tundra climate in the polar north; winters vary from cool along Black Sea coast to frigid in Siberia; summers vary from warm in the steppes to cool along Arctic coast
Terrain: broad plain with low hills west of Urals; vast coniferous forest and tundra in Siberia; uplands and mountains along southern border regions
lowest point: Caspian Sea -28 m
highest point: Gora El'brus 5,633 m
Natural hazards: permafrost over much of Siberia is a major impediment to development; volcanic activity in the Kuril Islands; volcanoes and earthquakes on the Kamchatka Peninsula; spring floods and summer/autumn forest fires throughout Siberia and parts of European Russia
Vaccination(s): No vaccination requirements for any international traveller.
Water temperature: 2°C/35.6F (Jan-Mar), 23°C/73.4F (July-Sept)
Hyperbaric chambers:
City Moscow
Telephone: (495) 785-45-38, 298-08-55*
Popular dive sites: Black Sea, White Sea, Japan Sea, Baikal Lake, Baltic Sea
Tourism information: Federal Tourism Agency (www.russiatourism.ru)
* SOURCE: CRASA (2005)

SABA (See Netherlands Antilles)

St. EUSTATIUS (See Netherlands Ant.)

SAINT KITTS AND NEVIS

▶ GENERAL

Capital: Basseterre
Government: constitutional monarchy with West-minster-style parliament
Population: 38,958 (July 2005 est.)
Ethnic groups: predominantly black; some British, Portuguese, and Lebanese
Language(s): English
Religion(s): Anglican, other Protestant, Roman Catholic
GDP per capita: $8,800 (2002 est.)
Currency: East Caribbean dollar (XCD) - East Caribbean dollars per US dollar - 2.7 (2004)
Time: GMT - 4
Electricity: 230V, 60Hz
National holiday: Independence Day, 19 September (1983)

▶ GEOGRAPHY

Location: Caribbean, islands in the Caribbean Sea, about one-third of the way from Puerto Rico to Trinidad and Tobago
Border countries: None
Area: 261 sq km (Saint Kitts 168 sq km; Nevis 93 sq km)
Coastline: 135 km
Climate: tropical tempered by constant sea breezes; little seasonal temperature variation; rainy season (May to November)
Terrain: volcanic with mountainous interiors
lowest point: Caribbean Sea 0 m

highest point: Mount Liamuiga 1,156 m
Natural hazards: hurricanes (July to October)
Vaccination(s): Yellow fever: A yellow fever vaccination certificate is required from travellers over 1 year of age coming from infected areas.

▶ DIVING

Number of certified divers: Mainly tourists
Dive federation(s): None
Dive regulations: Diver certification
Freediving federation(s): None
Major bodies of water: Caribbean Sea
Dive season: year-round
Water temperature: 24°C/75.2F (Jan-Mar), 27°C/80.6F (July-Sept)
Hyperbaric chambers: N/A
Closest: Barbados

Popular dive sites: Black Coral Reef, The Caves, Monkey Reef, River Taw Wreck, M.V. Talata Wreck
Tourism information: St. Kitts Tourism (www.stkitts-tourism.com); Nevis Tourism Authority (www.nevisisland.com)

SAINT LUCIA

▶ GENERAL

Capital: Castries
Government: Westminster-style parliamentary democracy
Population: 166,312 (July 2005 est.)
Ethnic groups: black 90%, mixed 6%, East Indian 3%, white 1%
Language(s): English (official), French patois
Religion(s): Roman Catholic 67.5%, Seventh Day Adventist 8.5%, Pentecostal 5.7%, Anglican 2%, Evangelical 2%, other Christian 5.1%, Rastafarian 2.1%, other 1.1%, unspecified 1.5%, none 4.5% (2001 census)
GDP per capita: $5,400 (2002 est.)
Currency: East Caribbean dollar (XCD) - East Caribbean dollars per US dollar - 2.7 (2004)
Time: GMT - 4
Electricity: 220V, 50Hz
National holiday: Independence Day, 22 February (1979)

▶ GEOGRAPHY

Location: Caribbean, island between the Caribbean Sea and North Atlantic Ocean, north of Trinidad and Tobago
Border countries: None
Area: 616 sq km
Coastline: 158 km
Climate: tropical, moderated by northeast trade winds; dry season from January to April, rainy season from May to August

Terrain: volcanic and mountainous with some broad, fertile valleys
lowest point: Caribbean Sea 0 m
highest point: Mount Gimie 950 m
Natural hazards: hurricanes and volcanic activity
Vaccination(s): Yellow fever: A yellow fever vaccination certificate is required from travellers over 1 year of age coming from infected areas.

▶ DIVING

Number of certified divers: Mainly tourists
Dive federation(s): None
Dive regulations: Diver certification
Freediving federation(s): None
Major bodies of water: North Atlantic Ocean, Caribbean Sea
Dive season: year-round
Water temperature: 26°C/78.8F (Jan-Mar), 28°C/82.4F (July-Sept)
Hyperbaric chambers:
Closest: Martinique & Barbados
Popular dive sites: Keyhole Pinnacles, Gros Piton, Anse Chastenet, Anse La Raye, the Waiwinette freighter
Tourism information: Saint Lucia Tourist Board (www.stlucia.org)

St. MAARTEN (See Netherlands Antilles)

SAINT-PIERRE AND MIQUELON

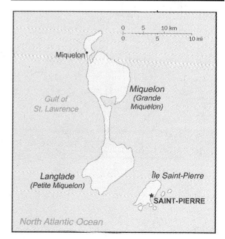

▶ GENERAL

Capital: Saint-Pierre
Government: self-governing territorial collectivity of France
Population: 7,012 (July 2005 est.)
Ethnic groups: Basques and Bretons (French fishermen)
Language(s): French (official)

Religion(s): Roman Catholic 99%
GDP per capita: $5,400 (2002 est.)
Currency: East Caribbean dollar (XCD) - East Caribbean dollars per US dollar - 2.7 (2004)
Time: GMT - 3
Electricity:
National holiday: Bastille Day, 14 July (1789)

▶ **GEOGRAPHY**

Location: Northern North America, islands in the North Atlantic Ocean, south of Newfoundland (Canada)
Border countries: None
Area: 242 sq km; *note:* includes eight small islands in the Saint Pierre and the Miquelon groups
Coastline: 120 km
Climate: cold and wet, with much mist and fog; spring and autumn are windy
Terrain: mostly barren rock
lowest point: Atlantic Ocean 0 m
highest point: Morne de la Grande Montagne 240m
Natural hazards: persistent fog throughout the year can be a maritime hazard
Vaccination(s): No vaccination requirements for any international traveller.

▶ **DIVING**

Number of certified divers: N/A
Dive federation(s): FFESSM
Dive regulations: Diver certification
Freediving federation(s): AIDA
Major bodies of water: Gulf of Saint-Lawrence
Dive season: year-round
Water temperature: 0°C/37.4F (Jan-Mar), 8°C/46.4F (July-Sept)
Hyperbaric chambers: N/A
Closest: Newfoundland Canada
Popular dive sites:
Tourism information: Tourism Agency of Saint-Pierre et Miquelon (www.st-pierre-et-miquelon.com)

ST-VINCENT AND THE GRENADINES

▶ **GENERAL**

Capital: Kingstown
Government: parliamentary democracy; independent sovereign state within the Commonwealth
Population: 117,534 (July 2005 est.)
Ethnic groups: black 66%, mixed 19%, East Indian 6%, Carib Amerindian 2%, other 7%
Language(s): English, French patois
Religion(s): Anglican 47%, Methodist 28%, Roman Catholic 13%, Hindu, Seventh-Day Adventist, other Protestant
GDP per capita: $2,900 (2002 est.)

Currency: East Caribbean dollar (XCD) - East Caribbean dollars per US dollar - 2.7 (2004)
Time: GMT - 4
Electricity: 220V, 50Hz
National holiday: Independence Day, 27 October (1979)

▶ **GEOGRAPHY**

Location: Caribbean, islands between the Caribbean Sea and North Atlantic Oceannorth of Trinidad and Tobago
Border countries: None
Area: 389 sq km (Saint Vincent 344 sq km)
Coastline: 84 km
Climate: tropical; little seasonal temperature variation; rainy season (May to November)
Terrain: volcanic, mountainous
lowest point: Caribbean Sea 0 m
highest point: Soufriere 1,234 m
Natural hazards: hurricanes; Soufriere volcano on the island of Saint Vincent is a constant threat
Vaccination(s): Yellow fever: A yellow fever vaccination certificate is required from travellers over 1 year of age coming from infected areas.

▶ **DIVING**

Number of certified divers: Mainly tourists
Dive federation(s): None
Dive regulations: Diver certification, no spear fishing within Vincentian waters, strict rules regarding water sports within the Tobago Cays* nothing can be removed from reefs in designated park areas**
Freediving federation(s): None*
Major bodies of water: Caribbean Sea
Dive season: year-round
Water temperature: 26°C/78.8F (Jan-Mar), 28°C/82.4F (July-Sept)

Hyperbaric chambers:
City: Bridgetown, Barbados
Telephone: (246) 436 6185
City: Martinique
Telephone (596) 751575**
Popular dive sites: Petit Byahaut, The Steps, Anchor Reef, Horseshoe Reef (Tobago Cays), The Wall (Bequia)* West Cay, The Boulders, Devil's Table, Moonhole, Middle Cay**
Tourism information: Department of Tourism (www.svgtourism.com)
* SOURCE: Indigo Dive (2006)
** SOURCE: Dive Bequia (2006)

SAMOA

▶ **GENERAL**

Capital: Apia
Government: mix of parliamentary democracy and constitutional monarchy
Population: 177,287 (July 2005 est.)
Ethnic groups: Samoan 92.6%, Euronesians 7% (persons of European and Polynesian blood), Europeans 0.4%
Language(s): Samoan (Polynesian), English
Religion(s): Congregationalist 34.8%, Roman Catholic 19.6%, Methodist 15%, Latter-Day Saints 12.7%, Assembly of God 6.6%, Seventh-Day Adventist 3.5%, other Christian 4.5%, Worship Centre 1.3%, other 1.7%, unspecified 0.1% (2001 census)
GDP per capita: $2,900 (2002 est.)
Currency: East Caribbean dollar (XCD) - East Caribbean dollars per US dollar - 2.7 (2004)
Time: GMT - 11
Electricity: 240V, 50Hz
National holiday: Independence Day Celebration, 1 June (1962)

▶ **GEOGRAPHY**

Location: Oceania, group of islands in the South Pacific Ocean, about one-half of the way from Hawaii to New Zealand
Border countries: None
Area: 2,944 sq km
Coastline: 403 km
Climate: tropical; rainy season (November to April), dry season (May to October)
Terrain: two main islands (Savaii, Upolu) and several smaller islands and uninhabited islets; narrow coastal plain with volcanic, rocky, rugged mountains in interior
lowest point: Pacific Ocean 0 m
highest point: Mauga Silisili (Savaii) 1,857 m
Natural hazards: occasional typhoons; active volcanism
Vaccination(s): Yellow fever: A yellow fever vaccination certificate is required from travellers over 1 year of age coming from infected areas.

▶ **DIVING**

Number of certified divers: 70*
Dive federation(s): None
Dive regulations: Diver certification, no spear fishing*
Freediving federation(s): None
Major bodies of water: South Pacific Ocean
Dive season: Best from March to November. Rainy season December to February: limited diving locations*
Water temperature: 24°C/75.2F (Jan-Mar), 21°C/69.8F (July-Sept)
Hyperbaric chambers:
City: Pago Pago, American Samoa
Telephone: (+684)2584965 or (+684)6334573*
Popular dive sites: Juno wreck (1881), Coral Gardens, Tiupili's Heaven, Lelepa Bay, Larva Fields*
Tourism information: Samoa Tourism Authority (www.visitsamoa.ws)
* SOURCE: **Dive Savaii (2006)**

SAN MARINO

▶ **GENERAL**

Capital: San Marino
Government: independent republic
Population: 28,880 (July 2005 est.)

Ethnic groups: Sammarinese, Italian
Language(s): Italian
Religion(s): Roman Catholic
GDP per capita: $34,600 (2001 est.)
Currency: euro (EUR) - euros per US dollar - 0.8054 (2004)
Time: GMT - 11
Electricity: 220V, 50Hz
National holiday: Founding of the Republic, 3 September (301)

▶ **GEOGRAPHY**

Location: Southern Europe, an enclave in central Italy
Border countries: Italy 39 km
Area: 61.2 sq km
Coastline: 0 km (landlocked)
Climate: Mediterranean; mild to cool winters; warm, sunny summers
Terrain: rugged mountains
lowest point: Torrente Ausa 55 m
highest point: Monte Titano 755 m
Natural hazards: NA
Vaccination(s): No vaccination requirements for any international traveller.

▶ **DIVING**

Number of certified divers: Mainly tourists
Dive federation(s): Federazione Sammarinese Attivita Subacquee
Dive regulations: Diver certification
Freediving federation(s): None
Major bodies of water: Adriatic Sea
Dive season: year-round
Water temperature: 13°C/55.4F (Jan-Mar), 23°C/73.4F (July-Sept)
Hyperbaric chambers: N/A
Closest: Bologna Italy
Popular dive sites:
Tourism information: Segreteria di Stato per il Lavoro e Cooperazione, Turismo, Sport e Poste (www.visitsanmarino.com)

SAO TOME AND PRINCIPE

▶ **GENERAL**

Capital: Sao Tome
Government: republic
Population: 187,410 (July 2005 est.)
Ethnic groups: mestico, angolares (descendants of Angolan slaves), forros (descendants of freed slaves), servicais (contract laborers from Angola, Mozambique, and Cape Verde), tongas (children of servicais born on the islands), Europeans (primarily Portuguese)
Language(s): Portuguese (official)
Religion(s): Catholic 70.3%, Evangelical 3.4%, New Apostolic 2%, Adventist 1.8%, other 3.1%, none 19.4% (2001 census)
GDP per capita: $1,200 (2003 est.)

Currency: dobra (STD) - dobras per US dollar - 9,900.4 (2004)
Time: GMT + 0
Electricity: 220V, 50Hz
National holiday: Independence Day, 12 July (1975)

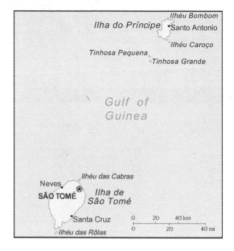

▶ **GEOGRAPHY**

Location: Western Africa, islands in the Gulf of Guinea, straddling the Equator, west of Gabon
Border countries: None
Area: 1,001 sq km
Coastline: 209 km
Climate: tropical; hot, humid; one rainy season (October to May)
Terrain: volcanic, mountainous
lowest point: Atlantic Ocean 0 m
highest point: Pico de Sao Tome 2,024 m
Natural hazards: NA
Vaccination(s): Yellow fever: A yellow fever vaccination certificate is required from all travellers over 1 year of age. **Malaria:** Malaria risk—predominantly due to *P. falciparum*—exists throughout the year. Chloroquine-resistant *P. falciparum* reported. Recommended prevention: IV

▶ **DIVING**

Number of certified divers: Mainly tourists
Dive federation(s): None
Dive regulations: Diver certification
Freediving federation(s): None
Major bodies of water: Gulf of Guinea
Dive season: year-round
Water temperature: 28.5°C/83F (Jan-Mar), 25°C/77F (July-Sept)
Hyperbaric chambers: N/A
Popular dive sites: Bom Bom Island

Tourism information: São Tomé and Principe (www.saotome.st)

SAUDI ARABIA

▶ GENERAL

Capital: Riyadh
Government: monarchy
Population: 26,417,599; *note:* includes 5,576,076 non-nationals (July 2005 est.)
Ethnic groups: Arab 90%, Afro Asian 10% **Language(s):** Arabic
Religion(s): Muslim 100%
GDP per capita: $12,000 (2004 est.)
Currency: Saudi riyal (SAR) - Saudi riyals per US dollar - 3.745 (2004)
Time: GMT + 3
Electricity: 127/220V, 60Hz
National holiday: Unification of the Kingdom, 23 September (1932)

▶ GEOGRAPHY

Location: Middle East, bordering the Persian Gulf and the Red Sea, north of Yemen
Border countries: Iraq 814 km, Jordan 744 km, Kuwait 222 km, Oman 676 km, Qatar 60 km, UAE 457 km, Yemen 1,458 km
Area: 1,960,582 sq km
Coastline: 2,640 km
Climate: harsh, dry desert with great temperature extremes
Terrain: mostly uninhabited, sandy desert
lowest point: Persian Gulf 0 m
highest point: Jabal Sawda' 3,133 m
Natural hazards: frequent sand and dust storms
Vaccination(s): Yellow fever: A yellow fever vaccination certificate is required from all travellers coming from countries, any parts of which are infected. **Malaria:** Malaria risk—predominantly

due to *P. falciparum*—exists throughout the year in most of the Southern Region (except in the high-altitude areas of Asir Province) and in certain rural areas of the Western Region. No risk in Mecca or Medina cities. Chloroquine-resistant *P. falciparum* reported. Recommended prevention in risk areas: IV

▶ DIVING

Number of certified divers: N/A
Dive federation(s): Saudi Divng Federation
Dive regulations: Diver certification
Freediving federation(s): None
Major bodies of water: Red Sea, Persian Gulf
Dive season: year-round
Water temperature: 23°C/73.4F (Jan-Mar), 29°C/84.2F (July-Sept)
Hyperbaric chambers:
City: Jeddah, Jeddah Decompression Chamber
Telephone (966-2) 682-3200
City: Riyadh. King Faisal Specialist Hospital & Research Centre,
Telephone: 00966 - 1 - 4647272 pager 8517
Popular dive sites: Plateau, Saudi Arabia Border, Farasan Banks, Yanbu
Tourism Information: Royal Embassy of Saudi Arabia
(www.saudiembassy.net); Supreme Commission for Tourism (www.sct.gov.sa)

SCOTLAND (See United Kingdom)

SENEGAL

▶ GENERAL

Capital: Dakar
Government: republic under multiparty democratic rule

Population: 11,126,832 (July 2005 est.)
Ethnic groups: Wolof 43.3%, Pular 23.8%, Serer 14.7%, Jola 3.7%, Mandinka 3%, Soninke 1.1%, European and Lebanese 1%, other 9.4% **Language(s):** French (official), Wolof, Pulaar, Jola, Mandinka
Religion(s): Muslim 94%, indigenous beliefs 1%, Christian 5% (mostly Roman Catholic)
GDP per capita: $1,700 (2004 est.)
Currency: Communauté Financière Africaine franc (XOF) - Communauté Financière Africaine francs (XOF) per US dollar - 528.29 (2004)
Time: GMT + 0
Electricity: 220V, 50Hz
National holiday: Unification of the Kingdom, 23 September (1932)

▶ **GEOGRAPHY**

Location: Western Africa, bordering the North Atlantic Ocean, between Guinea-Bissau and Mauritania
Border countries: Gambia 740 km, Guinea 330 km, Guinea-Bissau 338 km, Mali 419 km, Mauritania 813 km
Area: 196,190 sq km
Coastline: 531 km
Climate: tropical; hot, humid; rainy season (May to November) has strong southeast winds; dry season (December to April) dominated by hot, dry, harmattan wind
Terrain: generally low, rolling, plains rising to foothills in southeast
lowest point: Atlantic Ocean 0 m
highest point: unnamed feature near Nepen Diakha 581 m
Natural hazards: lowlands seasonally flooded; periodic droughts
Vaccination(s): Yellow fever: A yellow fever vaccination certificate is required from travellers coming from endemic areas. **Malaria:** Malaria risk—predominantly due to *P. falciparum*—exists throughout the year in the whole country. There is less risk from January through June in the central western regions. Resistance to chloroquine and sulfadoxine–pyrimethamine reported. Recommended prevention: IV

▶ **DIVING**

Number of certified divers: Mainly tourists
Dive federation(s): Federation Senegalaise Des Activites Subaquatiques
Dive regulations: Diver certification
Freediving federation(s): None
Major bodies of water: North Atlantic Ocean
Dive season: year-round, best: mid-May – Dec.
Water temperature: 16°C/60.8F (Jan-Mar), 26°C/78.8F (July-Sept)
Hyperbaric chambers: N/A
Popular dive sites: Goree island, l'île de la Madeleine, The Tacoma wreck
Tourism information: Ministry of Tourism (www.tourisme.gouv.sn)

SERBIA

▶ **GENERAL**

Capital: Belgrade
Government: Republic
Population: 10,829,175 (July 2005 est.)
Ethnic groups: Serb 62.6%, Albanian 16.5%, Montenegrin 5%, Hungarian 3.3%, other 12.6% (1991)
Language(s): Serbian 95%, Albanian 5%
Religion(s): Orthodox 65%, Muslim 19%, Roman Catholic 4%, Protestant 1%, other 11%
GDP per capita: $2,400 (2004 est.)
Currency: New Yugoslav dinar (YUM); note - in Montenegro the euro is legal tender; in Kosovo both the euro and the Yugoslav dinar are legal
Time: GMT + 1
Electricity: 220V, 50Hz
National holiday: National Day, 27 April

▶ **GEOGRAPHY**

Location: Southeastern Europe, bordering the Adriatic Sea, between Albania and Bosnia and Herzegovina
Border countries: Albania 287 km, Bosnia and Herzegovina 527 km, Bulgaria 318 km, Croatia (north) 241 km, Croatia (south) 25 km, Hungary 151 km, Macedonia 221 km, Romania 476 km
Area: 102,350 sq. km
Coastline: 199 km
Climate: In the north, continental climate (cold winters and hot, humid summers with well distributed rainfall); central portion, continental and Mediterranean climate; to the south, Adriatic climate along the coast, hot, dry summers and autumns and relatively cold winters with heavy snowfall inland
Terrain: Extremely varied; to the north, rich fertile plains; to the east, limestone ranges and basins;

to the southeast, ancient mountains and hills; to the southwest, extremely high shoreline with no islands off the coast
lowest point: Adriatic Sea 0 m
highest point: Daravica 2,656 m
Natural hazards: Earthquakes
Vaccination(s): No vaccination requirements for any international traveller.

▶ **DIVING**

Number of certified divers: 15,000* includes Montenegro
Dive federation(s): Serbia and Montenegro Divers Association
Dive regulations: None*
Freediving federation(s): AIDA
Major bodies of water: Adriatic Sea
Dive season: All year in Adriatic Sea*
Water temperature: 15°C/59F (Jan-Mar), 24°C/75.2F (July-Sept)
Hyperbaric chambers:
Popular dive sites: Cattaro submarine wrecks UC-24, U-72
Tourism information: Montenegro Official Tourist Site (www.visit-montenegro.com)

* SOURCE: Serbia and Montenegro Divers Association (2006)

SEYCHELLES

▶ **GENERAL**

Capital: Victoria
Government: Republic
Population: 81,188 (July 2005 est.)
Ethnic groups: mixed French, African, Indian, Chinese, and Arab
Language(s): Creole 91.8%, English 4.9% (official), other 3.1%, unspecified 0.2% (2002 census)

Religion(s): Roman Catholic 82.3%, Anglican 6.4%, Seventh Day Adventist 1.1%, other Christian 3.4%, Hindu 2.1%, Muslim 1.1%, other non-Christian 1.5%, unspecified 1.5%, none 0.6% (2002 census)
GDP per capita: $7,800 (2002 est.)
Currency: Seychelles rupee (SCR) - Seychelles rupees per US dollar - 5.5 (2004)
Time: GMT + 4
Electricity: 240V, 50Hz
National holiday: Constitution Day (National Day), 18 June (1993)

▶ **GEOGRAPHY**

Location: archipelago in the Indian Ocean, northeast of Madagascar
Border countries: None
Area: 455 sq km
Coastline: 491 km
Climate: tropical marine; humid; cooler season during southeast monsoon (late May to September); warmer season during northwest monsoon (March to May)
Terrain: Mahe Group is granitic, narrow coastal strip, rocky, hilly; others are coral, flat, elevated reefs
lowest point: Indian Ocean 0 m
highest point: Morne Seychellois 905 m
Natural hazards: lies outside the cyclone belt, so severe storms are rare; short droughts possible
Vaccination(s): Yellow fever: A yellow fever vaccination certificate is required from travellers over 1 year of age coming from infected areas or who have passed through partly or wholly endemic areas within the preceding 6 days. The countries and areas included in the endemic zones are considered as infected areas.

▶ **DIVING**

Number of certified divers: 650*
Dive federation(s): None*
Dive regulations: Diver certification
Freediving federation(s): None*
Major bodies of water: Indian Ocean
Dive season: year-round: best: March to mid-May and Oct. to mid-Dec.
Water temperature: 28°C/82.4F (Jan-Mar), 26°C/78.8F (July-Sept)
Hyperbaric chambers
City: Victoria Hospital, Mahe
Telephone: 388020
Popular dive sites: Shark Bank, South Marianne Island, Brissare Rocks, Ennerdale Wreck, Stork Patch*
Tourism information: Seychelles Tourist Office (www.seychelles.com)
* SOURCE: Dive Seychelles (2006)

SINGAPORE

▶ **GENERAL**

Capital: Singapore
Government: parliamentary republic
Population: 4,425,720 (July 2005 est.)
Ethnic groups: Chinese 76.8%, Malay 13.9%, Indian 7.9%, other 1.4% (2000 census)
Language(s): Mandarin 35%, English 23%, Malay 14.1%, Hokkien 11.4%, Cantonese 5.7%, Teochew 4.9%, Tamil 3.2%, other Chinese dialects 1.8%, other 0.9% (2000 census)
Religion(s): Buddhist 42.5%, Muslim 14.9%, Taoist 8.5%, Hindu 4%, Catholic 4.8%, other Christian 9.8%, other 0.7%, none 14.8% (2000 census)
GDP per capita: $27,800 (2004 est.)
Currency: Singapore dollar (SGD) - Singapore dollars per US dollar - 1.6902 (2004)
Time: GMT + 8
Electricity: 220/240V, 50Hz
National holiday: National Day, 9 August (1965)

▶ **GEOGRAPHY**

Location: Southeastern Asia, islands between Malaysia and Indonesia
Border countries: None
Area: 692.7 sq km
Coastline: 193 km
Climate: tropical; hot, humid, rainy; two distinct monsoon seasons - Northeastern monsoon from December to March and Southwestern monsoon from June to September; inter-monsoon - frequent afternoon and early evening thunderstorms
Terrain: lowland; gently undulating central plateau contains water catchment area and nature preserve
lowest point: Singapore Strait 0 m

highest point: Bukit Timah 166 m
Natural hazards: NA
Vaccination(s): Yellow fever: A yellow fever vaccination certificate is required from travellers over 1 year of age coming from infected areas. Certificates of vaccination are required from travellers over 1 year of age who, within the preceding 6 days, have been in or have passed through any country partly or wholly endemic for yellow fever.

▶ **DIVING**

Number of certified divers: N/A
Dive federation(s): Singapore Underwater Federation (SUF)
Dive regulations: Diver certification
Freediving federation(s): AIDA
Major bodies of water: South China Sea, Main Strait, Singapore Strait
Dive season: year-round
Water temperature: 28°C/82.4F (Jan-Mar), 28.5°C/83F (July-Sept)
Hyperbaric chambers:
Hyperbaric Medical Services
Camden Medical Centre
Tel: + (65) 6732 8552 / 6732 0068
Hyperbaric Medical Services
Tan Tock Seng Hospital Basement 1
Tel: + (43365) 63559021 / 63559022
Popular dive sites: Pulau Tioman, Pulau hantu, Kusu Island, Pulau Sudong, Pulau Kapas
Tourism information: Singapore Tourism Board (www.visitsingapore.com)

SLOVAKIA

▶ **GENERAL**

Capital: Bratislava
Government: parliamentary democracy
Population: 5,431,363 (July 2005 est.)
Ethnic groups: Slovak 85.8%, Hungarian 9.7%, Roma 1.7%, Ruthenian/Ukrainian 1%, other and unspecified 1.8% (2001 census)
Language(s): Slovak (official) 83.9%, Hungarian 10.7%, Roma 1.8%, Ukrainian 1%, other or unspecified 2.6% (2001 census)
Religion(s): Roman Catholic 68.9%, Protestant 10.8%, Greek Catholic 4.1%, other or unspecified 3.2%, none 13% (2001 census)
GDP per capita: $14,500 (2004 est.)
Currency: Slovak koruna (SKK) - koruny per US dollar - 32.257 (2004)

Time: GMT + 1
Electricity: 220V, 50Hz
National holiday: Constitution Day, 1 September (1992)

▶ **GEOGRAPHY**

Location: Central Europe, south of Poland
Border countries: Austria 91 km, Czech Republic 215 km, Hungary 677 km, Poland 444 km, Ukraine 97 km
Area: 48,845 sq km
Coastline: 0 km (landlocked)
Climate: temperate; cool summers; cold, cloudy, humid winters
Terrain: rugged mountains in the central and northern part and lowlands in the south
lowest point: Bodrok River 94 m
highest point: Gerlachovsky Stit 2,655 m
Natural hazards: NA
Vaccination(s): No vaccination requirements for any international traveller.

▶ **DIVING**

Number of certified divers: N/A
Dive federation(s): Slovak Divers Association
Dive regulations: Diver certification
Freediving federation(s): AIDA
Major bodies of water: Danube River
Water temperature: 0°C/32F (Jan-Mar), 21°C/69.8F (July-Sept)
Hyperbaric chambers: N/A
Popular dive sites:
Tourism information: Slovak Tourist Board (www.slovakiatourism.sk)

SLOVENIA

▶ **GENERAL**

Capital: Ljubljana
Government: Parliamentary democratic republic
Population: 2,011,070 (July 2005 est.)
Ethnic groups: Slovene 83.1%, Serb 2%, Croat 1.8%, Bosniak 1.1%, other or unspecified 12% (2002 census)
Language(s): Slovenian 91.1%, Serbo-Croatian 4.5%, other or unspecified 4.4% (2002 census)
Religion(s): Catholic 57.8%, Orthodox 2.3%, other Christian 0.9%, Muslim 2.4%, unaffiliated 3.5%, other or unspecified 23%, none 10.1% (2002 census)
GDP per capita: $19,600 (2004 est.)
Currency: Tolar (SIT) - tolars per US dollar - 192.38 (2004)
Time: GMT + 1
Electricity: 220V, 50Hz
National holiday: Independence Day/Statehood Day, 25 June (1991)

▶ **GEOGRAPHY**

Location: Central Europe, eastern Alps bordering the Adriatic Sea, between Austria and Croatia.
Border countries: Austria 330 km, Croatia 670 km, Italy 232 km, Hungary 102 km
Area: 20,273 sq. km
Coastline: 46.6 km
Climate: Mediterranean climate on the coast, continental climate with mild to hot summers and cold winters in the plateaus and valleys to the east.
Terrain: A short coastal strip on the Adriatic, an alpine mountain region adjacent to Italy and Austria, mixed mountains and valleys with numerous rivers to the east.
Lowest point: Adriatic Sea (0 m)
Highest point: Triglav (2,864 m)
Natural hazards: Flooding and earthquakes
Vaccination(s): No vaccination requirements for any international traveller.

▶ **DIVING**

Number of certified divers: 5,000*
Dive federation(s): Slovenian diving federation
Dive regulations: Diver certification, preliminary registration at local police station; diving prohibited in harbor and specially marked areas.
Freediving federation(s): AIDA
Major bodies of water: Adriatic Sea
Dive season: year-round*
Water temperature: 10°C/50F (Jan-Mar), 26°C/78.8F (July-Sept)
Hyperbaric chambers:
Ljubljana: +386 41 696 558
Ljubljana: +386 1 543 75 37*
Popular dive sites: Piran, Fiesa, Bled, Krka, Bohinj*
Tourism information: Slovenian Tourist Board (www.slovenia-tourism.si)
* SOURCE: SPZ (2005)

SOLOMON ISLANDS

▶ **GENERAL**

Capital: Honiara
Government: parliamentary democracy
Population: 538,032 (July 2005 est.)
Ethnic groups: Melanesian 94.5%, Polynesian 3%, Micronesian 1.2%, other 1.1%, unspecified 0.2% (1999 census)

Language(s): Melanesian pidgin in much of the country is lingua franca; English is official but spoken by only 1%-2% of the population; *note:* 120 indigenous languages
Religion(s): Church of Melanesia 32.8%, Roman Catholic 19%, South Seas Evangelical 17%, Seventh-Day Adventist 11.2%, United Church 10.3%, Christian Fellowship Church 2.4%, other Christian 4.4%, other 2.4%, unspecified 0.3%, none 0.2% (1999 census)
GDP per capita: $1,700 (2002 est.)
Currency: Solomon Islands dollar (SBD) - Solomon Islands dollars per US dollar - 7.4847 (2004)
Time: GMT + 11
Electricity: 240V, 50Hz
National holiday: Independence Day, 7 July (1978)

▶ **GEOGRAPHY**

Location: Oceania, group of islands in the South Pacific Ocean, east of Papua New Guinea
Border countries: None
Area: 28,450 sq km
Coastline: 5,313 km
Climate: tropical monsoon; few extremes of temperature and weather
Terrain: mostly rugged mountains with some low coral atolls
lowest point: Pacific Ocean 0 m
highest point: Mount Makarakomburu 2,447 m
Natural hazards: typhoons, but rarely destructive; geologically active region with frequent earth tremors; volcanic activity
Vaccination(s): Yellow fever: A yellow fever vaccination certificate is required from travellers coming from infected areas. **Malaria:** Malaria risk—predominantly due to *P. falciparum*—exists throughout the year except in a few eastern and southern outlying islets. *P. falciparum* resistant to

chloroquine and sulfadoxine–pyrimethamine reported. Recommended prevention: III

▶ **DIVING**

Number of certified divers: 150*
Dive federation(s): None*
Dive regulations: Diver certification*
Freediving federation(s): None*
Major bodies of water: South Pacific Ocean, Solomon Sea, Coral Sea
Dive season: year-round
Water temperature: 29°C/84.2F (Jan-Mar), 29°C/84.2F (July-Sept)
Hyperbaric chambers:
City: Honiara, Blue Zone Medical Centre
Telephone: 21205*
Popular dive sites: Toa Maru, Hellcat Fighter plane, Grand Central Station, Hot Spot, Yellow Corner*
Tourism information: Solomon Islands Visitors Bureau (www.visitsolomons.com.sb)
* SOURCE: Dive Gizo (2006)

SOMALIA

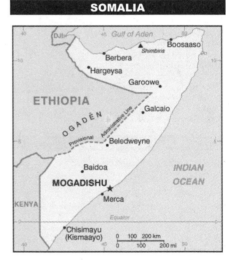

▶ **GENERAL**

Capital: Mogadishu
Government: no permanent national government; transitional, parliamentary federal government
Population: 8,591,629
Ethnic groups: Somali 85%, Bantu and other non-Somali 15% (including Arabs 30,000)
Language(s): Somali (official), Arabic, Italian, English
Religion(s): Sunni Muslim
GDP per capita: $600 (2004 est.)
Currency: Somali shilling (SOS) - Somali shillings per US dollar - 11,000 (November 2000)

Time: GMT + 3
Electricity: 220V, 50V
National holiday: Foundation of the Somali Republic, 1 July (1960)

▶ **GEOGRAPHY**

Location: Eastern Africa, bordering the Gulf of Aden and the Indian Ocean, east of Ethiopia
Border countries: Djibouti 58 km, Ethiopia 1,600 km, Kenya 682 km
Area: 637,657 sq km
Coastline: 3,025 km
Climate: principally desert; December to February - northeast monsoon, moderate temperatures in north and very hot in south; May to October - southwest monsoon, torrid in the north and hot in the south, irregular rainfall, hot and humid periods (tangambili) between monsoons
Terrain: mostly flat to undulating plateau rising to hills in north
lowest point: Indian Ocean *highest point:* Shimbiris 2,416 m
Natural hazards: recurring droughts; frequent dust storms over eastern plains in summer; floods during rainy season
Vaccination(s): Yellow fever: A yellow fever vaccination certificate is required from travellers coming from infected areas. **Malaria:** Malaria risk—predominantly due to *P. falciparum*—exists throughout the year in the whole country. Resistance to chloroquine and sulfadoxine–pyrimethamine reported. Recommended prevention: IV

▶ **DIVING**

Number of certified divers: Mainly tourists
Dive federation(s): None
Dive regulations: Diver certification
Freediving federation(s): None
Major bodies of water: Indian Ocean, Gulf of Aden
Dive season: year-round
Water temperature: 28°C/84.2F (Jan-Mar), 26°C/78.8F (July-Sept)
Hyperbaric chambers: N/A
Closest: Saudi Arabia
Popular dive sites: Bajuni Islands
Tourism information: NA

SOUTH AFRICA

▶ **GENERAL**

Capital: Pretoria
Government: republic
Population: 44,344,136
Ethnic groups: black African 79%, white 9.6%, colored 8.9%, Indian/Asian 2.5% (2001 census)
Language(s): IsiZulu 23.8%, IsiXhosa 17.6%, Afrikaans 13.3%, Sepedi 9.4%, English 8.2%, Setswana 8.2%, Sesotho 7.9%, Xitsonga 4.4%, other 7.2% (2001 census)

Religion(s): Zion Christian 11.1%, Pentecostal / Charismatic 8.2%, Catholic 7.1%, Methodist 6.8%, Dutch Reformed 6.7%, Anglican 3.8%, other Christian 36%, Islam 1.5%, other 2.3%, unspecified 1.4%, none 15.1% (2001 census)
GDP per capita: $11,100 (2004 est.)
Currency: rand (ZAR) - rand per US dollar - 6.4597 (2004)
Time: GMT + 2
Electricity: 220/230V, 50 Hz
National holiday: Freedom Day, 27 April (1994)

▶ **GEOGRAPHY**

Location: Southern Africa, at the southern tip of the continent of Africa
Border countries: Botswana 1,840 km, Lesotho 909 km, Mozambique 491 km, Namibia 967 km, Swaziland 430 km, Zimbabwe 225 km
Area: 1,219,912 sq km; note: includes Prince Edward Islands (Marion Island and Prince Edward Island)
Coastline: 2,798 km
Climate: mostly semiarid; subtropical along east coast; sunny days, cool nights
Terrain: vast interior plateau rimmed by rugged hills and narrow coastal plain
lowest point: Atlantic Ocean 0 m
highest point: Njesuthi 3,408 m
Natural hazards: prolonged droughts
Vaccination(s): Yellow fever: A yellow fever vaccination certificate is required from travellers over 1 year of age coming from infected areas. The countries or areas included in the endemic zones in Africa and the Americas are regarded as infected. **Malaria:** Malaria risk—predominantly due to *P. falciparum*—exists throughout the year in the low altitude areas of Mpumalanga Province (including the Kruger National Park), Northern Province and north-eastern KwaZulu-Natal as far

south as the Tugela River. Risk is highest from October to May. Resistance to chloroquine and sulfadoxine–pyrimethamine reported. Recommended prevention in risk areas: IV

▶ DIVING

Number of certified divers: N/A
Dive federation(s): South Africa Underwater Union
Dive regulations: Diver certification
Freediving federation(s): AIDA
Major bodies of water: Indian Ocean, South Atlantic Ocean
Dive season: year-round
Water temperature: 20°C/68F (Jan-Mar), 16°C/60.8F (July-Sept)
Hyperbaric chambers: Many
City: Capetown , National Hyberbarics
Klienmont Hospital
Telephone: 021-671-8655 (24 Hours)
City: Durban, St. Augustine's Hyperbaric Medicine Centre
Telephone: 031 2685000
Popular dive sites: Protea Banks, Sodwana bay, Alival Shoal, Cathedral, Smits Wrecks
Tourism information: South African Tourism (www.southafrica.net)

SPAIN

Canary Islands are not shown.

▶ GENERAL

Capital: Madrid
Government: parliamentary monarchy
Population: 40,341,462 (July 2005 est.)
Ethnic groups: composite of Mediterranean and Nordic types
Language(s): Castilian Spanish 74%, Catalan 17%, Galician 7%, Basque 2%; note - Castilian is the official language nationwide; the other languages are official regionally

Religion(s): Roman Catholic 94%, other 6%
GDP per capita: $23,300 (2004 est.)
Currency: euro (EUR) - euros per US dollar - 0.8054 (2004)
Time: GMT + 1
Electricity: 230V, 50Hz
National holiday: National Day, 12 October

▶ GEOGRAPHY

Location: Southwestern Europe, bordering the Bay of Biscay, Mediterranean Sea, North Atlantic Ocean, and Pyrenees Mountains, southwest of France
Border countries: Andorra 63.7 km, France 623 km, Gibraltar 1.2 km, Portugal 1,214 km, Morocco (Ceuta) 6.3 km, Morocco (Melilla) 9.6 km
Area: 504,782 sq km; *note:* there are 19 autonomous communities including Balearic Islands and Canary Islands, and three small Spanish possessions off the coast of Morocco - Islas Chafarinas, Penon de Alhucemas, and Penon de Velez de la Gomera
Coastline: 4,964 km
Climate: temperate; clear, hot summers in interior, more moderate and cloudy along coast; cloudy, cold winters in interior, partly cloudy and cool along coast
Terrain: large, flat to dissected plateau surrounded by rugged hills; Pyrenees in north
lowest point: Atlantic Ocean 0 m
highest point: Pico de Teide (Tenerife) on Canary Islands 3,718 m
Natural hazards: periodic droughts
Vaccination(s): No vaccination requirements for any international traveller.

▶ DIVING

Number of certified divers: 50,000 federated*
Dive federation(s): Spanish Federation of Underwater Activities (FEDAS)
Dive regulations: Diver certification
Freediving federation(s): AIDA
Major bodies of water: North Atlantic Ocean, Mediterranean Sea, Balearic Sea
Dive season: year-round
Water temperature: 12°C/53.6F (Jan-Mar), 23°C/73.4F (July-Sept)
Hyperbaric chambers: Many
City: Barcelona, CRIS-Unitat de Terapeutica Hiperbarica
Telephone : (34) 3 433 1551
City : Santander, INSALUD, Hospital Universitario
Telephone: 942-202520
Popular dive sites: Medes Islands, Costa Blanca, Costa del Sol, Majorca and Minorca islands, The Canaries Islands
Tourism information: Tourism in Spain (www.spain.info)

* SOURCE: Spanish Federation of Underwater Activities (2006)

SRI LANKA

▶ **GENERAL**

Capital: Colombo
Government: republic
Population: 20,064,776 (July 2005 est.)
Ethnic groups: Sinhalese 73.8%, Sri Lankan Moors 7.2%, Indian Tamil 4.6%, Sri Lankan Tamil 3.9%, other 0.5%, unspecified 10% (2001 census provisional data)
Language(s): Sinhala (official and national language) 74%, Tamil (national language) 18%, other 8%
note: English is commonly used in government and is spoken competently by about 10% of the population
Religion(s): Buddhist 69.1%, Muslim 7.6%, Hindu 7.1%, Christian 6.2%, unspecified 10% (2001 census provisional data)
GDP per capita: $4,000 (2004 est.)
Currency: Sri Lankan rupee (LKR) - Sri Lankan rupees per US dollar - 101.194 (2004)
Time: GMT + 5.5
Electricity: 230V, 50Hz
National holiday: Independence Day, 4 February (1948)

▶ **GEOGRAPHY**

Location: Southern Asia, island in the Indian Ocean, south of India
Border countries: None
Area: 65,610 sq km
Coastline: 1,340 km
Climate: tropical monsoon; northeast monsoon (December to March); southwest monsoon (June to October)
Terrain: mostly low, flat to rolling plain; mountains in south-central interior
lowest point: Indian Ocean 0 m

highest point: Pidurutalagala 2,524 m
Natural hazards: occasional cyclonesand tornadoes
Vaccination(s): Yellow fever: A yellow fever vaccination certificate is required from travellers over 1 year of age coming from infected areas. **Malaria:** Malaria risk—*P. vivax* (88%), *P. falciparum* (12%)—exists throughout the year, except in the districts of Colombo, Galle, Gampaha, Kalutara, Matara and Nuwara Eliya. *P. falciparum* resistant to chloroquine and sulfadoxine–pyrimethamine reported. Recommended prevention in risk areas: III

▶ **DIVING**

Number of certified divers: 10.000*
Dive federation(s): None
Dive regulations: Diver certification
Freediving federation(s): None*
Major bodies of water: Indian Ocean, Bay of Bengal, Gulf of Mannar
Dive season: year-round
Water temperature: 28°C/82.4F (Jan-Mar), 28°C/82.4F (July-Sept)
Hyperbaric chambers:
City: Trincomalee, Navy headquarters*
Popular dive sites: First oil tanker "Conch", Kiralagala, Black Coral Point, Coral Garden Cave, Godagala*
Tourism information: Sri Lanka Tourist Board (www.srilankatourism.org)
* SOURCE: International Diving School (2006)

SWEDEN

▶ **GENERAL**

Capital: Stockholm
Government: constitutional monarchy
Population: 9,001,774 (July 2005 est.)
Ethnic groups: indigenous population: Swedes and Finnish and Sami minorities; foreign-born or first-generation immigrants: Finns, Yugoslavs, Danes, Norwegians, Greeks, Turks
Language(s): Swedish, small Sami- and Finnish-speaking minorities
Religion(s): Lutheran 87%, Roman Catholic, Orthodox, Baptist, Muslim, Jewish, Buddhist
GDP per capita: $28,400 (2004 est.)
Currency: Swedish krona (SEK) - Swedish kronor per US dollar - 7.3489 (2004)
Time: GMT + 1
Electricity: 230V, 50Hz
National holiday: Flag Day, 6 June

▶ **GEOGRAPHY**

Location: Northern Europe, bordering the Baltic Sea, Gulf of Bothnia, Kattegat, and Skagerrak, between Finland and Norway
Border countries: Finland 614 km, Norway 1,619 km

Area: 449,964 sq km
Coastline: 3,218 km
Climate: temperate in south with cold, cloudy winters and cool, partly cloudy summers; subarctic in north
Terrain: mostly flat or gently rolling lowlands; mountains in west
lowest point: reclaimed bay of Lake Hammarsjon, near Kristianstad -2.41 m
highest point: Kebnekaise 2,111 m
Natural hazards: ice floes in the surrounding waters, especially in the Gulf of Bothnia, can interfere with maritime traffic
Vaccination(s): No vaccination requirements for any international traveller.

Major bodies of water: North Sea, Norwegian Sea, Baltic Sea
Dive season: year-round
Water temperature: 1°C/33.8F (Jan-Mar), 15°C/59F(July-Sept)
Hyperbaric chambers: Many
City: Stockholm, Karolinska sjukhuset
Telephone: 08-517 700 00
City: Goteborg, Ostra sjukhuset
Telephone: 031-3434000
Popular dive sites: Storholmen, Kammarskär, Bergeforsen River
Tourism information: Swedish Travel and Tourism Council (www.visit-sweden.com)
* http://www.abc.se/~pa/publ/swescuba.htm

► **DIVING**

Number of certified divers: 130,000*
Dive federation(s): Swedish Sportsdiving Federation
Dive regulations: Diver certification
Freediving federation(s): AIDA

SWITZERLAND

► **GENERAL**

Capital: Bern
Government: formally a confederation, but similar in structure to a federal republic
Population: 7,489,370 (July 2005 est.)
Ethnic groups: German 65%, French 18%, Italian 10%, Romansch 1%, other 6%
Language(s): German (official) 63.7%, French (official) 20.4%, Italian (official) 6.5%, Serbo-Croatian 1.5%, Albanian 1.3%, Portuguese 1.2%, Spanish 1.1%, English 1%, Romansch 0.5%, other 2.8% (2000 census)
Religion(s): Roman Catholic 41.8%, Protestant 35.3%, Orthodox 1.8%, other Christian 0.4%, Muslim 4.3%, other 1%, unspecified 4.3%, none 11.1% (2000 census)
GDP per capita: $33,800 (2004 est.)
Currency: Swiss franc (CHF) - Swiss francs per US dollar - 1.2435 (2004)
Time: GMT + 1
Electricity: 230V, 50Hz
National holiday: Founding of the Swiss Confederation, 1 August (1291)

► **GEOGRAPHY**

Location: Central Europe, east of France, north of Italy
Border countries: Austria 164 km, France 573 km, Italy 740 km, Liechtenstein 41 km, Germany 334 km
Area: 41,290 sq km
Coastline: 0 km (landlocked)

Climate: temperate, but varies with altitude; cold, cloudy, rainy/snowy winters; cool to warm, cloudy, humid summers with occasional showers
Terrain: mostly mountains (Alps in south, Jura in northwest) with a central plateau of rolling hills, plains, and large lakes
lowest point: Lake Maggiore 195 m
highest point: Dufourspitze 4,634 m
Natural hazards: avalanches, landslides, flash floods
Vaccination(s): No vaccination requirements for any international traveller.

▶ **DIVING**

Number of certified divers: N/A
Dive federation(s): Schweizer Unterwasser-Sport-Verband
Dive regulations: Diver certification
Freediving federation(s): ICARE-FSAS Switzerland (AIDA)
Major bodies of water: Lake Geneva, Neuchatel Lake, Lake of Lucerne, Zürichsee
Dive season: year-round, winter ice diving
Water temperature: 3°C/37.4F (Jan-Mar), 20°C/68F (July-Sept)
Hyperbaric chambers:
City: Basel, HBO-Zentrum Basel
Telephone: 061 265 25 25 (24 hr)
City: Geneva, HBO-Zentrum UNI Genf
Telephone: 022 372 67 50 (GE 144) (24 hr)
Popular dive sites: Bignasco, Verzasca Valley, Römerbrücke, Amsler Becken, Lake Zurich
Tourism information: Switzerland Tourism Office (www.myswitzerland.com)

SYRIA

▶ **GENERAL**

Capital: Damascus
Government: republic under military regime since March 1963
Population: 18,448,752
Ethnic groups: Arab 90.3%, Kurds, Armenians, and other 9.7%
Language(s): Arabic (official); Kurdish, Armenian, Aramaic, Circassian widely understood; French, English somewhat understood
Religion(s): Sunni Muslim 74%, Alawite, Druze, and other Muslim sects 16%, Christian (various sects) 10%, Jewish (tiny communities in Damascus, Al Qamishli, and Aleppo)
GDP per capita: $3,400 (2004 est.)
Currency: Syrian pound (SYP) - Syrian pounds per US dollar - (official rate): 11.225 (2004)
Time: GMT + 2
Electricity: 220V, 50Hz
National holiday: Independence Day, 17 April (1946)

▶ **GEOGRAPHY**

Location: Middle East, bordering the Mediterranean Sea, between Lebanon and Turkey
Border countries: Iraq 605 km, Israel 76 km, Jordan 375 km, Lebanon 375 km, Turkey 822 km
Area: 185,180 sq km
Coastline: 193 km
Climate: mostly desert; hot, dry, sunny summers (June to August) and mild, rainy winters (December to February) along coast; cold weather with snow or sleet periodically in Damascus
Terrain: primarily semiarid and desert plateau; narrow coastal plain; mountains in west
lowest point: location near Lake Tiberias -200m
highest point: Mount Hermon 2,814 m
Natural hazards: dust storms, sandstorms
Vaccination(s): Yellow fever: A yellow fever vaccination certificate is required from travellers coming from infected areas. **Malaria:** Limited malaria risk—exclusively due to *P. vivax*—exists from May through October in foci along the northern border, especially in rural areas of El Hasaka Governorate Recommended prevention in risk areas: I

▶ **DIVING**

Number of certified divers: N/A
Dive federation(s): Syrian Underwater Sport Federation
Dive regulations: Diver certification
Freediving federation(s): None
Major bodies of water: Mediterranean Sea
Dive season: year-round
Water temperature: 17°C/62.6F (Jan-Mar), 26°C/78.8F (July-Sept)
Hyperbaric chambers: N/A
Popular dive sites:
Tourism information: Ministry of Tourism (www.syriatourism.org)

TAIWAN

▶ **GENERAL**

Capital: Taipei
Government: multiparty democratic regime headed by popularly-elected president and unicameral legislature
Population: 22,894,384 (July 2005 est.)
Ethnic groups: Taiwanese (including Hakka) 84%, mainland Chinese 14%, aborigine 2%
Language(s): Mandarin Chinese (official), Taiwanese (Min), Hakka dialects
Religion(s): mixture of Buddhist, Confucian, and Taoist 93%, Christian 4.5%, other 2.5%
GDP per capita: $25,300 (2004 est.)
Currency: new Taiwan dollar (TWD) - new Taiwan dollars per US dollar - 33.422 (2004)
Time: GMT - 10
Electricity: 110V, 60Hz
National holiday: Republic Day (Anniversary of the Chinese Revolution), 10 October (1911)

▶ **GEOGRAPHY**

Location: Eastern Asia, islands bordering the East China Sea, Philippine Sea, South China Sea, and Taiwan Strait, north of the Philippines, off the southeastern coast of China
Border countries: Oman 288 km, Saudi Arabia 1,458 km
Area: 35,980 sq km; *note:* includes the Pescadores, Matsu, and Quemoy
Coastline: 1,566.3 km
Climate: tropical; marine; rainy season during southwest monsoon (June to August); cloudiness is persistent and extensive all year
Terrain: eastern two-thirds mostly rugged mountains; flat to gently rolling plains in west

lowest point: South China Sea 0 m
highest point: Yu Shan 3,952 m
Natural hazards: earthquakes and typhoons
Vaccination(s): No vaccination requirements for any international traveller.

▶ **DIVING**

Number of certified divers: 4,000*
Dive federation(s): None
Dive regulations: Diver certification
Freediving federation(s): None
Major bodies of water: Philippine Sea, Taiwan Strait
Dive season: year-round
Water temperature: 24°C/75.2F (Jan-Mar), 28.5°C/83F (July-Sept)
Hyperbaric chambers:
City: Kaosiung, Navy Hospital.
Telephone: 07 5812826
City: Changhua, Changhua Christian Hospital
Telephone: 886-4-7238595
Popular dive sites: Green Island, Kenting, Orchid Island, Penghu Islands
Tourism information: Taiwan Tourism Bureau (www.taiwantourism.org)
* SOURCE: Scuba Diving in Taiwan / Randal H. Garrett

TANZANIA

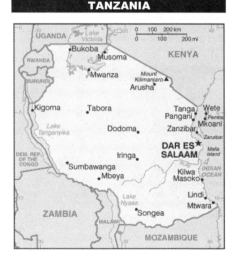

▶ **GENERAL**

Capital: Dar es Salaam
Government: republic
Population: 36,766,356
Ethnic groups: mainland - native African 99% (of which 95% are Bantu consisting of more than 130 tribes), other 1% (consisting of Asian, European, and Arab); Zanzibar - Arab, native African, mixed Arab and native African

Language(s): Kiswahili or Swahili (official), Kiunguja (name for Swahili in Zanzibar), English (official, primary language of commerce, administration, and higher education), Arabic (widely spoken in Zanzibar), many local languages
Religion(s): mainland - Christian 30%, Muslim 35%, indigenous beliefs 35%; Zanzibar - more than 99% Muslim
GDP per capita: $700 (2004 est.)
Currency: Tanzanian shilling (TZS) - Tanzanian shillings per US dollar - 1,089.33 (2004)
Time: GMT + 3
Electricity: 230V, 50Hz
National holiday: Union Day (Tanganyika and Zanzibar), 26 April (1964)

▶ **GEOGRAPHY**

Location: Eastern Africa, bordering the Indian Ocean, between Kenya and Mozambique
Border countries: Burundi 451 km, Democratic Republic of the Congo 459 km, Kenya 769 km, Malawi 475 km, Mozambique 756 km, Rwanda 217 km, Uganda 396 km, Zambia 338 km
Area: 945,087 sq km; *note:* includes the islands of Mafia, Pemba, and Zanzibar
Coastline: 1,424 km
Climate: varies from tropical along coast to temperate in highlands
Terrain: plains along coast; central plateau; highlands in north, south
lowest point: Indian Ocean 0 m
highest point: Kilimanjaro 5,895 m
Natural hazards: flooding on the central plateau during the rainy season; drought
Vaccination(s): Yellow fever: A yellow fever vaccination certificate is required from travellers over 1 year of age coming from infected areas. **Malaria:** Malaria risk—predominantly due to *P. falciparum*—exists throughout the year in the whole country below 1800 m. *P. falciparum* resistant to chloroquine and sulfadoxine–pyrimethamine reported. Recommended prevention: IV

▶ **DIVING**

Number of certified divers: Mainly tourists
Dive federation(s): None
Dive regulations: Diver certification
Freediving federation(s): None
Major bodies of water: Indian Ocean
Dive season: year-round, best: Oct-Mar
Water temperature: 28°C/82.4F (Jan-Mar), 25°C/77F (July-Sept)
Hyperbaric chambers: N/A
ClosestL South Africa or Réunion
Popular dive sites: Dar es Salaam Marine Reserve, Zanzibar, Pemba, 'Fungu Yasin' Reef, Lake Nyasa (Malawi)
Tourism information: Tanzania Tourist Board (www.tanzaniatouristboard.com)

THAILAND

▶ **GENERAL**

Capital: Bangkok
Government: constitutional monarchy
Population: 65,444,371
Ethnic groups: Thai 75%, Chinese 14%, other 11%
Language(s): Thai, English (secondary language of the elite), ethnic and regional dialects
Religion(s): Buddhist 94.6%, Muslim 4.6%, Christian 0.7%, other 0.1% (2000 census)
GDP per capita: $8,100 (2004 est.)
Currency: baht (THB) - baht per US dollar - 40.222 (2004)
Time: GMT + 7
Electricity: 220V, 50Hz
National holiday: Birthday of King PHUMIPHON, 5 December (1927)

▶ **GEOGRAPHY**

Location: Southeastern Asia, bordering the Andaman Sea and the Gulf of Thailand, southeast of Burma

Border countries: Burma 1,800 km, Cambodia 803 km, Laos 1,754 km, Malaysia 506 km
Area: 514,000 sq km
Coastline: 3,219 km
Climate: tropical; rainy, warm, cloudy southwest monsoon (mid-May to September); dry, cool northeast monsoon (November to mid-March); southern isthmus always hot and humid
Terrain: central plain; Khorat Plateau in the east; mountains elsewhere
lowest point: Gulf of Thailand 0 m
highest point: Doi Inthanon 2,576 m
Natural hazards: land subsidence in Bangkok area resulting from the depletion of the water table; droughts
Vaccination(s): Yellow fever: A yellow fever vaccination certificate is required from travellers over 1 year of age coming from infected areas. **Malaria:** Malaria risk—predominantly due to *P. falciparum*—exists throughout the year in the whole country below 1800 m. *P. falciparum* resistant to chloroquine and sulfadoxine–pyrimethamine reported. Recommended prevention: IV

► **DIVING**

Number of certified divers: Mainly tourists
Dive federation(s): Thailand Diving Association
Dive regulations: Diver certification
Freediving federation(s): None
Major bodies of water: Indian Ocean, South China Sea, Gulf of Thailand, Andaman Sea
Dive season: year-round
Water temperature: 27°C/80.6F (Jan-Mar), 29°C/84.2F (July-Sept)
Hyperbaric chambers:
City: Phuket, Hyperbaric Services Thailand
Telephone: +66 76 342-518
Popular dive sites: Breakfast Bend, East of Eden, Phuket
Tourism information: Tourism Authority of Thailand (www.tourismthailand.org)

Timor-Leste (See East Timor)

TONGA

► **GENERAL**

Capital: Nuku'alofa
Government: hereditary constitutional monarchy
Population: 112,422 (July 2005 est.)
Ethnic groups: Polynesian, Europeans about 300
Language(s): Tongan, English
Religion(s): Christian (Free Wesleyan Church claims over 30,000 adherents)
GDP per capita: $2,300 (2002 est.)
Currency: pa'anga (TOP) - pa'anga per US dollar - 1.9716 (2004)
Time: GMT + 13
Electricity: 240V, 50Hz
National holiday: Emancipation Day, 4 June (1970)

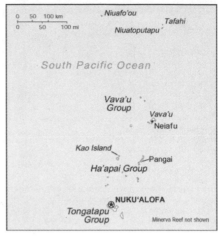

► **GEOGRAPHY**

Location: Oceania, archipelago in the South Pacific Ocean, about two-thirds of the way from Hawaii to New Zealand
Border countries: None
Area: 748 sq km
Coastline: 419 km
Climate: tropical; modified by trade winds; warm season (December to May), cool season (May to December)
Terrain: most islands have limestone base formed from uplifted coral formation; others have limestone overlying volcanic base
lowest point: Pacific Ocean 0 m
highest point: unnamed location on Kao Island 1,033 m
Natural hazards: cyclones (October to April); earthquakes and volcanic activity on Fonuafo'ou
Vaccination(s): Yellow fever: A yellow fever vaccination certificate is required from travellers over 1 year of age coming from infected areas.

► **DIVING**

Number of certified divers: 50*
Dive federation(s): None*
Dive regulations: Diver certification, no removal from sea*
Freediving federation(s): None
Major bodies of water: South Pacific Ocean
Dive season: year-round
Water temperature: 24°C/75.2F (Jan-Mar), 21°C/69.8F (July-Sept)
Hyperbaric chambers:
Closest: Fiji*
Popular dive sites: Cathedral, Colosseum, Lepardshark Rock, lost anchor, Hammerhead Point*
Tourism information: Tonga Visitors Bureau (www.tongaholiday.com)
* SOURCE: Deep Blue Diving (2006)

TRINIDAD AND TOBAGO

▶ **GENERAL**

Capital: Port-of-Spain
Government: parliamentary democracy
Population: 1,088,644 (July 2005 est.)
Ethnic groups: Indian (South Asian) 40%, African 37.5%, mixed 20.5%, other 1.2%, unspecified 0.8% (2000 census)
Language(s): English (official), Hindi, French, Spanish, Chinese
Religion(s): Roman Catholic 26%, Hindu 22.5%, Anglican 7.8%, Baptist 7.2%, Pentecostal 6.8%, Seventh Day Adventist 4%, other Christian 5.8%, Muslim 5.8%, other 10.8%, unspecified 1.4%, none 1.9% (2000 census)
GDP per capita: $10,500 (2004 est.)
Currency: Trinidad and Tobago dollar (TTD) - Trinidad and Tobago dollars per US dollar - 6.299 (2004)
Time: GMT - 4
Electricity: 110/220V, 60Hz
National holiday: Independence Day, 31 August (1962)

▶ **GEOGRAPHY**

Location: Caribbean, islands between the Caribbean Sea and the North Atlantic Ocean, northeast of Venezuela
Border countries: None
Area: 5,128 sq km
Coastline: 362 km
Climate: tropical; rainy season (June to December)
Terrain: mostly plains with some hills and low mountains
lowest point: Caribbean Sea 0 m
highest point: El Cerro del Aripo 940 m

Natural hazards: outside usual path of hurricanes and other tropical storms
Vaccination(s): Yellow fever: A yellow fever vaccination certificate is required from travellers over 1 year of age coming from infected areas.

▶ **DIVING**

Number of certified divers: Mainly tourists
Dive federation(s): Association of Tobago Dive Operators
Dive regulations: Diver certification
Freediving federation(s): None*
Major bodies of water: Caribbean Sea, North Atlantic Ocean
Dive season: year-round, visibility diminished September to November*
Water temperature: 26°C/78.8F (Jan-Mar), 28°C/82.4F (July-Sept)
Hyperbaric chambers:
City: Roxborough, Tobago
Telephone: 660 4000
Telephone: emergency 789 9682*
Popular dive sites: The MV Maverick, Flying Reef, Sisters, Japanese Gardens* Little Tobago, London bridge
Tourism information: Tourism and Industrial Development Company (www.visittnt.com)

* SOURCE: Association of Tobago Dive Operators (2006)

TUNISIA

▶ **GENERAL**

Capital: Tunis
Government: republic
Population: 10,074,951 (July 2005 est.)
Ethnic groups: Arab 98%, European 1%, Jewish and other 1%
Language(s): Arabic (official and one of the languages of commerce), French (commerce)
Religion(s): Muslim 98%, Christian 1%, Jewish and other 1%
GDP per capita: $7,100 (2004 est.)
Currency: Tunisian dinar (TND) - Tunisian dinars per US dollar - 1.2455 (2004)
Time: GMT + 1
Electricity: 230V, 50Hz
National holiday: Independence Day, 20 March (1956)

▶ **GEOGRAPHY**

Location: Northern Africa, bordering the Mediterranean Sea, between Algeria and Libya
Border countries: Algeria 965 km, Libya 459 km
Area: 163,610 sq km
Coastline: 1,148 km
Climate: temperate in north with mild, rainy winters and hot, dry summers; desert in south **Terrain:**

mountains in north; hot, dry central plain; semiarid south merges into the Sahara
lowest point: Shatt al Gharsah -17 m
highest point: Jebel ech Chambi 1,544 m
Natural hazards: NA
Vaccination(s): Yellow fever: A yellow fever vaccination certificate is required from travellers over 1 year of age coming from infected areas.

▶ DIVING

Number of certified divers: 800*
Dive federation(s): Federation Des Activites Subaquatiques De Tunisie
Dive regulations: Diver certification
Freediving federation(s): FAST*
Major bodies of water: Mediterranean Sea
Dive season: year-round, best from March to November*
Water temperature: 16°C/60.8F (Jan-Mar), 25°C/77F (July-Sept)
Hyperbaric chambers:
City : Ecole des peches zarzis, base militaires marine Bizerte
Telephone : 72 431700.
City : Ecole de peches Tabarka,
Telephone : 78 644344*

Popular dive sites: Rocher du merou, tabarka, Rocher de l'odysea hammamet, epave PLM mahdia, tunel 1 & 2, Tabarka*
Tourism information: Tunisian National Tourism Office (www.tourismtunisia.com)
* SOURCE: Odysea Diving School (2006)

TURKEY

▶ GENERAL

Capital: Ankara
Government: republican parliamentary democracy
Population: 69,660,559 (July 2005 est.)
Ethnic groups: Turkish 80%, Kurdish 20% (estimated)
Language(s): Turkish (official), Kurdish, Arabic, Armenian, Greek
Religion(s): Muslim 99.8% (mostly Sunni), other 0.2% (mostly Christians and Jews)
GDP per capita: $7,400 (2004 est.)
Currency: New Turkish lira (YTL) -
Time: GMT + 2
Electricity: 220V, 50Hz, European 2-pin plug
National holiday: Republic Day, 29 October (1923)

▶ GEOGRAPHY

Location: southeastern Europe and southwestern Asia (that portion of Turkey west of the Bosporus is geographically part of Europe), bordering the Black Sea, between Bulgaria and Georgia, and bordering the Aegean Sea and the Mediterranean Sea, between Greece and Syria
Border countries: Armenia 268 km, Azerbaijan 9 km, Bulgaria 240 km, Georgia 252 km, Greece 206 km, Iran 499 km, Iraq 352 km, Syria 822 km
Area: 780,580 sq km
Coastline: 7,200 km
Climate: temperate; hot, dry summers with mild, wet winters; harsher in interior
Terrain: high central plateau (Anatolia); narrow coastal plain; several mountain ranges
lowest point: Mediterranean Sea 0 m
highest point: Mount Ararat 5,166 m
Natural hazards: very severe earthquakes, especially in northern Turkey, along an arc extending from the Sea of Marmara to Lake Van

Vaccination(s): No vaccination requirements for any international traveller. **Malaria:** Malaria risk—exclusively due to *P. vivax*—exists from May to October mainly in the south-eastern part of the country, and in Amikova and Çukurova Plain. There is no malaria risk in the main tourist areas in the west and south-west of the country. Recommended prevention in risk areas: II

▶ **DIVING**

Number of certified divers: N/A*
Dive federation(s): TSSF (Turkiye Sualti Sporlari Federasyonu / Turkish Underwater Sport Federation)
Dive regulations: Diver certification, diving prohibited in certain areas*
Freediving federation(s): Part of TSSF (AIDA)
Major bodies of water: Mediterranean Sea, Aegean Sea, Black Sea
Dive season: North Aegean / Black Sea / Marmara Sea: April – September; South Aegean / Mediterranean Sea: year- round*
Water temperature: 16°C/60.8F (Jan-Mar), 26°C/78.8F (July-Sept)
Hyperbaric chambers:
City: Istanbul (Capa Tip Fakultesi Sualti Hekimligi)
Telephone: +90.212.414.2234
City: Kabatepe (Saroz) (Ozgur Teknesi Eceabat)
Telephone: +90.216.330.9839
City : Fethiye (Club Likya World / Oludeniz)
Telephone: +90.252.617.0200
City: Antalya (Hiperox)
Telephone: +90.242.322.0099
Popular dive sites: Bodrum, Saroz, Kas, Fethiye, Antalya*
Tourism information: Ministry of Tourism (www.tourismturkey.org)
* SOURCE: ARGOS Diving Club (2006)

TURKS AND CAICOS

▶ **GENERAL**

Capital: Grand Turk
Government: overseas territory of the UK
Population: 20,556 (July 2005 est.)
Ethnic groups: black 90%, mixed, European, or North American 10%
Language(s): English (official)
Religion(s): Baptist 40%, Methodist 16%, Anglican 18%, Church of God 12%, other 14% (1990)
GDP per capita: $11,500 (2002 est.)
Currency: US dollar (USD)
Time: GMT - 5
Electricity: 110/220V, 60Hz
National holiday: Constitution Day, 30 August (1976)

▶ **GEOGRAPHY**

Location: Caribbean, two island groups in the North Atlantic Ocean, southeast of The Bahamas, north of Haiti
Border countries: None
Area: 430 sq km
Coastline: 389 km
Climate: tropical; marine; moderated by trade winds; sunny and relatively dry
Terrain: low, flat limestone; extensive marshes and mangrove swamps
lowest point: Caribbean Sea 0 m
highest point: Blue Hills 49 m
Natural hazards: frequent hurricanes
Vaccination(s): No vaccination requirements for any international traveller.

▶ **DIVING**

Number of certified divers: Mainly tourists
Dive federation(s): WATCI*
Dive regulations: Diver certification
Freediving federation(s): None
Major bodies of water: North Atlantic Ocean
Dive season: year-round
Water temperature: 25°C/77F (Jan-Mar), 29°C/84.2F (July-Sept)
Hyperbaric chambers:
City: Providenciales
Telephone: (649) 946-4242*
Popular dive sites: The Crack at NW Point, Spanish Anchor at West Caicos, Aquarium in Grace Bay, Double D at French Cay, G Spot at French Cay*
Tourism information: Turks & Caicos Tourist Board (www.turksandcaicostourism.com)
* SOURCE: Dive Provo (2006)

TUVALU

▶ **GENERAL**

Capital: Funafuti
Government: constitutional monarchy with a parliamentary democracy; began debating republic status in 1992
Population: 11,636 (July 2005 est.)
Ethnic groups: Polynesian 96%, Micronesian 4%
Language(s): Tuvaluan, English, Samoan, Kiribati (on the island of Nui)
Religion(s): Church of Tuvalu (Congregationalist) 97%, Seventh-Day Adventist 1.4%, Baha'i 1%, other 0.6%
GDP per capita: $1,100 (2000 est.)
Currency: Australian dollar (AUD); Tuvaluan dollar - Tuvaluan dollars or Australian dollars per US dollar - 1.3598 (2004)
Time: GMT + 12
Electricity: 220V, 50Hz
National holiday: Constitution Day, 30 August (1976)

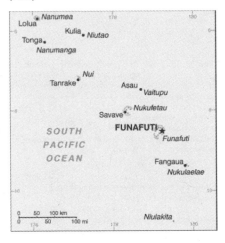

▶ **GEOGRAPHY**

Location: Oceania, island group consisting of nine coral atolls in the South Pacific Ocean, about one-half of the way from Hawaii to Australia
Border countries: None
Area: 26 sq km
Coastline: 24 km
Climate: tropical; moderated by easterly trade winds (March to November); westerly gales and heavy rain (November to March)
Terrain: very low-lying and narrow coral atolls
lowest point: Pacific Ocean 0 m
highest point: unnamed location 5 m
Natural hazards: severe tropical storms are usually rare, but, in 1997, there were three cyclones; low level of islands make them very sensitive to changes in sea level

Vaccination(s): No vaccination requirements for any international traveller.

▶ **DIVING**

Number of certified divers: Mainly tourists
Dive federation(s): None
Dive regulations: Diver certification
Freediving federation(s): None
Major bodies of water: South Pacific Ocean
Dive season: year-round
Water temperature: 28.5°C/83F (Jan-Mar), 28.5°C/83F (July-Sept)
Hyperbaric chambers: N/A
Closest: Solomon Islands
Popular dive sites: Funafuti Island, Nukufetau Reef
Tourism information: Government of Tuvalu (www.timelesstuvalu.com)

UKRAINE

▶ **GENERAL**

Capital: Kiev
Government: republic
Population: 47,425,336 (July 2005 est.)
Ethnic groups: Ukrainian 77.8%, Russian 17.3%, Belarusian 0.6%, Moldovan 0.5%, Crimean Tatar 0.5%, Bulgarian 0.4%, Hungarian 0.3%, Romanian 0.3%, Polish 0.3%, Jewish 0.2%, other 1.8% (2001 census)
Language(s): Ukrainian (official) 67%, Russian 24%; small Romanian-, Polish-, and Hungarian-speaking minorities
Religion(s): Ukrainian Orthodox - Kiev Patriarchate 19%, Orthodox (no particular jurisdiction) 16%, Ukrainian Orthodox - Moscow Patriarchate 9%, Ukrainian Greek Catholic 6%, Ukrainian Autocephalous Orthodox 1.7%, Protestant, Jewish, none 38% (2004 est.)
GDP per capita: $6,300 (2004 est.)
Currency: hryvnia (UAH) - hryvnia per US dollar - 5.3192 (2004)
Time: GMT + 2
Electricity: 220V, 50Hz
National holiday: Independence Day, 24 August (1991)

▶ **GEOGRAPHY**

Location: Eastern Europe, bordering the Black Sea, between Poland, Romania, and Moldova in the west and Russia in the east

Border countries: Belarus 891 km, Hungary 103 km, Moldova 939 km, Poland 526 km, Romania (south) 169 km, Romania (west) 362 km, Russia 1,576 km, Slovakia 97 km
Area: 603,700 sq km
Coastline: 2,782 km
Climate: temperate continental; Mediterranean only on the southern Crimean coast; precipitation disproportionately distributed, highest in west and north, lesser in east and southeast; winters vary from cool along the Black Sea to cold farther inland; summers are warm across the greater part of the country, hot in the south
Terrain: most of Ukraine consists of fertile plains (steppes) and plateaus, mountains being found only in the west (the Carpathians), and in the Crimean Peninsula in the extreme south
lowest point: Black Sea 0 m
highest point: Hora Hoverla 2,061 m
Natural hazards: NA
Vaccination(s): No vaccination requirements for any international traveller.

▶ DIVING

Number of certified divers: N/A
Dive federation(s): Ukrainian Underwater Sports Federation
Dive regulations: Diver certification
Freediving federation(s): AIDA
Major bodies of water: Black Sea, Sea of Azov
Dive season: year-round
Water temperature: 2°C/35.6F (Jan-Mar), 23°C/73.4F (July-Sept)
Hyperbaric chambers: N/A
Popular dive sites:
Tourism information: Travel Ukraine (www.wumag.kiev.ua)

UNITED ARAB EMIRATES

▶ GENERAL

Capital: Abu Dhabi
Government: federation with specified powers delegated to the UAE federal government and other powers reserved to member emirates
Population: 2,563,212
Ethnic groups: Emirati 19%, other Arab and Iranian 23%, South Asian 50%, other expatriates (includes Westerners and East Asians) 8% (1982); *note:* less than 20% are UAE citizens (1982)

Language(s): Arabic (official), Persian, English, Hindi, Urdu
Religion(s): Muslim 96% (Shi'a 16%), Christian, Hindu, and other 4%
GDP per capita: $25,200 (2004 est.)
Currency: Emirati dirham (AED) - Emirati dirhams per US dollar - 3.6725 (2004)
Time: GMT + 4
Electricity: 220V, 50Hz
National holiday: Independence Day, 2 December (1971)

▶ GEOGRAPHY

Location: Middle East, bordering the Gulf of Oman and the Persian Gulf, between Oman and Saudi Arabia
Border countries: Oman 410 km, Saudi Arabia 457 km
Area: 82,880 sq km
Coastline: 1,318 km
Climate: desert; cooler in eastern mountains
Terrain: flat, barren coastal plain merging into rolling sand dunes of vast desert wasteland; mountains in east
lowest point: Persian Gulf 0 m
highest point: Jabal Yibir 1,527 m
Natural hazards: frequent sand and dust storms
Vaccination(s): No vaccination requirements for any international traveller.

▶ DIVING

Number of certified divers: 6,000*
Dive federation(s): Emirates Diving Association
Dive regulations: Diver certification, no fishing*
Freediving federation(s): None
Major bodies of water: Persian Gulf, Gulf of Oman
Dive season: year-round
Water temperature: 24°C/75.2F (Jan-Mar), 27°C/80.6F (July-Sept)
Hyperbaric chambers:
City: Dubai,
Contact: Fraser Diving
City: Fujairah Port Clinic
Contact: local dive centre*
Popular dive sites: Martini Rock, Dibba Rock, Inchcape 10, Shark Island, Energy Determination*
Tourism information: Department of Tourism (www.dubaitourism.ae)
* SOURCE: Scuba International Diving College (2006)

UNITED KINGDOM

▶ GENERAL

Capital: London
Government: constitutional monarchy
Population: 60,441,457 (July 2005 est.)
Ethnic groups: white (English 83.6%, Scottish 8.6%, Welsh 4.9%, Northern Irish 2.9%) 92.1%, black 2%, Indian 1.8%, Pakistani 1.3%, mixed 1.2%, other 1.6% (2001 census)

Language(s). English, Welsh (about 26% of the population of Wales), Scottish form of Gaelic (about 60,000 in Scotland)
Religion(s): Christian (Anglican, Roman Catholic, Presbyterian, Methodist) 71.6%, Muslim 2.7%, Hindu 1%, other 1.6%, unspecified or none 23.1% (2001 census)
GDP per capita: $29,600 (2004 est.)
Currency: British pound (GBP) - British pounds per US dollar - 0.5462 (2004)
Time: GMT + 0
Electricity: 230V, 50Hz
National holiday: the UK does not celebrate one particular national holiday

▶ **GEOGRAPHY**

Location: Western Europe, islands including the northern one-sixth of the island of Ireland between the North Atlantic Ocean and the North Sea, northwest of France
Border countries: Ireland 360 km
Area: 244,820 sq km; *note:* includes Rockall and Shetland Islands
Coastline: 12,429 km
Climate: temperate; moderated by prevailing southwest winds over the North Atlantic Current; more than one-half of the days are overcast
Terrain: mostly rugged hills and low mountains; level to rolling plains in east and southeast
lowest point: The Fens -4 m
highest point: Ben Nevis 1,343 m
Natural hazards: winter windstorms; floods
Vaccination(s): No vaccination requirements for any international traveller.

▶ **DIVING**

Number of certified divers: 100,000*
Dive federation(s): BSAC (British Sub-Aqua Club)
Dive regulations: Diver certification
Freediving federation(s): British Freediving Association (AIDA)
Major bodies of water: North Atlantic Ocean, English Channel, North Sea, Irish Sea, Celtic Sea
Dive season: year-round
Water temperature: 7°C/44.6F (Jan-Mar), 12°C/53.6F (July-Sept)
Hyperbaric chambers:
City: Aberdeen Scotland
Aberdeen Royal Infirmary
Telephone: 0845 408 6008
City: Plymouth, Diving Diseases Research Centre
Hyperbaric Medical Centre
Telephone: +44(0)1752 209999
City: Isle of Man. Department of Hyperbaric Medicine

Fire Headquarters,
Telephone: 01624626394
City: London, Capital Hyperbarics
Highgate Hospital
Telephone: 020 8347 3883
Popular dive sites: The Breda in Oban, wreck of the Adam Smith in the Firth of Forth, The Farnes Islands, Jersey, Beadnell, Shetland Isles, Moray Coast, Devil's Point Plymouth
Tourism information: British Tourist Authority (www.visitbritain.com)
* SOURCE: Divernet news (2001)

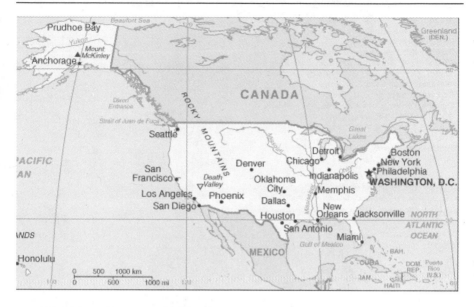

UNITED STATES

▶ **GENERAL**

Capital: Washington, DC
Government: constitution-based federal republic
Population: 295,734,134 (July 2005 est.)
Ethnic groups: white 81.7%, black 12.9%, Asian 4.2%, Amerindian and Alaska native 1%, native Hawaiian and other Pacific islander 0.2% (2003 est.)
Language(s): English 82.1%, Spanish 10.7%, other Indo-European 3.8%, Asian and Pacific island 2.7%, other 0.7% (2000 census)
Religion(s): Protestant 52%, Roman Catholic 24%, Mormon 2%, Jewish 1%, Muslim 1%, other 10%, none 10% (2002 est.)
GDP per capita: $40,100 (2004 est.)
Currency: US dollar (USD)
Time: GMT -10, -9, -8, -7, -6, -5
Electricity: 110/120V, 60Hz
National holiday: Independence Day, 4 July (1776)

▶ **GEOGRAPHY**

Location: North America, bordering both the North Atlantic Ocean and the North Pacific Ocean, between Canada and Mexico
Border countries: Canada 8,893 km (including 2,477 km with Alaska), Mexico 3,141 km
Area: 9,631,418 sq km; includes only the 50 states and District of Columbia
Coastline: 19,924 km
Climate: mostly temperate, but tropical in Hawaii and Florida, arctic in Alaska, semiarid in the great plains west of the Mississippi River, and arid in the Great Basin of the southwest; low winter temperatures in the northwest are ameliorated occasionally in January and February by warm chinook winds from the eastern slopes of the Rocky Mountains
Terrain: vast central plain, mountains in west, hills and low mountains in east; rugged mountains and broad river valleys in Alaska; rugged, volcanic topography in Hawaii
lowest point: Death Valley -86 m
highest point: Mount McKinley 6,194 m
Natural hazards: tsunamis, volcanoes, and earthquake activity around Pacific Basin; hurricanes along the Atlantic and Gulf of Mexico coasts; tornadoes in the midwest and southeast; mud slides in California; forest fires in the west; flooding; permafrost in northern Alaska, a major impediment to development
Vaccination(s): No vaccination requirements for any international traveller.

▶ **DIVING**

Number of certified divers: 16,184,240[52]
Dive federation(s): Underwater Society of America
Dive regulations: Diver certification
Freediving federation(s): Underwater Society of America
Major bodies of water: North Atlantic Ocean, North Pacific Ocean, Arctic Ocean

---

[52] Track on Scuba Diving (January 1998) / The Leisure Trends Group

Dive season: year-round in Florida, California, Texas and other southern states *
Water temperature:
NE: 3°/37.4FC (Jan-Mar), 8°C/46.4F (July-Sept)
NW: 8°C/46.4F (Jan-Mar), 15°C/59F (July-Sept)
S: 22°C/71.6F (Jan-Mar), 29°C/84.2F (July-Sept)
Hyperbaric chambers: Contact DAN *
Popular dive sites: Florida : The Duane, The Eagle, Tenneco Towers; San Diego CA, Monterey CA, lakes in Midwest/NE, Santa Barbara/Channel Island CA * Hawaii: Manta Ray Night Dive, The Caverns, Turtle Pinnacle
Tourism information: U.S. Government Portal (www.firstgov.gov)

URUGUAY

▶ GENERAL

Capital: Montevideo
Government: constitutional republic
Population: 3,415,920 (July 2005 est.)
Ethnic groups: white 88%, mestizo 8%, black 4%, Amerindian (practically nonexistent)
Language(s): Spanish, Portunol, or Brazilero (Portuguese-Spanish mix on the Brazilian frontier)
Religion(s): Roman Catholic 66% (less than half of the adult population attends church regularly), Protestant 2%, Jewish 1%, nonprofessing or other 31%
GDP per capita: $14,500 (2004 est.)
Currency: Uruguayan peso (UYU) - Uruguayan pesos per US dollar - 28.704 (2004)
Time: GMT - 3
Electricity: 220V, 50Hz
National holiday: Independence Day, 25 August (1825)

▶ GEOGRAPHY

Location: Southern South America, bordering the South Atlantic Ocean, between Argentina and Brazil
Border countries: Argentina 579 km, Brazil 985 km
Area: 176,220 sq km
Coastline: 660 km
Climate: warm temperate; freezing temperatures almost unknown
Terrain: mostly rolling plains and low hills; fertile coastal lowland
lowest point: Atlantic Ocean 0 m
highest point: Cerro Catedral 514 m
Natural hazards: seasonally high winds (the pampero is a chilly and occasional violent wind which blows north from the Argentine pampas), droughts, floods; because of the absence of mountains, which act as weather barriers, all locations are particularly vulnerable to rapid changes from weather fronts
Vaccination(s): No vaccination requirements for any international traveller.

▶ DIVING

Number of certified divers: N/A
Dive federation(s): None
Dive regulations: Diver certification
Freediving federation(s): AIDA
Major bodies of water: South Atlantic Ocean, Rio de la Plata
Dive season: year-round
Water temperature: 25°C/77F (Jan-Mar), 21°C/69.8F (July-Sept)
Hyperbaric chambers: N/A
Popular dive sites:
Tourism information: Ministry of Tourism (www.turismo.gub.uy)

VANUATU

▶ GENERAL

Capital: Port-Vila (Efate)
Government: parliamentary republic
Population: 205,754 (July 2005 est.)
Ethnic groups: Ni-Vanuatu 98.5%, other 1.5% (1999 Census)
Language(s): local languages (more than 100) 72.6%, pidgin (known as Bislama or Bichelama) 23.1%, English 1.9%, French 1.4%, other 0.3%, unspecified 0.7% (1999 Census)
Religion(s): Presbyterian 31.4%, Anglican 13.4%, Roman Catholic 13.1%, Seventh-Day Adventist 10.8%, other Christian 13.8%, indigenous beliefs 5.6% (including Jon Frum cargo cult), other 9.6%, none 1%, unspecified 1.3% (1999 Census)
GDP per capita: $2,900 (2003 est.)
Currency: vatu (VUV) - vatu per US dollar - 111.79 (2004)
Time: GMT + 11
Electricity: 241V, 50Hz

National holiday: Independence Day, 30 July (1980)

Îles Torres

South Pacific Ocean

Îles Banks

Espiritu Santo

Aoba   Maéwo

Luganville

Pentecôte

Malakula   Ambrym

Épi

Forari
PORT VILA   Éfaté

N e w   H e b r i d e s

Erromango   Ipota

Coral Sea   Tanna

Anatom

Matthew

Islands claimed by FRANCE and VANUATU   Hunter

0   50   100   150 km
0   50   100   150 mi

▶ **GEOGRAPHY**

Location: Oceania, group of islands in the South Pacific Ocean, about three-quarters of the way from Hawaii to Australia
Border countries: None
Area: 12,200 sq km; *note:* includes more than 80 islands, about 65 of which are inhabited
Coastline: 2,528 km
Climate: tropical; moderated by southeast trade winds from May to October; moderate rainfall from November to April; may be affected by cyclones from December to April
Terrain: mostly mountainous islands of volcanic origin; narrow coastal plains
lowest point: Pacific Ocean 0 m
highest point: Tabwemasana 1,877 m
Natural hazards: tropical cyclones or typhoons (January to April); volcanism causes minor earthquakes; tsunamis

Vaccination(s): No vaccination requirements for any international traveller. **Malaria:**Malaria: Low to moderate malaria risk—predominantly due to *P. falciparum*—exists throughout the year in the whole country. *P. falciparum* resistant to chloroquine and sulfadoxine–pyrimethamine reported. *P. vivax* resistant to chloroquine reported. Recommended prevention: III

▶ **DIVING**

Number of certified divers: 300*
Dive federation(s): Vanuatu Scuba Operators Assocation
Dive regulations: Diver certification
Freediving federation(s): None
Major bodies of water: South Pacific Ocean, Coral Sea
Dive season: year-round, peak season: March-Nov.*
Water temperature: 28°C/82.4F (Jan-Mar), 27°C/80.6F (July-Sept)
Hyperbaric chambers:
City: Port Vila, ProMedical Vanuatu facility
Telephone: +678 25566
Popular dive sites: SS President Coolidge, Million Dollar Point, Star of Russia, Tasman Flying Boat, Cathedral*
Tourism information: Vanuatu Tourism Office (www.vanuatutourism.com)

* SOURCE: Aquamarine Santo (2006)

VENEZUELA

Caribbean   Sea   ST. VINCENT AND THE GRENADINES
Aruba (NETH.)   Nath. Antilles (NETH.)
GRENADA
BARBADOS
Amuay
Maracaibo   Puerto Cabello   CARACAS   Cumaná   TRINIDAD AND TOBAGO
Barquisimeto   Maracay   Puerto La Cruz
Valencia
Andes
San Cristóbal   Llanos   San Fernando   Ciudad Guayana
Guiana Highlands   GUY.
Puerto Ayacucho
COLOMBIA
BRAZIL
0   100   200 km
0   100   200 mi

▶ **GENERAL**

Capital: Caracas
Government: federal republic
Population: 25,375,281 (July 2005 est.)

Ethnic groups: Spanish, Italian, Portuguese, Arab, German, African, indigenous people
Language(s): Spanish (official), numerous indigenous dialects
Religion(s): nominally Roman Catholic 96%, Protestant 2%, other 2%
GDP per capita: $5,800 (2004 est.)
Currency: bolivar (VEB) - bolivares per US dollar - 1,891.3 (2004)
Time: GMT - 4
Electricity: 110V, 60Hz
National holiday: Independence Day, 5 July (1811)

▶ **GEOGRAPHY**

Location: Northern South America, bordering the Caribbean Sea and the North Atlantic Ocean, between Colombia and Guyana
Border countries: Brazil 2,200 km, Colombia 2,050 km, Guyana 743 km
Area: 912,050 sq km
Coastline: 2,800 km
Climate: tropical; hot, humid; more moderate in highlands
Terrain: Andes Mountains and Maracaibo Lowlands in northwest; central plains (llanos); Guiana Highlands in southeast
lowest point: Caribbean Sea 0 m
highest point: Pico Bolivar (La Columna) 5,007 m
Natural hazards: subject to floods, rockslides, mudslides; periodic droughts
Vaccination(s): No vaccination requirements for any international traveller. **Malaria:** Malaria risk due to *P. vivax* exists throughout the year in some rural areas of Apure, Amazonas, Barinas, Bolívar, Sucre and Táchira states. Risk of *P. falciparum* malaria is restricted to municipalities in jungle areas of Amazonas (Atabapo), Bolívar (Cedeño, Gran Sabana, Raul Leoni, Sifontes and Sucre) and Delta Amacuro (Antonia Diaz, Casacoima and Pedernales). Chloroquine and sulfadoxine-pyrimethamine resistant *P. falciparum* reported. Recommended prevention: II in *P. vivax* risk areas; IV in *P. falciparum* risk areas.

▶ **DIVING**

Number of certified divers: N/A
Dive federation(s): Federacion Venezolana De Actividades Subacuaticas
Dive regulations: Diver certification
Freediving federation(s): AIDA
Major bodies of water: Caribbean Sea
Dive season: year-round
Water temperature: 26°C/78.8F (Jan-Mar), 28°C/82.4F (July-Sept)
Hyperbaric chambers:
Catia La Mar. Estado Vargas (North Coast)
Hospital Naval Raúl Perdomo (Operativa)
Telephone: (0212) 3504126
Lagunillas Norte. Estado Zulia. (West Coast)
Unidad De Buceo Pdvsa (Operativa)
Telephone: (0265) 805-3333

Popular dive sites: Los Testigos Islands, Los Roques, Henri Pittier National Park, Mochima National Park
Tourism information: Discover Venezuela (www.discovervenezuela.com)

VIETNAM

▶ **GENERAL**

Capital: Hanoi
Government: Communist state
Population: 83,535,576 (July 2005 est.)
Ethnic groups: Kinh (Viet) 86.2%, Tay 1.9%, Thai 1.7%, Muong 1.5%, Khome 1.4%, Hoa 1.1%, Nun 1.1%, Hmong 1%, others 4.1% (1999 census)
Language(s): Vietnamese (official), English (increasingly favored as a second language), some French, Chinese, and Khmer; mountain area languages (Mon-Khmer and Malayo-Polynesian)

Religion(s): Buddhist 9.3%, Catholic 6.7%, Hoa Hao 1.5%, Cao Dai 1.1%, Protestant 0.5%, Muslim 0.1%, none 80.8% (1999 census)
GDP per capita: $2,700 (2004 est.)
Currency: dong (VND) - dong per US dollar - 15,746 (2004)
Time: GMT + 7
Electricity: 220V, 50Hz
National holiday: Independence Day, 2 September (1945)

▶ GEOGRAPHY

Location: Southeastern Asia, bordering the Gulf of Thailand, Gulf of Tonkin, and South China Sea, alongside China, Laos, and Cambodia
Border countries: Cambodia 1,228 km, China 1,281 km, Laos 2,130 km
Area: 329,560 sq km
Coastline: 3,444 km (excludes islands)
Climate: tropical in south; monsoonal in north with hot, rainy season (mid May to mid-September) and warm, dry season (mid-October to mid-March)
Terrain: low, flat delta in south and north; central highlands; hilly, mountainous in far north and northwest
lowest point: South China Sea 0 m
highest point: Fan Si Pan 3,144 m
Natural hazards: occasional typhoons (May to January) with extensive flooding, especially in the Mekong River delta
Vaccination(s): Yellow fever: A yellow fever vaccination certificate is required from travellers over 1 year of age coming from infected areas. **Malaria:** Malaria risk—predominantly due to *P. falciparum*—exists in the whole country, excluding urban centres, the Red River delta, and the coastal plain areas of central Viet Nam. High-risk areas are the highland areas below 1500 m south of 18½N, notably the three central highlands provinces of Dak Lak, Gia Lai and Kon Tum, as well as the southern provinces of Ca Mau, Bac Lieu, and Tay Ninh. Resistance to chloroquine, sulfadoxine-pyrimethamine and mefloquine reported. Recommended prevention in risk areas: IV

▶ DIVING

Number of certified divers: 200 *
Dive federation(s): Hiep Hoi The Thao Duoi Nuoc Viet Nam (VASA) (Vietnam Aquatic Sports Association)
Dive regulations: Diver cerfitication
Freediving federation(s): None*
Major bodies of water: South China Sea, Gulf of Thailand, Gulf of Tonkin
Dive season: year-round
Water temperature: 25°C/77F (Jan-Mar), 29°C/84.2F (July-Sept)
Hyperbaric chambers:
City: Ha Noi
City Ho Chi Minh city*

Popular dive sites: Nha Trang, (Khanh Hoa province), Vung Tau province, Ho Chi Minh city, Hai Phong city, Quang Ninh province*
Tourism information: Vietnam National Administration of Tourism (www.vietnamtourism.com)
* SOURCE: VASA (Dec. 2005)

VIRGIN ISLANDS

▶ GENERAL

Capital: Charlotte Amalie
Government: organized, unincorporated territory of the US
Population: 108,708 (July 2005 est.)
Ethnic groups: black 76.2%, white 13.1%, Asian 1.1%, other 6.1%, mixed 3.5% (2000 census)
Language(s): English 74.7%, Spanish or Spanish Creole 16.8%, French or French Creole 6.6%, other 1.9% (2000 census)
Religion(s): Baptist 42%, Roman Catholic 34%, Episcopalian 17%, other 7%
GDP per capita: $17,200 (2002 est.)
Currency: US dollar (USD)
Time: GMT - 4
Electricity: 110V, 60Hz
National holiday: Transfer Day (from Denmark to the US), 27 March (1917)

▶ GEOGRAPHY

Location: Caribbean, islands between the Caribbean Sea and the North Atlantic Ocean, east of Puerto Rico
Border countries: None
Area: 352 sq km
Coastline: 188 km
Climate: subtropical, tempered by easterly trade winds, relatively low humidity, little seasonal temperature variation; rainy season September to November

Terrain: mostly hilly to rugged and mountainous with little level land
lowest point: Caribbean Sea 0 m
highest point: Crown Mountain 474 m
Natural hazards: several hurricanes in recent years; frequent and severe droughts and floods; occasional earthquakes
Vaccination(s): No vaccination requirements for any international traveller.

► **DIVING**

Number of certified divers: Mainly tourists
Dive federation(s): None
Dive regulations: Diver certification
Freediving federation(s): None
Major bodies of water: North Atlantic Ocean, Caribbean Sea
Dive season: year-round
Water temperature: 24°C75.2F (Jan-Mar), 27°C/80.6F (July-Sept)
Hyperbaric chambers:
City: St Thomas, USVI
Popular dive sites: Submarine Alley, Cow and Calf Rocks, Carval Rock, Dutchcap Cay, Wreck: Major General Rogers
Tourism information: United States Virgin Islands Department of Tourism (www.usvitourism.vi)

WALLIS AND FUTUNA

► **GENERAL**

Capital: Mata-Utu (on Ile Uvea)
Government: overseas territory of France
Population: 16,025 (July 2005 est.)
Ethnic groups: Polynesian
Language(s): Wallisian 58.9% (indigenous Polynesian language), Futunian 30.1%, French 10.8%, other 0.2% (2003 census)
Religion(s): Roman Catholic 99%, other 1%

GDP per capita: $3,800 (2004 est.)
Currency: Comptoirs Français du Pacifique franc (XPF) - Comptoirs Français du Pacifique francs (XPF) per US dollar - 96.04 (2004)
Time: GMT + 12
Electricity: 220V, 50Hz
National holiday: Bastille Day, 14 July (1789)

► **GEOGRAPHY**

Location: Oceania, islands in the South Pacific Ocean, about two-thirds of the way from Hawaii to New Zealand
Border countries: None
Area: 274 sq km
Coastline: 129 km
Climate: tropical; hot, rainy season (November to April); cool, dry season (May to October); rains 2,500-3,000 mm per year (80% humidity); average temperature 26.6 degrees C
Terrain: volcanic origin; low hills
lowest point: Pacific Ocean 0 m
highest point: Mont Singavi 765 m
Natural hazards: NA
Vaccination(s): NA

► **DIVING**

Number of certified divers: Mainly tourists
Dive federation(s): None
Dive regulations: Diver certification
Freediving federation(s): None
Major bodies of water: South Pacific Ocean
Dive season: year-round
Water temperature: 24°C75.2F (Jan-Mar), 21°C/69.8F (July-Sept)
Hyperbaric chambers: N/A
Popular dive sites:
Tourism information: Ministère de l'Outre-Mer (www.outre-mer.gouv.fr)

YEMEN

► **GENERAL**

Capital: Sanaa
Government: republic
Population: 20,727,063 (July 2005 est.)
Ethnic groups: predominantly Arab; but also Afro-Arab, South Asians, Europeans
Language(s): Arabic
Religion(s): Muslim including Shaf'i (Sunni) and Zaydi (Shi'a), small numbers of Jewish, Christian, and Hindu
GDP per capita: $800 (2004 est.)
Currency: Yemeni rial (YER) - Yemeni rials per US dollar - 184.78 (2004)
Time: GMT + 3
Electricity: 220/240V, 50Hz
National holiday: Unification Day, 22 May (1990)
► **GEOGRAPHY**

Location: Middle East, bordering the Arabian Sea, Gulf of Aden, and Red Sea, between Oman and Saudi Arabia
Border countries: Oman 288 km, Saudi Arabia 1,458 km
Area: 527,970 sq km
Coastline: 1,906 km
Climate: mostly desert; hot and humid along west coast; temperate in western mountains affected by seasonal monsoon; extraordinarily hot, dry, harsh desert in east
Terrain: narrow coastal plain backed by flat-topped hills and rugged mountains; dissected upland desert plains in center slope into the desert interior of the Arabian Peninsula
lowest point: Arabian Sea 0 m
highest point: Jabal an Nabi Shu'ayb 3,760 m
Natural hazards: sandstorms and dust storms in summer
Vaccination(s): Yellow fever: A yellow fever vaccination certificate is required from travellers over 1 year of age coming from infected areas. **Malaria:** Malaria risk—predominantly due to *P. falciparum*—exists throughout the year, but mainly from September through February, in the whole country below 2000 m. There is no risk in Sana'a city. Resistance to chloroquine reported. Recommended prevention in risk areas: IV

Water temperature: 25°C/77F (Jan-Mar), 26°C/78.8F(July-Sept)
Hyperbaric chambers:
City : Sanaa, Alhemed-Co
Telephone : 009671-231874
Popular dive sites: Kadman Island, Maha's Rock, Socotra Island, Middle Reef
Tourism information: Yemen Tourism Promotion Board (www.yementourism.com)

▶ **DIVING**

Number of certified divers: Mainly tourists
Dive federation(s): None
Dive regulations: Diver certification
Freediving federation(s): None
Major bodies of water: Red Sea, Arabian Sea, Gulf of Aden
Dive season: year-round

2005/2006 DIVING CHRONICLE

The Diving Chronicle section presents a monthly review of the last year's events[53]. News items are excerpted from a variety of information sources. The accuracy of every news item is verified whenever possible but cannot be guaranteed. When the exact date on an event is unavailable, the date used is that of the news item release.

If you would like to submit a news item for the 2008 edition, please contact us at: news@divingalmanac.com

SEPTEMBER

01
ALASKA – Court issues salvage rights
NOAA team in the Gulf of Mexico successfully films the fluorescent pattern of the world's first fluorescent shark, the chain cat shark, which the team had discovered the year before.

Fluorescent chain cat shark at about 1,820 ft (555 m) deep. This shark was no more than 3 ft (1 m) long and posed for a couple of minutes lying still on the bottom near the submersible. Photo: NOAA Operation Deep Scope 2006

01
PHILIPPINES – Spanish gunboat discovered

Archaeologists believe a vessel accidentally discovered by divers on August 24 off the town of Caramoan is the 19th century Spanish gunboat *Elcano*.

02
THAILAND – Sculptures to save reefs
Thai authorities set up plan to sink marine artwork in the form of concrete sculptures in order to lure divers away from endangered coral in the six Andaman provinces affected by the December 26 tsunami.

05
CANADA – *Empress of Ireland* reveals some of her secrets
Four expeditions led by Capt. Gary Kulisek during the summer reveal previously unseen items from the shipwreck, including human remains. Capt. Kulisek reported that for unknown reasons, the various objects were at least partially swept of the layer of accumulated silt which had gradually covered the surrounding bottom since the ship sank off Rimouski in 1914. Quebec law forbids the collecting of any items found on the ship or in the surrounding debris field.

08
AUSTRALIA – Divers rewarded
The Sydney Project, Keith Appleby and the fishermen of Bermagui receive an award from the Heritage Council of NSW for their discovery of three historic shipwrecks off the south coast (sydneyproject.com)

09
NORTH CAROLINA – Hunt for *Alligator*
NOAA and the Office of Naval Research conduct a week-long search for the lost

---

[53] News items mentioned elsewhere in the Diving Almanac & Yearbook, such as freediving records, are not repeated in the Diving Chronicle.

Civil War sub *Alligator* off Cape Hatteras in the "Graveyard of the Atlantic." The U.S. Navy's first submarine was lost during a fierce storm in 1863.

23
AUSTRALIA – NSW Government considers annual license for scuba divers
Primary Industries Minister Ian Macdonald announces that a licensing program administered by dive industry members may be established for scuba divers. Funds raised would be used to create improved amenities for scuba divers, and to dedicate funds towards environmental programs such as the preservation of the grey nurse shark.

26
JAPAN – Giant squid photographed alive
Japanese scientists release the first-ever photos of a live giant squid. The squid measuring approximately 25 ft (8 m) long was photographed over 500 times at a depth of 2,950 ft (900 m) on September 2004 using a baited fishing line. A tentacle that got snagged on the bait hook was recovered for analysis.

31
CANADA – Underwater arsenal found in Nova Scotia
Hundreds of arrowheads and tools were discovered last year in the Mersey River, near Kejimkujik National Park. Archaeologists have dated some of the items back to 8,000 years ago. The native Mi'kmaq artefacts were discovered in the mud when the water level of the Mersey River was lowered by Nova Scotia Power in order to conduct repairs on generating stations. In all, 109 campsites were found and searched. Archaeologists found pottery fragments, spear points, knives and even harpoons used for salmon fishing. The important discovery was kept secret and the RCMP was brought in to prevent looting until the water levels were brought back to normal and the settlements were once again submerged. The artefacts will be displayed at the Nova Scotia Museum.

OCTOBER

02
CROATIA – Herbert Nitsch sets new freediving record
Nitsch sets No Limit world record at 172 m off the town of Sibenik.

04
FLORIDA – *Oriskany* sinking to cost over 12 million USD
The planned cost of scuttling the USS *Oriskany* as an artificial reef is much higher than anticipated. Delays in obtaining a permit from the Environmental Protection Agency, towing expenses and other difficulties have made the cost of sinking the aircraft carrier soar from $2.8 million (€2.2 million EUR) to $12.73 million (€10 million EUR).

Tugboats turn the decommissioned aircraft carrier USS *Oriskany* (CVA 34) prior to mooring at Allegheny Pier onboard Naval Air Station Pensacola. Photo: U.S. Navy / Megan Kohr

05
GREECE – Law relaxed to allow more diving
Bill to lift restrictions on recreational scuba-diving passes in a parliamentary committee in order to stimulate diving tourism in Greece. Sport diving is Greece has long been strictly restricted to prevent the smuggling of antiquities.

10
ITALY – Wreck of the *Polluce* found
Italian divers discover the wreck of the *Polluce* that sank off the island of Elba in 1841. Divers have already recovered jew-

els and coins missed by the pirates who attacked the ship which sank in less than 15 minutes.

11
United States – SDI/TDI files lawsuit against PSA
ITI Holdings, Inc., the parent company of SDI[54], TDI[55] and ERDI[56], files lawsuit against PSA[57] for various claims including misappropriation of trade secrets and copyright infringement.

14
AUSTRALIA – Divers discover colonial shipwreck off Queensland
Ian Eberhardt and Kevin Denlay report the discovery of what could be Australia's oldest colonial shipwreck during the previous month. The divers recovered the ship's bell and bottles at a depth of 200 ft (60 m) about 37 miles (60 km) off Double Island Point. The evidence collected to date including the absence of boilers would indicate the ship may have sunk around 1860.

14
SOLOMON ISLANDS – Diving boycott lifted after minister is sacked
Fisheries Minister, Paul Maenu'u is forced to resign after divers launch a boycott of the Solomon Islands in response to the minister's vote in favour of commercial whaling at the International Whaling Commission (IWC) meeting in June.

16
FLORIDA – Mayor of Tarpon Springs goes for sponge dive
Mayor Beverley Billiris demonstrates sponge diving wearing traditional hard hat and canvass suit during Historical Diving Society's annual conference.

20
MASSACHUSETTS – Anti-diver device
Raytheon Corporation applies for a patent for an anti-diver device. The system for swimmer denial transmits low-frequency

underwater sound to stop divers from approaching any protected ship or installation. The amplified sound has sufficient peak pressure and/or impulse area to make human organs resonate, causing divers to vomit or suffer internal ruptures.

21
NORTH CAROLINA – Hurricane aids in archaeological recovery
Waters churned by Hurricane Ophelia off Atlantic Beach uncover an apothecary mortar from the wreck of Blackbeard's *Queen Anne's Revenge*.

22
BELIZE – Divers drift at sea for three days
An American woman dies and three friends drift for three days in stormy seas after the engine of their dive charter boat fails and they try to swim to shore. The deceased diver was the only person in the group not wearing a dive suit.

24
MEXICO – Yucatan Peninsula takes a beating from Hurricane Wilma
Dive operations and resorts at highly popular Cozumel Island and Cancun take a direct hit and are badly damaged by the Category 3 storm.

27
NORWAY – Norway hopes to protect heritage sites with u/w signs
Several shipwrecks are slated to be flagged with special signs from the Directorate for Cultural Heritage in order to prevent looting by divers.

27
CANADA – Freediving short takes the prize at Montreal festival
The 2005 edition of the Montreal International Adventure Film Festival (FIFAM) awards the Adventura Prize for Best Extreme Short Film to French freediver Loïc Leferme. FIFAM's Adventura prize goes to the short film that best illustrates an extreme sporting event. Leferme's short film, *Profondeur Absolue -171m* (France, 2004, 9 min.), is a condensed version of his record No Limits freedive to 561 ft (171 m) which

---

[54] SDI – Scuba Diving International
[55] TDI – Technical Diving International
[56] ERDI – Emergency Response Diving International
[57] PSA – Professional Scuba Association International

he set off Villefranche-sur-Mer in October 2004.

Photo: J. Strazzanti / Courtesy of Loïc Leferme (www.loicleferme.fr)

29
INDONESIA – Divers recover treasure from century-old shipwreck
An international team of divers present items recovered from the excavation of a 1,000-year-old shipwreck in the Java Sea. It took over 24,000 dives to recover hundreds of artifacts including ceramic pottery and jewels from a depth of 180 ft (54 m).

31
HAWAII – Charter operator may face fines
Coast Guard investigators recommend that a Kauai dive charter operator be fined $15,000 (€11,700 EUR) for letting two divers drift from his boat off Anahola on Oct. 30, 2003. One diver was later recovered by another boat and the other made it to shore after swimming for several hours. There was no divemaster on the boat to monitor diving activities at the time of the incident.

31
PHILIPPINES – Greenpeace fined for damaging reef
Environmental group Greenpeace is fined almost $7,000 (€5,500 EUR) for damaging World Heritage site Tubbataha Reef Marine Park in the Sulu Sea. Greenpeace officials agreed to pay the fine although they blame inaccurate charts supplied by

the government led their flagship *Rainbow Warrior II* to run aground.

NOVEMBER

07
EGYPT – Divers uncover foundation of ancient lighthouse
French underwater archeologists discover the base of the ancient lighthouse of Pharos in Alexandria, the seventh wonder of the world.

13
NEW ZEALAND – Warship scuttled for divers
HMNZS Wellington, a Leander class frigate decommissioned in 1999, is scuttled off the city of Wellington. The vessel sinks to the sea floor in 55 seconds. The wreck breaks into two sections during a storm in February.

F69/HMNZS *Wellington* being sunk. Photo: John Lewis[58]

18
CANADA – Giant octopus attacks ROV
A giant octopus attacks an ROV during a survey operation off Vancouver Island, British Columbia. The 100-lb (45 kg) cephalopod latches on to the $200,000 machine until the operator is able to blast it off by going in full reverse. Neither the octopus nor the ROV are seriously affected by the incident.

[58] Image licensed under the Creative Commons Attribution ShareAlike License v. 2.5

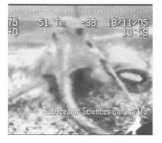

Giant octopus attacks ROV off Vancouver Island. Photo: SubOceanic Sciences Canada - www.suboceanic.net

19
NEW ZEALAND – Diver saved after drifting out to sea
A Japanese diver is saved by a police rescue boat after she gets separated from her group and drifts out of sight of land for nearly three hours. The police boat was making its way to the search zone several miles away when it unexpectedly came upon the lost diver.

21
CALIFORNIA – U/W noise harms animals
A study released by the Natural Resources Defense Council (NRDC) finds that ocean noise generated by military sonar, shipping, and oil and gas exploration threatens cetaceans that use sound for mating, finding food and avoiding predators.

21
GEORGIA – Largest aquarium in the world opens in Atlanta
The Georgia Aquarium opens exhibiting whale sharks, marine mammals and over 100,000 other animals in the world's largest fish tank (6.2 million gallons – 23,500,000 l)

21
FRANCE – Experienced divers disappear
Penny Glover, one of the British Sub Aqua Club's top instructors and one of the most experienced divers in the UK, disappears with her diving partner Jacques Filippi during a dive near the island of Porquerolles in the Mediterranean Sea. Their bodies were discovered using an ROV off Porquerolles

on January 5, 2006. Both were still fully clad in diving equipment.

22
AUSTRALIA – Abalone diver convicted
A diver is convicted for not declaring over 4.5 tonnes of abalone which he recorded on another diver's dockets and for which he received payment. The diver is given a suspended jail sentence after pleading guilty to a conspiracy charge. The diver had to repay the $35,000 AUD ($26,500 USD / €20,700 EUR) he received for the catch which had an estimated beach value of $200,000 AUD ($152,000 USD / €118,000 EUR).

24
FLORIDA – Zak Jones dies during dive
Zak Jones, a respected and popular course director, dies during a dive with friends on Thanksgiving Day.

27
AUSTRALIA – Japanese midget submarine located in Sydney Harbor
Filmmaker Damien is believed to have discovered the wreck of the M24, a midget-sub of the Japanese Imperial Navy which along with two other mini-subs sank HMAS *Kuttabul* killing 21 in May, 1942.

Japanese "Type A" midget submarine on an Hawaiian beach following attempts to enter Pearl Harbor in December 1941. Photo: U.S. Navy Naval Historical Center

DECEMBER

01
Under-ice weddings

The town council of Percé, one of Quebec's most picturesque coastal communities, approves project to allow the mayor of the community to celebrate underwater weddings, including ceremonies under pack ice during the cold winter months.

03
OHIO - Divers locate coveted Erie shipwreck
Divers announce the discovery of the wreck of the *Cortland*, a 173-ft (53 m), three-masted bark which was one of the largest sailing vessels on the Great Lakes when it sank on June 20, 1868. (See Aug. 22)

06
MASSACHUSETTS - Oceanographers discover submerged forest
Oceanographers mapping the bottom of Nantucket Sound discovered a submerged forest under 6 ft (2 m) of sediment. The debris was part of the seaside forest lining the coast before sea levels rose after the last ice age, 5,500 years ago.

08
ALABAMA – Diver convicted
A dive shop owner is convicted of misdemeanor third-degree theft for removing a Civil War-era musket from the Alabama River at Selma. (See April 14)

11
CALIFORNIA – Divers save whale
A group of divers and staff from the Marine Mammal Center in Sausalito rescue a 50-ft (15 m) humpback whale entangled in fishing gear near the Farallon Islands, a chain of rocky islands known as a haunt for the great white shark about 30 miles (50 km) west of San Francisco.

12
SPAIN – Exploration of HMS *Sussex*
Odyssey Marine Exploration begins operations on the shipwreck site believed to be HMS *Sussex*. HMS *Sussex* was a large 80-gun English warship lost in a severe storm in 1694. Historical research suggests a large cargo of money was carried by the *Sussex* when she sank. If the research is correct,

then the numismatic value estimates for the cargo range from several hundred million to a billion dollars or more.

A Remotely Operated Vehicle (ROV) is launched from the stern of the R/V *Minibex* on its way to investigate a shipwreck site discovered by Odyssey Marine Exploration nearly 3000 ft (900 m) below. Photo: Odyssey Marine Exploration - www.shipwreck.net

The *Carthaginian II* before and after being scuttled off Puamana, Hawaii. Photo: Atlantis Adventures - www.atlantisadventures.com

13
HAWAII – New artificial reef
The *Carthaginian II*, a 97-ft (30 m) vessel made to look like a 19th-century brig, was scuttled in 95 ft (30 m) of water off Puamana. The operation was conducted by Atlantis Adventures which offers a view of the new artificial reef aboard a passenger submarine equipped with large viewing ports.

14
ISRAEL – Inventor designs human gills
Alan Bodner announces the development of self-contained breathing apparatus that should allow breathing underwater without compressed air. Bodner's system instead extracts from sea water to supply divers and submarines with an unlimited supply of breathing gas. (www.likeafish.biz)

Image: www.likeafish.biz

21
AUSTRALIA – Airplane wreck discovered
Diver and underwater filmmaker Ben Cropp announces the discovery of a wrecked plane at a depth of 20 ft (6 m) at an undisclosed location off Cape York in November. The plane lost during World War II is likely an American or Japanese bomber. Further examination of the debris will reveal the nationality and type of aircraft.

23
MALTA – Divers charged for stealing
Police file charges against six divers accused of stealing and destroying Maltese underwater heritage. This is the first time a case of marine heritage pilfering is heard of in a Maltese court.

23
SOUTH AFRICA – Poachers part of tour
Poaching of endangered Perlemoen (a.k.a. abalone) has become so commonplace that a Port Elizabeth tour bus operator points out a group of poachers readying for a dive on his microphone as if they have become a regular attraction.

25
SINGAPORE – The longest dive
Khoo Swee Chiow emerges from a tank after spending 220 hours underwater in a controlled environment without surfacing, thus establishing a new world record. Chiow began his ten-day ordeal on December 16.
(www.daretodream.com.sg)

27
FLORIDA - Norine Rouse (1925-2005)
"If there's not an ocean in heaven, I'm not going." Norine Rouse, one of the country's first female diving instructors and an active environmentalist, dies at the age of 80.

30
NEW ZEALAND – Reefs good for business
Dive operators in Wellington report a large increase in business after the scuttling of the Leander class frigate HMNZS *Wellington* on November 13. Charters have jumped by over 50% and registration for scuba courses has jumped by up to 70%.

31
ALASKA – Court issues salvage rights
Steve Lloyd of Anchorage is a partner in Shoreline Adventures and the first diver to the wreck of the steamship SS *Aleutian* off the coast of Alaska. The ship sank in 1929 and was discovered by Lloyd in 2002.

SS *Aleutian*

Lloyd has been fighting the State of Alaska in court in order to gain access to the shipwreck and its cargo. The court's decision permits Shoreline Adventures to salvage the dishes, furnishings, fixtures and other objects remaining 76 years after the ship sank 200 ft (60 m) underwater.

Plates & light frame on wreck of SS *Aleutian*. Photos courtesy of Shoreline Adventures (www.divealeutian.com)

Shoreline Adventures cannot begin the retrieval process until an environmental assessment is completed, as per the agreement reached by both parties. In addition, Shoreline Adventures must share a "representative sampling" of the artifacts with the state Office of History and Archeology.

JANUARY

Photo: Franck Goddio / Hilti Foundation / Jérôme Delafosse (www.franckgoddio.org)

06
GERMANY – Egyptian artifact exhibit
The Franck Goddio Society announces that for the first time, objects re-covered from underwater archeological sites off Alexandria will be displayed to the public at an exhibition to be held in the Martin-Gropius-Bau in Berlin in 2006. The exhibition includes 20-ft (6 m) high statues, the largest stele (stone slab with inscriptions) ever

found in Egypt, and some 500 other objects.

Photo: Franck Goddio / Hilti Foundation/ Christoph Gerigk (www.franckgoddio.org)

06
FLORIDA – Centennial Epiphany Dive
Jack Vasilaros, 16, surfaces holding the white wooden cross lobbed into Tarpon Springs' Spring Bayou by his All Holiness Bartholomew of the Greek Orthodox Church. The winner of the yearly event held since 1906, is then blessed with a year's luck.

07
AUSTRALIA – Shark attack closes beaches
Australian police close several popular beaches in Queensland State after a shark attacks kills a scuba diver. It is reported that the 21-year-old female diver was attacked in waist-deep water by at least three bull sharks.

07
THAILAND – Diver killed by speedboat
A 27-year-old female diver from Bangkok was killed when she was struck by a speedboat in the Gulf of Thailand. The owner of the boat later turned himself in to police and was later charged with neglect resulting in death.

09
BONAIRE – Bonaire at the top again
Bonaire captures number one spot for the fourth straight year in *Scuba Diving* magazine's 2006 Readers' Choice Awards. Bonaire received the #1 rating in four Carib-

bean/Atlantic categories including, Top Caribbean Dive Destination (96.3%). Bonaire was also rated #1 for Underwater Photography (97.4%), Beginner Diving (95.7%) and Shore Diving (95.4%). Bonaire took second place in the categories of Marine Life (94.7%), Healthiest Marine Environment (94.7%), Visibility (92.3%) and Top Small Animals (89%), and placed in the top five in the Top Value (90.5%) and Top Snorkeling (85.1%) categories. (www.infobonaire.com)

12
SOUTH AFRICA – Boulder kills diver
A diamond diver is killed when a huge boulder falls on him. The victim was pumping diamondiferous gravel at a depth of 15 ft (5 m) at the time of the accident.

12
MALAYSIA – Shark foils record attempt
A nurse shark bumps into Ashrita Furman as he attempts to break his own underwater juggling world record of 48 minutes and 36 seconds. The brush with the shark at the Aquatheatre, Aquaria KLCC, broke Furman's momentum 13 minutes into the attempt. The diver was apparently standing at the shark's resting spot. Furman holds 32 world records. (www.ashrita.com)

15
AUSTRALIA – Diver fights off shark
A 46-year-old diver fights off an 11-ft (3.5 m) great white shark near Perth with a speargun after the shark bites his arm. Brian Williams escapes the attack with just lacerations.

16
SOUTH AFRICA – Divers must renew permit
The South African government announces that divers must renew permits in order to continue diving in marine protected areas.

19
UK – Hydrodome project may relocate
Promoter Andrew Sneath announces that the Hydrodome project may be relocated for lack of support. The £5,000,000 ($9.4 million USD / € 7.4 million EUR) Hydrodome, an indoor film studio and dive center

slated for construction in the town of Bromsgrove, would contain a giant aquarium for divers, tourists and researchers to observe Sneath's mechanical fish. (www.hydrodome.co.uk)

19
CALIFORNIA – DEMA elections
Results of DEMA's 2006 Board of Directors Election are announced. DEMA's 2006 Board of Directors consists of the following individuals:

A1-Manufacturers & Distributors
Dan Emke – Aeris
Susan Long – Diving Unlimited International

A2-Diver Certification and Training Agencies
Al Hornsby – PADI
Dan Orr – Divers Alert Network

A3-Dive Publishing, Media, Consulting and Non-Retail Service Providers
Ty Sawyer – Sport Diver Magazine
Rick Stratton – Northwest Dive News

A4-Retailers
Jim Byrem – Ocean Concepts Scuba
Dave Riscinti – Blue Water Divers

A5-Travel & Resorts
Wayne Hasson – Aggressor Fleet
Keith Sahm – Sunset House

In accordance with the DEMA Bylaws, Directors serve three-year terms. Directors cannot serve more than two consecutive three-year terms, but can be re-elected after a minimum break of one year. For more information on DEMA's Board of Directors and Bylaws visit: www.dema.org

22
NEW YORK – Divers find body of lost diver
Divers looking for the wreck of the *Sir Robert Peel* in the St. Lawrence River discover the body of a diver missing since 1981. Brett Schirmer disappeared 25 years earlier while searching for the *Sir Robert Peel*.

FEBRUARY

01
CANADA – Wrecks require dive permit
Ontario Government announces that a permit is now required to dive the deep-water wrecks the *Edmund Fitzgerald*, the *Hamilton* and the *Scourge*. The new regulation under the Ontario Heritage Act is intended to protect human remains.

01
AUSTRALIA – Shark repellent rejected
The Queensland Government announces it will not install a shark repellent device along its beaches for lack of scientific proof that it works. Known as Beach Barrier, the device would replace shark nets that also kills other marine life. The device developed by Seachange is meant to keep sharks away from beaches by creating an electrical field which causes discomfort to sharks.
(www.sharkshield.com)

02
GREECE – ROV explores ancient wreck
U.S. and Greek researchers from the Woods Hole Oceanographic Institution (WHOI), Massachusetts Institute of Technology (MIT), the Greek Ministry of Culture, and the Hellenic Centre for Marine Research (HCMR) announce the discovery of a sunken 4th century B.C. merchant ship off the coast of Greece. The wreck which was originally discovered at a depth of 200 ft (60 m) using sonar in 2004, was laden with a cargo of 400 amphoras containing white wine and olive oil.

05
BONAIRE – Top Caribbean dive destination
Bonaire rated the top dive destination in the Caribbean for the fourth year in a row by Scuba Diving magazine.

06
AUSTRALIA – Shark ends competition
The 10km Cole Classic race off Sydney, one of Australia's top ocean swimming races, is abruptly terminated when a 3-meter shark is observed stalking the 21 swimmers.

08
NEW ZEALAND – Diver found after 3 days
Former navy diver Robert Hewitt, 38, is found suffering from dehydration and hallucinations after going missing for three days (72 hours). Hewitt disappeared after going on a solo dive near Wellington. Robert survived without water on raw sea urchins and crayfish he caught while drifting at sea.

Graf Spee burns and sinks from self-inflicted wounds off Montevideo in December 1939.

09
URUGUAY – Graf Spee eagle recovered
Six decades after the pride of the German navy is scuttled during the Battle of the River Plate, divers salvage the 6.5-ft (2 m), 880-lb (400 kg) eagle statue from the *Admiral Graf Spee*.
(www.lummifilm.com/grafspee)

11
NEW JERSEY – Peter Benchley (1940-2006)
Peter Bradford Benchley, writer of *Jaws*, dies in Princeton, New Jersey.

25
MALDIVES – World record dive
979 divers aged between 10 and 73 set a new record for people scuba diving simultaneously at Sunlight Thila, North Male' Atoll The divers consist of tourists, Maldivians and expatriates from 37 resorts, 9 dive centres, the Coast Guard and 14 safari vessels.

MARCH

02
SWEDEN – 12TH century wreck discovered
Archeologists announce the discovery of a 12th century shipwreck buried in the mud at a depth of 30 ft (10 m) in Riddarfjarden Bay in Stockholm. The National Maritime Museum has tentatively dated the construction of the vessel to between 1350 and 1370, and it is believed to have sunk in the 1390s. (www.maritima.se)

Neil McDaniel filming jacks in Sipadan for an unrelated IMAX production. Photo: Jason Isley (www.neilmcdaniel.com)

03
CANADA - IMAX 3D Underwater Film

Deep Sea 3D debuts at select IMAX, IMAX 3D and IMAX Dome theatres. Audiences are transported below the ocean surface to swim with some of the planet's most unique, dangerous and colorful creatures, from the unusual Wolf Eel to the Giant Pacific Octopus. The film is directed by world-renowned underwater cinematographer, Howard Hall. Narrators are Johnny Depp and Kate Winslet, with an original score by Danny Elfman. (www.imax.com/deepsea)

08
NEW ZEALAND – No diving on F69
Authorities declare a prohibited area of 650 ft (200 m) around the site for both anchoring and diving after a one-in-fifty year weather event breaks the wreck of the HMNZN *Wellington* (F69) in two. The area is to remain off limits till March 16 or until damage to the artificial reef can be monitored by the Sink F69 Trust and police divers.

F69/HMNZS *Wellington* prior to being sunk as a dive wreck. Photo: Greg O'Beirne[59]

09
INDONESIA – Wreck pillagers arrested
Two men from France and Germany are arrested and accused of illegally salvaging treasure from a Java shipwreck. The French and German divers removed 150,000 Chinese ceramic pieces dating back to the 10th century. The items recovered from a depth of 178 ft (54 m) near the city of Cirebon are worth millions of dollars. If convicted, the two men face a jail term of up to 10 years.

---

[59] Image licensed under the Creative Commons Attribution ShareAlike License v. 2.5

11
SAUDI ARABIA – Ancient coins returned

U.S. customs officials have returned 132 lbs (60 kg) of 13th century coins to Saudi Arabia after seizing the stolen artifacts from a Florida diver who illegally removed them from a shipwreck in the Red Sea more than 10 years ago. "Artifacts such as these coins are not trinkets that can be pilfered and sold to the highest bidder," said Julie L. Myers, assistant secretary of homeland security for Immigration and Customs Enforcement (ICE). "To their rightful owners, these artifacts are priceless items that are cherished and proudly displayed as a testament to their cultural history." Saudi Ambassador to the United States Prince Turki Al-Faisal said the coins reflect "Saudi Arabia's unique history as an ancient trade center and as the birthplace of Islam." He said the return of the antiquities shows the United States' respect for cultural heritage. After being confronted by ICE agents, a Florida man admitted to stealing the coins during a recreational dive in Saudi territorial waters in 1994. He surrendered the artifacts to customs officials in April 2005.

11
AUSTRALIA – Ferry delayed by diver

A Melbourne ferry is evacuated and delayed by nearly three hours after a security officer spots a diver four hours before departure time. The vessel finally leaves at 10.45pm after police complete a search of the water and ship.

APRIL

05
UK – Dive shop owner convicted

The owner of a Leeds dive shop is convicted of secretly filming customers in a changing room. Victims include a 13-year-old girl and two women. After a three-day trial, the jury rejects his claim that he was trying to catch thieves. Conviction of three counts of voyeurism by recording another person doing a private act in order to obtain sexual gratification could lead to a prison sentence. He was suspended from conducting PADI courses in August and is now facing banishment.

10
FLORIDA – More *Atocha* treasure uncovered

Divers from Mel Fisher's Treasure recover two gold bars and 15 silver coins from the shipwreck of the *Nuestra Senora de Atocha*, a Spanish galleon that sank off Key West in 1622. The bars were discovered approximately 35 miles (56 km) offshore under 12 ft (3.6 m) of sand at a depth of 20 ft (6 m). The gold is worth an estimated $250,000 USD.

14
ALABAMA – Court relaxes regulations

The Alabama Historical Commission announces changes to regulations prohibiting divers from removing arrowheads and other manmade objects from the state's rivers without a permit.

25
FLORIDA – Court relaxes regulations

A diver is bit by a 9-ft (2.75 m) alligator while retrieving golf balls from a murky Boynton lake. The 43-year-old man is recovering from an injury which resembles a dog bite. The alligator bit Martinez's air tank and attempted to drag him underwater. The alligator bit his arm when the diver went for his knife. The alligator was later trapped and euthanized.

27
NORTH CAROLINA – DAN & SSS settlement

Divers Alert Network (DAN America) and clinic members of the SSS Network of Recompression Chambers (SSS) announce that they have reached a settlement in the recent legal action. Representatives of SSS announce that DAN America insurance is once again accepted as a result of the resolution of the outstanding claims that were the basis for the lawsuit. The terms of the settlement remain confidential. The SSS Network of Recompression Chambers and DAN America pledge to work closely together to ensure that injured divers will receive the most appropriate and effective medical care.

MAY

08
NEW YORK – Failed breath hold attempt
Illusionist David Blaine is pulled from the water unconscious during a breath-holding stunt in an 8-ft (2.4 m) aquarium. Blaine was nearly two minutes short of his goal of setting a breath hold world record.

Zebra mussels overwhelm native mussels of the St. Lawrence River in Lake St. Pierre, east of Montreal, Quebec. Photo: J. Gallant / D.A.Y.

11
VIRGINIA – Zebra mussels eradicated
Biologists conduct the first successful openwater extermination of the zebra mussel in a Virginia quarry. The invasive species was eliminated by injecting the quarry with thousands of gallons of potassium chloride solution over a three week period. The solution apparently does not pose a threat to the environment or humans but it is only feasible in small bodies of water and could not be used to treat the Great Lakes. Zebra mussels were first discovered in the United States in 1988, having been discharged from the ballast tanks of Trans-Atlantic vessels. They have since spread to all of the Great Lakes and St. Lawrence Seaway, and they have been documented in hundreds of lakes and rivers across the U.S. and Canada.

13
ALASKA – First artificial reef
NOAA Fisheries experts and their partners begin construction of Alaska's first pre-planned and monitored artificial reef in Prince William Sound near Whittier.

17
FLORIDA – Aircraft carrier sunk for divers
The ex-*Oriskany*, a decommissioned aircraft carrier, became the largest ship intentionally sunk as an artificial reef May 17 when it was sunk at a depth of 150 ft (46 m) approximately 24 miles off the coast of Pensacola, Florida. The 888-foot (270 m) ship took about 37 minutes to sink.

Smoke belches from the 888-ft (270 m) *Oriskany* after explosive charges rip through the ship. (U.S. Navy photo)

19
MALAYSIA – Sipadan to be shut down?
The government of Malaysia considers shutting down diving operations off the island of Sipadan due to extensive damage caused to the coral reef at three popular dive sites. The damage was caused by a barge carrying construction materials. Diving will be restricted in order to let the corals rest and regenerate.

20
HAWAII – 1.4 million death settlement
Three companies agreed to pay $1.4 million to the family of a West Virginia woman who died while scuba diving off Hawai'i Kai in July when her BCD malfunctioned. In-

experience and a lack of supervision also contributed to the fatal accident. Aqua-Zone, Sheico PKS and the equipment distributor are ordered to pay a total of 1.4 million USD in compensation.

25
TEXAS – Ralph Erickson (1922- 2006)
PADI co-founder passes away at the age of 84. Erickson and partner John Cronin founded the Professional Association of Diving Instructors (PADI) in 1966.

29
UNITED KINGDOM – HMS *Resolution*?
Culture Minister David Lammy announces that the remains of a shipwreck believed to be the 17th-century warship HMS *Resolution*, have been accorded protected status in a bid to deter wreck hunters. The vessel was recently discovered by a fisherman and a novice diver off the Sussex coast. The 70-gun HMS *Resolution* sank in the great storm of November, 1703.

29
HAWAII – Record judgment
Attorney Rick Lesser wins a multimillion dollar dive case for a PADI instructor critically injured in a dive accident in Hawaii. Instructor Matthew Isham and one of his students were run over by a catamaran, resulting in the loss of Isham's leg above the knee and rendering the student's dominant arm permanently disabled. The dive vessel had failed to raise any dive flag, and it was also determined later that the company did not even own the large Alpha flag required by Coast Guard regulations to be displayed during diving operations. The judgment entered for Isham of $2,975,000 USD is believed to be the largest single award to a dive instructor in any published case in the country. (www.divelaw.com)

JUNE

06
SOUTH AFRICA – Shark diving report
A technical report presented to the Cape Town city council says the granting of cage-diving permits should be reviewed. The council also recommends that growth in the shark cage-diving industry should be restricted until it can be scientifically proven that cage diving does not contribute to shark attacks on swimmers and does not affect the natural behaviour of great white sharks.

12
CALIFORNIA – Dick Anderson (1933-2006)
The equipment designer, writer and filmmaker saved the life of Swiss scientist Hannes Keller during a deadly world record bell dive to 1,020 ft (311 m) off Catalina Island in 1962. Another diver and Anderson's fellow safety diver died in the attempt.

12
GRAND BAHAMA – New artificial reef
Bradford Marine, Grand Bahama, in conjunction with the Grand Bahama Divers Association, sinks the tugboat *La Rose* in 80 ft (24 m) of water off the South Shore of Grand Bahama.
(www.grandbahamascuba.com)

12
UNITED KINGDOM – Diver was a spy
The BBC reports that famed Royal Navy diver Lionel 'Buster' Crabb vanished while spying on Soviet warships which had brought Nikita Khrushchev on a diplomatic visit in the city of Portsmouth in 1956. At the time of the incident, Crabb had falsely been reported killed while handling an experimental mine in nearby Stokes Bay. A search for Crabb was not attempted when he was reported missing in order not to alert the crew of the cruiser *Ordzhonikidze*.

12
UNITED KINGDOM – First shark cage dives
Over 1,000 people sign up for the first cage diving trip in Britain. Only 72 divers will actually get to look for blue, mako and hammerhead sharks with shark conservationist Richard Pierce off the city of Cornwall in July.

14
FLORIDA – Swimmer injured by CO_2

A 17-year-old swimmer is rushed to hospital after breathing in carbon dioxide while swimming in an underwater cave. It is believed the teen may have breathed from an air pocket.

15
HAWAII – New protected marine area

President Bush announces the creation of the world's largest protected marine area around the Northwestern Hawaiian Islands, an archipelago 1,400 miles (2,253 km) long and 100 miles (161 km) wide that's home to rare marine mammals, fish and birds.

16
MEXICO – New reefs for Cozumel

As part of Cozumel's ongoing commitment to create new and exciting dive and snorkeling sites off the coast of the world-famous island, two former Mexican Navy Patrol ships are sunk to become new underwater attractions for exploration by divers and snorkelers. The two patrol ships, the *Laguna Mandinga* and the *Patzcuaro*, measuring 85 ft (26 m) long and 42 ft (13 m) long, respectively, now rest at a depth of approximately 38 ft (12 m) some 370 yards (338 m) from shore.

The P-74 heads for the bottom off the coast of Cozumel. Photos: www.islacozumel.com.mx

17
THAILAND – Lost WWII submarine found

Divers from USS *Salvor* (ARS 52) conduct six-days of diving to positively identify wreck of the WWII submarine USS *Lagarto*. Photographs and video of the submarine are sent to the Naval Historical Center in Washington for further analysis.

Chief Navy Diver Jon Sommers performs diving supervisor checks on Gunner's Mate 2nd Bryan Zenoni, who is preparing to dive from USS Salvor (ARS 52) on what is presumed to be World War II-era USS Lagarto (SS 371). Salvor divers are assisting the Naval Historical Center in attempting to positively identify the wreck. Photo: U.S. Navy Lt. Erik Wells

20
FRANCE – Wreck of *Lancastria* off-limits

The French Government protects the wreck site of the *Lancastria*, a WWII troop-ship sunk by German aircraft while evacuating troops and civilians from France in 1940. Over 3,000 people died when the ship sank in only minutes. Diving is now entirely prohibited at the site.

23
CAYMANS – Dan Tibbetts (1953- 2006)

Pioneer Cayman Islands resort operator passes away. Tibbetts opened Little Cayman Beach Resort in 1993 and later built the Conch Club and The Club Condominiums. He also formed Reef Divers on both Little Cayman and Cayman Brac to become the only dive operator at the time on both islands.

30
PARIS – Cousteau's *Calypso* to be repaired

Équipe Cousteau and the FFESSM[60] launch a new fundraising campaign to repair Jacques-Yves Cousteau's oceanographic vessel the Calypso which has been steadily succumbing to decay at La Rochelle for nearly 10 years. (www.cousteau.org)

---

[60] FFESSM: *Fédération française d'études et de sports sous-marins* - www.ffessm.fr

The *Calypso* at La Rochelle in 1999. Photo obtained under GNU General Public License.

30
SOUTH AFRICA – Grannies dive with sharks
Four adventurous grannies including Bettie (86), Anne (85) and Babs Hitchcock, go shark cage diving at Gans Bay in the Western Cape where they observe three great white sharks.

30
SWEDEN – Poseidon sold
DP Scandinavia acquires equipment manufacturer Poseidon Industries, founded in 1958. DP Scandinavia is located in Marstrand (Sweden). The company recently acquired all rights to Cis-Lunar Closed Circuit Rebreather and related technology. (www.poseidon.se)

JULY

03
PALAU – Looters convicted
Matthew Young and Cameron James Avenell are sentenced to three-month and six-month jail terms after being convicted of stealing underwater artefacts. They were also respectively fined $5,000 USD and $12,000 USD.

08
NEW JERSEY – David Bright (1957-2006)
David Bright, a leading researcher into underwater exploration and shipwrecks, dies upon surfacing from a dive on the wreck of the *Andrea Doria*, off Nantucket.

15
MASSACHUSETTS – Live wreck exploration
NOAA scientists and archaeologists from the National Undersea Research Center at the University of Connecticut and the Stellwagen Bank National Marine Sanctuary explore the shipwrecks of the coal schooners *Frank A. Palmer* and *Louise B. Crary* via a remotely operated vehicle (ROV) during 30-minute live broadcasts from underwater.

Sonar image of coal schooners *Frank A. Palmer* and *Louise B. Crary*. Photo: NOAA/SBNMS and NURC-UConn

16
CANADA – Rare aircraft salvaged
A team of divers recovers the engine and propeller of a Fokker Standard Universal northern cargo transport from Lake Charron in Manitoba. The plane sank to a depth of 120 ft (37 m) after an emergency landing on the frozen lake in 1931. (www.fokkeraircraftrecovery.ca)

17
JAPAN – Lost divers rescued
Four scuba divers are rescued off the Uji islands off the coast of Kagoshima Prefecture (South China Sea) after going missing for 13 hours at sea.

25
USA – First black navy diver dies
Carl M. Brashear, a pioneer in the Navy as the first black deep-sea diver, the first black Master Diver and the first Navy diver

in naval history to be restored to full active duty as an amputee, dies at the age of 75.

Honor Guard salute as they bring retired Master Chief Boatswain's Mate (Master Diver) Carl M. Brashear into the base Chapel aboard Naval Amphibious Base Little Creek, Va., July 29. In May 1966, Brashear had the lower part of his left leg medically removed after suffering an accident at sea. After almost two years of rehabilitation, Master Chief Brashear became the first amputee to be certified as a U.S. Navy diver. Later in 1970 Master Chief Brashear was the first African American to become a U.S. Navy Master Diver. Brashear died from heart and respiratory failure at Naval Medical Center Portsmouth, Va., July 25, at the age of 75. Photo: U.S. Navy Mass Communications Specialist 3rd Class Matthew D. Leistikow

27
FLORIDA – Three divers die during hunt
Four divers die and several others are injured during the two-day lobster mini-season off the Florida coast.

27
POLAND – Wreck of *Graf Zeppelin* found
The Polish navy announces the discovery of the wreck of Nazi Germany's only aircraft carrier in the Baltic Sea. The Graf Zeppelin was discovered by the Polish oil company Petrobaltic earlier this month about 38 miles (61 km) north of Gdansk. Launched in December 1938, the lone German aircraft carrier never saw action. It was taken by the Soviet Union in 1945 and was later sunk for target practice in 1947.

28
CALIFORNIA – Bill Meistrell (1929-2006)
Body Glove founder who revolutionized water sports by designing a light and flexible wet suit passes away at age 77.

Chief Navy Diver Daniel Jackson completes a successful certification dive of the Atmospheric Diving System (ADS) aboard the special mission charter ship M/V *Kellie Chouest*. Photo: U.S. Navy Mass Communication Specialist Seaman Chelsea Kennedy

AUGUST

01
CALIFORNIA – New ADS record
Chief Navy Diver (DSW/SS) Daniel P. Jackson of Navy Reserve Deep Submergence Unit (DSU) submerges to 2,000 ft, (610 m) setting a record using the new Atmospheric Diving System (ADS) suit, off the coast of La Jolla, California.

05
FRANCE – Divers swim across Channel
Six men and one woman are the first people to swim across the English Channel from Britain to France in an under-water scuba relay. They cover the distance of 21 miles (34 km) from Dover to Cap Gris Nez in just over 12 hours.

10

HAWAII – Diver finds the 'Precious'

Lindsey Holt finds a graduation ring at a depth of 60 ft (18 m) in a series of caves known as The Cathedral. After removing the coral that had covered the ring, he found the owner's and his school's name engraved on one side. A brief search led to a phone call to the owner, William Bundy, who had lost the ring during a dive outing in 1988.

10

UNITED KINGDOM – Lobster finds wallet

Diver finds a wallet in a lobster's claw. The wallet was lost when its owner went for a drunken swim.

17

ALASKA – Coast Guard divers killed

Two Coast Guard divers are killed during a cold-water training dive 500 miles (800 km) north of Barrow.

18

MICHIGAN – Shipwreck bell stolen

Department of Natural Resources announces that it is offering a $500 USD reward for information leading to the arrest and conviction of the person or persons responsible for taking the bell of the *City of Detroit* shipwreck. A group of divers noticed the bell was missing on July 30. Taking artifacts without a permit is a punishable offence.

22

OHIO – Divers recover shipwreck bell

Divers from CLUE, the Cleveland Underwater Explorers, in conjunction with the Great Lakes Historical Society, recover the bell of the *Cortland*, which sank in 1868. (See Dec. 03)

22

AUSTRALIA – Shipwreck protected

Federal Environment and Heritage Minister, Senator Ian Campbell, announces that the wreck of the SS *Iron Knight* is to be protected as a war grave. The Austrian cargo ship was torpedoed and sunk by a Japanese submarine off the Narooma coast in New South Wales during World War II. It was recently discovered by a team of specialist divers from The Sydney Project dive team 22 miles (35 km) south of Montague Island, off the coast of NSW, at a depth of 400 ft (125 m). "I consider vessels such as SS *Iron Knight*, sunk during enemy action in the Second World War, to be a significant part of Australia's maritime heritage and so I have declared the vessel a historic shipwreck to ensure its protection now and for future generations." Senator Campbell said he made the declaration to ensure the vessel and its contents were protected from possible interference or damage by visitors. "It is important that we respect our underwater heritage. Shipwrecks hold valuable information that needs to be protected for the benefit of all Australians - both now and in the future." Under the *Historic Shipwrecks Act 1976*, historic shipwrecks are protected and preserved by the Australian Government. The Act aims to protect maritime archaeological sites, while encouraging public access to them. The Act prohibits damage, interference or removal of historic shipwrecks and their associated relics.

UNITS OF MEASUREMENT AND CONVERSIONS

1 **atm** = 1 bar = 14.7 psi = 1.0333 kgs/cm²
1 **bar** = 14.7 psi = 1 atm = 1.0333 kgs/cm²
1 **centimeter** = 0.3937 inch
1 **cubic foot** = 7.481 gallons = 0.28.316 cubic meters
1 **fathom** = 6 feet = 1.8288 meters
1 **foot** 0.3048 meter
1 **inch** = 2.54 centimeters
1 **gallon (British Imperial)** = 1.201 U.S. gallons = 4.546 liters = 160 British fluid ounces
1 **gallon (U.S.)** = 3.785 liters = 0.833 British gallon = 128 U.S. fluid ounces
1 **kilometer** = 0.621 mile
1 **liter** = 61.024 cubic inches
1 **meter** = 39.37 inches = 1.094 yards
1 **mile** (statute or land) = 5,280 feet = 1.609 kilometers
1 **nautical mile** (Intl) = 1.852 km = 1.151 statute miles = 0.999 U.S. nautical miles
1 **ounce**, liquid (U.S.) = 29.574 milliliters = 1.041 British fluid ounces
1 **pint**, liquid = 0.473 liter
1 **psi** = 0.068 atm = 0.068 bar
1 **square foot** = 929.030 square centimeters
1 **square inch** 6.4516 square centimeters
1 **square kilometer** = 0.386 square mile = 247.105 acres
1 **square meter** = 1.196 square yards = 10.764 square feet
1 **square mile** = 258.999 hectares
1 **square yard** = 0.836 square meters
1 **ton, gross or long** = 2,240 pounds = 1.12 net tons = 1.016 metric tons
1 **ton, metric** = 2,204.623 pounds = 0.984 gross ton = 1.102 net tons
1 **ton, net or short** = 2,000 pounds = 0.893 gross ton = 0.907 metric ton
1 **yard** = 0.9144 meter

To convert	Into	Multiply by
meters (m)	feet (ft)	3.280840
kilometers (km)	(statute) miles (mi)	0.621371
kilometers (km)	nautical miles (nm)	0.539612
kilograms (kg)	pounds (lbs)	2.204627
grams (g)	ounces (oz)	0.035274
atmospheres (atm)	feet of water (at 4°C)	33.90
atmospheres (atm)	kgs/cm²	1.0333
atmospheres (atm)	lbs/in²	14.70
atmospheres (atm)	tons/ft²	1.058
kilometers/hour (km/h)	meters/second (m/s)	0.277778
kilometers/hour (km/h)	miles/hour (mi/hr)	0.6214
knots(kn)	meters/second (m/s)	0.514444
Fahrenheit (°F)-32	Celsius (°C)	5/9
Celsius (°C)+17.7778	Fahrenheit (°F)	1.8
cubic meters (m³)	cubic feet (ft³)	35.31467

SOURCE:
NOAA-NESDIS-National Oceanographic Data Center

INDEX

NOTES

DIVING IN
CANADA 🍁

With the exception of British Columbia, Canada is one of the most underrated dive destinations in the world. Few divers outside the country know that Canada is home to a myriad of large and exotic species rarely observed anywhere else. This comes as no surprise when one knows that Canada has the longest coastline on the globe spanning three oceans and the Great Lakes. Canada also has the largest freshwater supply on the planet in the form of countless lakes of all sizes, as well as rivers and other bodies of water that host diverse and lively ecosystems.

Contrary to popular belief, all of Canada does not disappear under a sheet of snow and ice for six months of the year. The dense rain-forest coasts of British Columbia remain temperate year-round and offer some of the best-rated diving in the world. Although the east coast is colder during winter, the seasonally difficult conditions that have sunk thousands of ships make for incredible visibility along the shores of Canada's historical Maritime provinces.

For those who enjoy traveling off the beaten track, diving through ice in the Canadian Arctic is now accessible to adventurous divers seeking to explore the remote polar region. Northern Manitoba also offers the rare opportunity to swim alongside beluga whales in Hudson's Bay.

With the world's best freshwater wreck diving, as well as the St. Lawrence Seaway and Estuary, the Saguenay Fjord and the Gaspé Peninsula, the provinces of Quebec and Ontario offer enough diving opportunities to keep even the most demanding diver exploring during a lifetime. Canada is a diver's dream come true and it is waiting for you!

DIVER
The longest-established scuba diving magazine in North America
www.divermag.com

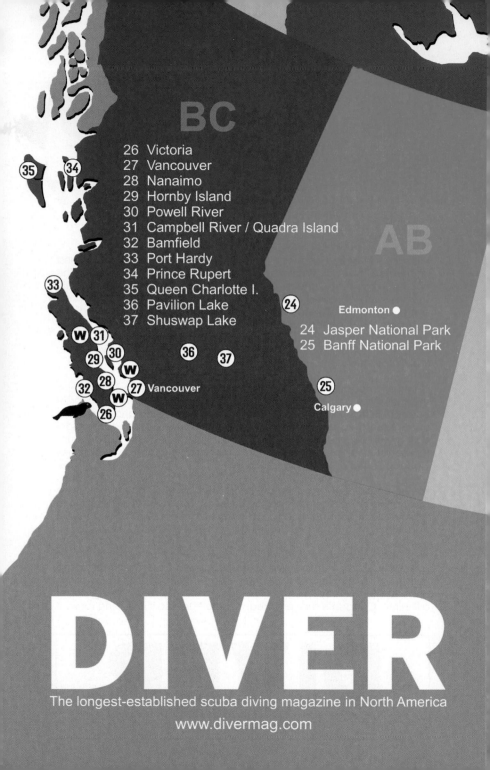

BC

26 Victoria
27 Vancouver
28 Nanaimo
29 Hornby Island
30 Powell River
31 Campbell River / Quadra Island
32 Bamfield
33 Port Hardy
34 Prince Rupert
35 Queen Charlotte I.
36 Pavilion Lake
37 Shuswap Lake

AB

24 Jasper National Park
25 Banff National Park

Edmonton ●

Calgary ●

Vancouver

DIVER

The longest-established scuba diving magazine in North America

www.divermag.com

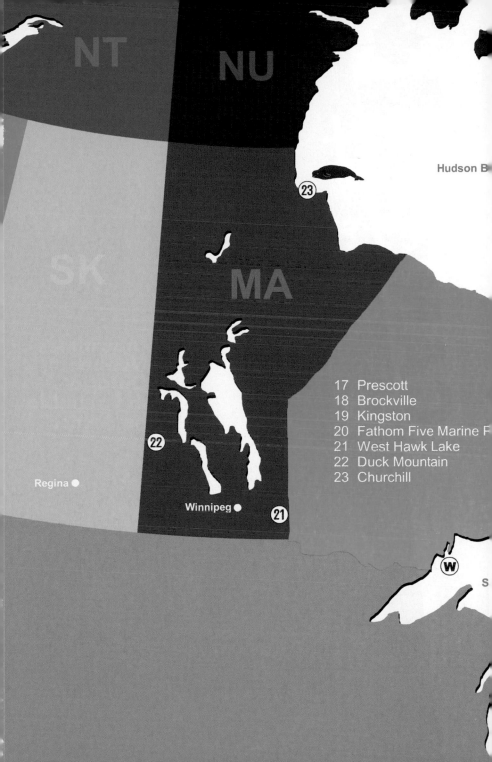

NT

NU

Hudson B

SK

MA

23

17 Prescott
18 Brockville
19 Kingston
20 Fathom Five Marine F
21 West Hawk Lake
22 Duck Mountain
23 Churchill

22

Regina ●

Winnipeg ●

21

W

S

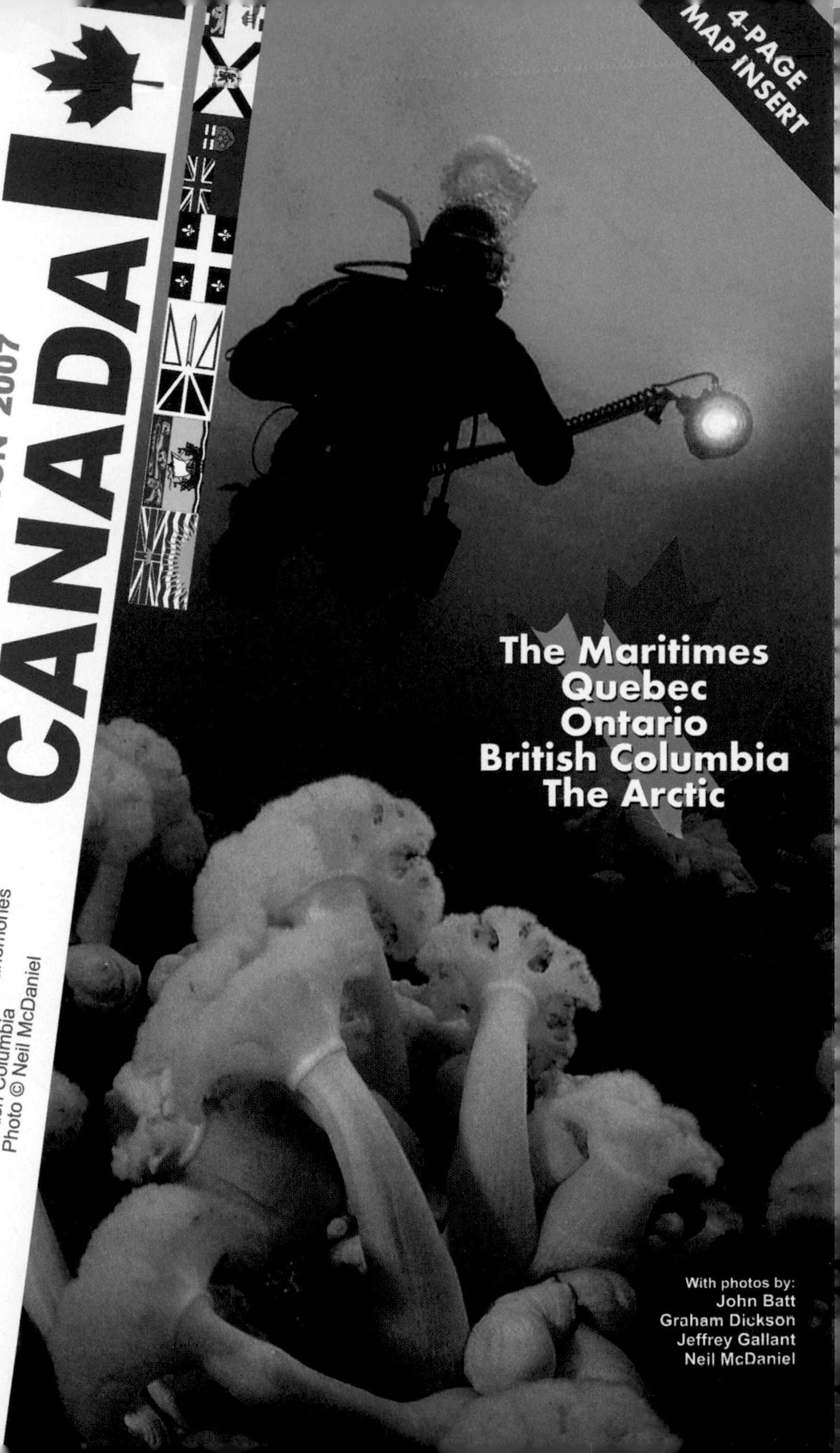

FEATURE DESTINATION 2007

CANADA

The Maritimes
Quebec
Ontario
British Columbia
The Arctic

Diver and plumose anemones
British Columbia
Photo © Neil McDaniel

With photos by:
John Batt
Graham Dickson
Jeffrey Gallant
Neil McDaniel

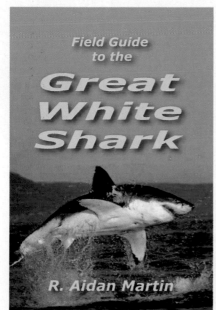

1 Baie-Comeau
2 Les Escoumins
3 Wreck of the *San Juan*
4 Wreck of the *Elizabeth & Mary*
5 Wrecks of Louisbourg
6 Wreck of *Empress or Ireland*
  and HMCS *Nipigon* artificial reef
7 Wreck of *Le Machault*
8 Forillon National Park and *Percé* Rock
9 Halifax Approaches
10 HMCS *Saguenay* artificial reef
11 Deer Island
12 Bell Island (Conception Bay)
13 Saguenay-St. Lawrence Marine Park
14 Flintkote Mine
15 Memphremagog Lake
16 Morrison Quarry

Ungava
Bay

LABRADOR

James
Bay

obermory

QC

CN

NB

Québec

Bay
Fun

World's H
Tide

Montréal

Ottawa

Huron

Toronto

Ontario

Erie

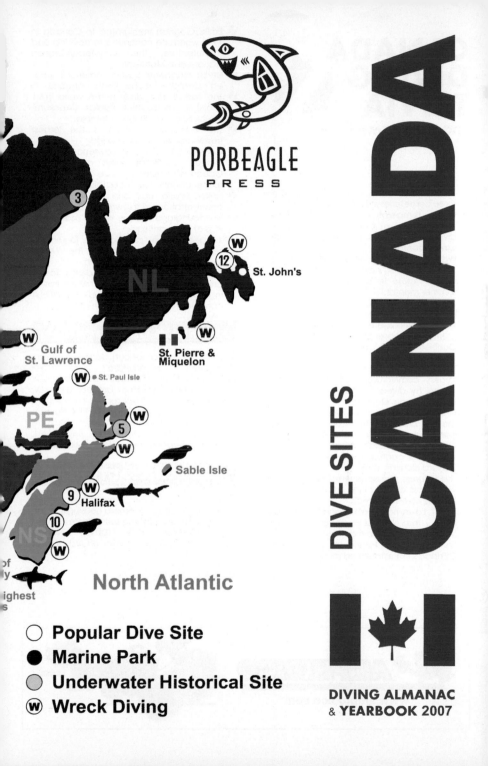

PORBEAGLE
PRESS

NL

③

St. John's

Ⓦ
⑫

Ⓦ
St. Pierre &
Miquelon

Ⓦ
Gulf of
St. Lawrence

Ⓦ ● St. Paul Isle

PE

Ⓦ
⑤

Ⓦ

Sable Isle

Ⓦ
⑨ Halifax

⑩

Ⓦ

of
...ly

...ighest
...s

North Atlantic

DIVE SITES

CANADA

○ **Popular Dive Site**
● **Marine Park**
◐ **Underwater Historical Site**
Ⓦ **Wreck Diving**

DIVING ALMANAC
& **YEARBOOK** 2007

CANADA DIVING TRIVIA

and little known facts

- 150 victims of the *Titanic* are buried in three cemeteries in Halifax, Nova Scotia.
- Water temperature at Les Escoumins, Quebec, one of Canada's most popular dive sites, reaches 28F (-2C) during the winter months.
- Water temperature off Brockville, Ontario, one of Canada's most popular dive sites, reaches close to 80 F (28 C) during the summer months.
- The Artificial Reef Society of British Columbia has scuttled 5 destroyers.
- The Blue whale, the world's largest animal, is regularly observed at Les Escoumins, Quebec, one of Canada's most popular dive sites.
- The Greenland shark, the world's second largest carnivorous shark, is often observed by divers at shallow depths near Baie-Comeau, Quebec.
- British Columbia's Hornby Island is one of the few places in the world where divers can regularly observe the six-gill shark.
- One of the world's largest great white sharks ever captured was taken off Prince Edward Island in 1983.
- The *Empress of Ireland* which sank in 1914 with a loss of 1,012 lives is Canada's most famous diveable wreck.
- The St. Lawrence Seaway and Great Lakes have the largest concentration of freshwater wrecks in the world.
- Fathom Five (off Tobermory, Ontario) was Canada's first established marine park.

- Émile Gagnan immigrated to Canada in 1947 where he continued to develop and manufacture the Cousteau/Gagnan Aqualung in Montreal.
- DIVER Magazine is North America's longest-established scuba diving magazine.
- The fastest drift dive in the world (16.1 knots) is at Sechelt Rapids (Skookumchuck Narrows), British Columbia.
- The *Edmund Fitzgerald* is the largest freshwater wreck in the world.
- Construction of the St. Lawrence Seaway linking the Great Lakes and Atlantic Ocean submerged entire villages and former canals now accessible to divers.
- Nova Scotia has one of the highest concentrations of shipwrecks in the world.
- Newfoundland has the world's most sightings of the giant squid.
- Jacques Mayol produced a journalistic report on a dolphin at the Miami Seaquarium for Radio-Canada.
- Canadian divers are considered to be among the best in the world when traveling abroad due to the sometimes difficult conditions in which they dive at home.

FAMOUS CDN DIVERS*

Roberta Bondar (astronaut), James Cameron (filmmaker), Mandy-Rae Cruickshank (freediver), Marc Garneau (astronaut), Dr. Robert Grenier (marine archeologist), Dr. Joseph MacInnis (hyperbaric researcher), Neil McDaniel (filmmaker), Dr. Phil Nuytten (submersible engineer), Julie Payette (astronaut), John Stoneman (filmmaker), Pierre Elliot Trudeau (former Prime Minister)

CDN MANUFACTURERS

Abyss (diving suits), Amphibico (video housings), Aquatica (camera housings), Atlan (diving suits), Bare (diving suits), Brooks (diving suits), Farallon USA (DPVs), Nuytco (submersibles), Shark Marine (ROVs), Whites (diving suits),

* Living or born in Canada

Tube-dwelling anemone
Pachycerianthus fimbriatus
British Columbia
Photo © Neil McDaniel

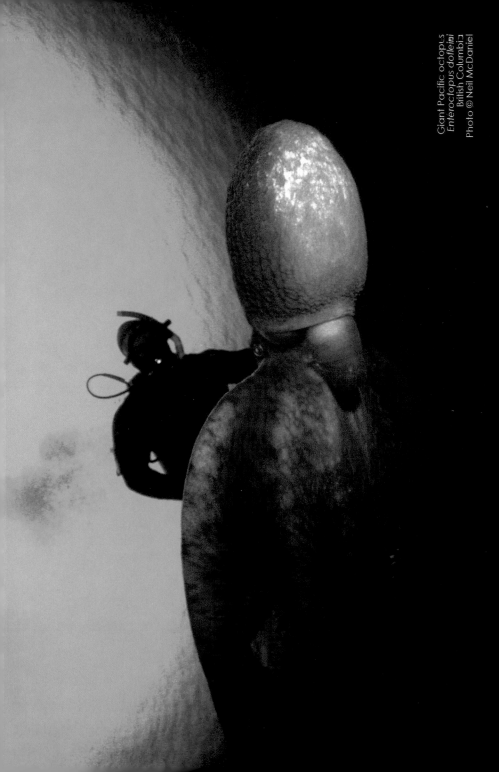

Giant Pacific octopus
Enteroctopus dofleini
British Columbia
Photo © Neil McDaniel

Basket star
Gorgonocephalus eucnemis
British Columbia
Photo © Neil McDaniel

ARCTIC

D.A.Y. 2007 FEATURE DESTINATION

Despite what many divers may believe, the Arctic Ocean is anything but a frozen wasteland devoid of life. In fact, Canada's Arctic territories are becoming one of the 'hottest' dive destinations in the world thanks to a few entrepreneurial pioneers who have shed light on the many unique natural wonders not found anywhere else. Diving or snorkeling with bowhead and beluga whales, the Greenland shark, walrus and seals are highly prized and rare entries in anyone's logbook. Experiencing Inuit culture while roughing it out at an ice camp floating over thousands of feet of water is an unforgettable experience for even the most adventurous traveler. Diving the Arctic is one of the few remaining dive destinations that offer a genuine feeling of discovery.

1. Arctic dive. Photo: NOAA
2. Seal. Photo: NOAA
3. Polar bear
   Photo: Paul Jackson
   www.arctickingdom.com
4. Walrus
   Photo: Graham Dickson
   www.arctickingdom.com

Diver and walrus
Photo © Graham Dickson
Arctic Kingdom Marine Expeditions
www.arctickingdom.com

D.A.Y. 2007 PROFILE

Dr.
PHIL
NUYTTEN (OBC, L.L.D.)

Dr. Phil Nuytten has spent his life in subsea exploration. He has logged many thousands of hours underwater world-wide as a working commercial diver and as a developer of underwater equipment and techniques. He is widely regarded as one of the pioneers of the modern commercial diving industry and a significant force in the creation of new technology.

In the 1960's and 70's, Nuytten was heavily involved in experimental deep-diving and the development of mixed gas decompression tables. In 1968 he was a member of the team that completed the first 600 foot ocean 'bounce' dives on 'Project Nesco', and in 1972 he wrote the protocol for 'Deep Work 1000', the first North American thousand foot saturation dive. These early projects helped set the international standards in use today. During this period, Phil Nuytten co-founded Oceaneering International Inc. Oceaneering International pioneered many early subsea development projects, and has gone on to become one of the largest underwater skills companies in the world.

In the 1970's, working with long-time colleague Dr. Joe MacInnis, Nuytten headed the equipment research component of a series of high arctic expeditions. Among the goals of these expeditions was the testing of his own designs of life-support gear for use in polar and sub-polar conditions. In 1984, Phil Nuytten appeared on the cover of National Geographic Magazine for his record dives through ice-covered arctic waters onto the *Breadalbane*, the northernmost known shipwreck. His involvement in underwater activities in virtually all of the world's oceans has resulted in articles on his work in Reader's Digest, Business Week, Newsweek, Time, Popular Science, Discovery, Fortune, and Scientific American, as well as dozens of dozens of diving and aerospace technical journals.

Dr. Phil Nuytten in the Newtsult.
Photo courtesy Nuytco Research Ltd

Nuytco Research
www.nuytco.com

Nuytten is a popular speaker at underwater conferences around the world and has published nu-merous technical papers on his leading-edge work in subsea technology

Dr. Phil Nuytten has been instrumental in the development and current acceptance of Atmospheric Diving System technology. In 1979, he began work on a revolutionary new one-atmosphere diving suit that resulted in a patented breakthrough in rotary joint design, and formed the basis for the world-famous 'Newtsuit'. The 'Newtsuit' is a thousand foot-rated hard suit that completely protects the wearer from outside pressure and eliminates the need for decompression while still maintaining mobility and dexterity - a "submarine that you wear". It is now standard equipment in many of the world's navies.

In 1997, Nuytten and his design team produced the two-thousand-foot-rated micro-submersible DeepWorker 2000: a revolutionary deep-diving system that has been called an "underwater sports car". Nuytten and Nuytco Research Ltd. received a five year contract from the National Geographic Society to provide DeepWorker 2000 submersibles and crews on Dr. Sylvia Earle's 'Sustainable Seas Expeditions': an initiative to study deep ocean en-vironmental impact. The use of the DeepWorker micro-subs to explore and monitor National marine sanctuaries has already increased scientists' understanding of underwater ecology, habitats, and biodiversity.

In 1999, NASA contracted a pair of DeepWorkers to study their possible use in the recovery of the Space Shuttle booster rockets, and in 2000 DeepWorkers successfully recovered the Space Shuttle booster rockets from the May flight to the U.S. Space Station. NASA is currently studying acquisition of a pair of titanium DeepWorkers specifically dedicated to booster rocket recovery. Nuytten's work with NASA spans more than twenty-five years, and he has published several papers on space applications of undersea technology. He is also a senior member of the American Association of Aeronautics and Astronautics, and a life member of the American Association of Underwater Scientists.

DIVER

The longest-established scuba diving magazine in North America

Also in the year 2000, Nuytten introduced a new concept for an ultralightweight, swimming, hard suit called the 'Exosuit'. Nuytten and his team recently completed a contract for the Canadian Department of National Defence to examine the feasibility of using the Exosuit as a submarine escape device. The Beta prototype of the Exosuit underwent swim testing in 2005 and target date for release is 2006. Plans to utilize a space version of the Exosuit are under discussion and Nuytten and his team are currently training astronauts from the Canadian Space Agency as pilots of the DeepWorker 2000 submersibles. In 2003, Nuytten and his design team completed the first side-by-side Dual DeepWorker, designed for a pilot and one observer. Designed with the use of deep-depth underwater tourism in mind, this 2000-ft rated submersible has commercial and scientific applications as well.

Dr. Phil Nuytten has earned many international honours and awards. These include commercial diving's highest award from the Association of Diving Contractors International, the Academy of Underwater Art and Sciences 'Nogi' award, induction into the 'Diving Hall of Fame', and the Explorer's Club's prestigious 'Lowell Thomas' Award. In 1992, Nuytten was awarded the Order of British Columbia, his home province's highest honour, in recognition of his role in making British Columbia one of the world centres of underwater technology.

His outstanding Canadian achievements were recognized again in 2000 when he received the Canadian Underwater Pioneer Award. In 2001 Nuytten received the Jules Verne Award in Paris for his international accomplishments in the subsea field.

Dr. Phil Nuytten has spent nearly forty years developing undersea systems that have the safety of the diving technician as their common theme. His goal has been to provide scientific, technical, military, and sport divers full access to continental shelf depths without the hazards of decompression, so that humans can explore, learn about, and, ultimately, protect the world's oceans

Dr. Phil Nuytten pilots DeepWorker. Photo: Nate Johnson / Courtesy: Nuytco Research Ltd

MARITIMES

D.A.Y. 2007 FEATURE DESTINATION

Canada's maritime provinces are steeped in history both topside and underwater. Thousands of wrecks, some dating back to the colonial period, await divers of all levels of experience. Thousands more are still waiting to be discovered. Add to this a myriad of marine species and you have what Nova Scotians call Canada's Atlantic Playground. The HMCS *Saguenay* artificial reef in Lunenburg has blossomed into an oasis of life since it was scuttled in 1994. Divers stare in disbelief at the incredible visibility in the pristine waters of Conception Bay, Newfoundland, where they come to explore wartime wrecks. Swept by the highest tides in the world, New Brunswick's Deer Island is one of the most biologically diverse and bountiful sites found anywhere; a photographer's dream come true. Those who have experienced Canada's maritime provinces keep coming again and again.

Labrador

NL

③

⑫ Ⓦ St. John's

Gulf of
St. Lawrence

Ⓦ St. Pierre & Miquelon

Ⓦ ● St. Paul Isle

PE

⑦

Ⓦ
⑤
Ⓦ

● Sable Isle

NB

Ⓦ
⑨ Halifax

⑪ NS

⑩ Ⓦ

Ⓦ

Bay of
Fundy

North Atlantic

World's Highest
Tides

1. Sambro Island
   Photo: Jeffrey Gallant
2. Flounder
   Photo: Jeffrey Gallant

3. Monkfish
   Photo: Chris Harvey-Clark
4. Lion's mane jellyfish
   Photo: Jeffrey Gallant

Sambro Island
Halifax approaches
Photo © Jeffrey Gallant

Sea raven
Hemitripterus americanus
Sambro Island
Photo © John Batt

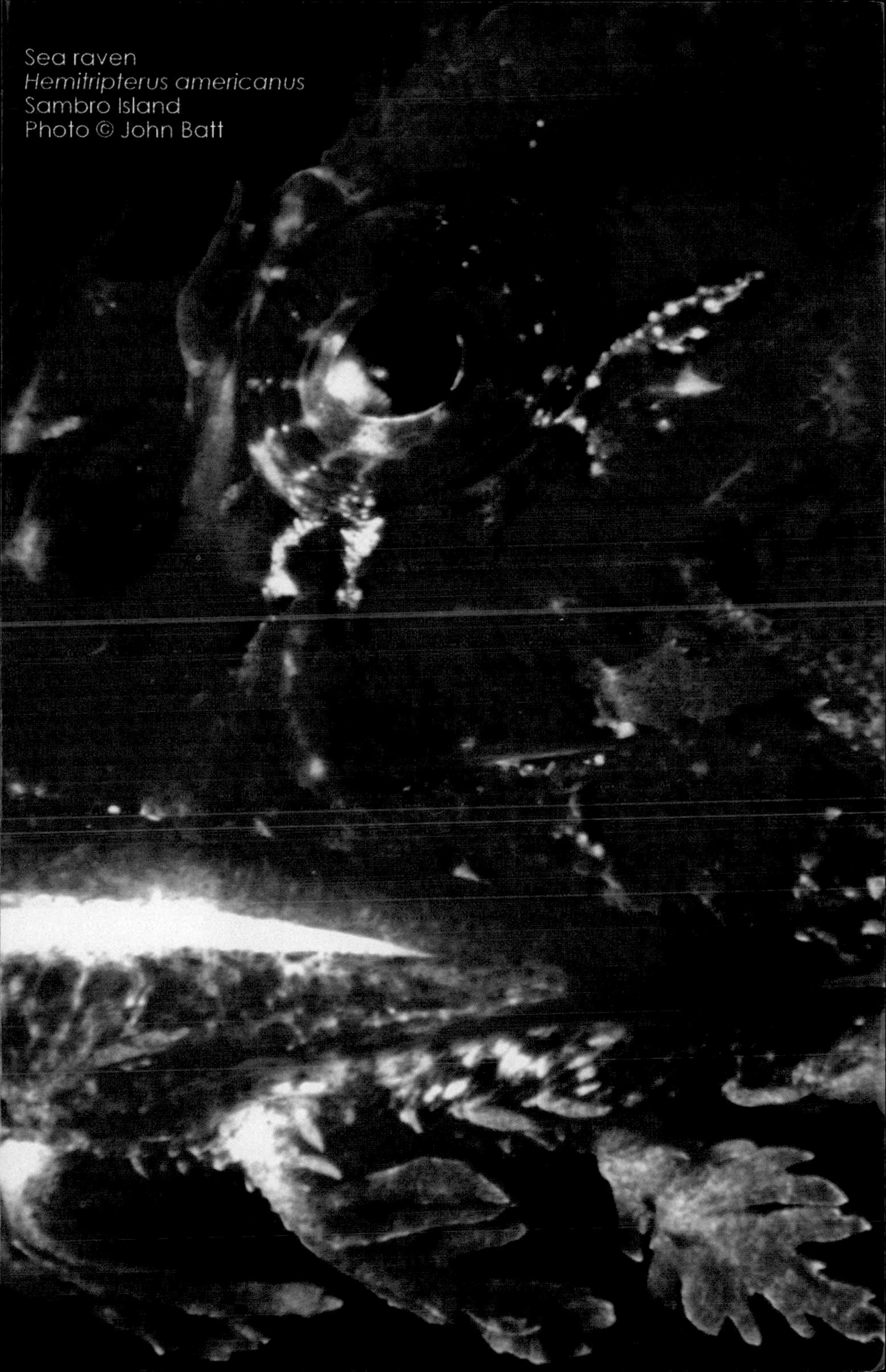

The province of Québec offers some of the best and coldest diving in the world. The waters of the St. Lawrence Estuary are among the richest in the world. Underwater photographers keep returning to record the seemingly unending marine biodiversity off the town of Les Escoumins, Quebec's most popular dive area. The little explored Saguenay Fjord reveals a unique northern ecosystem to the few that dare to explore its unseen depths. The wreck of the liner *Empress of Ireland*, Canada's worst maritime tragedy (1914), and the HMCS *Nipigon* artificial reef, attract divers from all over North America to the Rimouski area on the south shore of the St. Lawrence. Countless rivers and lakes offer limitless possibilities to freshwater enthusiasts.

1. Johnny Darter / St. François River
   Photo: Jeffrey Gallant
2. HMCS Nipigon
   Photo: Paul Boissinot
3. White-cross hydromedusa
   Photo: Jeffrey Gallant

4. Les Escoumins
   Photo: Jeffrey Gallant
5. Flintkote Quarry
   Photo: Jeffrey Gallant

Naked sea butterfly
Clione limacina
Les Escoumins
Photo © Jeffrey Gallant

Greenland shark
Somniosus microcephalus
St. Lawrence Estuary
Photo © Jeffrey Gallant

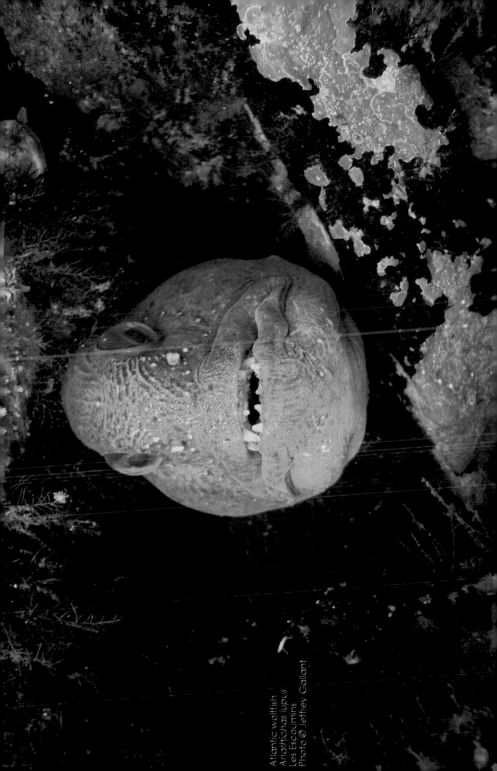

Atlantic wolffish
Anarhichas lupus
Les Escoumins
Photo © Jeffrey Gallant

ONTARIO

The province of Ontario is a beacon for turn-of-the-century wreck enthusiasts. The Great Lakes and the St. Lawrence Seaway contain the remains of thousands of well preserved wooden and steel vessels of all types and sizes lost to storms, human error and war. Several wrecks are in shallow water accessible from land even by beginner divers. Others are further from shore and require a boat and advanced or technical certification. The hundreds of wrecks located near the cities of Brockville and Kingston are mentioned most often although great wreck sites may be found all over the province. Fathom Five National Park at the mouth of Georgian Bay is Canada's first National Marine Conservation Area. The park preserves 22 shipwrecks in some of the clearest waters of the Great Lakes.

1 & 3. Fathom Five
Photos: Jeffrey Gallant
2 & 5. St. Lawrence Seaway
Photos: Jeffrey Gallant

4. Wreck of the *Rothesay*
Photo: Jeffrey Gallant

Wreck of the Sweepstakes
Fathom Five National Marine Park
Tobermory, Ontario
Photo © Jeffrey Gallant

Wreck of the *W.L. Wetmore*
Fathom Five National Marine Park
Tobermory, Ontario
Photo © Jeffrey Gallant

Mid-winter dive in a frozen lake
Eastern Ontario
Photo © Jeffrey Gallant

BRITISH COLUMBIA

D.A.Y. 2007 FEATURE DESTINATION

The province of British Columbia is known as one of the best diving regions in the world. Wreck enthusiasts revel on the many world-class artificial reefs that dot the coast. Underwater naturalists seek out exciting marine species that regularly appear at various sites: sixgill shark and stellar sea lion (Hornby Island), giant Pacific octopus and spiny dogfish (Quadra Island), and Pacific salmon runs in many rivers on Vancouver Island and the mainland. Sea life literally covers every inch of the rocky substrate in the nutrient-rich and current-swept waters of the Sunshine Coast, north of Vancouver. It's no wonder diver surveys have repeatedly placed B.C. at the top of the list for best diving in North America.

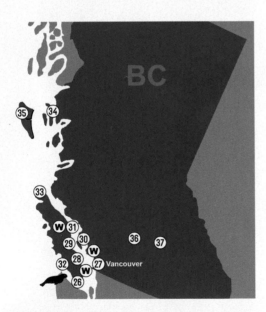

1. Kelp greenling
   Photo: Jeffrey Gallant
2. Fish-eating anemone
   Photo: Jeffrey Gallant

3. Howe Sound
   Photo:Jeffrey Gallant
4. Hooded nudibranch
   Photo: Jeffrey Gallant
5. Wolf eels
   Photo: Jeffrey Gallant